AF772358

Web-Based Green Products Life Cycle Management Systems: Reverse Supply Chain Utilization

Hsiao-Fan Wang
National Tsing Hua University, ROC

Information Science REFERENCE
INFORMATION SCIENCE REFERENCE
Hershey • New York

Director of Editorial Content: Kristin Klinger
Managing Development Editor: Kristin M. Roth
Editorial Assistant: Rebecca Beistline
Director of Production: Jennifer Neidig
Managing Editor: Jamie Snavely
Assistant Managing Editor: Carole Coulson
Typesetter: Carole Coulson
Cover Design: Lisa Tosheff
Printed at: Yurchak Printing Inc.

Published in the United States of America by
Information Science Reference (an imprint of IGI Global)
701 E. Chocolate Avenue, Suite 200
Hershey PA 17033
Tel: 717-533-8845
Fax: 717-533-8661
E-mail: cust@igi-global.com
Web site: http://www.igi-global.com

and in the United Kingdom by
Information Science Reference (an imprint of IGI Global)
3 Henrietta Street
Covent Garden
London WC2E 8LU
Tel: 44 20 7240 0856
Fax: 44 20 7379 0609
Web site: http://www.eurospanbookstore.com

Copyright © 2009 by IGI Global. All rights reserved. No part of this publication may be reproduced, stored or distributed in any form or by any means, electronic or mechanical, including photocopying, without written permission from the publisher.

Product or company names used in this set are for identification purposes only. Inclusion of the names of the products or companies does not indicate a claim of ownership by IGI Global of the trademark or registered trademark.

Library of Congress Cataloging-in-Publication Data

Web-based green products life cycle management systems : reverse supply chain utilization / Hsiao-Fan Wang, editor.

p. cm.

Summary: "This book is for those who have been working on supply chain management to gain an overall picture of the existing and potential developments on the issues related to life-cycle management of a green product"--Provided by publisher.

Includes bibliographical references and index.

ISBN 978-1-60566-114-8 (hardcover) -- ISBN 978-1-60566-115-5 (ebook)

1. Green products. 2. Business logistics. I. Wang, Hsiao-Fan.

HF5413.W43 2009

658.5--dc22

2008017754

British Cataloguing in Publication Data
A Cataloguing in Publication record for this book is available from the British Library.

All work contributed to this book set is original material. The views expressed in this book are those of the authors, but not necessarily of the publisher.

If a library purchased a print copy of this publication, please go to http://www.igi-global.com/agreement for information on activating the library's complimentary electronic access to this publication.

List of Reviewers

Anders Andrae
National Institute of Advanced Industrial Science & Technology, Japan

Ying-Yeng Chen
Naional Tsing Hua University, Taiwan, ROC

Alvin B. Culaba
De La Salle University-Manila, Philippines

Surendra M. Gupta
Northeastern University, USA

Hidetaka Hayashi
University of Tokyo, Japan

Hsuan Ethan Hong
National Chiao Tung University, Taiwan, ROC

Wei-Kuo Hong
Chunghwa Telecom, Taiwan, ROC

Jin-Li Hu
National Chiao Tung University, Taiwan, ROC

Nikos I. Karacapilidis
University of Patras, Greece

Dimitris Kiritsis
École Polytechnique Fédérale Lausanne cublens, Switzerland

Elif Kongar
University of Bridgeport, USA

H. Krikke
Tilburg, The Netherlands

Mattias Lindahl
Linköpings Universitet, Sweden

Sagisaka Masayuki
The LCA Research Center of Japan, Tokyo, Japan

Seamus M. McGovern
Aviation Systems Engineering Division, National Transportation Systems Center, MA, USA

Semih ÖNÜT
Yildiz Technical University, Istanbul, Turkey

Dimitris Papadias
Hong Kong University of Science and Technology, HK

Rajesh Piplani
Nanyang Technology University, Singapore

Kishore K. Pochampally
Southern New Hampshire University, USA

Karsten Schischke
Fraunhofer Institute for Reliability and Microintegration, Berlin, Germany

Julie M. Schoenung
University of California, Davis, USA

Vivek Sood
Global Supply Chain Group, Sidney, Australia

Th. Spengler
TU Braunschweig, Braunschweig, Germany

Jack Su
National Tsing Hua University, Taiwan, ROC

Halefsan Sumen
Istanbul Technical University, Turkey

R. R. Tan
De La Salle University-Manila, Philippines

Ching-Jun Ting
Yuan Ze University, Taiwan, ROC

Amy Trappey
National Tsing Hua University, Taiwan, ROC

Hsiao-Fan Wang
National Tsing Hua University, Taiwan, ROC

Ming-Yang Wang
National Tsing Hua University, Taiwan, ROC

U.P. Wen
National Tsing Hua University, Taiwan, ROC

C. T. Wu
National Tsing Hua University, Taiwan. ROC

Table of Contents

Foreword xv

Preface xvii

Section I
Life Cycle Assessment: Concept and Practice

Chapter I
Life Cycle Design, Planning, and Assessment 1
Raymond R. Tan, De La Salle University, Manila, Philippines
Alvin B. Culaba, De La Salle University, Manila, Philippines
Michael R. I. Purvis, University of Portsmouth, UK
Joel Q. Tanchuco, De La Salle University, Manila, Philippines

Chapter II
Industrial Metabolism: Materials and Energy Flow Studies.. 16
A. J. D. Lambert, Technische Universiteit Eindhoven, The Netherlands

Chapter III
Sustainability Constraints as System Boundaries: Introductory Steps Toward Strategic
Life-Cycle Management 51
Henrik Ny, Blekinge Institute of Technology, Sweden
Jamie P. MacDonald, Office of the Minister of the Environment, Ontario, Canada
Göran Broman, Blekinge Institute of Technology, Sweden
Karl-Henrik Robèrt, Blekinge Institute of Technology, Sweden

Chapter IV
Environmental Criteria in a MCDM Context 74
Ahmed Bufardi, Federal Institute of Aquatic Science and Technology (EAWAG), Switzerland
Dimitris Kiritsis, Ecole Polytechnique Fédérale de Lausanne, Switzerland

Chapter V
Sustainable Electronic Product Design: A Comparison of Environmental Performance Assessment Tools Derived from Life Cycle Thinking 93
Xiaoying Zhou, University of California–Davis, USA
Julie M. Schoenung, University of California–Davis, USA

Chapter VI
From Cleaner Production to Greening the Local Economy: A Case Study of Two European Programs Enhancing SMEs Competitiveness Through Environmental Approaches 129
Nobutaka Odake, Nagoya Institute of Technology, Japan
Satomi Furukawa, Fuluhashi Environmental Institutute Co., Ltd., Japan

Section II
Demand and Service Chain Management

Chapter VII
Does Trust Foster Sustainability? Results from a Management Simulation Game 149
Harold Krikke, Tilburg University, The Netherlands
Ruud Brekelmans, Tilburg University, The Netherlands
Hein Fleuren, Tilburg University,, The Netherlands
Cindy Kuijpers, Tilburg University, The Netherlands

Chapter VIII
Identifying and Clustering of Target Customers of Green Products 182
Miao-Ling Wang, Ming-Hsin University of Science & Technology, Taiwan, ROC

Chapter IX
Application of Fuzzy Analytic Network Process and Fuzzy TOPSIS to the Undesirable Location Selection Problem 208
Semih Önüt, Yildiz Technical University, Turkey
Selin Soner Kara, Yildiz Technical University, Turkey
Derya Tekin, Yildiz Technical University, Turkey

Chapter X
Sustainable Product Service Systems: Potential to Deliver Business and Social Benefits with Less Resource Use 232
David Ness, University of South Australia, Australia

Chapter XI
Strategic Decisions for Green Electricity Marketing: Learning from Past Experiences 250
Marta Pérez-Plaza, Universidad Pontificia Comillas, Spain
Pedro Linares, Universidad Pontificia Comillas, Spain

Section III
Supply Chain and Logistics Management

Chapter XII
Modeling of Green Supply Chain Logistics 268
Hsin-Wei Hsu, National Tsing Hua University, Taiwan, ROC
Hsiao-Fan Wang, National Tsing Hua University, Taiwan, ROC

Chapter XIII
Reverse Supply Chain Design: A Neural Network Approach 283
Kishore K. Pochampally, Southern New Hampshire University, Manchester, USA
Surendra M. Gupta, Northeastern University, Boston, USA

Chapter XIV
System Dynamics Modeling for Strategic Management of Green Supply Chain 301
Ying Su, Institute of Scientific and Technical Information of China, Beijing, P.R. China
Zhanming Jin, Tsinghua University, Beijing, P.R. China
Lei Yang, South China University of Technology, Panyu, Guangzhou, P.R. China

Chapter XV
A Vehicle Routing and Scheduling Model for a Distribution Center 334
Hsiao-Fan Wang, National Tsing Hua University, ROC
Yu-Chun Chiu, National Tsing Hua University, ROC

Chapter XVI
A Data Envelopment Analysis Approach for Household Appliances and Automobile
Recycling 367
Elif Kongar, University of Bridgeport, Bridgeport, CT, USA
Surendra M. Gupta, Northeastern University, Boston, USA

Section IV
Web-Based Management Technology

Chapter XVII
Green Product Retrieval and Recommendations Systems.. 379
Yi-Chun Liao, Hsuan Chuang University, Taiwan, R.O.C.

Chapter XVIII
Applying Web-Based Collaborative Decision-Making in Reverse Logistics: The Case of Mobile Phones 401
Giannis T. Tsoulfas, University of Piraeus, Greece
Costas P. Pappis, University of Piraeus, Greece
Nikos I. Karacapilidis, University of Patras, Greece

Compilation of References 416

About the Contributors 451

Index 459

Detailed Table of Contents

Foreword xv

Preface xvii

Section I
Life Cycle Assessment: Concept and Practice

Chapter I
Life Cycle Design, Planning, and Assessment 1
Raymond R. Tan, De La Salle University, Manila, Philippines
Alvin B. Culaba, De La Salle University, Manila, Philippines
Michael R. I. Purvis, University of Portsmouth, UK
Joel Q. Tanchuco, De La Salle University, Manila, Philippines

Chapter I provides an overall concept of life cycle assessment of green products and the quantitative method of measurement and ways of improvement for the industries. In particular, this chapter discusses life cycle assessment principles and its application in the design and planning of industrial supply chains. A specific case study on the production of biofuels from agricultural crops is used to illustrate the key concepts.

Chapter II
Industrial Metabolism: Materials and Energy Flow Studies.. 16
A. J. D. Lambert, Technische Universiteit Eindhoven, The Netherlands

Chapter II provides a rigorous method of life cycle assessment based on the concept of quantitative physical flow analysis, known as industrial metabolism. A discussion of the reverse product-process chain, which includes reuse and recycling, is presented from the transformation of both the materials and also the energy. In particular, the chapter summarizes available types of software with examples which are very useful and valuable for applications in practice.

Chapter III
Sustainability Constraints as System Boundaries: Introductory Steps toward Strategic Life-Cycle Management 51
Henrik Ny, Blekinge Institute of Technology, Sweden
Jamie P. MacDonald, Institute for Resources, Environment, and Sustainability, University of . British Columbia, Vancouver Canada
Goran Broman, Blekinge Institute of Technology, Sweden
Karl-Henrik Robèrt, Blekinge Institute of Technology, Sweden

Chapter III discusses the life cycle management from the sustainability viewpoint, and proposes a useful strategy to reach the global sustainability based on the continuous evaluation of numerous complex social, ecological, and economic factors. Thus, the article not only brings about the issues of sustainability in the framework of life cycle management, but also provides an approach to arrive at it with detailed illustration.

Chapter IV
Environmental Criteria in a MCDM Context 74
Ahmed Bufardi, Federal Institute of Aquatic Science and Technology (EAWAG), Switzerland
Dimitris Kiritsis, École Polytechnique Fédérale de Lausanne, Switzerland

Chapter IV discusses the environmental criteria which should be considered in green product management and presents a method of environment impact assessment from MCDM approach. Therefore, not only can the environmental criteria be accessed from both the forward and reverse supply chains, but also the weights of their importance can be measured. A comprehensive case study of *a vacuum cleaner* is presented for illustration.

Chapter V
Sustainable Electronic Product Design: A Comparison of Environmental Performance Assessment Tools Derived from Life Cycle Thinking 93
Xiaoying Zhou, University of California, Davis, USA
Julie M. Schoenung, University of California, Davis, USA

Chapter V is also a study which integrates the sustainability into life cycle management, while taking a system viewpoint toward environmental performance assessment. In particular, the chapter highlights the environmental issues in the framework of overall economic, geographical, and legislative factors so that the methodologies developed along this line have guidelines to reach system optimization.

Chapter VI
From Cleaner Production to Greening the Local Economy:
A Case Study of Two European Programs Enhancing SMEs Competitiveness through Environmental Approaches.. 129
Nobutaka Odake, Nagoya Institute of Technology, Japan
Satomi Furukawa, Fuluhashi Environmental Institutute Co., Ltd., Japan

Chapter VI introduces the concept of eco-efficiency, and in particular, provides two cases of European small and medium-sized enterprises for detailed illustration and demonstration. The article emphasizes the diffusion-oriented policy so that reducing environmental burden can be achieved by guiding the companies to improve their resource productivity and add production values.

Section II
Demand and Service Chain Management

Chapter VII
Does Trust Foster Sustainability? Results from a Management Simulation Game 149
Harold Krikke, Economics and Business Administration, The Netherlands
Ruud Brekelmans, Economics and Business Administration, The Netherlands
Hein Fleuren, Economics and Business Administration, The Netherlands
Cindy Kuijpers, Economics and Business Administration, The Netherlands

Chapter VII brings about a different and interesting view toward sustainability. Realizing the importance of marketing demand and customer response for green product development, this chapter presents a developed management game and concludes some propositions on the trust and sustainability in supply chains. The detailed description of the design of this game as well as the roles involved in this game along the overall supply chain have been provided, which facilitates practical implement. Also, further research along this line has been identified with a list of questions to be answered.

Chapter VIII
Identifying and Clustering of Target Customers of Green Products.. 182
Miao-Ling Wang, Ming-Hsin University of Science & Technology, Taiwan, ROC

Chapter VIII presents a methodology of identifying target customers of green products for market expansion purposes. Based on a data mining technique, the customers can be classified according to their preference, purchasing behaviour, and demographical factors. Then, by a developed bi-objective mathematical model, pricing strategies can be developed from win-win perspectives, which is beneficial for both the producers and the customers. The rigors analysis provides a tractable approach for market analysis and pricing development.

Chapter IX
Application of Fuzzy Analytic Network Process and Fuzzy TOPSIS to the Undesirable Location Selection Proble 208
Semih ÖNÜT, Yildiz Technical University, Turkey
Selin Soner Kara, Yildiz Technical University, Turkey
Derya Tekin, Yildiz Technical University, Turkey

Chapter IX tackles a different but important issue related to green supply chain management, the facility location problem. Regarding the environmental impact, the issue is tackled by considering the undesirable locations. Using fuzzy TOPSIS approach, the design of a group decision process is presented to find the criteria with their weights of undesirability. Measurement of conflict and vagueness among criteria and decision makers is presented with detailed illustration and numerical examples.

Chapter X
Sustainable Product Service Systems: Potential to Deliver Business and Social Benefits with Less Resource Use 232
David Ness, University of South Australia and Department for Transport Energy and Infrastructure, SA, Australia

Chapter X presents an overall system for green service chain management, namely sustainable product service systems (S-PSS). By taking the factors of sustainability, resource productivity, and eco-efficiency into account, the article shows how the developing countries, in particular, can apply the system to trade off among these factors. Many practical cases are presented which provide significant references for both concept clarification and practical applications.

Chapter XI
Strategic Decisions for Green Electricity Marketing: Learning from Past Experiences 250
Marta Pérez-Plaza, Universidad Pontificia Comillas, Spain
Pedro Linares, Universidad Pontificia Comillas, Spain

Chapter XI discusses the energy issues, in particular, green electricity and its renewability from historical development. Based on the literature review and the customer response, the article concludes a comprehensive approach toward green electricity utilization by identifying its development boundaries and past mistakes.

Section III
Supply Chain and Logistics Management

Chapter XII
Modeling of Green Supply Chain Logistics 268
Hsin-Wei Hsu, National Tsing Hua University, Taiwan, ROC
Hsiao-Fan Wang, National Tsing Hua University, Taiwan, ROC

Chapter XII opens another door toward green supply chain and logistics management. A mathematical model in the form of a 0-1 integer linear program is developed for close-loop logistics of which optimal solution for determining the facilities of manufactures, distribution centers, and dismantlers can be found with minimum cost. Sensitivity analyses on the recovery rate and land-filling rate on the reverse logistics have been carried out for managerial purposes.

Chapter XIII
Reverse Supply Chain Design: A Neural Network Approach 283
Kishore K. Pochampally, Southern New Hampshire University, Manchester, USA
Surendra M. Gupta, Northeastern University, Boston, USA

Chapter XIII provides an alternative method for reverse supply chain design. Realizing the efficiency issues of the collection facilities and recovery facilities chosen while designing a reverse supply chain, this chapter is based on the neural network approach to develop a four-stage procedure for evaluating the facilities. Group decision techniques are in-cooperated with successful applications.

Chapter XIV
System Dynamics Modeling for Strategic Management of Green Supply Chain 301
Ying Su, Tsinghua University, China
Zhanming Jin, Tsinghua University, China
Lei Yang, South China University of Technology, Panyu, Guangzhou, P.R. China

Chapter XIV takes a different approach of system dynamics methodology to develop a simulation model for evaluating different green supply chain management strategies. By measuring the total profit, the effectiveness of different strategies can be evaluated efficiently and successfully.

Chapter XV
A Vehicle Routing and Scheduling Model for a Distribution Center 334
Hsiao-Fan Wang, National Tsing Hua University, Taiwan, ROC
Yu-Chun Chiu, National Tsing Hua University, Taiwan, ROC

Chapter XV illustrates how to design a routing system for a distribution center to assign a number of limited-capacity vehicles to serve a given number of customers within the required time window with minimum service cost. An optimization model is formulated in the form of an integer linear program and a genetic algorithm is developed for efficient solution. Therefore, NP complexity problem embedded in such kinds of optimization problems have shown to be resolved with reasonable accuracy.

Chapter XVI
A Data Envelopment Analysis Approach for Household Appliances and Automobile Recycling..... 368
Elif Kongar, University of Bridgeport, Bridgeport, CT, USA
Surendra M. Gupta, Northeastern University, Boston, USA

Chapter XVI discusses a recovery issue in reverse supply chain. Criteria and the proposed data envelopment method are presented to evaluate the used house appliance and automobiles. It aims that the cost added to the process of the recycled products will be justified by their economic and environmental benefit.

Chapter XVII
Green Product Retrieval and Recommendations System 379
Yi-Chun Liao, Hsuan Chuang University, Taiwan, ROC

Chapter XVII introduces a preference-based recommendation procedure in a green product information retrieval system. The online procedure is based on an off-line database which includes the description of the green products with their green properties and prices and the relevant green regulations. The information retrieval procedure then is based on the preference of the users, and by a data mining technique, the products can be recommended and the database can be updated simultaneously. The system is useful for both the consumers and the producers. A prototype has been developed and illustrated in the chapter.

Chapter XVIII
Applying Web-based Collaborative Decision-making in Reverse Logistics: The Case of
Mobile Phones 401
Giannis T. Tsoulfas, University of Piraeus, Greece
Costas P. Pappis, University of Piraeus, Greece
Nikos I. Karacapilidis, University of Patras, Greece

Chapter XVIII discusses a different issue of Web-based green supply chain management. This online decision support system is developed for the stakeholders in reverse supply chain when they have different views, perspectives, and priorities. The end-of-life mobile phones are taken as an illustrative example to show how this system supports a collaborative decision-making process on the Web site.

Compilation of References 416

About the Contributors 451

Index 459

Foreword

Modern manufacturing is based on international supply chains. This is actually a rather new reality. Some 20 years ago, much of manufacturing was still very much a national, even a provincial, affair. When Henry Ford in the early 20th century optimised the logistics of car manufacturing, and when Taiichi Ohno, learning from Ford, since the 1950s created the Toyota Production System, international supply chains played no role.

One aspect figured prominently since the early days of the Toyota Production System: avoiding waste. Under the cramped conditions of ever more densely populated Japan, one of the principles of avoiding waste became the avoidance of space consuming storehouses, leading during the 1970s to the just-in-time delivery of parts into the assembly factory. This can be seen as the birth of supply chain management. At that time, however, the suppliers were mostly located in close vicinity of the assembly hall.

The idea of employing suppliers from far away, including from overseas, creeped in during the 1980s when transport costs plummeted and the international coordination of supply chains became technically feasible. During the 1990s, cost trimming and outsourcing, for cost reasons, became the undisputed mainstream of the economies of the world, giving birth to the new term of "globalization." Globalized capital markets and the rise of the Internet were additional driving forces for ever more globally integrated production chains.

During the euphoric 1990s, not much attention was given to potential downsides of this new kind of an international division of labour. The most important downside, it can be argued, has been the neglect of the environment. World-wide manufacturing systems involve enormous transportation, often by air cargo. World-wide distribution of goods makes recycling rather complicated. And generally, the rampant growth of mass manufacturing of all kinds of goods entailed swelling avalanches of waste. In parallel, gigantic mining schemes became ever more threatening to some of the last remaining natural habitats.

As environmental consciousness began spreading, the supply chains came under scrutiny by necessity. Environmentally minded consumers in the prosperous countries demanded increasing transparency on the part of the retailers, and soon a new kind of consultancy profession emerged: the ecological analysts of the supply chains.

Pressure is increasing on all countries that participate in the global supply chains to abide by ecological standards negotiated and agreed between manufacturers and governments or advocacy groups. Green life cycle certificates become strong sales arguments in some of the prosperous countries.

The Internet works in two important directions in this situation. On one hand, it allows advocacy groups to swiftly coordinate their research and their actions. On the other hand, it allows firms in all countries to optimize the use of resources and thereby to reduce their ecological footprints.

The National Tsing Hua University has taken the lead in addressing the challenges of the greening of the supply chains using modern communication technologies and the Web. I was proud to be invited to one of their pivotal conferences organized in Hsinchu by Professor Hsiao-Fan Wang, who also serves as editor of this volume.

The contributions to this book show an impressive and dynamic picture of what is going on world-wide in green supply chain management in general and in web-based improvements in particular. It is to be wished that this highly relevant new field of scientific inquiry and technological progress receives widest attention both in academia and in the globalized business world.

Ernst Ulrich von Weizsäcker
Dean, Donald Bren School of Environmental Science and Management,
UCSB, Santa Barbara, California, USA

Ernst Ulrich von Weizsäcker *received his physics diploma from the University of Hamburg, and his PhD in zoology from the University of Freiburg. He has numerous experience as a professor of biology at the University of Essen, president of the University of Kassel, director at the UN Centre for Science and Technology for Development in New York, director of the Institute for European Environmental Policy, Bonn-London-Paris, and president of the Wuppertal Institute for Climate, Environment, and Energy. From 1998-2005, he was a member of the German Parliament, chairman, Select Committee on Globalization, and later on the Environment Committee from 2002-2004. He was also a member of the World Commission on the Social Dimensions of Globalisation, dean of the Bren School for Environmental Science and Management, UCSB, Santa Barbara, California, USA, and co-chair of the UNEP International Panel on Resources. He has received many honors, including the Pfaff Prize in 1977 and Premio de Naturain in 1989, as well as becoming an honorary professor at the University of Valparaiso, Chile, in 1991. 1996. He received the Duke of Edinburgh Gold Medal in 1996, an honorary degree from Soka University, Tokyo, in 2000, and the Takeda Award in 2001. He is also listed in Who's Who in the World.*

Preface

Energy and environmental concerns are intricately linked to the supply chains of various goods. Increased public awareness of such issues is reflected in the contemporary business environment as well as government legislation. It is necessary to apply systematic techniques to quantify the environmental impacts of supply chains, and to identify opportunities for making improvements. This attributes to the life cycle management of a product. In particular, to urge a manufacturer to produce a product with higher production cost, which is the case for a green product; legislation is one way, and market demand is the other. Therefore, in order to develop effective marketing strategies under minimum environmental impact, investigation of life cycle management of green products from two aspects of supply chain management and demand chain management needs to be carried out.

Many companies today have a fairly good knowledge of the environmental impacts which their production causes, and they are experienced in preventing or limiting these impacts. However, very few have realized the environmental impacts in relation to their products through their lifecycle, from the production of raw materials to the production for use, and, in the end the disposal of the products. Therefore, the classification of green products based on their ready-made impacts to the environment is not effective to reduce the environmental impacts as the levels of pollution, consumed energy, and the amount of recycle. When regarding environment as natural resources, a product-centered environment management approach should be considered, as shown in Figure 1, such that the environmental impacts of a product throughout its life cycle will be measured as an accumulated effect. Then, not only can the overall impacts be realized, but also the stage-wise factors can be detected and integrated into the design stage of a product.

Figure 1. Ideas of green product environment management

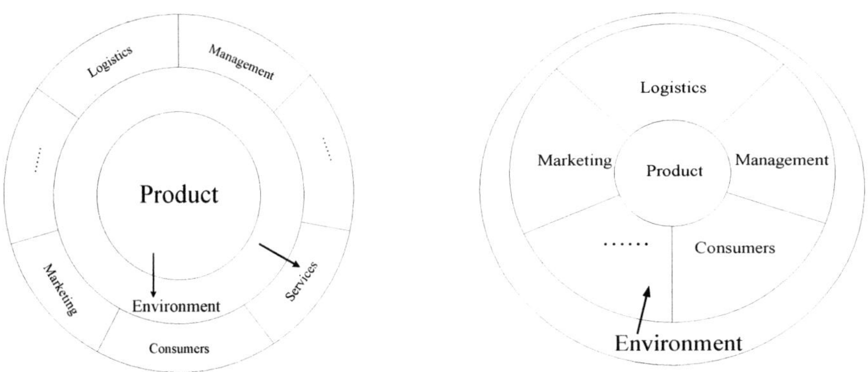

(a) Conventional environment management *(b) Product-centered environment management*

A strategic change such as the integration of product-centered environmental management in practice needs a solid basis for decision making. Therefore, it is important to both assess the environmental condition of the products, as well as the business opportunities, strategic intention, and market expectations. Market expectations are an essential motivation, which can be stimulated by focusing on the advantages gained by each party in the product chain. This leads to an important issue of establishing a channel between the customers and suppliers. Due to the rapid development of Internet technology, such a channel can be effectively built up on the Web site as a platform, of which a search engine for such information flow is thus important for both sides and the base for effective search relies on a well-established data base and efficient retrieval scheme.

Business opportunities are developed by realizing the recognition of green products of customers. Then, by identifying the targeted customers, effective marking strategies can be developed correspondingly. It has been considered as a critical difference between conventional supply chain management and green supply chain management that market demand for green products has been a push force for production, and its scale determines the success of recycled economy.

Since the 3Rs of Reduce, Recycle and Remanufacture are the basic requirement for green supply chain activities, a closed loop management from in-plant production to off-plant forward and reverse logistics has to be taken care of so that environmental impact and energy usage can be minimized.

Therefore, this book contains four main sections which include 18 chapters to address the different issues and solutions of a green product from its life cycle. After an overview of life cycle issues and concepts of green products is provided in Section I, methodologies and practice of green market and demand are discussed in Section II. Then, in Section III, issues of green supply chain management are tackled from both theoretical analysis and practical illustration. Finally, Web-based platforms for information retrieval and environmental management of a green product along its life cycle will be discussed in Section IV, which pave the way for effective supporting and cooperation between supply and demand. It can be noted from the well-balanced number of chapters related to demand and supply chains that methods related to Web site applications are comparatively rare and thus require the devotion of more researchers. The details of the content are described in the following.

There are six chapters in Section I: Life Cycle Assessment: Concept and Practice.

Chapter I provides an overall concept of life cycle assessment of green products and the quantitative method of measurement and ways of improvement for the industries. In particular, this chapter discusses life cycle assessment principles and its application in the design and planning of industrial supply chains. A specific case study on the production of biofuels from agricultural crops is used to illustrate the key concepts.

Chapter II provides a rigorous method of life cycle assessment based on the concept of quantitative physical flow analysis, known as industrial metabolism. A discussion of the reverse product-process chain, which includes reuse and recycling, is presented from the transformation of both the materials and also the energy. In particular, the chapter summarizes available types of software with examples which are very useful and valuable for applications in practice.

Chapter III discusses the life cycle management from the sustainability viewpoint, and proposes a useful strategy to reach the global sustainability based on the continuous evaluation of numerous complex social, ecological, and economic factors. Thus, the article not only brings about the issues of sustainability in the framework of life cycle management, but also provides an approach to arrive at it with detailed illustration.

Chapter IV discusses the environmental criteria which should be considered in green product management, and presents a method of environment impact assessment from MCDM approach. Therefore, not only can the environmental criteria be accessed from both the forward and reverse supply chains, but also the weights of their importance can be measured. A comprehensive case study of *a vacuum cleaner* is presented for illustration.

Chapter V is also a study which integrates the sustainability into life cycle management, while taking a system viewpoint toward environmental performance assessment. In particular, the chapter highlights the environmental issues in the framework of overall economic, geographical, and legislative factors so that the methodologies developed along this line have guidelines to reach system optimization.

Chapter VI introduces the concept of eco-efficiency, and in particular, provides two cases of European small- and medium-sized enterprises for detailed illustration and demonstration. The article emphasizes the diffusion-oriented policy so that reducing environmental burden can be achieved by guiding the companies to improve their resource productivity and add production values.

There are five chapters in Section II: Demand and Service Chain Management.

Chapter VII brings about a different and interesting view toward sustainability. Realizing the importance of marketing demand and customer response for green product development, this chapter presents a developed management game and concludes some propositions on the trust and sustainability in supply chains. The detailed description of the design of this game as well as the roles involved in this game along the overall supply chain have been provided, which facilitates practical implement. Also, further research along this line has been identified with a list of questions to be answered.

Chapter VIII presents a methodology of identifying target customers of green products for market expansion purposes. Based on a data mining technique, the customers can be classified according to their preference, purchasing behaviour and demographical factors. Then, by a developed bi-objective mathematical model, pricing strategies can be developed from win-win perspectives, which is beneficial for both the producers and the customers. The rigors analysis provides a tractable approach for market analysis and pricing development.

Chapter IX tackles a different but important issue related to green supply chain management, the facility location problem. Regarding the environmental impact, the issue is tackled by considering the undesirable locations. Using fuzzy TOPSIS approach, design of a group decision process is presented to find the criteria with their weights of undesirability. Measurement of conflict and vagueness among criteria and decision makers is presented with detailed illustration and numerical examples.

Chapter X presents an overall system for green service chain management, namely sustainable product service systems (S-PSS). By taking the factors of sustainability, resource productivity, and eco-efficiency into account, the article shows how the developing countries, in particular, can apply the system to trade off among these factors. Many practical cases are presented which provide significant references for both concept clarification and practical applications.

Chapter XI discusses the energy issues, in particular, green electricity and its renewability from historical development. Based on the literature review and the customer response, the article concludes a comprehensive approach toward green electricity utilization by identifying its development boundaries and past mistakes.

There are five chapters in Section III: Supply Chain and Logistics Management. The section can be regarded as the dual of the previous section.

Chapter XII opens another door toward green supply chain and logistics management. A mathematical model in the form of a 0-1 integer linear program is developed for close-loop logistics of which optimal solution for determining the facilities of manufactures, distribution centers and dismantlers can be found with minimum cost. Sensitivity analyses on the recovery rate and land-filling rate on the reverse logistics have been carried out for managerial purposes.

Chapter XIII provides an alternative method for reverse supply chain design. Realizing the efficiency issues of the collection facilities and recovery facilities chosen while designing a reverse supply chain, this chapter is based on neural network approach to develop a four-stage procedure for evaluating the facilities. Group decision techniques are in-cooperated with successful applications.

Chapter XIV takes a different approach of system dynamics methodology to develop a simulation model for evaluating different green supply chain management strategies. By measuring the total profit, the effectiveness of different strategies can be evaluated efficiently and successfully.

Chapter XV illustrates how to design a routing system for a distribution center to assign a number of limited-capacity vehicles to serve a given number of customers within the required time window with minimum service cost. An optimization model is formulated in the form of an integer linear program and a genetic algorithm is developed for efficient solution. Therefore, NP complexity problem embedded in such kinds of optimization problems have shown to be resolved with reasonable accuracy.

Chapter XVI discusses a recovery issue in reverse supply chain. Criteria and the proposed data envelopment method are presented to evaluate the used house appliance and automobiles. It aims that the cost added to the process of the recycled products will be justified by their economic and environmental benefit.

Finally, there are two chapters in Section IV: Web-based Management Technology. Current methodologies developed for Web site development and applications are presented.

Chapter XVII introduces a preference-based recommendation procedure in a green product information retrieval system. The online procedure is based on an off-line database which includes the description of the green products with their green properties and prices, and the relevant green regulations. The information retrieval procedure then is based on the preference of the users and by a data mining technique, the products can be recommended and the database can be updated simultaneously. The system is useful for both the consumers and the producers. A prototype has been developed and illustrated in the chapter.

Chapter XVIII discusses a different issue of Web-based green supply chain management. This online decision support system is developed for the stakeholders in reverse supply chain when they have different views, perspectives and priorities. The end-of-life mobile phones are taken as an illustrative example to show how this system supports a collaborative decision-making process on the Web site.

From the content described above, it can be noted that this book will be useful for both researchers and practitioners who are interested in receiving comprehensive views and insights from the variety of issues covered in this book in relation to green value chain management. In particular, those who have been working on supply chain management will have an overall picture of the existing and potential developments on the issues related to life-cycle management of a green product. Finally, it is expected that with different case studies introduced along with the presented concepts and methodologies, applications of green value chain management will be pushed forward a big step toward a cleaner globe.

Hsiao-Fan Wang
Tsing Hua Chair Professor
Hsinchu, Taiwan, ROC

ADDITIONAL READINGS

Baumgarten, H., Christian, B., Annerous, F., & Thomas, S.-D. (2003). Supply chain management and reverse logistics-integration of reverse logistics processes into supply chain management approaches. In *Proceedings of the International Symposium on Electronics and the Environment* (pp. 79-84).

Bowersox, D.J., & Closs, D.J. (1996). *Logistical management: The integrated supply chain process*. New York: McGraw-Hill.

De Groene, A., & Hermans, M. (1998). Economic and other implications of integrated chain management: A case study. *Journal of Cleaner Production*, 6, 199-221.

Fleischmann, M., Jacqueline, M.B.-R., Rommert, D., van der Laan, E., Jo, A.E.E., van Nunen, & van Wassenhove, L.N. (1997). Quantitative models for reverse logistics: A review. *European Journal of Operational Research, 16*, 1-17.

Hsu, P.Y., Chen, Y.L., & Ling, C.C. (2004). Algorithms for mining association rules in bag databases. *Information Sciences, 166*, 31-47.

Kohrs, K., & Meriadlo, B. (2001). Creating user adapted Web sites by the use of collaborative filtering. *Interacting with Computers*, 695-716.

Liu, D.R., & Shih, Y.Y. (2005). Integrating AHP and data mining for product recommendation based on customer lifetime value. *Information and Management, 42*, 387-400.

Montaner, L., López, B., & Rosa, J.L.D.L. (2003). A taxonomy of recommender agents on the Internet. *Artificial Intelligence Review, 19*(4), 285-330.

Salema, M.I.G., Barbosa-Povoa, A.P., & Novais, A.Q. (2007). An optimization model for the design of a capacitated multi-product reverse logistics network with uncertainty. *European Journal of Operational Research, 179*, 1063-1077.

Schultmann, F., Moritz, Z., & Otto, R. (2006). Modeling reverse logistic tasks within closed-loop supply chains: An example from the automotive industry. *European Journal of Operational Research, 171*, 1033-1050.

Wang, H.F., & Hong, W.K. (2006). Managing customer profitability in a competitive market by continuous data mining. *Industrial Marketing Management Journal, 35*, 715-723.

Wang, H.F., & Kuo, C.Y. (2006, April). 3-parameter fuzzy arithmetic approximation of L-R fuzzy number for fuzzy neural networks. *International Journal of Uncertainty and Knowledge-based Systems, 14*(2), 211-233.

Yang, H.W., Pan, Z.G., Wang, X.Z., & Xu, B. (2004). A personalized products selection assistance based on e-commerce machine learning. In *Proceedings of the 3rd International Conference on Machine Learning and Cybernetics*, Shanghai, China (pp. 26-29).

Zhu, Q., & Raymond P.C. (2004). Integrating green supply chain management into an embryonic eco-industrial development: A case study of the Guitang Group. *Journal of Cleaner Production, 12*, 1025-1035.

Acknowledgment

The editor would like to acknowledge the help of all involved in the collation and review process of the book, without whose support the project could not have been satisfactorily completed.

Deep gratitude is first sent to Professor Ernst Ulrich von Weizsäcke, dean of the Donald Bren School of Environmental Science and Management, UCSB, California, USA, for his foreword full of encouragement and kind support. We also would like to thank all authors for their excellent contributions to this volume. In particular, most of the authors of chapters included in this book also served as referees for chapters written by other authors. Thanks go to all those who provided comprehensive reviews and constructive comments. Special thanks also go to the publishing team at IGI Global, in particular, to Rebecca Beistline and Jessica Thompson, who continuously prodded via e-mail to keep the project on schedule, and to Mehdi Khosrow-Pour, whose enthusiasm motivated me to initially accept his invitation for taking on this project.

Special thanks go to National Tsing Hua University and the colleagues of the Department of Industrial Engineering and Engineering Management in Taiwan. Without their understanding and support, this volume would not be possible.

Finally, I wish to thank my boys, I-Fan (Daniel) and Tao-Fan (Ray), for their understanding and immense love during this project.

Editor,

Hsiao-Fan Wang
Tsing Hua Chair Professor
Vice Dean of the Engineering College
National Tsing Hua University
Taiwan, Republic of China
March 2008

Section I
Life Cycle Assessment:
Concept and Practice

Chapter I
Life Cycle Design, Planning, and Assessment

Raymond R. Tan
De La Salle University, Manila, Philippines

Alvin B. Culaba
De La Salle University, Manila, Philippines

Michael R. I. Purvis
University of Portsmouth, UK

Joel Q. Tanchuco
De La Salle University, Manila, Philippines

ABSTRACT

Energy and environmental concerns are intricately linked to the supply chains of various goods. Increased public awareness of such issues is reflected in the contemporary business environment as well as government legislation. Companies must not only comply with environmental regulations, but also contend with the need for increasingly green corporate practices in order to stay competitive in global markets. Thus, it is necessary to apply systematic techniques to quantify the environmental impacts of supply chains, and to identify opportunities for making improvements. This chapter discusses life cycle assessment principles and its application in the design and planning of industrial supply chains. A specific case study on the production of biofuels from agricultural crops is used to illustrate the key concepts.

Copyright © 2009, IGI Global, distributing in print or electronic forms without written permission of IGI Global is prohibited.

BACKGROUND

The past few decades have seen increased concern for environmental issues by companies, governments, and the general public. This trend was first apparent in regulatory limits on industrial pollutant discharges, which in turn led to the development of end-of-pipe treatment technologies. These techniques focus on the treatment and safe disposal of residues, and are still in use today when regulatory compliance needs to be ensured. However, such activities do not generate any savings or revenues, and are thus understandably viewed by companies as cost centers. In recent years, there has been considerable interest in pollution prevention (P2) or cleaner production (CP), in addition to pollution control. P2 or CP entails the use of strategies which attempt to give inherently clean solutions in order to minimize the need to treat wastes and residues. There is often the associated benefit of reducing the consumption of raw materials and utilities, which potentially generates cost savings in addition to environmental benefits. Examples of strategies used to achieve P2 or CP include:

- Use of environment-friendly materials;
- Product or process modifications to improve efficiency and reduce attendant environmental releases;
- Optimal operation of processes to minimize consumption of energy or raw materials and generation of waste; and
- Implementing exchange of waste streams between process or plants to achieve industrial symbiosis.

Any P2 or CP strategies to be implemented must be evaluated using systematic procedures to assess the potential environmental benefits

Figure 1. A generic life cycle system (Adapted from SETAC, 1991)

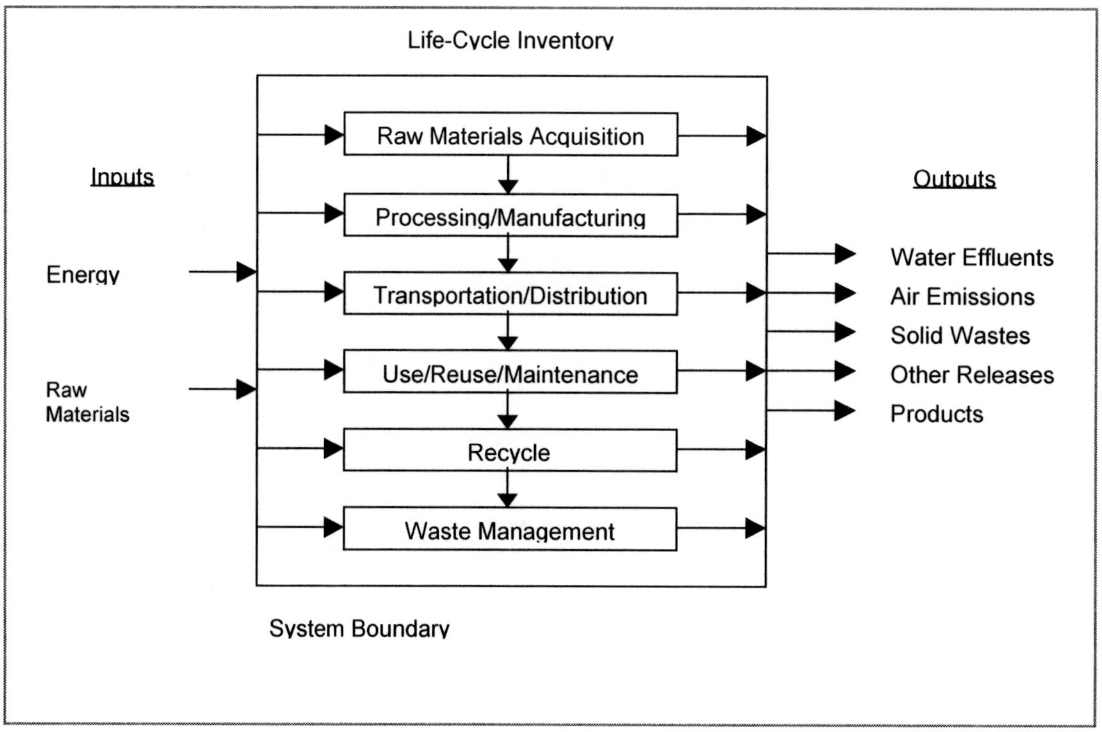

vis-à-vis investment costs. Such evaluations often implicitly require comparison of P2/CP options with each other, and with baseline technological choices. Normal profitability analysis techniques can be applied to deal with the economic considerations. On the other hand, systematic assessment methodologies must be applied to quantify the usage of natural resources, release of pollutants, and generation of environmental impacts of technology options being compared. One such methodology is known as life cycle assessment (LCA).

LCA is a methodology for assessing the cumulative material and energy flows and associated environmental impacts of industrial systems. In LCA, these flows and impacts are calculated on a *cradle-to-grave* basis, meaning that direct and indirect contributions over the entire supply chain are accounted for, as shown in Figure 1. The calculations are done relative to a unit of industrial output known as the *functional unit*, which serves as a basis for subsequent interpretation of environmental benefits. Furthermore, industrial activities generate multiple pollutants, which in turn result in different pathways for damaging the environment. LCA methodology takes into account these different environmental criteria. LCA can thus be used as a comprehensive and rigorous approach for evaluating different alternative P2/CP strategies.

Life cycle concepts are also essential in promoting the design of environment friendly products (Graedel & Allenby, 1996). For instance, manufacturers must consider not just environmental impacts arising directly from manufacture of such goods; the products must be designed to be environment friendly during use (for instance, by being energy efficient) and at the end of their useful lives (e.g., by being designed for ease of disassembly and recycling, or by being constructed out of materials that present no disposal difficulties). Legislation on extended producer responsibility (EPR) or product take-back, such as those specified for certain appliances in Japan or the European Union, are intended in part to encourage design of inherently clean products. Furthermore, such measures as the EU Directive for Setting Eco-Design Requirements for Energy-Using Products facilitate trading of manufactured goods across national borders. It is clear that environmental impacts occurring across the life cycle of a product will tend to be distributed geographically, and will also include time delays, and that the inherently distributed nature of these effects must be taken into account in the practice of green supply chain management.

HISTORICAL DEVELOPMENT OF LIFE CYCLE ASSESSMENT

The earliest forerunners of modern LCA methodology include resource and environmental profile analysis (REPA) and net energy analysis in the 1960s-1970s. These techniques focused on the quantification of material and energy flows over entire supply chains, without any formal consideration of environmental impacts. The oil crises of the 1970s triggered interest in alternative transportation fuels derived from agricultural products; for example, ethanol produced from corn or sugarcane can be used as a gasoline additive or extender. It was soon recognized that the farms and alcohol distilleries in the ethanol supply chains needed energy inputs themselves, and as a result a number of studies were done to determine whether or not such systems actually produced any net energy (Chambers, Herendeen, Joyce, & Penner, 1979; Weisz & Marshall, 1979). This debate continues to the present day, and net energy analysis is still used as a specialized form of LCA for such applications.

Modern LCA methodology is based on efforts in the early 1990s by the Society of Environmental Toxicology and Chemistry (SETAC) to develop a technical and methodological framework. The SETAC framework (1991) proposed four components of LCA methodology: goal and scope definition; inventory analysis; impact assessment; and improvement analysis. Each component in turn had a set of specific constituent activities. In the late 1990s, further developments toward standardization were established in the form of the ISO 14040 standards, which attempted to describe LCA principles and framework (ISO 14040), goal and scope definition and inventory analysis (ISO 14041), impact assessment (ISO 14043) and interpretation (ISO 14043). As a result of recent revisions, the latter three standards are no longer in use. Table 1 shows the current LCA standards.

Figure 1 shows the interaction of the four components of LCA under the ISO framework, along with potential direct applications of the methodology. More details of the methodology are described in the next section.

LIFE CYCLE ASSESSMENT METHODOLOGY

This section provides a brief description of LCA methodology. For further details, the interested reader is referred to Guinee (2002). The steps in conducting an LCA follow logically from the four components described in the ISO 14040 standards.

The goal and scope definition phase sets the parameters of the assessment. First, it is necessary

Table 1. The current ISO standards for LCA

Standard	Title and Content
14040	Principles and framework
14044	Requirements and guidelines
14047	Examples of application of ISO 14042
14048	Data documentation format

Figure 2. The framework of LCA (Adapted from ISO 14040, 1997)

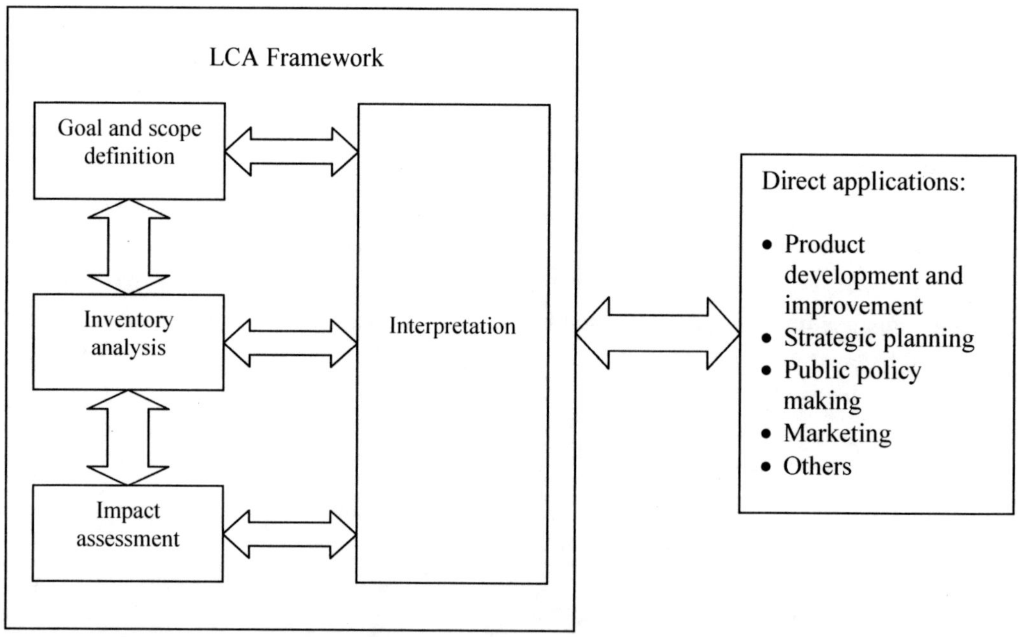

to define the purpose of the case study. The most common objectives are comparison of alternative technologies or strategies and the assessment of an existing system to identify opportunities to make to improvements. In some applications, the information may be used for marketing or product claim purposes, in which case review by an independent third party is called for. The scope of the study is also defined by identifying system boundaries, technological choices, and environmental flows and impacts of interest. Such choices require some background knowledge of the problem at hand; otherwise, a preliminary "screening" assessment may be necessary. Depending on the goals and context of the LCA, some steps may be omitted to expedite or *streamline* the assessment process. Finally, a functional unit that accurately reflects the goal of the LCA is selected.

Inventory analysis involves acquiring relevant flow data for processes that make up the life cycle system. The data can come from a combination of sources, such as theoretical material and energy balances, economic input-output tables, scientific publications, company records, or direct, site-specific measurements. In addition, databases are usually available in conjunction with commercial LCA software packages. These data are then put into a mathematical model that calculates the quantities of natural resources consumed and emission discharged per function unit. A summary of the calculations involved is given in the appendix, while a more comprehensive description of the computational theory of LCA can be found in Heijungs and Suh (2002). The calculations are normally done with the aid of computers, using either generic software (i.e., spreadsheets) or purpose-built LCA programs.

Impact assessment involves identifying which natural resource and emission flows contribute to environmental impact categories such as global warming, stratospheric ozone depletion, or acidification; this step is known as *classification*. The magnitudes, or potentials, of these contributions are also calculated (this step is called *characterization*) with the aid of characterization factors. For example, if a life cycle system generates 10g of carbon dioxide and 1g of methane emissions per functional unit output, the combined global warming potential of the two emissions streams can be calculated based on the relative potencies of the two substances in terms of global warming impact, as shown in Table 2. In this case, each g of methane causes as much global warming as 21g of carbon dioxide. Hence, the characterization factor of methane is said to be 21g carbon dioxide equivalents per gram (by definition, the characterization factor of carbon dioxide, which is used as the reference substance for global warming, is equal to unity; each gram of carbon dioxide is equivalent to one gram of itself). The given quantities of these two gases are thus equivalent to 31g of carbon dioxide, and the global warming impact is reported as 31g of carbon dioxide equivalents. Such a procedure is applied to all the relevant impact categories identified during the goal and scope definition phase. The impact potentials can then be normalized, for example, relative to background per capita impacts already being generated; and, finally, a measure of "total" or weighted average environmental impact can be

Table 2. Sample impact assessment calculations

Substance	Quantity Released (g)	GWP ($g\ CO_2$ eq./g)	Climate change impact ($g\ CO_2$ eq.)
Carbon dioxide (CO_2)	10	1	10
Methane (CH_4)	1	21	21
Total	11	---	31

calculated, if it is possible to identify weights that reflect the importance of these impact categories. This latter phase is known as *valuation*.

The final component of LCA is interpretation. This step is intended to see if the goals set forth are satisfied by the results of the inventory analysis and impact assessment phases. Because of uncertainties inherent in many of the steps of LCA, it is also necessary to assess the robustness of the findings by using techniques such as sensitivity analysis or Monte Carlo simulations. It is possible for the results of LCA to be inconclusive, in which case further assessment may be required with expanded scope or with new data. The next section describes a simple case study on a streamlined (i.e., simplified) LCA of clean fuels for automotive use.

ILLUSTRATIVE CASE: PRODUCTION OF BIOFUELS FROM AGRICULTURAL CROPS

Recent years have seen the revival of interest in alternative fuels derived from crops as substitutes for petroleum-based fuels such as gasoline in diesel. The interest is motivated in part by perennial volatility in global oil supplies, coupled with environmental concerns on the depletion of nonrenewable petroleum reserves and climate change. Oil-importing countries are understandably keen on reducing their dependence on foreign energy supplies by developing some substitutes derived from indigenous resources. The transportation sectors of such countries are particularly vulnerable, because these are almost entirely dependent on liquid, petroleum-based fuels. At the same time, carbon dioxide emissions from fuel use are prevalent in modern economies because transportation activities are involved in all industrial sectors.

To illustrate this point, Figure 3 shows carbon dioxide emissions of different sectors of the Philippine economy in the year 2000 per thousand pesos (approximately US$20) of contribution to GDP. These results were calculated from low-resolution economic input-output tables using the procedure shown in the appendix, and can thus be seen as carbon intensities of the different industrial sectors. Furthermore, these emissions are life-cycle

Figure 3. Sectoral carbon dioxide emissions in the Philippines

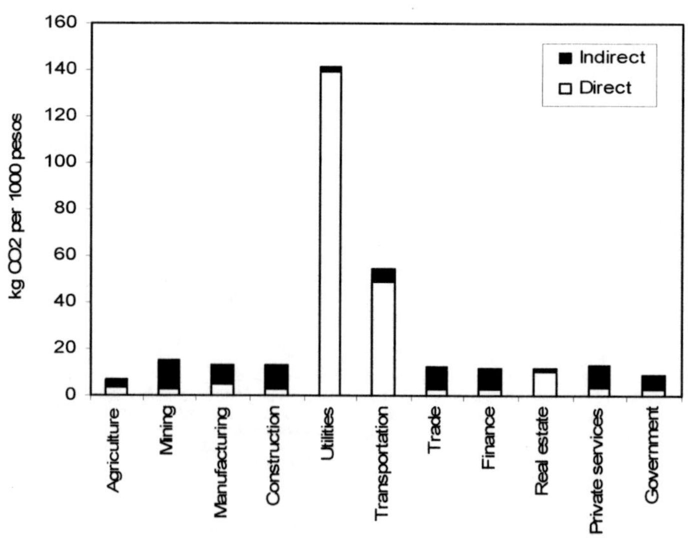

based; they include direct releases by a given sector, as well as indirect releases of the other parts of the economy that are part of the sector's supply chain. Life cycle principles are clearly linked to the interconnectivity inherent in modern economies. For instance, the manufacturing sector generates about 13kg of carbon dioxide per thousand pesos of output, but only about one-third of this total is generated directly by manufacturing activities; the remaining two-thirds is contributed by other sectors which supply inputs to manufacturing, for example, the utilities sector supplies electricity and water, agriculture and mining supply raw materials, and construction supplies capital goods such as buildings and factories. All these sectors contribute to the indirect emissions by virtue of supply chain linkages. It is notable that the utilities and transportation sectors have disproportionately high carbon intensities, and at the same time direct carbon dioxide emissions dominate these two sectors. Thus, there is considerable potential to reduce emissions in these sectors by modifying current fuel use patterns.

The use of agricultural crops to make liquid fuels for motor vehicles is not a new idea. For example, Brazil has sustained its *ProAlcool* program since the 1970s, and today about one-fifth of the fuel used in gasoline-powered vehicles is ethanol derived from sugarcane. Significant gains in agricultural and process yields have been realized over 3 decades through improvements in technology and management practices. While interest in such fuels has in the past fluctuated along with global oil prices, today concern about climate change provides additional incentive for such programs. Unlike fossil fuels like coal and petroleum, fuels derived from plant matter (often collectively known as *biofuels*) approach carbon neutrality, because the photosynthetic carbon fixation during crop growth offset the carbon dioxide emissions produced when the fuel product is burned. In practice, biofuel supply chains may require inputs (e.g., fertilizers, pesticides, and fuels for farm machinery) with associated carbon emissions, as illustrated in Figure 3. Nevertheless, net carbon dioxide emissions from biofuel supply chains can be significantly lower than those of conventional fuels. Use of the latter, by comparison, entails a net transfer of carbon from geological fossil fuel deposits into atmospheric carbon dioxide.

Despite economic gains associated with displacement of oil imports, and environmental benefits from reduced carbon dioxide emissions, biofuel initiatives have been criticized for diverting valuable land resources away from vital food production functions toward energy production (Nonhebel, 2005, 2007). Much work has been done to assess biofuel production potential by taking agricultural productivity and land availability into account. Developing countries, which are usually characterized by rapidly growing population, rising standards of living, and low agricultural productivities, must thus scrutinize biofuel alternatives carefully before committing valuable land resources to energy production. In the case of the Philippines, legislation has recently been passed by the government which mandates blending of biofuels into petroleum products at progressively higher percentages as production capacity is built up. The new law requires ethanol to be mixed with gasoline, and biodiesel derived from vegetable oil to be blended with diesel fuel.

Analysis of the issue is provided here under the assumption that ethanol is produced from sugarcane and biodiesel from coconut. The latter fuel is usually produced from coconut oil and methanol derived from fossil fuels (Tan, Culaba, & Purvis, 2004), but in this case we assume that case ethanol is used instead of methanol; the resulting product is a *coconut oil ethyl ester* (CEE). Note that the ethanol is used in gasoline-powered vehicles while the CEE is used in vehicles with diesel engines. Both types of vehicle can be assumed to provide comparable transportation service. At the same time, it is necessary to strike a balance between achieving reductions in carbon dioxide emissions, and minimizing use of valuable agricultural land for fuel production. Thus, a simple LCA is performed *to quantify carbon dioxide releases and land use per unit of transportation service delivered by each of the two biofuel supply chain options.*

Figure 4 shows the results for a system that makes use of biodiesel, or CEE, for vehicle propulsion. This supply chain requires 0.27 square meter-years of land use and generates 0.054kg of carbon dioxide per kilometer of transportation service output. Note that this scheme requires sugarcane farming and ethanol production as part of the biodiesel supply chain; however, none of the ethanol produced reaches the final consumer as it is fully consumed as a feedstock to make the CEE final product. The coconut and sugarcane farming activities contribute roughly equal amounts of carbon dioxide in this system. The biodiesel production system is partly dependent on external electricity supply, which in turn contributes to the system's fossil fuel usage and carbon dioxide emissions.

The corresponding result when ethanol is used for motor vehicle production is shown in Figure 5. This system generates 0.017kg of carbon dioxide emissions per kilometer (less than one-third of emission levels of the previous case, for the same level of final transportation output). On the other hand, the land usage is about 24% higher, at 0.34 square meter-years per kilometer. Note that many parts of the system are inactive. Large quantities of process residues in ethanol production, called *bagasse*, can be utilized to make the alcohol distillery energy self-sufficient (Oliverio, 2006), thus eliminating the need for an external electricity supply.

The fuel supply chain systems illustrated in Figures 4 and 5 represent the two extremes of a continuum. It is possible to have a system in which, on the average, each kilometer of transport service is produced by a mix of ethanol and CEE fuel products. Any intermediate mix will generate emissions and use land to degrees that fall between the corresponding values in the cases given here. The results can be summarized as follows:

- It is preferable to use ethanol instead of biodiesel (CEE) in order to minimize fossil carbon dioxide emissions
- It is preferable to use biodiesel instead of ethanol to minimize land use

Figure 4. Simplified biodiesel supply chain (Adapted from Tan, Culaba, & Aviso, 2008)

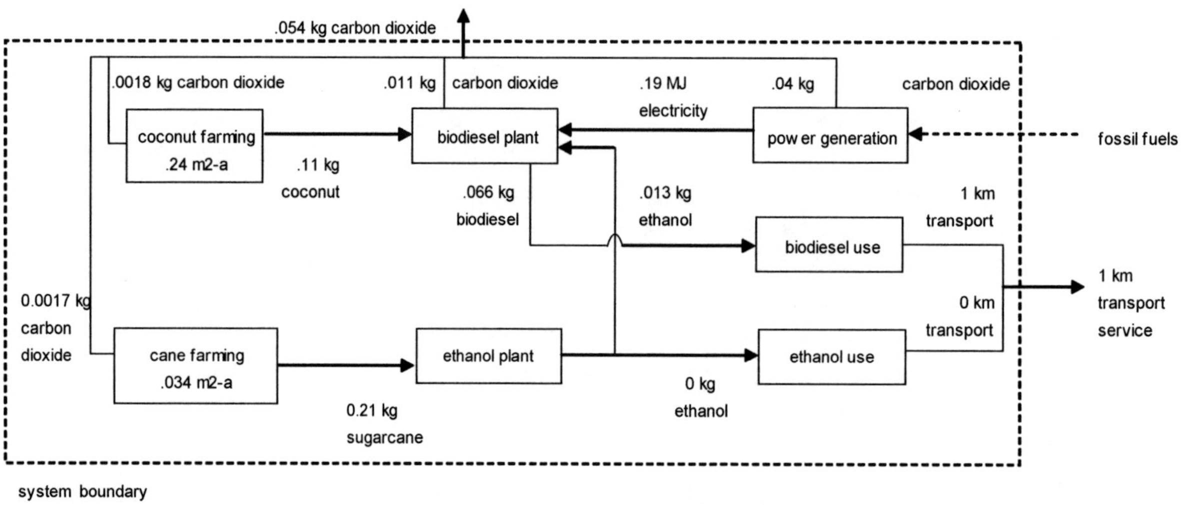

Figure 5. Simplified ethanol supply chain (Adapted from Tan et al., 2008)

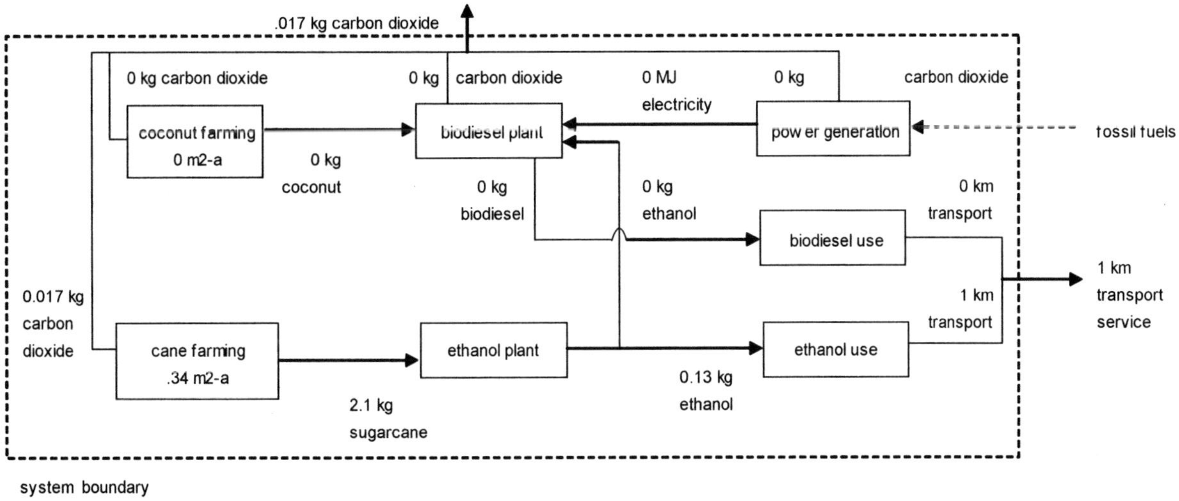

Results such as these often arise in LCA, in which no technological alternative emerges as a clear winner. In this instance, both options are Pareto optimal; however, in general dominated alternatives can be eliminated to allow for a reduced number of viable Pareto optimal ones to be compared further (Azapagic & Clift, 1999). Inherently conflicting results can arise in the presence of multiple environmental criteria, and they can only be resolved by providing quantitative measures of the relative values, or weights, of the criteria used. Various decision analysis techniques can be brought to bear on such problems (Seppala, Basson, & Norris, 2002).

FUTURE TRENDS AND RESEARCH DIRECTIONS

Although LCA methodology has progressed rapidly in the past decade, there are still considerable opportunities for methodological advances and new applications. For example, development of land use impact categories started only recently (Dubreuil & Muller-Wenk, 2007), and it is highly probable that new impact categories will be developed in the future. In applications involving crops or water-intensive industrial processes such as electricity generation, the concept of *virtual water* (Allan, 1997; Bouwer, 2000), which is the cumulative water embodied in all industrial activities in a supply chain, may become an important constraint in many production systems.

Conventional LCA methodology is *descriptive* in nature; it allows environmental flows and impact to be quantified for a given state of technology and system configuration. The flow of information is summarized in Figure 6. Some work has been done in the integration of life cycle thinking with optimization models (Azapagic & Clift, 1995, 1999; Tan, 2005; Tan et al., 2008). Unlike conventional LCA, these hybrid methodologies are *normative* (their solutions say what technological states and system configurations are needed to achieve desired environmental performance levels). These models have to contend with the fundamentally multicriterion nature of LCA, and more work needs to be done on improving these approaches. Furthermore, optimization has to be done even with the considerable uncertainties

Figure 6. Flow of information in conventional LCA

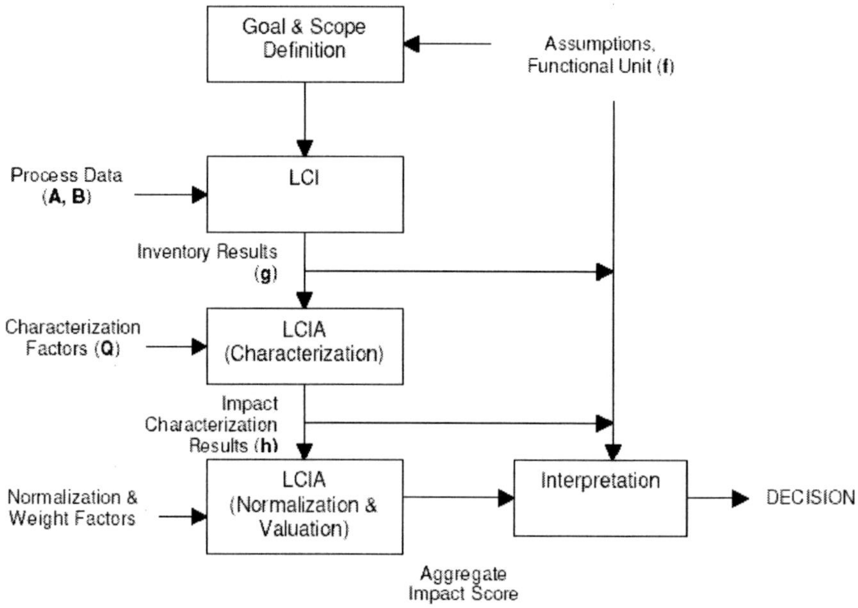

normally found in LCA data, which requires fuzzy or stochastic model formulations.

In practice, the use of LCA is often hindered by the extensive data requirements needed to implement the steps prescribed in the ISO 14040 standards. Alternative approaches that make use of life cycle concepts, but which are much less rigorous than full LCA, may have many applications. For example, economic input-output tables can be used as a basis for LCA computations (Heijungs & Suh, 2002; Hendrickson, Lave, & Matthews, 2006). Such an EIO-LCA approach is, of course, still limited by the availability of sufficiently disaggregated input-output tables and emissions inventory records. It has been demonstrated to be workable when such data is available, and interested readers are advised to use an online, open access EIO-LCA model developed in Carnegie-Mellon University at http://www.eiolca.net. EIO-LCA models can be used by themselves, or as components of much larger hybrid models. There is also interest in streamlined LCA (SLCA) methods, which attempt to simplify LCA methodology by omitting some steps, or reducing data requirements (Graedel, 1998). SLCA can, for example, be limited to a small number of highly important environmental flows or impact criteria, as in the biofuel case study used in the previous section. Such choices can be made during goal and scope definition, but there is always a risk that potentially important results may be missed in SLCA. In any case, SLCA will always entail a tradeoff between ease of implementation and reliability of results. Hence, some research is now needed on how to determine the degree to which LCA may be simplified, or streamlined, without unduly compromising the value of the assessment findings.

Furthermore, it is essential to integrate LCA methodology with other aspects of supply chain research; for example, there is plenty of opportunity to model the supply chains of emerging technologies, such as fuel hydrogen or nanotechnology, well before distribution networks and infrastructure are in place (Grossmann, 2004; Shah, 2005). This situation bypasses the technological inertia or "lock-in" now encountered with existing systems, and presents important opportunities for designing inherently sustainable life cycle systems or supply chains from the ground up. In such cases, dynamic LCA models will be needed to determine the environmental effects of technological development and market penetration over time; the models will also be useful for selecting the best policy intervention measures to give the most favorable economic and environmental trajectories over time.

Another trend that is to be expected as life cycle concepts become integral to decision-making in industry is the increased emphasis on training and education on its fundamental principles. In addition to specialized postgraduate programs on LCA and allied fields, life cycle thinking will become integrated into environmental management and design modules. Aside from its entry into formal curriculum, informal educational channels such as industrial seminars and e-learning packages should become increasingly prevalent, especially for practicing supply chain professionals.

CONCLUSION

LCA methodology allows resource consumption, emissions release, and environmental impact generation of industrial systems to be evaluated, while taking into account the inherent interconnectivity of the processes that comprise them. It thus yields valuable insights on how such environmental effects can be reduced by improving technology or network configuration. The concept of the industrial life cycle has evolved over 4 decades, with considerable advances toward standardization of methodology being made from the mid-1990s onward. There has thus been corresponding improvement in the reliability, consistency, and ease of interpretation of LCA findings. LCA is now used for many major environmental issues of global concern, as demonstrated here on the issue of land use and carbon emissions arising from the production of different alternative fuels. The future should see more LCA applications, as well as methodological advances, including life-cycle based optimization models, dynamic LCA, SLCA, and software implementations of these new computing approaches.

ACKNOWLEDGMENT

Some of the material used in this chapter was developed thanks to the support of the European Commission Asia Link Project Contract 2005/109-629, and from a grant by the University Research Coordination Office of De La Salle University, Manila, Philippines.

REFERENCES

Allan, J. A. (1997). *Virtual water: A long-term solution for water-short Middle Eastern economies.* Retrieved July 6, 2008, from www.soas.ac.uk/waterissues/occasionalpapers/OCC03.PDF

Azapagic, A., & Clift, R. (1995). Life cycle assessment and linear programming environmental optimization of product systems. *Computers and Chemical Engineering, 19*, 229-234.

Azapagic, A., & Clift, R. (1999). Life cycle assessment and multiobjective optimization. *Journal of Cleaner Production, 7*, 135-143.

Bouwer, H. (2000). Integrated water management: Emerging issues and challenges. *Agricultural Water Management, 45*, 217-228.

Chambers, R., Herendeen, R., Joyce, J., & Penner, P. (1979). Gasohol: Does it or doesn't it produce positive net energy? *Science, 206*, 790-795.

Dubreuil, Gaillard, G., & Muller-Wenk, R. (2007). Key elements in a framework for land use impact assessment within LCA. *International Journal of Life Cycle Assessment, 12*, 5-15.

Graedel, T. E. (1998). *Streamlined life cycle assessment.* NJ: Prentice Hall.

Graedel, T. E., & Allenby, B. (1996). *Design for environment.* NJ: Prentice Hall.

Grossmann, I. E. (2004). Challenges in the new millennium: Product discovery and design, enterprise and supply chain optimization, global life cycle assessment. *Computers and Chemical Engineering, 29*, 29-39.

Guinee, J. B. (Ed.). (2002). *Handbook on life cycle assessment: Operational guide to the ISO standards.* Dordrecht, The Netherlands: Kluwer.

Heijungs, R., & Suh, S. (2002). *The computational structure of life cycle assessment.* Dordrecht, The Netherlands: Kluwer.

Hendrickson, C. T., Lave, L. B., & Matthews, H. S. (2006). *Environmental life cycle assessment of goods and services. An input-output approach.* Washington, DC: RFF Press.

ISO 14040. (2006). *Environmental management—life cycle assessment—principles and framework.* Geneva, Switzerland: International Organisation for Standardisation.

ISO 14044. (2006). *Environmental management—life cycle assessment—requirements and guidelines.* Geneva, Switzerland: International Organisation for Standardisation.

ISO 14047. (2003). *Environmental management—life cycle assessment—examples of the application of ISO 14042.* Geneva, Switzerland: International Organisation for Standardisation.

ISO 14048. (2002). *Environmental management—life cycle assessment—data documentation format.* Geneva, Switzerland: International Organisation for Standardisation.

Nonhebel, S. (2005). Renewable energy and food supply: Will there be enough land? *Renewable and Sustainable Energy Reviews, 9*, 191-201.

Nonhebel, S. (2007). Energy from agricultural residues and consequences for land requirements for food production. *Agricultural Systems, 94*, 586-592.

Oliverio, J. L. (2006). Technological evolution of the Brazilian sugar and alcohol sector: Dedini's contribution. *International Sugar Journal, 108*, 120-126.

Parikka, M. (2004). Global biomass fuel resources. *Biomass and Bioenergy, 27*, 613-620.

Seppala, J., Basson, L., & Norris, G. A. (2002). Decision analysis frameworks for life cycle impact assessment. *Journal of Industrial Ecology, 5*, 45-68.

Shah, N. (2005). Process industry supply chains: Advances and challenges. *Computers and Chemical Engineering, 29*, 1225-1235.

Society for Environmental Toxicology and Chemistry. (1991). *A technical framework for life cycle assessments.* Washington, D.C.

Tan, R. R. (2005). Application of symmetric fuzzy linear programming in life cycle assessment. *Environmental Modelling and Software, 20*, 1343-1346.

Tan, R. R., Culaba, A. B., & Aviso, K. B. (2008). A fuzzy linear programming extension of the general matrix-based life cycle model. *Journal of Cleaner Production, 16,* 1358-1367.

Tan, R. R., Culaba, A. B., & Purvis, M. R. I. (2004). Carbon balance implications of coconut biodiesel utilization in the Philippine automotive transport sector. *Biomass and Bioenergy, 26*, 579-585.

Weisz, P. B., & Marshall, J. F. (1979). High grade fuels from biomass farming: Potentials and constraints. *Science, 206*, 24-29.

ADDITIONAL READING

Asif, M., & Muneer, T. (2007). Energy supply, its demand and security issues for developed and emerging economies. *Renewable and Sustainable Energy Reviews, 11*, 1388-1413.

Berndes, G., Hoogwijk, M., & van den Broek, R. (2003). The contribution of biomass in the future global energy supply: A review of 17 studies. *Biomass and Bioenergy, 25*, 1-28.

Fischer, G., & Schrattenholzer, L. (2001). Global bioenergy potentials through 2050. *Biomass and Bioenergy, 20*, 151-159.

Heijungs, R., & Suh, S. (2006). Reformulation of matrix-based LCI: From product balance to process balance. *Journal of Cleaner Production, 14*, 47-51.

Hoogwijk, M., Faaij, A., van den Broek, R., Berndes, G., Gielen, D., & Turkenburg, W. (2003). Exploration of the ranges of the global potential of biomass for energy. *Biomass and Bioenergy, 25*, 119-133.

Kondili, E. M., & Kaldellis, J. K. (2007). Biofuel implementation in East Europe: Current status and future prospects. *Renewable and Sustainable Energy Reviews, 11*, 2137-2151.

McCormick, K., & Kaberger, T. (2007). Key barriers for bioenergy in Europe: Economic conditions, know-how and institutional capacity, and supply chain co-ordination. *Biomass and Bioenergy, 31*, 443-452.

Suh, S. (2004). Functions, commodities and environmental impacts in an ecological-economic model. *Ecological Economics, 48*, 451-467.

Suh, S., & Huppes, G. (2005). Methods for life cycle inventory of a product. *Journal of Cleaner Production, 13*, 687-697.

von Blottnitz, H., & Curran, M. A. (2007). A review of assessments conducted on bio-ethanol as a transportation fuel from a net energy, greenhouse gas, and environmental life cycle perspective. *Journal of Cleaner Production, 15*, 607-619.

APPENDIX: SUMMARY OF COMPUTATIONAL ASPECTS OF LCA

Process-Based Life Cycle Inventory Analysis (LCI)

The content of this section is based on Heijungs and Suh (2002) and Tan et al. (2008). The basic model for inventory analysis describes the overall material and energy balances for a life cycle system. In the model, inflows and outflows are denoted with negative and positive values, respectively. For each process, the ratios of the energy and material flows remains fixed regardless of scale; thus, each process can be scaled up or down by multiplying all its flows with a scaling factor. The flow balances are such that the net output of the system is equal to the specified net output or functional unit:

$$\mathbf{As} = \mathbf{f} \tag{A.1}$$

where:

$\mathbf{A}$ = technology matrix
$\mathbf{f}$ = functional unit vector
$\mathbf{s}$ = scaling vector

The matrix **A** summarizes the flow of economic commodities. The columns of **A** correspond to processes, while its rows correspond to goods or services. Each element of the scaling vector **s** gives the factor by which the model expands or contracts a corresponding process column to ensure that the net output of the system is equal to the functional unit, given by **f**. Furthermore, for each process there are inflows of natural resources and outflows of emissions. The total inventory flows for the entire system is given by:

$$\mathbf{Bs} = \mathbf{g} \tag{A.2}$$

where:

$\mathbf{B}$ = intervention matrix
$\mathbf{g}$ = inventory vector

The matrix **B** contains extensions of the same processes as in **A**, but it lists environmental flows across the system boundaries. Scaling vector **s** applies to **B** as well, to yield the **g** which gives the total quantities of natural resource used and emissions generated by the system. If **A** is a square matrix, there is a one-to-one correspondence between processes and economic commodities, and Equations A.1 and A.2 combine to give:

$$\mathbf{g} = \mathbf{BA}^{-1}\mathbf{f} \tag{A.3}$$

It is possible for some systems to yield a nonsquare technology matrix **A**, in which case, different methodologies based on allocation or displacement can be used to yield a square **A** matrix; detailed discussion is given by Heijungs and Suh (2002). The latter case results in an underdetermined system, which provides opportunities for optimization once a suitable measure of overall performance can be specified.

continued on following page

APPENDIX: CONTINUED

Economic Input-Output-Based Inventory Analysis

The similarity between life cycle models and economic input-output models allows the latter to be used for inventory analysis applications. Details can be found in Heijungs and Suh (2002) and Hendrickson et al. (2006). The inventory vector **g** can be found alternatively using:

$$\mathbf{g} = \mathbf{R}(\mathbf{I} - \mathbf{Z})^{-1}\mathbf{y} \qquad (A.4)$$

where:

$\mathbf{R}$	=	sectoral intervention matrix
$\mathbf{I}$	=	identity matrix
$\mathbf{Z}$	=	technical coefficient matrix
$\mathbf{y}$	=	net output vector

Note the strong structural similarity between Equations A.3 and A.4.

Life Cycle Impact Assessment

This section is also based on Heijungs and Suh (2002). The characterization phase of impact assessment can also be expressed in compact matrix notation as:

$$\mathbf{h} = \mathbf{Q}\mathbf{g} \qquad (A.5)$$

where:

$\mathbf{h}$	=	impact vector in LCIA characterization model
$\mathbf{Q}$	=	characterization matrix in LCIA model

The matrix **Q** contains the characterization factors of the inventory flows listed in **g** with respect to impact categories listed in **h**. In principle, it is also possible to determine a single overall environmental performance index, provided that appropriate weight values are known:

$$e = \Sigma_i\, w_i\, h_i \qquad (A.6)$$

where:

e	=	aggregate environmental impact score
w_i	=	weight of impact category i
h_i	=	impact score with respect to category i

Chapter II
Industrial Metabolism:
Materials and Energy Flow Studies

A. J. D. Lambert
Technische Universiteit Eindhoven, The Netherlands

ABSTRACT

This chapter introduces the concept of quantitative physical flow analysis, known as industrial metabolism, which is a basis for modeling the environmental impact of products in the course of their life-cycles. This also includes a discussion of the reverse product-process chain, which includes reuse and recycling. Apart from transformation of materials, also transformation of energy is discussed. This is followed by the introduction of gross energy requirement. After this, the life-cycle assessment method is explained. After this, a section on available types of software is presented, followed by some examples from practice that illustrate the value of quantitative modeling. Finally, some future trends are discussed and a conclusion is given.

INTRODUCTION

Design and management of environmentally conscious products and production processes has various aspects that require a multidisciplinary approach. As the complete life-cycle of products has to be considered for a thorough analysis, which is a prerequisite in assessing the environmental performance of a product, the problem grows still more complicated. Because dealing with all those aspects in a satisfactory way is hardly possible, we are obliged to restrict our approach to those aspects of the reality that are particularly relevant to our purposes, thus simplifying the reality by means of modeling. Such models thus do not provide us with the complete truth, but modeling opens the way toward investigating some relationships that cannot be made available by other ways.

The aspects that are highlighted in this chapter refer to the physical basis that is inherent to the production of commodities and the impact that this has on the environment. This manifests itself by the fact that the relation of the product's life-cycle with its environment is understood in terms of materials and energy flows. In frequently used environmental analysis techniques, such as life-

Copyright © 2009, IGI Global, distributing in print or electronic forms without written permission of IGI Global is prohibited.

cycle assessment, the analysis of materials and energy flows is at the basis of these methods.

Such an approach is incorporated in *industrial metabolism*, which is a subdomain of *industrial ecology*, although some confusion on the precise use of these concepts can be detected in the literature.

INDUSTRIAL ECOLOGY AND INDUSTRIAL METABOLISM

The Origin of Industrial Ecology

Industrial ecology is an approach to minimize the environmental impact of human economic activities by means of mimicking the nature, which implies that no finite resources are consumed and no waste is produced.

The history of industrial ecology has its roots in growing consciousness about the finiteness of the natural resources that provide us with a supply of raw materials. Confronted with a growing population and with the globally rapidly increasing pro capita consumption, science has long attempted to quantify the impact of these phenomena. An early attempt has been made by Thomas R. Malthus, who published in 1798 a rather pessimistic vision in his principal work: *"An essay on the principle of population."* He argued that the linear growth in possible (agricultural) resources was never able to cope with the requirements of an exponentially growing population. Later on, other scientists have developed various alternative theories, some of them optimistic and other rather pessimistic. In the sixties of the 20th century, for instance, some extremely optimistic opinions were published, from which Herman Kahn was a notorious exponent (see, e.g., Kahn & Wiener, 1967).

In the same years, more worried authors, who observed overuse of natural resources, started to publish. Since the Apollo project brought men in space, who saw the Earth as a tiny and vulnerable sphere, called *"spaceship Earth,"* people such as Buckminster Fuller (1963) and Kenneth Boulding (1966) were inspired to formulate criticism on those optimistic and careless attitudes: *"Anyone who believes exponential growth can go on forever is either a madman or an economist."* Boulding's plea was to reconsider the physical roots of economy. These can be found in the first and second law of thermodynamics, which refer to energy conservation and to growing disorder, respectively. The way of thinking with regard to this postulate is called *neo-Malthusianism*.

The Report of the Club of Rome (Meadows, Meadows, & Randers, 1972) soon confronted a more extended public with the results of such studies. In this report, a dynamic modeling approach has been utilized aimed at forecasting the future according to a variety of scenarios. About in the same time, the term *"industrial ecology"* had been coined by Evan (1974), who advocated a broad, multi-disciplinary approach with an emphasis on social sciences.

Later on, possibly unaware of Evan's work, a more dedicated interpretation of this term had been proposed, particularly by Frosch and Gallopoulos (1989), who referred to a globally organized closed-cycle economy. The drastic restructuring of industrial processes was considered a crucial condition for attaining this objective. The term *"industrial ecology'* was assigned to the attempt for mimicking the natural processes in the industrial system, particularly the use of renewable energy resources and the closing of materials cycles. The authors stressed that no waste was produced in the natural environment, but instead, everything was recycled. The authors stated this as follows: *"Wastes from one industrial process can serve as the raw materials for another, thereby reducing the impact of industry on the environment."*

In the same couple of years, the related concept of *sustainability* was introduced by Brundtland (1987). Awareness of this originally came from development economics: It is intended to meet the needs of the present generation in such a way that the needs of the future generations will not become compromised by present-day consumption. Although often erroneously used for protecting the actual high level of consumption in industrialized countries instead of the environment and the poor, protection of the latter is nevertheless exactly what is meant by Brundtland, who emphasizes *"the essential needs of the world's poor, to which overriding priority should be given,"* and also stresses *"the preservation and protection of diverse ecosystems."* She stated that both of these aspects should have absolute priority in a sustainable economy.

The concept of industrial ecology, such as formulated by Frosch and Gallopoulis (1989), has been used in a broader sense, including the complete field of environmental consciousness in industry.

Industrial Metabolism

In order to confine the scope on physical flows, the term *"industrial metabolism"* was coined by Ayres and Simonis (1994). Other authors, particularly Graedel and Allenby (1995) still used the term *"industrial ecology"* for the same type of study that was intended to be covered by industrial metabolism.

Although the name of any approach might be of merely academic importance, a clear definition of concepts is useful to avoid confusion. Therefore, we agree that industrial metabolism refers to the physical flow approach. Apart from this, it uses the characteristics that are listed below, which are compiled from the work of various authors. We thus leave the term "industrial ecology" for the broader approach, including management issues and social sciences, such as defined by Evans.

The main characteristics of industrial metabolism are:

- It studies the anthropogenic materials and energy flows
- It is an integrated view
- It is based on systems theory
- It can be applied on various levels of aggregation, varying from process-oriented to global
- It has an emphasis on physical flows, which are materials and energy flows
- It is quantitatively oriented
- It is life-cycle oriented
- It attempts to minimize the environmental impact of these flows via mimicking the natural cycles

Although industrial metabolism can be carried out on a high level of aggregation, for example, globally, in a country of region, or in an industrial branch, it is also possible to apply the same approach to lower levels of aggregation. The basic ideal is always the closing of the cycles.

Industrial symbiosis and Process Integration

Industrial metabolism is sometimes confused with *industrial symbiosis*, which refers to the exchange of resources between companies that are located on the same site (eco-industrial park) or in the same region (eco-region). It thus is a subdomain of industrial metabolism. This concept has been derived from a promising case of exchange of materials and energy between some companies located in Kalundborg, Denmark (see Côté & Hall, 1995; Lowe & Evans, 1995). There are various examples of exchange of byproducts with nearby companies, such as that of the Corus plant in IJmuiden, The Netherlands. Byproducts are gases, slag, steam, and coal tar. The gases are combusted in a nearby power plant; the slag is partly processed to a fertilizer and partly used in the cement industries by plants (Mekog and Cemij) that are located at the same site; steam has been used as process steam in the pulp and paper industry. Coal tars from the coke plant are processed in a separate plant (Cindu) at a location about 20km distant. Although eco-industrial parks pretend to be based on this concept, the reality is often less far-reaching as the original concept: Apart from the establishment of some collective services such as waste management and the purchase of energy, there is often few left of the original idea.

Process integration is the use of resources from a process by another process at the same location of a company. From this, *heat integration* via heat-exchangers is widely used, which has resulted in considerable energy savings. This concept has been developed by crude oil refineries for optimizing their fuel efficiency. Another frequently applied technique is the integration of water flows inside a production plant, often called *water-pinch* (see Buehner & Rossiter, 1996).

BASIC CONCEPTS OF INDUSTRIAL METABOLISM

Systems Approach

System and Universe

As in every concept, the reality (called: *universe*) is mapped onto a model, which is always a simplification of reality. This modeling occurs according to a set of definite assumptions and rules. Usually, the modeler wants to consider only part of the reality and is restricted to a well-defined set of aspects he or she wants to consider. The part of the reality that appears in the model is separated from the rest of the universe by the *systems boundary*. The model is called a *system* because it is considered a set of *related objects*. If the structure of these components of the system is kept unclear, the system is called a *black box*. The systems boundary usually cannot be considered a spatially defined entity. Frequently, it is rather vague and ambiguous.

Obviously, the system is not completely isolated from the rest of the universe. However, the interaction between system and universe does not take place to every part of the universe, but rather to a specific part of it, which is called the *environment* of the system.

The relevant aspects of the reality that are positioned in the environment are said to be *externalized* from the system. Some of these aspects, however, can impose constraints to the behavior of the system itself. An example of this is legislation: the process of establishing legislation is not studied in industrial metabolism, but it can impose constrains on, for example, emissions.

System Structure

If one starts with a black box approach, the relevant relationships between the system and its environment must be considered. In some cases, this can be done indeed without any knowledge of the interior of the system. Often, however, the system's internal structure must be revealed to some extent. In particular, this is relevant when modifications of the system are investigated. In this case, we say that the *black box must be opened.*

As noticed before, a system consists of a set of related *objects*. These on their own can also be considered as systems. For this reason, the objects are called *subsystems*. These can be approached as black boxes that can be opened in turn, if desired. Self-evidently, this procedure can be applied repeatedly if desirable.

Opening a black box and considering the internal structure of a system is an example of *disaggregation*, which is a splitting up of an entity in its separate subentities. The reverse action is called *aggregation*.

Physical Systems

Physical systems are those systems in which the objects are *transformation processes* of materials and energy, and the relationships are *flows* of materials and energy. Materials and energy are subjected to the laws of physics, from which mass and energy conservation are the most fundamental ones. Additionally, the second law of thermodynamics (law of increasing disorder) is of crucial importance for physical systems. Besides this, other physical laws such as chemical reaction equations must also be considered. Notice that energy is involved in every kind of transformation process.

Technosystem and Ecosystem

Industrial metabolism focuses on the *technosystem.* The environment of the technosystem consists mainly of the *ecosystem* (biosphere, soil, hydrosphere, and atmosphere). Part of the lithosphere (the Earth's crust) can also be considered part of the technosystem's environment, as this is accessible via mining and drilling.

The *technosystem* is the entirety of materials and energy that is controlled by humans.

The *ecosystem* is the habitat of organisms. It is composed of the biosphere, which includes all living and dead biomass, and the abiotic environment in which organisms are living: the atmosphere, the hydrosphere (seawater, surface water, groundwater), and the soil.

It is unavoidable that the systems boundary between technosystem and ecosystem is rather abstract and arbitrary: it is not like a distinct spatial barrier. Strictly spoken, the technosystem is part of the ecosystem as it has been emerged from this, but in the systems approach, subsystems can be taken apart aimed at studying those aspects of it that are distinct from its environment, which is the rest of the system. In the industrial metabolism approach, the interaction between the ecosystem and the technosystem is studied in terms of physical flows. Flows that are entering the technosystem are said to be *extracted*, flows that are leaving the technosystem are said to be *discharged.*

Other crucial influences of the technosystem on the ecosystem, particularly the destruction of habitat and biodiversity, are not explicitly studied in industrial metabolism, although an efficient utilization of area must always be kept in mind.

Life-Cycle Approach

Introduction

In the actual industrial system one is aware of the fact that a single production process or plant cannot be considered isolated from preceding and subsequent processes. The majority of the products pass through various processes that are carried out in multiple companies. This is further emphasized by the current practices of globalization and outsourcing. The environmental impact of any product thus extends beyond a single process or company. The complete product life-cycle must be considered, not only upstream up to extraction but also downstream to include consumption and end-of life processing. This is called the "cradle to grave" approach.

This needs some clarification, as two concepts of life-cycle are frequently tangled up in the literature:

- **The conceptual life-cycle**, which runs from design via production and product maturity to product obsolescence.
- **The physical life-cycle**, which runs from extraction of raw materials via production and consumption to discharge.

In industrial metabolism, the physical life-cycle is considered. Life-cycle studies are frequently carried out aimed at improving product design, because good product design is crucial for a sound environmental performance.

Origin of the Life-Cycle Approach

First of all, we will trace back the efforts of determining the energy use over the complete life-cycle that have been triggered by the 1973 oil crisis and the 1979 energy crisis. These events forced the industrialized countries to realize how dependent they have become of oil, which mainly resides in rather politically unstable regions.

Aimed at quantifying the impact of raising energy prices on the economy as a whole, methods have been developed and advocated by the International Federation of Institutes of Advanced Studies (IFIAS) for the determination of the Gross Energy Requirement (GER) of a product (see IFIAS, 1973). The GER method follows the product from cradle to grave, that is, during its complete life-cycle. By this, substitution mechanisms could be studied by which the energy-intensive materials are replaced by substitutes that are produced at lower expense of energy. The GER method is explained in the section entitled Gross Energy Requirement.

Authors such as Chapman and Roberts (1983) applied this concept to metals, particularly those metals from which the ore grade was gradually decreasing because of depletion of the most abundant resources. They realized themselves that the GER of a product based on recycled materials was often far below that of the same product, made from primary materials. As metals can relatively easily be recycled without loss of quality, metals recycling has long been practiced in an economically feasible way.

GLOBAL PHYSICAL FLOWS

Cycles in the Ecosystem

Many cycles can be discerned in the ecosystem, some of them with a rather long, others with a rather short cycle time. Important cycles are: water cycle, carbon cycle, sulfur cycle, nitrogen cycle and so forth. A further principal cycle is that of erosion and sedimentation. In the course of industrial development of mankind, the anthropogenic materials flows have become sometimes of a similar order of magnitude than that of the equivalent natural flows. For specific materials these have even become larger. Apart from local effects caused by this, it also can result in a shift of the equilibrium concentration of definite substances in seawater or the atmosphere, which might result in major irreversible effects that can exert an unpredictable impact on the environment. Global warming is a typical example of such an influence. The mass of the materials displaced by humans is about equal to the mass that is displaced by natural erosion. For energy flows the situation is slightly different, as the energy flow due to the sun is quite large compared with the artificial energy flows.

Anthropogenic Materials Flows

Without accounting for the substructure of the technosystem, we can list some *global anthropogenic materials flows* (see Table 1). The figures presented here are crude estimates that give an impression of their order of magnitude.

Figures like these can also be presented on a regional basis, such as has been done first by Kneese, Ayres, and D'Arge (1974) for the U.S. For assessing these values, one must keep in mind that the transformation processes that take place in the technosystem also include "logistic" processes such as storage and transportation. The impact of these transformations is apparently low, as these do not result in any change in physical properties involved. Nevertheless, the displacement of such huge quantities of inert materials as water, soil, and rock has substantial effects on the environment. Apart from this, the impact of materials flows due to human-induced changes in the ecosystem, such as those caused by mineralization of organic soil, can also be impressive. Study of this falls beyond industrial ecology, which is confined to the technosystem in a more strict sense.

Global Energy Flows

Table 2 presents some important global energy flows. The figures in this table illustrate that the

Table 1. Global anthropogenic mass flows

Flow	Mass flow ($\times 10^6$ ton/yr)
Water (irrigation, cooling, processes)	
• Irrigation	2,500,000
• Industry	200,000
• Household	150,000
Oxygen from atmosphere	33,500
Sand, gravel, minerals	9,000
Broken stones, etc.	9,000
Coal	3,600
Wood	3,340
Oil	3,000
Agricultural production	2,500
Natural gas	2,000
Limestone for cement	1,800
Lignite	1,250
Iron ore (50% Fe)	920
Copper ore (2% Cu)	800
Cereals	601
Rice	524
Maize	480
Peat	266
Salt	190
Phosphorus ore	150
Limestone	120
Bauxite	100
Nitrogen for ammonia	96
Gypsum	90
Nickel ore (tailings included)	66
Clay	40
Pumice stone	12
Stone	10
Titanium concentrate	1,2
Gold	0.002

Table 2. Natural global energy flows that are derived from solar energy

Energy flow	**Power density** (mW/m^2)	**Global power** (TW)
Solar, reflection excluded:	*238,000*	*122,000*
Solar derived:		
Biomass fixation	150	78
Hydropower	20	10
Wave energy	6	3
Wind energy	70	364
Nonsolar:		
Geothermal	45	23
Tidal	6	3
Starlight, etc.	0.006	0.003
Fossil fuel consumption:	*25*	*13*

vast majority of Earth's energy input is solar radiation and the energy flows that are derived from it.

PHYSICAL FLOWS IN INDUSTRY

Introduction

In this section we start with presenting the basic structure of the technosystem. The subsystems are transformation processes and the relations between these processes are physical flows, called product flows, although they can also refer to raw materials, semifinished products, and waste. Products and processes are combined to product-process chains that represent the product life-cycle. In this section the principal phases in a product life-cycle are discussed.

Processes

Processes always include some transformation. Industrial metabolism focuses on transformation processes of physical flows. These can be subdivided in transformations with respect to time (storage), place (transport), and quality. Qualitative transformations are subdivided in nuclear, chemical, and physical processes.

Transformation processes always require *energy*. Although energy is apparently a well understood concept in physics, there exists neither an exact definition of this concept, nor an absolute measure for it. The quantity of energy is expressed with respect to some reference, which is usually some easily obtainable zero point, such as the ambient at a temperature of 0° Celsius. Even the concept of *energy conservation* is a hypothesis, but it has never been violated, neither in experiments nor in everyday observation. In spite of its vagueness, energy has proved to be an excellent concept in both physics and engineering. Energy conservation is usually referred to as the *First Law of Thermodynamics*.

Although energy is conserved, its quality inevitably changes when it is involved in transformation processes. This is expressed via the *Second Law of Thermodynamics*, which states that the quality of the energy, which is expressed as the maximum amount of mechanical energy (energy of motion) in which it can be converted, always decreases in the course of transformation processes. This can also be formulated by stating that the amount of disorder (called *entropy*) always increases.

When describing the technosystem, transformation always serves a specific purpose. In case of a *production process*, this aim is the increase of the *value* of some object, which can be either energetic or material. Although we can distinguish between *economic* and *functional* value, both have in common that they are determined by humans and thus are subjective to some extent. The ingoing and outgoing flows are called product flows, although the flows can include raw materials, semifinished products, utilities, products, by-products, and waste. Actually, virtually any process in the technosystem is a multi-input multi-output process.

From a physical point of view, a *consumption process* is not essentially different from a production process from a physical point of view. However, the consumption process serves a different purpose, as in consumption the functional value of the product is utilized for providing *services* to the consumer. In the course of this process, the product ultimately deteriorates. Therefore, consumption processes in general result in both process waste and product waste. The latter refers to discarded products.

Physical Flows

Introduction

We already noticed that processes are connected by physical flows. A picture of such a set of connected processes is presented in Figure 1. It can be observed that extraction and discharge are also processes of their own that have much in common with production processes. These processes also require utilities and generate additional waste.

Now we will discuss some of the specific physical flows in this scheme.

Resources

Resources originate from the environment. These include atmospheric gases, water, minerals, ores, and fossil fuels. Area is the resource that is required for agriculture, fishery, and forestry. Natural energy flows such as hydropower, wind, solar radiation, and geothermal energy are also considered resources. The availability of all of these resources is restricted.

Two types of resources can be distinguished:

- **Exhaustible resources:** These resources are reclaimed from a finite stock. The delivery rate, in units/time unit can be arbitrary, but the stock is not.
- **Renewable resources:** These resources are reclaimed from a finite flow. The delivery rate has a distinct upper bound, but delivery is assured for a virtually infinite period of time.

Utilities

Utilities involve ancillary materials, cooling water, steam, compressed air, electricity, and similar supplies.

Products

These can be discerned in *intended products* and *byproducts*. Byproducts are unintended, but nevertheless useful as they have both functional and economic value. Examples of byproducts are vegetable oil cake and blast furnace gas. The economic value of a byproduct can manifest itself via a *shadow price*, which is just below the price of its substitute, that is, the primary commodity that it replaces. This can be seen when considering

Figure 1. Schematic outline of the technosystem

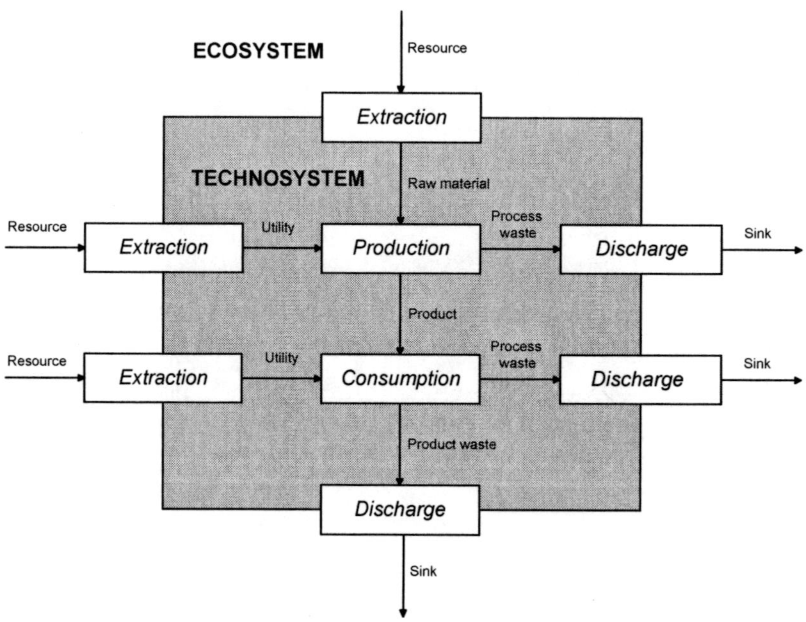

byproducts of the food industries that are used as cattle-feed.

Wastes or Residual Products

This refers to those flows that leave the production process and that have a negative value, which implies that the costs of upgrading these products for a useful purpose exceed their potential benefit. However, discharge of these products is usually connected with costs as well. Apart from this, legislation often enforces specific pretreatment prior to discharge. Damage that is inflicted to the environment is often not explicitly included in the costs of discharge, but an environmentally conscious enterprise should nevertheless be aware of these costs.

Two types of residual products can be distinguished:

- Process waste.
    - Process waste caused by production processes (industrial waste), or
    - Process waste caused by consumption processes (household waste).
- Product waste
    - Discarded capital goods, or
    - Discarded consumer goods.

Another categorization of waste is with regard to the component of the biosphere that is used as a sink:

- **Emissions**, most of them gaseous, some of them solid, such as soot. These are discharged to the atmosphere,
- **Effluent,** frequently consisting of polluted water, to the hydrosphere,
- **Leach,** emission to the soil, and
- **Solid waste,** including liquid waste that can be stored in a container.

PRODUCT-PROCESS CHAIN

Process Disaggregation

In this section we will describe a general product-process chain into more detail with complex products as an example, as these illustrate the most comprehensive set of processes. A rudimentary classification of processes will also be presented. We will start with discussing a linear chain, which is the most elementary configuration of a product-process chain, in which industrial metabolism principles are hardly incorporated.

Production Processes

Production processes are distinguished into those aimed at *production of services* and those aimed at *production of physical commodities*. We confine ourselves to the production of the latter, keeping in mind that physical commodities are in turn intended for the production of services, such as "transportation" or "feeling comfortable." Production of services, on the other hand, is also connected to physical production systems.

We recapitulate that Figure 1 depicts a typical linear product-life cycle, which is a chain of succeeding processes that are connected via physical flows. In general, the production process can be subdivided in multiple subprocesses. Performing such a division is called *vertical disaggregation*.

Although many subdivisions are possible, a frequently applied disaggregation is in:

- **Materials production**, which establishes the *intrinsic properties* of a product, such as the chemical and physical composition of materials. This takes place in the *process industries*.
- **Component production**, which establishes the *extrinsic properties* of a product, such as dimensions, shape, and surface condi-

tions. This takes place in the *manufacturing industries*.

- *Assembly*, which combines the components to complex products. This takes place in the *assembly industries*.

It is evident that not every product is produced by this sequence of processes. Some products are materials, and others are not more than a couple of combined components. We introduce the concept of *complex products*, which are those products that consist of many components as well as of a number of distinct materials, each contributing with its specific properties to the product's complex functionality.

The variety of possible processes is usually structured by classifying them via a distinct set of *unit operations*. This practice originates from the process industries, where numerous processes existed that had many characteristics in common. An example of such a unit operation is *distillation*. A suchlike categorization has been designed for the proper modeling of realistic processes and the initial list of unit operations has been composed from a more ore less eclectical point of view. From a general point of view, a more abstract classification can be made, which is able to incorporate all kinds of material processes.

We already encountered the transformation processes with respect to time and place (storage and transportation), which are combined to the concept of *logistic processes*.

Apart from this, we have to classify the processes with respect to qualitative transformations.

A thorough classification includes categories such as:

- Increase in coherence
- Decrease in coherence
- Coherence unchanged

Another classification is by:

- Physical processes
- Chemical processes
- Nuclear processes

These distinctions can be combined in a *matrix*. Increase in coherence, for example, can proceed both physically (such as via compression), chemically (such as via chemical binding), and in a nuclear way (via the capture of particles).

This categorization can be further refined. For instance, decrease in coherence can proceed via separation, resulting in two or more separate products, or via processes such as milling, resulting in a single product with altered properties.

We must realize ourselves that a real-world process combines the characteristics of multiple transformations. For instance, in every process a product is transformed both in time (as the process needs a finite lead time) and in place (as the product is always moved to some extent), and different types of process proceed in combination, for example, heating enables a chemical reaction.

Consumption Processes

Consumption processes can be subdivided in categories with essentially different characteristics. We already noticed that consumption of a product is aimed at providing services. These services can be provided via *irreversible destruction* of the product, such as in food, cosmetics, and forth. The other extreme is found in durable commodities that are used for an extended period of time. The lifetime of buildings and infrastructural constructions can even amount to centuries. Ultimately, these products are discarded because of wear and tear, such as cars, or because of becoming technically obsolete, such as PCs. For keeping a product in a good condition, or even for being able to use the product, one needs ancillaries, such as spare parts and gasoline in the case of a car. Somewhere in between both extremes is the gradual destruction of a product, such as in the case of a pencil.

Characteristic for many consumption processes is that these generate both process waste and product waste, such as exhaust gases and wrecks in the case of cars.

End-of-Pipe Processes

Since several decennia, consciousness has been developed on pollution damage, particularly by emissions to the atmosphere, contaminated water, and leaching to the soil and the groundwater. This resulted in incentives aimed at *pollution prevention*, which could be achieved via *end-of-pipe* measures, such as the installation of filters, cyclones, scrubbers, water purification units, impermeable floors, controlled waste disposal, and so forth. Already existing pollution had to be remediated via, for example, soil sanitation projects.

The waste, however, remained, albeit concentrated in filter residues, sludges, and so forth. This made the waste better manageable and was a prerequisite for waste processing aimed at a further reduction of the negative impact of these undesired substances.

THE REVERSE PRODUCT-PROCESS CHAIN

Introduction

As has been explained earlier, industrial metabolism studies the opportunities for waste reduction prior to, or in combination with, the application of end-of-pipe technologies. Waste reduction can be done both by waste prevention via enhanced process management, by process modification, and by utilizing waste as a resource, thus converting it into a byproduct. Some possible waste prevention measures are listed below.

Waste Prevention Measures

Process and Product Improvement

- **Good housekeeping**, which includes both optimum process management and optimum product management by consumers,
- Modification of the process environment, such as via insulation, which reduced the losses,
- In-process **recycling** of residual flows,
- In-process **cascading (downcycling)** of residual flows,
- **Process modification**,
- **Product improvement** aimed at increasing the useful lifetime of a product,
- **Product modification** aimed at making it more environmentally benign during its use, and
- **Dematerialization**, which results from product modification in such a way that the same *service* to the consumer is provided by a strongly reduced materials use (see, e.g., Herman, Ardekani, & Ausubel, 1990; Wernick, Herman, Govind, & Ausubel, 1996).

Optimal Use of Residual Flows

- **Process integration**, which includes the use of residual flows of a process in neighboring processes,
- **Industrial symbiosis,** which includes the use of residual flows in neighboring enterprises,
- Useful application of former waste flows, and
- Upgrading of residual flows to useful byproducts.

According to this hierarchy, waste prevention is considered superior to the utilization of residual flows. The waste that is produced in spite of these measures should be treated via end-of pipe techniques.

Processing of Product Waste

Apart from process waste, product waste is generated during a consumption process and discarded capital goods and rejected products are released in the course of production processes. Complex products exhibit all the production steps that are typical in reverse manufacturing. In products of a simpler type, not all these steps are present.

Listed below is a hierarchy of operations that are intended to properly upgrade the product waste, once it is available (see Dekker, Fleischmann, Inderfurth, & Wassenhove, 2004).

- **Rework.** This includes the upgrading of products that are rejected in the course of the production process to their proper specifications,
- **Maintenance** which include preventive tasks aimed at increasing the lifetime of a product,
- **Repair** is restoring the functionality of a product after it has been broken down,
- **Refurbishing.** This is the recovery of a discarded product via cleaning and repair,
- **Remanufacturing,** which might include partial disassembly and reassembly aimed at obtaining a new configuration of the product, which is reused in an "as new" state,
- **Disassembly,** which is the nondestructive removal of components or modules,
- **Dismantling,** which is the destructive removal of components or modules,
- **Unlocking,** which is the destructive breaking apart of a product in chunks, aimed at proper materials separation,
- **Separation,** which is the sorting out of materials according to definite criteria (separation can take place by a variety of physical and chemical methods), and
- **Materials recovery,** which includes the processes that are required to produce materials from scrap. These materials are called *secondary materials*, in contrast with *primary* or *virgin materials*, which result from processing of freshly extracted material.

Notice that we must clearly distinguish between *reuse*, which refers to the secondary use of products, modules, and components, and *recycling*, which refers to the secondary use of the materials. This is consistent with the vertical disaggregation of the production process that we have discussed in the preceding sections. However, the processing of discarded complex products is not exactly the reverted production process of these products because there exist essential differences between both. Not only is the incentive for performing the processing of discarded products different from that of producing new products, but there are also logistic, economical, and technical differences. Therefore, even the nondestructive operations in the disassembly processes are different from those that would appear if the assembly process was reverted.

The incentives for performing *disassembly* processes are:

- *Reuse* of products, modules, or components,
- Removal of hazardous components or materials,
- Recovery of materials with enhanced homogeneity aimed at *recycling*, and
- Preparation of the technical conditions for subsequent processes, for instance, the removal of components that might harm a shredder.

Further differences between assembly and disassembly are due to:

- Many processes in assembly, such as welding and press-fitting, are irreversible.
- The added value of disassembly processes is usually much lower than that of assembly processes.
- The chain of assembly processes must be executed to its end, that is, until the final product is established. Disassembly processes are performed until an arbitrary level that depends on environmental and economic criteria.
- Assembly processes are predictable and repetitive, with a determined supply of components. Disassembly processes are not predictable, because the discarded product is usually modified by wear, damage, or other causalities and the supply is also irregular.
- Products are produced in large production units, but consumed in a much more dilute way. They are also discarded in the course of a substantial time span. This means that the logistics of recollection is different, resulting in the supply of a mix of brands, types, configurations, and states of discarded products.

With these remarks in mind, we can depict a (simplified) scheme of a product-process chain with cycles included (see Figure 2).

Various cycles can be discerned in this picture: product reuse, component reuse, materials recycling via homogeneous components, and materials recycling via shredding and separation.

Influence of Recycling on Extraction and Discharge

With pictures such as in Figure 2, we are able to calculate the decrease in raw materials consumption and waste production when the relevant recovery rates are given. Usually, the unit of flow through the consumption process is normalized to 1, independent of the selected recovery rates. This is done because comparable systems must provide the same amount of products to the consumer.

Example:

We demonstrate such a calculation for the system in Figure 3, with recovery rates $a = 0.05$, $b = 0.15$, $c = 0.25$, and $d = 0.35$, respectively. The recovery rate is the share of the incoming flow of a process that is collected, recycled, or reused. We use node equations that reflect that the sum of the incoming flows of a process equals that of the outgoing flows, which is true when storage is not considered, that is, when the model is assumed stationary.

The simple calculation demonstrates that the combined effect of even modest recovery rates results in a substantial decrease (here 80%) in raw materials consumption and, simultaneously, in the reduction of the amount of waste that is discharged.

ENERGY TRANSFORMATIONS

Introduction

The discussion in the preceding sections focused on materials transformation. In a subsection of the section on product-process chain, we discussed production processes, and a subsection of the section on reverse product-process chains focused on the processing of discarded products. Although energy aspects play an important role in any transformation process, there are also processes of which the primary goal is the transformation of energy itself.

We noticed already that, although energy is conserved, the overall quality of energy tends to decrease. This is formulated by the second law of thermodynamics, stating that a measure of disorder, called *entropy*, steadily increases when transformations take place. This seems in contrast with everyday observation, where pro-

Figure 2. Disaggregated product-process chain, with cycles

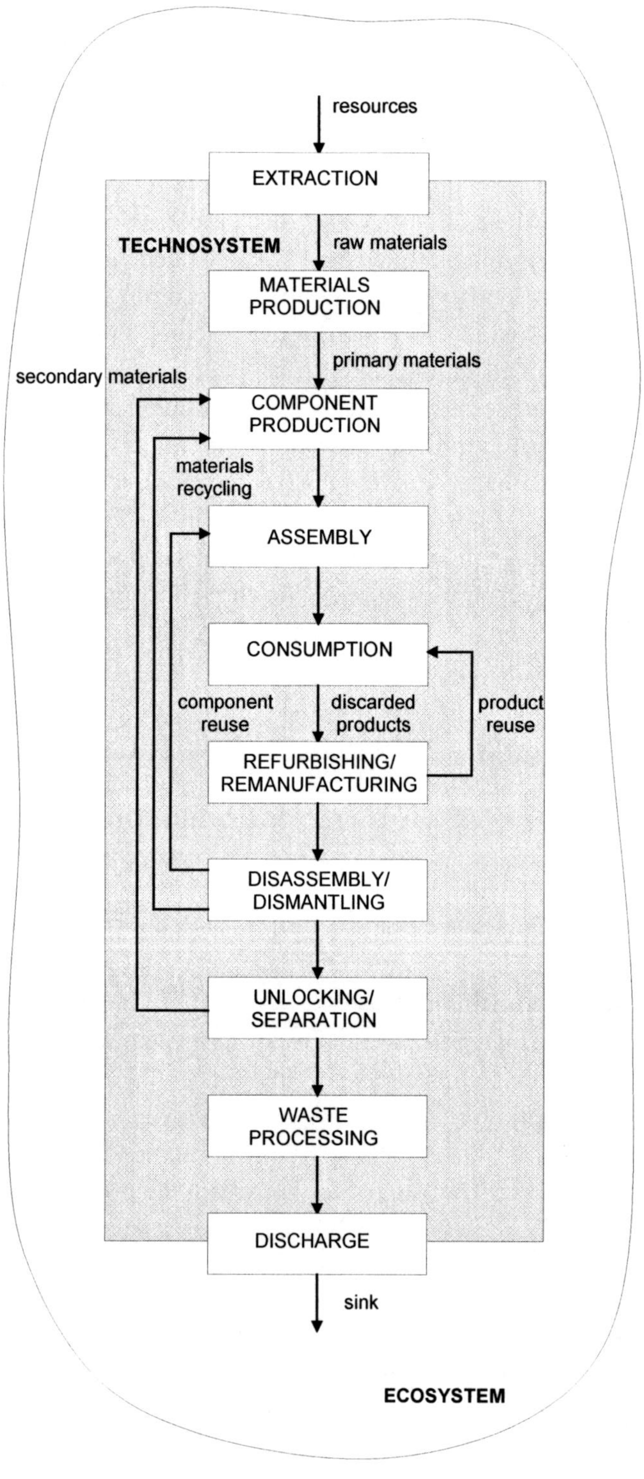

Figure 3. Calculation of decrease in raw materials consumption due to cycles

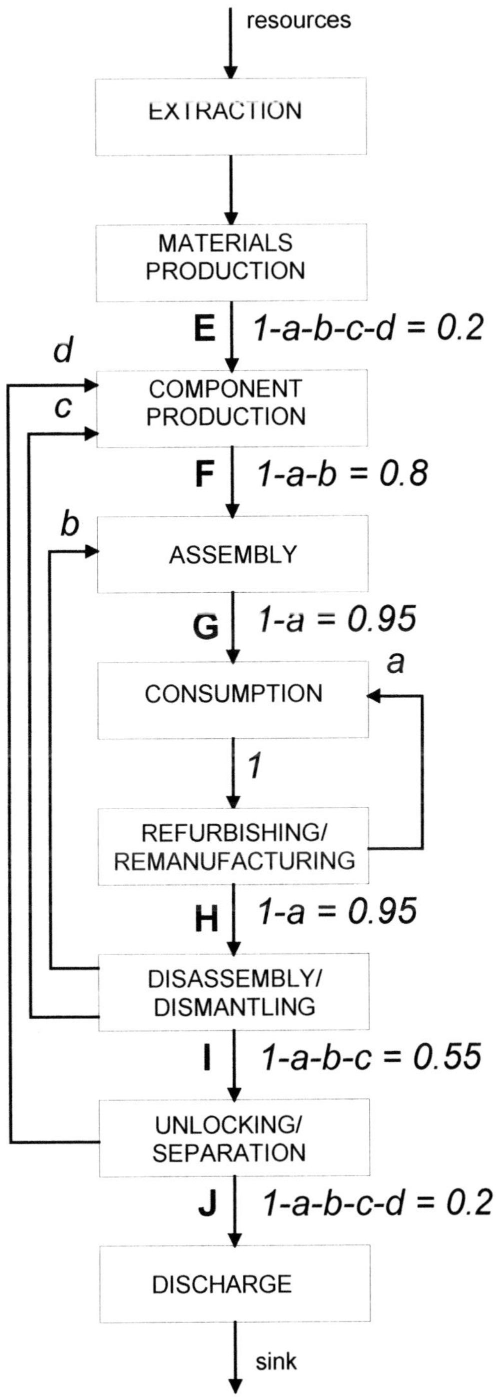

duction usually increases the order of materials. The apparent paradox is removed by the fact that such a transformation system not only produces the product, but also byproducts and, moreover, residual heat. It is mainly the latter that carries away the excess entropy of the system, together with combustion products such as CO_2, which have no chemical energy left.

The concept of order, or structure, always refers to an unlikely situation. An example is macroscopic motion or kinetic energy, which implies that all the molecules in an object move in the same direction. This distinguishes kinetic energy from thermal energy, or heat, in which the molecules move (or vibrate) in arbitrary directions, aand thus not ordered, which is a more likely situation. Moreover, we expect that a temperature that substantially differs from the temperature of the environment is more unlikely to appear than a temperature that is close to the ambient temperature. We know that motion can be converted in heat, for instance, via friction, but the reverse is less likely. We also observe that heat is always flowing from the higher to the lower temperature, which results in smoothening of the temperature differences until temperature is in equilibrium with the ambient temperature. We know that a high energy density or temperature is more useful, but less likely, than a state that is close to that of the ambient. We also can convert a larger share of high temperature heat in electricity than we can do with the same amount of low-temperature heat.

The energy sources that we exploit are in most cases of a high quality: chemical energy in fuels, mechanical energy in wind, and solar radiation. These must be converted to final energy which is the energy such as we want to directly apply, such as electricity or mechanical energy.

Even if the aim of a process is "energy production," such as in power plants, we are confronted with conversion processes that have an efficiency far below 50%.

Materials and energy transformation combined is presented via a more detailed scheme of a production process, such as depicted in Figure

Figure 4. A production process with energy flows included

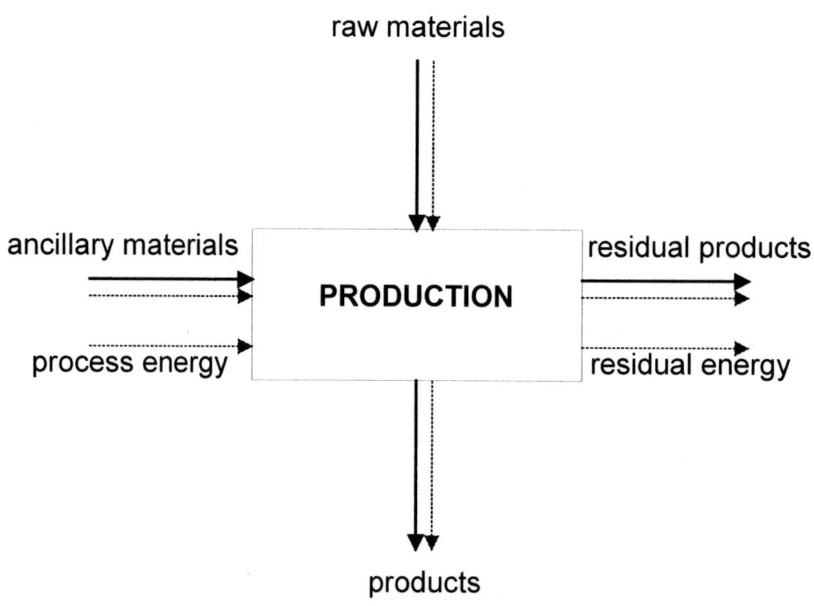

4. Notice that the dashed arrows represent energy flows. The materials flows in this figure are also accompanied by energy flows that reflect the fact that materials are energy carriers, which can contain chemical energy, thermal energy, and so forth. Both the materials flows and the energy flows must be balanced in a static approach.

An example is the heating of water for steam production. The water is the raw material that carries tangible heat when it has a temperature different from the ambient. The ancillary materials are a fuel that carries chemical energy, and combustion air. Residual products are flue gases, which carry both tangible heat and evaporation energy, and ash. Apart from this, residual energy is leaving the process via heat conduction and radiation. The product is steam that carries both tangible heat and evaporation energy. We observe that this process is aimed at an energy conversion process in which chemical energy of the fuel is converted to thermal energy of the steam.

Energy Forms and Kinds

Energy manifests itself in many ways. The most fundamental categorization is in energy *forms*: stored energy and energy flow or process energy. The latter is a transport phenomenon. Every energy form comes in different energy *kinds*:

- **Stored energy** is expressed in Joule (J), kiloJoule (kJ), and so forth. It is subdivided in the following categories:
- **Nuclear energy**, which is available in heavy nuclei such as uranium, and in light nuclei, such as hydrogen.
- **Chemical energy**, which is available in fossil fuels such as oil and coal, in biomass and in substances derived from hydrocarbons, such as plastics, or in batteries.
- **Mechanical energy,** which is available as *potential energy*, such as in a metal spring or in water at a definite altitude, as well as in kinetic energy, which is present in a moving fluid such as wind or water, in moving axles and wheels, and so forth.
- **Electromagnetic energy**, which is present in electric or magnetic fields, such as that of a solenoid or capacitor.
- **Thermal energy**, subdivided in *tangible heat*, which is present in a body of a definite temperature, and *latent heat*, which is due to phase transitions such as evaporation and is available, for example, in vapor.

Energy flow is expressed in power units: Watt (Joule per second) or kiloWatt (kW), and so forth. It is subdivided into:

- **Work**, which is the transport of mechanical energy.
- **Electricity**, which is the transport of electric current, that is, charged particles.
- **Radiation**, which is the transport via electromagnetic waves, such as thermal radiation (infrared), light, and so forth.
- **Heat,** which is the transport of thermal energy via conduction or convection.

Energy conversion is the transformation of energy from one form or kind into another form or kind. Transformation of energy from the available resources to the end user proceeds in the following phases:

- **Primary energy** is the energy such as it is put available via extraction. Some conditioning, such as cleaning or concentration, has already been performed. Examples are coal, crude oil, uranium, and also solar radiation, wind energy, and hydro energy.
- **Secondary energy** is the energy such as put available to end users. It includes gasoline, natural gas (pressurized and standardized), electricity, and so forth.
- **Final energy** is the energy such as actually used by the end user. This can be mechanical energy, lighting, heat, and so forth.

Direct conversion of primary energy in final energy is in general not feasible. If mechanical energy is desired by the end user, the fuel must be converted to electricity in large, centralized plants. The electricity can be transported and the final conversion, from electric to mechanical energy, is performed by the end user via an electric motor.

GROSS ENERGY REQUIREMENT (GER)

Backgrounds

In the wake of the 1973 oil crisis, it became evident that the prices of energy carriers evolved in an unpredictable way, but with an upward trend. Not only depletion of resources played a role, but also the dependence of a politically unreliable region with countries such as Saudi-Arabia, Iraq, and Iran. Therefore, quantitative insight on the response of the economy on energy prices became indispensable. For attaining knowledge on this subject, research was performed on the gross energy content of materials and products. This not only incorporated the *direct energy* that was involved via a specific production process, but also the *indirect energy* that was used in preceding production processes. An example is aluminum, which is reclaimed from bauxite in an energy-intensive process. Accounting for this type of energy, which is not directly present in the product, means that we must add all the energy that is required to obtain the aluminum such as it is present as the raw material for producing the final product, that is, we must consider the complete aluminum production chain, including mining, transport, conversion to alumina and next to metallic aluminum, processing, and so forth. If a company applies aluminum to a product, it thus must not only account for the direct energy in its own processes. When the energy price increases, this also touches the prices of the raw materials in a way that is proportional to the gross energy requirement of these materials.

Because the aluminum production chain also requires ancillaries and capital goods, we have to account for the production of these commodities as well. Apart from this, the processes that are connected with discharge have to be included too. If we would perform such a calculation in detail, we would end up with a task that is not manageable, so we have to make some guesses in this kind of calculation and we also have to make some restrictions by imposing some boundary on the system that we are considering in detail. With this in mind, we define the *gross energy requirement* (GER) of a product as the energy that is required to produce a unit of this product with regard to its complete life-cycle.

This implies that energy conservation measures, if considered within the framework of a subsystem, might result in a suboptimum solution for the system as a whole. When, in an enterprise that applies aluminum in discrete products, a new process is introduced that requires less energy but more aluminum, it depends on a tradeoff whether this modification is beneficial from an energy point of view. This can be done via the GER method.

Presently, the GER method is incorporated in life-cycle assessment (LCA) calculations, which are standardized in the ISO 14000 series. In contrast to GER, an LCA study includes various environment-related aspects of a product's life-cycle, not only energy consumption.

Allocation Problems

A problem that long has been recognized in GER is the allocation of resources in multi-output systems that also produce byproducts. It is not correct to assign all the energy to the intended product only. A naïve approach could result in an allocation key with respect to the mass of the product (in kg), but this results in a rather unrealistic outcome, because the mass of the byproducts can be much higher than that of the intended product. Examples are: the extraction of vegetable oil from seeds, which leaves us with the byproduct oil cake, used as cattle feed; and uranium enrichment, which leaves us with depleted uranium in much larger amounts than the amount of enriched uranium, which is the intended product. We already noticed that the price of a byproduct is often established as a shadow price, which is always below that of the product for which the byproduct serves as a substitute. A byproduct as oil cake, for instance, is a substitute for cattle feed from dedicated agricultural products.

Allocation of energy use proportional to the market value of the product apparently gives a reasonable outcome. However, if processes are encountered that are exclusively aimed at the upgrading of the byproducts to the standards that are required by the market, the energy consumption of these processes must be completely assigned to the byproduct.

Energy Analysis: Beet Sugar Industry

The Production Process

We will demonstrate the principle of allocation with the beet sugar industry as an example. Beet sugar production units produce sugar from sugar beets, which are agricultural products. Beets are grown, harvested, and shipped to the factory. Here the beets are cleaned, such that the attached clay is removed. Next, the beets are sliced and fed to a diffuser, where the beet's sugar content is dissolved in water. This solution is called juice. The remaining pulp has a dry mass of only 5% and must be prepared for use as cattle-feed via an energy-intensive drying process.

The juice is fed to a carbonation and a subsequent sulfonization process. Both processes are intended for the removal of impurities. Carbonation sludge is produced as a byproduct. This sludge has no significant market value, but it can be applied as a fertilizer.

The remaining purified juice is concentrated via evaporation. Next, a multistage crystallization process takes place, in which sugar crystals are formed. These are separated via a centrifuge and finally dried. The remaining syrup, which is loaded with impurities, is called molasses. This is a byproduct that is used in the feed industry, as a substrate for biotechnological industries, and as a feedstock for the production of alcohol and related substances.

The main ancillaries for the process are coke and lime, for enabling the carbonation process, and electricity and fuel, for providing the required energy. Fuel is also used for the raising of steam.

Apart from residual water and residual energy, we can distinguish three major byproducts: dried pulp, carbonation sludge, and molasses. The raw material is sugar beet, and the intended product is sugar. A simplified mass balance of the sugar beet industries is depicted in Figure 5. Notice that free water is not included in this scheme, which causes the unbalance. Water is present in sugar beets (76%), in the wet pulp (95%), in dried pulp (12%), in carbonation sludge (50%) and in molasses (24%).

Energy Analysis

Introduction

Next, we will account for the energy that is incorporated in the process. The direct energy that is required for sugar production can roughly be estimated by comparing the energy consumption of the complete beet sugar industry with its production rate.

However, when we want to allocate the energy consumption to the various byproducts, we must open this black box and we must consider the subprocesses that are hidden inside of it. For

Figure 5. Inputs, products, and by-products in the beet sugar industry

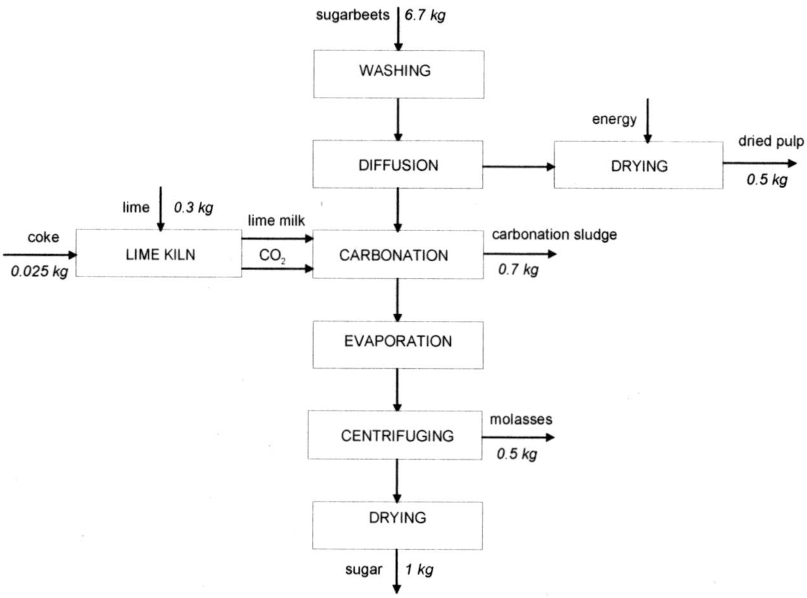

Table 3. Data on products in the beet sugar industry

	Price (€/kg)	Mass (kg)	Value (%)	GER (kJ/kg)	Internal energy (kJ/kg)
Sugar beet	0.10	6.7	n.a.	340	3,700
Dried pulp	0.36	0.5	10	12,300	12,500
Molasses	0.18	0.5	5	1,790	10,500
Sugar	1.50	1.0	85	15,000	15,000

the subdivision of the energy over the processes we rely on data by Brown, Hamel, and Hedman (1985).

With these data, the GER of sugar, molasses, and dried pulp can be calculated, once the market prices are known. Some data on the different products are summarized in Table 3.

The establishment of the GER of dried pulp, molasses, and sugar is discussed in the next subsections.

Sugar Beets Growing

In determining the GER of sugar, we have to start with the GER of sugar beet production. Data on this are available via chain analyses that have been carried out by the agricultural sector. The GER of sugar beets, shipped to the production plant, is about 340 kJ/kg beet, which is subdivided into: fuel (24%), fertilizer (70%), and herbicides (6%).

The chemical energy that is incorporated in the beet is about 3,600 kJ/kg beet, but this is usually not included in GER calculations, as it is not reclaimed from fossil fuels. Although electricity generation is also not completely based on fossil fuels, this exception is not quite logical, but stems from the era in which depletion of fossil fuels was the principal issue to account for. The required area for beet production is about 0.25 m^2/kg beets per year. We need 6.7 kg sugar beet for producing

1 kg of sugar. This accounts for 2,278 kJ, from which 228 kJ to the pulp, 114 kJ to the molasses, and 1,936 kJ to the sugar.

All the figures in the subsequent subsections refer to the production of 1 kg sugar. Assignment of the energy proceeds with respect to the value of the various products.

GER of Dried Pulp

The first process in the sugar production plant is *washing (and slicing).* This requires 120 kJ of electricity which leaves the process as heat loss. This amount must be assigned to all the products and byproducts according to their value. One also must account for the efficiency of electricity production, which assumed about 40%. This means that 300 kJ primary fuels is applied, from which 30 kJ is assigned to dried pulp and 270 kJ to the juice.

The second process is *diffusion.* This requires 870 kJ of hot water, 495 kJ of steam, and 30 kJ of electricity. From this, 72 kJ leaves the process as heat loss, 470 kJ is assigned to the heated wet pulp, and 805 kJ to the heated juice, while 48 kJ is in the condensate and is returned in the steam circuit, which means that only 447 kJ of external heat is needed for the production of steam. Here, we notice a physical aspect: The product flows have a distinct temperature which determines their energy content. Some arbitrariness is encountered. If the pulp were useless, the 470 kJ was considered a loss, but actually it is useful energy that appears helpful when drying the pulp. We have to account here both for the efficiency of electricity production and for that of heat production. The latter is assumed 80%.

This means that 1646 kJ of primary energy is needed for heating of water and steam, and 75 kJ for energy production. This is divided via the key: 470/(470 + 805) for the pulp and the rest for the juice (according to heat content of the respective flows). This reveals an amount of 606 kJ primary fuels for the pulp, and 1040 kJ for the juice.

As the pulp is now separated from the juice, subsequent processing of the pulp is exclusively assigned to it. This refers to the processes:

- **Dewatering.** This requires 105 kJ electricity. There is converted to 105 kJ heat loss. From the heat that was originally in the pulp, 315 kJ is spoiled in the wastewater, and still 155 kJ is present in the dewatered pulp. For electricity production, an amount of 263 kJ primary fuel is required, which is assigned to the dried pulp.
- **Drying.** This requires 4,800 kJ of fuel and 30 kJ of electricity. The latter corresponds to 75 kJ of primary fuel. 4,490 kJ is lost in the stack. 450 kJ are thermal losses, and 45 kJ is left in the dried pulp.
- **Pelletizing.** This requires 60 kJ of electricity. This corresponds to 150 kJ primary fuel. This is converted to residual heat, together with the heat still present in the dried pulp, which spontaneously cools down to ambient temperature.

These three processes together require 5,288 kJ of primary fuel, which is completely assigned to dried pulp. Increased with 606 kJ of primary fuel of the diffusion, and 30 kJ of washing and slicing, this adds to 5,924 kJ for the production of 0.5 kg of dried pulp, or 11,848 kJ/kg dried pulp.

Part of the energy that is required for growing and harvesting of the sugar beet must be also added to the GER of the various products and byproducts. For producing 1 kg of dried pulp, 13.4 kg of sugar beet is required, which accounts for 4,556 kJ, from which 10% is assigned to the dried pulp. This means that about 12,300 kJ/kg is assigned to the dried pulp.

GER of Molasses and Sugar

Next, the juice flow is considered, which is subjected to the following processes:

- **Heating.** The incoming juice accounts for 805 kJ, and 900 kJ of steam is introduced that leaves as condensate with still contains 96 kJ of energy, which is returned to the steam raising system. This means that 804 kJ only is added to the steam, which corresponds to 1005 kJ of primary fuel. The juice contains 1385 kJ, and 225 kJ is heat loss.
- **Liming and carbonation** needs the lime and CO_2 that has been formerly produced, the juice is entering and its energy content increases slightly from 1385 kJ to 1403 kJ. 30 kJ of electricity is needed. 594 kJ is in the vented CO_2 and 201 kJ heat loss is observed. The electricity corresponds to 75 kJ of primary fuel.
- The **lime kiln** produces lime (CaO) and carbon dioxide (CO_2) from limestone ($CaCO_3$). 870 kJ of fuel is needed, from which 22 kJ is in the lime, 761 kJ is assigned to the (hot) CO_2, and 87 kJ leaves the system as heat loss.
- **Sulfonation and filtering** is a process in which water and SO_2 is added, and sludge is removed. Heat losses account for 120 kJ, the sludge accounts for 23 kJ, and the juice still has a heat content of 1260 kJ. The carbonation sludge has no significant market value, and therefore no energy is assigned to the sludge.
- After this purification process, the juice is **heated** again, which requires 1500 kJ of steam, from which 158 kJ is returned as condensate. The heat content of the juice increases to 2,378 kJ. 225 kJ is due to heat losses. Heating of the steam requires 1678 kJ of primary fuel.
- **Evaporation** of the juice takes place with steam as a heat transfer medium. This steam has a heat content of 5,850 kJ. From this, 525 kJ is returned as condensate, so 5,325 kJ is effectively needed, which corresponds to 6656 kJ of primary fuel. The water that is evaporated has a heat content of 375 kJ, the juice contains 375 kJ, and cooling water removes 6,324 kJ. Heat losses account for 629 kJ.
- The **vacuum pans** need 1,500 kJ of steam, from which 158 kJ is returned as condensate. The remaining juice still contains 270 kJ, wastewater 15 kJ, heat losses 375 kJ, and 1058 kJ is in the cooling water. Steam generation requires 1,678 kJ of primary fuel.
- The **crystallization process** needs 75 kJ of electricity. The heat content of the remaining juice is 120 kJ, and a loss of 225 kJ is observed. Generating the electricity requires 188 kJ.
- After this, the final separation process takes place by **centrifugation**. It requires

Table 4. Primary energy use of subprocesses in the sugar industry

Process	Primary energy (kJ/kg sugar)
Washing/slicing	270
Diffusion	1,040
Heating	1,005
Lime kiln	870
Liming/carbonation	75
Reheating	1,678
Evaporation	6,656
Vacuum pan	1,678
Crystallization	188
Centrifugation	300
Granulation	84
Total	**13,844**

120 kJ electric energy. As a byproduct, 0.5 kg of molasses is produced that contain 8 kJ thermal energy, which is lost when the molasses is cooled down. It also produces sugar, which still has to be dried. This sugar has an energy content of 15 kJ. The heat loss is 218 kJ. Electricity production requires 300 kJ of primary fuel.

- The sugar is dried in a **granulator**, for which 75 kJ of steam is needed, from which 8 kJ is returned as condensate. One needs 84 kJ of primary fuel to generate this steam. This is completely assigned to the sugar.

We thus have the following need for primary energy that is assigned to molasses and sugar as shown in Table 4.

From this, 12,981 kJ is assigned to the sugar, and 779 kJ to the molasses.

The energy of 84 kJ due to the granulator is completely assigned to the sugar, which means that 13,065 kJ of primary fuel is required for producing 1 kg of sugar, and 1558 kJ for producing 1 kg of molasses.

The energy that is required for the primary production of sugar beet must be added to these figures. For the molasses, this is 5% of the energy required for growing 13.4 kg sugar beet, which is 228 kJ/kg molasses. For the sugar, this is 85% of the energy required for growing 6.7 kg of sugar beet, which is 1936 kJ/kg sugar.

Therefore, the GER of sugar is about 15,000 kJ/kg, and 1 kg of molasses has a GER of 1,786 kJ/kg.

It is interesting to compare the GER figures with the internal chemical energy of the products, which is *not* incorporated in the GER. These are listed in Table 3. We can observe that for both dried pulp and sugar the needed primary energy has the same order of magnitude than the internal energy. For sugar beet and molasses, the situation is different: the value added to these products is modest.

Energy Conservation Measures

Although GER analyses originally were used for assessing the influence of increasing energy prices on the economy, it appeared that these were also useful in detecting the most effective energy conservation options. In the beet sugar industry, for example, the majority of energy consumption takes place in evaporation and pulp drying, which are thus important targets for improvement.

LIFE CYCLE ASSESSMENT (LCA) AND ECO-INDICATOR

Backgrounds

The concept of life-cycle assessment (LCA) is an extended version of the GER method. It not only reveals the GER, but also includes various other environmental impact parameters, such as the release of greenhouse gases and the ozone depletion potential. Therefore, it is called a multicriteria approach. Application of a forerunner of LCA, called resource and environmental profile analysis (REPA) took place in 1969. This study, which has never been published, was performed by H.E. Teastley of the Coca-Cola Company for assessing the type of bottling (glass or plastic), the choice between internal and external beverage container production, and the preferable end-of life option. The study resulted in a preference for plastic bottles. After this, a similar study was carried out by the beverage container firm TetraPak, in 1985, which revealed cartons as the best solutions. This all made it suspect that the outcome could be biased to reveal a predefined option. This could only be avoided by an absolute transparency in the used method and in the origin of the applied data.

Due to the involvement of the Society of Environmental Toxicology and Chemistry (SETAC), at the beginning of the 1990s of the 20th century, the method became more accepted and ultimately standardized.

The first scientific paper on LCA that could be traced so far is due to Klöpffer and Rippen (1992). This paper was also focused on beverage packing systems. A systematic and methodologically-oriented approach can be found in the papers by Guinée, Udo de Haes, and Huppes (1993), Guinée, Heijungs, Udo de Haes, and Huppes (1993), and Heijungs (1994), who elaborated the method in a more general way. Since then, LCA evolved to an internationally accepted method, which has been laid down in 1997 in the ISO 14040 series. Various software tools are nowadays available to support LCA studies. These include extended databases for materials and processes, which also include the results of former GER studies. A restriction of LCA appears when dealing with topics such as product cycles, downcycling, and so forth. Attempts to cope with this problem, which is related to the appropriate selection of systems boundaries, is discussed by Tillman, Ekvall, Baumann, and Rydberg (1994).

The Society for Promotion of Life-cycle Assessment Development (SPOLD) has developed a standardized procedure for the exchange of data between researchers, industries, and software developers. This took place in the years 1995-1997.

Basic Methodology

Although the LCA method is described extensively in the literature and in ISO 14040 guidelines, we will give a brief summary and also discuss some basic characteristic of this method.

LCA is typically a *cradle-to-grave* method, which accounts for the impact of a product to the environment in the course of its complete life-cycle: From the extraction of the required raw materials via production and consumption to disposal. It is also a *quantitative* study: The results are expressed in figures. The results can, however, not be interpreted as absolute figures, but have a rather comparative character.

LCA studies consist of four phases:

1. **Goal and scope definition.** For a correct interpretation of the results of the analysis, it is indispensable to enunciate the objective of the study. This includes a proper definition of the system boundaries.
2. The **life-cycle inventory** is the phase in which all the relevant physical flows that are entering or leaving the system under consideration are listed and quantified. Self-evidently, there are many kinds of such flows.
3. The *i***mpact analysis** assigns the impact on human health, and on environmental and resource issues of the various materials and energy flows that are involved. As there is only a restricted set of impact parameters (see the list below), the impact of the different flows is assigned to these parameters by means of weight factors, which are based on physical data. Some flows cause multiple effects. Chlorofluorocarbons (CFCs), for example, add to both ozone depletion and global warming. In contrast with a GER analysis, the impact analysis results in multiple figures that reflect effects that are not quite comparable. Usually, the impact is subdivided in the contributions of the different processes that are involved in the product life-cycle.
4. The **improvement analysis** translates the results of the study into practical measures aimed at improving production processes, the choice of raw materials, the mix of product types, and so forth. The quantitative analysis reveals the bottlenecks in the product life-cycle, and is a tool for selection of the measures that have to be implemented.

The following types of *impact parameters* are usually incorporated in the analysis:

1. Depletion of natural resources,
2. Ozone depletion potential (ODP), a measure that accounts for degradation of the ozone layer,
3. Global warming potential (GWP), a measure that accounts for contribution to the anthropogenic greenhouse effect,
4. Eutrophiciation, which is the non-natural enrichment of the environment with nutrients,
5. Acidification, which occurs in soils and surface waters due to precipitation of substances such as ammonia and sulfur dioxide,
6. Energy use, which is equivalent to the GER,
7. Photochemical smog, such as via the release of volatile hydrocarbons,
8. Solid waste production,
9. Human toxicity, and
10. Ecotoxicity.

In general, there is no need to perform the full calculation, because a lot of data are available from previous studies. Specifically, there exist databases on the LCA results of many commonly used raw materials and production processes. Apart from this, existing parameter values for the impact of multiple materials can be applied. These do not account for the impact of the complete life-cycle but can be considered building blocks in carrying out a life-cycle assessment study.

Eco-Indicator

As an LCA study results in multiple figures, one has to make a tradeoff between the different types of impact that result from the product life-cycle. This can be done by intuition, but it can also take place via a predefined set of weight factors. In this case all the different effects are condensed into a single figure, which is called eco-indicator. Such a single figure is typically used as a management tool, for the results can be clearly presented. The weight factors, however, are inevitably based on subjective criteria to a great extent. This subjectivism can be related to political and criteria, interests, and even fashion. The issue of depletion, for example, played a major role in the wake of the energy crises, acidification has been a major issue after this, followed by an emphasis on ozone depletion and, presently, on the release of greenhouse gases. To cope with this, the set of weight factors can be regularly adapted. The selection of the weight factors must remain transparent, of course.

Advantages and Drawbacks

The principal advantage of LCA is that the method is standardized and that it must be presented in a transparent way, which means that both sources and methodology must be made clear to the user of the study. Apart from this, results of LCA studies enable a clear and illustrative presentation of the environmental impact of a product or process in the course of its complete life-cycle.

A principal drawback of LCA is that it relies on the bookkeeping model rather than on network analysis. This puts restrictions on the analysis of byproducts and recycling in the method. The systems that are studied are essentially tree structures, that is, convergent and linear, with the addition of the contributions of the different resources, such as is also done in the determination of the GER. This implies that LCA cannot appropriately deal with divergent and cyclic structures. Accounting for those materials that are crossing the systems boundary without being discharged is not obvious in LCA. Usually, this is accounted for in a somewhat artificial and inflexible way, via assigning fixed percentages to those outgoing flows that are reused, disposed, combusted, and discharged, and assigning negative environmental impact figures to these flows.

A further drawback lies in the values that are used in the databases. Rather than a static and linear chain, the product-life-cycle manifests itself in a dynamic network. Nevertheless, one must be satisfied with some average value. Notorious is the supply of electric energy from which the environmental impact can substantially vary with the mix of power plant types that is used. In case of materials, transport issues play a significant role, as does the type of resource, the reclamation technology, and so forth. Apart from this, data are frequently obsolete because of gradual modernization of production units.

Other drawbacks are inherent to all methods of quantitative determination of environmental effects, such as the fact that the impact of discharge depends on the place where discharge occurs. For instance, in an alkaline environment the influence of acidification is, because of buffering, less serious than in an acidic environment. This implies that local effects and global effects such as global warming and ozone depletion are treated similarly although their impact is completely different. Moreover, the LCA analysis assumes implicitly that environmental impacts of a specific kind are additive and do not influence each other in a nonlinear way, for instance, via thresholds.

LCA suffers from incompleteness in so far that usually no complete mass balances are considered, and so not all effects are included. This is different from a full network analysis based on the principles of industrial metabolism.

In spite of this, LCA offers a valuable tool that also facilitates the exchange of data in a standardized way.

MATHEMATICAL MODELS AND SOFTWARE TOOLS

There are many types of mathematical models and software tools. Some of the most important of them are listed below.

Process simulation goes in technical detail and is mainly a tool for process engineers. Process simulation software is usually accompanied by a detailed database of physical properties of various substances and process types. Although closest to the real world, models of this kind are usually not appropriate for environmental analyses. Example packages are ProSim, Chemsim, Aspen, and many others.

Product-process chain analysis is a technique that is not as detailed as process simulation, but that nevertheless provides materials and energy balances on a firm physical basis. On the rather high level of aggregation, approximations such as linearization must be carried through and relationships must be simplified. This implies that aberrations from "normal" working points or base cases can only be modest. In the case of *dynamic* analysis, storage effects are incorporated in the mass balances, and in the case of *static* analysis, these are not, as these are considered small with respect to the flows that are considered. In the static case, the models are expressed as a set of linear equations, and in the dynamic case, as a set of linear differential equations. In the dynamic case, one also uses *simulation* techniques.

Optimization techniques are used when decisions must be analyzed. One discerns exact, metaheuristic, and heuristic methods:

- **Exact methods** are typically based on linear programming (LP) or mixed-integer linear programming (MILP) methods. If many (0,1)-variables or even integer variables are required, which occurs if complex models are considered, the needed processor time (CPU-time) tends to increase exponentially, which makes exact methods often inappropriate for these models. To deal with nonlinearity, one must use non-linear programming (NLP) methods that further complicate the calculation. The advantage of exact methods is that these reveal the optimum value.
- **Metaheuristic methods** are based on algorithms that are basically independent on the type of problem. These involve techniques such as genetic algorithms, neural networks, simulated annealing, ant colony simulation,

and so forth. The algorithms are less time-consuming than exact methods, but there is no guarantee that an optimum solution is retuned.

- **Heuristic methods** are more or less sophisticated rules-of-thumb that are incorporated in problem-specific algorithms. It is often possible to design quick and efficient algorithms that give satisfactory solutions even in the case of complex problems, but obtaining the optimum solution is also not guaranteed here. Heuristics can often be successfully applied to online applications, such as scheduling issues. A principal drawback of heuristic methods is that these have to be separately designed and tested for every type of problem. Apart from this, convergence of the calculation can strongly depend on the instance of the problem that is considered.

Environmental information systems are usually connected to materials resource planning (MRP) and enterprise resource planning (ERP) systems. This involves the addition of environmental information to recipes in case of process industries, and to the bill of materials (BOM) in case of manufacturing industries. Quantitative information on mass and composition of materials is incorporated here and information on chemical reactions and other processes is also considered. Apart from this, qualitative information can be added, such as rules and instructions on product safety, and so forth. Other qualitative information, for example, for supporting environmental management systems, is also part of such systems. Here also, many software tools are available, with SAP and Oracle as important purchasers of these packages.

LCA software usually comprises an extended database of environmental impacts of multiple basic materials and processes, and a set of weight factors. This is completed by a program in which mainly convergent product-process chains can be built and made visible. The calculation essentially consists of bookkeeping of the multiple relevant materials flows and their environmental impact. The result of the calculation is represented via illustrative graphs that can be used for identifying bottlenecks and improvement options. The software is also used for comparison of different options with respect to materials and processes. Multiple software tools that support both LCA and Eco-Indicator are available, such as SimaPro, GaBi, LCAit, KCL-ECO, Team, and Life-Cycle Advantage.

Web-based environmental software is not quite well developed, but a considerable potential might be in sharing statistical data and results of, for example, already conducted environmental studies, such as already has been realized by SPOLD. A prerequisite for Web based applications is the standardization and interchangeability of the data.

CASES

Packaging Industry: Laminated foil

The integration of the principles of industrial metabolism in the MRP system of a plant for aluminum foil packaging materials has been analyzed. This plant consists of a rolling mill for the production of aluminum foil, which is a semicontinuous roll-to-roll process. As oil is required in the rolling process for lubricating and cooling, the foil must be cleaned after the rolling process, which requires chemicals and which generates wastewater. After cleaning, some rolls are laminated, which involves the addition of a paper sheet by gluing. This process generates both aluminum waste and paper waste, in which the aluminum waste is contaminated by the glue. Next, the roll might be printed via a subsequent roll-to-roll process. Finally, the foil is slitted to form the items of the required packaging materials. By this process, laminated aluminum foil waste is generated that cannot be directly reused as recycled aluminum unless some preparatory process is performed in which paper and glue is removed.

The required ink, in contrast, is prepared in a separate department of the plant via a batch process. The main environmental issue in the plant is the emission of volatile hydrocarbons and the generation of solid waste from the ink production facility.

The available MRP software was only supporting the roll-to-roll processes and did even not account for the waste. By introduction of data on the mass flow of the substances in the MRP system, instead of only expressing the relevant quantities in "items," "square meters," and so forth, the amount of the different categories of waste could be predicted and deviations in waste production could be easily detected and rectified (see Lambert, Jansen, & Splinter, 2000).

Formerly, the production unit had to carry out separate registrations of both materials and waste, which could only be laboriously interpreted, and resulted in a complex administration that was prone to errors.

Packaging Industry: Reels in the Electronics Industries

A company produces reels on which tapes are wrapped that bear surface mounted devices (SMDs), which are small electronic components such as resistors and capacitors based on semiconductor technology. These are mounted to electronic circuit boards by pick-and-place machines.

For a proper operation of the components precautions have to be made. The most important from these is that the plastic reels should be treated such that friction cannot result in static electricity. Apart from this, the dimensions of the reels must be kept within narrow limits.

The company wanted to consider a recycling system for these reels, and to this purpose a quantitative analysis of multiple options had to be carried out. The major problem here was the complex downstream supply chain: The reels are wrapped with SMD-bearing tape in multiple companies all over the world and are unwrapped in still more companies that are different from the wrapping plants. The customers are owners of the reels, and contamination or damage frequently occurs. So the question arose of how a recollection system could be established, to what extent the reels could be reused, for example, via application of a coating via a spraying technique, in how far materials recycling would be feasible, and whether down cycling could be a feasible option.

A model based on the product-process chain has been established (see Lambert, Boelaarts, & Splinter, 2004). The model applied LP and MIP techniques for searching the optimum configuration of the chain. This resulted in a tool that supported decision making and sensitivity analyses. There appeared to exist a lot of uncertainty, however, on the distribution of the reels over the globe and over the customer's behavior. Tracking and tracing would be an important tool in establishing a proper recycling system here.

Truck Manufacturing: Anticipating Future Legislation

A truck manufacturer wanted to be informed about the composition of the product that it produces. This was required for avoiding future liability for hazardous substances in case the product should become discarded. As the life-cycle of a truck is over 25 years, in which period the truck is handed over to multiple owners, legislation is expected to be tightened and liability is expected to be assigned to the original equipment manufacturer (OEM). The problem here is that the product, a truck, consists of tens of thousands of parts that are supplied by many suppliers and that suppliers can change over time. If one considers the presence of hazardous substances such as Cadmium or Cr^{6+}, used for surface improvement of many small parts such as bolts, it is unclear where these substances can exactly be found in a truck and in what quantity. The existing MRP system only lists items such as "bolts" and their specifications or code, but not their mass and composition. Apart from this, data from suppliers is not available. To change this, databases have to be coupled and data has to be extended with physical characteristics in a transparent and standardized way that enables coupling, that reveals the needed information, and that can be easily extended to include more substances when this would become required.

FUTURE TRENDS

When studying the recent literature on industrial metabolism, we see that the progress in this field has virtually come to a halt. No systematic and thorough study on the meso-level, such as that of Brown et al. (1985), has been carried out in more recent years. This makes recent sets of quantitative data hardly available, which is regrettable, as many figures in this study have to be revised, because of energy conservation measures and new technologies that have been introduced since then. The only data available are related to LCA studies that are still carried out frequently.

The concept of industrial ecology has moved away from the visionary idea that has been formulated by Frosch and Gallopoulos (1989). A lot of, mainly qualitatively-oriented, environmental management issues have been included in the term "industrial ecology," which makes the concept a little confusing and more such as the original idea suggested by Evan (1974). The clearly stated aim of closing the cycles and, particularly, that of a systematic and integral approach, has thus been partly abandoned. Environmental issues still are rather considered isolated topics such as, presently, the reduction of environmental harm to CO_2-related topics only, without including a more complete set of environmental aspects. This reflects itself in the present literature, where an emphasis can be observed on renewable energy resources. These are often called "sustainable," often without providing any quantitative data on the actual sustainability of these resources, sometimes even with the energy use to provide these resources being underexposed, particularly in case of primary biofuel that requires substantial amounts of fertilizer and fuel for harvesting, transport, and processing.

For a proper management of global environment, however, an integrated view must be reestablished, aimed at detecting and validation of the measures that have to be taken for attaining true sustainability on all the environment-related aspects of massively introduced technologies, without putting a growing occupation of natural resources as a prerequisite for human development. As an example only of the devaluation of some concepts, we observe, a proliferation of industrial parks that call themselves sustainable," but without implementing any radical measure to conserve materials and energy. This manifests itself, for instance, in the fact that residual heat is still spoiled on a large scale, rather than being upgraded via heat pumps or being used for spatial or greenhouse heating.

Another point that deserves attention is the proper reuse and recycling of complex electric and electronic products, which contain various hazardous components and materials and that are apparently notoriously difficult to disassemble. Exportation of these products to developing countries is still an actual and underexposed issue that should be consciously and effectively monitored. The construction of recycling factories in industrialized countries with enhanced recovery rates should be stimulated further, which requires extensive research. The appropriate design for life-cycle must also deserve increasing attention. The beneficial aspects of this kind of design will not only become visible at the end of the product life-cycle, which can take several decennia, but also appear in the domain of assembly, maintenance, and repair. Investigating the impact of technical progress on recycling issues is highly desirable.

As an illustration, the introduction of flatscreens imposes a constraint on the recovery of cathode ray tube-glass for the production of new tubes, as nowadays the production rate of cathode ray tubes has been collapsed.

In spite of this, progress has been made via the standardization of the life cycle assessment method in the ISO 14000 environmental management series. LCA studies are performed for many types of product, which provides a better insight in the environmental impact of these products.

CONCLUSION

In this chapter, we marked off the field of industrial metabolism from other, related, subjects. We have also given some explanation on how this domain has been emerged from societal needs.

Although we could not present here an exhaustive discussion of the complete field of industrial metabolism, we outlined the principal aspects of this field, and we also have worked out some simple numerical examples to illustrate how this concept can be used in modeling and quantifying of physical flows and their related environmental impact.

We also presented an overview of the GER and LCA methods that are used for quantitative analyses of the environmental impact of products in the course of their life-cycle. This has been accompanied by an overview of the available software solutions.

A couple of case descriptions qualitatively illustrated some types of problem where companies presently are confronted with, and the role of quantitative modeling and exchange of information for coping with these problems.

REFERENCES

Ayres, R.U., & Simonis, U.E. (Eds.). (1994). *Industrial metabolism.* Tokyo, Japan: United Nations University Press.

Boulding, K.E. (1966). The economics of the coming spaceship Earth. In H. Jarrett (Ed.), *Environmental quality in a growing economy* (pp. 3-14). Baltimore, MD: John Hopkins Press.

Brown, H.L., Hamel, B.B., & Hedman, B.A. (1985). *Energy analysis of 108 industrial processes.* U.S. Department of Energy.

Brundtland, G.H. (1987). *Our common future.* Oxford, UK: Oxford University Press.

Buckminster Fuller, R. (1963). *Operating manual for spaceship Earth.* New York: Dutton & Co.

Buehner, F.W., & Rossiter, A.P. (1996, April). Minimize waste by managing process design. *Chemtech, 26,* 64-72.

Chapman, P.F., & Roberts, F. (1983). *Metal resources and energy.* London: Butterworth.

Côté, R., & Hall, J. (1995). Industrial parks as ecosystems. *Journal of Cleaner Production, 3*(1-2), 41-46.

Dekker, R., Fleischmann, M., Inderfurth, K., & Wassenhove, L.N. (Eds.). (2004). *Reverse logistics: Quantitative models for closed-loop supply chains.* Heidelberg, Germany: Springer-Verlag.

Evan, H.Z. (1974). Socio-economic and labour aspects of pollution control in the chemical industries. *Journal for International Labour Review, 110*(3), 219-233.

Frosch, R.A., & Gallopoulos, N.E. (1989, September). Strategies for manufacturing. *Scientific American, 261,* 144-152.

Graedel, T.E., & Allenby, B.R. (1995). *Industrial ecology.* Englewood Cliffs, NJ: Prentice Hall.

Guinée, J.B., Udo de Haes, H.A., & Huppes, G. (1993). Quantitative life cycle assessment of products 1: Goal definition and inventory. *Journal of Cleaner Production, 1*(1), 3-13.

Guinée, J.B., Heijungs, R., Udo de Haes, H.A., & Huppes, G. (1993). Quantitative life cycle assessment of products 2: Classification, valuation and improvement analysis. *Journal of Cleaner Production, 1*(2), 81-91.

Heijungs, R. (1994). A generic method for the identification of options for cleaner products. *Ecological Economics, 10*, 69-81.

Herman, R. Ardekani, S.A., & Ausubel, J.H. (1990). Dematerialization. *Technological Forecasting and Social Change, 38*, 333-347.

IFIAS. (1973). *Report of the International Federation of Institutes for Advanced Study* (Workshop n° 6 on Energy Analysis). Guldsmedshyttan, Sweden.

Kahn, H., & Wiener, A.J. (1967). *The year 2000: A framework for speculation on the next thirty-three years*. New York: MacMillan.

Klöpffer, W., & Rippen, G. (1992). Life cycle analysis and ecological balance: Methodological approach to the assessment of environmental aspects of products. *Environment International, 18*(1), 55-61.

Kneese, A.V., Ayres, R.U., & D'Arge, R.C. (1974). Economics and the environment: A materials balance approach. In H. Wolozin (Ed.), *The economics of pollution*. Morristown: General Learning Press.

Lambert, A.J.D., Boelaarts, H.M., & Splinter, M.A.M. (2004). Optimal recycling system design: With an application to sophisticated packaging tools. *Environmental and Resource Economics, 28*, 273-299.

Lambert, A.J.D., Jansen, M.H., & Splinter, M.A.M. (2000). Environmental information systems based on enterprise resource planning. *Integrated Manufacturing Systems, 11*(2), 105-111.

Lowe, E.A., & Evans, L.K. (1995). Industrial ecology and industrial ecosystems. *Journal of Cleaner Production, 3*(1-2), 47-53.

Meadows, D.H., Meadows, D.L., & Randers, J. (1972). *The limits to growth: A report for the Club of Rome's project on the predicament of mankind.* New York: Universe books.

Tillman, A., Ekvall, T., Baumann, H., & Rydberg, T. (1994). Choice of system boundaries in life cycle assessment. *Journal of Cleaner Production, 2*(1), 21-29.

Vaccari, G., Tamburini, E., Sgualdino, G., Urbaniec, K., & Klemeš, J. (2005). Overview of the environmental problems in beet sugar processing: Possible solutions. *Journal of Cleaner Production, 13*(5), 499-507.

Wernick, I.K., Herman, R., Govind, S., & Ausubel, J.H. (1996). Materialization and Dematerialization: Measures and Trends. *Daedalus, 125*(3), 171-198.

ADDITIONAL READING

As the textbooks on industrial metabolism have been referred to in the Reference List, a list of scientific publications on this field is presented below.

Allen, D. T., & Rosselot, K. S. (1994). Pollution prevention at the macro scale: Flows of wastes, industrial ecology and life-cycle analyses. *Waste Management 14*(3-4), 317-328.

Butler, J., & Hooper, P. (2005). Dilemmas in optimising the environmental benefit from recycling: A case study of glass container waste management in the UK. *Resources Conservation and Recycling, 45*(4), 331-355.

Bystrom, S., & Lonnstedt, L. (1995). Waste paper usage and fiber flow in Western-Europe. *Resources Conservation and Recycling, 15*(2), 111-121.

Bystrom, S., & Lonnstedt, L. (1997). Paper recycling: Environmental and economic

impact. *Resources, Conservation and Recycling, 21*(2), 109-127.

Bystrom, S., & Lonnstedt, L. (1997). The economic and environmental impact of paper recycling. *Critical Reviews in Environmental Science and Technology, 27*, S193-S211 (Special Issue).

Cooper, J. S. (2003). Specifying functional units and reference flows for comparable alternatives. *International Journal of Life Cycle Assessment, 8*(6), 337-349.

Decker, E. H., Elliott, S., & Smith, F. A. (2000). Energy and material flow through the urban ecosystem. *Annual Review of Energy and the Environment 25*, 685-740.

Eriksson, I. S., Elmquist, H., & Stern, S. (2005). Environmental systems analysis of pig production: The impact of feed choice. *International Journal of Life Cycle Assessment, 10*(2), 143-154.

Geyer, R., Davis, J., Ley, J., He, J., Clift, R., Kwan, A., Sansom, A., & Jackson, T. (2007). Time-dependent material flow analysis of iron and steel in the UK. Part 1: Production and consumption trends 1970-2000. *Resources Conservation and Recycling, 51*(1), 101-117.

Ginley, D. M. (1994). Material flows in the transport industry: An example of industrial metabolism. *Resources Policy, 20*(3), 169-181.

Graedel, T. E., van Beers, D., & Bertram, M. (2005). The multilevel cycle of anthropogenic zinc. *Journal of Industrial Ecology, 9*(3), 67-90.

Hischier, R., Baitz, M., & Bretz, R. (2001). Guidelines for consistent reporting of exchanges from/to nature within life cycle inventories (LCI). *International Journal of Life Cycle Assessment, 6*(4), 192-198.

Huang, S. L., Lee, C. L., & Chen, C. W. (2006). Socioeconomic metabolism in Taiwan: Emergy synthesis versus material flow analysis. *Resources Conservation and Recycling, 48*(2), 166-196.

Kandelaars, P. P. A. A. H., & van Dam, J. D. (1998). An analysis of variables influencing the material composition of automobiles. *Resources, Conservation and Recycling, 24*(3-4), 323-333.

Kennedy, C., Cuddihy, J., & Engel-Yan, J. (2007). The changing metabolism of cities. *Journal of Industrial Ecology, 11*(2), 43-59.

Korhonen, J. (2002). A material and energy flow model for co-production of heat and

power. *Journal of Cleaner Production, 10*(6), 537-544.

Korhonen, J. (2004). Industrial ecology in the strategic sustainable development model: Strategic applications of industrial ecology. *Journal of Cleaner Production, 12*(8-10), 809-823.

Korhonen, J. (2005). Industrial ecology for sustainable development: Six controversies in theory building. *Environmental Values, 14*(1), 83-112.

Kytzia, S., Faist, M., & Baccini, P. (2004). Economically extended - MFA: A material flow approach for a better understanding of food production chain. *Journal of Cleaner Production, 12*(8-10), 877-889.

Lambert, A. J. D. (2001). Life-cycle chain analysis, including recycling. In J. Sarkis (Ed.), *Greener manufacturing and operations* (pp. 36-55). Sheffield, UK: Greenleaf Publishing.

Lambert, A.J.D., Boelaarts, H.M., & Splinter, M.A.M. (2004). Optimal recycling system design: With an application to sophisticated packaging tools. *Environmental and Resource Economics, 28*, 273-299.

Lifset, R. (2006). Differing approaches to energy flow accounting. *Journal of Industrial Ecology, 10*(4), 149-150.

McLaren, J., Parkinson, S., & Jackson, T. (2000). Modelling material cascades: Frameworks for the environmental assessment of recycling systems. *Resources Conservation and Recycling, 31*(1), 83-104.

Michaelis, P., & Jackson, T. (2000). Material and energy flow through the UK iron and steel sector. Part 1: 1954-1994. *Resources, Conservation and Recycling, 29*(1-2), 131-156.

Michaelis, P., & Jackson, T. (2000). Material and energy flow through the UK iron and steel sector - Part 2: 1994-2019. *Resources, Conservation and Recycling, 29*(3), 209-230.

Mulder, E., de Jong, T. P. R., & Feenstra, L. (2007). Closed cycle construction: An integrated process for the separation and reuse of C&D waste. *Waste Management, 27*(10), 1408-1415.

Narayanaswamy, V., Scott, J. A., & Ness, J. N. (2003). Resource flow and product chain analysis as practical tools to promote cleaner production initiatives. *Journal of Cleaner Production, 11*(4), 375-387.

Narodoslawsky, M., & Krotscheck, C. (2000). Integrated ecological optimization of processes with the sustainable process index. *Waste Management, 20*(8), 599-603.

Neset, T. S. S., Bader, H. P., & Scheidegger, R. (2006). Food consumption and nutrient flows: Nitrogen in Sweden since the 1870s. *Journal of Industrial Ecology, 10*(4), 1-75.

Nyland, C. A., Modahl, I. S., & Raadal, H.L. (2003). Application of LCA as a decision-making tool for waste management systems: Material flow modelling. *International Journal of Life Cycle Assessment, 8*(6), 331-336.

Sendra, C., Gabarrell, X., & Vicent, T. (2007). Material flow analysis adapted to an industrial area. *Journal of Cleaner Production, 15*(17), 1706-1715.

Sinclair, P., Papathanasopoulou, E., & Mellor, W. (2005). Towards an integrated regional materials flow accounting mode. *Journal of Industrial Ecology, 9*(1-2), 69-84.

Streicher-Porte, M., Widmer, R., & Jain, A. (2005). Key drivers of the e-waste recycling system: Assessing and modelling e-waste processing in the informal sector in Delhi. *Environmental Impact Assessment Review, 25*(5), 472-491.

Sundkvist, A., Jansson, A., & Enefalk, A. (1999). Energy flow analysis as a tool for developing a sustainable society: A case study of a Swedish island. *Resources, Conservation And Recycling, 25*(3-4), 289-299.

Uihlein, A., Poganietz, W. R., & Schebek, L. (2006). Carbon flows and carbon use in the German anthroposphere: An inventory. *Resources Conservation And Recycling, 46*(4), 410-429.

Vogtlader, J. G., Brezet, H. C., & Hendriks, C. F. (2001). Allocation in recycling systems: An integrated model for the analyses of environmental impact and market value. *International Journal of Life Cycle Assessment, 6*(6), 344-355.

Wang, M., Lee, H., & Molburg, J. (2004). Allocation of energy use in petroleum refineries to petroleum products: Implications for life-cycle energy use and emission inventory of petroleum transportation fuels. *International Journal of Life Cycle Assessment, 9*(1), 34-44.

Wernick, I. K., & Ausubel, J. H. (1995). National materials flows and the environment. *Annual Review of Energy and the Environment, 20*, 463-492.

Young, D., Scharp, R., & Cabezas, H. (2000). The waste reduction (WAR) algorithm: Environmental impacts, energy consumption, and engineering economics. *Waste Management, 20*(8), 605-615.

Zhang, B. J., & Hua, B. (2007). Effective MILP model for oil refinery-wide production planning and better energy utilization. *Journal of Cleaner Production, 15*(5), 439-448.

Chapter III
Sustainability Constraints as System Boundaries:
Introductory Steps Toward Strategic Life-Cycle Management

Henrik Ny
Blekinge Institute of Technology, Sweden

Jamie P. MacDonald
Office of the Minister of the Environment, Ontario, Canada

Göran Broman
Blekinge Institute of Technology, Sweden

Karl-Henrik Robèrt
Blekinge Institute of Technology, Sweden

ABSTRACT

Sustainable management of materials and products requires continuous evaluation of numerous complex social, ecological, and economic factors. Many tools and methods are emerging to support this. One of the most rigorous is life-cycle assessment (LCA). But LCAs often lack a sustainability perspective and bring about difficult trade-offs between specificity and depth, on the one hand, and comprehension and applicability, on the other. This article applies a framework for strategic sustainable development to foster a new general approach to the management of materials and products, here termed "strategic life-cycle management." This includes informing the overall analysis with aspects that are relevant to a basic perspective on (1) sustainability, and (2) strategy to arrive at sustainability. Early experiences indicate that the resulting overview could help avoiding costly assessments of flows and practices that are not critical from a sustainability or strategic perspective and help in identifying strategic knowledge gaps that need further assessment.

Copyright © 2009, IGI Global, distributing in print or electronic forms without written permission of IGI Global is prohibited.

INTRODUCTION

This chapter presents the previously published strategic life-cycle management approach (Ny, MacDonald, Broman, Yamamoto, & Robèrt, 2006) and some early experiences of its use in industry.

A Troubled History

Historically, many "safe" materials have been commercialized, followed by a later realization of negative effects on humans and the environment. This has led to subsequent large costs to redress the damage. Freons (CFCs), for example, were initially introduced as safe substances (Geiser, 2001), but are now known to be powerful ozone depleting substances. Unfortunately, society continues to repeat similar mistakes. Lessons that should have been learned for future planning are that impacts from societal activities typically occur through very complex interactions in the biosphere and often can be clearly related to certain activities only long after they have occurred, and then with great scientific difficulty. Consequently, an approach based on detailed knowledge of causes and impacts usually results in significantly delayed corrective actions.

A Complex Mix of Tools and Methods

The increasing complexity of social, ecological, and economic impacts from society's current unsustainable course has led to the development of a growing number of tools and methods to address the situation, each with its own unique assumptions and perspectives. Some of the most influential are related to or fall within the emerging field of industrial ecology and include the ecological footprint (Rees & Wackernagel, 1994); material intensity per service unit (MIPS) and Factor 10 (Schmidt-Bleek, 1997); cleaner production (Aloisi de Larderel, 1998); natural capitalism (Hawken & Lovins, 1999); zero emissions (Pauli, 1998; Suzuki, 2000); and life-cycle assessment (LCA) (International-Organization-for-Standardization-(ISO), 1997; Lindfors et al., 1995). Such tools and methods have become so numerous and poorly linked to each other that decision makers are now increasingly confused about how they fit together and should be used. Several attempts have been made to bring clarity and direction to future research (e.g., van Berkel, Willems, & Lafleur, 1997; Wrisberg, Udo de Haes, Triebswetter, Eder, & Clift, 2002). Another influential effort was made by several pioneers—representing their own tools and methods—attempting to build a consensus on the best use of each and potential synergies between them (e.g., Holmberg, Lundqvist, Robèrt, & Wackernagel, 1999; Korhonen, 2004; Robèrt, 2000; Robèrt, Daly, Hawken, & Holmberg, 1997; Robèrt, Holmberg, & Weizsacker, 2000; Robèrt et al., 2002).

Life-cycle assessment is one of the most rigorous and frequently used tools, with the objective of evaluating impacts of materials and products from the "cradle" (resource extraction), through transport, production, and use, to the "grave" (fate after end-use). Obviously, this leads to a more comprehensive view of the full impact than if only the material or product itself is evaluated. As will later be discussed, though, LCAs often lack a sustainability perspective and bring about difficult trade-offs between specificity and depth on the one hand, and comprehension and applicability on the other. In response, a new field of research and practice, called life-cycle management (LCM), is emerging, in which the focus is shifted toward the relationship between sustainability issues and life-cycle thinking in practice (e.g., Heinrich & Klopffer, 2002; Wrisberg et al., 2002).

Moving Forward with Strategic Life-Cycle Management

Instead of applying a problem-oriented approach to planning where impacts are dealt with one by one as they appear in the system, it is possible and desirable to plan ahead with the ultimate objective of sustainability in mind. Doing so requires a *backcasting* approach whereby a successful outcome is imagined, followed by the question, "What shall we do today to get there (Dreborg, 1996; Robinson, 1982)?" We argue that this approach could inform life-cycle management, allowing coverage of the full scope of sustainability for material and product life-cycles.

This chapter aims to: (i) highlight the need for management of materials and products through a lens of basic principles for sustainability, and (ii) apply this new perspective to life-cycle management techniques, bringing forward a new approach we term strategic life-cycle management (SLCM). Its objective is to identify viable investment paths toward social and ecological sustainability.

The underlying framework for strategic sustainable development based on backcasting from basic principles for sustainability is first described briefly in preparation for the discussion on SLCM.

BACKCASTING FROM BASIC SUSTAINABILITY PRINCIPLES

Backcasting was first elaborated as *scenario planning*, a planning methodology based on envisioning a simplified future outcome (Robinson, 1990). A games metaphor for this method of planning would be *jigsaw puzzles*, where the picture on the game's box provides guidance and helps the player deal with its complexity. Although backcasting from scenarios is a more strategic, that is, goal-oriented, methodology than fixing problems as they appear, and often encourages people to merge forces around shared visions, it also suffers from three potential shortcomings. First, given differing values, it can be difficult for large groups to agree on relatively detailed descriptions of a desirable distant future. Second, given technological evolution, it is best to avoid overly specific assumptions of the future. And third, if basic principles for sustainability are not explicit, it is difficult to know whether a scenario is sustainable or not.

It has been argued that it should be possible to backcast directly from a principled definition of sustainability, or from scenarios that are scrutinized by such principles (Holmberg & Robèrt, 2000). This method of "backcasting from basic sustainability principles" builds on a framework for strategic planning (Robèrt, 2000) and general experiences from the strategic management field (e.g., Mintzberg, Lampel, & Ahlstrand, 1998). More specifically, this framework for planning lets five interdependent but distinct levels communicate with each other as their respective contents and relationships are explored (Robèrt, 2000):

1. **The system.** The overall principles of functioning of the system, in this case the biosphere and the human society, is studied enough to arrive at a...
2. **Basic definition of success** within the system, in this case sustainability, which, in turn, is required for the development of...
3. **Strategic guidelines,** in this case a systematic step-by-step approach to comply with the definition of success (backcasting) while ensuring that financial and other resources continue to feed the process of choosing the appropriate...
4. **Actions,** that is, every concrete step in the transition toward sustainability should follow strategic guidelines, which, in turn, require...
5. **Tools** for systematically monitoring the (4) actions to ensure they are (3) strategic to arrive at (2) success in the (1) system.

Developing basic principles for success from an understanding of the system, then systematically planning ahead with those principles in mind, resembles chess more than jigsaw puzzles, in that principles of success (i.e., principles for checkmate, or basic principles for sustainability) guide the game instead of a single fixed outcome. Chess represents a dynamic planning method with each move taking the current situation of the game into account, minimizing the risk of losing pieces, while at the same time optimizing the possibility of arriving at compliance with the principles for checkmate. A large number of winning combinations (i.e., checkmates) exist. Similarly, rather than agreeing on detailed descriptions of a desirable distant future, it might be easier to agree on basic principles for sustainability and some initial concrete steps that can serve as flexible stepping-stones toward compliance with those principles. Thereafter, each new step of the transition should be continuously reevaluated as the "game" unfolds.

To be useful, we argue that the sustainability principles should be:

1. ... based on a scientifically agreed upon view of the world,
2. ... necessary to achieve sustainability,
3. ... sufficient to cover all aspects of sustainability,
4. ... concrete enough to guide actions and problem solving, and preferably,
5. ...mutually exclusive to facilitate comprehension and monitoring.

It has been argued elsewhere that the principles behind ecological footprints (Holmberg et al., 1999), Factor 10 (Robèrt et al., 2000), natural capitalism, zero emission, and cleaner production (Robèrt et al., 2002), and Daly's five principles (Robèrt et al., 1997) do not meet these criteria. This meant that something new was needed.

A process of scientific consensus building was therefore convened by Karl-Henrik Robèrt and led to the initial formulation of four basic principles for sustainability (Holmberg, Robèrt, & Eriksson, 1996). First, basic principles of socio-ecological *non*sustainability were identified by clustering the myriad of downstream socioecological impacts into a few well-defined upstream mechanisms. Thereafter, a "not" was inserted in each to direct focus to the underlying system errors of societal design. They form the basic sustainability principles (SPs), also known as The Natural Step (TNS) System Conditions (SCs), after the nongovernmental organization (NGO) promoting them.

In the sustainable society, nature is *not* subject to systematically increasing

I. Concentrations of substances extracted from the Earth's crust,
II. Concentrations of substances produced by society,
III. Degradation by physical means, and, in that society...
IV. People are *not* subject to conditions that systematically undermine their capacity to meet their needs.

Experience has been gathered from a variety of companies (Anderson, 1998; Nattrass, 1999; Robèrt, 2002) and municipalities (Gordon, 2004; James & Lahti, 2004) on applying these principles and creating a bird's-eye perspective on an array of sustainability-related problems. A metaphor has been identified, in which society is seen as moving into a "funnel" of declining opportunities. This metaphor mirrors long-term "enlightened self-interest" in backcasting from basic sustainability principles. As long as societal structures do not prevent unsustainable system behavior, increasing pollution and decreasing economic accessibility of natural resources will represent the walls of a funnel and function as dynamic constraints for human activities. Actors that contribute significantly to global unsustainability are therefore exposed to a systematically higher relative risk of economically hitting these funnel walls. This translates into higher costs for waste management, insurances, taxes, bad publicity, and so forth (Holmberg & Robèrt, 2000).

The parts of the planning process are (Figure 1): (A) sharing and discussing the suggested framework with all participants of the planning exercise, (B) assessing current material and energy flows and practices in relation to the basic sustainability principles (SPs) (rather than relying solely on today's perception of impacts), (C) creating options and visions that support society's compliance with the basic SPs, and (D) prioritizing early actions from the C-list that not only take care of the short term challenges but also prepare for coming actions to eventually make society comply with the SPs.

RATIONALE FOR STRATEGIC LIFE-CYCLE MANAGEMENT

The Dynamics of Dematerialization and Substitution Under Each Sustainability Principle

The backcasting planning process results in a set of measures that can be divided into dematerialization and substitution/change under each SP (Robèrt et al., 2002).

Dematerialization measures should here be taken in their widest possible meaning and include

Figure 1. Backcasting from Principles as illustrated by A-B-C-D-Planning. A. Agree on (1) the object of study, (2) the sustainability challenge (a funnel of declining opportunity), (3) the future sustainable landing place for planning (defined by compliance with Sustainability Principles [SPs, denoted by roman numerals]) and (4) the method of study - ABCD. B. For each SP (I-IV), list critical practices from the perspective of SPs. C. Develop a list of possible solutions and investments ('brainstorming'). D. Use guiding questions to prioritize early solutions and investments from C. The procedure is repeated as the development unfolds.

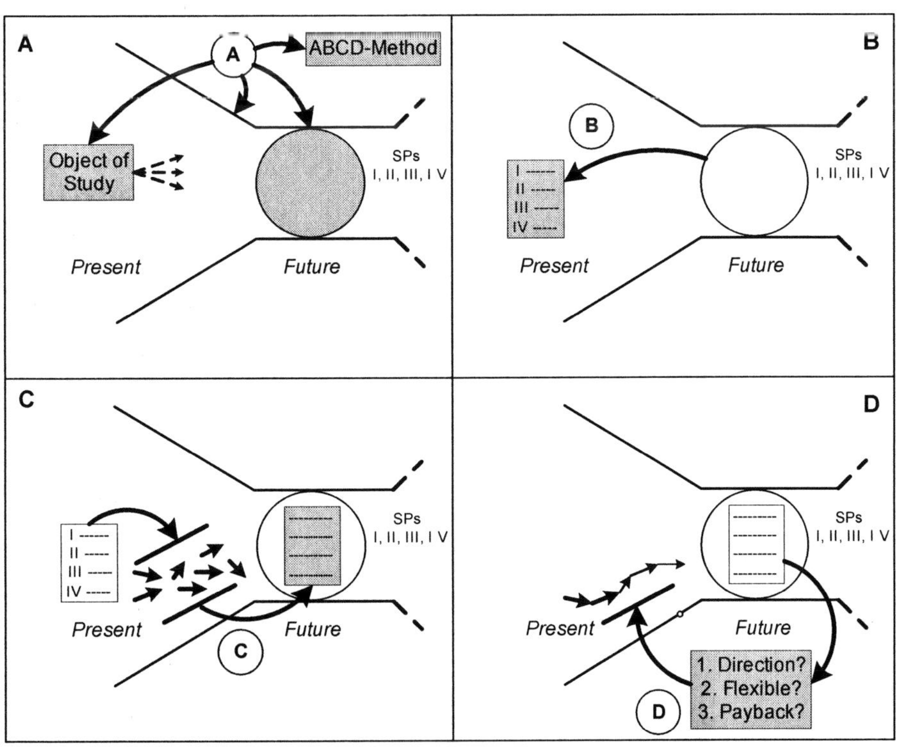

not only leaner production (Romm, 1994) but also recycling, new business models such as leasing (Fishbein, McGarry, & Dillon, 2000), and completely new innovations outside the box that meet human needs at higher material performance per unit of utility. Such measures are helpful in avoiding accumulation of elements and compounds (SP I and SP II) and reducing physical pressure on productive ecosystems (SP III). Increasing resource productivity and reducing waste are also ways of ensuring sufficient resources for people on the global scale (SP IV).

Substitution/change is sometimes required or preferred over and above dematerialization. Examples include replacing metals that are scarce in ecosystems (ones that consequently pose a greater risk of increasing in concentration in ecosystems if not kept in essentially closed societal loops)—for example, cadmium—with the use of more abundant metals (Broman, Holmberg, & Robèrt, 2000; Electrolux, 1994) (SP I); replacing chemicals that are relatively persistent and foreign to nature, such as certain plasticizers (Leadbitter, 2002) and CFCs, with more biodegradable chemicals (SP II); replacing materials from poorly managed ecosystems and mining areas where natural systems are not restored after mine-decommissioning (Holmberg et al., 1999) with materials from well-managed ecosystems and mines (SP III); and replacing narrowing rationales for meeting market needs with a wider humanized perspective given human needs at the global scale (Cook, 2004; Max-Neef et al., 1989) (SP IV). New materials and practices should, of course, be selected by considering all SPs collectively.

It is also possible that some materials may at times be required to increase in use to replace other materials. For example, the use of biofuels will probably increase as fossil fuels are gradually phased out. Moreover, photovoltaics may play a key role in the transition to sustainability, probably leading to expanded need for certain scarce metals (Andersson, Eide, Lundqvist, & Mattsson, 1998). Such materials then must, of course, be safeguarded by essentially closed-loop societal processes to ensure compliance with the SPs (Karlsson, 1999). Thus, it must be assured that such closed loops are economically viable or at least realistic over time. For photovoltaics, the material turnover is rather small, the use is inherently fairly nondissipative, and the long-term economic potential is probably large enough to carry the costs of the closed loops But again, if more abundant metals or other materials could provide the same function, those may be preferred.

Economic relationships also exist between dematerialization and substitution/change. Sometimes economically viable dematerialization is insufficient, because involved materials are relatively nondegradable (e.g., CFCs or PCBs [polychlorinated biphenyls]), or have already surpassed thresholds in natural systems due to the size of their flows (e.g., nitrogen oxides [NO_x]). In this case, substitution/change, rather than extensive and expensive closed-loop recycling may be the best option, even though it may be relatively expensive if economies of scale are lacking. Furthermore, substitution/change often requires investment in new infrastructure. An example is the development of substitutes for CFC refrigerants, as well as new refrigerators that accept new refrigerants. But profitable implementation of new technologies can often be supported or made possible through *dematerialization*, that is, higher resource productivity and less waste within the new production lines and products (Byggeth, 2001; Robèrt et al., 2002).

In summary, the SPs inform a dynamic (economic) relationship in this regard: Dematerialization may support certain substitutions/changes, substitution/change may prompt certain dematerializations, and substitution/change may eliminate some need for dematerialization. These linkages are essential when strategic investment paths are considered, and will surface if the applied method(s) allow(s) the transparency that follows from basic principles (in contrast to methods that either build on aggregation into one-dimensional information or certain selected impacts).

Practical Experiences from Applying Backcasting from Sustainability Principles

Practical experiences come from businesses such as Electrolux and IKEA (Broman et al., 2000), Interface, Scandic Hotels and Collins Pine (Nattrass, 1999), and Hydro Polymers (Everard, Monaghan, & Ray, 2000) as well as from regions and municipalities (James & Lahti, 2004; Resort-Municipality-of-Whistler-[RMOW], 2005). There have been assessments of agriculture (Andersson et al., 1993; Robèrt, 2002), forestry (Robèrt, 2002), and alternative sets of policies, technologies, and behaviours to arrive at sustainable transport systems have been modeled (Robèrt, 2005). The community-building aspects of applying backcasting from sustainability principles as a shared mental model have also been studied (Nattrass, 1999; Nattrass, & Altomare, 2002). It has been applied to academic education (Broman, Byggeth, & Robèrt, 2002; Robèrt et al., 2004; Waldron, 2005; Waldron, Byggeth, Ny, Broman, & Robèrt, 2004). Experiences from three industrial adopters of backcasting from sustainability principles, Electrolux, IKEA and Hydro Polymers, will be dealt with in some detail below.

The Electrolux Example: Solving Existing Problems While Planning for the Future

An example of how the dynamic of substitutions and dematerializations has been handled in practice is the phasing out of CFCs by the Swedish-based, multinational appliance producer, Electrolux (Robèrt, 1997). Introducing HydroChloroFluoroCarbons (HCFCs) would have meant an improvement in relation to CFCs as regards ozone destruction potential. HCFCs, though, just like CFCs, are relatively nondegradable in nature and therefore also potentially problematic as regards SP II. This meant that HCFCs, even though less damaging than CFCs, were not seen as a permanent solution (considering also the amounts necessary and type of use). Instead, a different strategy using the refrigerant R134a as a flexible platform was undertaken (Electrolux, 1994). Given the relatively low degradability of R134a and the fact that it is foreign to nature, it was not thought of as a long-term solution in itself. It could for technical reasons, though, be used as a step—linked to far lower subsequent investments than an HCFC-step would have required—in preparation for the next generation of hydrocarbon cooling agents. Electrolux expected to have the technology to ensure safe use of those agents (they are explosive) within a few years. With the chosen strategy, detailed LCAs comparing CFCs and HCFCs were unnecessary because these substances, using the overview assessment described above, could be ruled out as less viable paths to sustainability than R134a. The phase out plan for R134a also made a detailed LCA unnecessary for that substance. Electrolux then became the first company to launch an entire family of Freon-free refrigerators and freezers, resulting in increased market shares. The company also presented a new overall business strategy based on the SPs (Broman et al., 2000). It came to encompass a subtle balance of strategically chosen dematerializations and substitutions/changes for a number of product families.

The IKEA Example: Negotiating Trade-Offs When Introducing Low Energy Lamps

The market introduction of compact fluorescent lamps (CFLs) by IKEA, the Swedish-based multinational home furnishings retailer, is another example of this type of systematic planning. CFLs are energy efficient, but contain mercury, meaning that they are not sustainable in their present form unless the mercury is kept in a closed loop (which is very difficult). The head of environmental affairs at that time, Russel Johnson, presents an abridged version of the story (Broman et al., 2000; Johnson, 2004):

The trade-off problem here was between higher use of mercury (SP I), lower expenditure of energy (mainly SPs I and II), and higher costs for the lamps, thereby lowering their availability to the public (SP IV). A more creative methodology than trying to estimate whether the impacts outweighed the benefits was to start the planning procedure from a point where the trade-offs no longer existed – that is, backcasting from the system conditions [the SPs] to find a strategy to comply with them. In short, the following actions resulted:

1. *A producer who could provide an adequate combination of the listed criteria to serve as a platform was identified. A reliable CFL with max. 3 mg Hg (mercury)/lamp – comparable to the EU environmental labelling system requirement of max 10 mg on the global market (i.e. a reduction to one third of previous levels or a factor 3) for such lamps – was then selected as the standard. A Chinese manufacturer, outstanding both from product design and production technology perspectives met the requirements while also being price-competitive.*
2. *This producer and its competitors were notified that as long as they were ahead of the competitors on price, energy expenditure and mercury content, they would continue to do business with IKEA. Backcasting from the system conditions [the SPs] had allowed the trade off problem to support a process to arrive at principally sustainable low-energy lamps.*

The Hydro Polymers Example: Redefining Business Challenges by Backcasting from Sustainability Principles

We chose one example: the manufacturing and use of polyvinylchloride (PVC) and the environmental problems it causes (other examples are in the supplemental materials.) Environmental and social organizations (such as Greenpeace and Healthcare Without Harm) launched campaigns against this plastic. Hydro Polymers, a leading manufacturer of PVC in Europe, initially used two defensive counterarguments. The first was that other materials besides their product were associated with environmental problems. The second was that the company had made progress in comparison to previous practices.

Supported by the UK's Environmental Agency, backcasting from sustainability principles was used to assess PVC (Everard et al., 2000). Based on this, Hydro Polymers chose an alternative, proactive strategy (Leadbitter, 2002). It built on an analysis of the existing gap to full compliance with the four sustainability principles and included a commitment to systematically bridge the gap. The challenges included becoming carbon neutral through use of renewable raw materials and energy, and halting emissions and additives of any chemicals or elements that might contribute to any accumulation in natural systems, regardless of whether there were known eco-toxic impacts or not.

The debate has now switched from short-term trade-offs between various actions to whether Hydro Polymers is likely to succeed with its long-term commitment. There is now a clearly defined set of science-based objectives, so one can communicate whether there has been sufficient progress or not. An interesting spin-off of this reflects another challenge for sustainability. What Hydro Polymers puts in its products, and the way those products are used by customers, all influence whether the whole system is sustainable. Hydro Polymers has realized that it is relatively easier and more effective to consider approaches throughout the entire product life-cycle value-chain, from raw materials to the eventual disposal of the product, than to try to monitor detailed performance in isolation at each value-chain company. Business partners are sensitised through three questions: Is "sustainability" defined? What are the main challenges to becoming sustainable? With reference to these challenges, what are you doing at the strategic level? Thereafter, the backcasting from sustainability principles framework is used to co-create solutions across the value chain.

The Complexity of Making Detailed Priorities

How can trade-offs and uncertainties during the transition be managed? Some trade-off dimensions include potential seriousness of the social/ ecological impacts of the issue, the individual actor's relative contribution to the issue, and the temporal perspective of impacts. Together, such issues present themselves within areas of varying ambiguity ("gray areas") along these and other dimensions (Figure 2). Sustainability issues should be dealt with more urgently and vigorously the closer they are estimated to be to the max extreme. Furthermore, uncertainty about where to put the issue along the different

Figure 2. Gray Areas of Ambiguity for Prioritization Criteria for Sustainability Issues. Competent decision making often relies on strategic trade-offs where sustainability issues are evaluated against criteria such as potential magnitude, relative contribution to issue, and time perspective. Two extreme points exist for each, with gray areas between them. Three dimensions may already create considerable complexity, but more dimensions are often in play. Furthermore, uncertainty due to knowledge gaps may speak in favour of adding safety-zones along the dimensions (the precautionary principle). Issues between the extreme points should be given an increasing degree of priority the closer they are to the max-extreme.

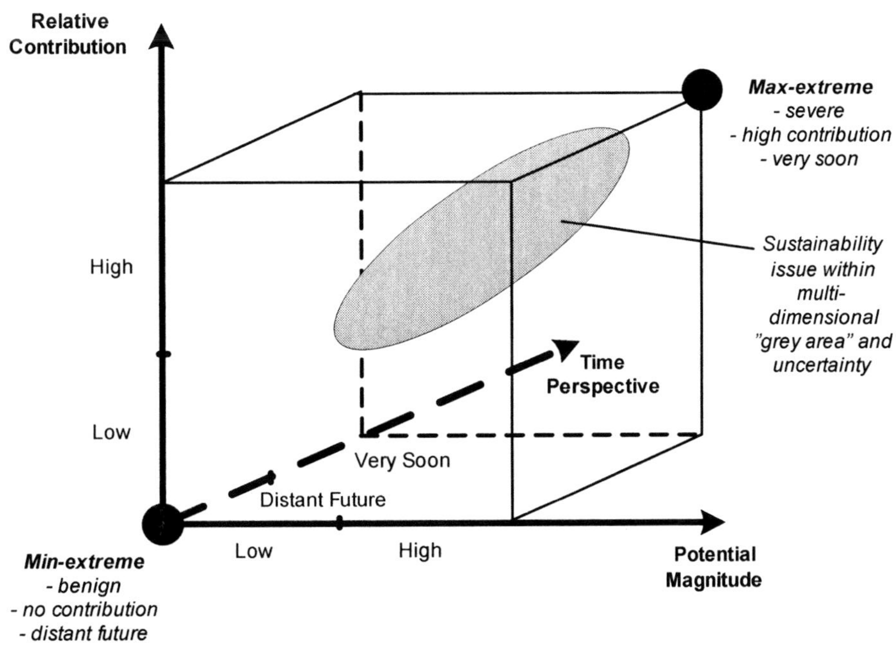

dimensions adds yet another trade-off dimension. This implies that greater uncertainty surrounding these and other dimensions (larger gray areas) is generally a rationale for undertaking proactive measures, as dealt with by the so-called precautionary principle.

Simultaneously, the economic dimension must be considered. It may be wise to schedule early measures that pay off quickly ("low hanging fruit") to obtain the economic power necessary to deal with the more severe challenges. This chapter presents an approach to comprehensively accomplish this through a framework based on a large enough systems perspective. Without such a framework, the uncertainties regarding the respective relationships between the issues, each presented in a multidimensional gray area, will make trade-offs and prioritizations unmanageable from a strategic systems perspective.

So far, most LCAs have been performed without a generally accepted framework for discussing impacts beyond the environmental perspective (Brattebø, 1996; Hoagland, 2001; Pennington et al., 2004). It is important that sustainability-related life-cycle methods (including social life-cycle assessment) use the same, and sufficiently wide, system boundaries (Klopffer, 2003). But to limit the complexity and size of studies, most of today's commonly applied forms of LCA use geographic and time-related system boundaries, focusing on a few ecological impact categories such as emissions of greenhouse gases, acidification, and eutrophication (Figure 3).

Many authors have discussed the complexity of, and difficulties related to, the assessment of impacts from societal activities. Efforts have been made to streamline LCA to make the results easier to interpret (Christiansen, 1997; Graedel,

Figure 3. System Boundaries in Traditional Life-Cycle Assessment (LCA) - Based on Selected Known Issues. The sustainability arena of a company starts with the strategic business dimension under company control, and continues with the surrounding societal and ecological dimensions that the company ultimately depends upon. The gray areas represent hot-spots, that is, impacts and issues that are essential from a sustainability perspective within those dimensions. Traditional LCA focuses mainly on a selection of known environmental impacts.

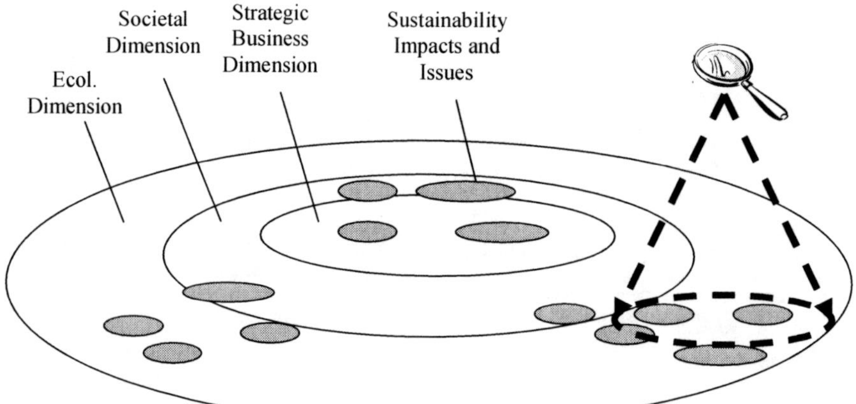

1998; Todd, 1996; Udo de Haes, Heijungs, Suh, & Huppes, 2004). A recent survey of available environmental evaluation tools in the EU concluded, though, that there are many approaches for simplified LCAs but they are not always clearly and consistently defined (Widheden, 2002). This therefore likely translates into inconsistencies when they are used.

A Swedish study on the implementation of environmental management systems in Swedish companies concluded that only 10% of corporations have allowed the results from LCAs to influence the measures taken (Zackrisson, Enroth, & Wilding, 1999). The study did not explain why, but others have discussed the issue (Frankl & Rubik, 2000; Heiskanen, 2000) and after talking to business leaders (e.g., Johnson, 2004) we suggest some presumptive reasons for the (as yet) relatively low use of LCA by decision makers in business.

- The results from LCA, performed by scientists to evaluate a scientific question, may be too complex to interpret from a business perspective.
- Efforts to aggregate information from different categories of impacts into simplistic figures for decision makers may be perceived as questionable.
- The impact perspective may be too narrow, that is, missing important aspects of sustainability such as social aspects, unsustainable management routines of ecosystems, and unsustainable emissions of compounds with yet undiscovered impacts.
- The commonly applied LCA methods generally lack a strategic business perspective.

In conclusion, it is possible that the relatively low impact of LCAs on business decisions is not only related to relatively low *use* of the method by decision makers in business, but also to relatively low *relevance* of traditional LCA for such purposes. LCA as currently practiced is neither complete from the sustainability perspective, nor business-oriented, nor practical from a user-friendly perspective. But as discussed in the next section, this does not mean that LCA cannot evolve to embody these characteristics.

PRELIMINARY GUIDELINES FOR STRATEGIC LIFE-CYCLE MANAGEMENT

Experience from Management of Complex Systems

It seems difficult to create comprehensible and user-friendly detailed checklists or manuals to detect optimal investment paths toward sustainability. Experience from management of any complex system (e.g., chess, traffic, or medical practice), though, points toward some guidelines for the selection of strategic paths:

- Once basic principles for the ultimate goal are clear, the individual's potential for dealing with trade-offs and for optimizing chances in multidimensional and complex situations (e.g., medical treatment) grows with experience.
- The complete investment path need not necessarily be determined up-front, only smart flexible steps followed by continuous reassessment as the "game" unfolds.
- Beyond a certain level of specificity, checklists may confuse more than help decision makers.

The overall recommendation from this would be to: (1) establish clear basic principles for sustainability up-front; (2) develop smart overall strategies and guidelines for how to approach societal compliance with these principles (i.e., to apply a framework for decisions as a shared mental model among team members); and then (3) proceed with the learning, that is, play the game and getting experienced in seeing the big picture goals and selecting stepping-stones in that direction. Once the need for more sophisticated tools, like multidimensional decision support (Figure 2), and other support systems, evolves, (4) *those too ought to be selected and designed in line with the structured overview that the basic principles provide.*

The capacity of basic principles to directly inform relatively advanced strategic decisions has been seen in many cases, such as the previously presented Electrolux, IKEA, and Hydro Polymers examples. Could this inform LCA and provide a method for assessing materials and products, and developing new products, from a full sustainability and life-cycle perspective?

Desired Features of Strategic Life-Cycle Management

Preliminary ideas for strategic life-cycle management, connecting current LCA methodology to a strategic sustainability perspective, are indicated in Table 1, Figure 4, and Table 2).

Instead of further narrowing the LCA scope, as is done in streamlined LCA, a sustainability-related LCA approach, such as SLCM, would require a systems view that tackled the problems from the broadest possible perspective (Bucciarelli, 1998). The four steps in a traditional LCA would then need to reflect the following:

Goal/Scope

The goal/scope of the study should be clearly linked to the ultimate purpose of *society reaching sustainability.* It should be recognized, for example, that for some purposes certain materials will probably ultimately not be used at all, given the large investments such use would require to assure society's compliance with the SPs. The goal/scope should also include consideration of indirect impacts that come from, for example, how ecosystems such as forests, agriculture, and fisheries are managed. Attempts should be made to include issues not yet known to harm the environment (Had CFCs been scrutinized through a SP lens, it could have been determined already upfront that large scale use, outside of tight technical loops, was not compatible with SP II).

Inventory Analysis

The inventory analysis should start from the top, with essentially no other system boundaries but the ones that apply for the whole biosphere.

Table 1. Strategic life-cycle management (SLCM) compared to other life-cycle related sustainability assessment approaches

Approach	Abridged description	Analysis specificity	Sustainability issues covered	Objective
Streamlined LCA	Overview of life-cycle environmental aspects or impacts.	Mainly overview analysis.	Focus on known environmental problems.	To give decision makers a simplified picture of system environmental load.
Traditional LCA	Detailed compilation and evaluation of materials and energy flows between a chosen system and its environment.	Detailed analysis.	Resource consumption and emissions of known pollutants within chosen scope.	To facilitate a choice of material or product with lowest environmental load values within chosen scope.
Strategic LCM	Sustainability assessment of a product life-cycle using backcasting from sustainability principles.	First overview then detailed analysis, as required.	Potential socioecological and economic problems from a full systems perspective.	To identify strategic pathways towards sustainability.

Figure 4. Strategic life-cycle management (SLCM) – sustainability principles as system boundaries. This approach starts with an overview of the whole system through the lens of the four Sustainability Principles (SPs). The large gray areas denote related hot spots, that is, impacts and issues found to be in conflict with the SPs and therefore essential for winning in the system. The smaller areas (black, or gray enclosed by a dashed line) may partly be impacts and issues newly discovered using the SPs, and partly the same impacts that were identified in figure 2, but now put in context. Some of these impacts and issues may be sufficiently described from the overview, while others (the solid black areas) may require deeper analysis using tools such as comprehensive life-cycle assessment. Other hot spot areas may not require any further analysis if, for example, the initial overview analysis reveals a strategic need to completely phase out a flow regardless of its exact size.

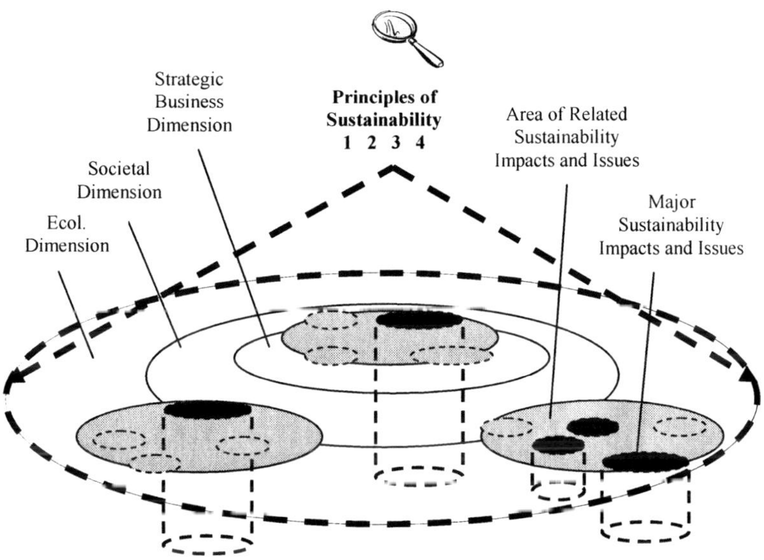

This means asking how a certain organisation or product, throughout its life-cycle, *contributes* to society's violation of the SPs. This overview will identify important issues ("hot spots") that may later require more detailed mapping, to give more information on priorities. Morevoer, other issues may be identified as less important and therefore omitted from further studies by *conscious* decisions (not a priori from gaps in methodological design).

Impact Assessment

A full LCA normally uses the inventory analysis as input, divides consumption and emissions into categories, and assigns quantitative indices according to their perceived threat to the environment. This results in one or several environmental impact indices that are presented to the decision maker. This could be valuable provided that the scope was wide enough, and includes areas where society's violations of basic SPs are also registered as impacts, regardless of whether documented damage had surfaced or not.

Results Interpretation and Improvement Assessment

The results interpretation and improvement assessment should include the full scope of options available given the full context of impacts identified above, and should also incorporate the business perspective. In a systematic way, it should deal with the complex trade-offs and prioritization exercises that are inevitable parts of choosing options. The strategic focus should be "smart stepping-stones towards sustainability" rather than relying solely on "the least harmful option right now." Although ISO 14040 (1997) and ISO 14043 (2000) refer to this component as an "interpretation" stage, a wider meaning is proposed here, implying that an improvement assessment (or a gap analysis) in relation to the SPs. should also take place at this stage.

Introductory Steps Toward Strategic Life-Cycle Management

LCA has previously been discussed in relation to a sustainability perspective. Cooper (2003) suggests using the traditional LCA approach but focusing more on impacts that are directly or indirectly linked to certain sustainable development indicators of national interest. Andersson et al. (1998) use an approach similar to the one put forward in this chapter. They also state that this perspective would open up for a more strategic approach to LCA, but they do not elaborate this idea, nor deal with the issue of complexity. The use of backcasting from sustainability principles can overcome these shortcomings and make LCA tools and instruments more useful for strategic decision making. A current example is Imperial Chemical Industries plc. (ICI), a large UK-based chemical company. They have developed, with funding from the UK government, a "Sustainability Life Cycle Analysis" (Imperial-Chemical-Industries-(ICI), 2007). This tool uses the SLCM approach and revolves around a sustainability performance matrix that scrutinizes violations of each of the four sustainability principles for each activity in the life-cycle. Other companies like Hydro Polymers and Rohm&Haas also use this tool to study life-cycle activities in their supply chains.

The framework for strategic sustainable development that is presented here has also been integrated with a traditional model for product development (Byggeth, 2001; Byggeth, Broman, & Robert, 2007). Product development teams from 10 small- and medium-sized enterprizes (SMEs) were exposed to guiding questions under each

Table 2. How a framework for sustainability can add to traditional LCA

LCA Stage	A-B-C-D Analysis Step	Benefits of Integration
1. Overall process	A-B-C-D	Provides a structured A-B-C-D manual and a set of questions with which one can "backcast from basic principles".
2. Scope/goal definition	A	Relates the exercise to the sustainability principles (SPs) so that scope is not limited to certain and/or known impacts.
3. Inventory analysis	B	Focuses on flows and practices relevant to the broadened sustainability-related scope.
4. Impact assessment	B	Impacts from contributions to violation of basic principles make it possible to not only fix known problems, but to avoid yet unknown ones.
5. Interpretation and Improvement assessment		
(i) Option generation	C	Provides overall strategic organizational objectives and improvements based on the four SPs, and categorizes them into two distinct and useful mechanisms for option generation - dematerialization and substitution/change.
(ii) Option analysis and option choice	D	Provides a set of questions (that are particularly useful at this stage) to ensure that the full context of sustainability, including the strategic business/economic dimension, is taken into account.

SP and under each stage of the product development process. With this experience, a Web-based method for sustainable product development (MSPD) is under development, aimed at creating a generic approach that can be applied for any product category. The method encompasses problem-related questions referring to the B-step with its current flows and practices (Figure 1), and solution-related questions referring to the C-step (option and vision creation). Both question types refer to the full life-cycle. These questions are run in a brainstorming session format where the answers under B and C are listed, and smart early moves from C are selected to form a strategic plan (D). Each question may trigger further extensive/quantitative analysis and the creation of indicators that would be suitable to monitor the phase out of critical flows and practices. Examples of B-questions under SP I, for instance, are: "Does our project/process/product systematically decrease its economic dependence on fossil fuels? Is it economically dependent on dissipative use of materials from the lithosphere and/or mined materials that are relatively scarce in ecosystems? Are elements from those materials currently increasing in concentration anywhere in the biosphere?"

The MSPD has also been used to produce templates for sustainable product development (TSPDs), where groups of sustainability and product experts develop tailored descriptions of various product categories. Thus, the TSPDs are

Figure 5. A future design space. Tools and concepts that are all informed by the strategic life-cycle management (SLCM) perspective constitute the design space. Tools that are already under development are the method for sustainable product development (MSPD), a library of expert templates for sustainable product development (TSPDs), a practitioners' good examples and support tools.

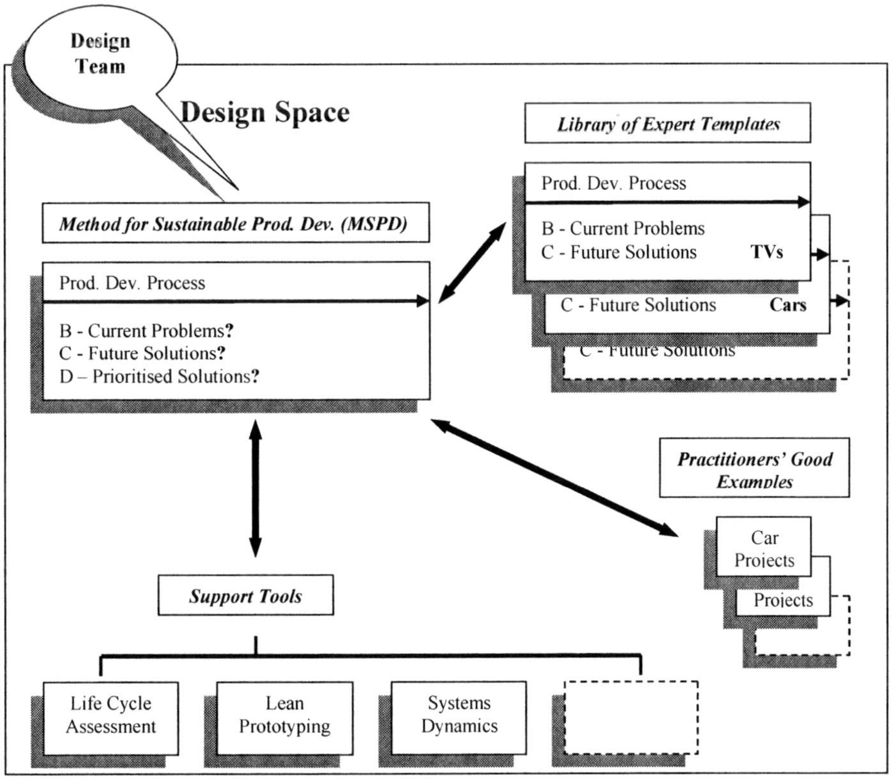

product-category-specific, but still general within the categories. Industrial designers can use the templates for filling the general sustainability gaps with innovative solutions for TVs, refrigerators, and so forth. This is intended to provide businesses with a time- and resource-efficient opportunity to see the sustainability contexts of their respective products and services. Templates have been tested in a beta-study of Matsushita's TVs, refrigerators, and for their recycling plant (METEC) in an effort to produce sustainability reports for those items (Matsushita, 2002). The TV case study is described in detail by Ny, Byggeth, MacDonald, Robert, and Broman (2008). Both new ideas and potential hot spots requiring incorporation into strategic planning and future detailed assessments (e.g., by LCA) were identified.

Future Steps Toward Strategic Life-Cycle Management

Recent MSPD and TSPD experience is suggested as a basis for developing more concrete guidelines for SLCM. We aim at a computer-based working environment ("design space") containing tools that are all informed by a framework for strategic sustainable development, thereby providing more synergistic decision support for sustainable products and services (Figure 5).

CONCLUSION

This chapter argues that a framework for sustainable development based on backcasting from basic principles for sustainability (often referred to as The Natural Step framework) could and should be used to foster a new general approach to the management of materials and products that allows the overall analysis to be informed by: (1) all issues that are essential from a basic sustainability perspective, and (2) all suggestions that can serve as flexible actions to eventually arrive at sustainability. It is suggested that this combination of framework and life-cycle assessment and management techniques, such as LCA and other support tools, be termed "strategic life-cycle management." Introductory applications of this approach suggest that it makes it possible to avoid costly assessments of flows and practices that are not critical from a sustainable development perspective, and to identify strategic gaps in knowledge or potential problems that need further assessment. Benefits are discussed particularly in relation to product development and LCA tools, but this approach could probably also improve the performance of other existing tools for the management of materials and products as well as facilitate the identification of need for, and the development of, new tools.

It is also argued that analysis dealing with system boundaries should start with an overview of the whole system, allowing *all* issues that are found to be in conflict with basic sustainability principles (SPs), as described earlier, to be taken into account. This requires a perspective that: (1) is large enough in time and space (humanity and ecosystems on Earth, both now and in the future); (2) supports assessment of products and services through the full life-cycle, where the lens is the SPs, and only thereafter are detailed studies on specific impacts undertaken by means and tools that are selected and designed for the purpose; (3) includes the strategic dimension of senior management and decision makers, that is, views innovations and design changes as economically feasible platforms and strategic trade-offs toward sustainability; (4) supports handling of complexity in a feasible and simple enough way to be practical, yet not simplistic in such a way that essential aspects of sustainability are inherently lost in the process; and (5) catalyzes innovation so that problems as well as solutions can be dealt with in a way that frees creativity from traditional constraints.

A more traditional assessment of targets might, for example, suggest that a corporation recycle 30% more than before or set recycling targets based on global best practices, instead of the more rigorous standard of recycle as much as is required to prevent the organization's contribution to the societal problem of systematic accumulations of minerals anywhere in the biosphere." Although the latter does not always give immediate answers as to how much recycling of a certain mineral is therefore required, given that there are so many possible solutions to this objective, the difference is still fundamental. Not maintaining continuous sight of the ultimate objective continuously deprives the creative process of its ultimate driver. Such a bird's-eye perspective probably also increases the potential for leapfrogging and for preventing investments that may lead to dead ends in which present problems are replaced with other ones in the future is also probably greater with the bird's-eye perspective.

ACKNOWLEDGMENT

Invaluable points of view on the manuscript from Sophie Byggeth and David Waldron are gratefully acknowledged. We also owe a special thanks to Renaud Richard for advice on some of the illustrations. This research was made possible through support from the Blekinge Institute of Technology, Karlskrona, Sweden, the Swedish Knowledge Foundation, NUTEK (the Swedish Business Development Agency), and the Center for Integrated Study of the Human Dimensions of Global Change at Carnegie Mellon University, established as a Center of Excellence in a cooperative agreement with the U.S. National Science Foundation (SBR-9521914).

REFERENCES

Aloisi de Larderel, J. (1998, October 14). *What is a sustainable enterprise?* Paper presented at the UNEP Workshop, Paris, France.

Anderson, R. C. (1998). *Mid course correction: Toward a sustainable enterprise: The Interface model.* Atlanta, USA: The Peregrinzilla Press.

Andersson, K., Eide, M. H., Lundqvist, U., & Mattsson, B. (1998). The feasibility of including sustainability in LCA for product development. *Journal of Cleaner Production, 6*(3-4), 289-298.

Andersson, R., Aronsson, M., Bucht, E., Le Clerq, L., Ebbersten, S., Edling, P., et al. (1993). *Agriculture from a scientific perspective.* Stockholm: The Federation of Swedish Farmers, Det Naturliga Steget.

Brattebø, H. (1996). *Industrial ecology—interdisciplinary perspectives and challenges. NTVA-report 2: Industrial ecology and sustainable product design.* Trondheim, Norway: The Norwegian Academy of Technological Science.

Broman, G., Byggeth, S. H., & Robèrt, K.-H. (2002). Integrating environmental aspects in engineering education. *International Journal of Engineering Education, 18*(6), 717-724.

Broman, G., Holmberg, J., & Robèrt, K.-H. (2000). Simplicity without reduction: Thinking upstream towards the sustainable society. *Interfaces, 30*(3), 13-25.

Bucciarelli, L. (1998). Project-oriented learning as part of the curriculum development. *Industrial ecology and curriculum.* Troyes, France: NTVA (Norwegian Academy of Technological Science).

Byggeth, S. H. (2001). *Integration of sustainability aspects in product development.* Unpublished Licentiate, Göteborg University, Göteborg, Sweden.

Byggeth, S. H., Broman, G. I., & Robert, K. H. (2007). A method for sustainable product development based on a modular system of guiding questions. *Journal of Cleaner Production,* (15), 1-11.

Christiansen, K. (1997). *Simplifying LCA: Just a cut?* Brussels, Belgium: SETAC (Society of Environmental Toxicology and Chemistry)-Europe.

Cook, D. (2004). *The natural step towards a sustainable society.* Dartington, UK: Green Books.

Cooper, J. (2003). Life-cycle assessment and sustainable development indicators. *Journal of Industrial Ecology, 7*(1), 12-15.

Dreborg, K. H. (1996). Essence of backcasting. *Futures, 28*(9), 813-828.

Electrolux. (1994). *Electrolux annual report 1994.* Stockholm: Electrolux.

Everard, M., Monaghan, M., & Ray, D. (2000). *2020 vision series No2: PVC and sustainability.* The Natural Step UK/UK Environment Agency.

Fishbein, B., McGarry, L. S., & Dillon, P. S. (2000). *Leasing: A step toward producer responsibility.* New York: Inform.

Frankl, P., & Rubik, F. (2000). *Life-cycle assessment in industry and business: Adoption patterns, applications and implications.* Heidelberg, Germany: Springer-Verlag.

Geiser, K. (2001). *Materials matter: Toward a sustainable materials policy.* Cambridge, MA, USA: MIT Press.

Gordon, S. (2004, March 15). *The natural step and Whistler's journey towards sustainability.* Retrieved July 6, 2008, from www.whistler.ca

Graedel, T. E. (1998). *Streamlined life-cycle assessment.* Upper Saddle River, NJ, USA: Prentice Hall.

Hawken, P. A., & Lovins, H. L. (1999). *Natural capitalism: Creating the next industrial revolution.* Snowmass, CO, USA: Rocky Mountain Institute.

Heinrich, A. B., & Klopffer, W. (2002). Integrating a new section in International Journal of LCA. *International Journal of Life Cycle Assessment, 7*(6), 315-316.

Heiskanen, E. (2000). Institutionalization of life-cycle thinking in the everyday discourse of market actors. *Journal of Industrial Ecology, 4*(4), 31-45.

Hoagland, N. T. (2001). Non-traditional tools for LCA and sustainability. *The International Journal of Life Cycle Assessment, 6*(2), 110-113.

Holmberg, J. (1998). Backcasting: A natural step in operationalising sustainable development(*). *Greener Management International,* (23), 30-52.

Holmberg, J., Lundqvist, U., Robèrt, K.-H., & Wackernagel, M. (1999). The ecological footprint from a systems perspective of sustainability. *International Journal of Sustainable Development and World Ecology, 6*(1), 17-33.

Holmberg, J., & Robèrt, K.-H. (2000). Backcasting: A framework for strategic planning. *International Journal of Sustainable Development and World Ecology, 7*(4), 291-308.

Holmberg, J., Robèrt, K.-H., & Eriksson, K.-E. (1996). Socio-ecological principles for sustainability. In R. Costanza, O. Segura, & J. Martinez-Alier (Eds.), *Getting down to Earth: Practical applications of ecological economics, International Society of Ecological Economics* (pp. 17-48). Washington DC, USA: Island Press.

Imperial-Chemical-Industries-(ICI). (2007). *ICI sustainability review 2006.* London, UK: ICI.

International-Organization-for-Standardization-(ISO). (1997). *Environmental management-life-cycle assessment: Principles and framework. ISO 14040.* Geneva, Switzerland: ISO.

International-Organization-for-Standardization-(ISO). (2000). *Environmental management--life-*

cycle assessment–lifecycle interpretation. ISO 14043. Geneva, Switzerland: ISO.

James, S., & Lahti, T. (2004). *The natural step for communities: How cities and towns can change to sustainable practices*. Gabriola Island, British Columbia, Canada: New Society Publishers.

Johnson, R. (2004). *Interview with director of Environmental Affairs at IKEA during 1989-1998.*

Karlsson, S. (1999). Closing the technospheric flows of toxic metals: Modeling lead losses from a lead-acid battery system for Sweden. *Journal of Industrial Ecology, 3*(1), 23-40.

Klopffer, W. (2003). Life-cycle-based methods for sustainable product development. *The International Journal of Life Cycle Assessment, 8*(3), 157-159.

Korhonen, J. (2004). Industrial ecology in the strategic sustainable development model: Strategic applications of industrial ecology. *Journal of Cleaner Production, 12*(8-10), 809-823.

Leadbitter, J. (2002). PVC and sustainability. *Progress in Polymer Science, 27*(10), 2197-2226.

Lindfors, L.-G., Christiansen, K., Hoffman, L., Virtanen, Y., Juntilla, V., Hanssen, O.-J., et al. (1995). *The Nordic guidelines for life-cycle assessment. Nord 1995:20*. Copenhagen, Denmark: Nordic Council of Ministers.

Matsushita. (2002). *Environmental sustainability report 2002*. Osaka, Japan: Matsushita Electric Industrial.

Max-Neef, M., Elizalde, A., Hopenhayn, M., Herrera, F., Zemelman, H., Jataba, J., et al. (1989). Human scale development: An option for the future. *Development Dialogue Journal, 1989*(1).

Mintzberg, H., Lampel, J., & Ahlstrand, B. (1998). *Strategy safari: A guided tour through the wilds of strategic management*. New York: Free Press.

Nattrass, B. (1999). *The natural step: Corporate learning and innovation for sustainability*. Unpublished doctoral thesis, The California Institute of Integral Studies, San Francisco, California, USA.

Nattrass, B., & Altomare, M. (2002). *Dancing with the tiger*. Gabriola Island, British Columbia, Canada: New Society Publishers.

Ny, H., Byggeth, S. H., MacDonald, J. P., Robèrt, K.-H., & Broman, G. (2008). *Introducing templates for sustainable product development through an evaluation case study of televisions at Matsushita Electric Group*. In press.

Ny, H., MacDonald, J. P., Broman, G., Yamamoto, R., & Robèrt, K.-H. (2006). Sustainability constraints as system boundaries: An approach to making life-cycle management strategic. *Journal of Industrial Ecology, 10*(1).

Pauli, G. (1998). *UpSizing: The road to zero emissions, more jobs, more income, and no pollution*. Sheffield, United Kingdom: Greenleaf Publishing.

Pennington, D. W., Potting, J., Finnveden, G., Lindeijer, E., Jolliet, O., Rydberg, T., et al. (2004). LCA Part 2: Current impact assessment practice. *Environment International, 30*, 721-739.

Rees, W. E., & Wackernagel, M. (1994). Ecological footprints and appropriated carrying capacity: Measuring the natural capital requirement of the human economy. In A. M. Jansson, H. M., C. Folke, & R. Costanza (Eds.), *Investing in natural capital: The ecological economics approach to sustainability*. Washington, DC, USA: Island Press.

Resort-Municipality-of-Whistler-(RMOW). (2005). *Whistler 2020: Moving toward a sustainable future*. RMOW.

Robèrt, K.-H. (1994). *The natural challenge*. Stockholm: Ekerlids Publisher.

Robèrt, K.-H. (1997, June 5-7). *ICA/Electrolux: A case report from 1992.* Paper presented at the 40th CIES Annual Executive Congress, Boston, MA.

Robèrt, K.-H. (2000). Tools and concepts for sustainable development: How do they relate to a general framework for sustainable development, and to each other? *Journal of Cleaner Production, 8*(3), 243-254.

Robèrt, K.-H. (2002). *The natural step story: Seeding a quiet revolution.* Gabriola Island, British Columbia, Canada: New Society Publishers.

Robèrt, M. (2005). Backcasting and econometrics for sustainable planning: Information technology and individual preferences of travel. *Journal of Cleaner Production, 13*(8), 841-852.

Robèrt, K.-H., Broman, G., Waldron, D., Ny, H., Byggeth, S. H., Cook, D., et al. (2004). *Strategic leadership towards sustainability* (3rd ed.). Karlskrona, Sweden: Psilanders grafiska.

Robèrt, K.-H., Daly, H. E., Hawken, P. A., & Holmberg, J. (1997). A compass for sustainable development. *International Journal of Sustainable Development and World Ecology, 4*, 79-92.

Robèrt, K.-H., Holmberg, J., & Weizsacker, E. U. v. (2000). Factor X for subtle policy-making. *Greener Management International*, (31), 25-38.

Robèrt, K.-H., Schmidt-Bleek, B., Aloisi de Larderel, J., Basile, G., Jansen, J. L., Kuehr, R., et al. (2002). Strategic sustainable development: Selection, design and synergies of applied tools. *Journal of Cleaner Production, 10*(3), 197-214.

Robinson, J. B. (1982). Energy backcasting: A proposed method of policy analysis. *Energy Policy, 10*(4), 337-344.

Robinson, J. B. (1990). Future under glass: A recipe for people who hate to predict. *Futures, 22*(9), 820-843.

Romm, J. (1994). *Lean and clean management.* New York: Kodansha International.

Schmidt-Bleek, F. (1997). *MIPS and factor 10 for a sustainable and profitable economy.* Wuppertal, Germany: Wuppertal Institute.

Suzuki, M. (2000). The zero emission concept in the 21st century. In U.-E. Simonis (Ed.), *Ecology yearbook 2001* (pp. 129-135). Munich, Germany: Verlag C. H. Beck.

Todd, J. A. (1996). Streamlining. In M. A. Curran (Ed.), *Environmental life cycle assessment* (pp. 4.1-4.17). New York: McGraw-Hill.

Udo de Haes, H. A., Heijungs, R., Suh, S., & Huppes, G. (2004). Three strategies to overcome the limitations of LCA. *Journal of Industrial Ecology, 2*(3), 19-32.

Waldron, D. (2005). *A new education: Strategic leadership towards sustainability.* In Paper presented at the Seminar on Education for Sustainable Development, Stockholm, Sweden.

Waldron, D., Byggeth, S. H., Ny, H., Broman, G., & Robèrt, K.-H. (2004). *Structured comprehension for systems thinking, learning and leadership towards sustainability: Environmental Management for Sustainable Universities (EMSU).* Tecnológico de Monterrey, Mexico.

van Berkel, R., Willems, E., & Lafleur, M. (1997). The relationship between cleaner production and industrial ecology. *Journal of Industrial Ecology, 1*(1), 51-66.

Widheden, J. (2002). *Methods for environmental assessments: Useful to the DANTES project.* Retrieved July 6, 2008, from http://www.dantes.info/Publications

Wrisberg, N., Udo de Haes, H. A., Triebswetter, U., Eder, P., & Clift, R. (Eds.). (2002). *Analytical tools for environmental design and management in a systems perspective* (Vol. 10). Dordrecht, The Netherlands: Kluwer Academic Publishers.

Zackrisson, M., Enroth, M., & Wilding, A. (1999). *Environmental management systems: Paper tiger or powerful tool. IVL-Report B 1351.* Stockholm: IVL Swedish Environmental Research Institute.

ADDITIONAL READING

Life-Cycle Assessment (LCA)

Andersson, K., Eide, M. H., Lundqvist, U., & Mattsson, B. (1998). The feasibility of including sustainability in LCA for product development. *Journal of Cleaner Production, 6*(3-4), 289-298.

Baumann, H., Boons, F., & Bragd, A. (2002). Mapping the green product development field: Engineering, policy and business perspectives. *Journal of Cleaner Production, 10*(5), 409-425.

Baumann, H., & Tillman, A.-M. (2004). *The hitch hiker's guide to LCA: An orientation in LCA methodology and application.* Lund, Sweden: Studentlitteratur.

Graedel, T. E. (1997). Designing the perfect green product: SLCA in reverse. In *ISEE-1997: Proceedings of the 1997 IEEE International Symposium on Electronics and the Environment* (pp. 317-321).

Graedel, T. E. (1998). *Streamlined life-cycle assessment.* Upper Saddle River, NJ, USA: Prentice Hall.

International-Organization-for-Standardization-(ISO). (1997). *Environmental management-life-cycle assessment: Principles and framework. ISO 14040.* Geneva, Switzerland: ISO.

Lindfors, L.-G., Christiansen, K., Hoffman, L., Virtanen, Y., Juntilla, V., Hanssen, O.-J., et al. (1995). *The Nordic guidelines for life-cycle assessment. Nord 1995:20.* Copenhagen, Denmark: Nordic Council of Ministers.

Backcasting

Anderson, K. L. (2001). Reconciling the electricity industry with sustainable development: Backcasting, a strategic alternative. *Futures, 33*(7), 607-623.

Dreborg, K. H. (1996). Essence of backcasting. *Futures, 28*(9), 813-828.

Robinson, J. B. (1982). Energy backcasting: A proposed method of policy analysis. *Energy Policy, 10(*4), 337-344.

Robinson, J. B. (1990). Future under glass: A recipe for people who hate to predict. *Futures, 22*(9), 820-843.

Robinson, J. B. (2003). Future subjunctive: Backcasting as social learning. *Futures, 35.*

A Framework for Strategic Sustainable Development (FSSD)

Broman, G., Holmberg, J., & Robèrt, K.-H. (2000). Simplicity without reduction: Thinking upstream towards the sustainable society. *Interfaces, 30*(3), 13-25.

Holmberg, J. (1998). Backcasting: A natural step in operationalising sustainable development(*). *Greener Management International,* (23), 30-52.

Holmberg, J., & Robèrt, K.-H. (2000). Backcasting: A framework for strategic planning. *International Journal of Sustainable Development and World Ecology, 7*(4), 291-308.

Robèrt, K.-H. (1994). *The natural challenge.* Sweden: Ekerlids Publisher.

Robèrt, K.-H. (2000). Tools and concepts for sustainable development, how do they relate to a general framework for sustainable development, and to each other? *Journal of Cleaner Production, 8*(3), 243-254.

Established Sustainable Development Tools and Concepts in Relation to FSSD

Byggeth, S. H., Broman, G. I., & Robert, K.-H. (2007). A method for sustainable product development based on a modular system of guiding questions. *Journal of Cleaner Production,* (15), 1-11.

Byggeth, S. H., & Horschorner, E. (2006). Handling trade-offs in ecodesign tools for sustainable product development and procurement. *Journal of Cleaner Production, 14*(15-16), 1420-1430.

Byggeth, S., Ny, H., Wall, J., & Broman, G. I. (2007). Introductory procedure for sustainability. In *Proceedings of Driven Design Optimization, International Conference on Engineering Design (ICED'07).* Paris, France: The Design Society, AIP-PRIMECA and GDR-MACS.

Holmberg, J., Lundqvist, U., Robèrt, K.-H., & Wackernagel, M. (1999). The ecological footprint from a systems perspective of sustainability. *International Journal of Sustainable Development and World Ecology, 6*(1), 17-33.

Korhonen, J. (2004). Industrial ecology in the strategic sustainable development model: Strategic applications of industrial ecology. *Journal of Cleaner Production, 12*(8-10), 809-823.

MacDonald, J. P. (2005). Strategic sustainable development using the ISO 14001 Standard. *Journal of Cleaner Production, 13*(6), 631-644.

Ny, H. (2006). *Strategic life-cycle modeling for sustainable product development.* Unpublished Licentiate, Blekinge Institute of Technology, Karlskrona, Sweden.

Ny, H., MacDonald, J. P., Broman, G., Yamamoto, R., & Robèrt, K.-H. (2006). Sustainability constraints as system boundaries: An approach to making life-cycle management strategic. *Journal of Industrial Ecology, 10*(1).

Robèrt, K.-H., Daly, H. E., Hawken, P. A., & Holmberg, J. (1997). A compass for sustainable development. *International Journal of Sustainable Development and World Ecology, 4,* 79-92.

Robèrt, K.-H., Holmberg, J., & Weizsacker, E. U. v. (2000). Factor X for subtle policy-making. *Greener Management International,* (31), 25-38.

Robèrt, K.-H., Schmidt-Bleek, B., Aloisi de Larderel, J., Basile, G., Jansen, J. L., Kuehr, R., et al. (2002). Strategic sustainable development: Selection, design and synergies of applied tools. *Journal of Cleaner Production, 10*(3), 197-214.

Rowland, E., & Sheldon, C. (1999). *The natural step and ISO 14001: Guidance on the integration of a framework for sustainable development into environmental management systems British Standards Institute (BSI).*

Policy Applications of FSSD

Cook, D. (2004). *The natural step towards a sustainable society.* Dartington, UK: Green Books.

James, S., & Lahti, T. (2004). *The natural step for communities: How cities and towns can change to sustainable practices.* Gabriola Island, British Columbia, Canada: New Society Publishers.

Robèrt, K.-H., Strauss-Kahn, D., Aelvoet, M., Aguilera, I., Bakoyannis, D., Boeri, T., et al. (2004). *Building a political Europe: 50 proposals for tomorrow's Europe. "A sustainable project for tomorrow's Europe."* Brussels: European Commission.

Industrial Applications of FSSD

Anderson, R. C. (1998). *Mid course correction: Toward a sustainable enterprise: The Interface model.* Atlanta, GA, USA: The Peregrinzilla Press.

Electrolux. (1994). *Electrolux annual report 1994.* Stockholm: Electrolux.

Leadbitter, J. (2002). PVC and sustainability. *Progress in Polymer Science, 27*(10), 2197-2226.

Matsushita. (2002). *Environmental sustainability report 2002.* Osaka, Japan: Matsushita Electric Industrial.

Nattrass, B. (1999). *The natural step: Corporate learning and innovation for sustainability.* Unpublished doctoral thesis, The California Institute of Integral Studies, San Francisco, California, USA.

Nattrass, B., & Altomare, M. (2002). *Dancing with the tiger.* Gabriola Island, British Columbia, Canada: New Society Publishers.

Robèrt, K.-H. (1997, June 5-7). *ICA/Electrolux: A case report from 1992.* Paper presented at the 40th CIES Annual Executive Congress, Boston, MA.

Robèrt, K.-H. (2002). *The natural step story: Seeding a quiet revolution.* Gabriola Island, British Columbia, Canada: New Society Publishers.

Chapter IV
Environmental Criteria in a MCDM Context

Ahmed Bufardi
Federal Institute of Aquatic Science and Technology (EAWAG), Switzerland

Dimitris Kiritsis
Ecole Polytechnique Fédérale de Lausanne, Switzerland

ABSTRACT

This chapter addresses the main issues that are worth considering when using environmental criteria in a multiple criteria decision making (MCDM) context and provides some guidance for a proper and efficient use of environmental criteria in a MCDM context. Among the main issues considered in this chapter, we can mention the definition and representation of criteria, their weighting, and their selection. The relation of criterion to other notions such as attribute, objective, goal, and indicator is also explained. Regarding the environmental criteria, we emphasize their main characteristics and indicate how these characteristics can support the users in selecting appropriate MCDM methods. An illustrative example about the selection of the best scenario for the treatment of a vacuum cleaner at the end of its life cycle is given. It shows the type of reverse supply chain problems in which environmental criteria can be used to evaluate and compare alternatives.

INTRODUCTION

Several factors such as the continuously increasing harm caused to the environment by the industry, the increasing interest of the populations in the environmental issues, and the reinforcement of the regulations regarding the protection of the environment raised the great importance of considering environmental criteria for the evaluation of alternatives in product life cycle decision mak-

Copyright © 2009, IGI Global, distributing in print or electronic forms without written permission of IGI Global is prohibited.

ing problems. Consequently, the development and design of products with reduced environmental impact during their whole life cycle is one of the important challenges toward a more sustainable society.

In a recent research work by Palme and Tillman (2007), the authors reported that sustainable development indicators are well used by companies for accounting and reporting purposes, whereas their use in planning and decision making situations is rare despite the importance recognized for the use of sustainable development indicators in planning and decision making.

A product causes negative environmental impacts during each of its life cycle phases. Consequently, the environmental impact of products should be considered throughout their whole life cycle from design until their final destination (recycling, remanufacturing, reuse, incineration, etc.).

The recovery of products when they reach the end of their useful life is a main concern in end-of-life (EOL) product planning and management. The main concept related to the recovery and processing of EOL products is that of reverse supply chain. Among the factors that have favoured the emergence of reverse supply chain as an important research field figures the increasingly constraining legislation with regard to the responsibility of companies toward their products throughout the whole lifecycle, including take-back and recycling. Examples of that are the European Union Directive on Waste Electrical and Electronic Equipment (WEEE Directive) and the European Union Directive on End-of-Life Vehicles (ELV Directive).

The aim of using environmental criteria is to enable the evaluation of environmental impacts both beneficial and harmful of a set of alternatives in a planning or decision making problem (Wang, Yang, & Xu, 2006).

In contrast to the methods addressing only the environmental impact indicators and which are mostly based on the use of impact indicators taken from life cycle assessment (LCA) methods and the cost based models such as cost benefit analysis (CBA), which are based exclusively on minimizing cost or maximizing profit, the MCDM approach considers various types of criteria such as environmental, economic, and social criteria.

Reverse supply chain involves a number of MCDM problems among which we can mention the selection of collection centers and recovery facilities (Pochampally, Gupta, & Gupta, 2004) and the selection of appropriate scenarios for treating EOL products (Bufardi, Gheorghe, Kritsis, & Xirouchakis, 2004).

It is worth recalling that a MCDM problem consists of comparing a number of alternatives (design concepts, materials, manufacturing processes, maintenance strategies, EOL scenarios, etc.) with respect to multiple criteria in order to choose a subset of best alternatives, to rank them from the best to the worst or to sort them according to predefined norms (Roy, 1996).

The comparison of alternatives in a MCDM context can be made according to different types of criteria: environmental, economic, technical, social, institutional, and so forth. Hence, environmental criteria can be considered alone or simultaneously together with other types of criteria. In this chapter, we focus on environmental criteria, even though we will consider their relation to the other types of criteria and we will address some issues related to the concept of criterion in general.

In the past, the MCDM approach suffered from the problem of not being adopted by official organizations. This is now changing positively. Indeed, recently, a number of European Union and United Nations' documents recommended the use of multicriteria analysis for applications where criteria cannot be easily expressed in terms of monetary values (Camper & Turcanu, 2007). According to the same authors, well-known institutions such as the World Bank and the United

Nations have applied multicriteria analysis in a number of projects, mainly those involving environmental and public health issues.

In general, the environmental criteria that are suitable for the evaluation of alternatives in a product life cycle context are those that are usually used in LCA applications. Most of the environmental criteria are related to: (i) the resources consumption which includes raw materials, energy and water, (ii) the production of wastes both solid and liquid, (iii) emissions of noise, and pollutants to the air, water, and soil, and (iv) health and safety issues. Sometimes health and safety issues are considered within the social dimension.

The chapter is organized as follows. First, we give the definition, characteristics, and representation of criteria and their relation to attributes, objectives, goals, and indicators in addition to the presentation of the specific characteristics of environmental criteria. Next, we deal with the important problem of weighting of criteria. We indicate the main existing weighting techniques and emphasize the importance of knowing the role and meaning of weights in a MCDM problem. The selection of environmental criteria is presented after that, and an illustrative example about the selection of the best EOL scenario for treating a vacuum cleaner at the end of its life cycle is provided. Then, some important directions of research and future trends related to the topic addressed in this chapter are presented. Finally, concluding remarks about the chapter are given.

CRITERIA, ATTRIBUTES, OBJECTIVES, GOALS, AND INDICATORS

Definition and Characteristics of Criteria

For Zeleny (1982), criteria are measures, rules, and standards that guide decision making. Bouyssou (1990) defined a criterion as "a tool allowing comparison of alternatives according to a particular point of view." According to Bana e Costa, Stewart, and Vansnick (1997) "Bouyssou's definition of a criterion not only incorporates a common-language sense of a criterion as defined by Zeleny (1982) but also the more technical notion of a criterion as a model i.e. a model of preferences between elements of a set of real or fictitious alternatives."

Theoretically, a criterion can be defined as a function, defined on a set of alternatives, and taking its values in a totally ordered set (i.e., a set for which all elements are comparable) and representing the decision maker's preferences according to some point of view (Vincke, 1992). A criterion can be quantitative if it is expressed in a numerical scale or qualitative if it is expressed in a linguistic scale (such as very high, high, medium, low, very low).

To be used in a MCDA context, the following characteristics of a criterion should be specified:

- **Direction of preferences**: The direction of preferences can be either minimization or maximization. Minimization means that alternatives with low performances are preferred to those with higher performances, that is, the higher the performance of an alternative is, the worse this alternative is, and maximization means that alternatives with high performances are preferred to those with lower performances, that is, the higher the performance of an alternative is, the better this alternative is.
- **Scale of measurement**: A criterion can be measured on different scales depending on the data available. It can also be measured qualitatively or quantitatively. Generally, qualitative evaluations are used when quantitative evaluations cannot be obtained. However, there exist some criteria which are purely qualitative such as comfort, customer satisfaction, and so forth.

- **Unit of measurement**: A criterion can be measured in different units depending on the nature of data at hand. For example, to measure weight, one can use grams for small weights, kilograms for medium weights, or tons for big weights. Only one unit of measurement should be chosen for a criterion. The unit of measurement should be specified for quantitative criteria. There is no unit of measurement for qualitative criteria.

In a MCDA context, Roy (1996) proposes the use of a coherent family of criteria, that is, criteria that satisfies properties of exhaustiveness, cohesiveness, and nonredundancy. Nonredundancy is defined below. Exhaustiveness is closer to the completeness condition defined below and cohesiveness concerns coherence between local preferences of each criterion and global preferences.

Among the conditions that the family of criteria should satisfy, we can quote:

- **Completeness** (Keeney & Raiffa, 1976). Completeness means that all important points of view (criteria) are covered by the considered family of criteria;
- **Nonredundancy** (Keeney & Raiffa, 1976). Nonredundancy means that two or more criteria should not measure the same thing;
- **Minimality** (Keeney & Raiffa, 1976). Minimality means that the dimension of the problem should be kept to a minimum;
- **Operationality** (Keeney & Raiffa, 1976). Operationality means that the set of criteria can be measured and meaningfully used in the analysis. Even if a criterion is important for the problem under consideration, if there is no way to measure it cannot be used efficiently to solve the problem; and
- **Discriminality**. Discriminality means that the criteria should discriminate between alternatives: Indeed, if all alternatives have the same value on a certain criterion, then this criterion will not play any role in the comparison of these alternatives.

The completeness property can be achieved by considering all points of view that can have an influence on the decision-making problem under consideration. It is difficult to have a set of completely independent criteria. There often exists some interaction (positive or negative) between two criteria. The objective is to use less correlated criteria which can be considered as nonredundant to some extent. According to Hokkanen, Lahdelma, and Salminen (2000), when trying to achieve completeness, it is difficult to avoid partial overlapping criteria and one way of reducing overlapping consists of introducing a larger set of more restricted criteria which contradicts the minimality requirement.

There exist in general various types of criteria such as environmental, economic, social, and technical, and depending on the particular domain of application some specific types of criteria can be considered. For example, in the case of product development, criteria related to the functionality, ergonomics, and geometry aspects can be considered.

Environmental criteria as well as economic and social criteria are present in almost all domains of activity and especially in the manufacturing industry.

Once the criteria are well defined with their characteristics, then they are used to evaluate and compare the alternatives. Often, in the form of a table or a matrix of evaluation, the alternatives are disposed on the rows and the criteria on the columns.

Sometimes to account for constraints in some MCDM applications, elimination thresholds are associated to criteria to eliminate those alternatives with very bad scores. This can be used as a first filter such that only those alternatives that do not fail to have on any criterion a value worse than the associated elimination threshold are selected for further consideration.

It is worth recalling that the evaluation of all alternatives with respect to a given criterion should be realized in the same conditions in terms of procedures (e.g., formula, measurement tool, etc.), boundaries (e.g., temporal, spatial, etc.), and so forth.

Threshold vs. Evaluation Criteria

In a decision making problem, there are some characteristics which are necessary to meet and others which should be met as much as possible. The criteria related to the necessary characteristics are called threshold criteria and criteria which are related to the desirable characteristics (i.e., those to be satisfied as much as possible) are called evaluation criteria.

Threshold criteria are used in the phase of screening alternatives to eliminate infeasible solutions and can be called *screening* criteria. They often reflect technical, regulatory, policy, cost, time, imperatives, and so forth.

The evaluation criteria are used in the selection phase where the alternatives are evaluated and compared on the basis of their performances with respect to the evaluation criteria.

In the MCDM literature, the evaluation criteria are the most used because it is often assumed that a set of feasible alternatives is already given, whereas in real-case applications, the set of feasible alternatives is one of the important and difficult tasks of the decision making process where the threshold criteria can play a crucial role. Indeed, Belton, Ackerman, and Shepherd (1997) mentioned that "work in the field of multiple criteria analysis has generally focused on evaluation procedures where it is assumed that there already exists a well-defined problem with specified alternatives and a set of criteria against which these are to be evaluated whereas for real-world applications, problems are rarely so well structured."

Some criteria such as cost can be both threshold and evaluation criteria. Indeed, a threshold on the cost criterion can be used to eliminate alternatives that are not economically feasible and at the same time among the alternatives that are economically feasible, as decision makers still prefer those which have a lower cost.

Relation to Attributes, Objectives, Goals, and Indicators

There are other notions such as attribute, objective, goal, and indicator which are closely related to that of criterion.

There is no common agreement between researchers about a clear definition of these notions and the main differences between them. However, all of them consider that these notions are tools that allow the evaluation and comparison of alternatives in a planning or decision making problem.

Some authors such as Triantaphyllou, Shu, Sanchez, and Ray (1998) consider that attributes, goals, and criteria designate the same notion. However, other researchers claim that there is a difference between them.

According to Sen (2001) an objective is an attribute with a direction of preferences (maximization or minimization). For example, the minimization of energy use and the maximization of percentage of recyclable materials in a product are objectives, whereas energy use and percentage of recyclable materials are attributes/criteria.

The main difference between criterion and attribute is that attribute has not necessarily a direction of preference. For example, color is an attribute and there is no common agreed preference distinction between different colors. The preferences about color are not only different from one application to another, but also from one decision maker to another.

Keeney and Raiffa (1976) gave a more detailed definition of objective, attribute, and goal: "an objective usually indicates the direction in which we should strive to do better and is measured using an attribute whereas a goal consists of fixing a certain target to achieve on the objective." For example, CO_2 emission is a criterion, the minimization of CO_2 emission is an objective, and a reduction of 10% of CO_2 emission is a goal.

Sometimes the evaluation of attributes/criteria requires their decomposition into elementary indicators which are easy to measure. Roy (2000) defined an indicator as "an instrument (parameter, variable, etc.) which synthesizes, in qualitative or quantitative terms, certain information intended to formulate a judgment on an alternative with respect to some of its characteristics, attributes, criteria or effects (consequences) that can result from its execution."

The key issue is not the appellation itself, but rather its right understanding and its proper use in a decision making context.

Definition and Representation of Criteria

There are two main approaches to define and represent environmental criteria: a top-down approach starting from a general view of the problem and then narrowing down into more specific issues (Belton & Vickers, 1990; Keeney & Raiffa, 1976; Saaty, 1980) and a bottom-up approach starting from specific issues of the problem and ending with a more general view (Roy, 2000).

A convenient approach to define criteria to compare alternatives is to follow what is called a top-down approach starting from a general view of the problem and then narrowing down into more specific issues, as shown in Figure 1.

The most general view which is mentioned in Figure 1 is that of dimension. There are 4 main dimensions which represent 4 different points of view from which alternatives can be assessed and compared: technical and the 3 dimensions of sustainability: economic, environmental, and social. It is worth noticing that other dimensions such as institutional and managerial can be considered if relevant. Within each dimension there can be various categories of criteria. For example, in the environmental dimension, a category can be natural resources. Within each category, there can be various aspects. For example, within the category "natural resources," the energy consumption is an aspect and within this aspect "total nonrenewable energy consumption" is identified as a criterion. A criterion can be measured by means of one or more indicators.

If Roy (2000) advocates a bottom-up approach to represent criteria, other authors such as Keeney and Raiffa (1976), Satty (1980), and Belton and Vickers (1990) consider a top-down approach called a hierarchical approach, where an overall point of view is decomposed into subpoints of view which are in their turn decomposed into sub-subpoints of view until relevant points of view are reached. According to Bouyssou (1990) the bottom-up approach and the hierarchical approach are not exclusive. Other approaches can be used. A detailed hierarchical presentation of criteria under the form main objective/dimension/aspect/criterion/indicator is shown in Figure 2.

In the hierarchical representation, the main objective designates the main reason of performing the decision making activity. In the case of the treatment of EOL products, the objective can be the selection of the best compromise scenario for treating a product at the end of its life cycle

Figure 1. From dimensions to indicators

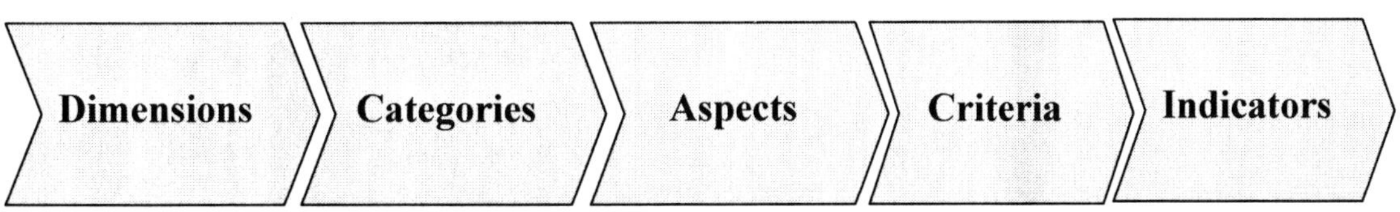

Figure 2. Hierarchical definition of criteria

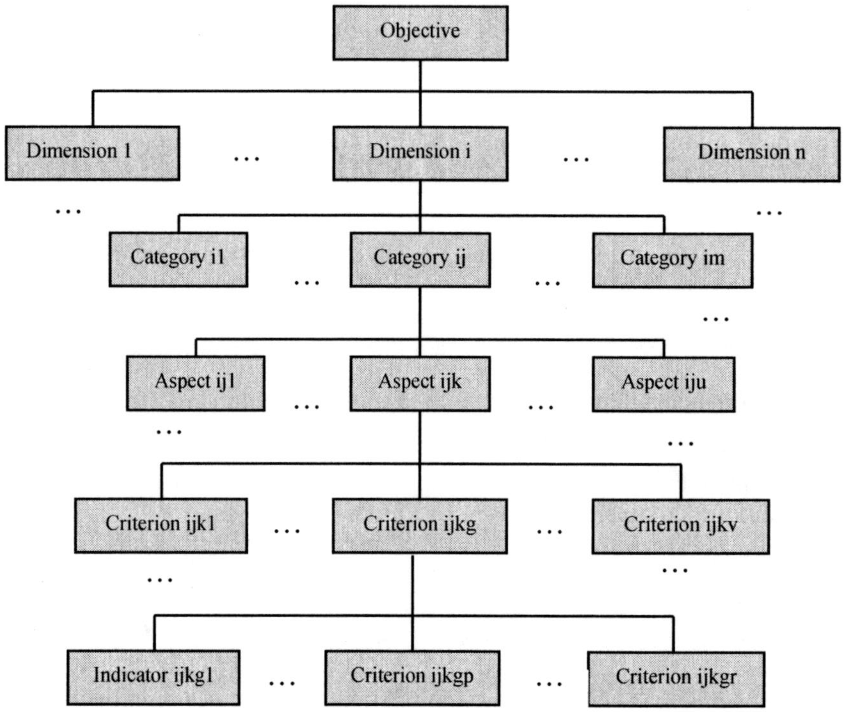

Figure 3. The main categories of the environmental dimension

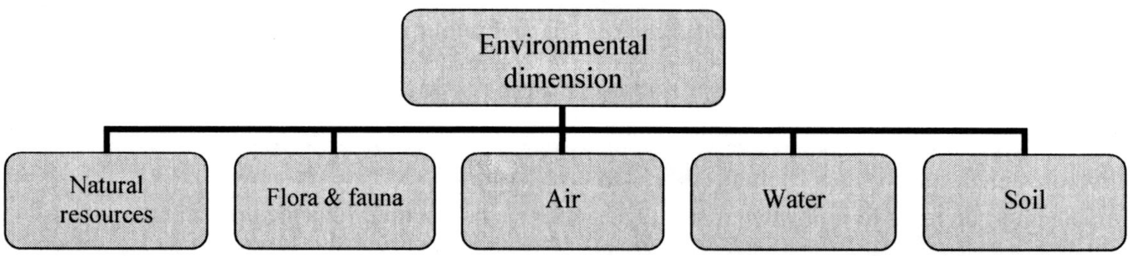

(Bufardi et al., 2004). The elements of the other levels of the hierarchy, that is, dimensions, aspects, criteria, and indicators, are explained above.

For the definition of environmental criteria/indicators, we adopt the concept-specification (also called dimensional analysis) method where the environmental dimension is decomposed into categories, the categories are decomposed into aspects, and the aspects are decomposed into criteria and the criteria into indicators.

The environmental dimension can be decomposed into five different categories: natural resources, flora and fauna, air, water, and soil (Figure 3). Health and safety is considered as being part of the social dimension even though some researchers consider it within the environmental dimension.

The main aspects associated to the environmental categories in Figure 3 are shown in Figure 4 (adapted from Adda et al., 2002, and Bufardi, Sakara, & Kiritsis, 2002).

Figure 4. The aspects of the environmental categories

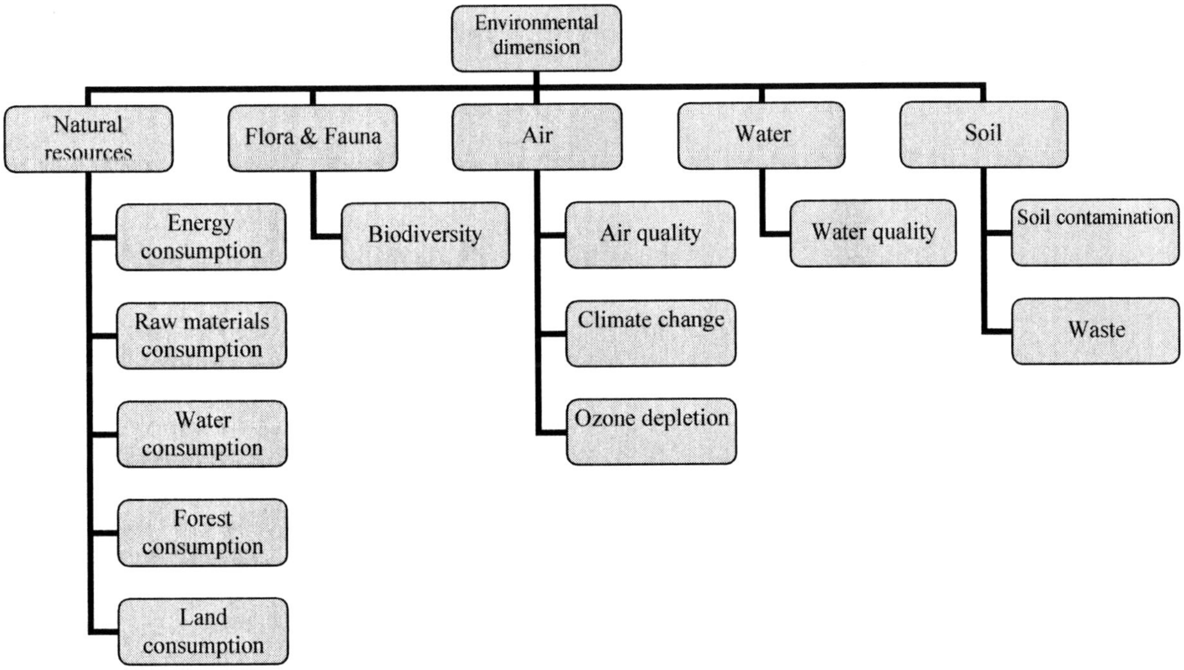

Figure 5. The criteria associated to the aspects of the category "natural resources"

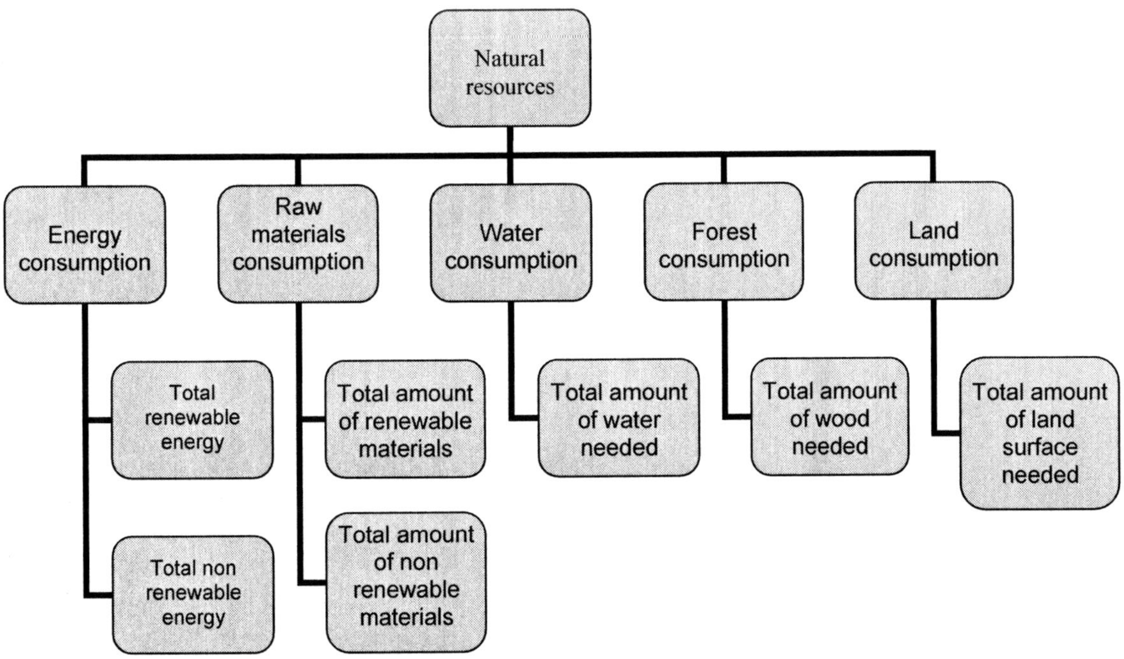

The categories air, water, and soil are related to the pollution generated by the product/system under consideration. If we replace these 3 categories by a larger category *pollution* we get the usual 3 categories of environmental issues: natural resources, biodiversity, and pollution.

The criteria associated to the environmental aspects of the category "natural resources" are provided in Figure 5 (adapted from Adda et al., 2002, and Bufardi et al., 2002).

Due to limitation in the space available for the chapter, the definition of criteria for other environmental categories will not be shown. Indeed, the objective is just to show the procedure followed to obtain the criteria. There exists an abundant literature proposing environmental indicators/criteria for different planning and decision making purposes.

Characteristics of Environmental Criteria

The main characteristics of environmental criteria are summarized as follows:

- **Incommensurability**. In the domain of environmental evaluation, it is not reasonable to assume the commensurability of criteria because in general it involves various aspects such as raw materials, energy and water consumption, solid and liquid wastes, emissions of noise and pollutants to the air, water and soil, and health and safety issues, and consequently the corresponding criteria are incommensurable.
- **Dependence**. In the domain of environmental evaluation, it is not reasonable to assume the independence between criteria because there is often some kind of positive or negative interaction between different criteria. For example, hazardous wastes and emissions, and health and safety issues are strongly related. The analytic network process (ANP) (Saaty, 1996) is suitable for handling this kind of issues.
- **Uncertainty**. The evaluation of alternatives on environmental criteria is affected by various types of uncertainty such as imprecision and vagueness induced for example, by the choice of measurement tools and the special and temporal boundaries and assumptions. Sometimes, the evaluations are based on judgments of experts which involve a high degree of subjectivity. It is important to know the type of uncertainty in order to determine the right method for modeling uncertainty.
- **Quantitative/qualitative**. Some of the environmental criteria such as pollution noise are qualitative. Hence, when the set of relevant environmental criteria considered involves qualitative criteria, only MCDM methods that can handle qualitative criteria can be used to solve the MCDM problem under consideration.

These characteristics provide a valuable support for the selection of an appropriate MCDM method. Indeed, the noncommensurability, for example, implies that methods that directly aggregate criteria using, for example, a weighted sum are not suitable. Also, the nonindependence between criteria implies that methods which assume the independence of criteria such as multiple attribute utility theory (MAUT) methods (Keeney & Raiffa, 1976) with additive utility functions are not appropriate. Regarding the handling of uncertainty, it is worth mentioning that in the case of imprecision, the MCDM methods using thresholds such as ELECTRE (Roy, 1996) and PROMETHEE (Brans & Vincke, 1985) methods are the most appropriate, in the case of stochastic uncertainty MCDM methods, using probability theory such as the analytic hierarchy process (AHP) (Saaty, 1980) are the most appropriate, and in the case of vagueness the MCDM methods using fuzzy sets theory such as the method of Gheorghe, Bufardi, and Xirouchakis (2004) are the most appropriate.

WEIGHTING OF CRITERIA

The weighting of criteria is recognized to be a difficult task by both decision makers and researchers in the domain of MCDM. That is why some guidance to the decision maker in the task of assigning weights to criteria is very useful.

Schenkerman (1991) distinguished two types of criteria weights: exogenous and endogenous. The endogenous weights are those that are strictly developed within the decision making model used to solve the decision making problem under consideration, as in AHP (Saaty, 1980) and the exogenous weights are those that are assigned by or elicited from the decision maker as in ELECTRE (Roy, 1996) and PROMETHEE (Brans & Vincke, 1985) methods. It is obvious that the weights whose determination needs investigation and guidance are the exogenous weights.

According to Zeleny (1982) the weights of criteria involve both objective and subjective information because they reflect: (i) the preferences of the decision maker which are often subjective, and (ii) the characteristics of the criteria which are objective.

Some approaches to the determination of criteria weights involve the intervention of the decision makers. As different decision makers may have different value systems, interests, and perceptions of a given decision making situation, it is not surprising that they assign different weights to the same family of criteria within a same decision making problem. In the domain of MCDM, it is recognized that the attribution of weights to criteria reflecting their relative importance is dependent on the decision maker.

According to Diakoulalaki, Mavrotas, and Papayannakis (1995), different methods of eliciting criteria weights used to obtain the criteria weights from the same decision maker will provide different results. Consequently, the consideration of an appropriate method for eliciting criteria weights is crucial for the accuracy of the decisions to be made.

According to Choo, Schoner, and Wedley (1999), the role and meaning of criteria weights vary from one method to another. The role of criteria weights in an MCDM method depends mainly on the aggregation rule used by the method. Consequently, the true meaning and validity of criteria weights are crucial in order to avoid improper use of the MCDM methods. Hence, the choice of a procedure to define the criteria weights should be based on its compatibility with the meaning and the role of the criteria weights used in the MCDM method under consideration.

In some MCDM methods such as ELECTRE, the weights of criteria are intrinsic, that is, they do not depend neither on the range of the scale nor on the encoding to express the evaluation on this scale, whereas in some other MCDM methods such as MAUT, the weights of criteria have not this intrinsic characteristic (Figueira & Roy, 2002).

Some well known techniques for eliciting criteria weights for the most important MCDM methods have been proposed in the literature. They are summarized in Table 1.

Hokkanen and Salminen's procedure (Hokkanen & Salminen, 1994) and Rogers and Bruen's procedure (Rogers & Bruen, 1998) are mainly used for weighting environmental criteria.

Except the AHP and MAUT techniques, the other techniques have theoretical interest and are difficult to use in practice.

There exist other weighting techniques such as SMART (Simple Multiattribute Rating Technique), SWING, SMARTER, and CONJOINT. These techniques are described in Alaja (1998).

When two or more decision makers are involved, two cases of defining criteria weights can be distinguished:

Table 1. Eliciting criteria weights techniques for important MCDM methods

Type of method	Elicitation criteria weights technique	Reference
ELECTRE type	Simos' procedure	Simos (1990)
	Mousseau's procedure	Mousseau (1995)
	Revised Simos' procedure	Figueira and Roy (2002)
	Hokkanen and Salminen's procedure	Hokkanen and Salminen (1994)
	Hinkle's "resistance to change" grid	Rogers and Bruen (1998)
AHP	Eigen values of the matrix of ratios obtained from the pairwise comparison of criteria	Saaty (1980)
MAUT	Indifference tradeoffs	Keeney and Raiffa (1976)

- The group of decision makers agrees on a common finite set of alternatives and a common finite set of criteria. Then, they determine together through negotiation, lobbying, or compromising, the evaluations of alternatives on criteria, the weights of criteria, and perhaps some other parameters if required by the procedure used to aggregate the preference structures. In this case, the decision makers act as a unitary entity (Khélifa, Martel, & Kiss, 1997). Then, the problem is treated as a multiple criteria decision making problem with a single decision maker. This situation implies that consensus is established on every aspect of the decision making process before performing any kind of synthesis (Khélifa et al., 1997). That is why a common finite set of criteria is assumed here, which is not the case for group decision making problems in general.
- Each decision maker provides his preferences on criteria separately and possibly in different formats. In this case two different approaches are possible: (i) obtaining criteria weights from the preferences of the different decision makers on criteria and in this case the decision makers should consider the same set of criteria, and (ii) the criteria weights of each decision maker are considered separately to obtain the global preferences (by taking into account all criteria) of each decision maker regarding the set of alternatives. In this case the individuals forming the group consider a common set of alternatives but do not necessarily share a common set of criteria. The objective of the group decision making methods considering this case is the determination of group preferences from the global individual preferences.

It is important to recall that the procedure of assigning weights to criteria should be considered after the selection of the MCDM method because the role and the meaning of the weights of criteria are totally dependent on the type of MCDM method used.

SELECTION OF CRITERIA

The selection of relevant criteria is a difficult task in a MCDM problem. More often, the decision maker needs some guidance during the process of selecting criteria. However, the problem of selecting the relevant criteria in general did not receive from the MCDM community the attention it deserves. That is why we address in this section the problem of selecting appropriate environmental criteria for a given MCDM problem. We will present three different techniques that can be used and provide some guidelines regarding the cases to which each technique is suitable. These techniques are: (i) direct selection, (ii) use of templates, and (iii) use of criticality matrix.

The direct selection technique is simply what is done when no guidance is provided to the decision maker or the analyst working on his behalf about the selection of relevant criteria. This is suitable to the situation where the user knows the problem very well and is able to select the relevant criteria without resorting to any support.

The existence of a predefined set of criteria and its hierarchical presentation are very helpful in the selection of relevant criteria, as it provides a top-down search technique for the user. Indeed, the user can select first the categories he or she considers as relevant. This means that if a category is considered as not relevant, the aspects composing this category and the criteria related to these aspects will not be investigated. If a category is considered as relevant, then the aspects composing this category are investigated. If an aspect is considered as relevant by the user, then he or she looks at the criteria composing this aspect to see which of them are relevant. If a criterion is considered as relevant, it is evaluated for each alternative using the related indicators.

Another way to select relevant criteria is to use templates. In this technique, a predefined list of criteria is associated with a certain domain of application, a certain type of decision making problem, a certain sector of activity, and so forth. For example, a template can be associated to each product life cycle phase, to each sector of industry, or to both. This technique requires the constitution of these predefined lists of criteria. These lists can be established by specialists of the domain of application, on the basis of past experience, characteristics of the application, and so forth.

A more sophisticated technique for selecting relevant criteria is the criticality matrix. It is a well known technique in operations research and engineering that is basically used to represent failure modes according to their probabilities of occurrence on the one hand and their severities on the other hand. It allows selecting the critical failure modes that is those with high severities and high probabilities of occurrence. However, this technique can also be used in other domains of application for other selection problems provided that the elements among which to select are represented according to 2 dimensions: one representing the likelihood of occurrence and the other one the severity.

Figure 6. Criticality matrix for selecting relevant environmental criteria

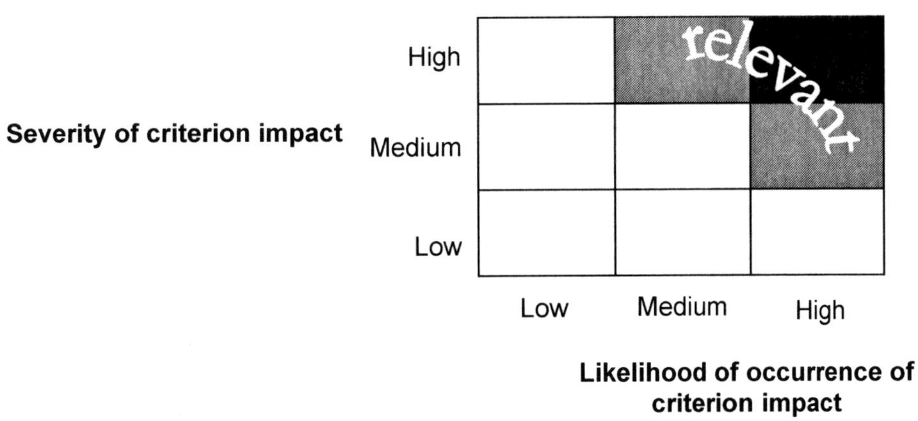

Figure 7. Options for selecting criteria

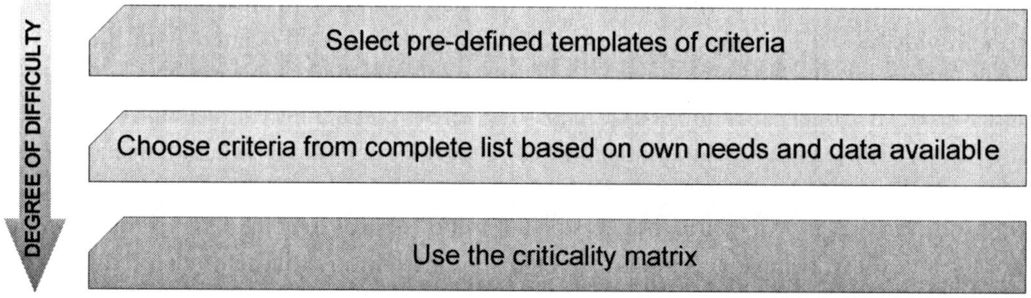

The selection of relevant environmental criteria through the use of criticality matrix is done on the basis of: (i) the likelihood of occurrence of the impacts of criteria in the decision making problem under consideration and (ii) the severity of these impacts.

In the case of Figure 6, only three levels of evaluation for the likelihood of occurrence and the severity of impacts, low, medium, and high, are considered. This is not a restriction and more levels can be considered if their evaluation is possible.

The different degrees of difficulty associated with the different techniques of selecting criteria are shown in Figure 7.

ILLUSTRATIVE EXAMPLE

The illustrative example focuses on one of the main activities of the reverse supply chain which is the treatment of EOL products where EOL products undergo one or more of the following options: remanufacturing, parts/components reuse, material recycling, incineration with or without energy recovery, and landfill.

The objective of this example is just to illustrate the type of decision making problems for which the consideration of environmental criteria is suitable.

The problem considered consists of selecting the best compromise EOL scenario to treat a vacuum cleaner at its EOL taking into account environmental and economic criteria (Bufardi et al., 2004).

The first step consists of selecting a set of potential alternatives among which the solution is to be found. Theoretically, the number of potential EOL scenarios that can be considered for this particular problem is very high because of the number of components in the vacuum cleaner and various options that each component can undergo. In general, only a few EOL scenarios are worth considering, and there is no general rule to identify them. Indeed, users have thier own ways for defining relevant EOL scenarios depending on their activity, their objectives, their experience and constraints from market, legislation, and available technology.

In this illustrative example, only five EOL scenarios are considered as potential alternatives and are described in Table 2.

The second step consists of selecting a set of relevant criteria against which the alternatives will be evaluated. The criteria selected for the evaluation of EOL scenarios are the three criteria of Eco-indicator 99 method: human health (HH), ecosystem quality (EQ), and resources (R), in addition to the EOL Treatment Cost (C). The detailed description of these environmental criteria can be found in Goedkoop and Spriensma (2000).

In this example, the four criteria are considered to be equally important. Hence, the environmental dimension received an overall weight of 75%

Table 2. EOL scenarios description

EOL scenario	Description	Main focus
EOL scenario 1	EOL scenario 1 consists of recycling as much as possible and incinerating the rest.	Recycling
EOL scenario 2	EOL scenario 2 consists of recycling only parts with benefits and incinerating the rest.	Benefit
EOL scenario 3	EOL scenario 3 consists of recycling all metals which cannot be incinerated and incinerating all the rest.	Incineration
EOL scenario 4	EOL scenario 4 consists of reusing the motor, recycling metals, and incinerating the rest.	Reuse of valuable components
EOL scenario 5	EOL scenario 5 consists of landfilling all	Landfill

Table 3. Ranking of EOL scenarios w.r.t. criteria

	Ranking			
	EOL Treatment Cost (C)	Human Health (HH)	Ecosystem Quality (EQ)	Resources (R)
EOL scenario 1	2	4	2	5
EOL scenario 2	3	2	3	2
EOL scenario 3	4	3	4	3
EOL scenario 4	1	1	1	1
EOL scenario 5	5	5	5	4

and the economic dimension an overall weight of 25% only.

According to Table 3, EOL scenario 4 is the best ranked EOL scenario because it dominates all the other EOL scenarios.

In Bufardi et al. (2004), we used the ELECTRE III method (Roy, 1978) to this problem and we obtained the following ranking: EOL scenario 4 is the best ranked EOL scenario, followed by EOL scenario 2, which is preferred to EOL scenario 3, which in its turn is preferred to EOL scenario 1, and EOL alternative 5 is the worst ranked EOL scenario as it can be predicted in advance.

The choice of relevant criteria should be driven by the satisfaction of the objectives of the problem under consideration. In our case the choice of criteria is mainly driven by the availability of a method that allows their evaluation, namely Eco-indicator 99 (Goedkoop & Spriensma, 2000).

IMPORTANT DIRECTIONS OF RESEARCH AND FUTURE TRENDS

Most of the references considering a multicriteria approach assume the existence of a well structured decision making problem with a finite set of alternatives and a finite set of criteria, whereas in real world applications, the definition of appropriate alternatives and the selection of relevant criteria are not only important for the decision making process but are also among the most difficult tasks to achieve. These issues should receive more attention from the multicriteria analysis community and should be integrated into MCDM procedures. More guidance on this issue is among the directions of research, and solid developments on it will strengthen multicriteria decision making from both theoretical and practical points of view.

From a technological view point, the development of product embedded information devices

(PEIDs) with a strong storage capability, communication possibilities, and long lifespan integrated to products and able to measure data related to important environmental criteria during the whole product life cycle is one of the most challenging issues in the near future (Kiritsis, Bufardi, & Xirouchakis, 2003).

The weighting of criteria is an important issue in multicriteria analysis. However, until now there is no convincing technique to deal with this issue. The development of appropriate procedures for allocating weights reflecting the relative power of each criterion is an important direction of research in the domain of multicriteria decision making.

The development of semi-automatic decision support systems with intensive guidance to the user about the most important issues discussed in this chapter, such as the selection of relevant criteria and their weighting, and an important library containing the most important existing techniques, is also one of the things that can bring a valuable support to the application of a multicriteria approach in the domain of environmental evaluation.

CONCLUSION

In this chapter, we dealt with the most important issues related to criteria in general and environmental criteria in particular to be considered when these criteria are used in a MCDM context. We presented these issues and provided some guidance regarding the way they should be tackled in order to ensure a proper and efficient use of (environmental) criteria in a decision making problem.

The use of environmental criteria in a MCDM context requires the consideration of a number of issues such as the selection of relevant environmental criteria and their weighting. We presented some techniques for selecting criteria and emphasized the efforts required for the use of each of them. Regarding the problem of defining the weights of criteria, we indicated some of the existing techniques for defining the weights of criteria and underlined how important it is to know the meaning of these weights and their role in the decision making problem under consideration in order to use the appropriate technique for determining the weights of criteria.

All that is valid for general criteria is also valid for environmental criteria. That is why for some issues, we used the term "criteria" and not the term "environmental criteria." The reason is that the reader can consider the related information for other types of criteria such as social, economic, and technical criteria.

Regarding the environmental criteria, we presented some of the main characteristics, such as incommensurability, dependence, and uncertainty, and indicated how these characteristics can help in the selection of appropriate MCDM methods.

An example about the selection of the best EOL scenario for the treatment of a vacuum cleaner at the end of its life cycle is given in this chapter in order to illustrate the type of decision making problems in which the environmental criteria together with other types of criteria can be used to evaluate and compare alternatives.

ACKNOWLEDGMENT

We would like to express our gratitude to two anonymous reviewers, whose useful comments and suggestions helped to improve significantly this work.

REFERENCES

Adda, S., Dahl, T., Gjerstad, T. B., Lamvik, T., Miljeteig, G., Molden, T. H., et al. (2002, November 1). *Environmental/social cost/value assessment methodology* (AEOLOS D4.1). WP4 D4.1, Version 2.

Alaja, S. (1998). *Structuring effects in environmental decision models.* Unpublished master's thesis, Helsinki University of Technology, Helsinki.

Bana e Costa, C. A., Stewart, T. J., & Vansnick, J.-C. (1997). Multicriteria decision analysis: Some thoughts based on the tutorial and discussion sessions of the ESIGMA meetings. *European Journal of Operational Research, 99*(1), 28-37.

Belton, F., Ackermann, F., & Shepherd, I. (1997). Integrated support from problem structuring through to alternative evaluation using COPE and V.I.S.A.. *Journal of Multi-Criteria Decision Analysis, 6,* 115-130.

Belton, V., & Vickers, S. (1990). Use of a simple multi-attribute value function incorporating visual interactive sensitivity analysis for multiple criteria decision making. In C.A. Bana e Costa (Ed.), *Readings in multiple criteria decision aid* (pp. 319-334). Berlin: Springer-Verlag.

Bouyssou, D. (1990). Building criteria: A prerequisite for MCDA. In C.A. Bana e Costa (Ed.), *Readings in multiple criteria decision aid* (pp. 58-80). Berlin: Springer-Verlag.

Brans, J.-P., & Vincke, P. (1985). A preference ranking organization method. *Management Science, 31,* 647-656.

Bufardi, A., Gheorghe, R., Kiritsis, D., & Xirouchakis, P. (2004). A multicriteria decision-aid approach for product end-of-life alternative selection. *International Journal of Production Research, 42*(16), 3139-3157.

Bufardi, A., Sakara, D., & Kiritsis, D. (2002, March 14). *Environmental/social cost/value software methodology and tool* (AEOLOS D4.2). WP4 D4.2, Version 1.

Camper, C. D., & Turcanu, C. (2007). On the governmental use of multi-criteria analysis. *Ecological Economics, 62,* 298-307.

Choo, E. U., Schoner, B., & Wedley, W. C. (1999). Interpretation of criteria weights in multicriteria decision making. *Computers & Industrial Engineering, 37*(3), 527-541.

Diakoulaki, D., Mavrotas, G., & Papayannakis, L. (1995). Determining objective weights in multiple criteria problems: The critic method. *Computers and Operations Research, 22*(7), 763-770.

Figueira, J., & Roy, B. (2002). Determining the weights of criteria in the ELECTRE type methods with a revised Simos's procedure. *European Journal of Operational Research, 139*(2), 317-326.

Gheorghe, R., Bufardi, A., & Xirouchakis, P. (2004). Construction of a two-parameters outranking relation from fuzzy evaluations. *Fuzzy Sets and Systems, 143,* 391-412.

Goedkoop, M., & Spriensma, R. (2000): *The Eco-indicator 99: A damage oriented method for life cycle impact assessment: Methodology report* (2nd rev. ed). Amersfoort, The Netherlands: PRé Consultants.

Hokkanen, J., Lahdelma, R., & Salminen, P. (2000). Multicriteria decision support in a technology competition for cleaning polluted soil in Hilsinki. *Journal of Environment Management, 60*(4), 339-348.

Hokkanen, J., & Salminen, P. (1994). The choice of a solid waste management system by using the ELECTRE III decision-aid method. In M. Paruccini (Ed.), *Environmental management: Applying multiple criteria aid for decision to environmental management* (Vol. 3, pp. 111-153). Dordrecht, Germany: Kluwer Academic Publishers.

Keeney, R. L., & Raiffa, H. (1976). *Decisions with multiple objectives: Preferences and value tradeoffs.* New York: John Wiley & Sons.

Khélifa, S. B., Martel, J. -M., & Kiss, L. N. (1997). Synthesizing decision-makers' preferences by taking into account their relative importance. In *Proceedings of the IEEE International Confer-*

ence on Systems, Man and Cybernetics (Vol. 2, pp. 1896-1899).

Kiritsis, D., Bufardi, A. & Xirouchakis, P. (2003). Research issues on product lifecycle management and information tracking using smart embedded systems. *Advanced Engineering Informatics, 17*(3-4), 189-202.

Mousseau, V. (1995). Eliciting information concerning the relative importance of criteria. In P. M. Paradalos, Y. Siskos, & C. Zpounidis (Eds.), *Advances in multicriteria analysis: Nonconvex optimization and its applications* (pp. 17-43).

Palme, U., & Tillman, A. M. (2007). Sustainable development indicators: How they are used in Swedish water utilities? *Journal of Cleaner Production.* In press.

Pochampally, K. K., Gupta, S. M., & Gupta, S. K. (2004). Selection of collection centers and recovery facilities for designing a reverse supply chain. In *Proceedings of SPIE: The International Society for Optical Engineering* (Vol. 5583, pp. 127-137).

Rogers, M., & Bruen, M. (1998). A new system for weighting environmental criteria for use within ELECTRE III. *European Journal of Operational Research, 107*(3), 552-563.

Roy, B. (1978). ELECTRE III: Algorithme de classement basé sur une représentation floue des préférences en présence des critères multiples. *Cahiers du* CERO, *20*, 3-24.

Roy, B. (1996). *Multicriteria methodology for decision aiding.* London: Kluwer Academic Publishers.

Roy, B. (2000). Supplement No. 1: A French-English decision aiding glossary. *Newsletter of the European Working Group "Multicriteria Aid for Decisions," Series, 3*(1), 1-10.

Saaty, T. L. (1980). *The analytic hierarchy process.* New York: McGraw-Hill.

Saaty, T. L. (1996). *Decision making with dependence and feedback: The analytic network process.* Pittsburgh, PA: RWS Publications.

Sen, P. (2001). Communicating preferences in multiple-criteria decision-making: The role of the designer. *Journal of Engineering Design, 12*(1), 15-24.

Simos, J. (1990). *Evaluer l'impact sur l'environement: Une approche originale par l'analyse multicritère et la négociation.* Lausanne, Presses Polytechniques et Universitaires romandes.

Triantaphyllou, E., Shu, B., Sanchez, S. N., & Ray, T. (1998). Multi-criteria decision making: An operations research approach. In J. G. Webster (Ed.), *Encyclopedia of electrical and electronics engineering* (pp. 175-186). New York: John Wiley & Sons.

Vincke, P. (1992). *Multicriteria decision-aid.* New York: John Wiley & Sons.

Wang, Y.-M., Yang, J.-B., & Xu, D.-L. (2006). Environmental impact assessment using the evidential reasoning approach. *European Journal of Operational Research, 174*(3), 1885-1913.

Zeleny, M. (1982). *Multiple criteria decision making.* New York: McGraw-Hill.

ADDITIONAL READING

Barbiroli, G., & Raggi, A. (2003). A method for evaluating the overall technical and economic performance of environmental innovations in production cycles. *Journal of Cleaner Production, 11*(4), 365-374.

Calcott, P., & Walls, M. (2005). Waste, recycling, and "Design for Environment": Roles for markets and policy instruments. *Resource and Energy Economics, 27* (4), 287-305.

Emblemsvåg, J., & Bras, B. (2000). *Activity-based cost and environmental management: A different approach to the ISO 14000 compliance*. Boston: Kluwer Academic Publishers.

French, S., & Geldermann, J. (2005). The varied contexts of environmental decision problems and their implications for decision support. *Environmental Science & Policy, 8*(4), 378-391.

Geldermann, J., Spengler, T., & Rentz, O. (2000). Fuzzy outranking for environmental assessment: Case study: Iron and steel making industry. *Fuzzy Sets and Systems, 115*(1), 45-65.

Gungor, A., & Gupta, S. M. (1999). Issues in environmentally conscious manufacturing and product recovery: A survey. *Computers & Industrial Engineering, 36*(4)811-853.

Handfield, R. B., Melnyk, S. A., Calantone, R. J., & Curkovic, S. (2001). Integrating environmental concerns into the design process: The gap between theory and practice. *IEEE Transactions on Engineering Management,* 48(2), 189-208.

Hauschild, M., & Wenzel, H. (1997). *Environmental assessment of products: Scientific background* (Vol. 2). London: Chapman & Hall.

Hofstetter, P. (1998). *Perspectives in life cycle impact assessment: A structured approach to combine models of the technosphere, ecosphere and valuesphere*. Boston: Kluwer Academic Publishers.

Hokkanen, J., Lahdelma, R., Miettinen, K., & Salminen, S. (1998). Determining the implementation order of a general plan by using a multicriteria method. *Journal of Multi-Criteria Decision Analysis, 7*(5), 273-284.

Huang, G. Q. (Ed.). (1996). *Design for X: Concurrent engineering imperatives*. London: Chapman & Hall.

Hundal, M. S. (Ed.). (2000). *Mechanical life cycle handbook: Good environmental design and manufacturing*. New York: Marcel Dekker.

Janssen, R. (2001). On the use of multi-criteria analysis in environmental impact assessment in The Netherlands. *Journal of Multi-Criteria Decision Analysis, 10*(2), 101-109.

Labuschagne, C., Brent, A. C., & van Erck, R. (2005). Assessing the sustainability performances of industries. *Journal of Cleaner Production, 13*(4), 373-385.

Nagel, M. H. (2003). Managing the environmental performance of production facilities in the electronics industry: More than application of the concept of cleaner production. *Journal of Cleaner Production, 11*(1), 11-26.

Papamichail, K. N., & Robertson, I. (2003). Supporting societal decision making: A process perspective. *Multi-Criteria Decision Analysis, 12*(2-3), 203-212.

Park, J.-H., & Seo, K.-K. (2006). A knowledge-based approximate life cycle assessment system for evaluating environmental impacts of product design alternatives in a collaborative design environment. *Advanced Engineering Informatics, 20*(2), 147-154.

Rauschmayer, F. (2001). Reflections on ethics and MCA in environmental decisions. *Journal of Multi-Criteria Decision Analysis, 10*(2), 65-74.

Rautenstrauch, C., & Patig, S. (Eds.). (2001). *Environmental information systems in industry and public administration.* Hershey, PA: IGI Publishing.

Sarkis, J. (1995a). Manufacturing strategy and environmental consciousness. *Technovation, 15*(2), 79-97.

Sarkis, J. (1995b). Supply chain management and environmentally conscious design and manufacturing. *International Journal of Environmentally Conscious Design and Manufacturing, 4*(2), 43-52.

Sarkis, J. (1998). Evaluating environmentally conscious business practices. *Journal of Operational Research, 107*(1), 159-174.

Steen, B. (1999). *A systematic approach to environmental strategies in product development (EPS). Version 2000: Models and data of the default methods*. CPM report 1999:5.

Thierry, M., Salomon, M., van Nunen, J., & van Wassenhove, L. (1995). Strategic issues in product recovery management. *California Management Review, 1*(2), 114-135.

Thoresen, J. (1999). Environmental performance evaluation: A tool for industrial improvement. *Journal of Cleaner Production, 7*(5), 365-370.

Wenzel, H., Hauschild, M., & Alting, L. (1997). *Environmental assessment of products: Methodology, tools and case studies in product development* (Vol. 1). London: Chapman & Hall.

Zhang, Y., Wang, H.-P., & Zhang, C. (1999). Green QFD-II: A life cycle approach for environmentally conscious manufacturing by integrating LCA and LCC into QFD matrices. *International Journal of Production Research, 37*(5), 1075-1091.

Chapter V
Sustainable Electronic Product Design:
A Comparison of Environmental Performance Assessment Tools Derived from Life Cycle Thinking

Xiaoying Zhou
University of California – Davis, USA

Julie M. Schoenung
University of California – Davis, USA

ABSTRACT

The ability to concretely and quantitatively measure the environmental performance of a product system is essential to support the establishment of objectives, the selection among alternatives, and continuous improvement in environmental management. Integration of the life cycle perspective into the assessment tools is one of the key challenges. On the basis of an extensive literature review, the authors describe the state-of-the-art of assessment tools available for product systems in the electronics industry. The intent is to enable the informed use of these product assessment tools with life cycle thinking so that a tool is chosen for the optimal application given specific goals. Furthermore, the classification scheme, the business initiatives, the economic, geographical, legislative factors, and the methodological challenges of the emerging industrial practice are thoroughly examined. Through these discussions, the authors hope to facilitate the methodological development that moves beyond discrete product boundaries toward system optimization and standard guidelines that best meet the needs of corporations in a global and societal context.

Copyright © 2009, IGI Global, distributing in print or electronic forms without written permission of IGI Global is prohibited.

BACKGROUND

In the past 2 decades, the logic of life cycle thinking within environmental impact assessment (EIA) and the concept of sustainability have extended beyond the traditional focus of specific projects with long service life, such as infrastructure construction for transportation, to the field of consumer products with short life cycles. Taking environmental aspects into consideration creates new challenges for managers accustomed to focusing on engineering performance and cost elements. Such strategic and life cycle orientations need new measurement tools or quantitative indicators to simultaneously assess environmental, technical, and economic performance of products and product systems. Although there are many existing management methods and engineering tools, they do not allow the cross-functional integration to evaluate trade-offs between environmental performance, technical characteristics, and economic impact for product systems. An important quantitative analytical tool, life cycle assessment (LCA), has been developed and utilized for the evaluation of potential environmental impacts of product systems. Although the conceptual "from cradle to grave" framework is widely acknowledged, LCA has some methodological limitations to constrain its widespread application in industrial sectors, such as the expensive purchase price of LCA commercial software, the time-consuming procedure, the complexity of assumptions, the involvement of uncertainties in each evaluation process, the dependence on extensive databases, and the failure to satisfy the special requirements and priorities of individual companies. Because, thus far, industry employs different approaches to fulfill various objectives, there is a clear need to summarize the innovations and development in currently available tools and to discuss their strengths and limitations so that we can improve the overall implementation of a consistent set of operational tools by integrating the discrete approaches and better address the challenges associated with this field of study.

MOTIVATIONS FOR METHODOLOGICAL DEVELOPMENT

- **Legislative compliance:** Rapid technological advances have led to dramatic reductions in the time-to-market for new electronic products. The consequential reduction in useful product life can cause long-term environmental impacts associated with the disposal of electronic wastes. The European Union (EU), China, Japan, and various states within the United States, have announced new environmental protection laws aimed at the electronics industry (Schoenung, Ogunseitan, Saphores, & Shapiro, 2005). Accordingly, the companies need to adjust their strategies in the field of product design, selection of raw materials, and availability of re-use or recycling options for end-of-life products. The integration of environmental considerations into the design of product systems is difficult without standard reference systems or metrics to assess environmental performance of products. Concrete and quantitative measurement of product performance at all stages of the life cycle will facilitate legislative compliance and provide a foundation for establishing policy targets.
- **Benchmarking products and company activities:** Benchmarking activities for environmental management in industry means the process of identifying the best practice and the external reference with which to carry out the product performance assessment. To evaluate the current business performance and improve competitiveness by adapting the best practice, performance needs to be quantified into a single value indicator for comparison purposes. Few

analytical evaluation tools for benchmarking have been fully developed and a consensus on the best method does not exist.

- **Promote eco-design:** Tangible economic benefits from implementing eco-design practices are recognized by more and more corporations. In the design phase for products, the performance at all stages of the life cycle for these product systems should be accounted for to determine potential trade-offs associated with alternatives and to support decision making. The evaluation tools for the environment will ensure eco-design activities move toward a sustainable direction.
- **Extended product/producer responsibility:** The growing trend toward environmental responsibility and control is not only driven by legislation but also by public expectations. Establishing a good relationship with the community and improving the company image through extended producer responsibility are effective ways to increase market share. Knowing and disclosing the information on environmental performance not only at a firm level but also at the product system level is an essential part of external communications with different stakeholders. The evaluation and reporting procedures have already been required in some international or regional standards and guidelines Furthermore, the policies on eco-labels and environment index trading between companies create additional motivation for the development and implementation of sound scientific approaches within corporations to assess potential or actual environmental impacts of products and to ensure common interpretation and execution of environmental management.

Given the variability in the goals for product environmental assessment, it is not surprising that disparate approaches are employed by different actors for different applications. It is of interest to characterize different methods in order to better understand their common features and the appropriateness of different tools for different applications. There are numerous publications, most of which rigorously examine the approaches used by academia (Baumann & Cowell, 1999; Dale & English, 1999; Daniels & Moore, 2002; Finnveden & Moberg, 2005; Sonnemann, Castells, & Schumacher, 2004; Wrisberg, Udo de Haes, Triebwetter, Eder, & Clift, 2002), but little attention is given to the feasible practices in industry. Currently, there is no unambiguous universal method or indicator for measuring environmental performance within product systems in industry. Actually, for specific goals, even slightly different, there should be various versions of methods generated under real application situations, which is in fact the current case. The purpose of this chapter is not to enumerate all of the assessment methods exclusively, but rather to identify the similarities and trends for future development through analysis of various state-of-the-art methods. By identifying the structure and relationships in this jungle of methods, no matter qualitative or quantitative, simplistic or sophisticated, we can extract the necessary characteristic for a "good" method and enable the informed use of appropriate methods so that an optimal method can be chosen for a given application situation. In one way, this will contribute to the methodological development. In another way, when we have to compare two indicators derived from different methods, we will know the fundamental methodological differences behind the "black" toolbox, allowing for comparison based on one common conceptual framework, that is, a comparable reference system, to convey meaningful information to decision makers.

OVERVIEW OF METHODS

On the basis of the level of detail and the key players implementing the assessment, we roughly divide the emerging performance assessment methods into three categories: simplified industrial approaches, mid-level collaborative approaches and comprehensive academic approaches. As shown in the classification scheme provided in Table 1, the methods can be further classified into several subcategories within each category based on the goals of the application and the types of measurement indicators. Some examples from each category are explored in the following paragraphs.

Type I: Simplified Industrial Approaches

The electronics industry is using a variety of metrics to track environmental performance and management, as described in a series of published corporate environmental reports (Ericsson Corporation, 2004; IBM Corporation, 2002; LG Electronics Corporation, 2004; Motorola, Inc., 2004; Nokia Corporation, 2004; Siemens Corporation, 2003; Sony Corporation, 2006; Samsung Electronics, 2004). These reports regularly audit and publish the company's performance with regard to environmental, health, and safety policies and strategies. Different streamlined life cycle approaches are applied as a means of determining significant environmental impacts. The goal of this category of methods is usually to comply with the rigorous requirements of national and regional legislation, to meet the company's needs for internal evaluation and external communication. The goal of management is to minimize resource depletion, energy consumption, toxic substances usage, and emissions of greenhouse gases. From the perspective of a corporation, simplicity and concreteness are the important factors for the successful application of an environmental assessment of a product system. Thus, the performance of the product at the level of the firm is most likely to be assessed typically by using some basic inventory related indicators and methods. We classify these methods into three subcategories: materials flow indicators, energy flow indicators, and checklists.

Materials Flow Indicators

This subcategory of methods focuses on the analysis of materials flows and associated environmental burdens in industrial activities, and of the effect of these flows on the state of the environment. Manufacturing a single product involves a variety of different processes. For a business sec-

Table 1. Product environmental performance assessment tools classification schemes

Levels	Main Goals	Approaches	Characteristics
Type I: simplified industrial approaches	Legislative compliance	• Materials flow indicator • Energy flow indicator • Checklists	• Inventory data based • Easy to implement
Type II: mid-level collaborative approaches	Business strategy-environmental improvement	• Design for Environment (DfE) aid tools • End-of-Life (EOL) oriented tools • Benchmarking type tools	• Objective oriented or function driven • Specific life cycle focused
Type III: comprehensive analytical approaches	Policy making-environmental management	• Materials balance based environmental assessment analysis • Integrated economic analysis • Combined engineering tools	• In-depth sophisticated analysis • Blend of expertise needed • Uncertainties introduced by valuation

tor, an input-output materials inventory analysis can reveal the transformation of materials during sequential processes. The primary indicators in this subcategory include resource consumption, materials usage, waste, and pollutants generated. Most methods accounting for inputs and outputs of environmental performance for processes focus on certain chemical substances, compounds and bulk materials, pollutant emissions, and water usage (Ericsson, 2004; IBM, 2002; LG, 2004; Motorola, 2004; Nokia, 2004; Siemens, 2003; Sony, 2006; Samsung, 2004). Key environmental performance indicators (KEPIs) accounting for physical and chemical characteristics of environmental performance of products, such as the amount of precious metals, the amount of solder paste, and so forth, are developed by Singhal, Ahonen, Rice, Stutz, Terho, and van der Wel (2004). Most of these substances, usage, or emissions are identified as high priorities to improve environmental quality. Usually, they are regulated by environmental laws and require regional or local monitoring programs. For instance, some emissions standards (air, water, and solid waste), worker exposure standards, and banned materials and reporting requirements, such as the toxic release inventory (TRI) system, are mandated by the U.S. Environmental Protection Agency (EPA). Toxic pollutants, recycling rate and waste generation rate from facilities are quantified on the basis of the rule of material balance and process flowcharts (U.S. EPA, 2002). These performance indicators can be measured in absolute volumes or normalized with respect to production volume or annual revenue.

Energy Flow Indicators

This subcategory of methods is similar to the material flow indicator but addresses energy flow only. Energy use impacts are quantified on the basis of relevant inventory data: fuel oil, natural gas, and electricity consumption (Intel, 2005). The aggregated sum of all primary energy inputs to a product's life cycle is used as an indicator for these impacts. Because much of the environmental burden during a product's life cycle is related to the outputs of the energy conversion processes, the emissions from energy production are also calculated and compiled into an inventory list. Some emerging approaches apply energy equivalents. For instance, using fuel energy equivalents provides the assessor with a common dimensional unit for gauging consumption of various renewable and nonrenewable energy resources against a known constant for comparison (Ogallachoir, Oleary, Bazilian, Howley, & Mckeogh, 2006).

The life cycle of a product begins with the extraction of raw materials and ends with recycling and waste treatment. The environmental aspects of electronic products are linked to the materials and energy flows at the different stages of their life cycle. The corresponding environmental impacts are mainly associated with toxic substance usage; waste and pollutants released into the air, water, and soil; and energy efficiency. These physical measurement metrics involve little uncertainty because they rely directly on the numerical inventory data. Additionally, these data can be easily tracked and monitored objectively. However, absolute comparisons between these indicators may be misleading among two or more different product systems and corporations. The relative comparison based on a common reference is generally less biased (Fiksel, 1996).

Checklists

A checklist is a method in which every item is compared with the standards and criteria, so that specific environmental aspects of a product or company can be reviewed and audited internally and externally. This method provides a convenient summarized format that can be rapidly read by managers. A checklist provides a screening process for evaluating the environmental performance of products, so it is commonly used to verify the status and compliance of a system.

The items on a checklist can be either quantitative threshold requirements of materials content mandated by regulations or qualitative criteria of various aspects of environmental management. Upon completion, each checklist must be reviewed and approved by an Expert System. One typical checklist example for the identification of significant environmental aspects of products is "Ecolist" (Chung, Lee, Koh, & Hur, 2003). The Ecolist consists of checklist type questionnaires and assessment criteria for each questionnaire. Another example is the seven broad categories that make up a performance-based model called the Baldrige Criteria (Hussey, Eagan, & Pojasek, 2002). A company can utilize this checklist type model to improve their environmental performance and identify applicable environmental issues. Although a qualitative checklist type of assessment does not require a large amount of data, these methods implicitly incorporate subjective information and are therefore difficult to validate (Fiksel, 1996).

The checklist method also can be applied in the phase of product planning. The comprehensive system OneDFE developed by Alcatel-Lucent Corporation includes mandatory requirements, guidelines, and checklists that are employed during product realization processes (Donnelly & Boehm, 2003). OneDFE checklists are Web-based forms that developers complete to assess the characteristics for each hardware product. These checklists help to ensure that environmental requirements and improvements have been considered during design. They also provide a record for auditing purposes.

Type II: Mid-Level Collaborative Approaches

Industry is beginning to be aware of the priority of environmental management with life cycle thinking for long-term business policies and strategies. Life cycle impact evaluations can help to improve the environmental performance of products at the early stages of their product development cycle where improvements are most effective and can be achieved cost-effectively, especially for complex electronic products.

Tools suitable for the assessment of environmental impacts focusing on different life stages of products are being developed through significant collaborations between industry and researchers and specialists in the field of industrial ecology. These methods do not directly quantify and measure the environmental performance of product systems based on "observable" inventory data. Instead, the judgment of experts on the environmental performance relative to a given product function and the consequential environmental impacts are incorporated into the assessment tools. Not only the environmental burden of a product system from its design through to production and then final disposal is determined; concurrently, the potential environmental impact, the technological attributes, economic constraints, quality and reliability requirements, and stakeholders' interests are also systematically taken into consideration by a procedure of partial synthesis. Instead of being very complicated tools, the methods in this category are usually simplified or start with some easily targeted indicators to facilitate the wide application in industry without too much expertise required.

Design for Environment (DfE) Aid Tools

The decisions during the conceptual design stage have the greatest effect on multiple aspects such as resource availability, manufacturing process selection, manufacturability, reliability, profitability, and environmental impact. But traditional design tools such as CAD software are only available to support the routine work of traditional design engineers. Currently, environmental considerations such as recyclability, product end-of-life fate, and latent human hazards have migrated from secondary constraints to integral design objectives. The final task in the assessment of eco-products for designers is to choose the best alternative from all the available solutions according to the comprehensive assessment of technological, economic, and environmental aspects instead of emphasizing only one single facet. Therefore, there is a need for tools that can be used to evaluate trade-offs at the early product design and development phase. Launched in 2001, the 3-year grEEE project involving both academic institutions and industrial partners seeks to develop a DfE model for the electronics industry sector. The case study of a shift to halogen-free printed wiring boards illustrates the grEEE costing system has the advantage to locate environmental costing and savings as a standard electronic product design tool (Bergendahl, Lichtenvort, Johansson, Zackrisson, & Nyyssonen, 2005). Park, Lee, and Wimmer (2006) proposed an eco-design model linking the top-down guidelines, that is, general ecodesign principles, and bottom-up methods, that is, LCA, and so forth, for identification of environmental weak points of a product in the key life cycle stage. The application of this model to mobile phones shows its potential to improve the efficiency of identifying design solutions for product designers.

Some tools have been developed that estimate the quantitative relationship between environmental impact and design parameters with life cycle thinking, such as Eco-Pas (Dewulf & Duflou, 2004), a multilayered environmental influence diagram (Siddhaye & Sheng, 2000), and simplified LCA using a response surface method for multidisciplinary design of eco-products (Chen & Chien, 2004). The principle of these methods is to establish a relationship between the functional requirements or design parameters and the environmental impact of products. Different mathematical models based on theoretical and empirical data are employed in these methods to derive this relationship. LCA scores are the most popular representation of environmental impact for these approaches.

In contrast, the following methods use qualitative relationships between environmental impact and product functions. These eco-design assessment tools are company internal and objective-oriented. For instance, the EcoScan® series of software basically provides a user-friendly format and interface to integrate an environmental impact database, global warming potential and energy consumption into the product life cycle database (Eikelenberg, Kok, & Tempelman, 2004). "Eco-value analysis" is developed to identify the opportunities for environmental improvement from the components and processes subject to technical functional requirements and cost constraints (Oberender & Birkhofer, 2004). Both methods adopt Eco-indicator 99® as a built-in method for environmental impact assessment of products. Systematic environmental assessment (SEA) is a methodology used by IBM to investigate and document the known technical, political, and environmental issues associated with design options and their potential impacts on its business operations. An SEA follows a prescribed process flowchart and generates an ultimate ranking of possible design alternatives based on their environmental benefits (IBM, 2002). In Sweden, the Swedish Environmental Research Institute developed its Environmental Priority Strategies in Product Design (the EPS system) to allow designers to assess the total impact of a product system from cradle to grave (Steen, 1999).

Quality function deployment for environment (QFDE) (Sakao, Kaneko, Masui, & Tsubaki, 2004) and green quality function deployment (GQFD) (Christopher, Deshmukh, & Wang, 1996) are methods capable of determining the priority values for components, when considering their functional roles from an environmental viewpoint. These tools integrate LCA, life cycle costing (LCC) and qualify function deployment (QFD) into an efficient tool and deploy environmental, financial and customers' requirements throughout the entire product development process. Environmental aspects are taken into account as the desired customer requirements as well as other function-related customer requirements. This approach allows the user to choose the most environmentally friendly design alternatives on the basis of the correlation between the environmental attributes and the engineering attributes, and the priority values for customers' requirements. An advantage of these tools derived from the quality management tool of QFD is the capability of integrating the value system of stakeholders into the product system's performance assessment.

To evaluate the potential environmental impacts, some simple environmental indicators are implemented in the DfE aid tools as the first indication of environmental weak points. Particularly for the electronics industry, the designers of products and processes prefer one single score from the assessment (i.e., an indicator) to keep pace with innovation cycles. The indicator is likely to connect the material content of products or the input/output inventory of a process with some potential environmental performance measure, such as toxicity impact or recyclability. These methods attempt to capture the health impact assessment of a product's complete life cycle in one indicator. For example, the toxicity potential indicator (TPI) is a screening indicator used during the design phase of a product, and is based on the environmental properties of the materials contained in the final product (Mueller, Griese, Hageluken, Middendorf, & Reichl, 2003). It is a quick assessment method designed to address the potential toxicity issues of different materials. The TPI is based on health and safety rules, maximum allowable workplace concentrations, and German water pollution classes. Different ecological impacts are aggregated into one score, so the numerical result expresses the harmful potential to both humans and the environment when the substances in the product are released uncontrolled. Aiming as a simplistic screening tool, TPI does not involve the exposure-fate environmental impact mechanisms on the basis of concentration, dissipation, and transformation of input and output of materials flow.

End-Of-Life (EOL) Oriented Tools

Issues associated with the end-of-life treatment of electronic products have been driven by the upcoming take-back regulations (Kang & Schoenung, 2005). In some situations, however, the disassembly and recycling of spent products may not be the optimal end-of-life scenario even from the viewpoint of the environment. For example, energy consumption and other relevant environmental impact that occur during collection, distribution, delivery, and recycling processes may offset the partial consequential environmental benefits (Hischier, Waeger, & Gauglhofer, 2005). Some approaches aim to determine the recycling potential and consequential environmental and economic benefit of recycling activities for end-of-life electronic/electrical products. An evaluation method designed to assess recycling potential taking into consideration both the environmental and economic aspects was suggested for home appliance wastes (Kim, Hwang, Matthews, & Kwangho, 2004). In this method, LCA was applied to obtain an environmental score - SEnv, and the actual value and static economic model was used to obtain the economic score - SEco. The recycling potentials for the recyclable materials were calculated by weighting SEnv and SEco with factors obtained from the Analytical Hierarchy Process (AHP) method. Herrmann, Eyerer, and Geidiga (2004) proposed the economic and ecological materials index to evaluate the benefits and feasibility of different recycling routes according to contained materials in electronic wastes. Quotes for environmentally weighted recyclability (QWERTY) have been proposed in order to quantify the environmental and economic gain that can be realized per unit of financial investment in establishing take back and recycling systems for consumer electronic products (Huisman, 2003). The built-in LCA score is used as the environmental impact indicator.

Multiple-criteria decision aid methods are particularly well suited for the selection of the optimal EOL scenarios. Alternative options for management of spent products and materials at the end-of-life include some responsible disposal options in addition to recycling and reuse. Choices are affected greatly by the mix of products, recovery technologies, and economics. These trade-offs must be evaluated from not only the environmental perspective, but also the viewpoint of sustainability measured by some new decision supporting tools. An assessment method used for these decisions is usually constructed on the basis of an objective function of economic profit maximization. Then, the disassembly level and end-of-life fate of individual subassemblies and components can be determined with mixed integer linear programming. The optimal part disposal (OPD) model is one example (Das & Yedlarajiah, 2002). Some German electronic scrap recycling enterprises already utilize this program in their daily recycling program planning. The Watson Implosion Technology (WIT) optimization tool developed by IBM's TJ Watson Research Center can be used to determine a theoretical optimal cost scenario through a reverse logistics supply chain model for cost-benefit estimation of different product end-of-life options (IBM, 2002). An end-of-life of product systems (AEOLOS) method is another comprehensive example to evaluate product end-of-life treatment options with regard to environmental, economic, and social criteria. In this method, the environmental criterion is based on the CO_2 emissions, the economic criterion is based on the disassembly cost, and the social criterion is based on the number of employees (Kiritsis, Bufardi, & Xirouchakis, 2003). Although the premise of these methods is to choose an optimal product scenario by considering EOL options on the basis of multifaceted criteria, they do not explicitly focus on environmental impact evaluation, but rather on the economic criterion.

The EOL-oriented tools can be incorporated with DfE tools to improve the recycling potential of new products. Masanet and Horvath (2004) introduced the Take-Back Planning Advisor for the environmental and economic planning of take-back systems for plastic components from end-of-life electronics. This method is based on a comprehensive unit process modeling approach that characterizes the energy consumption, energy-related air emissions, solid waste generation, material state transformation, and processing costs of the discrete process steps. In the work of Rose, Stevels, and Ishii (2000), the end-of-life design advisor (ELDA) method was developed for a product designer to predict the end-of-life strategies within a product system. This method integrates six product features into the product design and is capable of analyzing and judging the suitable end-of-life treatment strategies. The focus of this method is the technical performance of products in the EOL treatment processes. Green Design Advisor shows another beneficial cooperation between industry and academia in the area of integration of end-of-life simulation and DfE (Feldmann, Meedt, Trautner, Scheller, & Hoffman, 1999).

Benchmarking Type Tools

The methods in this subcategory are mostly eco-efficiency-based assessment tools that focus on the field of industrial processing and manufacturing activities. To find the best practice for environmental improvement from a business perspective, the economic benefit is an explicit performance indicator. Eco-efficiency evaluation targets the interface of the economic and environmental aspects of a product system. A quantitative definition of eco-efficiency is the ratio between economic value added during a production process or service and the consequent environmental impact caused during this process or service. An improvement in eco-efficiency can not only be caused by environmental impact reduction, but also by technological progress and an increment in economic value added. Especially in Japan, many firms introduce this indicator and disclose it in their environmental reports to quantitatively assess their annual environmental activities. The Factor X tool (Ueno et al., 2001) is a tool invented and developed in Japan to calculate the ratio of eco-efficiency between the evaluated product and the reference product. The environmental impact reduction can be achieved by the efficient utilization of energy, the reduced usage of toxic materials, and reduced emission of greenhouse gases. The sustainability target method (STM) presently is being developed through collaboration of the Multi-Lifecycle Engineering Research Center at the New Jersey Institute of Technology and industry partners (Dickinson, Mosovsky, & Houthuysen, 2003). The key and unique feature of the STM is that it links the economic value of a product with its environmental impact to provide a practical business criterion for sustainability. This method defines the relative indicator, resource productivity (RP), for environmental impact and the absolute indicator, eco-efficiency (EE), for sustainability. In eco-efficiency assessment methods, environmental impacts are typically difficult to analyze properly due to the lack of unambiguous definitions, distinct procedures, and sufficient input data. Instead of conducting full scope impact assessment, there is a need to develop practical indicator systems for assessing environmental impact relevant to the case concerned. Therefore, the differences in different benchmarking methods usually lie in the choice of various indicators representing the environmental performance of product systems. The basic indicators used by some firms include simple materials flow or energy flow associated metrics, such as "energy use," "resource use," and "pollutant emissions."

Some benchmarking activities are not implemented with a quantified framework, but rather are holistic. For example, developed by the European Foundation for Quality Management (EFQM) in 1992, the EFQM Excellence Model is a holistic self-assessment tool to help managers establish an appropriate quality management system by measuring where they are on the path to excellence. Also, this model is extended to environmental aspects and can be used to help organizations develop tangible and measurable goals for their environmental management system (Pascual, Boks, & Stevels, 2003).

Type III: Comprehensive Academic Approaches

There is a rich diversity of analytical tools developed by academia and nongovernment organizations (NGOs) for environmental management and full scope impact assessment backed by extensive discussions and theoretical considerations, such as environmental accounting (EA), cost-benefit analysis (CBA), environmental risk assessment (ERA), impact pathway analysis (IPA), material flow analysis (MFA) and life cycle assessment (LCA) (Sonnemann et al., 2004). A good review of these available tools and related concepts can be found within works of Baumann and Cowell (1999), Dale and English (1999), Daniels and Moore (2002), Finnveden and Moberg (2005), Sonnemann et al. (2004), and Wrisberg et al. (2002). Among the available analytical tools, LCA is the most widely accepted approach to assure that all relevant environmental information for a product or production system is considered. The ISO 14040 series of reference standards provide guidelines on the principles and methods to conduct each phase of LCA (ISO 14040, 1997). Most of the available commercial LCA software packages are based on the damage oriented Eco-indicator 99® methodology and its corresponding database (Goedkoop, Oele, & Effting, 2004). SEEbalance®, which is a methodology developed in Germany, extends life cycle type environmental assessment to the economic and societal dimensions with the goal of measuring the integrated sustainability of a product system (Schmidt, Meurer, Saling, Kicherer, Reuter, & Gensch, 2004). Menke, Davis, and Vigon (1996) and Fruhbroadt (2001) have summarized and evaluated the general features and quality of various LCA software programs that have been available in the market for years. Both reports reveal the high diversity of these software tools in terms of the multiple criteria discussed, that is, system definitions, database and data management, flexibility and transparency, calculation methods and comparisons, and outputs and exports. In contrast to the first two categories of methods (i.e., simplified industrial approaches and mid-level collaborative approaches), these analytical tools have gone through methodological development and peer review over a long period of time (Goedkoop & Spriensma, 2001). Some guidelines and standardized detailed procedures come into being for the practice of identification, measurement, accumulation, analysis, preparation, interpretation, and communication of environmental and economic information used by management to plan, evaluate, and control the environmental performance of a corporation. Usually, a large amount of high quality data, complex and transparent procedures, and strict satisfaction of miscellaneous assumptions are necessary to support the validity of conclusions derived from these tools.

In practice, however, complicated assumptions, incomplete data, weak adaptability, and high cost are the limitations that prevent these approaches from becoming a practical tool widely applied in industry. In order to make these tools more practical, the trend is to move toward streamlined or simplified methods. For instance, the streamlined LCA methods focus on either one or some significant environmental impact indicators during the product system's whole life cycle or focus on only one significant life cycle stage. A new evaluation method in this area named "the most of the most" (Liu, Liu, & Fung, 2003) has been developed. In addition, the limited range and function of LCA relative to environmental measures reduces its strength as a comprehensive method, as it cannot provide the full picture of sustainable performance. Several tools and methods developed through collaboration between government, professional organizations, and environmental institutions have emerged to assess the economic, social, and environmental impacts associated with sustainability. Generally, these approaches take into account a systematic point of view and the high dimensional requirements associated with multiple stakeholders. For example, the Product Sustainability Indicator for cellular phones has been developed for the strategic optimization of product systems, which integrates the economic, ecological, social, and technical aspects (Scrutz, Graulich, & Ebinger, 2004). This indicator can be used to understand both the technical performance and the life cycle environmental impact of processes and facilities. It is recommended that the information on environmental performance should be complemented with data from other engineering tools, such as process modeling and quality management tools. Life cycle engineering (LCE), developed and applied by IKP since 1989, offers the combined assessment of ecological, economic, and technical aspects. LCE allows a consistent modeling of process chain economics and a better inclusion of technical properties into the ecological LCA model (Pascual et al., 2003). The approach is based on life cycle costing, activity based costing theory, ISO 14040, quality function deployment, and total quality management. In a recent version of LCE, social impacts of product systems have also been included.

To be consistent with the classification scheme used in previous subsections of this chapter, we divide this category of methods into three subcategories: materials balance based environmental impact analysis, integrated economic analysis, and combined engineering tools. Because most of the methods in this category have been established for decades and have been discussed extensively in the literature, we limit our discussion of these

Table 2. Further details, examples and reference sources for all classified environmental performance assessment tools

Main Categories	Subcategories	Applications / tasks	Examples	References
Simplified industrial approaches	Materials flow indicator	Input-output physical flow analysis; inventory management; legislation compliance report; pollution prevention indicator.	Toxic release inventory report (Annual publicly available information mainly on absolute volume of toxic chemical releases and waste generation at facility level)	http://www.epa.gov/tri/index.htm
	Energy flow indicator	Starting point for energy analysis; relevant environmental impact assessment; pollution prevention indicator.	CO_2 emissions from direct energy use (CO_2 emission due to combustion of fossil fuel is the main cause of global warming.) Direct energy consumption indicators at facility level or product level, such as electricity usage, fuel usage, gas usage etc.	Annual company environmental reports Annual company environmental reports
	Checklist type	Checklist type of questionnaire for product design alternative assessment and qualitative assessment criteria based on six ecodesign strategic categories	Ecolist	Chung et al., 2003
		Seven categories of award criteria for companies/organizations to improve overall environmental performance	Baldrige Criteria	Hussey et al., 2002
		Web-based forms that developers complete to assess product's characteristics during product planning phase	OneDFE	Donnelly & Boehm, 2003
Mid-level collaborative approaches	Design for Environment (DfE) aid tools	Tools to estimate quantitative relationship between environmental impacts and design parameters of products based on theoretical and empirical data	• Eco-Pas • Multilayered environmental influence diagram • Simplified LCA by response surface method	• Dewulf & Duflou, 2004 • Siddhaye & Sheng, 2000 • Chen & Chien, 2004
		Tools to estimate qualitative relationships between environmental impacts and product functions	• EcoScan • Eco-value analysis • SEA methodology • EPS system	• Eikelenberg et al., 2004 • Oberender & Birkhofer, 2004 • IBM, 2002 • Steen, 1999
		Tools to identify environmentally friendly design alternatives based on the correlation between environmental attributes and engineering attributes and the priorities of customer requirements	• Quality Function Deployment for Environment (QFDE) • Green Quality Function Deployment (GQFD)	• Sakao et al. 2004 • Christopher et al. 1996
		Eco-design tools to identify economic cost and savings	• grEEE costing system	
		Product design screening indicator based on the environmental properties of the materials contained in the final product	• Toxicity Potential Indicator	
	End-of-Life (EOL) oriented tools	Tools to evaluate recycling potential and consequential environmental and economic benefit of recycling activities at end-of-life for products	• Methodology for recycling potential evaluation of waste home appliances • Quotes for Environmentally Weighted Recyclability • Green Design Advisor	• Kim et al., 2004 • Huisman, 2003 • Feldmann et al., 1999
		Multi-criteria decision supporting tools to assess and select the optimal EOL scenarios	• Optimal Part Disposal (OPD) • WIT optimization tool • AEOLOS method	• Das & Yedlarajiah, 2002 • IBM, 2002 • Kiritsis et al., 2003
		Tools employed in the phase of product design to improve the recycling potential and EOL strategies of new products	• Take-Back Planning Advisor • End-of-Life Design Advisor (ELDA)	• Masanet & Horvath, 2004 • Rose et al., 2000
	Benchmarking type tools	Quantitative eco-efficiency based method to improve environmental and economic performance	• Factor X tools • Sustainability Target Method (STM)	• Ueno et al., 2001 • Dickinson et al., 2003

continued on following page

Table 2. continued

Comprehensive analytical approaches	Materials balance based environmental impact analysis	A tool standardized according to ISO series 14040 for product-oriented environmental impact assessment	Life Cycle Assessment • (e.g damage-oriented Eco-Indicator 99®)	Various literature sources • Goedkoop et al., 2003
		A category of sophisticated approach to evaluate materials and energy flow into, throughout, and out of a system.	Materials Flow Analysis	Various literature sources
		Site-specific environmental impact analysis	• Environmental Risk Assessment • Impact Pathway Analysis	Various literature sources
	Integrated economic analysis	A life cycle tool to quantify all environmental cost both internally and externally	Life Cycle Costing / Total Cost Assessment	Various literature sources
		An internal tool to measure the environmentally associated activities (cost and benefit) in a monetary term	Environmental Accounting	Various literature sources
		Extend LCA to eco-efficiency and social-efficiency analysis	SEEbalance®	Schmidt et al., 2004
	Modified engineering tools	A tool to offer the combined assessment of ecological, economic and technical aspects	Life Cycle Engineering	Various literature sources
		A tool to explore potential of process improvement with environmental considerations	Process simulation	Various literature sources

Figure 1. Application of environmental performance assessment along the supply chain. DfE: design for environment; LCA: life cycle assessment; EA: environmental accounting; EOL: end of life

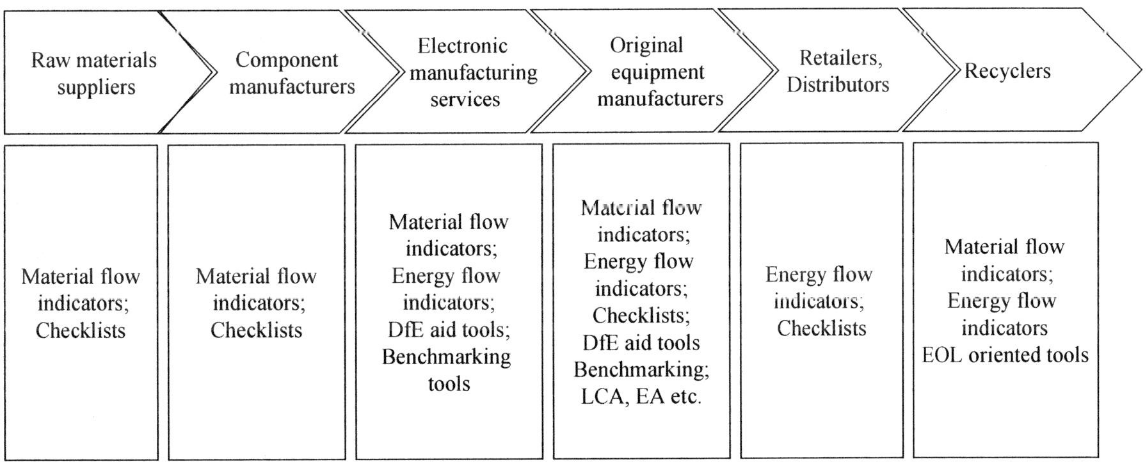

methods by providing an overall summary of our classification with key examples and some references in Table 2.

Additionally, there are some other tools for product environmental assessment, which cannot be classified into the above categories due to their particular application and actors or economy wide system boundaries. For instance, the goal of electronic product environmental assessment tool (EPEAT) is to help institutional purchasers to identify and evaluate environmentally preferable electronic products among all the products in the marketplace on the basis of environmental performance. The complete set of EPEAT criteria includes 22 mandatory criteria and 33 optional criteria, which must be satisfied comprehensively (Katz, Rifer, & Wilson, 2005). These tools will not be discussed in this chapter due to space limitations, but it should be recognized that they have some overlap and similarities in motivation and methodological design with assessment approaches used within product systems.

To summarize, on the basis of the actors and the goals of the application, as discussed in this section, we present in Figure 1 frequently used product assessment tools, as they would be applied along the supply chain in the electronics sector. The electronics sector supply chain includes the raw materials and component suppliers at the early life stage, the Electronic Manufacturing Service Companies (EMSs), the Original Equipment Manufacturers (OEMs), the distributors, the retailers, and the recyclers at the end-of-life. From a business perspective, each level in the supply chain will prefer to adopt specific types of environmental performance assessment methods. For example, for EMS companies, there is a need to adopt an integrated method or tool, one that satisfies the requirements of regulation through materials flow indicators, seeks opportunities to reduce the operating cost through energy flow indicators, generates the additional value through DfE aid tools, and improves the competitiveness as contractors through benchmarking tools.

SOCIETAL IMPETUS TO INFLUENCE THE DIRECTION OF METHODOLOGICAL DEVELOPMENT

The primary motivation that influences the corporate management strategy and the application of environmental performance assessment tools include geographical, political, economic, societal, and ethical facets. The analysis of the roles of these elements on the development of methodology deserves more attention in order to completely understand these methods and consolidate a methodological basis.

International Legislative Focus and Orientation

The legislative focus is the most important factor to influence the environmental strategy and selection of sustainable indicators and tools for measurement of performance of product systems. Overflowing landfills and the potential environmental risk of leaching materials, such as mercury, lead, and cadmium, from discarded electronic products have become targets of government intervention. Policymakers have generally advocated two regulatory approaches to solve these problems: increasing efficiency of recycling and EOL management, and restricting the use of specific substances in products. Thus, the performance assessment tools reflect these interventions and provide comprehensive identification of linkages between environmental performance, production activities, and economic demands.

Launched in 1996 by the International Organization for Standardization (ISO), the ISO 14001 Standard has been undergoing rapid growth and is apt to impose itself as a new standard of reference for issues of environmental management, especially in Europe and in Asia (Lamprecht, 1997). It is expected that, analogous to the ISO 9000 series quality standards, the ISO 14000 series will move their way toward indispensable certification for entrance into the international market. Conformability of product performance assessment with these international standards and integration of management systems is provident business strategy and can reduce economic risk of noncompliance.

Although there is currently no legislation or regulation requiring the application of DfE within companies, DfE can be used to achieve compliance and even some tangible benefits for corporations. In addition, ISO 14062, *Environmental Management: Integrating Environmental Aspects into Product Design and Development,* has been cited within several policy documents as a guide for companies seeking to integrate DfE into their activities (Quella & Schmidt, 2003). It is anticipated that there will be an increasing focus in the early design stages of products and services to achieve more sustainable production and consumption. The increasing array of environmental regulations across the world makes it clear that compliance should not be viewed as a one-time event. Meanwhile, the tools capable of providing the essential quantitative information for minimizing adverse environmental impact are very helpful to aid formulating effective policies.

Regional Compliance and Societal Implications

The European Union (EU), Japan, South Korea, various states within the United States, and China have announced new environmental protection laws aimed at manufacturers of electronic equipment and related products. The broad scope and strict nature of these environmental policies will influence the development of sustainable product assessment. In this section, we compare the characteristics and societal implications with respect to economic, political and cultural perspectives for the assessment method evolution in five regions: European countries, Japan, South Korea, the United States, and China.

European Union (EU)

In February 2003, the EU passed sweeping legislation, known as the Directive 2002/95/EC on the Restriction of certain Hazardous Substances Directive (RoHS) and the Directive 2002/96/EC on Waste Electrical and Electronic Equipment (WEEE). In addition, the European Commission has commenced a number of other environmental policy initiatives that will have a significant impact on the electronic industry, including regulation of chemicals, product eco-design requirements, and integrating environmental requirements into product standards. For example, the Eco-Design for Energy-Using Products (EuP) requires manufacturers of electronic devices to perform an assessment of the environmental impact of the product throughout its life cycle and report on how they are integrating environmental considerations into their product design processes and environmental management systems. On October 30, 2003, the European Commission proposed a regulation on the Registration, Evaluation, and Authorization of Chemicals (REACH). Different countries in Europe also passed related pieces of environmental legislation for the electronics industry including liquid waste, solid waste, packaging, atmospheric emissions, and statutory subtle variations (Envirowise, 2005). Together, these laws seek to control the presence of environmentally unfriendly substances during the product design and manufacturing processes, as well as during the end-of-life treatment processes.

Nature conservation is of great economic importance to European countries. The profound environmental policy and legislation system and strong environmental awareness rooted in the public and in industry provide an effective atmosphere for implementation and enforcement of environmental protection measures. Europe has been a leader in promoting sustainable development internationally and at the national level. European regulators are going upstream to product manufacturers to eliminate perceived risk. In the EU, this is called the"Precautionary Principle," which is driven by the perception that pollution prevention and control must be integrated into corporate management for sustainable economic development. International cooperation promotes methodological investigation and research among universities, institutions, and NGOs. The vast field of knowledge related to sustainable product performance assessment has been accumulating. For instance, currently the EU leads the world in LCA studies. In short , the environmental and economic interface and environmental-social integration provide an advantageous platform for improvement of assessment tools. The institutional and legal framework, the regulatory instruments, economic instruments (e.g., environmental taxes), and government expenditures in this region provide tremendous motivation and support for methodological development in the issues of environmental management.

Japan

Japan takes the leadership in the integration of the electronics industry and environmental management. Japan occupies a small geographic area but has a high population density. Limited space and resources have led Japan to improve the efficiency of treatment of end-of-life products. Both industry and government intensify and continue efforts on the efficient production and end-of-life take-back infrastructure to ensure that various environmental management activities are organized in an environmentally sound and economically efficient manner. The polluter-pays and extended producer responsibility principles have been implemented in Japan for years. There is indirect pressure from Japanese legislation. In Japan, only certain landfill sites permit dumping of hazardous substances, such as lead (Pb), which carries a cost premium. The Electric Household Appliance Recycling Law passed on the obligation for collection and recycling of waste appliances to the producers. The appliance law is part of "The Basic Law" for establishing the Recycling-based Society in Japan (Inform, 2003). In addition, to maintain the leadership in technology innovation and to pursue the best practices to achieve added value of products, Japanese industry tends to employ the DfE aid, EOL-oriented, and benchmarking performance assessment tools within product systems.

South Korea

The economy in South Korea has a strong international orientation. Exports contribute to a high percentage of the gross domestic product (GDP). In the year 2005, the electronics sector alone achieved $100 billion in exports in South Korea; 17% of these electronics are exported to the EU's 25 countries (Lee, 2006). In an effort to ensure that its electronics industry has access to the EU market, before the Korea "RoHS" type legislation takes effect, approximately 340 companies, representing 95% of South Korea's electronics industry, signed a voluntary declaration that they would participate (IPC, 2005). Most likely the motivation for companies to develop product performance tools is the permission for entrance of their products in the worldwide market and the industrial initiatives to reduce operation and production costs (Lee & Whang, 2006). Export-oriented Korean industries therefore prefer eco-design aid and in-depth analytical performance assessment tools, not only to cope with the regulatory framework, but also to contribute to strengthening the competitiveness of products by satisfying market demand.

The United States

Despite links between health and the environment, which are usually incorporated into environmental policy making in the United States, there are no existing or pending federal regulations similar to the EU RoHS/WEEE directives. While many U.S. states are actively developing waste electronics legislation, California is the only state currently restricting the importation, manufacture, or sale of lead (Pb) containing electronics and banning landfill disposal of electronic waste (IPC, 2005). California's leadership in the field of environmental management is probably a direct consequence of its economic vitality and population pressure (Lamprecht, 1997). Industry is more realistic about the long-term challenge to incorporate environmental awareness into business, yet most companies still remain firmly in the category of "wait and see" toward environmental management with some concerns about potential risk, while some large international corporations take action in response to offshore legislation. Without sufficient pressure from legislation, in order to convince industry to take action, such as to prepare for the radical changes caused by RoHS, a comprehensive cost-benefit analysis is a necessity. Some leading environmental impact assessment practitioners in industry have developed streamlined approaches and sustainability indexes parallel to those being used in Europe (Graedel, 1998; IBM, 2002). Some approaches incorporate environmental, health, safety, and recycling costs and considerations into a traditional cost and performance analysis. The environmental management system adopted by large firms typically is a hybrid of various management models that currently exist, or that have evolved over the years to show their effectiveness and efficiency (IBM, 2002). But there is still room for further improvement, such as extending the usefulness of a more consistent set of operational assessment tools in order to be implemented industry wide.

China

China is experiencing high economic growth, which benefits particularly from increasing revenues from the manufacturing sector. In response to growing pressure and concern on nature conservation and pollution prevention, China has strengthened its institutional framework for environmental management. Many efforts have been made to enhance the implementation of extended producer responsibility schemes in various industrial sectors. Environmental concerns are more and more integrated into economic policies, in response to domestic environmental problems as well as international commitments. Without an established infrastructure, the Chinese Government is looking to the EU for inspiration on environmental policy. In 2003, the Chinese Government initiated four major environmental policy initiatives that affect the energy efficiency, hazardous material content, and end-of-life disposition of high-tech products, as well as the collection and recycling of spent batteries (AeA, 2006). In 2006, China announced the "Administrative Measure on the Control of Pollution Caused by Electronic Information Products," (RPCEP), the so-called China RoHS. In addition to new restrictions on industry, the directives propose new policies and practices to help domestic manufacturers meet specific objectives. China is on the fast track because its government recognizes that compliance with global environmental regulation is important to maintaining the nation's competitiveness in the international arena. Academic researchers have also focused on learning from the European experience and conceptual framework so that they can provide government and industry the modified tools suitable for the situations in China. Therefore, the choice for environmental performance assessment methods is to seek extended analytical models that can identify and quantify infrastructure needs and promote environmentally conscious technologies within the Chinese domestic industry.

METHODOLOGICAL CHALLENGES AND RECOMMENDATIONS

There are some general methodological challenges associated with environmental performance assessment of electronic product systems, for example, the collection of life cycle inventory data, the uncertainty analysis, and simplification of assessment tools (Andrae, 2005). In this section, we attempt to summarize several of the common challenges in methodological development; we do not attempt to provide a conclusive solution.

Selection of Appropriate Impact Indicators

The performance indicators used in practice in different assessment methods cover a wide range of options. Some focus only on a single environmental aspect or a specific life cycle stage; some are too comprehensive and complicated to be applicable and understandable in practice; some are quantitative and objective; and some involve a value system. Direct "recordable" stressors from input/output inventory sheets and gate-to-gate analyses, such as CO_2, NO_x, and SO_2 emissions and water usage appear often in corporate annual environmental reports (Ericsson, 2004; IBM, 2002; Intel, 2005; LG, 2004; Motorola, 2004; Nokia, 2004; Siemens, 2003; Sony, 2006; Samsung, 2004). These "elementary flows," as defined by ISO, or "environmental interventions," as defined by the Society of Environmental Toxicology and Chemistry (SETAC) (Udo de Haes et al., 1999), are easy to implement in industry because they do not need much expertise to track down, and do not involve any characterization modeling or value system elicitation, which usually requires the documentation of well-defined procedures, specification of underlying assumptions, and strong scientific validations. In different locations and under different conditions, however, the same absolute volume of inputs or outputs may or may not contribute to the same degree of environmental impact. The term "midpoint" category, for example, global warming, ozone depletion, and acidification, is used in classic LCA methods because this type of impact category lies within the cause-effect chain between stressor at the source and damage to receptors. The "safeguard subjects," the areas of protection, being the impact categories in damage-oriented assessment, such as human health, ecosystem damage, and resource depletion applied in Eco-indicator 99®, reflect the final environmental effect (Udo de Haes et al., 1999). The inter-relationships between stressors, midpoint indicators, safeguards subjects, and a single-value indicator are shown in Figure 2. Through a cause-effect chain on environmental mechanisms, materials balance analysis and inventory sheets can provide information on stressors; fate analysis, resource analysis, exposure, and effect analysis are procedures to derive midpoint categories; damage analysis leads to environmental impact at the damage level; and valuation steps (normalization and weighting) aggregate the impact categories into a single value indicator (Goedkoop & Spriensma, 2001). During these procedures and analysis, the rules of allocation and aggregation are employed to various degrees.

The selection of midpoint indicators is suggested by Hertwich and Hammitt (2001) to be suitable for comparing similar impacts. To some extent, analysis at a midpoint category can minimize the extent of modeling required and avoid the incorporation of the valuation procedure, thereby generating results that are appropriate for communication and comparison, particularly for similar product or production systems. The derivation of environmental impact to the damage level requires information on exposure and sources-pathway-receptors mechanisms, which introduces more subjective choice and uncertainty into the analysis. For example, the ecotoxicity is expressed as the percentage of all species present in ecosystem under toxic stress (PAF) in Eco-indicator 99®. As this is not an observable damage, a rather crude conversion factor is applied in calculation. Without spatial and temporal definitions, the fate-exposure-effect-damage analysis cannot provide robust comparisons. Because the damage-oriented indicators express more environmental relevance, however, they facilitate including the value system of interest groups at the assessment stage by estimation of weighting factors for the various impact categories, and are therefore suitable for leading to a single value comparison. The current tendency aims at reconciling these two types of approaches, which is presented in Vienna Workshop 2003 of the UNEP/SETAC Life Cycle

Fig. 2. Impact chain in environmental performance assessment. CFC: chlorofluorocarbons; VOC: volatile organic compounds; HAP: hazardous air pollutants

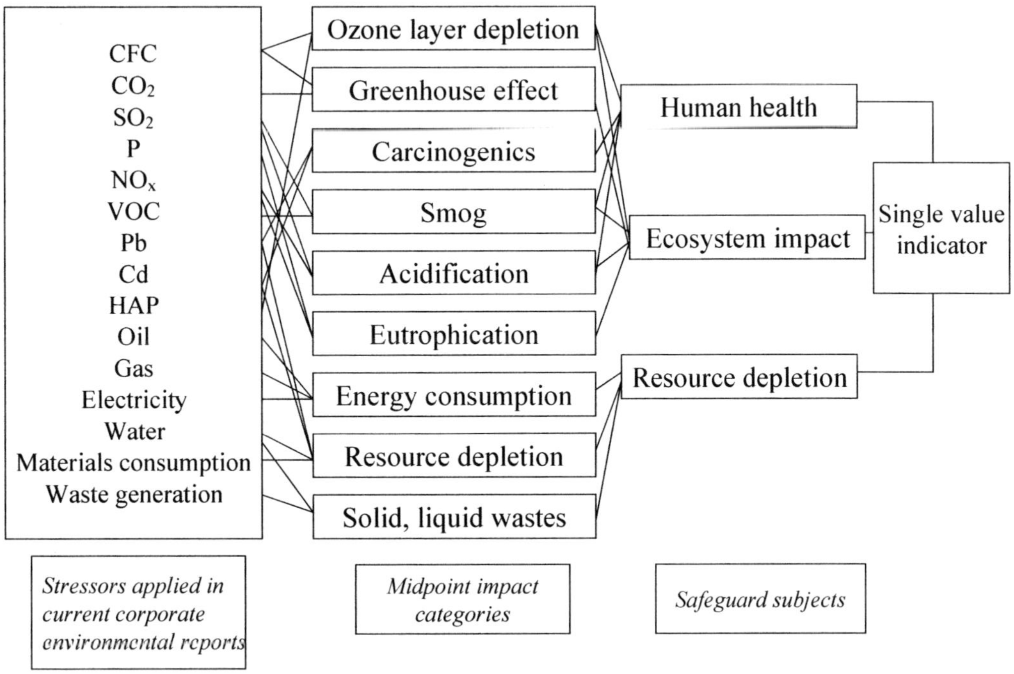

Initiative (Jolliet et al., 2004). It is important to evaluate the effectiveness of impact indicators on the basis of the availability and quality of data, and the purpose of measurement and environmental relevance, and to carefully select the best set of indicators, because they can potentially influence the consequential results and decisions. Careful evaluation of appropriate indicators should take place both before data collection and as part of the product assessment. A SETAC workshop on the issues of impact categories and category indicators summarized the criteria for choosing performance indicators as environmental relevance, independence, completeness, and so forth (Udo de Haes et al., 1999). It is also agreed that the selection of indicators and categories can be anywhere in the cause-effect chain of environmental mechanisms, but for comparative assertions they should be modeled in a technically valid way and open to further scientific progress (Jolliet et al., 2004).

Here we have emphasized the complexity associated with the proper selection of impact indicators in the dimension of environmental impact. Furthermore, the selection of appropriate indicators or metrics in the dimensions of economics and engineering performance also need to be addressed, as described below. The underlying principle for the choice of an indicator is practicality, meaning it needs to be easily interpreted and it can serve as a target for improvement by design engineers and managers.

Assessment of Economic Impacts

The relevant economic impacts associated with environmental activities are not always obvious, especially some indirect, intangible, and hidden costs. For a company's or an organization's decision making process, we suggest the incorporation of an environmental accounting system (EPA, 1995) into the conventional management system, which is particularly valuable for management initiatives with a specific environmental focus. The most practical way to simulate the environmental improvement activities is by showing that there are substantial economic benefits. There is a publicly available report on Total Cost Assessment, providing a methodological approach and practical guidelines (AIChE, 2003) to estimate five categories of relevant economic impact caused by corporate environmental activities. It must be noted, however, that most available database sources on energy and materials as inputs to production and final demand, and the generation of pollutants and solid waste are at the national level or industrial sector level. What is needed is a process-oriented indicator that can be applied to a comparison within a product system. Therefore, further investigations into micro-level allocation are necessary to obtain reliable estimations. In the international arena of environmental accounting, Japanese organizations implement the practice of environmental accounting successfully based on the guidelines developed by the Japanese Ministry of Environment (MOE, 2002). Based on the experience of Austrian companies adopting the environmental accounting approach developed by the United Nations Division of Sustainable Development (UN DSD), Jasch (2006) describes in detail how to evaluate data consistency within different information systems.

Furthermore, the internalization of environmental externalities is essential for a sustainable economy because some changes in activities, processes, and technologies required by environmental regulations and policies are very costly and unpredictable at the starting point. Theoretically, if externalities could be internalized, we could use a monetary value to represent the relative importance of different environmental impacts and overcome the methodological shortcoming (noncommensurability). However, a monetary measurement for each environmental impact is not readily available and monetary valuation bears a large margin of error and variability. Agreeing upon the relevant social costs and benefits is often controversial and requires justification between interest groups and legislators, on the presumption that one should not adopt standards, technologies, controls, or policies if the corresponding social costs exceed benefits (Delucchi, Murphy, & McCubbin, 2002). Currently, however, it is not possible to achieve a high level of societal consensus. For example, estimates of the social cost of air pollutant emissions have proven to be highly variable, often differing by an order of magnitude or more (Delucchi et al., 2002). The success of internalization of environmental costs requires more contributions from the political and scientific communities. Furthermore, the time-value-of-money needs to be taken into account when we attempt to internalize the environmental cost because, in general, the public tends to care more about the current crisis and discount potential long-term impacts, in part because of the anticipation of new technology development that would solve or reduce the future environmental problems. Thus, assumptions on temporal scale, discount rate, and spatial specificity of a study need to be consistently well defined and documented.

Integrated Methodology and Interdisciplinary Collaboration

Many facets of manufacturing operations, design of a product, selection of materials use, transport and delivery of products, and feasibility of re-use and recycling options all influence the environment. As has been stated in the previous section, the change and consequences of environmental performance have important economic implications. It is worthwhile emphasizing that economic, technical, and environmental effects are often interrelated, and should not be evaluated in isolation from each other (see Figure 3). Along the diagonal line of the matrix in Figure 3, the conventional analytical tools are listed in the traditional environmental, economic, and engineering domains. Other spaces within

Figure 3. Interconnections between environmental, economic and engineering facets and emerging interdisciplinary analysis

	Environment	Economic	Engineering
Environment	Multi-step exposure-pathway-damage environmental mechanisms. *{EIA; LCA; MFA; IPA; environmental hazard risk assessment etc.}*	Relevant cost and benefit associated with environmental activities; environmentally relevant economic instrument, *e.g.*, environmental fees and taxes.	Composition formula and process parameters affecting physical material and energy flows; lean manufacturing; closed-loop supply chain design.
Economic	*{Social cost model; EA, LCC (or total cost assessment); CBA; EIO-LCA; eco-efficiency tools etc.}*	Direct and indirect expenses and revenues. *{Conventional financial accounting; econometrics; revealed/stated preference model etc.}*	Process optimization with profitability; capacity planning with budget constraints; process economics; value stream management.
Engineering	*{Clean technology; DFE tools; hybrid LCA; energy footprint; modified quality management tools for environmental improvement; life cycle thermodynamics etc.}*	*{Technical cost modeling; activity based cost modeling; operations research; CBA etc.}*	Material balances; functionality and reliability; unit operations; reaction efficiency and yield; supply chain design. *{Process control simulation; TQM tools; technology-efficiency tools etc.}*

Note: Upper right matrix above diagonal: generally conceptual focuses and mechanisms; Lower left matrix below diagonal: generally adaptive tools and methodologies; Italic inside parenthesis: models and tools applied within or across domains; EIA: Environmental Impact Assessment; LCA: Life Cycle Assessment; MFA: Materials Flow Analysis; IPA: Impact Pathway Analysis; LCC: Life Cycle Cost; EA: Environmental Accounting; CBA: Cost – Benefit Analysis; DFE: Design for Environment; TQM: Total Quality Management.

this schematic matrix represent the important issues to be addressed and examples of emerging approaches that cross the traditional domain boundaries. When the common theme is to solve a complex environmental management issue, the collaboration of different disciplines contributes different perspectives to methodological development, synthesis of data, and technology innovation. The practitioners will benefit from more research at these interfaces of traditional disciplines. While the broader perspective has been recognized for some time, the interdisciplinary approaches and collaborative activities are quite limited so far.

Many useful, sophisticated tools and methods from extensive traditional engineering disciplines are available for measurement and analysis of product performance, but many of these tools focus upon one single issue or one interest group. An open source assessment framework is able to accumulate and diffuse the know-how of diverse disciplines. Hybrid methods and performance indicators that combine various aspects and various practices may serve for the better application of multicriteria environmental evaluations for various scenarios. Instead of a single predetermined procedure by one method, practitioners should be able to choose applicable methods from a variety of harmonized approaches and unify their advantages and knowledge in different disciplinary fields. For example, the environmental indicators developed in Germany for ICT products use an adapted method, which converts qualitative information inputs such as customer requirements and desired technical functions into technical parameters through QFD (Takahashi, Tatemichi, Tanaka, & Kunioka, 2004). Various approaches that apply collaborative research across different areas should be employed to derive the underlying correlations with environmental improvements based on empirical data and theoretical science, such as the established statistical modeling, modified quality management tools, eco-efficiency tools, environmental accounting, and operations research methods. There is also some overlap between these emerging approaches, as they usually tend to address the challenges crossing traditional disciplines (SETAC, 1993). It is important to aggressively consider new competent or complementary methodology initiatives from different disciplines to synthesize the efforts and avoid reinventing the wheel. The optimal application of these approaches either individually or in combination depends on the product design objectives, the application actors, the management focus, and other factors.

Aggregation of Different Environmental Impacts into a Single Value Environmental Performance Score

A common purpose for which the numerous methodologies for environmental impact assessment within product systems methodologies serve is to benchmark the products or processes and to identify the optimal design options. From the users' viewpoint, aggregation of the information is needed to provide decision makers with a single value assessment conclusion. To compare across environmental impact categories (e.g., a lower global warming indicator for one alternative, but a lower toxicological indicator for another), practitioners attempt to use a single dimension and single value criterion. We can use the perspective of a mathematical optimization problem to formulate the aggregation of environmental impacts into a single value environmental performance score based on the theory of multi-attribute decision analysis (Zhou & Schoenung, 2006), as follows:

Given a set of product systems X, each alternative x within the set possessing unique environmental impact potentials, select the alternative x that gives the best set of characteristics Z*(x) to reduce the total environmental impact. The formula is expressed as (Seppala, 2003):

$$Z^*(x) = F\,[V_1(I_1), \ldots, V_n(I_n), W_1, \ldots, W_n, \ldots W_s]$$

F: the overall single function value;

V_i: single value function with impact indicator I_i within each impact category i (i=1, …n);

$W_1 \sim W_n$: weighting factor representing the relative significance of each impact category i (i=1, …n);

$W_{n+1} \sim W_s$: interaction between weighting factors.

According to multi-attribute decision theory (MADT), the performance assessment model is expressed by one linear combination of weighted input variables (Field, 1985) with the assumptions of mutual independence of impact categories and no interaction between weighting factors. However, these assumptions are used only because of the need to simplify the complex mathematical form. Furthermore, we assume the shape of the single value function curve is linear and goes through the origin, so that no threshold data are required (Seppala, 2003).

Generally speaking, there are three steps required for aggregation. The first step is normalization, to determine how much each alternative contributes to the environmental impact within each impact category and to convert different units into one comparable base. The second critical step is the calculation of the weighting factors to determine the relative priority of the different impact categories, meaning how important each category is from the perspective of decision makers. There are two main categories of weighting methods: generic (external) and case-specific (internal). There are many different sets of generic weighting factors available, for example, environmental design of industrial products (EDIP) (Wenzel, Hauschild, & Alting, 1997), Swedish Environmental Tax and Fees method (Johnsson, 1999), Eco-indicator 99® (Goedkoop & Spriensma, 2001) and so forth. These weighting methods are based on different assumptions and various local or regional reference and value systems. However, there has been no universal drop-in replacement identified so far. Generally, there are different approaches used to develop generic weighting factors in a regional context: *damage-oriented impact assessment*, *distance to target method*, and *monetary valuation method* (Schmidt & Sullivan, 2002). In the case study of desktop display technology environmental evaluation, the case-specific considerations are integrated into the joint framework of analytic hierarchical process (AHP) (Satty & Vargas, 2001) to objectively capture and quantify the value system (Zhou & Scheonung, 2007). When assigning the priority values to each category within the pairwise comparison of AHP, the properties of each impact category and five factors of potential risk are carefully considered, as follows: (i) *value* (the average willingness to pay to avoid the potential impact), (ii) *distribution* (spatial and geographic scales of impact), (iii) *frequency* or *intensity* (the extent of impact in the affected environmental area), (iv) *duration* (duration of impact and remediation or reversibility time), and (v) *contribution* (severity of potential hazard, magnitude and degree of exposure, size of population and mobility of substance) as required by the streamlined life cycle assessment methodology (Graedel, 1998). The joint framework for pairwise comparisons, along with specific temporal and spatial boundaries as refinement, is shown schematically in Figure 4. The final step is the aggregation of each impact category output, which is calculated by weighting each normalized output with the obtained priority. A complimentary discussion, with additional details of underlying principles and numerical examples, is available in Zhou and Schoenung (2007).

The Integration of Trade-Offs Between Environmental, Economic, and Technical Aspects of Product Systems

For most product systems, one alternative is generally not superior to the others in all of the important characteristics, that is, technical performance, environmental impact, and economic feasibility. The challenge associated with respect to the integration of trade-offs between environmental, economic, and technical aspects of product systems lies in the combination of three important and often-conflicting issues; sometimes the social impact adds more complexity. A decision maker is confronted with the question of setting priorities. For example, the development of an alternative process may reduce environmental impact but extra capital investment and reliability issues during the launching period may bring an

Figure 4. The flowchart of joint pairwise comparison on the basis of generic weighing factors and case-specific considerations

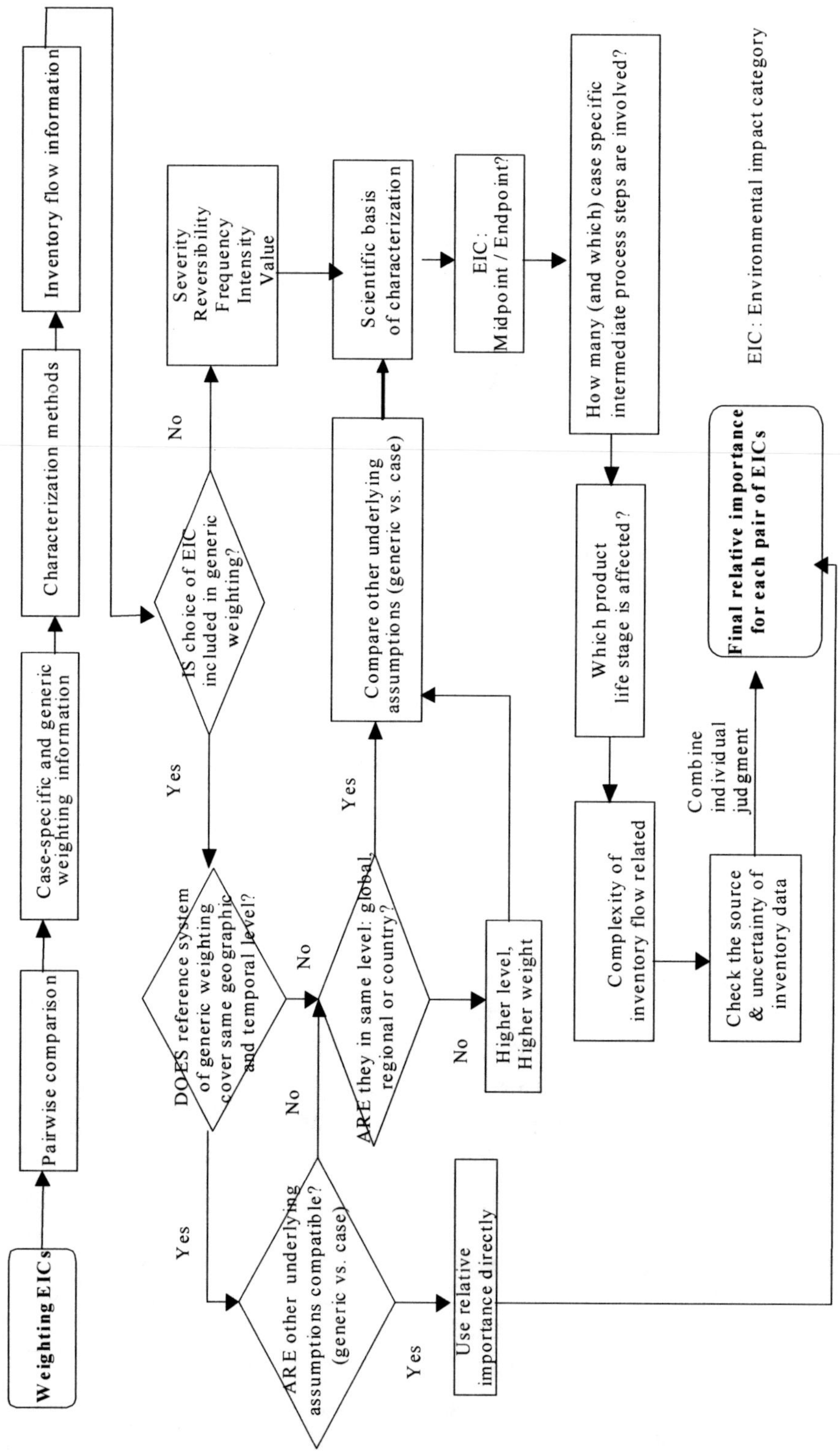

apparent reluctance from managers to adopt new technologies. To be able to integrate trade-offs between economic, technical, and environmental impacts with a single indicator, one must determine the relative importance of the multiple aspects or formulate the objective function and corresponding constraints within an optimization framework. For example, the conflict between economic and environmental issues can be formulated as one optimization problem with the objective of profit maximization (or cost minimization) and with the constraint of environmental regulatory targets. The value system, the preference of different stakeholders to determine the relative importance of achieving one objective vs. another, must be quantitatively incorporated into the evaluation framework at the early stage. The opinions from the design engineers, manufacturing engineers, representatives from purchasing, marketing, production, quality assurance, customers, suppliers, the field, and other functional groups need to be considered simultaneously. Concurrent and rapid communication across disciplinary boundaries and the combination of top-down and bottom-up hierarchical-structured approaches are proposed to be an effective and efficient option to resolve this challenge. There are some sophisticated tools and techniques available for measurement and analysis of trade-offs between different dimensions. Eco-efficiency analysis aims at creating an integrated indicator of the environmental burden intensity per unit of economic value (or production output), that is, the ratio between environmental impact and determined economic value. However, this ratio value representing "efficiency" cannot reflect fully the information in two dimensions and lacks a mechanism to assign different priorities to different dimensions of the objective. Thus, trade-off graphic portfolios are often used. Another type of approach is monetarization. The stated preference and revealed preference approaches (Whitehead, Pattanayak, Van Houtven, & Gelso, 2005) are examples of this category. Stated preference approaches such as conjoint analysis and contingent valuation are based on the assumption that all the attributes evaluated can be represented by some value due to a change within a utility system. This type of method invites people's direct statement of a product's characteristics. Because each individual's utility function is estimated independently, the technique is useful for determining the marginal value of characteristics to various consumer segments in the market. The difficulty is in how to design the questionnaire to obtain values for attributes. The revealed preference approaches rely on the observed behavior to derive the relative values for attributes. Thus, it can only be successfully applied to a few product systems that are not only widely available on the market, but for which there are robust statistics and well-informed descriptions of characteristics in the different domains. The data envelopment analysis (DEA) eco-efficiency approach proposed by Kuosmanen and Kortelainen (2005) has the potential to accommodate variable effects of a product system into a single value efficiency index as well. In the DEA framework, the approach is to measure the distance from the observed points to the curve of technically feasible options, the so-called "efficient frontier." The efficient production unit is defined as "it is impossible to decrease any environmental pressure without simultaneously decreasing the economic value added" (Kuosmanen & Kortelainen, 2005). DEA does not require subjective or normative judgment about priorities, yet can incorporate the predetermined weighting structure if necessary.

Information Declaration and Database Management

No matter which method we adopt, all environmental performance assessment methods rely on a common source of data describing activities to be managed. There are clear benefits that could be derived if all interests groups could effectively collaborate and share data (SETAC, 1993). Global availability of information on product bills, process bills, and material declaration sheets would certainly promote eco-design activities and support research on methodological development. There is also a need for standardization or consensus from industry to report, track, update, and organize materials declaration databases. In the context of the coming EU-directives and policy initiatives, such as REACH and EuP, the companies must disclose the information about the constituent substances in their products and establish product eco-profiles. In some regions, central life cycle inventory databases containing adequate ecological data relevant to the materials and processes used in the electronics industry have been established, for example, the Swiss "ecoinvent" database (Frischknecht et al., 2005) and the Korean Web-based eco-database (Chung et al., 2003). Even so, there is still a data gap that results from these efforts. For example, only generic component and process data are available for certain industrial economic sectors (e.g., energy, building materials, metal, paper and board, agriculture, transport, etc.) and they are hardly suitable for the eco-design of a product. The current "ecoinvent" is only valid for Western European and Swiss conditions. In order to apply this database directly in Asia or the U.S. economy, the robustness needs to be examined. To combine the specific process and product information, one approach is to expand the data provided in a bill of materials (BOM). In industry, the material inventory analysis is routinely performed in the format of BOMs. Generally, BOMs only reflect the usual information of supply chain with the list of components, functionality, and suppliers' information provided. For support of environmentally-oriented decisions, BOMs need to be complemented with essential information on mass and composition (Lambert, 2001); in addition, the amount of hazardous substances, the amount of recycled materials used in components and products, and so forth, need to be provided. Keeping the format consistent with that of a BOM has another advantage, that of allowing the information on materials composition to be trackable to the specific component, part, or functional family, which provides quick and efficient responses to internal references or external inquires about the material specifications. Because of the uncertainty associated with data collection, data integration, and data analysis, uncertainty analysis and risk assessment methods should be integrated into such approaches.

Uncertainty Check and Sensitivity Analysis

In the face of uncertainty, statistical methods can facilitate the interpretation of data, diagnosis of variance, and making inference. Sensitivity analysis evaluates the effect that variations in data, quality of data, methodological assumptions, threshold or reference values, the use of subjective judgment, and so forth, have on final outcomes to understand which of these factors may most influence the results and to check the robustness of the results.

The uncertainty usually comes from two sources: the model and the data. Usually, the more simplified models inherently contain more uncertainty in the methodology and model construction because they involve multiple assumptions on environmental processes and mechanisms that vary spatially and temporally in a wide range. The uncertainty from the model itself also derives from the definition of the system boundary, selection of impact categories, and the set up of the valuation method, such as the determination of a normalization reference, equivalency factors and weighting factors. Because uncertainty in itself is a risk, when our goal is just comparison of two products or considering improving processes for the same application, we can avoid this risk to a large extent by employing a relative assessment, for example, internal normalization, instead of absolutely determining or measuring the performance. The combination of absolute and relative approaches will contribute to the decision making together (SETAC, 1998). Another type of uncertainty comes from data quality, which derives from missing data, outdated data, unrepresentative data, and measurement errors. The uncertainty in inventory data can have a significant effect on the credibility of the final results. The simplistic models based on a small number of readily available input data, thus possibly involve less uncertainty than complex models. However, the lower uncertainty in some cases does not assure the validity of the result and, in the extreme case, will mislead the decision maker with a false sense of confidence. Applying probability distributions, stochastic models, and numerical simulation methods can help to discern the degree of uncertainty and improve the robustness and stability of the final results (Steen, 1999). In particular, Monte Carlo simulation is considered the most effective quantification method currently available for characterization of uncertainties and variability among the environmental system analysis tools (Sonnemann et al., 2004).

Peer Review

As observed from the references cited in previous sections, a large number of the environmental performance assessment tools adopted by practitioners (mainly Type I and Type II, see Table 2) are described only in conference proceedings instead of peer-reviewed journals. There are some reasons for this. First of all, while passing the peer-review process is often considered in the scientific community to be a certification of validity, there is no objective standard against which to compare the assessment methods to determine their validity because we have very limited experience with the complexities involved in environmental systems. At present, some academic conferences and professional symposia, such as the International Symposium of Environment and Electronics sponsored by IEEE and Electronics Goes Green in Germany, provide a forum for dialog among practitioners and those developing new methodologies in an effort to encourage interdisciplinary efforts and to solve specific but complex problems. Second, for industrial practitioners, impact and actual effect are more important than validity, as their assessment methods are being used to satisfy a deadline from upcoming legislation. Third, it is challenging to find appropriate peer-reviewed journals that cross the boundaries of this integrated discipline, yet will serve the need of the design engineers making decisions. Despite these reasons, there is a need for increased peer-review in order to find the flaws in methodologies, to check the validity and robustness of data and results, and to create a synthesis of both practical and theoretical knowledge.

Teaching Sustainable Product Assessment Methods

There is yet another challenge facing the successful design of product systems with sustainability in mind: education of future design engineers. As the demand for measuring environmental performance and progress has exploded in industry, the conventional engineering curriculum is faced with new challenges. The general objectives of an up-to-date curriculum that incorporates sustainability need to provide future engineers with an understanding of the quantitative methods used for environmental performance assessment and to introduce some available computer aided ecodesign tools in engineering design applications. There are a handful of programs in the U.S. that have begun to tackle this challenge, including Rochester Institute of Technology (RIT), Carnegie Mellon University and California Polytechnic State University San Luis Obispo (Cal Poly). At the University of California Davis, we have implemented various aspects of sustainability into the chemical engineering and materials science curriculum. Specifically, a graduate course in green engineering is now available and curriculum modifications have been made in various undergraduate courses, including those in chemical engineering plant design and in materials selection. The focal point has been in the latter course, in which the curriculum modification has been guided by four principles (Zhou & Schoenung, 2006): 1) consideration of the entire life-cycle, 2) consideration of the multiple objective nature of the selection decision, 3) application of various databases and software packages, and 4) a focus on the open-ended nature of these selection decisions.

CONCLUSION AND FURTHER DIRECTIONS

Historically, environmental aspects have not been highlighted in the framework of corporate management, but some leading companies in electronics have included environmental performance assessment results in the corporate societal responsibility reports or annual environmental reports. The current changes in the consumer electronics industry, such as the short business cycle, reduced life of products, and globalization of marketing and manufacturing activities, provide the background spurring the sweeping emergence of the transparent decision making framework and assessment approaches for evaluating material selection and technology substitution within this industry. Meanwhile, resource optimization and environmental issues in the life cycle context are taken very seriously by both the general public and government agencies. New environmental regulations are cropping up around the world. Industry-wide communication and cooperation on a global basis regarding environmentally friendly product innovations and end-of-life strategies need a comprehensive and standardized framework or quick reference system to quantify the environmental performance of a product system. Thus, product environmental performance assessment, which is designated to help companies evaluate, plan for, and integrate sustainable policies into business, has, over the last decade, become more quantitative. The trend is to integrate materials and energy input-output inventory analysis, environmental impact and life cycle cost assessment, trade-off and multi-attribute analysis from conceptual design to the launch and manufacturing, until end-of-life of products, through the upstream to the downstream activities along the whole supply chain. The industry is using various tools that allow the establishment of relationships among environmental, societal, technical, and economic aspects to communicate the performance of products and evaluate trade-offs. By no means does this chapter intend to explore the entire spectrum, but rather to inform the appropriate selection of life cycle analytical tools used in a certain context and by a concrete cluster of actors. The goals of application include:

- Legislative compliance
- Declaration of environmentally friendly technologies in products and production
- Measurement of products and processes to improve the efficiency and identify bottlenecks to environmental management
- Support of eco-design and quick identification of preferred design alternatives at the early design stage
- Optimization of end-of-life processes and level of disassembly
- Decisions on end-of-life product scenarios
- Benchmarking of products, product generations, processes, and companies
- In-depth comprehensive analytical assessment for setting feasible policy objectives
- Environmentally preferable purchasing
- Environmental supply chain management
- Environmental life cycle assessment/costing/design

The major factors that influence the corporation's management strategy and application of environmental assessment tools include geography, policies, culture, economics, and business. These elements play an important role on the development of methodology, as described for five key representative geographic regions that have provided leadership in environmental management within the electronics industry. Some methodological challenges still exist. Although there is no definitive answer or strategy on how to deal with them, there is a need for industry to be more involved in multi-attribute and multi-objective analysis and integrated adapted methods so that the assessment will reflect trade-offs inherent in environmental management of product systems. We recommend the following approaches to resolve some of the problems:

- Evaluate the effectiveness of impact indicators based on the availability and quality of data, purpose of measurement, and environmental relevance.
- Incorporate an environmental accounting system into the conventional management system. Process-oriented indicators and product-level allocation need more effort.
- Various approaches should be employed to derive the underlying correlation for environmental improvements based on both empirical and theoretical data.
- A single value environmental performance score can be achieved by the combined use of ecological, social science, and economic instruments.
- Concurrent and rapid communication across disciplinary boundaries and the combination of top-down and bottom-up hierarchical-structured approaches are proposed to objectively quantify the preferences of different stakeholders.
- Global availability of information on product bills, process bills, and material declaration sheets should be promoted to support research on methodological development.
- Practitioners should be able to choose applicable methods from a variety of harmonized approaches and unify their advantages and knowledge in various disciplinary fields.
- Easier access and a mechanism to easily track the underlying data and assumptions will contribute to the public debate and future methodological innovation and development.

ACKNOWLEDGMENT

Financial support of this work was provided by the U.S. National Science Foundation under the grant number CMS-0524903.

REFERENCES

American Electronic Association (AeA). (2004). *Update: International environmental regulations affecting high-tech companies*. Retrieved July 8, 2008, from http://www.aeanet.org/GovernmentAffairs/gaet_EnvUpdate042704.asp?bhcp=1

Andrae, A. S. G. (2005). *Environmental life-cycle assessment in microelectronic packaging*. ISBN 91-7291-607-9, doctoral dissertation, Chalmers University of Technology, Gothenburg, Sweden.

Baumann, H., & Cowell, S. (1999). An evaluative framework for conceptual and analytical approaches used in environmental management. *The Journal of Corporate Environmental Strategy and Practice, 26*, 109-122.

Bergendahl, C. G., Lichtenvort, K., Johansson, G., Zackrisson, M., & Nyyssonen, J. (2005). Environmental and economic implications of a shift to halogen-free printed wiring boards. *Circuit World, 31*(3), 26-31.

Chen, J. L., & Chien, H. W. (2004). Simple LCA by response surface method for multidisciplinary design of eco-product. In H. Reichl, H. Griese, & H. Potter (Eds.), *2004 Proceedings of the Elec-*

tronics Goes Green: Driving Forces for Future Electronics (pp. 515-520). Stuttgart, Germany: Fraunhofer IRB, IRB Staz-und Druckcenter.

Christopher, M., Deshmukh, A., & Wang, B. (1996). Green quality function deployment. In *Proceedings of the 4th International Conference on Environmentally Conscious Design and Manufacturing* (pp. 297-304).

Chung, J., Lee, H., Koh, Y., & Hur, T. (2003). Web based ecodesign supporting system for electronic product. In *Proceedings of the 2003 IEEE International Symposium on Electronics and the Environment* (pp. 246-250). The Institute of Electrical and Electronics Engineers, Inc.

Dale, V. H., & English, M. R. (Eds.). (1999). *Tools to aid environmental decision making*. New York: Springer-Verlag.

Daniels, P. L., & Moore, S. (2002). Quantifying the metabolism of physical economies, Part I: Methodological overview. *Journal of Industrial Ecology, 5*(4), 69-93.

Das, S., & Yedlarajiah, D. (2002). An integer programming model for prescribing material recovery strategies. In *Proceedings of the 2002 IEEE International Symposium on Electronics and the Environment* (pp. 118-122). The Institute of Electrical and Electronics Engineers, Inc.

Delucchi, M. A., Murphy, J. J., & McCubbin, D. R. (2002). The health and visibility cost of air pollution: A comparison of estimation methods. *Journal of Environmental Management, 64*, 139-152.

Dewulf, W., & Duflou, J. (2004). Estimating environmental impact scores and related uncertainties using the Eco-Pas methodology. In H. Reichl, H. Griese, & H. Potter (Eds.), *2004 Proceedings of the Electronics Goes Green: Driving Forces for Future Electronics* (pp. 447-452). Stuttgart, Germany: Fraunhofer IRB, IRB Staz-und Druckcenter.

Dickinson, D. A., Mosovsky, J. A., & Houthuysen, S. D. (2003). Assessing integrated circuit manufacturing for environmental performance and sustainability: A full scale IC business application. In *Proceedings of the 2003 IEEE International Symposium on Electronics and the Environment* (pp. 214-219). The Institute of Electrical and Electronics Engineers, Inc.

Donnelly, K., & Boehm, T. (2003). Implementing DFE through a product-based environmental management system. In *Proceedings of the 2003 IEEE International Symposium on Electronics and the Environment* (pp. 111-113). The Institute of Electrical and Electronics Engineers, Inc.

Eikelenberg, N. L. W., Kok, I. C., & Tempelman, E. (2004). Implementation ecodesign for EEE-products. In H. Reichl, H. Griese, & H. Potter (Eds.), *2004 Proceedings of the Electronics Goes Green: Driving Forces for Future Electronics* (pp. 469-474). Stuttgart, Germany: Fraunhofer IRB, IRB Staz-und Druckcenter.

Environmental Protection Agency (EPA), U.S. (1995). An introduction to environmental accounting as a business management tool: Key concepts and terms. Retrieved July 8, 2008, from http://www.epa.gov

Environmental Protection Agency (EPA), U.S. (2002). *The Toxics Release Inventory (TRI) and factors to consider when using TRI data.* Retrieved July 8, 2008, from http://www.epa.gov/tri

Envirowise, Electronics Sector. (2005). *Relevant legislation/regulations*. Retrieved July, 8, 2008, from http://www.envirowise.gov.uk/page.aspx?o=Ref165

Ericsson Corporation. (2004). *Ericsson sustainability report: Bridging the digital divide with communication for all.* Stockholm, Sweden.

Feldmann, K., Meedt, O., Trautner, S., Scheller, H., & Hoffman, W. (1999). The "Green Design

Advisor": A tool for design for environment. *Journal of Electronics Manufacturing, 9*(1), 17-28.

Field, F. R. (1985). *Application of multi-attribute utility analysis to problems in materials selection*. Doctoral dissertation, Massachusetts Institute of Technology, Cambridge, MA.

Fiksel, J. (Ed.). (1996). *Design for environment: Creating eco-efficient products and processes*. McGraw-Hill.

Finnveden, G., & Moberg, A. (2005). Environmental systems analysis tools: An overview. *Journal of Cleaner Production, 13*(12), 1165-1173.

Frischknecht, R. et al. (2005). The ecoinvent database: Overview and methodological framework. *International Journal of Life Cycle Assessment, 10*(1), 3-9.

Fruhbrodt, E. (2001). *LCA software review: An up-to-date overview of European market*. Germany: Heidelberger Druckmaschinen AG.

Goedkoop, M., Oele, M., & Effting, S. (2004). Simapro *6 database manual: Methods library*. PRé.

Goedkoop, M., & Spriensma, R. (2001). *The Eco-indicator 99: A damage oriented method for Life Cycle Impact Assessment*.

Graedel, T. E. (1998). *Streamlined life-cycle assessment*. Upper Saddle River, NJ: Prentice Hall.

Hageluken, M., & Schichke, K. (2004). Welcome to the jungle: Survival of the fitted environmental screening indicators. In H. Reichl, H. Griese, & H. Potter (Eds.), *2004 Proceedings of the Electronics Goes Green: Driving Forces for Future Electronics* (pp. 501-508). Stuttgart, Germany: Fraunhofer IRB, IRB Staz-und Druckcenter.

Herrmann, C., Eyerer, P., & Geidiga, J. (2004). Economic and ecological materials index for end-of-life and design of electronic products. *IEEE Transactions on Electronics Packaging Manufacturing, 27*(1), 2-8.

Hertwich, E. G., & Hammitt, J. K. (2001). A decision-analytic framework for impact assessment, part 2: Midpoints, endpoints and criteria for method development. *International Journal of Life Cycle Assessment, 6*(5), 265-272.

Hischier, R., Waeger, P., & Gauglhofer, J. (2005). Does WEEE recycling make sense from an environmental perspective? The environmental impacts of Swiss take-back and recycling systems for waste electrical and electronic equipment (WEEE). Environmental Impact Assessment Review, 25, 525-529.

Huisman, J. (2003). The QWERTY/EE concept, quantifying recyclability and eco-efficiency for end-of-life treatment of consumer electronic products. Doctoral dissertation, Delft University of Technology, The Netherlands.

Hussey, D. M., Eagan, P. D., & Pojasek, R. B. (2002). A performance model for driving environmental improvement down the supply chain. In *Proceedings of the 2002 IEEE International Symposium on Electronics and the Environment* (pp. 107-112). The Institute of Electrical and Electronics Engineers, Inc.

IBM Corporation. (2002). *IBM Corporation responsibility report*. USA.

INFORM, Inc. (2003). *Electric appliance recycling in Japan* (pp. 1-3).

Intel Corporation. (2005). *Intel Corporate responsibility report*. USA.

IPC (Association Connecting Electronics Industries). (2005). *Legislation and regulation*. Retrieved July 8, 2008, from http://leadfree.ipc.org

ISO 14040. (1997). *Environmental management: Life cycle assessment—principles and framework, ISO 14040: 1997(E).* Geneva, Switzerland: International Organization for Standardization.

Jasch, C. (2006). How to perform an environmental management cost assessment in one day. *Journal of Cleaner Production, 14(*14), 1194-1213.

Johnsson, J. (1999). *A monetary valuation weighting method for life cycle assessment based on environmental taxes and fees.* Master thesis, Natural Resource Management, Stockholm University, Sweden.

Jolliet, O. et al. (2004). The LCIA midpoint-damage framework of the UNEP/SETAC life cycle initiative. *International Journal of Life Cycle Assessment, 9*(6), 394-404.

Katz, J., Rifer, W., & Wilson, A. R. (2005). EPEAT: Electronic product environmental tool: Development of an environmental rating system of electronic products for governmental/institutional procurement. In *Proceedings of the 2005 IEEE International Symposium on Electronics and the Environment* (pp. 1-6). The Institute of Electrical and Electronics Engineers, Inc.

Kim, J., Hwang, Y., Matthews, H. S., & Kwangho, P. (2004). Methodology for recycling potential evaluation criterion of waste home appliances considering environmental and economic factor. In *Proceedings of the 2004 IEEE International Symposium on Electronics and the Environment* (pp. 68-73). The Institute of Electrical and Electronics Engineers, Inc.

Kiritsis, D., Bufardi, A., & Xirouchakis, P. (2005). Multi-criteria decision aid for product end of life options selection. In *Proceedings of the 2005 IEEE International Symposium on Electronics and the Environment* (pp. 48-53). The Institute of Electrical and Electronics Engineers, Inc.

Kuosmanen, T., & Kortelainen, M. (2005). Measuring eco-efficiency of production with data envelopment analysis. *Journal of Industrial Ecology, 9*(4), 59-72.

Lambert, A. J. D. (2001). Life-cycle chain analysis, including recycling. In J. Sarkis (Ed.), *Greener manufacturing and operations: From design to delivery and back* (pp. 36-55). Sheffield, UK: Greenleaf Publishing.

Lamprecht, J. L. (1997). *ISO 14000: Issues and implementation guidelines for responsible environmental management.* American Management Association.

Lee J. (2006, December). *Ecodesign movement in the Korean industries.* Paper presented on EcoDesign at the 2006 Asia Pacific Symposium, Tokyo, Japan.

Lee, J., & Whang, J. (2006). *Identifying complementary measures to ensure the maximum realization of benefit from the liberalization of trade in environmental goods and serves case study: Korea.* OECD Trade and Environment Working Paper No. 2004-03 (JT03212028).

LG Electronics Corporation. (2004). *LG 2004 environmental report.* Seoul, Korea.

Liu, L., Liu, Z., & Fung, R. (2003). "The most of the most:" Study on a new LCA method. In *Proceedings of the 2003 IEEE International Symposium on Electronics and the Environment* (pp. 177-182). The Institute of Electrical and Electronics Engineers, Inc.

Masanet, E. R, & Horvath, A. (2004). A decision-support tool for the take-back of plastics from end-of-life electronics. In *Proceedings of the 2004 IEEE International Symposium on Electronics and the Environment* (pp. 51-56). The Institute of Electrical and Electronics Engineers, Inc.

Menke, D. M., Davis, G. A., & Vigon, B. (1996). *Evaluation of life cycle tools.* Ottawa, Ontario: Environmental Canada, Hazardous Waste Branch.

Ministry of Environment (MOE), Japan. (2002). *Environmental accounting guidelines*. Tokyo, Japan.

Motorola, Inc. (2004). *Motorola global corporate citizenship report* (RC-99-2067). Schaumburg, Illinois.

Mueller, J., Griese, H., Hageluken, M., Middendorf, A., & Reichl, H. (2003). X-free mobile electronics-strategy for sustainable development. In *Proceedings of the 2003 IEEE International Symposium on Electronics and the Environment* (pp. 13-18). The Institute of Electrical and Electronics Engineers, Inc.

Nokia Corporation. (2004). *Environmental report of Nokia Corporation*. Finland.

Oberender, C., & Birkhofer, H. (2004). Designing environmentally friendly products in conformity with the market: A holistic analysis of product characteristics. In H. Reichl, H. Griese, & H. Potter (Eds.), *2004 Proceedings of the Electronics Goes Green: Driving Forces for Future Electronics* (pp. 481-486). Stuttgart, Germany: Fraunhofer IRB, IRB Staz-und Druckcenter.

Ogallachoir, B., Oleary, F., Bazilian, M., Howley, M., & Mckeogh, E. J. (2006). Comparing primary energy attributed to renewable energy with primary energy equivalent to determine carbon abatement in a national context. *Journal of Environmental Science and Health, Part A, 41*, 923-937.

Park, P., Lee, K., & Wimmer, W. (2006). Development of an environmental assessment method for consumer electronics by combining top-down and bottom-up approaches. *International Journal of Life Cycle Assessment, 11*(4), 254-264.

Pascual, O., Boks, C., & Stevels, A. (2003). Communicating eco-efficiency in industrial contexts: A framework for understanding the lack of success and applicability of eco-design. In *Proceedings of the 2003 IEEE International Symposium on Electronics and the Environment* (pp. 303-308). The Institute of Electrical and Electronics Engineers, Inc.

Quella, F., & Schmidt, W.-P. (2003). Integrating environmental aspects into product design and development: The new ISO TR 14062, Part 2: Contents and practical solutions. In *Proceedings of the 2003 Gate to EHS: Life Cycle Management – Design for Environment* (pp. 1-7).

Rose, C. M., Stevels, A., & Ishii, K. (2000). A new approach to end-of-life design advisor (ELDA). In *Proceedings of the 2000 IEEE International Symposium on Electronics and the Environment* (pp. 99-104). The Institute of Electrical and Electronics Engineers, Inc.

Sakao, T., Kaneko, K., Masui, K., & Tsubaki, H. (2004). Analysis of the characteristics of QFDE and LCA for ecodesign support. In H. Reichl, H. Griese, & H. Potter (Eds.), *2004 Proceedings of the Electronics Goes Green: Driving Forces for Future Electronics* (pp. 495-500). Stuttgart, Germany: Fraunhofer IRB, IRB Staz-und Druckcenter.

Samsung Electronics Co. Ltd. (2004). *Samsung electronics 2004 green management report: Respecting nature serving communities*. South Korea.

Satty, T. L., & Vargas, L. G. (2001). *Models, methods, concepts & applications of the analytic hierarchy process*. Kluwer Academic Publishers.

Schmidt, I., Meurer, M., Saling, P., Kicherer, A., Reuter, W., & Gensch C. O. (2004). SEEbalance: Managing sustainability of products and processes with the socio-eco-efficiency analysis by BASF. *Greener Management International, 45*, 79-94.

Schmidt, W.-P., & Sullivan, J. (2002). Weighting in life cycle assessment in a global context. *International Journal of Life Cycle Assessment, 7*(5), 5-10.

Schoenung, J. M., Ogunseitan, O. A., Saphores, J-D. M., & Shapiro, A. A. (2005). Adopting lead-free electronics: Policy differences and knowledge gaps. *Journal of Industrial Ecology, 8*(4), 59-85.

Scrutz M., Graulich, K., & Ebinger, F. (2004). Mind your steps towards sustainability: Developing product sustainability indicators for cellular phones. In H. Reichl, H. Griese, & H. Potter (Eds.), *2004 Proceedings of the Electronics Goes Green: Driving Forces for Future Electronics* (pp. 453-458). Stuttgart, Germany: Fraunhofer IRB, IRB Staz-und Druckcenter.

Seppala, J. (2003). *Life cycle impact assessment based on decision analysis.* Doctoral dissertation, Helsinki University of Technology, Finland.

SETAC (Society of Environmental Toxicology and Chemistry) - Europe Working Group. (1993). *Life cycle assessment and conceptually related programs.* CRP Report.

SETAC (Society of Environmental Toxicology and Chemistry). (1998). *Evolution and development of the conceptual framework and methodology of life cycle impact assessment.* SETAC Press.

Siddhaye, S., & Sheng, P. (2000). Environmental impact and design parameters in electronics manufacturing: A sensitivity analysis approach. In *Proceedings of the 2000 IEEE International Symposium on Electronics and the Environment* (pp. 39-45). The Institute of Electrical and Electronics Engineers, Inc.

Siemens Corporation. (2003). *Siemens corporate responsibility report.* Berlin/Munich, Germany.

Singhal, P., Ahonen, S., Rice, G., Stutz, M., Terho, M., & van der Wel, H. (2004). Key environmental performance indicators (KEPIs): A new approach to environmental assessment. In H. Reichl, H. Griese, & H. Potter (Eds.), *2004 Proceedings of the Electronics Goes Green: Driving Forces for Future Electronics* (pp. 697-702). Stuttgart, Germany: Fraunhofer IRB, IRB Staz-und Druckcenter.

Sonnemann, G., Castells, F., & Schumacher, M. (2004). *Integrated life-cycle and risk assessment for industrial processes.* Lewis Publishers.

Sony Corporation. (2006). *Corporate social responsibility report.* Japan.

Steen, B. (1999). *A systematic approach to environmental priority strategies in product development (EPS): Version 2000—general system characteristics.* Sweden: Chalmers University.

Takahashi, K. I., Tatemichi, H. T., Tanaka, N. S., & Kunioka, T. (2004). Environmental impact of information and communication technologies including rebound effects. In *Proceedings of the 2004 IEEE International Symposium on Electronics and the Environment* (pp. 13-16). The Institute of Electrical and Electronics Engineers, Inc.

Udo de Haes, H. A., Jolliet, O., Finnveden, G., Hauschild, M., Krewitt, W., & Mueller-Wenk, R. (1999). Best available practice regarding impact categories and category indicators in life-cycle impact assessment, Part 1. *International Journal of Life-Cycle Assessment, 4*, 66-74.

Ueno, K., et al. (2001, December). *Efforts to improve the eco-efficiency for products of Mitsubishi electronic corporation: Factor X by using MET indicators.* Paper presented at the 2001 EcoDesign Conference, Tokyo, Japan.

Wenzel, H., Hauschild, M., & Alting, L. (1997). *Environmental assessment of products, volume 1: Methodology, tools and case studies in product development.* London, UK: Chapman & Hall.

Whitehead, J. C., Pattanayak, S. K., Van Houtven, G. L., & Gelso, B. R. (2005). *Combining revealed and stated preference data to estimate the nonmarket value of ecological services: An assessment of the state of the science.* Series Working Paper (No. 05-19). Department of

Economics, Appalachian State University, USA.

Wrisberg, N., Udo de Haes, H. A., Triebwetter,U., Eder, P., & Clift, R. (2002). *Analytical tools for environmental design and management in a systems perspective*. Dordrecht, The Netherlands: Kluwer Academic Publishers.

Zhou, X., & Schoenung, J. M. (2006). Integrating eco-design into the university curriculum. In *Proceedings of the 2006 Ecodesign Asia and Pacific Symposium*, Tokyo, Japan (pp. 105-110).

Zhou, X., & Schoenung, J. M. (2007). An integrated impact assessment and weighting methodology: Evaluation of the environmental consequences of computer display technology substitution. *Journal of Environmental Management, 83*(1), 1-24.

ADDITIONAL READING

The books and journal articles listed below identify the life cycle concepts and environmental management opportunities at the level of companies and product systems, present further scientific background on the associated theories and methods, and explore the various applications and case studies for all phases of the life cycle for various product systems.

Asiedu, Y., & Gu, P. (1998). Product life cycle cost analysis: State of the art review. *International Journal of Product Research, 36*(4), 883-908.

Azapagic, A. (1999). Life cycle assessment and its application to process selection, design and optimisation. *Chemical Engineering Journal, 73*(1), 1-21.

Curran, M. A. (Ed.). (1996). *Environmental life cycle assessment*. New York: McGraw-Hill.

Giudice, F., La Rosa, G., & Risitano, A. (2006). *Product design for the environment—a life cycle approach*. Boca Raton, FL: CRC Press, Talor & Francis Group.

Guinee J. B. (Ed.). (2002). *Handbook on life cycle assessment: Operational guide to the ISO standards*. Dordrecht, The Netherlands: Kluwer Academic.

Huppes, G., & Ishikawa, M. (2005). A framework for quantified eco-efficiency analysis. *Journal of Industrial Ecology, 9*(4), 25-42.

Ishii, K., Eubanks, C. F., & Marks, M. (1993). Evaluation methodology for post manufacturing issues in life-cycle design. *Concurrent Engineering: Research and Applications, 1*(1), 61-68.

Joshi, S. (2000). Product environmental life-cycle assessment using input-output techniques. *Journal of Industrial Ecology, 3*(2&3), 95-120.

Keoleian, G. A., & Menerey, D. (1994). Sustainable development by design: Review of life-cycle design and related approaches. *Journal of the Air & Waste Management Association, 44*(5), 645-668.

Kobayashi, Y., Kobayashi, H., Hongu, A., & Sanehira K. (2005). A practical method for quantifying eco-efficiency using eco-design support tools. *Journal of Industrial Ecology, 9*(4), 131-144.

Lindahl, M. (2006). Engineering designers' experience of design for environment methods and tools: Requirement definitions from an interview study. *Journal of Cleaner Production, 14*(5), 487-496.

Lye, S. W., Lee, S. G., & Khoo, M. K. (2001). A design methodology for the strategic assessment of a product's eco-efficiency. *International Journal of Production Research, 39*(11), 2453-2474.

O'Shea, M. A. (2002). Design for environment in conceptual product design: A design model to reflect environmental issues of all life-cycle phases. *Journal of Sustainable Product Design, 2*, 11-28.

Rahimi, M., & Weidner, M. (2004). Decision analysis utilizing data from multiple life cycle assessment methods, part I: A theoretical basis. *Journal of Industrial Ecology, 8*(2), 93-118.

Rahimi, M., & Weidner, M. (2004). Decision analysis utilizing data from multiple life cycle assessment methods, part II: Model development. *Journal of Industrial Ecology, 8*(2), 119-141.

Rebitzer, G., & Seuring, S. (2003). Methodology and application of life cycle costing. *International Journal of Life Cycle Assessment, 8*(2), 110-111.

Rudenauer, I., Gensch, C-O., Grieβhammer, R., & Bunkc, D. (2005). Integrated environmental and economic assessment of products and processes: A method for eco-efficiency analysis. *Journal of Industrial Ecology, 9*(4), 105-116.

Sarkis, J. (Ed.). (2001). *Greener manufacturing and operations: From design to delivery and back*. Sheffield, UK: Greenleaf Publishing.

Schaltegger, S., & Burritt, R. (2000). *Contemporary environmental accounting: Issues, concepts and practice*. Sheffield, UK: Greenleaf Publishing.

Udo de Haes, H. A., et al. (Eds.). (2002). *Life-cycle impact assessment: Striving towards best practice*. Brussels, Belgium: SETAC Press.

Underwriters Laboratories Inc. (2006). *A summary of global restricted substances directives*. Retrieved July 8, 2008, from http://www.ul-rscs.com/pdf/RoHS_Directives_Update_08282006.pdf

United Nations Environment Programme (UNEP), Division of Technology, Industry and Economics Production and Consumption Branch. (2003). *Evaluation of environmental impacts in life cycle assessment* (meeting report). Brussels November 29-30, 1998, and Brighton, May 25-26, 2000. United Nations Publication.

Zhang, Y., Wang, H. P., & Zhang, C. (1999). Green QFD-II: A life cycle approach for environmentally conscious manufacturing by integrating LCA and LCC into QFD matrices. *International Journal of Production Research, 37*(5), 1075-1091.

Chapter VI
From Cleaner Production to Greening the Local Economy: A Case Study of Two European Programs Enhancing SMEs Competitiveness Through Environmental Approaches

Nobutaka Odake
Nagoya Institute of Technology, Japan

Satomi Furukawa
Fuluhashi Environmental Institute Co., Ltd., Japan

ABSTRACT

As interests in the impacts of business activities on environment have been growing, environmental policy is now shifting from the "end of pipe" stage to the next stage, which factor in the life cycles and social efficiency. An increasing trend in environmental departments of state and municipal governments in Europe is that these departments have outgrown their restriction-based environmental measures. Their concept of environmental policy has shifted to management support programs that helps small- and medium-sized enterprises (SMEs) increase their competitiveness through improving their environmental efficiency. This chapter discusses and compares two environmental programs: the case of die Effizienz Agentur NRW (EFA) and the case of der ÖkoBusinessPlan Wien, the Eco Business Plan Vienna (EBP). The goal of this chapter is to extract the conveyed meanings of partnerships and the role of public sectors through the activities of local intermediaries such as agents need to play in fostering environmental conservation. The focus of discussion is on the partnerships among the parties involved in the programs and on the program operations.

Copyright © 2009, IGI Global, distributing in print or electronic forms without written permission of IGI Global is prohibited.

INTRODUCTION

One of the downsides of industrial agglomeration is the affect on the environment caused by discharge of a large quantity of waste and pollutants beyond self-purification capacity and large volumes of energy consumption. Ashford (2005) presents his concept of triple sustainability[1] that include the following: (1) improvement in competitiveness (or productivity) and long-term dynamic efficiency, (2) social cohesion (labor/employment), and (3) environmental sustainability (based on resource productivity together with measures for combating environmental pollution, damage to ecosystems, and climate disruption). Eco-efficiency aims at creating economic values by reducing the impact of industrial activity on the environment and limiting resource consumption. Improving resource productivity leads us to review the cost of the entire production system and added value at the same time (Porter & van der Linde, 1995).

Due to a growing interest of the impact of business activities on the environment, environmental policy is now shifting from the "end of pipe" stage to the next stage. In this stage, prominence is given to environmentally sound designs that feature in the life cycle of the products and lead to social efficiency. We have seen an increasing number of cases where government departments dealing with environmental issues in states and municipalities across Europe have gone beyond their restriction-based environmental measures. In many cases, they have shifted their support programs in favor of private enterprises, in particular small- and medium-sized enterprises (SMEs), by inducing them to reform their production processes based on environmental friendliness and social efficiency. These programs are aimed at reducing the environmental burden, not by forcing SMEs to follow government imposed measures, but by supporting SMEs' own efforts to reduce the burden. This can be categorized as a diffusion-oriented policy.

In this chapter, two cases are examined and compared. The first case is the environmental program model of utilizing *Produktionsintegrieter Umweltschutz* (PIUS), which refers to "environmental conservation incorporated into production," that is, cleaner production. This program, PIUS-Check has been implemented by the agency of *die Effizienz Agentur NRW* (EFA), which was established by the State Government of North Rhine-Westphalia (NRW) in Germany. The second case is *der ÖkoBusinessPlan Wien*, the EcoBusinessPlan Vienna (EBP) operated by the Environmental Protection Department of Vienna City in Austria. This chapter focuses on the partnerships among the parties involved in the programs and on the program operations. The goal of this chapter is to extract the conveyed meanings of the roles local agents need to play in fostering environmental conservation. Proceeding with this research, we conducted hearings with the following groups: (1) the Ministry of the Environment, Nature Conservation, Agriculture and Consumer Protection of North Rhine-Westphalia, (2) EFA, (3) the SMEs that have adopted the PIUS-Check, (4) the Environmental Protection Department of Vienna City Government, and (5) the SMEs and the technical consultants that have participated in EBP.

ACTIVITIES OF EFA NRW FOR CLEANER PRODUCTION

NRW[2], the largest German state in terms of economy with large industrial agglomeration areas, has been conducting the project which is intended for SMEs to pursue both environmental conservation and economic growth. EFA, located in Duisburg, is a nonprofit agency that was founded by the State of NRW in 1998. 403 projects were executed or are now ongoing as of April of 2007.

The Establishment of EFA/NRW and the Concept of the PIUS-Check

It was the state general election in 1995 that led to EFA's foundation. The Social Democratic Party of Germany (SPD) and German Green Party (*Die Grün*) formed a coalition[3] and agreed on policies such as the following: (1) accelerating the development of environment friendly technology, (2) speeding up the reformation of economic structure as well as recognizing critical technology that can be applied to meet the project's goals, and (3) reconciling environmental needs with the needs of public. When this agreement came into effect, the Ministry of Environment, Nature Conservation, Agriculture and Consumer Protection of North Rhine-Westphalia approved the proposal submitted by a private consulting firm, thereby establishing the basis for EFA. An independent body of EFA, designed only to undertake EFA's tasks, was formed. EFA set out to employ new staff members as the qualified staff of the consulting firm were already engaged in their existing work at that time. It was also their large-budget program that allowed them to employ new members. EFA is composed of personnel from various backgrounds such as engineering, enterprise consortium, marketing research, and job training.

The core tenet of EFA is PIUS, which is an abbreviation of German word, *Produktions- integrieter Umweltschutz*, which refers to "environmental conservation incorporated into production," that is, cleaner production. By utilizing the PIUS, EFA has placed consulting and supporting activities at the center of their services in the field of cleaner production. In addition to the PIUS-Check, EFA has developed management tools such as the resource cost accounting tool called "RKR," and the eco-design tool called "JUMP." EFA has also been extending local cooperation. The Duisburg's Business Promotion Agency plays a leading role in local cooperation to meet the goal of the PIUS, whereas EFA engages in educational programs and workshops in the greater area. EFA also distributes about 10,000 copies of their newsletters to other related enterprises and organizations. These newsletters are issued four times a year. While consulting knowledge was already there before EFA, it was basically for big companies. SMEs were not used to working with external consultants. The second goal of EFA seems the formation of the environmental consulting market for SMEs. The State Environment Ministry, the authority concerned, has regular meetings with EFA. EFA also commissions a marketing office to evaluate customers' satisfaction of programs of EFA to ensure the quality of their programs and customers' satisfaction.

EFA, an agency of the State Environmental Ministry, uses a program called the PIUS-Check to support SMEs in cooperation with consultants. The PIUS-Check, one of the major programs of EFA, consists of a simple tool of material flow analysis and consulting service using that tool. Through the PIUS-Check, efficiency in production is identified within the scope of a process-oriented material flow analysis[4]. Resource efficiency also means improved production process management, waste reduction, avoidance of use of hazardous chemicals together with cost reduction. It helps SMEs increase economic competitiveness and decrease environmental burden through improved resource efficiency. The PIUS-Check consists of the following four steps as shown in Figure 1:

1. **Initial meeting:** An EFA staff member, together with a technical engineer, visits an enterprise to assess how much improvement the PIUS-Check can possibly generate. Understanding the overall manufacturing processes and the interest of managing director of the company, the staff estimates the potential of cost reduction and the enterprise's way of thinking. For the project to be successful, the managing director's commitment to the project and willingness to improve their production process,

Figure 1. PIUS-Check: Four steps to improve resource efficiency

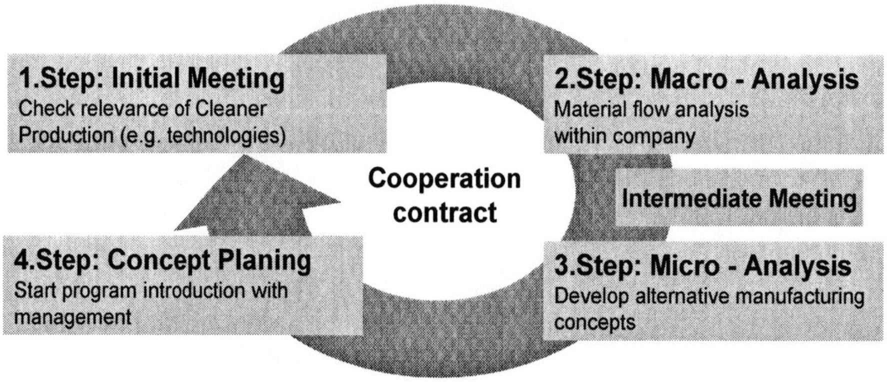

Source: EFA

that is, make changes to it, are important because of two reasons. Firstly, without the director's commitment, employees might not eagerly participate in the project as they are too busy dealing with their daily tasks. Secondly, with the director's willingness to change, it is more likely that the proposed improvement measures are implemented on the ground as a result of the PIUS-Check. The PIUS-Check's emphasis is more on making differences than on analysis and report writing.

2. **Macro-analysis:** The technical consultant, who is selected by the enterprise, conducts macrolevel analyses on its production processes. During the macro-analysis process, she or he describes material flow analysis and energy flow analysis through the macro-analysis of the whole factory. Intermediate meeting is held at this stage. In the meeting, the data collected at the company is examined and qualified by all three parties, including the EFA staff, the technical consultant, and representatives of the company. Based on the result of macro-analysis and the interest of the company manager, a few focus areas for micro-analysis that have most potential for improvement are determined. Participation of the company representatives is essential, as a reform plan produced through micro-analysis has to be in line with the company's current situation and future plan. If the focus area is decided only from an engineering viewpoint without company representation, the actual reform plan might never be realized.
3. **Micro-analysis:** The consultant conducts microlevel analyses of the focus areas determined through the macro-analysis. This is pursued to find specific solutions and to estimate the impact that the solutions will have on the entire production process. The concept of alternative processes is discussed, including specific solutions with potential impacts on the entire production processes.
4. **Concept planning:** Based on the results from the PIUS-Check, the consultant will then develop reform measures for production processes. The cost of this series of consulting processes is paid to the consultant. The SME covers 30% of the cost, and the state government subsidizes the rest of it through EFA.

Material flow analysis and energy flow analysis used in the PIUS-Check are not new concepts, but are seldom used in ordinary manufacturing firms except chemical plant engineering firms, and much less are utilized by SMEs. Even though this kind of analysis is not a complicated tool, it is rather difficult for SMEs to utilize it by themselves, as they often have limited resources, including employees' time and knowledge. EFA enabled SMEs to utilize these analyses in the form of the PIUS-Check, as it is a package of simplified tool and consultancy tailored to specific situations that each SME has. Working with an external consultant is also a very important factor, as it provides support to proceed with the processes of problem finding and then problem solving. It is often difficult for SMEs to proceed with the process without external consultant's support, as they are too busy to engage in "extra" work on top of their routine work. The total process must be completed in 9 days for a technical consultant because the amount of subsidies is limited for each project.

Now, we will discuss the advantages that enterprises have through cooperation with EFA. The PIUS-Check allows enterprises to reduce the cost of production through energy saving, water saving, reduction in discharged water, and curbing waste generation. It leads to improved energy efficiency through less input resources, and to the company's satisfaction that they contribute to the reduction of the environmental burden. Many of the enterprises that were initially hesitant to participate in the project find themselves largely satisfied and continue to engage in it. Among the three parties involved in the project, EFA, a technical consultant, and a SME, each party holds responsibilities for its own part. The external annual evaluation of EFA's program is very important, and is performed by a marketing firm.

Example of the Enterprises that Participated in the PIUS-Check

As of December 2007, over 400 PIUS-Check projects have been implemented in Germany. Detailed explanation and discussion of the application of PIUS-Check to a company is shown in this section. The authors participated in the PIUS-Check implementation in the Tokai Region, as a staff member and an advisor of the consulting company, the Fuluhashi Environmental Institute.

Since 2001, Japan-Germany PIUS Conference has been held in Berlin, Osaka, Düsseldorf, and Kitakyushu. Fortunately, Japan-Germany PIUS Conference in Nagoya was held in September of 2005. Nagoya is located in Tokai Region[5], the central part of Japan. The cases of eco-products and the processes on the theme of PIUS in Germany and the cases of zero-emission concept in Japan were introduced there. During the German Year in Japan 2005/2006, EFA sought participants of the PIUS-Check pilot projects in Japan. Three companies participated in Tokai Region and one in Kitakyushu.

The Fuluhashi Environmental Institute Co., Ltd. (FEI), coordinated the three PIUS-Check pilot projects in Tokai Region. The staff members of EFA visited Japan several times to support FEI to carry out the PIUS-Check in four steps, as carried out in Germany. The result of the three cases of PIUS-Check performed in Tokai Region is shown in the Table 1.

Company A: Metal Working

Here the case of Company A is shown as a sample of PIUS-check in steps, especially macro-analysis (Figure 2) and micro-analysis (Figure 3).

Company A is a medium-sized enterprise with about 1,600 employees. In the macro-analysis of the whole plant, it was found that the company had not paid close attention to some data. Even though the company has ISO14001 certification and collects environmental data, it was not well

Table 1. The three cases of PIUS-Check in Tokai region in Japan

	Company A Metal working	Company B Pipe-chair manufacturer	Company C Noodle manufacturer
Corporate profile*1	Annual sales: $440 million 1,641 employees ISO14001 certification	Annual sales: $21 million 64 employees ISO14001 certification	Annual sales: $30 million 78 employees
Description of business	Door locks, door closers and architectural hardware. security systems and related items	Pipe-chairs and folding chairs	Fresh noodle, boiled noodle, steamed noodle for pan fried noodle and pre-packaged noodle meal set
PIUS-Check Focus Areas	Plating & painting process	Plating & painting process	Noodle making process
Issues	Improvement of plating process and painting process	Improvement of painting process	Overuse of ground water, heat recovery of overflowing boiling water
Results	$0.2 million/ year cost savings by reducing the frequency of color change	Potential of $0.1 million/ year cost savings through waste water treatment process improvement and change of coloring process organization.	$0.2 million/ year cost savings through reduction in heavy oil consumption by installing heat exchanger. The investment in heat exchanger can be recovered within one year.
CO2 reduction*2	0.9 ton / year	19 ton / year	143 ton / year

*Notes: *1 Corporate profile data is as of April, 2007, 1US$=110JPN, *2 On-site greenhouse gas (CO2) emission reduction*2 (ton / year).Rough conversion from reduced amount of water, electricity, heavy oil, and butane gas.*

utilized for material flow improvement purposes prior to the PIUS-Check. Macro-analysis and discussions were held between EFA staff, the FEI consultant, and the company environmental manager. The focus area for the micro-analysis was to be the electroplating and painting processes. These areas were the ones that the company saw the possibility of making changes according to the recommendations of the PIUS-Check. In addition, the three parties could see the cost and material savings potential.

In conducting the micro-analysis, the FEI started from figuring out the material flow by tracking the input and output of the resources and energy in the focus area, for example, electro plating (Figure 2). Then, the material flow was plotted to each process, and then broken down into production steps. From the facility and equipment plan and the procedure manual that the company had, the FEI consultant drew micro-analysis production process flow (Figure 3). The FEI consultant drew the micro-analysis flow and plotted the numbers provided by the company. In order to determine accurate numbers and process steps, the consultant and the company staff member discussed and corrected the chart back and forth. Such material flow did not exist in the company at the time. Even the manager who was in charge of the electroplating process did not know in detail how much water was in which bath, how much flows into the bath, and how much is discharged from which bath. He only had a general overview of the process. The operation manual was made more than 10 years ago, and no revisions had been made, as there was no longer staff in the company with the required technical knowledge of electroplating.

The plant has various metal work processes and the plating has been considered as peripheral process. The plating line was designed over 20 years ago, and neither examination, nor improvement has been made on the line since, as there has

Figure 2. Macro-analysis of Company A

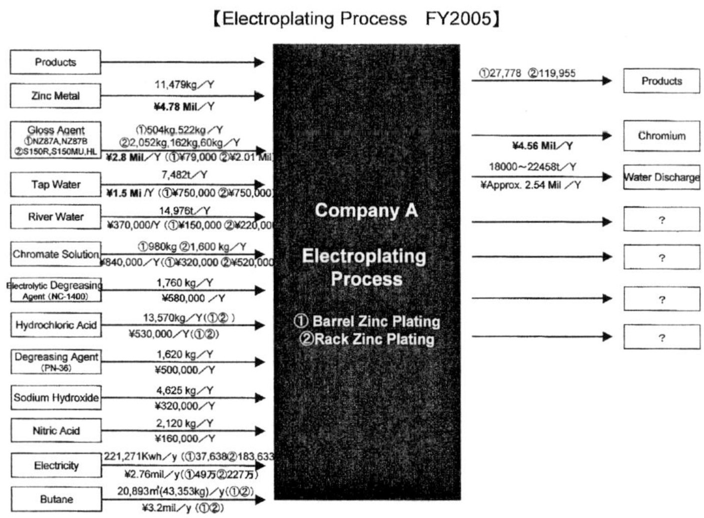

Figure 3. Micro-analysis of the rack plating process in Company A

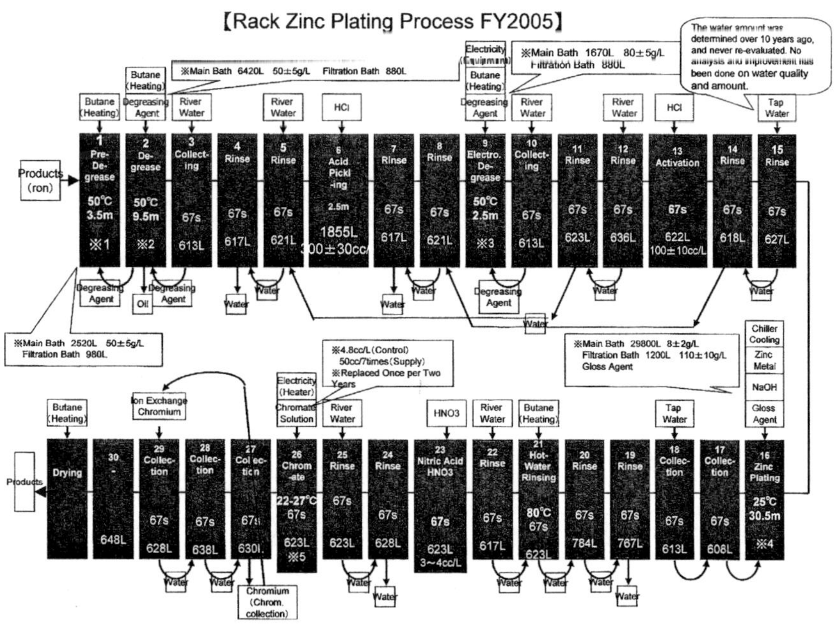

been no expert on the plating process in-house. Through the PIUS-Check analysis, potential for reducing water, energy and raw material consumption, as well as waste generation, was found that result in $0.2 million/year cost savings without any significant investment.

Prior to the PIUS-Check, the environmental manager of Company A was not fully convinced that great cost and material savings would be identified from the check, as they had already been working hard on cost savings. However, Company A decided to participate, as they were interested in learning about measures to find loss points for improvement. The reasonable cost setting that Company A had to pay to receive the consulting service was another factor that contributed to the company's decision to participate. As 70% of the consulting fee was subsidized by the NRW State government, the company was only to cover 30% of the cost.

Another essential factor is building a trusting working relationship among the three parties: the company, the consultant, and EFA. In the case of Company A, the company had a prior working relationship with the FEI. Existence of a certain degree of trust prior to the PIUS-Check was another factor contributing to the company's participation. When the FEI was recruiting SMEs to participate in the PIUS-Check, there are a greater number of companies who declined to participate, as there were no guarantees that any cost and material savings would be made as a result of the PIUS-Check. There also were companies that would not welcome external consultants looking closely at the company's production processes, nor did they expect to find measures for improving material flows. To overcome these barriers a trusting working relationship is an essential factor; a lack of such a relationship makes SMEs reluctant to work with external consultants.

An important aspect is that SMEs see the government and agencies of the government as helpful and supportive partners, as opposed to the inspection and controlling powers for enforcing regulations. Under the restriction-based environmental measures, SMEs and environmental governmental agencies often do not have a trusting relationship, as government is the entity that enforces the regulation.

Despite the fact that the two companies in the three cases are already certified according to ISO14001, in each plant significant points for improvement have been found through the PIUS-Check. The PIUS-Check based on material flow analysis and energy flow analysis basically stems from the concept of chemical engineering. It is rare that SMEs carry out material flow analysis even at the plant-wide level on their own, the micro-analysis of process-level, or equipment-level. SME managers and employees are too busy in dealing with their own daily tasks, such as production management and quality control, which leaves limited resources, including time, to engage in anything beyond their daily tasks. The data obtained from PIUS-Check has significant value and has become a resource for the management policies of SMEs, as it suggests points for improvement with cost/benefit factor. Tokai Region is recognized as a competitive manufacturing region; however, there is big room for improvement in peripheral processes, especially in SMEs. These three pilot projects in Tokai Region suggest that the PIUS-Check program can be applied outside of Germany, and it is a very effective tool to improve resource efficiency, especially at SMEs, where such improvement is difficult to be made on their own initiative.

Review of EFA's Attempts

As EFA has attempted to incorporate environmental conservation into production, their activities have been gradually permeating in the state, as well as abroad. In order for each project to be successful, however, SMEs themselves need to have an ardent determination and attitude to reform themselves. It is noteworthy that the PIUS-Check imposes certain financial burden on SMEs. The presence of a technical consultant between EFA and a SME makes it possible to provide detailed services for SMEs, which can ultimately promote the dissemination of the PIUS. In the meantime, in order for SMEs to provide the data from their working sites, it is necessary to have relationships of mutual trust between EFA staff, the consultant, and SME managers. The processes of nurturing the relationships are a hidden key to success of the projects. EFA is considered to be an evolutional initiative developing consultancy and management tools.

From the viewpoint of technology transfer, there are two types of technology transfer: (1) the mission-oriented type, which is intended to create innovations and their derivatives, and (2) the diffusion-oriented type, which is designed to diffuse innovations. In Germany, there have been technology transfers in the form of contract-type research and intermediary services, which have been conducted by specialized agencies (Abramson et al., 1997). Those research institutes are represented by the Steinbeis Foundation (StW) and the Fraunhofer Society (FhG), which has been widely seen as a role model for the latter type. Out of the three companies we interviewed in Germany, two SMEs are currently working in collaboration with FhG. It is important to note that these collaborations have given one another the opportunities to outsource the research and development. EFA, an agency of the state government, fosters the latter type, the diffusion-oriented technology transfer. While it does not belong to the type of contract research institute, it is the model based upon the cooperation among the company, the agent of the government and consulting offices, or engineering offices. The uniqueness of the model of EFA can be attributed to the agency system. The State Ministry of Environment set up its policy implementation agency, EFA, instead of implementing its policy program by itself. EFA, as an agency of the State Ministry of Environment, not only implements the policy program of production efficiency improvement consulting, but also develops unique programs best suited to achieve their mission of promoting cleaner production and improving economic competitiveness of SMEs.

ACTIVITIES OF THE EcoBusinessPlan Vienna (EBP)

The Municipal Government of the City of Vienna[6] has been taking unique approaches toward environmental issues. Their approaches are not confrontational types of environmental measures such as restrictions. The ultimate goal of their approaches is to detach economic growth from natural resources consumption and environmental contamination. The government has been implementing the supporting program for SMEs to reform their business managements through reducing environmental burdens in their business activities. The program has been successful so far.

There are 85,000 SMEs located in Vienna, but only 55,000 SMEs are currently running their businesses. In terms of the cumulative total for the 7 years, from 1998 to 2005, 527 out of 5,500 enterprises with more than one employee have participated in the program conducted by the Vienna City Administration Municipal Department for Environmental Protection. In this section, we discuss EBP implemented by the Vienna City. In particular, we focus on the partnerships between the parties involved in the program and their organizational operations.

The Concept of the EBP Vienna

The core of the Vienna City Government's activities of reducing environmental burden is the EcoBusinessPlan Vienna (EBP). EBP is based not on forcing SMEs to defer environmental measures but on supporting SMEs'own efforts to decrease environmental burden. The primary objectives of EBP are to enhance Vienna's competitive edge and to create medium-term sustainable employment. These objectives are achieved by reducing negative industrial impacts on environment and improving natural resource efficiency. The secondary objectives are to develop the relationships between the government and private enterprises, to contribute to sustainable development of the city, and to detach its economic growth from natural resource consumption (Symposium fact sheets, 2005). These objectives are linked to the concept of creating economic values through eco-efficiency, which include increasing productivity of natural resources. EBP consists of five modules: (1) ISO14001, (2) EMAS, (3) Ecoprofit[7], (4) Eco Bonus, and (5) Eco-label Tourism (Magistrat der Stadt Wien, 2005). The Ecoprofit, which is the third module stated above, is a program developed in Graz, Austria, tailored to manufacturing companies which aim at a rapid reduction of resource inputs; the way to achieve this is the efficient use of resources and input materials, optimization of production processes and prevention of waste generation. The Eco Bonus, which is the forth module also mentioned earlier, is targeted specifically for personal businesses and micro enterprises. It also focuses upon waste control and energy reduction. Eco-label Tourism is the fifth module, and is unique to Austria. This program supports tourism-related businesses, such as hotels and restaurants, to obtain the Eco-label Tourism, an Austrian eco-label for tourism-related businesses.

Out of 750 enterprises with more than 100 employees, 302 enterprises have somehow been involved in EBP. EBP of Vienna was awarded the best practice by the UN-HABITAT.

EBP is a coordinating type of program which is running on several different financial resources. These resources are composed of the seed money from the city's financial resources, participation fees from companies, and funding from various organizations such as the Federal Ministry of Environment, the European Union (EU), and the Vienna Business Promotion Institute (VBPI). According to the city government, the economic effect of EBP, which includes business investment in the count, is estimated to be 5 times larger than that the public sectors disburse for EBP. The Ecoprofit Module, which plays a major role in EBP, was developed in the City of Graz. The selected technical consultant and a SME are cooperating on the program of the Ecoprofit Module. The SME covers certain portion of the cost of the program. In addition to the SME's disbursement, the subsidy from Vienna City will be paid to the consultant. The Ecoprofit Module is the program combining consulting and workshops on environmental management, and SMEs' attending to the workshops is compulsory.

The program of Ecoprofit proceeds in the following manner: (1) to find a technical consultant, and the city examines if the consultant meets standards of the program, (2) to find a SME and decide whether or not the SME will participate in the program after a brief consulting, (3) to apply the Ecoprofit Module, and (4) to honor the SMEs and to certify the results of their program.

The Vienna City Government has a reserve pool of technical consultants who have met standards for the program. The selected consultant then finds a SME. The registered consultants, however, are divided for each of five modules. The methodologies employed in each program are compiled in a database. The city government provides the SMEs involved in EBP with technical public services, PR support and special information services. In running the program, EBP places emphasis on the importance of PR. According to the criteria of the EU, 20% of the program budget should be spent on publicity activities. The advisory board is in charge of evaluating the compatibility between development of modules, subsidy issues, industrial classification of enterprises, and roles that supporting programs need to play. The ultimate goal of EBP is to increase the number of successful cases of SMEs, environmentally and economically through EBP.

A certification scheme functions as an incentive for SMEs to participate in EBP. The SMEs, whose EBP programs have made achievements, are certified as being successful in a recognized ceremony. This ceremony is held in a luxurious banquette room inside the Vienna City Hall. Such an opportunity for rewarding the participating SMEs serves as an incentive for increasing motivation of SMEs and their employees.

The external annual evaluation of EBP has an important role performed by the Vienna University of Business Studies and Economics. One part of the evaluation is based on standardized interviews. The other part is based on the statistics of the planned and realized environmental measures, which are documented in the database of EBP.

To examine if the subsidies spent by EBP, which in turn is financed by taxes, have an adequate effect, the multiplier of the total public expenses in relation to the total expenses of the companies is calculated. The public parts are direct and indirect subsidies, as well as program independent resources. The company expenses include the financial investments, the time resources needed, the participation fees, corrected by the reduction of the running costs. The evaluation calculated a ratio of one to five; for every euro invested by the government, companies invest five euros.

Case of an Enterprise that Participated in EBP Vienna

Company D: Catering Service

Placing organic goods and fair trade at the core policy of their business, Company D, which comprises nine staff members, is running catering services. From the very beginning, the company has intended to differentiate themselves from other enterprises. The owner's motivation to participate in the Eco-label Tourism module of EBP was to enhance their business competitiveness. Being certified has contributed greatly to the increase in the number of catering contracts and the sales of their sandwiches. For example, a company with Eco-label Tourism has a better chance to deliver services to the municipal government, as the city is committed to green procurement. Eco Business Club, a platform of companies who obtain EBP certification, is one of the places where the company expands the business opportunities, as environmentally conscious company managers gather at the meetings of the Eco Business Club, share their experiences and challenges, and network. New business matching is made there.

Through EBP program, Company D has started to garner information on other enterprises and environmentally sound services and products from their technical consultant. The company owner's experience with the consultant and the program has been positive. He recounted that the program is intended not to find fault with the staff members and then give them directions for reforming, but to motivate them to reform their business in an encouraging manner. In the very initial stage of the program, the staff members were not very responsive to the program. However, they have changed their attitudes after the company was certified. The employees' attitudes have shifted from complacency about their routine work activities to innovation-seeking attitudes. The company has now become a community-conscious enterprise. Participation in EBP contributed to strengthened management and employee motivation.

Related Programs in the Vienna City

As projects related to EBP, the Vienna City Government has been conducting the following programs, initiatives to contribute to sustainable development as local government: (1) Initiative "Waste Prevention in Vienna," (2) "ÖkoKauf Wien-Green Public Procurement in Vienna"[8], and (3) Programme Environmental Management in the Municipality "PUMA" (Symposium fact sheets, 2005). These projects make us recognize that the city government not only requests enterprises to reduce their environmental burdens, but also makes its own efforts to lead environmental initiatives by example.

Initiative "Waste Prevention in Vienna" is organized by the Strategy Group Waste Prevention, the main goals of which are reduction of waste amount by increasing quantitative and qualitative waste prevention and generating innovative ideas and actions. Through 12 demonstration projects, 17 research studies and awareness project for 2003 and 2004, more than 2,000 tons per year of nonhazardous waste and 4.5 tons per year of hazardous waste are reduced.

The project "ÖkoKauf Wien," EcoBuy Vienna, aims to advance the application of ecological criteria in procurement, that is, the purchase of goods, products, and services, in all fields of the City Administration. "ÖkoKauf Wien" is based on the Vienna Climate Programme KliP Wien[9]. It makes a substantial contribution to reaching the KliP targets. Experts from relevant departments as well as external environmental experts are brought together in working groups to develop ecological criteria specific to products or product groups. By the decree of the Chief Executive Director of the Vienna City Administration, the results of the "ÖkoKauf Wien" projects have been adopted as mandatory criterion for public procurement and contracting in Vienna.

By forming a team of experts, the Programme Environmental Management in the Municipality, "PUMA" developed guidelines and recommendations for municipal government as an organization to commit itself to better environmental management of their business activities.

Their experiences and lessons learned from PUMA provide feedback to the planning and implementation of other environmental programs and services, such as EBP Vienna. It works the other way around as well, that the experiences and lessons learned from other programs such as "ÖkoKauf Wien" and EBP also contribute to running PUMA. These multilayered programs reinforce each other.

Review of the Programs in the Vienna City

The environmental activities of the Vienna City Government are designed for SMEs to maximize their potential and strengthen their competitiveness, which eventually leads to bolstering up competitive power of the local community. EBP has adopted the evaluation process conducted by the outsiders from various local organizations. The Environment Department of the Vienna City Government maintains its close interactions with economic organizations, labor organizations, and private technical consultants. In addition to the program of the EU and that of the national Government, EBP has also adopted the program developed in University of Graz and utilizes it as the core module. This open-mindedness in organizational operations is one of the essential traits of EBP. In reference to the open-mindedness of EBP, the technical consultants in Graz play significant roles in the implementation of EBP. It is often the case in Japan that municipal governments are hesitant to employ external experts or partners from outside of their municipal boundary. The concept of modules is an effective tool to diffuse the activities of eco-efficiency. Because the five different modules are available within Vienna City, which is a relatively small area, micro-enterprises can also participate in EBP. EBP is a program run by the government in principle, but private consultants, including those who developed the Ecoprofit, play supporting roles. The consultants serve as an agent to provide SMEs with detailed services that the city government cannot cover. The consultants are thus a diffusion-type agent of the city government, and EBP also belongs to diffusion-oriented type policy.

DISCUSSIONS AND IMPLICATION: TOWARD GREENING THE LOCAL ECONOMY

The environmental policies of NRW and those of the Vienna City are both aimed at reducing the environmental burden and lift up the competitiveness of SMEs by improving the natural resource and energy efficiency. These are the PIUS-Check implemented by EFA, which was established by the State NRW in Germany, and EBP promoted by the Vienna City. Similarities and differences in these programs are summarized in the Table 2.

EFA was established as an agency of the state, against the backdrop of diffusion-oriented type policy being rooted in German policy practices as well as its targeted area being large. Not being complacent about acting as an agent for the state government, EFA has also been increasing its own leverage over the local communities by developing new programs, such as the PIUS-Check, from the viewpoint of eco-efficiency. In the case of Vienna City, Vienna City Administration Municipal Department for Environmental Protection functions as the actor of operating their programs. In both cases of EFA's PIUS-Check and Vienna City's EBP, the orchestration of the programs, including technical consultants, becomes a crucial point. Both of the programs rest upon the cooperative learning organization that consists of a local government, or an agency of government, technical consultants and SMEs. It is thus essential for these two programs to build up the trusting relationships among the three of them. For many SMEs, government tends to be the entity that restricts and controls environmental and other regulations, sometimes to the point that it is difficult for the company to deal with. These supporting programs for SMEs strengthen their competitiveness through eco-efficiency, allowing the government and government agencies to build trusting relationships with SMEs. In general, the problem finding process is essential before the problem solving process, and visualization of on-site issues or problems; these are the important aspects that make the PIUS-Check very successful to actually find problems and to make a difference at SMEs. Managing the quality of consultancy is essential, not only for the success of the programs, but also from the technical knowledge transfer perspective. Consultancy is considered to be a kind of knowledge transfer in some sense, externalizing in-house knowledge to the other firms.

These supporting programs for SMEs utilizing technical consultants can be seen as an empowerment policy. Both programs require SMEs to share a certain portion of the cost of the consulting services. From the standpoint of SMEs, the programs allow them to receive consulting services for low charges due to the subsidies. In the case of the PIUS-Check of EFA, for example, the subsidy covers 70% of the cost of the services. These consultancy services can be seen as "supporting business" and the subsidies contribute to nurturing the market of "supporting business," even though this type of market in the environmental sector has not been matured yet, neither in NRW nor in Vienna City. By nurturing "supporting enterprises," the governments can help form more innovative business communities, which will result in boosting their local industries, and hence empowerment policy. In addition to empowering SMEs, the secondary objective of both of the local governments can be said to increase the number of the technical consultants who have a community-conscious mind. An additional point about the cost sharing scheme to note is that letting SMEs bear a portion of the fee, even small portion, helps make SMEs responsible about their active participation to the program, as they would want to make sure to gain positive result in return to their "investment."

The corporate climate must enable the following in order to lead these programs to success: (1) good governance system with learning attitudes, (2) marketing activities (market sensitivity), and (3) open-mindedness of the enterprise. Without

Table 2. Similarities and differences of the programs EFA and EBP Vienna

Classification		EFA (the PIUS-Check)	EBP Vienna
Differences	Organizational structure	Run by an agency of the state government.	The Vienna City Government runs the program.
	Program development	Consulting based on the original program developed by EFA.	A combination of workshops and consulting programs including those developed by other organizations.
	Target group	The main target group is manufacturer.	A variety of groups including small businesses and service industry.
	Focus	Technology and engineering oriented program aiming to improve material and energy efficiency.	The focus is more on reforming the environmental management of the companies.
	Funding source	Solely by the NRW State Government.	Combination of the Federal government, EU, the city of Vienna, and the VBPI.
	Characteristic	Model for industrial districts with a large concentration of manufacturing.	Model for urban areas with concentration of service industries.
Similarities		- Link increased business competitiveness and economic benefit, and reduced environmental burden. - Promote concept of eco-efficiency. - 3 parties cooperation program of government or an agency of government, technical consultants, and SMEs. - Qualified consultants plays essential role in the program and the program supports development of consultants. - Consists of simple tools and consulting services. - The results of the consulting and improvement measures are recorded in a database. The accumulation of the improvement is shown as region-wide environmental improvement. - A certain portion of the program participation fee is born by SMEs; although the rest is subsidized.	

the open-mindedness of the enterprise, to let the consultant examine details of the company's business operation or production processes and to learn from the consulting, these programs could not have been materialized. For example, a staff member of EFA recounted that it was a challenge at the beginning of the program to build trust with enterprise managers in order to get them to participate. Over time, however, the accumulation of successful cases and company managers satisfied with their participation contributed to the programs' good reputation and better PR material. Trust must be established between the local government, technical consultants, and SMEs for successful implementation of the program. The three elements in a trust relationship are "trust in contract," "trust in capability," and "trust in sincerity" (Sako, 1992). A trust relationship comprising these three elements must be accumulated in order to build the trust in the entire business community.

It is necessary to note that there are some differences between the two programs, one of which is institutional set up of the two programs (Figure 4). In the case of NRW where targeted area is larger, the State Ministry does not directly operate their environmental programs but commissions it to EFA, which is a nonprofit agency, and is considered to be an evolutionary initiative developing consultancy and management tool. EFA also acts as an agency for the ministry to provide detailed public services, which is usually

Figure 4. Models of two programs

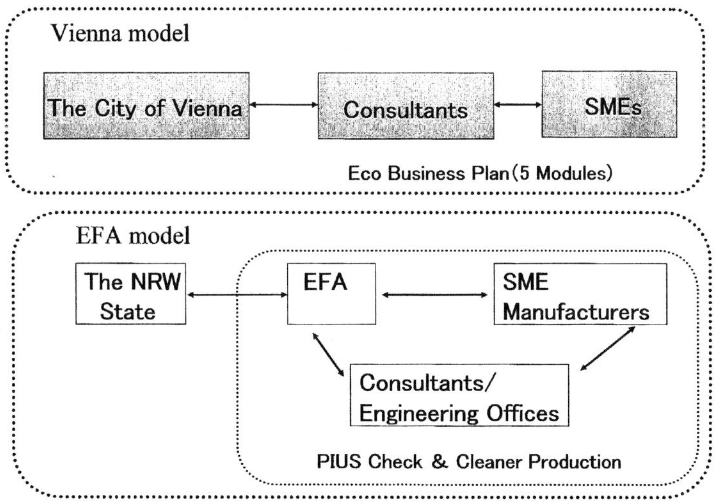

hard for a government to deal with. The success of EFA can be attributed to its set up whereby EFA acts as an independent agency, developing and delivering the best suited programs to achieve its mission of promoting cleaner production while increasing economic competitiveness of the businesses. Specialized agency systems proved to be effective, especially when technical expertise is needed and the service area is large. On the other hand, in the case of Vienna City where intended area is relatively small, the city government itself takes the main role of developing and promoting their environmental programs. Behind this scene, a great number of independent technical consultants and engineering experts play vital and valuable roles. They can be considered as subagents. Funded fully by the government of NRW, EFA has the networks with the city government of Duisburg, Universities, FhG, and so forth. EBP of Vienna City is funded by various organizations such as the EU and the Austrian Federal Ministry of Environment. EBP is also supported by the local network system based upon a good variety of the partnerships among the parties involved in EBP. It is thus regarded as a coordinating-type administration model. Even with different institutional set up, both programs work very well in their own ways. Both programs have external evaluation systems to secure quality of their programs.

Another difference between EFA and EBP is the focus and style of technical consulting. EFA provides the depth of technical consulting in maximizing efficiency of production processes, and introducing and developing cleaner production processes and measures best suited and specific to various production processes in different industries. Measures of EBP Vienna are more general in resource saving that could be applied to many offices or plants with the state-of-art motivating system provided by the Vienna City. Such difference derives partially from the difference in the target of the two programs; the major target group of EFA is limited to industries with production processes, while target of the EBP includes service industries. EFA is a model suited for industrial districts with a large concentration of manufacturing industries, while EBP Vienna is a model for urban areas with a concentration of service industries. EBP Vienna has specific modules for different target groups: Eco Bonus for small individual businesses, and Eco-label Tourism for the service industry, including hotel and restaurant business which are major elements of the Viennese local economy. The case of the city of Vienna can be seen as a model for greening the local economy, involving multilayered programs, such as Initiative "Waste Prevention in Vienna," Programme Environmental Management in the Municipality "PUMA," and "ÖkoKauf Wien."

The difficulties and challenges in setting up such programs are to deliver a certain level of achievement in return for the public funds invested, and the needs or potential needs of such services existing prior to setting up such programs.

CONCLUSION

In this chapter, we have discussed and compared the two environmental programs. Both programs contribute to the two significant aspect of eco-efficiency. The first is the achievement of individual firms that increase their competitiveness by cost reduction through an increase in resource and energy efficiency. The second is the regional level achievement by reduced negative environmental impact and improved economic competitiveness of the region as a whole. The accumulation of quantitative data of saved resources and energy is the evidence of the regional level achievement, leading to sustaining of public funding for the programs. In both programs the government plays an important role in increasing SMEs' competitiveness through improving their environmental performance.

A key of the success of the two programs is the composition of the programs. Both programs, the PIUS-Check and EBP, consist of a package of simple tool and consultancy service. The package of these two factors is quite indispensable, as these two make it possible for SMEs to actually improve the efficiency of their businesses. The analysis tool and the framework enabled various technical consultants to pursue the program in a limited time and to apply it to various sectors of industries. Without the consultancy component, the SMEs would have had a great difficulty in actually proceeding with the program, the problem finding and reforming process. In addition to the package; both programs are composed of various different elements such as legal system and control, financial methods, consulting system, and multifaceted partnerships. Creating partnerships among agency, technical consultants, and SMEs are another important aspect. Supporting and developing consultants and their market leads to incremental promotion of innovation.

Mechanisms to reward SMEs for their commitment to environmental improvement is also vital, as seen in the case of Vienna City, where SMEs have become certified as having achieved results and continue to keep motivation through staging effects such as certification ceremonies. This comprehensive system can be a model of community-empowering policy in an attempt for local governments to implement the bottom-up type measures for boosting local industries and revitalizing local business communities toward greening the local economy.

FUTURE RESEARCH DIRECTIONS

Regional Policy Perspective

Several municipal governments in the Tokai Region are about to start pilot projects of PIUS-Checks so as to develop policies suited to their own municipalities. The authors are leading these initiatives as a researcher and advisor of the Fuluhashi Environmental Institute in cooperation with municipal governments. We will continue research on the pilot projects and policy design in the form of action research. When accumulating data on the measures and results, development and application of data base will be important issues.

The role of consultants is the key factor to foster eco-innovation in the case of PIUS-Check and the EBP. Assurance of high quality consultants is essential for the success of the programs. Further research needs to be done on how development of high quality consultants will be assured and how it could be linked to development of consulting industry as a supporting industry, as well as how to assure fostering of trust among business communities and consultants and encouraging formal company interactions.

Another point for future research concerns the tool itself. Various tools concerning Life Cycle Assessment have been developed. Interrelation between these tools and consultancy needs to be researched from innovation promotion policy perspectives.

Industrial Cluster and Economic Development Perspective

In developed and mature industrial clusters, it is often the case that agents and intermediaries concerned with regional economic development play essential roles. Continuous innovation leads to the formation of clusters and regional economic development. Eco-innovation discussed in this chapter is mainly process improvement. Research and analysis on innovation or factors for innovation leading to new products development are also essential.

Strategic CSR Perspective

This chapter discussed introduction of eco-efficiency and corporate competitiveness. Eco-efficiency could be analyzed using CSR perspective. About the strategic characteristics of CSR, Porter and Krammer (2006) state that by taking a step further in shifting passive CSR to strategic CSR, corporate becomes able to establish competitive advantage leading to a sustainable growth and to internalize social issues to its own business. These benefit both society and the corporate. Further research and analysis on this point, that internalization of eco-efficiency into the corporate management and culture, might lead to the strengthened corporate competitiveness, similar to such a theory of CSR.

REFERENCES

Abramson, H., et al. (1997). *Technology transfer systems in the United States and Germany* (pp. 241-348). Washington, DC, USA: National Academy Press.

Ashford, N. (2005). Pathways to sustainability: Evolution or revolution? In M. Geenhuizen, D. Gibson, & M. Heitor (Ed.), *Regional development and creation for innovation in the network society* (pp. 35-59). West Lafayette, IN, USA: Purdue University Press.

Magistrat der Stadt Wien (Ed.). (2005). *Öko Business Das Buch- die Besten der Wiener Wirtschaft 2005.* Unpublished material, Wiener Umweltschutzabteilung, Vienna, Austria.

Porter, M. E., & Krammer, M. R. (2006, December). *Strategy and society: The link between competitive advantage and corporate social responsibility* (pp. 1-17). Harvard Business Review.

Porter, M. E., & van der Linde, C. (1995, September-October). *Green and competitive/ending the stalemate* (pp. 120-134). Harvard Business Review.

Sako, M. (1992). *Prices, quality and trust.* Cambridge, UK: Cambridge University Press.

Symposium fact sheets. (2005, October 27-28). *Symposium on public initiatives to promote environmental business performance: Greening the local economy.*

ADDITIONAL READING

Barney, J. B. (2002). *Gaining and sustaining competitive advantage* (2nd ed.). Upper Saddle River, NJ: Prentice Hall.

Battelle, J. (2005). *The search, how Google and its rivals rewrote the rules of business and transformed our culture*. New York: Portfolio.

Bornstein, D. (2004). *How to change the world: Social entrepreneurs and the power of new ideas*. New York: Oxford University Press.

Chesbrough, H. (2006). *Open innovation*. Boston: Harvard Business School Press.

Collins, J. (2001). *Good to great*. HarperBusiness.

Cleff, T., & Rennings, K. (1999). *Determinants of environmental product and process innovation. European Environment, 9*, 191-201.

DeSimone, L.D., & Popoff, F. (1997). *Eco-efficiency: The business link to sustainable development*. MIT Press.

Georg, S., Røpke, I., & Jørgensen, U. (1992). Clean technology: Innovation and environmental regulation. *Environmental and Resource Economics, 2*(6), 533-550.

Granovetter, M. (1985). Economic action and social structure: The problem of embeddedness. *American Journal of Society, 91*(3), 481-510.

Keijzers, G. (2002). The transition to the sustainable enterprise. *Journal of Cleaner Production, 8*(3), 179-200.

Kemp, R. (1994). Technology and environmental sustainability: The problem of technological regime shift. *Futures, 26*(10), 1023-1046.

Kotter, J. P. (1996). *Leading change*. Harvard Business School Press.

Lester, R.K., & Piore, M.J. (2004). *Innovation: The missing dimension*. Harvard University Press.

Mowery, D.C., & Rosenberg, N. (1989). *Technology and the pursuit of economic growth*. Cambridge University Press.

Nelson, R.R., & Rosenberg, N. (1993). *National innovation systems: A comparative analysis*. Oxford University Press.

Nonaka, I., & Takeuchi, H. (1995). *The knowledge-creating company: How Japanese companies create the dynamics of innovation*. Oxford University Press.

Paytas, J.P., Gradeck, R., & Andrews, L. (2004). *Universities and the development of industrial clusters*. Carnegie Melon University, Center for Economic Development, Prepared for Economic Development Administration U.S. Department of Commerce. Retrieved July 7, 2008, from http:// www. smartpolicy.org/pdf/ ucluster.pdf

Pernick, R., & Wilder, C. (2007). *The clean tech revolution*. New York: HarperCollins Publisher.

Reijnders, L. (1998). The factor X debate: Setting targets for eco-efficiency. *Journal of Industrial Ecology, 2*(1), 13-22.

Rogers, M.E. (1995). *Diffusion of innovations* (5th ed.). New York: Free Press.

Rosenbloom, R.S., & Spencer, W.J. (Eds.). (2006). *Engine of innovation*. Harvard Business School Press.

Savitz, A.W., & Weber, K. (2006). *The triple bottom line*. San Francisco: Jossey-Bass.

Saxenian, A. (1994). *Regional advantage: Culture and competition in Silicon Valley and Route 128*. Cambridge, MA, London: Harvard University Press.

Senge, M. P. (1990). *The fifth discipline: The art & practice of the learning organization.* New York: Currency Doubleday.

Vollenbroek, F.A. (2002). Sustainable development and the challenge of innovation. *Journal of Cleaner Production, 10*(3), 215-223.

Wenger, E., McDermott, R., & Snyder, W.M. (2002). *Cultivating communities of practice.* Boston: Harvard Business School Press.

ENDNOTES

1 A commitment to corporate social responsibility (CSR) implies a commitment to some form of triple bottom line reporting. The triple bottom line captures an expanded spectrum of values and criteria for measuring organizational (and societal) success; economic, environmental, and social. Triple sustainability is considered to be a dynamic change of the concept from the triple bottom line.

2 The State of North Rhine-Westphalia (NRW) has the area of 34,082km^2 and the population of 18.1 million. NRW also has the largest GDP among the 16 states in Germany and holds 22% of the national GDP.

3 The coalition of the Christian Democratic Union (CDU) and the Free Democratic Party (FDP) has taken over the power from the coalition of the Social Democratic Party of Germany (SPD) and the Green Party of Germany (DG) in the provincial general election of May 2005. However, the current administration has acknowledged the achievements of EFA and continues to support the program.

4 Interviewed Mr. Matthias Graf and Mr. Michael Niemczyk, staff members of EFA, during 2005-2007 in Duisburg, Germany, and Nagoya, Japan

5 Brief introduction of Tokai Region is described here. A very high percentage of manufacturing industries are concentrated in Tokai Region that consists of three prefectures: Aichi, Gifu, and Mie. Tokai region also contributes 17.8% of Japan's overall manufacturing shipment value (as of 2004). Composition of industry in the region is unique, as the share of transportation machinery is extremely high around the automobile industry, with 42% share of total shipment value of the region. Some other industries such as general machinery, including machine tool, iron and steel, plastic products, and so forth, are deeply related to the automobile industry.

6 Vienna, the capital city of Austria, has a population of 1.6 million with the area of 415 km^2. Out of the area, the city has its green space as large as 201 km^2. Vienna has long been known for sightseeing with 7.7 million tourists per year, but it has not been seen as an environmentally advanced area.

7 The Ecoprofit (ÖKOlogistics PROjekt Fur Integriete Umwelt-Technik), an environmental program developed in Graz City, aims to help local communities make sustainable economic development through improving the eco-efficiency of enterprises. It also attempts to empower both local governments and enterprises.

8 PUMA is intended to contribute to the Climate Protection Program. It also provides "ÖkoKauf Wien" with the feedback on the procurement.

9 The KliP, Climate Protection Program of the city of Vienna, is designed to help the city of Vienna act in accordance with the commitments subscribed to by joining the Climate Alliance as early as 1991 in order to put a greater emphasis on climate protection.

Section II
Demand and Service Chain Management

Chapter VII
Does Trust Foster Sustainability?
Results from a Management Simulation Game

Harold Krikke
Tilburg University, The Netherlands

Ruud Brekelmans
Tilburg University, The Netherlands

Hein Fleuren
Tilburg University, The Netherlands

Cindy Kuijpers
Tilburg University, The Netherlands

ABSTRACT

Successful supply chain collaboration is one of the principal means of achieving competitive advantage. New concepts such as vendor managed inventory, efficient consumer response, and factory gate pricing, among others, have been developed to optimize supply chains. The dual focus of supply chain collaboration has traditionally been customer service and cost. Sustainability is now also a primary focus. In this chapter, we study how trust impacts sustainability. Trust is often seen as a key moderator in supply chain performance. Yet, little is known about the role it plays in achieving sustainable supply chains. The ongoing debate about the greenhouse effect highlights the relevance of this topic. We look at trust and sustainability in supply chains using an advanced management game played by master students. We present the empirical data collected and then develop tentative propositions. We conclude with a discussion of the potential impact of the results for business and make suggestions for further research.

Copyright © 2009, IGI Global, distributing in print or electronic forms without written permission of IGI Global is prohibited.

INTRODUCTION

Supply chain management can be defined as the systematic strategic coordination and integration of traditional business processes across companies and of business functions along the supply chain to improve performance of individual companies and the supply chain as a whole (see e.g., Krikke, 1999). Its practical implementation boils down to concepts such as vendor managed inventory, efficient consumer response, factory gate pricing, outsourcing, and so forth. These concepts have been developed to counter phenomena such as the bullwhip effect, to create economies of scale, or to elicit better customer response. Collaboration is often the key to supply chain optimization.

Traditionally, an efficient supply chain was seen as a way to maximize customer service and minimize costs. Now, environmental considerations must also be taken into account. Al Gore (2006) has managed to focus attention on the green house effect and its underlying causes, especially CO_2 emissions, and has been recognized for his efforts with the Nobel Peace Prize. New EU directives and national environmental laws on emissions and recycling have led to closed loop supply chains.

Environmental impact is measured by (simplified) life cycle assessment (LCA). LCA in its pure form serves to assess the total environmental impact of a product and its supply chain in full detail. To reduce complexity, energy and waste-based environmental footprint measurements as proposed by Krikke, Bloemhof-Ruwaard, and van Wassenhove (2003) are an alternative. Measuring environmental aspects and LCA in the supply chain is dealt with in more detail later.

We believe that only by managing the full life cycle and hence the forward and reverse supply chain in their integrality can there be sustainability. Therefore, prevention is the first step toward achieving green solutions. *This chapter focuses on minimizing energy and materials wasted in the forward chain to reduce pressure on the reverse supply chain.* We emphasize the role of trust in this and also take cost and customer service into account.

Successful collaboration within supply chains appears to depend on several factors. Most existing theory looks at collaboration exclusively from one single angle be it product/technology, power/directorship, information/transparency, alignment/coordination, or performance. Some authors link these perspectives and describe the dynamics of the variables.

Possibly the most difficult, and yet the most important, variable to grasp is trust. McCutcheon and Stuart (2000) define trust as the belief that a party will act in a firm's best interest in circumstances where that party could act opportunistically at the expense of the firm. Amanor-Boadu and Starbird (2004) show convincingly that supply chains with high trust levels allow partners to cooperate more effectively and in so doing improve supply chain performance. Our own experience working in the area of logistics optimization has borne this out. Lack of trust often causes optimization projects and strategies to fail.

There is a considerable volume of literature on the relationship between trust and performance. Yet, the impact of trust on the sustainability of supply chains remains largely unexplored. We look at the role of trust in the greening of supply chains and collaboration. In Appendix IV, we show that most management games ignore this relationship altogether. Adding green objectives to supply chains adds complexity to decision making. As such complexities can only be resolved through good collaboration, in the end they can actually strengthen the relationship between supply chain players. We aim to develop tentative propositions using two cases. Case-based research is increasingly accepted as a way to develop new theory, provided it builds on existing constructs (Yin, 2003). We use constructs from established supply chain collaboration theory and closed loop supply chain theory.

Cases are often written by persons not directly involved precisely because they have the advantage of distance. A drawback of case research is that replication and comparability for purposes of validation and generalization is more difficult. To have the best of both worlds, we use the NetChain Game (NCG), which can readily be used by other researchers. More detail on the NCG is found in the appendices.

The game serves to face game participants with trade-offs and experience tensions much as they would be in real life, but the simulation model provides a safe and retractable environment. Moreover, a software-based game such as NCG provides researchers an opportunity to collect data in an organized manner. In order to gather sufficient data to develop our initial theory, we play two games, one involving automotive parts and the other cucumbers. We appreciate that our empirical database is not yet sufficient for ultimate generalization, but believe that we have made a good start.

We review the literature in the following section. We also build our research framework, using in part the work of van Leeuwen (2006). In our first results section, we use that framework to interpret the outcome of our experiment with an automotive industry-based supply chain simulation game, and discuss shortcomings of the case. We then develop propositions on the correlation between trust and supply chain sustainability. In the second results section, we detail changes in the game parameters. We then report on the playing of the game, this time involving a product with a short shelf life. Finally, we refine our propositions. We take a step toward generalization in the conclusion with a discussion about possible applicability of our results to business practice. We also make suggestions about additional cases and games that might be used in the future to further validate and strengthen our propositions.

TRUST AND GREEN SUPPLY CHAINS

Different Kinds of Trust

Along with other researchers, Boersma (1999) divides trust into contractual, competence, and goodwill trust. Contractual trust is characteristic of new relationships, when the partners to an agreement, be it oral or written, do not share a common history. If there are no sanctions put in place, and if one partner does not meet the expectations of the other, then trust will immediately deteriorate, causing the relationship to break down. Collaboration depends strongly on the benefits both parties expect before entering into a relationship. In the absence of a track record with the potential partner, the parties make their decisions on what information is available which consists mostly of quantified risks and performance measures (Williamson, 1993). Lewicki and Bunker (1996) see contractual trust as the first step in an evolutionary three-stage trust relationship development model.

Competence trust, also known as knowledge-based trust (Lewicki & Bunker, 1996), exists when the parties are confident that their counterparts have the knowledge and the ability to achieve targets successfully and will fulfill their part of the agreement completely. Competence trust engenders a closer relationship. Although contracts are needed, less time and resources go into drawing them up as the level of detail need not be as great when the partners have confidence in the ability of one another to deliver. As a result less structure is required, affording the partners more freedom, which translates into working more efficiently and effectively. According to Hartman (2000), competence trust reduces the frequency of reporting as the partners are expected to perform tasks properly.

Finally there is goodwill trust. Based no longer only on contracts or competencies, this kind of trust is characterized by an expectation that the parties will protect the interests of their counterparts and may exceed the terms of a contract to do so. It is expected that neither party will damage the other; moreover, if an opportunity arises the parties will attempt to increase the benefits of their counterparts. Such commitment reinforces goodwill-based relationships, but this kind of trust is the most difficult to build in the first place (Miyamoto & Rexha, 2004). The parties may have diverging expectations and objectives. These must be aligned before partners will concentrate on opportunities beneficial to their counterpart. This requires the partners to know each other very well, and that takes time. Therefore, goodwill-based trust exists only in long-term relationships.

Trust and Performance

Generally speaking, trust reduces transaction costs such as lengthy negotiations and time-consuming conflict resolution, but there is an element of risk as well. Companies must carefully weigh both the costs and the benefits beforehand as, although most researchers find a positive relation between trust and performance, the cumulative result is not unambiguously positive. Indeed, not all researchers have found significant results (Alesina & La Ferrara, 2000).

The impact of trust on performance is most clearly seen in instances of contractual trust, as this form of trust is based on expectations of performance set out in black and white in contractual agreements. Good financial performance strengthens the level of trust given the fact that the purpose of the collaboration is to make a profit. When both financial and logistics performance are satisfactory over a given period, competence trust will most likely follow. When the supplier has shown the capability to develop the dyad successfully, this second type of trust will rapidly develop. When one of the players fails to fulfill obligations in a certain period, competence trust may be negatively affected. It takes time to demonstrate that a failure to meet expectations is not systemic and then to repair damage to this type of trust. Goodwill-based trust, on the other hand, seems to be unrelated to immediate performance as such a construct primarily involves informal aspects of collaboration. However, in the long run its good performance improves moderating factors such as transparency, power, and alignment.

Therefore, financial performance predominately influences the level of contractual trust, logistical performance principally affects competence trust, and overall positive performance over a period of time leads to goodwill-based trust.

One might argue that efficient logistics, which are one of the hallmarks of goodwill-based relationships, help to reduce negative environmental impact by reducing waste of materials and energy. On the other hand, such intense relationships are often developed to improve the level of responsiveness. For example, suppliers might increase the frequency of deliveries. Such a move would increase congestion and exhaust pollution. To the best of our knowledge, there are no studies on how trust affects the sustainability of supply chains. This prompted us to conduct this explorative study.

Measuring Environmental Impact of Supply Chains

The environmental impact of a closed loop supply chain can be measured through a so-called life cycle assessment (LCA). LCA can be defined as an input-output analysis of resources or materials and of energy requirements in each phase of the life cycle of a product. LCA evaluates the environmental burden associated with a product, process, or activity by identifying and quantifying the energy and materials used and the waste released into the environment. By definition, LCA only considers environmental issues. In reality, economic and technical issues must also be taken into account. Therefore, LCA should be seen in a broader context, as a tool to be used by decision makers for evaluating the environmental impact of a product.

LCA is a tedious process that requires extensive, often impractical, data acquisition. Therefore, although we acknowledge that a full LCA gives a more comprehensive picture of the environmental impact of a given supply chain, we argue that measurement of energy use and waste provides a good approximation. We refer to this construct as simplified LCA. The lower data requirements of simplified LCA make it more practical, especially when combined with logistics optimization. The combined optimization of simplified LCA and economics is referred to as eco-efficiency.

RESEARCH FRAMEWORK AND GAME SET UP

The self-reinforcing power of trust is essential in supply chains (Gao, Sirgy, & Bird, 2005). Akkermans, Bogerd, and van Dorenmalen (2004) identify a cycle of causal loops where, representing *supply chain dynamics*. Based on this model we deduce a cascade relationship between various types of trust and performance. We show these relationships in Figure 1. Five categories of combined variables lead to good contracts, which improve the quality of short-term decision making. This results in a boost in the financial performance of the supply chain. According to Akkermans et al. (2004), when performance is satisfactory over multiple consecutive periods, a history of successful collaboration is established. At this point, competence trust will increase and in turn stimulate logistical performance. Trust improves communication between partners and that in turn builds goodwill. This leads to habituation, a process characterized by partners becoming used to one another and understanding each other better. If the relationship continues, the level of contract trust eventually increases. The process can be positively influenced by travail, namely working together and surmounting difficulties jointly. Still, the framework makes clear that the impact of trust on sustainability remains unknown.

The NetChain Game (NCG) is a generalized business simulator as described in Appendix I. The product in one case is automotive parts and in the other it is cucumbers. Players form supply chain networks by negotiating contracts, based on their formulated strategy and logistics structure. A strategy can focus on efficiency, be it customer-driven or eco-friendly. Subsequently, in a real-time simulation, actual operations take place and results are fed back to the participants. Participants are human players (e.g., masters students) of the game or virtual, that is, played by a computer, to differentiate between human and artificial intelligence (AI). Each player has a role: producer, wholesaler, or retailers can be either human or AI, but end-users and material suppliers are always AI. Unlike participants, AI-players do not attempt to optimize their decisions but have a fixed set of choices. More information on the game and its underlying simulation model is found in Appendix I.

The constructs reflected in the framework shown in Figure 1 need to be operationalized in the NetChain Game in order to be measured. As argued before, sustainability is measured using simplified LCA methods. Financial performance is measured by a profit and loss account for each participant, and logistics performance is measured by the reliability of the supplying party. This is fairly standard in measuring supply chain practices.

Contract trust is measured by counting the number of times a contract is extended, competence trust by the number of partners (human and AI) a participant has, and goodwill trust by a popularity poll taken among participants. A player can spread volume and hence risk, or rely on a few partners only. All trust measurements are bilateral, that is, between duos of partners and not throughout a supply chain.

The Lobus++ automotive parts case has a divergent network with two producers, three wholesalers, and four retailers having at least one AI player per role. This makes it possible for participants who are unable to come to an agreement with one of the other participants to exit to an AI-player who accepts any standard (nonoptimized) contract at all times. It also ensures sufficient competition in the game. Producers obtained goods from two virtual material suppliers (AI-suppliers). End customers (also AI) represent four product market combinations (PMCs), each of which covers a different segment of the market, at a different location, characterized by different demand behavior.

Note that participants are called on to make multiple decisions on the financial level (contract volume and price), and on logistics (structure, inventory management, delivery frequency, etc.), and also to take corrective action. Participants also decide for themselves what information they would share with partners, but only on a bilateral level. Appendix II describes the Lobus++ automotive parts case extensively, including a detailed role description.

Initially, sustainability is mostly influenced by logistical decisions in the Lobus++ automotive

Figure 1. Research model, the role of trust in supply chain performance

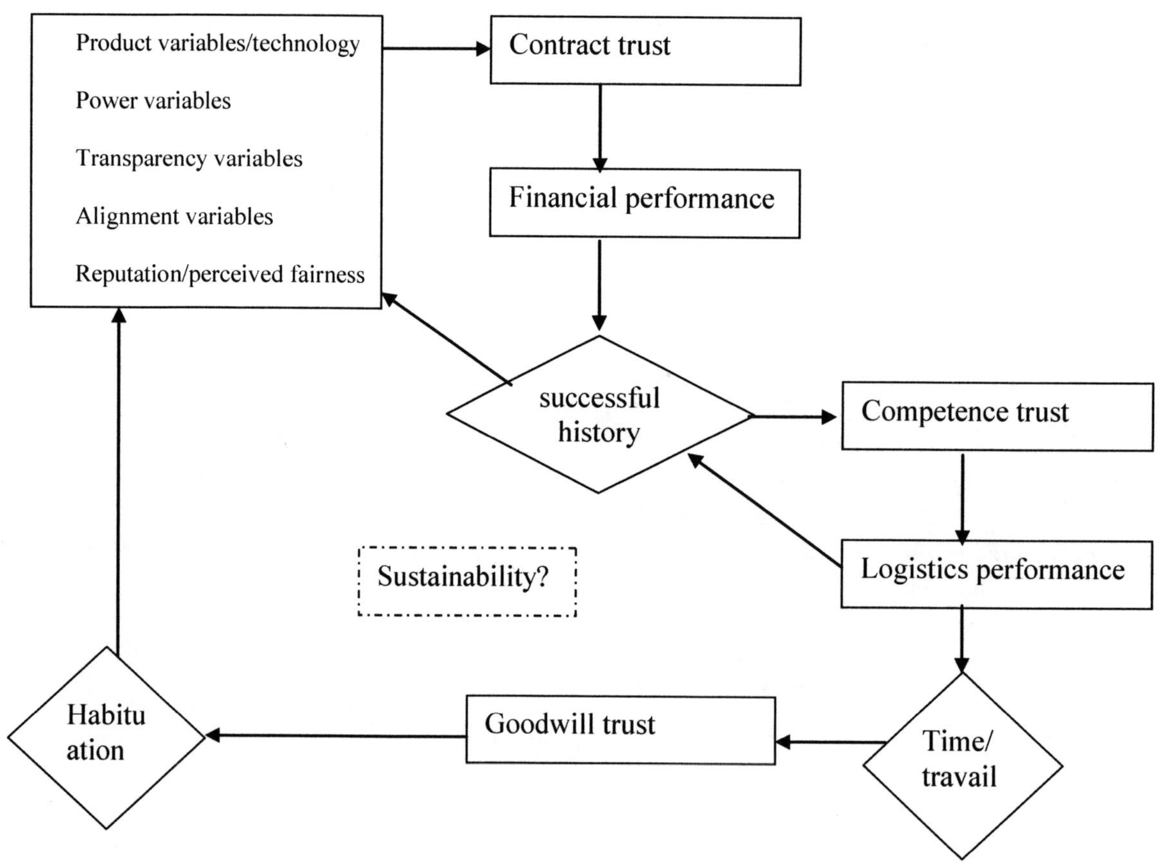

parts case. We use the number of kilometers driven in the supply chain as our measure of energy use. The underlying assumption being that the number of kilometers is a proxy for environmental impacts such as CO_2 emissions (Krikke et al., 2003). For example, a centralized logistics structure with high delivery frequencies would lead to a low sustainability score. This is implemented in the automotive case.

The participants, all of whom were students, were asked to prepare themselves for the game by reading case descriptions. Each participant prepared and then presented a "plan of attack" before the game began. In essence, they had to analyze their projected behavior and its impact (see Appendix III).

We learned from Lobus++ that the number of decisions that impact environmental performance needed to be increased. Thus, for the next case, we add energy use in the production process, which, in the case of cucumbers, consists of seed selection, planting, growing, and harvesting. We also introduce waste disposal at all stages of the supply chain. Because cucumbers are perishable, a shelf life factor and a yield factor are introduced on the supply side. The values of these parameters also depend on energy use decisions, particularly in the breeding and transportation processes. The limited shelf life of cucumbers is another added feature and increases time pressures. The matching of supply and demand becomes more critical in preventing waste materials, minimizing energy use, and maximizing reliability. Retailer pricing policies affect the elasticity of demand. Also, retailers can now buy a weather-and-sales forecast and share this (combined with other data on, for example, inventories) throughout the supply chain. This is an important difference between the two cases.

In the cucumber case, transparency is triangular, that is to say that crucial data are shared among more than two players. It enables participants to better coordinate decisions in multiple echelons both horizontally and vertically. Logistics choices and inventory management remain largely the same. To keep the case manageable, one PMC instead of four is implemented. A full description and analysis of the cucumber case, including a detailed role description, is given in Appendix V.

We develop propositions based on our observations and on the participant's responses to a survey taken at the end of play (see Appendix III).

RESULTS OF THE LOBUS++ AUTOMOTIVE PARTS CASE

The automotive parts game was played over three sessions. At the start of each session the participants were given additional information. In some sessions the game leader intervened using the gaming software, for instance, interrupted the supply of raw materials from the open market. Each session consisted of two rounds (referred to as a. and b.) meaning six negotiations and possibly contract extensions or cancellations and two popularity polls.

Performance and Sustainability

There was no clear financial winner of the game, as all the players were by and large equally successful. However, there were striking differences in the way participants collaborated in due course and in the related logistical performance levels at the supply chain level. The most striking difference was in the impact that various interventions on logistics reliability and sustainability made. Reliability is calculated as the total volume delivered divided by the total volume ordered, not including backorders. Figure 2 summarizes the conduct of the game throughout the three sessions that we describe in detail below.

The initial session was characterized by considerable confusion. In some cases, cheating sabotaged collaboration. Mostly such instances of cheating were actually not intentional but rather

Figure 2. The impact of interventions on logistics reliability and km driven (Lobus++)

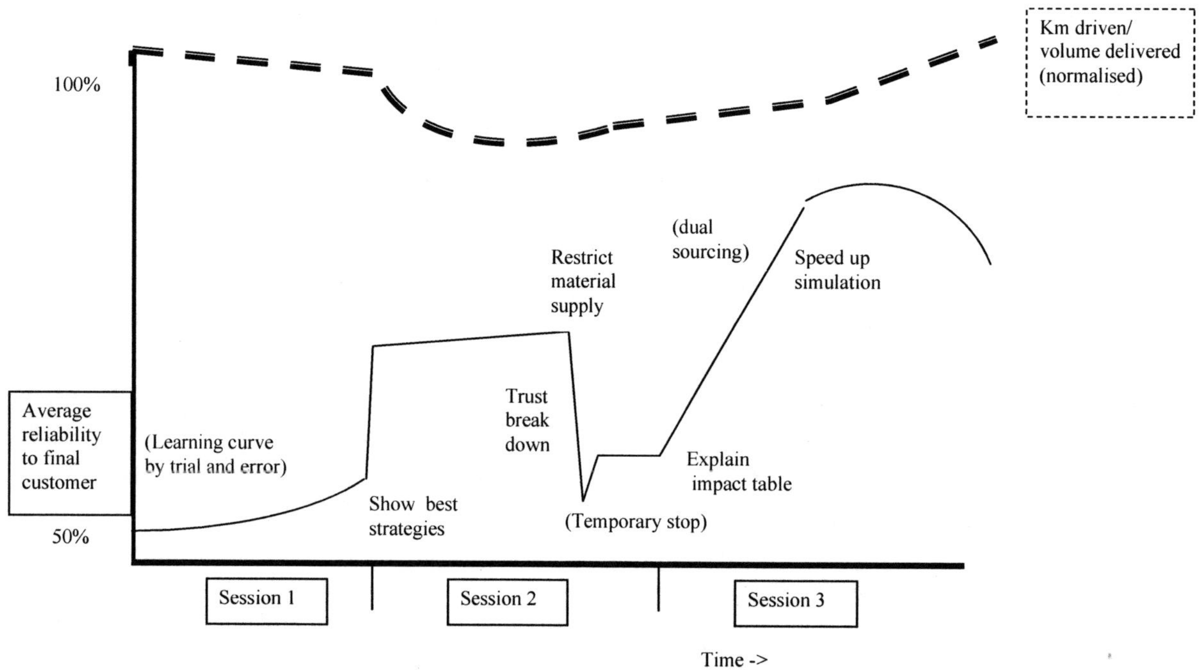

the result of poor decision making. Given the amount of data to be processed by participants during the initial, real-time phase of the game, this was not surprising. As expected, it was difficult for participants to establish a good overall point of view. They also found it difficult to handle the complexity of dealing with many potential partners during the negotiation phase. This was particularly true for participants in the wholesaler role that had to negotiate both upstream and downstream. In retrospect, most participants were working through a learning curve during these phases. At first, they were unable to effectively assess the impact of their decisions on performance and so they relied primarily on trial and error. Later, they were able to set parameters for inventory management and as a result contracts were closed a lot quicker. Sustainability, measured by the number of kilometers driven per unit, remained more or less constant, with some small efficiency improvements due to a learning curve.

In the second of the three sessions, the participants were told about optimal strategies on the strategic, tactical, and operational levels, but were given little detail. They were simply told that there were two basic strategies: one that would serve their own, short term interest, and another that would create a better overall supply chain performance but only if all partners collaborated, an option that required a long-term point of view. At that point, there were visible signs of improvement in logistics performance in particular due to better alignment of logistics structures throughout the supply chain. However, in the aftermath (in post-game interviews) most participants said that they thought that better alignment was seen only at the strategic level and had not been sufficiently followed up upon at the tactical and operational levels. For example, a participant might select a low cost logistical structure at the strategic level promising responsiveness in contracts, but fail to deliver in the operational real-time phase.

The number of kilometers driven per unit decreased due to efficiency and increased volumes, but not to the extent possible as there was a tendency to increase the frequency of deliveries in order to reduce stocks. This in turn had a negative sustainability impact because no full truckloads were realized. It should be noted that a significant reduction in mileage could only be achieved when delivery vehicle space is optimized, hence when relatively large batches are ordered and delivered. All of the participants initially focused on the traditional optimization goals of customer service and control of costs. Sustainability became an issue only after the relationship had been in place for some time. The game leader decided to increase the level of difficulty for the players by restricting the amount of raw materials available in the game. The participants were quick to single out the producer as being at fault, but it took significantly more time for them to find out that the material supplier was not delivering raw materials to the producers. Not even the producers themselves were aware of that fact! After fierce negotiations the wholesalers made some, though insufficient, emergency buys, angrily accepting the additional cost and irate with the general situation (the NCG allows the possibility of buying extra material in the open market as a costly emergency option). One participant increased safety stock levels to reduce risk but regretted this later when it resulted in increased cost. Because volumes and hence batch sizes dropped as well, the kilometers driven per volume unit increases were also relatively high; in other words, the conflicts created more inefficiencies and less sustainability. Performance declined precipitously, and game leaders decided to temporarily halt the game in order to reset some of the parameters to restore material supplies to the game. It took before any impact from the restoration of material supplies was seen. The incident also changed the balance of power. In principle retailers have the most power as they have the best access to final customers, but not many participants in that role were able to exploit that advantage as they devoted resources to competing for access to producers and wholesalers who had sufficient raw materials.

At the start of the final session, participants were given a so-called impact table, which mapped the impact of all of the decision variables on the key performance indicators, or objective functions, including sustainability. Clearly, this helped participants to better understand the situation. Performance improved markedly and the final customer was served well. We expected sustainability also to improve as soon as relationships stabilized, but this did not happen to the degree we believed it would. Spreading orders over multiple suppliers (dual sourcing) led to relatively small batches and hence the number of kilometers per unit increased moderately.

Possibly as a result of the material supply incident, many retailers turned to dual sourcing in order to reduce uncertainty, that is, they used multiple wholesalers and producers. Later on, in such a multisupplier situation, preferred suppliers (because of price or quality) got all orders and some contracts remained "un-used." Producers and wholesalers concerned became dissatisfied and they started canceling contracts and lowering

Table 1. Trust in sessions

Session	1		2		3	
Round	1a	1b	2a	2b	3a	3b
Contract trust (# of extended contracts)	0	+	+	+	+	NA
Competence trust (degree dual sourcing)	0	0	+	+	-	NA
Goodwill trust (popularity poll)	0	0	+	-	+	-

their inventories. Soon the performance curve flattened, but not as dramatic as before.

At this point, we increased the clock-speed of the game. As soon as that was done, participants complained that time pressures coupled with the still complex performance indicators did not allow them to assess what was happening. Some participants panicked and began to play more aggressively. One of the participants totally blocked deliveries and bill payments.

The Impact of Trust

Table 1 shows data on the three kinds of trust. The learning curve in phase 1 gradually leads to improvement in contract trust. Since the strategies tried by participants seem to work for them in session 2, all kinds of trust grow. All of the performance indicators are positive as well. The confusion that resulted from the first intervention first erodes goodwill trust and later competence trust (represented by increased dual sourcing to spread risk). It is especially worthy of note that an escape route to suboptimal AI-players is used often at this stage. In the end, dual sourcing in the third session also destroys goodwill trust due to the neglect of many contracts of "nonpreferred" suppliers.

We conclude then that the interventions set in motion a downward spiral leading to mistrust.

Most participants concluded afterwards that supply chain performance was the dependent variable and that trust, and sometimes power, were the main independent variables. They felt further that sustainability was no more than a byproduct of a good relationship. All of the participants were rather good at monitoring the performance variables of their supplying partner(s) and at assessing their own supply chain position, in particular when it related to power. Still, they largely did not monitor their own performance indicators, but rather looked at what their partners performed, nor did they realize where a given action might lead to. Most participants acknowledged that in retrospect they could have done a better job, but that the level of stress and the time constraints prompted them to act selfishly and to concentrate on local rather than supply chain optimization. Most participants felt that they could have been more successful had they had more feedback on the variables and a better understanding of their impact table. More insight in their own performance indicators, but also internal variables of their partners (e.g., with respect to inventory) would help improve performance and sustainability.

We see that overall, desirable levels of both performance and sustainability are best achieved by integral supply chain optimization and not by local optimization of individual participants. It is essential that supply chain strategies take into account the need to maintain inventories that allow for delivery batches large enough to meet the demand of a couple of days. Otherwise delivery frequency negatively impacts sustainability. Such a strategy only works when all three kinds of trust are present. In the automotive parts case, this was only the case in session 2. The ultimate indicator of success would have been to have created a positive spiral. This did not happen, and the question remains how to elicit this positive trust spiral.

Propositions Formulated

It is time to tie everything together and condense the discussion into three propositions.

Proposition P1: Strategies with supply chain optimization focus only work when all three types of trust are present. This by default requires long lasting relationships.

Proposition P2: Creating these long lasting relations requires time and travail, hence goodwill trust. It proves to be relatively easy to create a negative spiral, breaking down trust rapidly, but the opposite proves difficult.

Proposition P3: Even when all trust conditions are met, sustainability can only be achieved when the earlier mentioned supply chain strategies aim for minimal delivery frequencies, hence large batches.

The implications of these propositions for business practice can be serious. In today's responsive Just-In-Time strategies, the tendency is to create small batches. Moreover, e-business makes it possible to quickly switch supplier without incurring high transaction cost.

In order to further refine our propositions we need to find out how a positive trust spiral might be created, diversify the settings in which the game is played and create opportunities for synergy between economical, logistical, and environmental objectives. More feedback was given by the so-called tri-angular transparency to enable participants to judge their own performance better in view of total supply chain performance. To this end, we decided to develop the cucumber case, which is described in Appendix V.

RESULTS OF THE CUCUMBER CASE

As in the automotive parts case, the game was played over three sessions. Similar information was given to the participants and game leaders made more or less the same sorts of interventions. A major difference is that the supply of materials intervention is less critical. It should be noted that the limited shelf life of cucumbers augmented time pressure, which had an enormous impact on the game. The response to this was a desire for detailed planning and forecasting. Matching supply to demand was critical in maximizing reliability, limiting energy use, and minimizing waste. Again, positive performance hinged on multiple decisions made by several players. In fact, coordination and collaboration became still more important than in the automotive parts case because the window of opportunity is smaller.

All these factors aside, the trial and error stage of the game was not appreciably different from that of the previous game. We observed a gradual change in attitude from "I just want to win" to "If I am going to win, I need to collaborate." The way in which trust developed and the impact of trust on performance too were similar. Hence, Proposition 1 is maintained.

There were, however, definitely differences. The triangular transparency enabled participants to recover more quickly when trust was low. This has implications for our second proposition. Since material supply is not essential to plant-growers, we intervened to break down trust by at some point removing the possibility of AI-plant-growers to serve as backups. As shown in Appendix V, the normal breeding period was 91 days, and there were two such periods per year. Participants in the plant-grower role often chose to start planting and growing on January 1 or, in an effort to save on energy use, during periods when favorable weather was expected. Consequently, they frequently found themselves producing during the same periods as their competitors and often in May-June and November-December no product was available because no AI-plant-growers were available to fill the gap. Nonetheless, the impact of such shortfalls was less disastrous than was the shortage of materials in the automotive parts case, because it was possible for the participants to recover trust more quickly.

The triangular transparency enabled horizontal coordination and the breeding periods were staggered. Participants did spread supply over the semester; however, it was the cooperation who controlled the process, not the plant-growers themselves. Batch sizing was also better and aimed at full truckloads. Although not explicitly research, the impact of transparency suggests a key role for Web-based supply chain information systems.

There was a striking synergy between reliability, energy use, and waste. This can be explained by the fact that all the parties benefited from an optimal match of supply and demand. Indeed, although logistics and inventory costs did increase overall, they were overcompensated for by savings made in preventing waste. Not only were disposal costs minimized, but also the destruction of obsolete products was prevented, meaning that no capital is lost. Better logistical performance in terms of batch size and delivery frequency followed. In essence, supply chain management and integration helped to create sustainability as part of logistical optimization. Balanced solutions that integrated energy, logistics, production, and inventory management led to the highest levels of success. Again, the improved insight in each other's variables (triangular transparency) in the supply chain improved all kinds of trust.

The staggering of production periods did have a negative impact on some plant-growers, namely those who attempted to produce in periods when outside temperatures were either too warm or too cool and so extensive use of energy was needed to maintain an optimal 23°C greenhouse temperature. Little or no compensation was given to those plant-growers by the cooperation, bringing some of them to the brink of bankruptcy. One solution to this dilemma would have been for those plant-growers to organize as to negotiate collectively with the cooperation. This did not happen, possibly because they are members of that same organization. Reduced trust was found among these participants.

All together we suggest the following adaptations to the propositions:

- **Proposition P1:** None
- **Proposition P2' (addition):** "The negative spiral can be quickly reversed with triangular transparency as it enables the cooperation to act as chain director."
- **Proposition P3' (revised):** "Given trust is present in supply chains, to achieve sustain-

Figure 3. The impact of interventions on logistics reliability and km driven (Cucumber case)

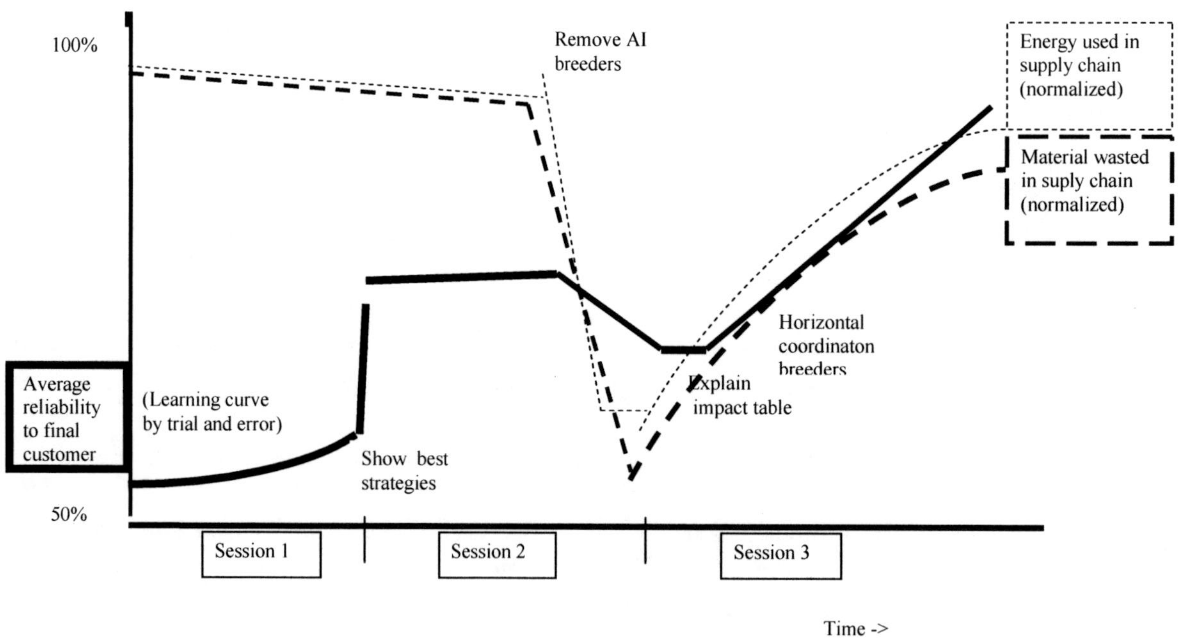

ability, strategies need to be eco-balanced on many decision variables, requiring vertical collaboration and horizontal coordination between players."

It is good news for business and the society as a whole that there is synergy between ecological and economic objectives in the supply chain. Eco-efficiency works, provided that vertical collaboration (between plant-grower, cooperation, and retailer) and horizontal coordination (especially among plant-growers) are present. At the same time, selfish behavior by which a player hopes to enjoy short-term financial success often hampers the process. *Only a positive spiral of trust can prevent the latter and enable the first.*

CONCLUSION

We conclude that trust has a major impact on supply chain sustainability, and that the benefits of trust may be maximized with the right supply chain strategies. Unfortunately, trust build-up is not an easy task for three main reasons. First, strategies designed to build and maintain trust are complex, involving many variables. Second, a long-lasting supply chain relationship seems to be a prerequisite for a high degree of trust. Although long and difficult to build, trust can quickly and easily be broken. However, triangular transparency appears to help. Third, including sustainability objectives in supply chain optimization efforts adds complexity and decision making stress because they add another variable to be coordinated.

Strengthening and validating Proposition P1 through P3 requires the playing of more games under different conditions and with different products. We concluded that behavior that might normally have been interpreted as cheating was not necessarily due to efforts to get ahead by any means, but rather the consequence of poor decision making due to inexperience. Still, it should be noted that the participants were students in a master of logistics program and so, although they had little to no management experience, they were familiar with the latest concepts in the field and were used to thinking at a relatively high level of abstraction. Experienced managers might in turn lack those attributes. It would be interesting to see the outcome of games tailor-made for managers and for different industries.

We suspect that in some cases, the development of trust was more the result of relationships outside of the classroom than an outgrowth of the game. It is difficult to control for this as, despite the fact that goodwill was measured by taking a poll and that the game was played over a period of time in multiple sessions, genuine long-lasting relationships are built over much longer periods, sometimes years. We believe that the results would be different if in the future games were played by persons brought together using the Web, possibly internationally, and over a longer period of time.

FUTURE TRENDS AND FURTHER READING

Further research should focus on ways of creating positive spirals that lead to long-lasting relationships that enable sustainable supply chain strategies. Given the importance of tri-angular transparency in trust development, the role of Web-based applications should receive more attention in the future. The use of advanced planning, including gain-sharing models, is an option to further make use of transparency in the supply chain.

Clearly, the role of trust in collaboration needs to be further worked out. Post-game interviews led to an impressive list of additional variables including uncertainty, time pressure, bypassing wholesalers, benevolence, learning curve, and participation. It is to be expected that these variables need to be integrated in the framework as presented in Figure 1, in order to create the wanted positive spiral.

The urge for sustainability will definitely put pressure on integrating environmental and economical objectives in a supply chain. In particular, it proves necessary to maximize transport batches size, which leads to stock keeping. To avoid obsolescence, the matching of supply and demand is critical. In a globalizing economy, this is not an easy thing to solve. New, trust-based supply strategies are needed to achieve sustainability.

For future trends and challenges in supply chains, we refer to Stadler (2005) for further reading. The use of agent-based modeling is discussed in Arunachalam and Sadeh (2005). More on trust and learning in supply chains can be found in the special issue of production planning and control (2006), edited by Hofstede and more on sustainability aspects is written in Krikke et al. (2004).

REFERENCES

Akkermans, H., Bogerd, P., & van Dorenmalen, J. (2004). Travail, transparency and trust: A case study of computer-supported collaborative supply chain planning in high tech electronics. *European Journal of Operational Research, 153*(2), 445-456.

Alesina, A., & La Ferrara, E. (2000). *The determinants of trust* (working paper 7621). Cambridge: National Bureau of Economic Research.

Amanor-Boadu, V., & Starbird, A. (2004). Minimizing the value of anonymity in supply chains. In Hofstede et al. (Ed.), *Hide or confide, the dilemma of transparency* (pp. 35-40). The Hague: Reed Business Information.

Boersma, M.F. (1999). *Developing trust in international joint ventures.* Doctoral thesis on Systems, Organization and Management, Groningen, Rijksuniversiteit.

Bots, P.W.G., & Hofstede, G.J. (2004). The Takeover Trio. *Simulation and Gaming, an International Journal of Theory, Practice, and Research, 35*(4), 505-516.

Gao, T., Sirgy, M.J., & Bird, M.M. (2005). Reducing buyer decision-making uncertainty in organizational purchasing: Can supplier trust, commitment, and dependence help? *Journal of Business Research, 58*, 397-405.

Gore, A. (2006). *An inconvenient truth* (Dutch version). Amsterdam: Meulenhoff.

Grubstrom, R.W. (2007). *The international logistics management game*. Retrieved July 7, 2008, from http://www.ipe.liu.se/rwg/ilmg/ilmg.htm

Hartman, F. (2000, June 21-24). The role of trust in project management: Managing business by projects. In *Proceedings of the PMI Research Conference*, Paris.

Hofstede, G.J., Kramer, M., Meijder, S., & Wijdemans, J. (2001). A chain game for distributed trading and negotiation. In *Proceedings of the IFIP Conference/Workshop Games in Production Management*, Madrid.

Hofstede, G.J., & Trienekens, J.H. (2000). Food for thought. In J.H. Trienekens & P.J.P. Zuurbier (Eds.), *Proceedings of the Fourth International Conference on Chain Management in Agribusiness and the Food Industry*, Wageningen Pers (pp. 41-45).

Krikke, H.R. (1999). Ketenlogistiek. In de Boer (Ed.), *Vraagbaak Inkoop en Logistiek.* Deventer: Kluwer.

Krikke, H.R., Bloemhof-Ruwaard, J.B., & Van Wassenhove, L.N. (2003). Concurrent product and closed loop design with an application of refrigerator. *International Journal of Production Research, 41*(16), 3689-3719.

Lewicki, R.J., McAllister, D.J., & Bies, R.J. (1996). Trust and distrust: New relationships and realities. *The Academy of Management Review, 23*(3), 438-458.

McCutcheon, D., & Stuart, F.I. (2000). Issues in the choice of supplier alliance partners. *Journal of Management, 18*(3), 279-301.

Miyamoto, T., & Rexha, N. (2004). Determinants of three facets of customer trust: A marketing model of Japanese buyer–supplier relationship. *Journal of Business Research, 57*, 312-319.

Sterman, J. (1992, October). Teaching takes off: Flight simulators for management education. *OR/MS Today*, 40-44.

Van Leeuwen, G. (2006). *Trust inside the NetChain game: The role of trust in the simulation of supply chain collaboration.* Masters thesis, Tilburg University.

Williamson, O.E. (1993). *The economic institutions of capitalism: Firms, markets, relational contracting.* New York: Free Press.

Yin, R.K. (2003). *Case study research: Design and methods* (3rd ed.). Thousand Oaks, CA: Sage Publications.

FURTHER READING

Arunachalam, R., & Sadeh, N.M. (2005). The supply chain trading agent competition. *Electronic Commerce Research and Applications, 4-1*, 66-84.

Hofstede, G.J. (Ed.). (2006). Experimental learning in chains and networks. *Special Issue of Production Planning and Control*, ISSN 0953-7287 print/ISSN 1366-5871.

Retrieved July 16, 2008, from Taylor & Francis, www.tandf.co.uk/journals

Krikke, H.R., le Blanc, H.M., & van de Velde, S. (2004), Product modularity and the design of closed-loop supply chains. *California Management Review, 46-2*, 23-39.

Stadtler, H. (2005). Supply chain management and advanced planning: Basics, overview and challenges. *European Journal of Operational Research, 163-3*, 575-588.

APPENDIX I. THE GENERIC SIMULATION MODEL OF THE NETCHAIN GAME

The case-based NetChain Game (NCG) is applicable to different logistical domains and rules. The generic nature of NCG allows other game developers to readily build on the platform it provides as opposed to programming an entirely new game. Researchers can use NCG to look at a broad range of behaviors and to meet a wide array of learning objectives. For our research we chose to use the Lobus++ case on the supply chain of automotive parts and an agribusiness case that featured a product with a short shelf life. The mechanics of the games were the same in both cases.

Model Structure

The model structure of the NetChain Game is made up of three key elements: participants, roles, and applications.

- The game leader and the players of the game, either human of virtual, are the participants. Note that we use the term player usually for human participants.
- The supply chain roles include raw material suppliers, producers, transporters, wholesalers, retailers, and end-users.
- The NetChain Game software *applications* that provide the interface of the participants to the game.

All participants of the game require a computer application to participate in the game. The game leader will require different options, and hence, a different interface than the players. Because one of the starting-points of the NetChain Game is that players should be able to compete with other (networks of) supply chains, we require the presence of Artificial Intelligence (AI) supply chains. This implies that the roles of producers/plant-growers, wholesalers/cooperation, and retailers can be either real or virtual. To structure the relationships between these three elements we have used the concept of *agents* and created the NetChain Game as a multi-agent application. The NCG is a multi-agent application. In such applications agents communicate via messages sent and received on the computer network. They then perform independently on behalf of the participants: (human players) or virtual (AI).

The NetChain Game has been developed in the computer package AIMMS. AIMMS is an advanced development environment for building decision support applications and advanced planning systems. One of key features of AIMMS is the possibility to create multi-agent applications. In the NetChain Game these agents include:

- The Game Manager controls the game set-up and game play. The game leader or teacher controls the game manager.
- The supply market controls the suppliers of raw materials used by the producers in the supply chain.
- The demand market controls the end-user market that generates the demand at the end of the supply chain.
- The Transportation Manager handles the timing of transports in the supply chain, that is, the logistics of getting materials to producers and the product to wholesalers and retailers.
- The human players are the producers, wholesalers, and retailers controlled by the human players

continued on following page

APPENDIX I. CONTINUED

of the game. Of course there are differences between the decisions that a producer, a wholesaler, or a retailer can make. On the other hand, there are a lot of similarities as well, and that is why they have been modeled as one agent type.

- The AI-players are the artificial producers, wholesalers, and retailers, and are the agents of last recourse. Combined they can form a network of supply chains, or offer collaboration with human players. Once initialized their (sub optimal) behavior is controlled by a fixed set of decision rules.
- The AI-controller initializes the AI-players upon request by the game manager.

The following figures show the relationships between the three key elements of the NetChain Game. The rectangles represent applications, the rounded rectangles participants, and the ellipses agents.

It should be noted that in the application diagramed above, AI-players are not included so as to reduce workload from the main game leader's application.

Figure 4. Game leader-controlled applications

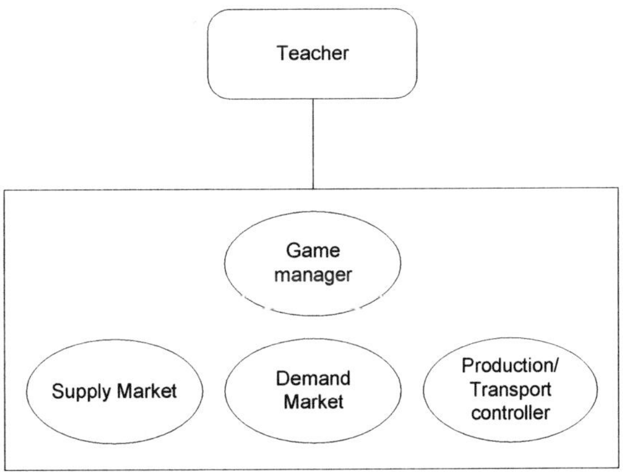

Figure 5. Game leader- AI applications

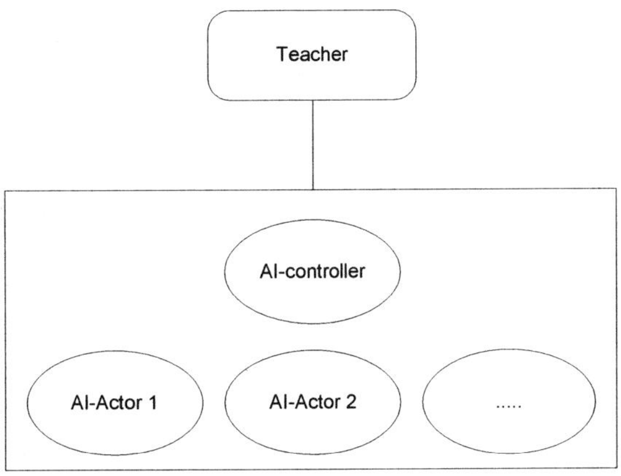

continued on following page

APPENDIX I. CONTINUED

Figure 6. Player applications

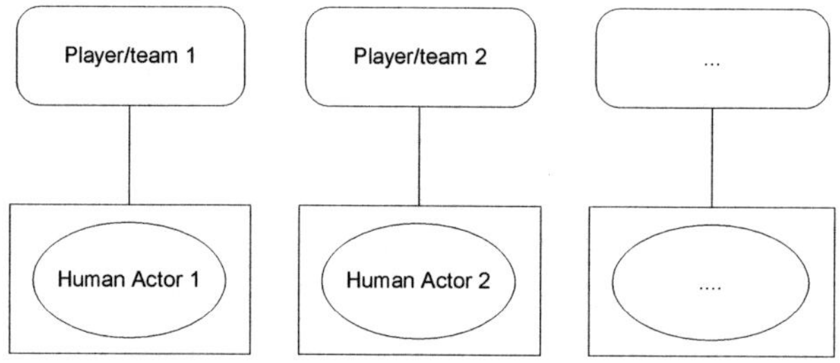

In this case, the game leader only initializes the application. The AI-agents function independently.

There are as many applications as there are participants. The game leader only affects the game via demand and supply market agents, the game phases, and the clock speed of the simulation.

Game set-up

The game leader, using the game manager agent, takes to several steps to initialize the game. First, a predefined case (Lobus++ or cucumber) loaded. This involves the definition of product-market combinations and their properties, characteristics of suppliers of raw materials, characteristics of the demand market, transportation and production rules, contract elements and negotiation topics for the participants, performance indicators, and so forth.

Second, players log in and connect to the multi-agent application and are assigned a role. AI-players are also created and one or more [AI-] supply chains formed. The rules of collaboration between human players and AI-players are set. It is possible for the game leader to create initial contracts. Such a so-called *warm boot* speeds up the starting process of the game and enhances the understanding of the game by the players.

Game Phases

Once the game is set up, the game manager controls transitions between three different NCG phases, strategic, tactical, and operational, each of which is characterized by the kind of decisions players will make during the phase. Each of the phases has different timing characteristics and a different set of options. The timing characteristics are twofold: one with respect to the *content of the game*, and the other with respect to the *playing of the game*. The former concerns the timeline of the game and can be either a fixed moment, or continuous time. The latter concerns the available time players have to perform their actions.

The following table shows the timing characteristics and the user actions for each phase.

continued on following page

APPENDIX I. CONTINUED

Table 2. Game phases

Phase	Timing characteristics	User actions
Strategic	• Fixed moment in timeline. • Fixed or game leader controlled duration.	• Set strategic goals. • Choose activity in product-market combinations. • Choose logistic structure.
Tactic	• Fixed moment in timeline. • Fixed or game leader controlled duration.	• Relationship management with other human players. • Negotiate contracts with other human players. • Collaborate with AI-players.
Operational	• Continuous time. • Game leader controlled speed (game timeline vs. real-time) determines duration.	• Monitor upstream and downstream product flow. • Monitor contract fulfillment. • Perform emergency actions. • Relationship management with other human players.

The NetChain Game usually begins with the strategic game phase. This phase will be played less frequently than the others. The tactical and operational phases are played in succession a number of times. In between a phase transition, the players are given a summary of performance indicators that can be used to evaluate the latest performance in the previous phase so as to plan a course of action for the next phase.

APPENDIX II. THE NCG LOBUS ++ CASE

Automotive parts business customers have become increasingly demanding as increased transparency has shifted the balance of power more in their favor. In this case, we distinguish between two major product groups, commodities that are fast movers of a fairly standard nature, and specialties that are specialized slow movers. The first accounts for the majority of turnover, but the second enjoys the highest margins. There are also two kinds of customer markets: urban and rural, which differ in terms of physical location and demand volumes. Thus, there are four product-market combinations (PMC), each characterized by a different level of demand. The case focuses on markets in the BENELUX and Western Germany, a combined area of about 100.000 km2 (or 62,000 square miles) with a total annual sales volume of about 120 million pieces. The Lobus++ supply chain consists of three roles: producers, wholesalers, and retailers. Retailers generally serve end-user markets, but they may buy directly from producers or wholesalers. Producers obtain their raw materials from material suppliers. In the NCG both end-users and material suppliers are always AI agents, while the other roles may be either AI or human participants. The supply chains formed may be linear, but also more complex network structures may emerge, depending on the behavior of the participants.

On the strategic level, game participants may or may not enter certain PMCs and set their logistics structure. Commodity markets have price-based competition while specialties are more service-oriented (expressed in reliability, order lead-time, and delivery frequency). The choice of logistics structure is paramount as both customer service and logistics costs are impacted. For each PMC, wholesalers and retailers can choose for centralized stock, regionalized stocks, cross docking structures or transit storage. Producers may choose to produce to stock or to order. Changing logistical structures or implementing new ones can be costly, but the result may be reduced logistics costs or improved customer service, which can lead to increased turnover. The preferred strategy depends on market characteristics (price vs. service competition). Thus, producers must strike a delicate balance between pursuing their own goals and safeguarding the interests of their partners.

After making these strategic (logistics) choices, the game leader (teacher) sets the next phase in motion. This phase concerns the negotiation on contracts, which ultimately determines the configuration of the network. Contracts can be renegotiated during each round, relationships with existing partners may be abandoned, and new partnerships may be formed. Contracts cover price and volume and also logistics requirements (reliability, delivery frequency, and order lead-time). It is essential that sales volumes match purchasing volumes. Moreover, it is essential that the promises made (high customer service at a higher price or lower customer service at lower prices) are in line with the logistics structures chosen.

Figure 7 shows that without a contract there is no link. In this game, participants configure and reconfigure supply chains and supply chain networks by closing contracts. There is de facto no relationship if there is no contract. Retailer-Harold denotes a human player, while AI indicates virtual players. After the negotiation phase, the game leader starts up the "real-time" phase.

Figure 8 shows the main screen of the game leader over different phases of the game. Every quarter, after negotiations are closed, real market demand is simulated and the supply chain partners have to fulfill that demand. The game is driven by end-user demand, and a chain of reaction leads to activities throughout the supply chain (network).

In the "real-time cockpit" (Figure 9), the players can observe the actual orders going in and out. A more aggregated management information overview serves to compare the contract deals made (white) and the actual performance delivered (black). Strategic and tactical decisions have now to be fulfilled

continued on following page

APPENDIX II. CONTINUED

Figure 7. An example of a supply chain network in development, i.e. relationships are built by closing contract (only 1 here)

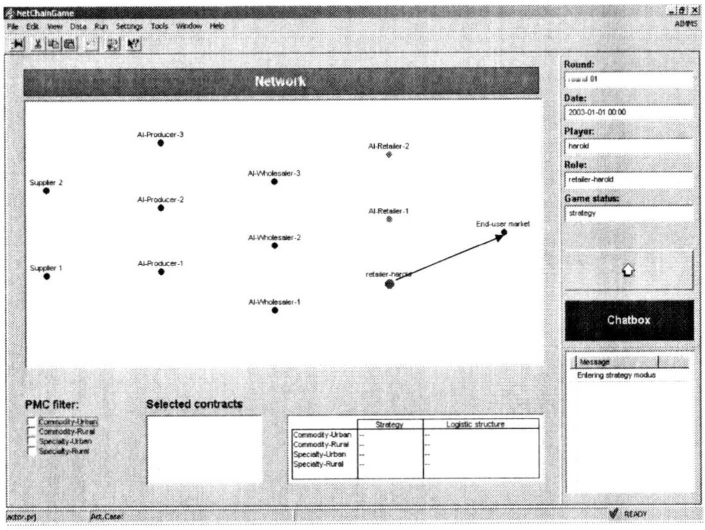

Figure 8. The game leader guiding the steps through the game

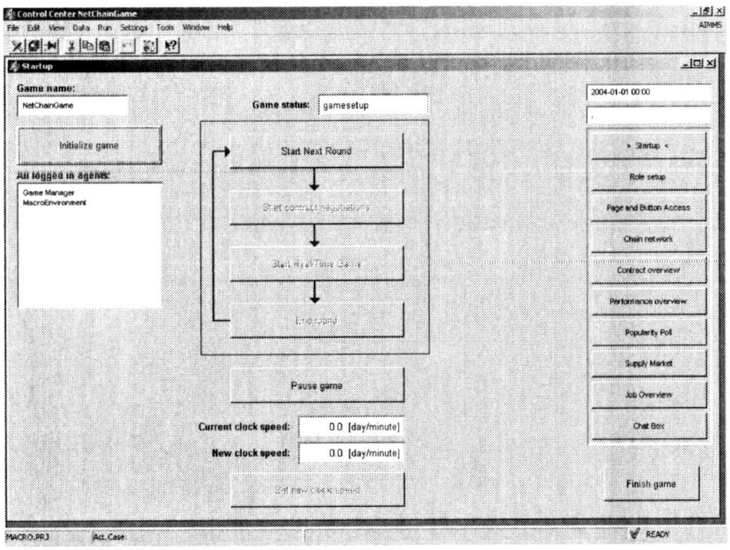

operationally. All operational parameters are initialized by the system, depending on choices made on the strategic and tactical level. During the real-time simulation the players can change these settings. For example, the inventory (s,S) policy can be adapted. Urgent problems like stock-outs must be solved immediately by so-called *exception handling* (e.g., rush orders or speeding up transportation). Problems can occur accidentally by unexpected events possibly generated by the game leader or by uncoordinated decisions of the players.

The logistics structures, contract agreements and the real-time cockpit cover the "hard" logistics issues of the NCG. But note how trust and collaboration issues are merged into it. Actors can cheat in

continued on following page

APPENDIX II. CONTINUED

Figure 9. Real time cockpit with management information of contracts agreements (white) versus real performance (black)

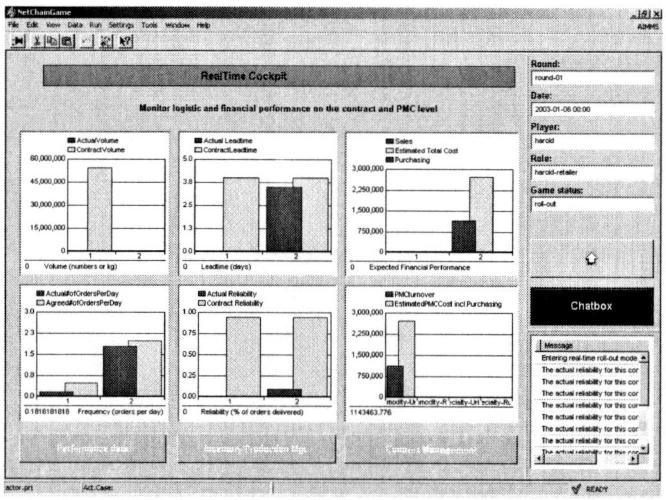

many ways. For instance, a player can cheat its partner: a player might delay making payments, put orders on the backburner, postpone deliveries and so forth.

Retailers have access to 90% of the end-user market, which puts them in a relatively strong position. However, there are scenarios in which the wholesaler and the producer have more direct access to the end-user market or otherwise increase their power. Wholesalers add value to the supply chain by creating economies of scale. However, the wrong logistical choices can jeopardize their position as producers may attempt to bypass them and deliver directly to retailers.

In addition to the formal simulation model, there is a chat box which facilitates informal communication. The chat box can be used at any time. Finally, popularity polls give insight in the strategic relationships every semester: players are asked if they want to do business with each other again.

As in any other industry, supply chain players in the automotive parts industry attempt to improve their equity. Obviously, they need to make a profit to do so, and for this they need the cooperation of their supply chain partners. A financial balance sheet and a Profit/Loss statement are drawn up each year. Financial performance and market share are compared among the participants and fed back to the strategy formulated. The winners of the game are players who realize their strategy. Figure 10 shows financial results.

In summary, the producers buy raw materials from AI-suppliers with which they produce automotive parts to be sold either directly to the retailer or via a wholesaler. A producer can produce to order or to stock in various batch sizes. The wholesaler has a trading role between producer and retailer and can provide logistics advantages through economies of scales. Other than stock keeping or cross docking there is no other role, and there are a variety of logistics structures a wholesaler can pick. The retailer buys from the producer or the wholesaler and then sells to the final customer. The retailer also decides on logistics and how and which PMCs will be served.

All orders and deliveries take place under a contract that determines price, volume, reliability, frequency (hence batch size), and delivery lead-time. These are agreements made between the supplier

continued on following page

APPENDIX II. CONTINUED

and the buyer. Fulfillment of such agreements depends on how each player optimizes the operational variables on inventory management and logistics structures. Table 3 summarizes all decisions and their impact.

Figure 10. Balance sheets and profit/loss account

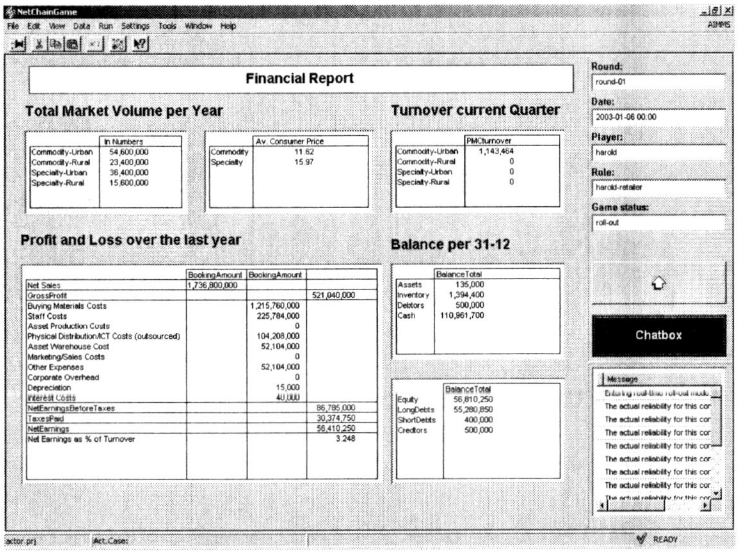

Table 3. Impact table of Lobus++ case

KPI	Producer PtO/PtS	Wholesaler L.structure	Retailer L.strucutre	Producer P.batch	Wholesaler Inv.mgt / batching	Retailer Inv.mgt order size	Retailer choosePMC
Cost	Pts ⇑ PtO ⇓	Centr. ⇓ Decentr. ⇑	Direct del. ⇓	Large ⇓ Small ⇑	Large ⇓ Small ⇑	Large ⇓ Small ⇑	More PMCs, more cost
Energy	-	Centr. ⇑ Decentr. ⇓	Direct del. ⇓	Large ⇓ Small ⇑	Large ⇓ Small ⇑	Large ⇓ Small ⇑	More PMCs more energy
Reliability	-	-	Direct del. ⇓	Large ⇓ Small ⇑	Large ⇓ Small ⇑	Large ⇓ Small ⇑	
Leadtime	PtO⇑ PtS ⇓	Centr. ⇑ Decentr. ⇓	Direct del. ⇓	Large ⇑ Small ⇓	Large ⇑ Small ⇓	Large ⇑ Small ⇓	
Sales	-	-	-	Large ⇓ Small ⇑	Large ⇓ Small ⇑	Large ⇓ Small ⇑	More PMCs, more sales

APPENDIX III. PARTICIPANT QUESTIONNAIRE

Key Problem Statement:

How would you manage the human factor in supply chains in order to achieve optimal supply chain performance?

Research Questions:

- **Part A. Human factors:** Trust, transparency, learning behavior, etc.
    1. What is/are the key human factor(s) in the supply chain for both games?
    2. What are moderating human factors, that is, which factors have an indirect impact only on supply chain performance?
    3. How do these moderating factors impact the key variable(s)?
    4. How could we measure these factors and their relationships (other than the popularity poll)?
- **Part B. Supply chain performance** (logistics, financial, quality, sustainability)
    1. Describe the most important variables (e.g., inventory policy) and key performance indicators (e.g., reliability) in both games with respect to supply chain performance?
    2. How can you describe their relationships?
    3. Which tensions did you experience, which trade-offs needed to be made between various goals in the game as well as between your own interest and that of the overall supply chain?
- **Part C. Impact of the human factor on supply chain performance**
    1. How did your behavior change while playing the game(s)?
    2. Was it good or bad for your performance and the supply chain performance?
    3. Construct *dynamic* relationship diagrams about the impact of your behavior, the human factor(s) on SC performance.
    4. Which (additional) incentives (carrot and stick) would you propose for both games to achieve optimal supply chain performance? These can be both financial and "soft" incentives. Or would you develop other measures to achieve optimal supply chain performance?

APPENDIX IV. MANAGEMENT GAMES OVERVIEW

The NetChain game was developed by a consortium of Tilburg University, Wageningen University, Erasmus University Rotterdam, TIAS Business School, Paragon Decision Technology, Nederland Distributieland, Van Heck Autoonderdelen, the Dutch Ministry of Transport, Public Works and Water Management (Ministerie van Verkeer & Waterstaat) and KLICT. It is a generic business simulator that can be applied to multiple cases.

Some aspects of games that were developed by others were incorporated into the design of the NetChain Game. Those games are described below.

- *The International Logistics Management Game* (ILMG) is a computer-based management game which can encompass one to four markets. Between one and seven companies can participate in the game, but ideally at least three will take part. Each company manufactures only one product and the manufacturing takes place in one of the four market regions. Each company decides in which regions products are to be marketed and produced, and the products may be shipped between these regions. The markets are characterized by different properties illustrative of different countries with different economic characteristics. ILMG was originally developed at Linkoping University in Sweden (Grubstrom, 2007). The game has a number of interesting characteristics from a logistic point of view, but does not explicitly include collaboration.
- *The strawberry game* (Hofstede & Trienekens, 2000) deals with the production of patisserie from fruit, cream, biscuits, and other ingredients. Three teams of participants will play the role of raw material suppliers, three teams will produce fruit treats from these materials, and three will sell the patisserie on the market. All teams have different strategies as well as different national cultures. The remaining participants play the consumers. The game's aim is to introduce phenomena that occur in international food chains. The delicate nature of food products and the uncertain supply of these products due to typical production circumstances can make distances in time and space to important barriers for trade. Also, differences in regulations between nations and cultural differences are to be overcome. Combinations of these factors can lead to problems such as throughput delays, bullwhip effects, unstable quality, or trust breakdowns. One specific purpose of the game is to bring intercultural differences to the participants' minds (see Hofstede, Kramer, Meijder, & Wijdemans, 2001). The game developed by Wageningen University has many relevant aspects from our point of view, but it is not computerized and no hard (logistics) data are available on the case. The interesting aspect of this game is the introduction of trust and cultural aspects.
- *A Daughter in Danger* is another game developed at Wageningen University. It is a simulation game designed by Bots and Hofstede (2004) about a business takeover. Three teams made up of four members each represent three organizations. An affiliate of a large industrial firm is making huge losses and the parent firm is looking for a good takeover candidate. The most likely one is a rich company that may undertake a reorganization not wanted by the parent firm and the affiliate. The three teams need to negotiate the terms of a possible takeover. Again, cultural differences play a significant role (see Hofstede et al. 2001). We find the contracting feature of the game particularly interesting, and have patterned the contracting aspect of the NetChain Game on it.

continued on following page

APPENDIX IV. CONTINUED

- *The beer game* developed by MIT and described by Sterman (1992) among others, deals with a highly simplified linear supply chain including a factory, a distributor, a wholesaler, and a retailer. The game leader manually generates demand. As players are only informed about the demand (forecast) of their predecessor in the chain, demand changes result quickly. There is a so-called bullwhip effect as a result of overcompensation in ordering. More transparency in the supply chain reduces this effect. Other than the bullwhip effect, neither collaboration issues nor logistics aspects are really incorporated in the beer game.

APPENDIX V. CUCUMBER CASE DESCRIPTION

In this appendix, we look at an agrifood sector case and in particular at the cucumber business. The cucumber business has some specific characteristics. Three different types of players are distinguished and only one product-market combination (PMC) is considered. We define the roles as follows: the plant-growers grow cucumbers, the corporation buys the cucumbers from the plant-growers and then sells them on retailers who in turn sell them to consumers.

Plant-Growers

Prior to the growing season, plant-growers negotiate with the corporation the conditions under which buying and selling will take place. Those conditions are detailed in a contract.

The length of the breeding period is 91 days, that is, the plant-grower is able to deliver the product at the end of a 3-month semester. A plant-grower can breed twice a year in 50% of the time. For this reason, most corporations enter into contracts with at least two plant-growers. The game is played in 2 semesters and each plant-grower is only productive for 3 months.

The yield is a function of production volume and production quality, both of which depend on the temperature at which the cucumbers are grown. The temperature in the greenhouse must be kept at an optimal 20-25°C (68-77 degrees Fahrenheit) which means heating in winter and cooling in summer. While growing at a higher temperature results in more cucumbers (more production volume), it shortens shelf life (less quality). When outside temperatures are low, the glass houses are heated to the perfect climate, but at the cost of increased energy use.

Although plant-growers may determine the optimal breeding period, they must reckon with additional energy costs outside of season.

Corporation

The corporation buys cucumbers from plant-growers and sells them on to retailers. It matches supply and demand and organizes logistical activities such as stock keeping and transportation. The corporation is a not-for-profit organization.

As mentioned above, the corporation and the plant-growers hammer out a contract prior to the growing season, and that contract sets out the conditions under which buying and selling will take place. It may happen that retailer demand outstrips the supply for which the corporation contracted. In this case, the corporation buys extra cucumbers from a third party, typically an AI-player abroad or from plant-growers not under contract. This generally results in higher purchase prices. Moreover, reliability cannot be guaranteed. Notice that cucumbers bought from a third party arrive 1 day later at the corporation than cucumbers bought from a plant-grower with whom the corporation has a contract. Hence, there is some risk of stock depletion.

Conversely, cucumber demand may be less than the available supply. This is also problematic, as not only is income reduced, but it costs money, especially in terms of energy costs, to keep the cucumbers temporarily in stock. In this case, the corporation disposes of the cucumbers as waste. Disposal to another AI-player adds still further to costs.

In the NCG both the buying of cucumbers from a third party and the disposal of cucumbers are automated actions. The corporations do not make specific decisions or take action in this regard.

continued on following page

APPENDIX V. CONTINUED

For the corporation, it is not very desirable to have to buy cucumbers from a third party very often, because of the high prices and the risk of stock-out.

To avoid these unwished situations, a corporation can decide to keep a safety stock. For determining the adequate level of safety stock the corporation uses (s,S)-inventory management. Note that order volume and hence transport batches have size Q=S-s in the NCG. If Q equals a full truckload (FTL), then transport costs are low and vice versa.

The corporation is responsible for the transport of the cucumbers from the plant-growers to the customers. High volumes can best be transported by the FTL directly from the plant-grower to the retailer. For lower volumes, cross docking to smaller vehicles at the corporation warehouse is more cost efficient. Direct plant-grower to retailer deliveries reduces transportation cost and energy use, but they also increase retailer inventories. Moreover, direct deliveries increase logistical complexity: direct delivery can take place only when the plant-grower has the volume needed at exactly the right moment. When cucumbers are brought to the corporation warehouse, they must be stored. This reduces the shelf life. The warehouse will attempt to reduce the impact of this using a First In, First Out (FIFO) inventory strategy.

Retailers

The retailer buys the cucumbers from the corporation and sells them to customers. In the NCG, the retailers are national-level chains, not individual supermarkets.

Before the cucumber breeding season starts, the retailer negotiates with the corporation the conditions under which a buying-selling transaction will take place. These are described in a contract.

Retailers cannot sell more cucumbers to their customers than they have bought from the corporation. If the demand for cucumbers is greater, they are unable to fill the order of their customers and so lose the sale.

If the demand for cucumbers is less than the supply, the retailer has unsold stock. Obviously, unsold inventory does not yield revenue. In addition, once the shelf life of the cucumbers is past, they must be disposed of.

Retailers cannot disappoint their customers often without suffering consequences. Not only do they miss out on a sale that day, but also an unhappy customer may decide to shop elsewhere tomorrow. Rather than risk running out of stock, a retailer might decide to over order. The retailer uses (s,S)-inventory management to determine how much more to keep on hand. Note that order volume, hence transport batches, have size Q=S-s in the NCG. If Q equals a FTL, then transport cost is low and vice versa.

Triangular Transparency

Of course, it is very important that the retailers make good decisions about how many cucumbers to buy in order to maximize their profits. Because market research shows that there are more cucumbers the warmer it is, the retailers may decide to buy access to a weather forecasting service to help them in making their decisions. The forecasts are reliable for 2 weeks out.

Having the forecasts costs 100 euros a day, but they are very reliable and so, in fact, a bargain. Moreover, the retailers might be able to get the plant-growers (or the corporation) to buy the forecasts

continued on following page

APPENDIX V. CONTINUED

from them. It would be to the benefit of them all. The plant-grower could use the forecasts can make better decisions about when to start breeding periods, and the corporation could use them to improve matching supply and demand. Actors can also share inventory information, contract data, and logistical insights.

Tactical Phase

Before the cucumber breeding season starts, contracts are drawn up between the plant-growers and the corporation, and between the corporation and the retailers. Those contracts include the conditions under which buying and selling transactions will take place. The contracts cover:

- Volume per year, that is, the number of cucumbers per annum;
- Reliability, as measured by the minimum percentage of cucumbers that must be delivered; and
- Shelf life.

Contract decisions are made every semester before the start of the real-time simulation. Other tactical decisions and operational decisions are made by the players at the beginning of every simulation interval (of equal length to the simulation step size; 2-8 weeks).

Decisions

At the beginning of the game, before the first simulation, the players determine the overall strategy for playing the game. They decide jointly whether they will play a primarily commercial strategy, making as much profit as possible, or largely an ecological strategy with as much care as possible being taken to minimize negative effects on the environment, and their decision is recorded so that there is no disagreement about it later.

Plant-Growers

Tactical Decisions

- At the start of the breeding period, the plant-growers decide on what day they will begin. The breeding period lasts 91 days. The outside temperature during the breeding period will determine energy use.
- The contract with the corporation is negotiated.

Operational Decisions

- The plant-growers weigh whether they will use low levels of energy which will result in less volume, but produce cucumbers with a longer shelf life, or whether they will use high levels of energy which will lead to a higher yield, but negatively impact shelf life. They might also choose to go for the middle ground and opt for medium energy consumption.

continued on following page

APPENDIX V. CONTINUED

Corporation

Tactical Decisions

- The corporation decides for each case whether it is best to deliver the cucumbers directly to the retailer from the plant-grower or not.
- The contract(s) with the plant-growers are negotiated.
- The contract(s) with the retailers are negotiated

Operational Decisions

- The corporation decides if it will use the (s,S) strategy or not.

Retailers

Tactical Decisions

- The retailers decide whether they will buy weather forecasts at 100 euros a day or not.
- The contract with the corporation is negotiated.

Operational Decisions

- The price is determined: low, medium, or high.
- The retailers decide whether they will use the (s,S) strategy or not.

Key Performance Indicators

The performance of the various players is measured during the game using a set of key performance indicators (KPIs). We distinguish between logistical, financial, and social KPIs.

Logistical KPIs

- *Reliability:* The percentage of the demand volume of cucumbers that was actually delivered
- *Remaining shelf life:* The average shelf life measured over all cucumber stock
- *Sales volume:* The number of cucumbers sold

Environmental KPIs

- *Energy use by the plant-grower:* the total amount of energy that is used for breeding the cucumbers in gigajoules? (GJ)

continued on following page

APPENDIX V. CONTINUED

- *Energy use by the corporation:* the total amount of energy that is used for transporting the cucumbers; the total number of kilometers driven multiplied by 0.85 megajoules (MJ) per ton per kilometer
- *Disposal volume:* The number of waste cucumbers

Financial KPIs

- *Total costs:* The sum of what a player spends on buying cucumbers, waste disposal, transport, energy use, and inventory keeping
- *Sales:* The total revenue from the sale of cucumbers
- *Revenue:* Sales less costs

Social KPIs

- *Trust:* A popularity poll is run every 3 months to determine the extent of goodwill, number of extended contracts for contract trust, and dual sourcing for competence trust

Table 4. Impact of decisions on the KPI

		"Buttons"/Decisions					
		Strategic/tactical decisions			**Operational decisions**		
		plant-grower	cor-poration	Retailer	plant-grower	cor-poration	retailer
- -Key Performance Indicators (KPI)		Change standard breeding moment	Direct delivery	Buying weather forecast	Extra energy (lower energy is vice versa)	Inventory management ((s,S) optimized)	Price reduction
	Costs	↑	↓	↑	↑	↓	
	Energy use	↑	↓	-	↑	-	-
	Reliability	↑	-	↑	↓	↑	-
	Remaining shelf life	-	↑	-	↓	↑	-
	Sales	↑	-	↑	↑	↑	↑

continued on following page

APPENDIX V. CONTINUED

The Balance Sheet

Every year, a profit and loss account is made and a balance sheet is drawn up. Quarterly reports of both financial and logistical performance indicators are also compiled. The values of the KPI are displayed for each individual player, and also for the total supply chain.

Table 4 summarizes the decisions taken in the cucumber game per player and their impact.

Real-Time Simulation: Operations Phase

The NCG looks at a demand driven supply chain network. Consumer markets are fully automated. The main mechanisms take into consideration pricing and allocation of demand.

Five different market prices are considered:

- Corporation market price (what the corporation pays to the plant-growers),
- Retailer market price (what the retailer pays the corporation),
- Consumer market price (what consumers pay the retailer),
- Third party buy price (what the third party is willing to pay for surplus from the corporation), and
- Third party sell price (what the third party is willing to take from the corporation).

The actual price paid is determined by the corresponding market price and specific contract specifications, or operational decisions (in the case of the consumer market price). The players, specifically the corporations, have no influence on the third party prices.

The market prices are set using the following method. Each day the total supply from all plant-growers is tallied and the total demand of all retailers is also computed by aggregating all retailer order sizes from the previous day. If possible, these orders have to be delivered on this day, or otherwise as soon as possile. If supply and demand is balanced, then the retail market price is equal to the default retailer price. However, if supply exceeds demand, then the retail market price drops below the default retailer price. The corporation market price is equal to the retail market price corrected by a certain percentage (the so-called "corporation markdown percentage"). The third party buying and selling prices are determined by markdown and mark up percentages on the corporation market price. The consumer market price for a given day is equal to the retail market price increased by a consumer mark up percentage. Note that the consumer market price is delayed by 1 day. The reason for this is that consumer demand, which we need for the computation, is partly determined by the consumer market price. Moreover, it is reasonable to assume that retailers cannot immediately change the price they charge consumers.

Next, for each retailer, a factor is computed which is the product of several elasticity components:

- The offered price level (low, medium, high)
- The offered remaining shelf life
- The price charged by competitors
- The remaining shelf life of the product of competitors

continued on following page

APPENDIX V. CONTINUED

A factor is determined such that a higher value means that the deal offered by the retailer at hand is found more attractive than the deal offered by competitors. Next, an allocation is computed which is proportional to the factor.

The allocation of consumer demand among all retailers is determined as follows. First, the default consumer demand is calculated. Second, the total supply by all retailers is computed. This is simply the sum of the inventory levels at the start of the day. This is equal to the product of an amount proportional to the number of plant-growers in the game, and a factor, which depends on the temperature, such that a higher temperature generates higher demand.

If a retailer is allocated more than his inventory, then the allocation is set equal to the inventory and the procedure above is repeated with this retailer removed. Note that, because of these factors, the total consumer demand depends on the offered prices and remaining shelf life, and not just the temperature, as well as inventory management.

From the retailer back to the plant-grower the ordering behavior is determined by the inventory management and ordering of the buying party and the reliability of the supplying player.

Chapter VIII
Identifying and Clustering of Target Customers of Green Products

Miao-Ling Wang
Ming-Hsin University of Science & Technology, Taiwan, ROC

ABSTRACT

The number of consumers concerned about the environment is growing. Although the promotion of green products is recognized as a basic method for solving the waste crisis and improving the environment, resources for producing or serving green products are relatively limited, causing inconveniences and elevated prices for the consumer. Therefore, it becomes significant that those customers who are willing to sacrifice convenience in order to purchase higher priced green products be identified. Through the affirmation of target customers in an effective marketing system, enterprises can recycle used products efficiently, increase profits and successfully transmit advertising information to consumers who are disposed to buy green products. In this chapter, we apply data mining techniques to cope with this problem. After clustering the customers, a bi-objective nonlinear problem is constructed with multiple attribute utility theory; the target customers form the foundation of marketing.

INTRODUCTION

Due to the potential depletion of raw materials in the near future, environmental protection issues have become increasingly important; likewise, the numbers of consumers who are concerned about the environment are also increasing. Green products can reduce the negative environmental impact while still maintaining or improving costs and quality needs. Promotion of green products is recognized as an access for solving resource waste and improving environmental pollution. In consequence, green marketing becomes a business management trend requiring frequent

Copyright © 2009, IGI Global, distributing in print or electronic forms without written permission of IGI Global is prohibited.

interactions between consumers and producers to ensure the 3R's of reusing, remanufacturing, and recycling.

Initially, green products and traditional products were sold in the market simultaneously. Most peripheral equipment or environments, however, mainly rely on traditional products as resources for serving green products are relatively limited and inconvenience and higher prices are associated with obtaining these products. Therefore, apart from setting up a complete recycling system, it becomes essential that customers who are willing to pay higher initial prices for products not widely used be identified. The affirmation of target customers and a complete marketing channel can not only assist enterprises in recycling effectively, but can transmit advertising information to customers who are willing to buy new products or services and thereby increase their profit.

For our purposes, a "target customer" refers to a consumer who is willing to purchase higher priced green products even though his/her convenience may be sacrificed. Investigating the product value with respect to such target customers will provide companies with good reference points for future pricing of such products.

To achieve the above goals, we need to efficiently cluster customers into various segmentations according to their preferences for green products. The multiattribute utility theory (MAUT) was used to develop the aggregated fulfillment of obtaining such a product. Based on the win-win concept, a bi-objective model was constructed to derive the optimal price that satisfies both the customers' utility and the producers' benefit simultaneously. Based on the characteristics of the customers' clusters, the target customers can be identified and this will be the foundation for marketing. Therefore, we can sell the right goods to the right person with value gained to the company.

In this chapter, we first introduce the background of related researches. Then, the theoretical development and the basic structure of the model are constructed, and the first part of a case study is used to illustrate the procedures of selecting suitable segmentation variables. Next, the optimal prices of a hybrid electric vehicle are used to illustrate the procedures for obtaining segmenting optimal prices by MAUT. Finally, discussion and conclusions are drawn. This chapter will be the foundation of a Web site for the marketing of green products.

LITERATURE REVIEW

The rapid development of information technology and the Internet has changed traditional business environments. Companies are realizing that they can use the Web to effectively communicate with customers, making their business easier. The author had proposed a Web mining system that incorporates both online efficiency and off-line effectiveness to provide the "right" information, based on users' preferences (Wang & Wang, 2005). To efficiently construct a Web site that will provide information about green products, we first need to identify customers according to their preferences, so that Web customers' behavior can be characterized.

Based on the above ideas we will first introduce the different demands of green marketing and in order to cope with these different demands, the existing research about the customer features will be investigated. Facing the customer heterogeneity and for a successful marketing, the suitable variables for profiling the green customers are discussed. Furthermore, MAUT and related techniques are introduced to construct a compromised model of the consumers between alternatives with conflicting objectives. Finally, the solution procedures for the proposed model are presented.

Supply-Derived Market

As environmental protection issues have become important around the world, consumers who are concerned about the environment are increasing. Businesses have been quick to accept concepts like environmental management systems and waste minimization, and have integrated environmental issues into all organizational activities. Businesses and industries need to provide products and services which promise environmental responsibility to preserve their markets and safeguard their reputation for a cleaner Earth (Ottman, 1998). Ottman (1998) indicated the differences between conventional and green marketing. The objective of conventional marketing is to develop products that meet consumers' needs at affordable prices and then to communicate the benefits of those products in a compelling way. The objectives of green marketing are first to develop products that balance consumers' needs for quality, performance, affordable pricing, and convenience with minimal impact on the environment; and the second is to project an image of high quality relating to both a product's attributes and its manufacturer's track record for environmental achievement (Ottman, 1998). Therefore, how to meet the consumers' need is an important issue.

Lummus and Vokurka (1999) suggested that companies must learn to pull products through a supply chain, that is, to learn to manage "demand chain," rather than to push products. A demand chain can be defined as a complex Web of business processes and activities which help firms to understand, manage, and ultimately create customer demand (Langabeer & Rose, 2001). It can help managers to analyze and understand overall demands for markets within the firm's current and potential product range. Supply chains emphasize the efficiencies in the production and logistics processes; the demand chains emphasize the effectiveness in the business (Walters & Rainbird, 2004).

Customer Features and Classification

Initially, green products and traditional products were sold in the market simultaneously, but because most peripheral equipment or environments rely mainly on traditional products, resources for serving green products are relatively limited which causes inconvenience and higher prices for obtaining them. Therefore, aside from setting up a complete recycling system, it is important that customers who would endure inconveniences or pay higher prices for green products are identified. It has been proven that the demand for green products is quite different between different markets (Ottman, 1998).

The consumer who is likely to be concerned about environmental issues and is willing to pay higher prices for green products needs to be identified, and such a green customer is called as a "target customer." Through a perfect marketing channel, moreover, through a perfect tracing system where target customers are identified, enterprises can recycle used products successfully, can accurately convey advertising information to the consumer and can generate additional profit. Therefore, we need to segment the customers and to provide different marketing strategies, which will meet their requests.

There have been many studies focused on the profiling of the green customers by using different kinds of segmentation variables (Bohlen, Schlegelmilch, & Diamantopoulos, 1993a, 1993b; Diamantopoulos, Schlegelmilch, Sinkovics, & Bohlen, 2003; Schlegelmilch, Bohlen, & Diamantopoulos, 1996; Straughan & Roberts, 1999; Tilikidou & Delistavrou, 2001; Tilikidou, 2007). Kolter (1997) suggested that an efficient segmentation needs to satisfy measurability, substantiality, accessibility, and actionability. Traditionally, the measures used to segment are the socio-demographics, such as age, location, social class, and the psychological variables, such as personality, and behavior variables such as purchasing frequency (Green, Tull, & Albaum, 1993; Kolter, 1997). The most widely and relatively easily used variables for profiling are the socio-demographics. Diamantopoulos et al. (2003) summarized the associations in the past studies between socio-demographics: gender, martial status, age, number of children, education, and social class. They addressed shortcomings identified in previous studies and concluded that the weak utility of socio-demographic variables for profiling green consumers according to their pro-environmental purchasing behavior by statistical hypothesis inferences in their serial studies (Bohlen et al., 1993a, 1993b; Diamantopoulos et al., 2003; Schlegelmilch et al., 1996). The more suitable variables for profiling green purchases on all components of environmental consciousness were suggested to be the knowledge about green issues, attitudes towards environmental quality, and levels of environmentally sensitive behavior (Bohlen et al., 1993a; Diamantopoulos et al., 2003; Roberts, 1996). Tanner and Kast (2003) uncovered personal and contextual factors that influence green food purchases by Swiss consumers; four categories of measures of specific attitudes, perceived barriers, knowledge, and personal norm are used to check the relevant impact on environmental behavior. Their study confirmed that personal norms and perceived monetary barriers were not significant, place of residence, household size, education, occupational level, employment status, and household income were not among the relevant predictors, and personal attitudes and beliefs are power predictors of green purchases (Tanner & Kast, 2003). Straughan and Roberts (1999) examined the characteristics of ecologically conscious consumer behavior and indicated that demographics, including age, sex, income, and academic classification, are not as useful as psychographic variables: environmental concern, altruism, and perceived consumer effectiveness for profiling and segmenting college students. Tilikidou and Delistavrou (2001) and Tilikidou (2007) presented an examination of pro-environmental purchasing behavior and how it was influenced by demographics, environmental knowledge, and attitudes (environmental unconcern). It was indicated that there were potentials for success in business offerings that focused on energy conservation or reassurance that products were free of GMOs and that Greek customers were less concerned with respect to environmental problems. Based on the above discussions, it can be concluded that we should incorporate both socio-demographic factors and environmental consciousness as segmentation variables in this study.

Multiattribute Utility Theory and Weight Elicitation

Facing a purchasing decision, consumers often need to select between some alternatives with conflicting objectives. Different utilities are obtained by various types of customers with diverse preferences. Multi-attribute utility theory (MAUT), which is a part of the multiple criteria decision making (MCDM), is a widely used tool to assist a decision maker (DM) to make such choices (van Calker, Berentsen, Romero, Giesen, & Huirne, 2006; Clemen, 1991; Keeny & Raiffa, 1976). There are four major tasks in the multiattribute utility measurement: to structure objectives, to develop attributes, to derive some single attribute utility function, and finally to aggregate utility functions with different weights of attributes (van Calker et al., 2006). There are some assumptions regarding MAUT, preferential independence, utility independency, and additive independence. Different models are constructed for different situations satisfying the above assumptions (Canbolat, Chelst, & Garg, 2007; Keeny & Raiffa, 1976; Malakooti & Subramanian, 1999). Keeny and Raiffa (1976) developed a procedure for determining an appropriate model. Among them, the additive utility model is the most well known and widely used (van Calker et al., 2006). Stewart (1996) constructed a simulation model to test the assumptions of the completeness, transitivity, and additive independence of criteria and the use of additive value functions which has been proven consistent and reliable, even if the nonlinearities exist.

Regarding the weight elicitation, there are many researches focused on the comparison of different weighting methods (Borcherding, Eppel, & von Winterfeldt, 1991; Bottomley & Doyle, 2001; Doyle, Green, & Bottomley, 1997; Harte & Koele, 1995; Jaccard, Brinberg, & Ackerman, 1986; *Schoemaker, Waid, & Carter*, 1982; Srivastava, Connolly, & Beach, 1995). Different results were obtained from different viewpoints; most studies indicated that different ways of eliciting attribute weights yield similar results. For example, Jaccard et al. (2001) evaluated the convergent validity of six methods of measuring attribute importance (elicitation measure, information-search measure, direct rating, conjoint measure, subjective probability measure, and Thurstone measure). They concluded that there was relatively little convergence between methods and the conclusion made about attribute importance may be quite different depending on the methods used to assess importance. Bottomley and Doyle (2001) compared the properties and performances of three weight elicitation methods: direct rating (DR), Max100, and Min10. They found that the weights produced by Max100 were somewhat more reliable than by DR and people actually preferred using Max100 and DR rather than Min10.

When a set of individual weights is obtained by DMs, a compromised ranking needs to be determined. González-Pachón and Romero (1999) reviewed past studies and proposed a methodology EGP based on goal programming (GP) that allowed the aggregation of individually ordinal preferences. An extended model of a weighted bi-objective programming was proposed to derive a compromised solution of minimization of aggregated disagreement between DMs and maximum disagreement (González-Pachón & Romero, 1999). Based on their study in 1999 and MAUT, Linares and Romero (2002) developed an overall sustainability function for Dutch dairy farming systems. Their approach consisted of four steps: determination of attribute utility functions, assessing attribute weights to determine utility functions per aspect, assessing aspect weights to determine the overall sustainability function per stakeholder group, and determination of the overall sustainability function for society by aggregating preferences of stakeholders and experts. When preferences provided by several social groups from different criteria and the EGP is used, optimal solutions with tradeoffs between maximum average agreement solutions and the most balanced solution are obtained.

Nonlinear Programming

Facing the different characteristics of a demand chain, enterprises should not only consider making profit but should also pay attention to their customers' requests regarding similar and inexpensive environmental-friendly products. Based on the win-win concept, this study constructs a bi-objective nonlinear problem to derive the optimal price satisfying both the customers' utility and the product's utility. When the weights are given by a DM, it will be transformed into a weighted problem. There are many methods focused on the solution of general constrained optimization problems (Bazaraa & Shetty, 1990; Hillier & Lieberman, 2005). According to different shapes and forms of nonlinear programming problems, different types are categorized and solution procedures were proposed accordingly. For example, the gradient search procedure for a multivariable unconstrained convex problem; the Karush-Kuhn–Tucker conditions for constrained problems; an extension of the simplex method for separable programming problems; and some sequential-approximation algorithms for convex programming problems. With the assumptions of convex programming, it was proved that any local optimum is also a global one, but it is not true for a nonconvex programming problem (Hillier & Lieberman, 2005). Therefore, a common approach is to apply an algorithmic search procedure, for example, sequential unconstrained minimization technique, to find a local optimum and to repeat the procedure to find more local ones as possible and generate a global one (Hillier & Lieberman, 2005). Regarding the recent studies, Meng, Hu, Dang, and Yang (2004) reviewed the existing penalty functions and proposed an objective penalty function method for solving this kind of problem. They developed a new algorithm to generate a globally optimal solution to a constrained nonlinear problem, called OPFM algorithm. With some special conditions, OPFM is proved a convergent algorithm and the global optimal solutions are guaranteed (Meng et al., 2004). Nesterov (1997) compared the methods and complexity of the existing interior-point methods to solve nonlinear programming. Potra and Wright (2000) reviewed the key developments of some existing interior-point methods and gave comments about the complexity for some types of problems. Zhu (2005) presented a new interior-point algorithm for nonconvex nonlinear programming; two linear equation systems need to be solved for iteration. Numerical experiments were used to illustrate the effectiveness of their algorithm. Zhou and Shi (1997) proposed a numerical algorithm to solve the local optimum by solving an ordinary differential equation, and this algorithm provides a great possibility for solving large-scale problems. Many authors devoted themselves to the approximate methods, for example, Padberg (2000) compared two existing literatures and proposed an improved method of approximating separable functions to mixed integer problems.

METHODOLOGY

In order to identify the target customers, we need to first collect customer information. The completion of the customer data will reveal personal information and preferences for some green products. Different groups of customers will generate different patterns of demand. After clustering, each utility function for each cluster can be obtained by MAUT. Incorporating the objective function of suppliers, bi-objective nonlinear integer programming problems will be constructed to obtain compromised prices of different clusters. The target customers from the different characteristics of consumers can be identified and the segmenting prices can be performed to gain more benefits for both customers and producers.

The framework of the proposed method is shown and illustrated in the following:

Figure 1. Framework of the proposed method

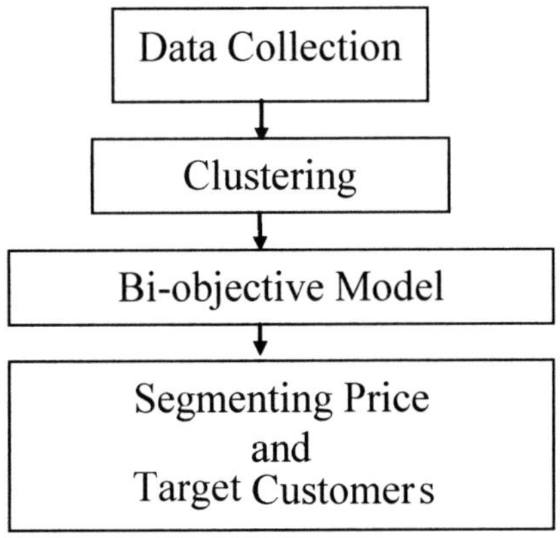

Data Collection

As shown above, there is weakness in the socio-demographics for profiling green consumers. Weak linkages between attitudes and behavior have often been noted in the environmental and social marketing literature; positive attitudes towards the environment are not necessarily indicative of high levels of environmental knowledge (Diamantopoulos et al., 2003). Furthermore, the large majority of environmental studies focusing on socio-demographic characteristics are U.S.-based, but the U.S. findings are not replicated in UK and it is country-specific.

Therefore, the first part of the questionnaires contains summarized questionnaires from the existing researches (Bohlen et al., 1993b; Roberts, 1996; Tanner & Kast, 2003; Tilikidou, 2007) with a selection of questions chosen from three dimensions suitable for Taiwan: knowledge, attitude, nonpurchasing behavior as segmentation variables and a set of purchasing behavior as the dependent variables for checking the effectiveness of segmentation. The second part of the questionnaires contains the questions of multi-attribute utility in purchasing a green product. The third and final part of the questionnaires contains questions dealing with socio-demographics.

Clustering Analysis

Data mining is the exploration and analysis of large quantities of data in order to discover meaningful patterns and rules and the main tasks are defined as classification, estimation, prediction, affinity grouping, clustering, and description (Barry & Linoff, 1997; Groth, 1999). Data mining, including some statistical techniques, can help us to verify the concerning relationships in the data and discover useful information, to improve strategic and operational planning activities and to excavate the hidden knowledge effectively and efficiently, and has been wisely used in direct marketing, customer acquisition, customer retention, cross-selling, trend analysis, fraud detection, and forecasting (Groth, 1999). Clustering algorithm, which can be used to organize, categorize, and compress data and construct models, is one of the most fundamental issues in data mining (Barry & Linoff, 1997). By clustering, a data set can be partitioned into several groups; the degree of similarity within a group may be high, whereas the similarity between the groups may be low. There are various kinds of clustering methods (Wang & Wang, 2005). Among these methods, the *c*-Means algorithm (Tamura, Higuchi, & Tanaka, 1971) is a most commonly used clustering method. By defining the distance from each datum to the center as the Euclidean distance, the model ensures that each datum is assigned to exactly one cluster.

When dealing with the vague data, elements may belong to several clusters with different degrees of belonging. Bezdek (1973) developed a flexible algorithm, Fuzzy *c*-Means (FCM) of which each datum belongs to a cluster is a degree specified by a membership value (Klir, 1988) between 0 and 1 as shown in Model (1).

$$\text{(FCM):}\quad \begin{aligned} &Min \quad Z(U;V)=\sum_{i=1}^{c}\sum_{k=1}^{K}(\mu_{ik})^2\left\|Y_k - v_i\right\|^2 \\ &\text{subject to} \quad \sum_{i=1}^{c}\mu_{ik}=1, \quad \forall k=1,\ldots,K \\ &\qquad \mu_{ik}\geq 0, \quad \forall i=1,\ldots,c, k=1,\ldots,K \end{aligned} \qquad (1)$$

where c is number of the clusters, $\|\cdot\|$ is an inner product norm, $Y_k, k=1,\ldots,K$, denote K elements, $v_i, i=1,\ldots,c$ is the center of cluster i and $\mu_{ik}, i=1,\ldots,c; k=1,\ldots,K$ are the membership values of Y_k belonging to cluster i. In this study, the Fuzzy c-Means algorithm is used to cluster the customers so that the total spread around the centers of the clusters is minimized.

Utility Function Construction

After clustering analysis, suppose we have N attributes $a_1,\ldots,a_N$ and denote x_j be the payoff under attribute a_j and $u^i_j(x_j)$ be the corresponding utility value of cluster i, j=1,…,N. A continuously-type exponential utility function of each cluster is defined as follows:

$$u^i_j(x_j)=\delta^i_j+\gamma^i_j e^{\rho_{ij}x_j} \tag{2}$$

The utility function u^i_j can be obtained by first setting the mean utility value of the best payoff $\overline{x}_j$ of attribute a_j as $\overline{u^i_j(\overline{x}_j)}$ and the mean utility value of the worst payoff $\underline{x}_j$ of attribute j as $\overline{u^i_j(\underline{x}_j)}$, and using the mid-value-splitting technique (Keeny & Raiffa, 1976) to obtain the parameter ρ_{ij} by asking DM a third point, for example, for which payoff value $x_{j,fair}$ he/she fells "fair" and computing $u^i_j(x_{j,fair})=0.5$, or the current spec utility. If the domain of variable x_j is a discrete one, therefore, the utility function can be set as the linear combination of three points with binary variables, for example, if attribute a_j has three levels of payoff as: $(\overline{x}_j, \overline{u^i_j(\overline{x}_j)})$, $(x'_j, \overline{u^i_j(x'_j)})$ and $(\underline{x}_j, \overline{u^i_j(\underline{x}_j)})$, we have:

$$\begin{aligned}
&u^i_j(x_j)=\overline{u^i_j(\overline{x}_j)}y_{j,1}+\overline{u^i_j(x'_j)}y_{j,2}+\overline{u^i_j(\underline{x}_j)}y_{j,3},\\
&y_{j,1}+y_{j,2}+y_{j,3}=1, y_{j,k}\in\{0,1\}, k=1,\ldots,3.
\end{aligned} \tag{3}$$

Weight Elicitation

Suppose we have T_i customers in cluster i and w^i_{jn} be the preference weight of attribute j of the nth member of cluster i by using Max100 method. The EGP model (van Calker et al., 2006; Linares & Romero, 2002) is used to obtain the aggregated weights W_{ij} of attribute j, j=1,…,N. For example, by solving the following system, we have the aggregated weights W_{ij} (van Calker et al., 2006):

$$\begin{aligned}
&\min\ (1-\lambda)D+\lambda\sum_{j=1}^{N}\sum_{n=1}^{T_i}(g_{jn}+h_{jn})\\
&s.t. \sum_{j=1}^{N}(g_{jn}+h_{jn})-D\le 0, n=1,\ldots,T_i,\\
&\quad W_{ij}+g_{jn}-h_{jn}=w^i_{jn}, n=1,\ldots,T_i,\\
&\quad \sum_{j=1}^{N}(g_{jn}+h_{jn})-D_n=0, n=1,\ldots,T_i,\\
&\quad \sum_{j=1}^{N}\sum_{n=1}^{T_i}(g_{jn}+h_{jn})-Z=0,
\end{aligned} \tag{4}$$

where λ is a weight of the tradeoff between maximum average agreement solution and the most balanced solution; D represents the maximum disagreement of individual customers; $D_n, n=1,\ldots,T_i$ represent the disagreement for each customer in cluster i; g_{jn} and $h_{jn}, j=1,\ldots,N, n=1,\ldots,T_i$ are the positive and negative deviation variables. Larger λ represents that more importance is given to the objective that minimizes the sum of individual disagreement; different λ will obtain different compromised solution.

Bi-Objective Model Construction

By setting the lower bound of the requested greenness $b_{i,greenness}$ of customers and the cost with regard to set up such a green product of the supplier, we have the following bi-objective model:

$$\begin{aligned}
&\max U^i_c(x_1,\ldots,x_{price},x_{greenness},\ldots,x_N)\\
&\quad =\sum_{j=1}^{N}W_{ij}(\delta^i_j+\gamma^i_j e^{\rho_{ij}x_j})\\
&\max U_s(z)\\
&s.t.\ z=x_{price}-COST(x_1,\ldots,x_{price},x_{greenness},\ldots,x_N)\\
&\quad x_{greenness}\ge b_{i,greenness},\\
&\quad \underline{x}_j\le x_j\le\overline{x}_j,\\
&\quad j=1,\ldots,N.
\end{aligned} \tag{5}$$

where U^i_c denotes the aggregated utility function of the customers of cluster i and is the weighted sum of utility functions of attributes; the function $COST(x_1,\ldots,x_N)$ is the total cost of different combination of components which can be represented as a linear combination of individual cost function by introducing some binary or integer variables; U_s denotes the utility of supplier's profit z of the first constraint and it can also be obtained by mid-value-splitting technique, that is, the supplier is asked to answer the following questions: "what is the current posting price?," and the utility is set as 1; "what is the lowest price you are willing to sell?," and we set the utility being 0.5; finally, "what is the lowest price you have no willingness to sell?" and the utility is set as 0. Similarly, we can obtain the supplier's utility function as shown in Eq. (2).

Solution Procedure of the Nonlinear Problem

After introducing the weights of the objectives, $\alpha_i, 1-\alpha_i, \alpha_i \in [0,1]$, we have the following nonlinear problem as shown in Box 1 (Problem 6).

Problem (6) can be solved by some well known software, for example, LINGO, or general nonlinear algorithm. The algorithm OPFM developed by Meng et al. (2004) as follows can help us to find the optimal solution:

Step 1: Choose parameters $p>1, \varepsilon>0, \mathbf{x}^0 \in S$ and $q_1 < f_0^i(\mathbf{x}^0)$. Let k=1, $r_1 = f_0^i(\mathbf{x}^0)$ and $M_1 = \frac{q_1+r_1}{2}$, go to Step 2.

Step 2: Solve the objective penalty function $\min_{\mathbf{x}\in L} F^i(\mathbf{x},M_k)$ where L is a N-dimensional set containing S and $F^i(\mathbf{x},M_k) = (f_0^i(\mathbf{x})-M_k)^2 + \sum_{j=1}^{2N+3} \max\{0, f_j^i(\mathbf{x})\}^p$.

Step 3: If $\mathbf{x}^k$ is not a feasible solution to problem (6), let $r_{k+1}=r_k$, $q_{k+1}=M_k$, $M_{k+1}=\frac{q_{k+1}+r_{k+1}}{2}$ and go to Step 5. Otherwise $\mathbf{x}^k \in S$ and go to Step 4.

Step 4: If $F^i(\mathbf{x}^k,M_k)=0$, let $q_{k+1}=q_k$, $r_{k+1}=M_k$, $M_{k+1}=\frac{q_{k+1}+r_{k+1}}{2}$ and go to Step 5. Otherwise, $F^i(\mathbf{x}^k,M_k)>0, \mathbf{x}^k$ is an optimal solution to problem (6) and the algorithm terminates.

Step 5: If $|r_{k+1}-q_{k+1}|<\varepsilon$, then the algorithm terminates and $\mathbf{x}^k$ is an approximately optimal solution to problem (6). Otherwise, let k=k+1 and go to Step 2.

Since S is a connected and compact set, and all f_j^i are continuous and the level set of f_0^i is bounded, it is proved that the OPFM algorithm converges and derives the optimal solution to problem (6). If there are some integer variables in the proposed model, the mixed integer programming technique, branch and bound algorithm (Hillier & Lieberman, 2005), will be used to find the solution.

Box 1. Problem 6

$$\min f_0^i(x_1,\ldots,x_N) = -\alpha_i \sum_{j=1}^{N} W_{ij}(\delta_j^i + \gamma_j^i e^{\rho_{ij}x_j}) - (1-\alpha_i)U_s(z)$$

s.t.

$$\mathbf{x} \in S = \left\{ (x_1,\ldots,x_N) \;\middle|\; \begin{array}{c} f_1^i(x) = z - x_{price} + COST(x_1,\ldots,x_{price},x_{greenness},\ldots,x_N) \le 0, \\ f_2^i(x) = -z + x_{price} - COST(x_1,\ldots,x_{price},x_{greenness},\ldots,x_N) \le 0, \\ f_3^i(\mathbf{x}) = b_{i,greenness} - x_{greenness} \le 0, \\ f_{j+3}^i(\mathbf{x}) = \underline{x}_j - x_j \le 0, j=1,\ldots,N, \\ f_{j+N+3}^i(\mathbf{x}) = x_j - \overline{x}_j \le 0, j=1,\ldots,N \end{array} \right\}.$$

Therefore, the target customers of different characteristics of customers can be identified and segmenting price can be performed to gain more profit for enterprises.

CLUSTERING ANALYSIS OF CASE STUDY

In order to demonstrate the proposed methodology and to collect data, a list of questionnaires was presented. The three main parts of the questionnaires are enclosed.

Questionnaire Content and Hypotheses

In part one, the first question is about the "Greenmark" in Taiwan. This is used to filter the individual who has no idea about environmental issues, and the answer is discarded in this study. Following are nine items about levels of environmental knowledge on global warming, greenhouse effect, acid rain, ozone layer depletion, nonrenewable resource, intergenerational equity principle, and so forth. The respondents were to fill in their self-reported level of knowledge within a five-point itemized scale, from "know nothing about" to "know very well."

Ten items are concerned with environmental cognition and attitudes. The level of agreement about the statements vary from, "I believe that there is no difference between the pollutions from general product and environmental product," to "The environment is one of the most important issues facing society today, we should pay a considerable amount of money to preserve our environment," to "I don't think we should sacrifice economic development just to protect the environment." Ten items are concerned with environmentally nonpurchasing behavior, such as "What is your level of recycling activities (paper, glass, plastics, metal) undertaken?," "I often visit or read environmental-related Websites or articles." Fourteen items are about environmentally purchasing behavior, for example, "What is your frequency of choosing the environmentally-friendly alternative regardless of price when purchasing?" and "I prefer environmentally friendly products, even if they are not equally effective."

The second part of the questionnaires is about the satisfaction of a hybrid electric vehicle (HEV) and finally, the third part contains the socio-demographic items: gender, age, martial, education, occupation, and income.

Part two of the questionnaires contains revised items from the past studies (Bohlen et al., 1993b; Roberts, 1996; Tanner & Kast, 2003; Tilikidou, 2007); we aim to check the utility of socio-demographic variables for profiling green consumers and to derive the suitable segmentation variables. Therefore, the alternative hypotheses are:

a. **Gender:**
   - *H1-1:* Females are more knowledgeable about environmental issues;
   - *H1-2:* Females are more concerned about environmental equality;
   - *H1-3:* Females are more willing to undertake environmentally nonpurchasing activities;
   - *H1-4:* Females are more willing to purchase green products.

b. **Age:**
   - *H2-1:* Older people are more knowledgeable about environmental issues;
   - *H2-2:* Older people are more concerned about environmental equality;
   - *H2-3:* Older people are more willing to undertake environmentally nonpurchasing activities;
   - *H2-4:* Older people are more willing to purchase green products.

c. **Martial status:**
   - *H3-1:* Married people are more knowledgeable about environmental issues;
   - *H3-2:* Married people are more concerned about environmental equality;

H3-3: Married people are more willing to undertake environmentally nonpurchasing activities;

H3-4: Married people are more willing to purchase green products.

d. **Education:**

H4-1: Better-educated people are more knowledgeable about environmental issues;

H4-2: Better-educated people are more concerned about environmental equality;

H4-3: Better-educated people are more willing to undertake environmentally nonpurchasing activities;

H4-4: Better-educated people are more willing to purchase green products.

f. **Occupation:**

H5-1: Different occupations have different levels of knowledge about environmental issues;

H5-2: Different occupations have different levels of concern about environmental equality;

H5-3: Different occupations have different levels of willingness to undertake environmentally nonpurchasing activities;

H5-4: Different occupations have different levels of willingness to purchase green products.

g. **Income:**

H6-1: People with higher income are more knowledgeable about environmental issues;

H6-2: People with higher income are more concerned about environmental equality;

H6-3: People with higher income are more willing to undertake environmentally nonpurchasing activities;

H6-4: People with higher income are more willing to purchase green products.

Four hundred respondents were proportionally and randomly sampled from northern cities of Taiwan, Taipei, Tao-Yuan, and Hsin-Chu according to the total number of residents in each area. 392 usable responses were finally collected. Approximately 85% of respondents gave correct answers to the filtering question; 12% of respondents gave a wrong but environmentally-dependent answer and 11 respondents gave a complete environmentally- independent answer and were deleted; therefore, 379 valid responses were used as the database in this study.

Measure Construction

Bohlen et al. (1993b) suggested that in order to construct a useful environmental measure to profile green consumers, the following tests need to be performed and established first: dimensionality, reliability analysis, and validity.

(i)*Knowledge about environmental problems*

All components in this domain were highly correlated and through exploratory factor analysis, two factors resulted. The first factor accounts for 49% of the total variance while the second accounts for only 14%. Therefore, we can treat these items as a single conceptually meaningful dimension, which purifies the measure solely based on internal consistency as suggested in Bohlen et al. (1993b). Using Cronbach's alpha for reliability analysis, a value of 0.8656 is obtained which indicates a high degree of internal consistency. When the "alpha if item deleted" statistics are computed, item eight is deleted and the alpha value is improved to 0.8664. Individuals' responses to the variables are examined for an aggregate measure of their knowledge about environmental problems. The summary statistics show a mean score of 26.14 (out of maximum score 40), indicating that the respondents perceive themselves to be generally educated on environmental issues.

(ii) *Cognition and Attitudes about the environment*

No significant correlation was found between items 2, 7, 9, and 10 and the others in this area as more than one dimension exist in this domain. Three factors result from exploratory factor analysis accounting for 24%, 17%, and 14% of the total variance. The Cronbach's alpha obtained is 0.4576. Similarly, when the "alpha if item deleted" statistics are computed, items 4, 5, and 9 are deleted and the alpha value is improved. A two-factor structure with seven variables, items 1, 2, 3, 6, and 8 form the first factors, named "Cognition" and items 7 and 10 form the second, named "Initiative." The two factors account for 54% of total variance and the Cronbach's alpha achieved is 0.6474. Responses to the variables are encapsulated for aggregate measures of their cognition and initiative; the summary statistics show mean scores of 18.91 (out of maximum score 25) and 6.22 (out of maximum score 10), respectively indicating that the respondents have favorable attitudes toward environmental protection, and a high willingness to obtain new information about green products or the environment.

(iii)*Environmentally-nonpurchasing behavior*

All items in this domain are significantly correlated. Exploratory factor analysis reveals two factors with 42% and 13% of the total variance, respectively. It appears that the latter is a subsidiary of the former, that is, we can treat the nonpurchasing behavior as a one-dimensional measure. The Cronbach's alpha is obtained as 0.8433 with no item needing to be deleted after computing the "alpha if item deleted" statistics. The summative measure of the individuals' responses show mean scores of 35.44 (out of maximum score 50), indicating that the respondents are generally favorable toward undertaking recycling activities or the other environmentally friendly activities.

(iv) *Environmentally-purchasing behavior*

With the exception of item 9, all items in this domain are significantly correlated. Through exploratory factor analysis, three factors arise with 44%, 10%, and 7% of the total variance, respectively. The Cronbach's alpha is obtained as 0.8881. Similarly, when the "alpha if item deleted" statistics are computed, item 9 is deleted and the alpha value is improved. A two-factor structure with 13 variables is obtained; items 1 through 12 form the first factor, named "Pragmatist" with items 13 and 14 forming the second , named "Activist." The two factors account for 58% of total variance and the Cronbach's alpha is achieved as 0.9012. The summative measure of the individuals' responses show mean scores of 38.33 (out of maximum score 50) and 6.41 (out of a maximum 10), respectively. That is, they view the levels of themselves as a pragmatist or an activist being 79% and 64%, respectively. These indicate that most of the respondents in Taiwan are not so highly environmentally friendly before making purchases, which suggests that this issue needs further attention.

Measure Validation and Reliability

A validation test can help to ensure whether a scale accurately reflects the specific concept that the researcher is attempting to measure. In this subsection, the correlations of the measure are examined first; ANOVA and multivariate analysis are used to capture the effects of the input profiling variables.

(i)*Validity test*

In order to check the validity of the measures, the inter-item and total-item correlations are calculated. Regarding the knowledge measure, all inter-item correlations are significant at p-value <0.001 with a mean of 0.4509. The item-total correlations range from 0.5212 to 0.6944, which indicates a high degree of validity. Although the inter-item correlation of item 2 of the cognition measure is not significant (p-value=0.056), the others are significant and the item-total cor-

Table 1. Inter-item correlations and item-total ranges of each aspect

	Inter-item correlations				Item-total range	
Constructs	Mean	Minimum	Maximum	Variance	Minimum	Maximum
Knowledge	0.4509	0.3275	0.7579	0.0096	0.5212	0.6944
Cognition	0.2723	0.0819	0.4924	0.0144	0.2708	0.5470
Initiative	0.5508	0.5508	0.5508	0	0.5508	0.5508
Non-purchasing behavior	0.3560	0.1756	0.6669	0.011	0.4453	0.5948
Pragmatist	0.4525	0.2267	0.7235	0.008	0.5145	0.7422
Activist	0.7612	0.7612	0.7612	0	0.7612	0.7612

relations have an acceptable degree of validity within a range of 0.2708 to 0.5470. Two items in the initiative measure are highly correlated with a correlation of 0.5508 and a p-value<0.001. Regarding the nonpurchasing behaviors, all inter-item correlations are significant at p-value <0.001 with a mean of 0.356. The item-total correlations range from 0.4453 to 0.5948 which indicates a sufficient degree of validity. Finally, the inter-item correlations of the first measure of purchasing behavior, pragmatist, have a mean of 0.4525 and is significantly correlated. The item-total correlations indicate a high degree of validity. The inter-item correlations of the second measure of purchasing behavior, activist, have a mean of 0.7612 indicating a high degree of validity.

Cooperating with the socio-demographics, we have 10 measures (gender, age, marital status, education, occupation, income, knowledge, cognition, initiative, and nonpurchasing behavior) as independent variables and the two purchasing variables, pragmatist and activist, as dependent variables. The correlations are calculated and show that "gender" is not significantly correlated with all measures of environmental concepts, a conclusion which conflicts with those of past studies (Diamantopoulos et al., 2003), that "Females paid more attention than males to the environmental issues" and hypotheses H1-1 – H1-4 are rejected. "Age" and "marital status" are significantly correlated with "nonpurchasing behavior" and the degree of being a "pragmatist" means that those older and married have more willingness to support recycling and environmental protection activities, H2-3, H2-4, H3-3, and H3-4 are accepted. Hypotheses H2-1, H2-2, H3-1 and H3-2 are rejected. "Education" is correlated with "cognition" and "initiative," meaning that higher educated people have higher degrees of attitude toward environmental behaviors. H4-1 and H4-2 are rejected and H4-3 and H4-4 are accepted. "Occupation" is significantly correlated with all environmental measures except "knowledge" and "initiative," meaning that the degree of self reported knowledge and the degree for getting more green information are not significantly different between occupations. H5-1 is rejected; H5-2 is partly accepted; H5-3 and H5-4 are accepted. Different degrees of income present different degrees of knowledge, nonpurchasing behavior and the likelihood of being a pragmatist. People with higher incomes would likely be more understanding and would support environmental issues. H6-1 – H6-2 are accepted. All environmental measures are highly correlated with each other. The results provide more powerful evidence of the usefulness of environmental measures as segmentation variables rather than the socio-demographics as mentioned in the past researches' results.

(ii)*Segmentation variable selection*

Although the socio-demographics variables provide a limited value for profiling the green consumers, they provide easily attainable data, which play important roles in segmentation (Diamantopoulos et al., 2003). The multiple regression analyses are performed to ascertain the joint explanations of socio-demographics and environmental measures independently and simultaneously. The dichotomous and multi-chotomous variables need to be transformed into interval variables first, and k category needs k-1 dummy variables. Six socio-demographic variables have been placed into 20 dichotomous variables and six regressions are obtained as shown in the following table. Small proportions of the variances in all environmental measures, less than 5.7%, are explained by the socio-demographic variables. Furthermore, cooperating with the environmental measures: knowledge, cognition, initiative, and nonpurchasing behavior as the independent variables, it is obtained that an impressive proportion, 49.6%, of the variances in "pragmatist" is explained significantly while 28.5% of the variances in "activist" is explained significantly. This indicates the power of using knowledge, attitudes, and nonpurchasing behavior as independent variables to predict environmentally purchasing behaviors.

To further select useful segmentation variables to reduce complexity, the step-wise multiple regression analysis is performed. The variables: nonpurchasing behavior, cognition, education (undergraduate), and knowledge are selected successively into the regression model with 50% of the variances in "pragmatist" and the variables: nonpurchasing behavior, initiative, and knowledge are selected successively into the regression model with 23.5% of the variances in "activist." Therefore, nonpurchasing behavior, cognition, initiative, education, and knowledge are used as segmentation variables in our following study.

Clustering Analysis

The two-stage clustering analysis was performed in this study. First, the Ward's method with Euclidean distance, which tries to minimize the variance of the differences in attributes within a cluster based on the sum of squares of the difference of the attributes, was used to determine the optimal cluster number. The largest incremental proportion in the agglomerative value was found when the cluster number was reduced form four to three, therefore, using the FCM, we clustered the data into four clusters by the five segmentation variables derived in the last step.

There were 97, 72, 96, and 114 persons in the clusters, respectively. The ANOVA presented the mean values of each variable in different clusters to be significantly different with a p-value<0.001, as shown in Table 4. The multiple comparison procedures of Scheffe were used to show the differences between each cluster. It was found that the mean level of education in cluster 4 was

Table 2. Results of ANOVA

	Adjusted R^2	F-value	p-value
Knowledge	0.023	1.439	0.101
Cognition	0.057	2.132	0.003
Initiative	0	1.004	0.456
Nonpurchasing	0.011	1.215	0.239
Pragmatist	0.029	1.564	0.059
Activist	0	0.998	0.463

Table 3. Part result of agglomeration schedule

	Cluster combined		Coefficient	Stage cluster 1st appears		Next	Incremental proportion
Stage	Cluster 1	Cluster 2		Cluster 1	Cluster 2		
375	1	2	16.63066	367	372	378	0.098697
376	3	83	18.27028	374	363	377	0.09859
377	3	7	22.48993	376	373	378	0.230957
378	1	3	27.80578	375	377	0	0.236366

Table 4. Results of ANOVA and multiple comparisons of different factors and clusters

	Cluster 1	Cluster 2	Cluster 3	Cluster 4	F-value	Scheffe
Education	3.73	4.07	3.95	2.88	161.419	2 , 3> 1>4
Knowledge	30.47	24.85	24.20	24.92	53.383	1>4, 2, 3
Cognitive	20.69	18.74	18.51	17.89	25.892	1>2, 3, 4
Initiative	7.61	6.49	4.54	6.27	167.421	1>2, 4 >3
Non-purchasing	40.16	35.67	31.45	34.62	72.491	1>2, 4 >3

less than that of cluster 1, cluster 3, and cluster 2; the mean level of knowledge of cluster 2 was not significantly larger than that of cluster 3; the mean values of knowledge, cognitive, and initiative of cluster 1 were significantly larger than the others and those in cluster 3 had the least mean values. Therefore, we should describe cluster 1 as a "High motivation group," cluster 2 as a "Medium motivation but high education group," cluster 3 as a "Low motivation group," and cluster 4 as a "Medium motivation but low education group."

Most of the respondents in the "High motivation" group were undergraduates or above. Their self-reported knowledge was high, scoring greater than 21 (out of maximum score 40); high cognitive, scoring greater than 21; high initiative, scoring greater than 7 (out of maximum score 10); medium level of nonpurchasing behavior, scoring from 31 to 40 (out of maximum score 50); medium level of pragmatist and high level of activist. Most of the respondents in the "Medium motivation but high education" group were undergraduates or above. Their self-reported knowledge was low, scoring less than 20; medium level of cognitive, scoring from 16 to 20; medium level of initiative, scoring from 5 to 6; medium level of nonpurchasing behavior, scoring from 31 to 40 (out of maximum score 50); medium level of pragmatist and activist. Most of the respondents in the "Low motivation" group were undergraduates or above. Their self-reported knowledge was low, scoring less than 20; medium level of cognitive, scoring from 16 to 20; medium level of initiative, scoring from 5 to 6; medium level of nonpurchasing behavior, scoring from 31 to 40; lower level of pragmatist and high level of activist. The major differences between cluster 2 and cluster 3 were the distribution degrees of initiative; the nonpurchasing behaviors made the differences in the purchasing behaviors. Finally, most of respondents in the "Medium motivation but low education" group were high-school or lower educated; medium level of cognitive, scoring from 16 to 20; medium level of initiative, scoring from 5 to 6; medium level of nonpurchasing behavior, scoring from 31 to 40; medium level of pragmatist. The major difference

Table 5. Characteristics of each group

		High motivation	Medium motivation but high education	Low motivation	Medium motivation but low education	c^2-value	p-value
Education	High school and lower	31 32.0%		11 11.5%	114 100.0%	251.692	<0.001
	Undergraduate and above	66 68.0%	72 100.0%	85 88.5%			
Knowledge	<=20	3 3.1%	39 54.2%	56 58.3%	58 50.9%	79.204	<0.001
	>=21	94 96.9%	33 45.8%	40 41.7%	56 49.1%		
Cognitive	<=15	1 1.0%	7 9.7%	12 12.5%	17 14.9%	54.885	<0.001
	16-20	46 47.4%	47 65.3%	66 68.8%	85 74.6%		
	21-25	50 51.5%	18 25.0%	18 18.8%	12 10.5%		
Initiative	<=4			43 44.8%	1 .9%	235.706	<0.001
	5-6	15 15.5%	41 56.9%	53 55.2%	71 62.3%		
	>=7	82 84.5%	31 43.1%		42 36.8%		
Non-purchasing	<=30	2 2.1%	2 2.8%	39 40.6%	22 19.3%	121.135	<0.001
	31-40	57 58.8%	64 88.9%	55 57.3%	85 74.6%		
	41-50	38 39.2%	6 8.3%	2 2.1%	7 6.1%		
Pragmatist	<=32	10 10.3%	21 29.2%	54 56.3%	34 29.8%	93.486	<0.001
	33-44	55 56.7%	48 66.7%	40 41.7%	74 64.9%		
	45-55	32 33.0%	3 4.2%	2 2.1%	6 5.3%		
Activist	<=4	2 2.1%	6 8.3%	29 30.2%	16 14.0%	51.412	<0.001
	5-6	36 37.1%	35 48.6%	48 50.0%	50 43.9%		
	>=7	59 60.8%	31 43.1%	19 19.8%	48 42.1%		

between cluster 2 and cluster 4 was the distribution of educated levels as named.

PRICE SETTING FOR THE TARGET CUSTOMERS

In order to demonstrate the proposed methodology, the second part of the questionnaire dealt with about a hybrid electric vehicle (HEV). HEVs typically combine the internal combustion engine of a conventional vehicle with the battery and electric motor of an electric vehicle. Therefore, the optimal price for the target customers can be obtained from the win-win concept.

Utility Function Construction of an HEV

Unlike electric vehicles, the batteries in HEVs do not need to be plugged in to recharge. Instead, they are recharged using regenerative braking or by using an on-board generator. HEVs have lower emissions than conventional vehicles because an electric motor is used with an internal combustion engine, which offsets how often the engine is used and, therefore, reduces fuel use and emissions. A hierarchical utility function of an HEV is constructed from the viewpoint of multiple criteria decision making (MCDM) as follows:

Eight main attributes, several subattributes, and five cars with different conditions but similar

Figure 2. Hierarchical utility function of an HEV

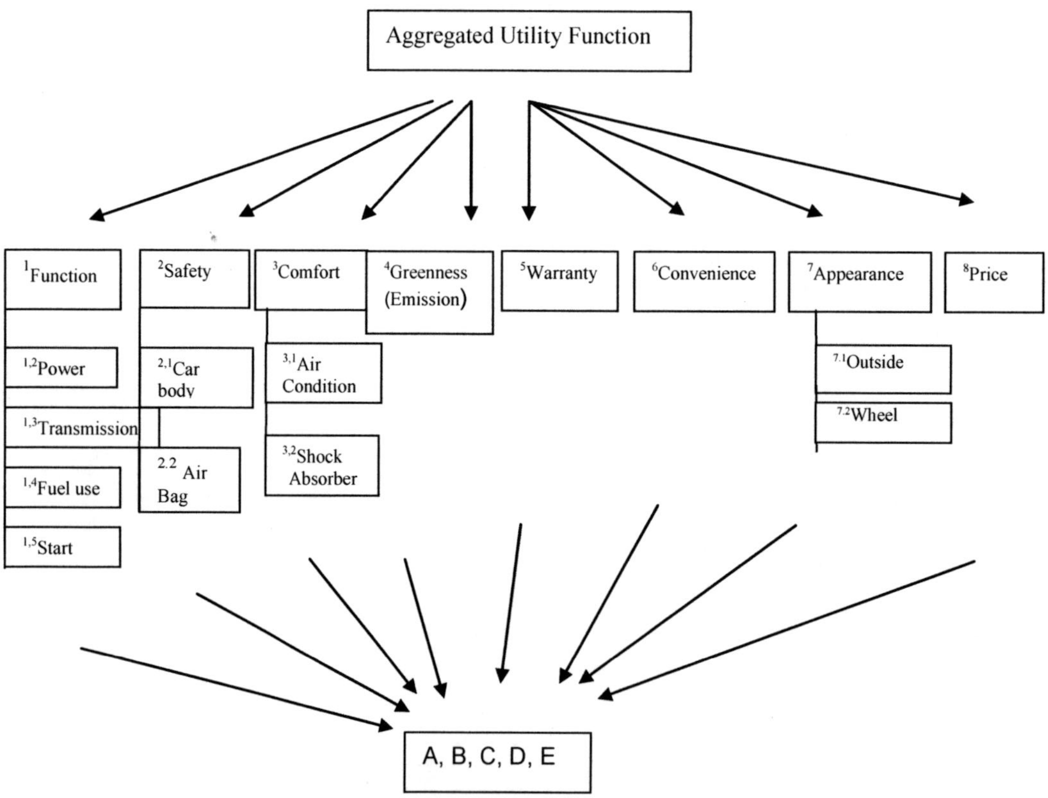

interior equipments were used for comparison. Car A is a 1500CC HEV with 77 horsepower, fuel use- 23.3 kilometers per liter and emission- 2 grams per kilometer. The respondents were asked to choose the satisfactory levels of current specs corresponding to car A and fill in the relative importance of each attribute if the most important one is given as a score of 100. Among them, we have 9 discrete variables and 4 continuous variables. Regarding the collected data, by ANOVA, it is found that the mean degrees of satisfaction of fuel use of cluster 1 and 3 are higher than that of cluster 4; the mean degree of satisfaction of the given emission of CO_2 of cluster 1 is higher than that of cluster 4; but the mean degrees of satisfaction of the current price are not significantly different between the four clusters, the mean degree of satisfaction is about 0.36 meaning that the current price is not acceptable for most of the respondents. Therefore, the exponential utility functions for each attribute can be found by solving δ^i_j, γ^i_j and ρ^i_j of Eq. (2). For example, in our case, the best horse power for a 1500CC car is set as 140, fair being set at 110 with a mean utility of the current spec for cluster 1, 77 hp, obtained as 0.4871. Therefore, by solving the following system:

$$\begin{cases} \delta^1_{1,1} + \gamma^1_{1,1} e^{140\rho^1_{1,1}} = 1 \\ \delta^1_{1,1} + \gamma^1_{1,1} e^{110\rho^1_{1,1}} = 0.5 \\ \delta^1_{1,1} + \gamma^1_{1,1} e^{77\rho^1_{1,1}} = 0.4871 \end{cases}, \qquad (7)$$

we have the utility function for the sub attribute, horsepower, of function as

$$u^1_{1,1}(x_{1,1}) = 0.4869 + 1.912 \times 10^{-8} e^{0.1222 x_{1,1}}, x_{1,1} \in [77,140] \qquad (8)$$

it is a convex increasing function of horsepower. Furthermore, from the three levels of car body material, the utility of the current spec is the lowest one from the viewpoint of safety and we have the mean utility being 0.3. The utility of the second level is set as 0.5 and the utility of the highest level is set as 1, and we have

$$u^1_{2,1}(x_{2,1}) = y_{2,1,1} + 0.5 y_{2,1,2} + 0.3 y_{2,1,3},$$

$$y_{2,1,1} + y_{2,1,2} + y_{2,1,3} = 1, y_{2,1,k} \in \{0,1\}, k = 1,...,3. \qquad (9)$$

The aggregated weights W_{ij} are determined by solving the EGP models. As we have mentioned, larger λ represents that more importance is given to the objective that minimizes the sum of individual disagreement, equal weights of maximum average agreement solution, and the most balanced solution are chosen in this study, that is, $\lambda = 0.5$. After input of the derived preference w^i_{jn} of attribute j of the nth member of cluster i, the aggregated weights can be obtained by using the software LINGO. For example, the weights of subattributes of "Function" of cluster 1 are obtained as 0.2405, 0.3167, 0.2658 and 0.2532; the weights of attributes are 0.1267, 0.1264, 0.1265, 0.1223, 0.123, 0.1231, 0.12382 and 0.1283, respectively. Therefore, we have the aggregated utility function of customers in cluster 1 as shown in Equation 10.

On the other hand, the supplier provided us with the lowest price that he/she is willing to sell to be about NTS 950000, the lowest price that he/she is not willing to sell is about NTS 900000, therefore, we have the utility function for the supplier as:

$$U_s(z) = 1.002 - 14.2391 e^{-0.1382 z}, \qquad (11)$$

where z denotes the profit of the supplier, it can be represented as the price minus a linear combination of costs of different specifications, for example, it costs about NTS 425 to improve by one additional horsepower; it costs NTS 160000, 120000 and 90000 for levels 1, 2, and 3 of different car body materials, therefore, we have what is illustrated in Box 2 (12).

Equation 10.

$$U_c^1(\mathbf{x},\mathbf{y}) = 0.11197 + 5.82\times10^{-10} e^{0.1222x_{1,1}} + 0.01995y_{1,2,1} + 0.02005y_{1,2,2} + 0.04011y_{1,2,3} - 10166.22e^{-0.8292x_{1,3}} + 0.01603y_{1,4,1} + 0.01699y_{1,4,2} + 0.0205y_{1,4,3} + 0.03207y_{1,4,4} + 0.02207y_{2,1,1} + 0.03078y_{2,1,2} + 0.06153y_{2,1,3} + 0y_{2,2,1} + 0.03242y_{2,2,2} + 0.04478y_{2,2,3} + 0y_{3,1,1} + 0.02657y_{3,1,2} + 0.03767y_{3,1,3} + 0.04464y_{3,2,1} + 0.07339y_{3,2,2} - 5.175\times10^{-12} e^{11.1562x_4} + 0.0437e^{0.0577x_5} + 0.06154y_{6,1} + 0.07645y_{6,2} + 0.1231y_{6,3} + 0.03167y_{7,1,1} + 0.04278y_{7,1,2} + 0.06334y_{7,1,3} + 0.03024y_{7,2,1} + 0.03772y_{7,2,2} + 0.06047y_{7,2,3} + 2.5551e^{-0.06918x_8}.$$

Box 2. Equation 12

$$z = x_8 - 3.89 - 18 - 0.04248(x_{1,1} - 77) - 12.6y_{1,2,1} - 13.3y_{1,2,2} - 14.7y_{1,2,3} - (3.08 - \frac{x_{1,3} - 15.6}{0.1}\times 0.4) - 0.6y_{1,4,1} - 0.7y_{1,4,2} - 1.2y_{1,4,3} - 1.3y_{1,4,4} - 16y_{2,1,1} - 12y_{2,1,2} - 9y_{2,1,3} - 0y_{2,2,1} - 4.5y_{2,2,1} - 6y_{2,2,3} - 1.2y_{3,1,1} - 1.5y_{3,1,2} - 1.8y_{3,1,3} - 1y_{3,2,1} - 1.6y_{3,2,2} - 0.6\times\frac{(x_4 - 1.64)}{0.1} - 0.00354\times(x_5 - 6) - 4.5y_{6,1} - 6y_{6,2} - 9y_{6,3} - 1.2y_{7,2,1} - 1.8y_{7,2,2} - 2y_{7,2,3}.$$

Bi-Objective Model Construction of an HEV

In cooperating with the required greenness $b_{greenness}$ of the customers, we have the bi-objective nonlinear integer problem of cluster 1 as model (13). To meet the required greenness of customers, a constraint of the inverse function is transformed as the first constraint in the model and the fuel use is constrained by the weights of the car body, we use the big-M technique to represent the relationship between them.

Max Eq. (10)

Max Eq. (11)

Please refer to Box 3 for model (13).

Optimal Solutions with Sensitivity Analysis

By introducing the weights of the objectives, we can obtain the noninferior solution set. Because of the different scales of the two objectives, they must be transformed into the same scale before weighting. For example, if the greenness is required as 0.6 and we have the weighted model as shown in Box 4.

Different values of α_1 will generate different optimal solutions; if we systematically change the value of α_1, we can obtain the noninferior solution set of the problem. Furthermore, since the feasible region of model (14) is determined dependently on the required greenness, ranges of utility functions of both customers and suppliers are changed simultaneously, sensitivity analysis of the greenness and weights is performed. From the view point of a win-win concept, when the

Box 3. Model 13

$$
\begin{aligned}
s.t.\ & (u_4^1)^{-1}(b_{greenness}) - x_4 \geq 0; \\
& \text{Eq.(12)}; \\
& 77 - x_{1,1} \leq 0; \\
& y_{1,2,1} + y_{1,2,2} + y_{1,2,3} = 1; \quad 15.6 - x_{1,3} \leq 0; \\
& y_{1,4,1} + y_{1,4,2} + y_{1,4,3} + y_{1,4,4} = 1; \quad y_{2,1,1} + y_{2,1,2} + y_{2,1,3} = 1; y_{2,2,1} + y_{2,2,2} + y_{2,2,3} = 1; \\
& x_{1,3} - 20 \leq My_{2,1,1}; x_{1,3} - 18 \leq My_{2,1,2} + My_{2,1,1}; 20 - x_{13} \leq My_{2,1,2} + My_{2,1,3}; 18 - x_{1,3} \leq My_{2,1,3}; \\
& y_{3,1,1} + y_{3,1,2} + y_{3,1,3} = 1; \quad y_{3,2,1} + y_{3,2,2} = 1; \\
& 1.64 - x_4 \leq 0; \quad x_5 \in \{6,..,25\}; \quad y_{6,1} + y_{6,2} + y_{6,3} = 1; \quad y_{7,1,1} + y_{7,1,2} + y_{7,1,3} = 1; \\
& y_{7,2,1} + y_{7,2,2} + y_{7,2,3} - 1; \quad 50 - x_8 \leq 0; \\
& x_{1,1} - 140 \leq 0; x_{1,3} - 23.3 \leq 0; x_4 - 2.11 \leq 0; x_8 - 118 \leq 0; \\
& y_{1,2,1} = 1, y_{i,j,k} \in \{0,1\}, \forall i,j,k.
\end{aligned}
$$

Box 4. Model 14

$$
\text{Max } \alpha_1\left(\frac{\text{Equ.(10)} - 0.38686}{0.83144 - 0.38686}\right) + (1 - \alpha_1)\left(\frac{\text{Equ.(11)} - 0}{0.99989}\right)
$$

$$
\begin{aligned}
s.t.\ & 1.941 - x_4 \geq 0; \\
& \text{Eq.(12)}; \\
& 77 - x_{1,1} \leq 0; \\
& y_{1,2,1} + y_{1,2,2} + y_{1,2,3} = 1; \quad 15.6 - x_{1,3} \leq 0; \\
& y_{1,4,1} + y_{1,4,2} + y_{1,4,3} + y_{1,4,4} = 1; \quad y_{2,1,1} + y_{2,1,2} + y_{2,1,3} = 1; y_{2,2,1} + y_{2,2,2} + y_{2,2,3} = 1; \\
& x_{1,3} - 20 \leq My_{2,1,1}; x_{1,3} - 18 \leq My_{2,1,2} + My_{2,1,1}; 20 - x_{13} \leq My_{2,1,2} + My_{2,1,3}; 18 - x_{1,3} \leq My_{2,1,3}; \\
& y_{3,1,1} + y_{3,1,2} + y_{3,1,3} = 1; \quad y_{3,2,1} + y_{3,2,2} = 1; \\
& 1.64 - x_4 \leq 0; \quad x_5 \in \{6,..,25\}; \quad y_{6,1} + y_{6,2} + y_{6,3} = 1; \quad y_{7,1,1} + y_{7,1,2} + y_{7,1,3} = 1; \\
& y_{7,2,1} + y_{7,2,2} + y_{7,2,3} = 1; \quad 50 - x_8 \leq 0; \\
& x_{1,1} - 140 \leq 0; x_{1,3} - 23.3 \leq 0; x_4 - 2.11 \leq 0; x_8 - 118 \leq 0; \\
& y_{1,2,1} = 1, y_{i,j,k} \in \{0,1\}, \forall i,j,k.
\end{aligned}
$$

weight of the customer's utility is greater than 0, in order for suppliers to sell this car at the current price, they must improve the existing spec to the higher level to satisfy the customer; otherwise, the customers' utility is relatively low and the willingness to purchase the car is low too. Secondly, if the weight of customers is placed to be sufficiently high, for example, larger than 0.93 in cluster 1, the price has to be reduced with the highest mix of specifications.

Optimal Price Setting and The Target Customer Identification

Regarding our case, from the viewpoint of the supplier, the current specifications are the lowest power, the highest fuel use, continuous variable transmission system , the lowest level of car body material with respect to safety, the highest level of air bags, the highest level of air conditioner, the lower level of shock absorber, the least emission of CO_2, 20 service centers in Taiwan, the second level of warranty duration, the most preferred look, the second level of wheel size, and the price at NTS 1.18 million; the utilities of customers are 0.5973, 0.5525, 0.5432, and 0.5490 with respect to each cluster and the supplier gains a utility of 0.9864. Different weights will derive different optimal solutions as shown in Table 6. When the weight of the customers is chosen as 0.2, the weight of the supplier is 0.8, that is, less importance is give to the satisfaction of customers. The optimal price for cluster 1 is about NTS 1160000, with the supplier gaining about NTS 476000. Customers are less satisfied, only 59.74% but suppliers are more satisfied; therefore, the willingness to pay for this car should be lower. Increasing the weight of customers will cause the lower optimal price. If the weight of customers is 0.8, the optimal price will be reduced as the lowest acceptable supplier price, and the satisfaction of customers will be increased.

From the win-win concept, if equal weights are selected, from the optimal prices of each cluster shown in Table 6, the highest price is obtained from cluster 2; therefore, those in cluster 2 will be referred to as the target customers in our study. They are undergraduates with medium motivation but high education. Furthermore, from the viewpoint of the objective of green marketing, that is, "to develop products that balance consumers' needs for quality, performance, affordable pricing, and convenience with minimal impact on the environment," customers usually feel important when they have the ability to negotiate their own price. That feeling of control contributes to their feelings about the deal they are getting. Therefore, we suggest that the posting price can be set as 970000 NT dollars, which is a little higher than the optimal price of our target customers. Rooms for the negotiated price for each cluster are NTS 11427, 6314, 8378, and 9804, respectively.

Promotion Strategies

For gaining sales and more profit, different promotion strategies can be set for different clusters of customers by ranking the weights of the attributes. For example, the largest weight

Table 6. Optimal prices and profits of different weights for each cluster

Weights	(customers, suppliers)					
	(0.2, 0.8)		(0.5, 0.5)		(0.8, 0.2)	
Unit: 10000 NTD (utility)	Optimal prices (utility of customers)	Profits (utility of supplier)	Optimal prices (utility of customers)	Profits (utility of supplier)	Optimal prices (utility of customers)	Profits (utility of supplier)
Cluster 1	115.8847 (0.5974)	47.5947 (0.9814)	95.85724 (0.6)	27.56724 (0.6866)	87.49094 (0.6026)	19.2 (0)
Cluster 2	112.25 (0.5535)	43.96003 (0.9686)	96.36855 (0.5582)	28.67855 (0.7081)	87.49094 (0.5630)	19.2 (0)
Cluster 3	113.4562 (0.5437)	45.16624 (0.9736)	96.16215 (0.5477)	27.87215 (0.6996)	87.49094 (0.5517)	19.2 (0)
Cluster 4	114.4767 (0.5492)	46.18644 (0.9771)	96.01955 (0.5538)	27.72955 (0.6936)	87.49094 (0.5550)	19.2 (0)

Table 7. The ranking of weights of different clusters

	Function	Safety	Comfort	Greenness	Convenience	Warranty	Appearance	Price
Cluster 1	2	4	3	8	7	6	5	1
Cluster 2	3	1	4	8	7	5	6	2
Cluster 3	3	1	4	8	7	5	6	2
Cluster 4	2	1	3	8	7	6	5	4

Table 8. Points for promotion of different clusters

Cluster 1	1. Price can be negotiated. 2. Hybrid system net power can reach 110hp. 3. Comfortable 4. Safety: Global Outstanding Assessment, the most top one safety design
Cluster 2	1. Safety: Global Outstanding Assessment, the most top one safety design 2. Price can be negotiated. 3. High performance of fuel use, then save money 4. Comfortable
Cluster 3	1. Safety: Global Outstanding Assessment, the most top one safety design 2. Price can be negotiated. 3. High performance of fuel use then save money 4. Comfortable
Cluster 4	1. Safety: Global Outstanding Assessment, the most top one safety design 2. High performance of fuel use then save money 3. Comfortable 4. Price can be negotiated.

of attributes given by customers of cluster 1 is "Price," and successive ones are "Function" and "Comfort" as shown in Table 7.

That is, customers of cluster 1 are mostly concerned about the price at which they can purchase such a car; therefore, we can first inform them that the price is negotiable. Secondly, customers are also concerned about the "Function" of this car, especially the horsepower. Unfortunately, it is only 77 hps, so the point for promotion will focus on the limit of the net power, which is as large as a general one. Regarding "Comfort," and "Safety," to increase fuel use, the car body is the lightest, which makes it a lower utility from the viewpoint of safety, so the supplier needs to provide arguments for safety. Different strategies, as shown in Table 8, need to be proposed for different clusters to make the largest profit.

CONCLUSION

In this chapter, we first pointed out the different characteristics of green marketing and reviewed the existing researches for profiling green customers. Due to the country-specific results, we used a list of questionnaires to investigate the suitable segmentation variables for clustering analysis. After clustering the customers, a bi-objective nonlinear integer problem was constructed using MAUT and EGP models, and many types of utility functions were obtained from groups of customers which generated different optimal prices. By comparing the cluster centers, various types of customers can be classified into clusters and charged different prices. Therefore, based on this study, a supplier can provide active services and differential promotion strategies to different kinds of customers to create the highest sales. Target customers establish the foundation of marketing, and thus the right goods can be sold to the right people in the right way.

FUTURE RESEARCH DIRECTIONS

In many real situations, it is not appropriate to reflect people's judgments with quantitative terms, and ambiguity results due to differences in the meanings and interpretations that people may attach to words. They use linguistic terms, such as "good" or "very good" to reflect their preferences. Therefore, further study can be focused on this kind of uncertainty; the concept of fuzzy set theory can be incorporated to solve the question by converting a linguistic term into a fuzzy number. Then, the most flexible and noninferior solution set can be found. Thus, this study can help the producers to effectively target on different green consumers by market segmentation analysis to promote marketing strategies and sell green products.

ACKNOWLEDGMENT

The author acknowledges the financial support from National Science Council, ROC with project number NSC 95-2221-E-159-019.

REFERENCES

Barry, M.J.A., & Linoff, G.S. (1997). *Data mining technique for marketing, sale, and customer support.* Wiley Computer.

Bazaraa, M.S., & Shetty, C.M. (1990). *Nonlinear programming, theory and algorithms.* John Wiely & Sons.

Bezdek, J.C. (1973). *Fuzzy mathematics in pattern classification.* Unpublished doctoral dissertation, Cornell University.

Bohlen, G.M., Schlegelmilch, B.B., & Diamantopoulos, A. (1993a). Consumer perceptions of the environmental impact of an industrial service. *Marketing Intelligence & Planning, 11*(1), 37-48.

Bohlen, G.M., Schlegelmilch, B.B., & Diamantopoulos, A. (1993b). Measuring ecological concern: A multi-construct perspective. *Journal of Marketing Management*, 415-430.

Borcherding, K., Eppel, T., & von Winterfeldt, D. (1991). Comparison on weighting judgments in multiattribute utility measurement. *Management Science, 37*(12), 1603-1619.

Bottomley, P.A., & Doyle, J.D. (2001). A comparison of three weight elicitation methods: Good, better and best. *Omega, 29*, 553-560.

van Calker, K.J., Berentsen, P.B.M., Romero, C., Giesen, G.W.J., & Huirne, R.B.M. (2006). Development and application of a multi-attribute sustainability function for Dutch dairy farming systems. *Ecological Economics, 57*, 640-658.

Canbolat, Y.B., Chelst, K., & Garg, N. (2007). Combining decision tree and MAUT for selecting a country for a global manufacturing facility. *Omega, 35*(3), 312-325.

Clemen, R.T. (1991). *Making hard decisions: An introduction to decision analysis.* Boston: PWS-Kent Publishing Company.

Diamantopoulos, A., Schlegelmilch, B.B., Sinkovics, R.R., & Bohlen, G.M. (2003). Can socio-demographics still play a role in profiling green consumers? A review of the evidence and an empirical investigation. *Journal of Business Research, 56*(6), 465-480.

Doyle, J.R., Green, R.H., & Bottomley, P.A. (1997, April). Judging relative importance: Direct rating and point allocation are not equivalent. *Organizational Behavior and Human Decision Processes, 70*(1), 65-72.

González-Pachón, J., & Romero, C. (1999). Distance-based consensus methods: A goal programming approach. *Omega, 27,* 341-347.

Green, P.E., Tull, D.S., & Albaum, G. (1993). *Research for marketing decisions* (5th ed.). Prentice Hall.

Groth, R. (1999). *Data mining: Building competitive advantage.* Prentice Hall.

Harte, J.M., & Koele, P. (1995, October). A comparison of different methods for the elicitation of attribute weights: Structural modeling, process tracing, and self-reports. *Organizational Behavior and Human Decision Processes, 64*(1), 49-64.

Hillier, F.S., & Lieberman, G.J. (2005). *Introduction to operations research* (8th ed.). McGraw-Hill.

Jaccard, J., Brinberg, D., & Ackerman, L.J. (1986). Assessing attribute importance: A comparison of six methods. *Journal of Consumer Research, 12*(4), 463-468.

Keeny & Raiffa. (1976). *Decision with multiple objectives: Preferences and value tradeoffs.* New York: John Wiley.

Klir, G.J. (1988). *Fuzzy sets, uncertainty and information.* Prentice Hall.

Kolter, P. (1997). *Marketing management: Analysis, planning and control* (9th ed.). NJ: Prentice Hall.

Langabeer, J., & Rose, J. (2001). *Creating demand driven supply chains.* Oxford: Chandos Publishing.

Linares, P., & Romero, C. (2002). Aggregation of preferences in an environmental economics context: A goal-programming approach. *Omega, 30,* 89-95.

Lummus, R.R., & Vokurka, R.J. (1999). Managing the demand chain through managing the information flow: Capturing "moment of information." *Production and Inventory Management Journal, 1,* 16-20.

Malakooti, B., & Subramanian, S. (1999). Generalized polynomial decomposable multiple utility functions for ranking and rating multiple criteria discrete. *Applied Mathematics and Computation, 106,* 69-102.

Meng, Z., Hu, Q., Dang, C., & Yang, X. (2004). An objective penalty function method for nonlinear programming. *Applied Mathematics Letters, 17,* 683-689.

Nesterov, Y. (1997). Interior-point methods: An old and new approach to linear programming. *Mathematical Programming, 79,* 285-297.

Ottman, J.A. (1998). *Green marketing: Opportunity for innovation* **(2nd ed.).** Lincolnwood, IL: NTC Business Books.

Padberg, M. (2000). Approximating separable functions via mixed zero-one programs. *Operations Research Letters, 27,* 1-5.

Potra, F.A., & Wright, S.J. (2000). Interior-point methods. *Journal of Computational and Applied Mathematics, 24,* 282-302.

Roberts, J. A. (1996). Green consumers in 1990s: Profile and implications for advertising. *Journal of Business Research, 36,* 217-231.

Schlegelmilch, B.B., Bohlen, G.M., & Diamantopoulos, A. (1996). The link between green purchasing decisions and measures of environmental consciousness. *European Journal of Marketing, 30*(5), 35-55.

Schoemaker, P.J.H., Waid, C., & Carter, W.C. (1982). An experimental comparison of different approaches to determining weights in additive utility models. *Management Science, Linthicum, 28*(2), 182-196.

Srivastava, J., Connolly, T., & Beach, L.R. (1995, July). Do rank suffice? A comparison of alternative weighting approaches in value elicitation. *Organizational Behavior and Human Decision Process, 63*(1), 112-116.

Stewart, T.J. (1996). Robustness of additive value function methods in MCDM. *Journal of Multi-Criteria Decision Analysis, 5*(4), 301-310.

Straughan, R.D., & Roberts, J.A. (1999). Environmental segmentation alternatives: A look at green consumer behavior in the new millennium. *The Journal of Consumer Marketing, 16*(6), 558-575.

Tamura, S., Higuchi, K., & Tanaka, K. (1971). Pattern classification based on fuzzy relations. *IEEE Trans. SMC, 1*, 61-66.

Tanner, C., & Kast, S.W. (2003, October). Promoting sustainable consumption: Determinants of green purchases by Swiss consumers. *Psychology & Marketing, 20*(10), 883-902.

Tilikidou, I. (2007). The effect of knowledge and attitudes upon Greeks' pro-environmental purchasing behaviour. *Corporate Social Responsibility and Environmental Management, 14***(3), 121-134.**

Tilikidou, I., & Delistavrou, A. (2001). Utilization of selected demographics and psychographics in recycling behavior understanding: A focus on materialism. *Greener Management International, 34*, 75-93.

Walters, D., & Rainbird, M. (2004). The demand chain as an integral component of the value chain. *The journal of Consumer Marketing, 21*(7), 465-475.

Wang, M.L., & Wang, H.F. (2005). Web mining system for mobile-phone marketing. In K. Voges & K.L. Nige (Eds.), *Business applications and computational intelligence* (pp.113-129). Hershey, PA: Idea Group Publishing.

Zhou, Z., & Shi, Y. (1997). An ODE method of solving nonlinear programming. *Computers & Mathematics with Applications, 34*(1), 97-102.

Zhu, Z. (2005). A feasible interior-point algorithm for nonconvex nonlinear programming. *Applied Mathematics and Computation, 163*, 745-753.

ADDITIONAL READING

Allnoch, A. (1997). Demand-chain software allows wholesale distributor to compete more effectively. *IIE Solutions, 29*(9), 60-66.

Baugh, K., Byrnes, B., Jones, C., & Rahimzadeh, M. (1995). Green pricing: Removing the guesswork? *Public Utilities Fortnightly, 133*(15), 26-29.

Bordley, R.F., & Kirkwood, C.W. (2004). Multiattribute preference analysis with performance targets. *Operations Research, 52*(6), 826-835.

Christopher, M. (1992). *Logistics: The strategic issues.* Chapman and Hall.

Cooper, M.C., Lambert, D.M., & Pugh, J.D. (1997). Supply chain management: More than a new name for logistics. *The International Journal of Logistics Management, 8*(1), 1-14.

Cristina da Costa, M., Deliza, R., Reenthal, A., Hedderley D., & Frewer, L. (2000). Non conventional technologies and impact on consumer behavior. *Trends in Food Science & Technology, 11*, 188-193.

Fotopoulos, C., & Krystallis, A. (2002). Purchasing motives and profile of the Greek organic consumer: A countrywide survey. *British Food Journal, 104*,730-765.

Gadiesh, O., & Gilbert, J.L. (1998). How to map your industry's profit pool. *Harvard Business Review, 76*(3), 149-162.

Hagel, J., III. (2002, October). Leveraged growth: Expanding sales without sacrificing profits. *Harvard Business Review*, 68-77.

Hagel, J., III, & Singer, M. (1999, March-April). Unbundling the corporation. *Harvard Business Review*, 133-141.

Hammer, M. (2001). *The agenda.* New York: Crown Publishing Group.

Hsu, H. (2006). An empirical study of Web site quality, customer value, and customer satisfaction based on e-shop. *The Business Review, 5*(1), 190-193.

Jaccard, J., Brinberg, D., & Ackerman, L.J. (1986). Assessing attribute importance: A comparison of six methods. *Journal of Consumer Research, 12*(4), 463-468.

Jain, S.K., & Kaur, G. (2004). Green marketing: An attitudinal and behavioural analysis of Indian consumers. *Global Business Review, 5*(2), 187-205.

Kainuma, Y., & Tawara, N. (2006). A multiple attribute utility theory approach to lean and green supply chain management. *International Journal of Production Economics, 101*, 99-108.

Katrin, E., Thomas, E., & Von Winterfeldt, D. (1991). Comparison of weighting judgments in multiattribute utility. *Management Science, 37*(12), 1603-1618.

Langabeer, J., & Rose, J. (2001). *Creating demand driven supply* chains. Oxford: Chandos Publishing.

Lockie, S., Lyons, K., Lawrence, G., & Grice, J. (2004). Choosing organics: A path analysis of factors underlying the selection of organic food among Australian customers. *Appetite, 43*, 135-146.

Magretta, J. (2002). Why business models matter. *Harvard Business Review, 80*, 86-92.

Malakooti, B., & Subramanian, S. (1999). Generalized polynomial decomposable multiple attribute utility functions for ranking and rating multiple criteria discrete alternatives. *Applied Mathematics and Computation, 106*, 69-102.

Martinez, S., & Stewart, H. (2003). From supply push to demand pull: Agribusiness strategies for today's consumers. *Amber Waves, 1*(5), 22-29.

Mascarenhas, O.A., Kesavan, R., & Bernacchi, M. (2004). Customer value-chain involvement for co-creating customer delight. *The Journal of Consumer Marketing, 21*(7), 486-496.

McDonald, S., & Oates, C.O. (2006). Sustainability: Consumer perceptions and marketing strategies. *Business Strategy and the Environment, 15*, 157-170.

Moxnes, E. (2004). Estimating customer utility of energy efficiency standards for refrigerators. *Journal of Economic Psychology, 25*, 707-724.

Normann, R. (2001). *Refraining business.* Chichester: John Wiley.

Porter, M. (1985). *Competitive strategy.* New York: The Free Press.

Chapter IX
Application of Fuzzy Analytic Network Process and Fuzzy TOPSIS to the Undesirable Location Selection Problem

Semih Önüt
Yildiz Technical University, Turkey

Selin Soner Kara
Yildiz Technical University, Turkey

Derya Tekin
Yildiz Technical University, Turkey

ABSTRACT

In this chapter, a combined fuzzy multiple criteria decision making (MCDM) methodology for supporting the undesirable location selection process is presented. The undesirable location selection process is formulated by using the fuzzy analytic network process (FANP), one of MCDM methods, which is used to evaluate the most suitable alternatives of undesirable facility locations. Then, the fuzzy TOPSIS (technique for order performance by similarity to ideal solution) is used to rank competing locations in terms of overall performances. Since different alternatives and various quantitative, qualitative, tangible, and intangible criteria should be considered in the selection process, fuzzy MCDM methods have been found to be a useful approach to solve this kind of location selection problems including vagueness and imprecision in the human judgments.

Copyright © 2009, IGI Global, distributing in print or electronic forms without written permission of IGI Global is prohibited.

INTRODUCTION

The term facility involves that a particular establishment offers some kind of service to a certain group of customers. Hence, in the context of facility location, it can be argued that all facilities are necessary because of the service they provide. A facility location problem deals with the evaluation of the different kinds of points for taking into account different criteria. As technology and industrialization make our lives easier by offering new services or products, some of the facilities needed to produce these services or products may also create some byproducts that people do not find desirable. If a facility does not have any significant detrimental effects, it is usually referred to as a desirable facility; otherwise it is called an undesirable facility. For example, police stations, shopping centers, hospitals, or educational centers are facilities that people like nearby and all of these facilities are desirable to the nearby inhabitants. However, on the other hand, there are some other facilities such as nuclear reactors, garbage dump locations, chemical plants, power plants, landfills, military installations, and mega-airports that inhabitants prefer to be as far as possible and these kinds of facilities are undesirable for the surrounding population. Noxious and obnoxious facilities can be simply regarded as undesirable facilities. While noxious facilities, like nuclear reactors, involve a potential risk to public health, obnoxious facilities are less of a health risk. Despite these undesirable facilities being necessary to the community, the location of such facilities might cause a certain disagreement in the community. Such disagreement has become an opposition of people toward the installation of undesirable facilities close to them. However, most facilities cannot be considered as totally undesirable. Even if it creates some undesirable products, every facility is built to meet some need for people to maintain some standard of living. These kinds of facilities might be named as semidesirable, as those that provide valuable services to the community but at the same time cause inconveniences to the neighboring areas. For example, if a train station, an airport, or any other noisy facility is located too far from populated areas, the transportation costs to/from this semidesirable facility become heavy; on the other hand, if it is too close to populated areas, the noise and traffic density may cause important problems (Colebrook & Sicilia, 2007; Erkut & Neuman, 1989).

In recent years, environmental regulations and public opposition have increasingly forced new landfills to be allocated away from urban areas. The extra distance to these landfills has encouraged the development of regular solid waste storage locations and solid waste transfer stations. The obnoxious externalities of these storage and transfer locations (odor, noise, traffic, unsightliness) have increased public opposition. Selection of the appropriate undesirable facility location is a complex problem and requires an extensive evaluation process considering with the requirements of municipal, governmental, environmental regulations, and so forth. Inappropriate and inefficient selection causes several problems, such as social opposition, environmental problems, cost increases, and so forth. Selecting the undesirable facility locations is also one of the most complicated problems for local governments because of the availability of several potential locations for a certain type of facility in general. The determination and evaluation of positive and negative characteristics of one location relative to others is a difficult task. The increase in the popularity of using environmental design criteria in municipal planning has brought about the need to fully identify the principles to determine the best location of this kind of undesirable facilities. This environmental management issue has received considerable attention because of its applications in urban and rural infrastructure planning, industrial development planning as well as health, housing, transportation, and agricultural schemes. The planning and design of a regional waste management system involves selection of treatment and disposal facilities, allocation of wastes and waste residues from generator to the treatment and disposal locations, and selection of the transportation routes (Yeşilnacar & Cetin, 2005). Furthermore many potential criteria, such as proximity to residential area, distance from the main roads, investment costs, climate, land slope, and so forth, must be considered in the selection procedure of an undesirable facility location. Therefore, undesirable facility location selection can be viewed as a multiple criteria decision making (MCDM) problem. MCDM is a well known method of the decision making procedure.

Many researchers have studied to determine the suitable location and the transportation routes in waste management using different mathematical and heuristic models. To deal with decision making problems that involve both quantitative and qualitative considerations, MCDM can be used because it provides a systematic procedure to help decision makers identify suitable alternatives under uncertainty. In general, decision making processes where multiple conflicting criteria involved can be classified into two types: multiple objective decision making (MODM) methods, which have an infinite number of feasible alternatives and multiple attribute decision making (MADM) methods, which have a finite set of alternatives (Cheng, Chan, & Huang, 2002). This chapter focuses on the latter type of problem. The main distinction between the two groups of methods is based on the number of alternatives under evaluation. These methods share common characteristics of conflict among criteria, incomparable units, and difficulties in selection of alternatives. In MODM, the alternatives are not predetermined, but instead a set of objective functions is optimized subject to a set of constraints (Pohekar & Ramachandran, 2004). The most satisfactory and efficient solution is sought. In MADM, a small of alternatives are to be evaluated against a set of attributes which are often hard to quantify. Hence, these two methodologies can be effectively used in the different waste management problems according to the number of the selection alternatives. In municipal planning, planners may not have complete access to explicit information on some issues. A decision maker is required to choose a number of quantifiable or nonquantifiable and multiple criteria. Hence, performing different analysis and evaluations may not be feasible. Since objectives are usually conflicting, the solution is highly dependent on the preferences of decision makers. In most cases, different groups of decision makers are involved in the process. This is where MCDM can be used to help decision makers minimize conflicts among various considerations in the decision making process. It presupposes a balanced treatment of too many details and too little information. Hence, it has been widely used for urban planning in the last years.

There are a number of methods in each of the above mentioned categories. Multiple attribute utility methods, priority based outranking methods, distance based methods, interactive methods, and hybrid methods are also applied to different waste management problems. Each method has its own characteristics. Tuzkaya, Onut, Tuzkaya, and Gulsun (2008) presented comprehensive literature review about used methods related to the undesirable location selection problem. According to the authors, multiple objective decision making methods have been used in a number of studies. Some of them are presented as follows. Erkut and Neuman (1992) pointed out the multiple objective nature of the problem. In this study, three objectives are considered as to minimize total costs, to minimize total opposition to nuisances and to maximize equity. Similar to these objectives, generally, most common objectives considered are the minimization of cost, the maximization distance between facilities and customers and the equitable treatment of customers, that is, the equitable distribution of the disutility imposed by the facilities (Avella et al., 1998). Stowers and Palekar (1993) developed a model that selects the location of treatment facility for a single type of hazardous material. They assumed that the facility can be located anywhere in the region. On the other hand, as an important weakness of this study, only a few candidate sites in practice will be available because of the landuse pattern of the region. In 1998, Giannikos proposed a multiple objective model for locating disposal or treatment facilities and transporting hazardous waste along the links of a transportation network. In this study goal programming is used for the satisfaction of the multiple objectives. Nema and Gupta (1999) proposed an improved formulation based on multi-objective integer programming approach to arrive at the optimal configuration of regional hazardous waste management system. They use a composite objective function and purpose two constraints. But, as a weakness, they were not able to implement these constraints in their proposed mathematical model. In another work, Chang and Wei (2000) presented a model to optimize siting aspects in the solid waste collection network using a fuzzy multi objective nonlinear integer programming. In 2004, Rakas, Teodorovic, and Kim developed a multiple objective programming model utilizing from fuzzy linear programming for determining undesirable facility locations. Al-Jarrah and Abu-Qdais (2006) focused the problem of siting a new landfill using an intelligent system based on fuzzy inference.

Some examples related with the multi objective optimization applications in the undesirable location selection literature were summarized above. Due to the complexity of undesirable location selection problems, multi objective approaches are often used in the literature. However, the process of obtaining solution through this method is complex, because there are several objectives that are conflicting. In MODM, the decision maker's objective, such as optimal utilization of resources, remain explicit and are assigned weights reflecting their relative importance (Kahraman, Cevik, Ates, & Gulbay, 2007b). Contrary to single objective optimization, the solution of a multi objective problem is not unique. The notion of optimality cannot be used in multi objective problems generally and the optimal value of all the objectives cannot be achieved simultaneously, because a solution that maximizes/minimizes one objective will not, in general, maximize/minimize any other objective due to their conflicting nature. The notion of optimality is replaced by the concept of nondominance and pareto optimal. In general, there can be an infinite number of efficient solutions for an MODM problem. The objective is to find the best compromise solution, which is the efficient solution that is best with respect to the decision makers' preferences (Wadhwa & Ravindran, 2007). The choice of a solution compared to another requires the knowledge of the problem and many factors related to the problem. Hence, a solution chosen by the decision maker may not be acceptable for another. To cope with these problems there are several methods to transform the multi objective problem into single objective problem, such as the aggregation method and the compromise method. As an important weakness in MODM method is that after the result from MODM has been generated, further analysis may still be required. Furthermore, a MODM model cannot support input parameters for landfill selection which are based on the subjective opinions of the decision maker or analyst and which can change over time (Cheng, Chan, & Huang, 2003). For these reasons, an integration of MCDM methods with those models can be proposed to deal with the landfill allocation problems. MODM models are largely used in the literature with also different metaheuristics, such as genetic algorithms, simulated annealing, and so forth, to obtain the most suitable and the most efficient solution. Using a population of solutions to evolve towards several nondominated solutions in each run makes metaheuristics popular in solving multi objective optimization problems. As can be seen above mentioned difficulties in the solution procedure of the MODM methods, these methods are not easy to implement to the complex environmental planning problems. The decision makers or analyst may not have enough knowledge about the complex mathematical methodologies and heuristic algorithms. Additionally, there are two important problems with this approach; first the criteria, which are considered as constraints, are weighted equally, which rarely happens in practice, and second, they have significant problems in considering qualitative criteria (Wadhwa & Ravindran, 2007).

MADM techniques have also been widely used for the undesirable facility site selection problem. Salminen, Hokkanen, and Lahdelma (1998) presented an analysis of the use of ELECTRE III, PROMETHEE I, II, and SMART decision aids in the context of different real applications to environmental problems such as land use planning problem, waste treatment facility location problem, and choosing of a municipal solid waste management system in two districts of Finland. In another study, a fuzzy MCDM approach was developed to solve the landfill selection problem in Canada (Cheng et al., 2002). Simple weighted addition (SWA) method, weighted product (WP) method, TOPSIS, cooperative game theory, and ELECTRE as the MCDM methods were used to evaluate the landfill location alternatives in this study. In environmental planning, instead of searching for the optimal solution, analysts often try to minimize the risks involved. Similar to TOPSIS, an indifference threshold can also be set to group alternatives within the same preference level. These alternatives are likely to be similarly preferred by decision makers. This is one of the main emphasizes of the study. As a very similar work, same authors analyzed an integration of MCDM and inexact mixed-integer linear programming methods to support selection of an optimal landfill location in the solid waste management (Cheng et al., 2003). The five MCDM methods of SWA, WP, cooperative game theory, TOPSIS, and ELECTRE were used again to evaluate the landfill location alternatives. In these studies, the authors use more than one method to enhance confidence and reliability of the rankings. This approach can be seen as the strength of these studies. But, since different multi criteria methods may result in different ranking of alternatives, this approach may cause some misunderstandings for the decision makers. Mahler and Lima (2003) discussed a value analysis and fuzzy logic based methodology for assessing the selection of suitable waste filling areas. The most important contribution of the above mentioned approaches is to consider the uncertainties embedded in the waste management processes. The uncertainty plays an important role in planning waste management problems. The possible sources of uncertainty may be the vagueness of planning objectives and constraints, the estimation errors in parameter values and the random character governing waste generation (Chang & Wei, 2000). In a recently studied paper, Önüt and Soner (2008) applied a fuzzy TOPSIS based methodology to solve the solid waste transshipment site selection problem in Istanbul, Turkey. As a real world environmental application, the main contribution of this study is that the results guide municipality authorization to choose the best solid waste site effectively among the candidate sites.

It can be observed from surveyed literature that outranking methods are commonly used to solve environmental problems. The primary reason for the popularity of these methods is that the approaches are very easy to implement within the waste management problems. The methods are also easy to understand and intuitively appealing to decision makers. Among these methods ELECTRE is widely utilized for waste management. This method is capable of handling discrete criteria of both quantitative and qualitative in nature. However, it is sometimes unable to identify the preferred alternative and especially suitable while encountering a few criteria with a large number of alternatives. The SWA and WP methods are the simplest methods for the analysts. TOPSIS is developed as an alternative to ELECTRE and assumes that each attribute has a monotonically increasing or decreasing utility.

This makes it easy to locate the ideal and negative ideal solutions. In MADM, all objectives of decision maker are unified under a superfunction termed decision maker's utility which depends on location attributes. The main advantage of MADM models is their ability to consider a large amount of location attributes. Although MCDM models provide systematic approaches for analysts to evaluate and score alternative locations with multi criteria, these models are not easy to implement such a complex municipal planning problems. These models require the decision makers to exogenously specify the exact values of weights of individual criteria. It is sometimes very difficult to obtain precise values. Sometimes a large number of pairwise comparisons should be performed by decision makers and this situation become impractical the usage of the MADM methods in some cases. Since different MADM methods have been developed, using more than one method can enhance confidence and reliability of the rankings. A hybrid MADM methodology is used in this chapter to cope with these problems. Since undesirable location selection problems usually involve mixtures of deterministic and fuzzy data, more extensive integration of fuzzy set theory within the MCDM framework would help to more effectively handle uncertainties in the data.

Additionally, different decision making techniques and combinations of them have also been utilized to make a decision for selecting the most appropriate undesirable location. Ramuu and Kennedy (1994) has developed a heuristic algorithm for locating a solid waste disposal location. Kao and Lin (1996) proposed a siting model to obtain a landfill location using a mixed-integer programming model. A combined geographical information system (GIS) and the analytical hierarchy process (AHP) procedure to aid in location selection problem firstly used by Siddiqui et al. (1996). Similarly Charnpratheep, Zhou, and Garner (1997) utilized fuzzy set theory with GIS for the screening of landfill locations in Thailand. Wey (2005) aimed to develop an integrated decision support system for the optimization of waste incinerator siting problems. In this integrated approach, both expert system and operations research techniques are used to model the siting problems of waste incinerator. Yeşilnacar and Cetin (2005) proposed a method to determine how to locate suitable locations for hazardous waste landfilling area by using the location screening study in Turkey. The problem of locating collection areas for urban waste management in Barcelona was modeled and solved using a genetic algorithm and a GRASP heuristic (Bautista & Pereira, 2006).

As mentioned before, it is not easy to develop a selection criterion that can exactly describe the preference of one location over another. Many precision-based methods for location selection in waste management have been investigated as given above. Most of these methods have been developed based on the concepts of accurate measurements and crisp evaluation (Chu & Lin, 2003). However, most of the selection parameters cannot be given precisely and this makes fuzzy logic a more natural approach to this kind of problems. MCDM methods deal with the process of making decisions in the presence of multiple objectives. A decision maker is required to choose among quantifiable or nonquantifiable and multiple criteria. The objectives are usually conflicting and therefore the solution is highly dependent on the preferences of the decision maker and must be a compromise. MCDM methods can also be integrated with fuzzy set theory which is suitable for modeling vagueness and imprecision (Pohekar & Ramachandran, 2004). Many researchers have attempted to use fuzzy MCDM methods for selection problems. The technique for order preference by similarity to ideal solution (TOPSIS) is one of the well known classical MCDM methods (Hwang & Yoon, 1981). TOPSIS method is a popular approach to multiple criteria decision making and widely used in the literature. This technique is based on the concept that the ideal alternative has the best level for all criteria, whereas the negative ideal the one with all the worst criteria values. TOPSIS is a widely accepted multi-attribute decision making technique due to its sound logic, simultaneous consideration of the ideal and the anti-ideal solutions, and easily programmable computation procedure (Karsak, 2002). Also, linguistic preferences can be easily converted to fuzzy numbers and TOPSIS admits of using these fuzzy numbers in the calculation. In fuzzy TOPSIS, criteria values are represented by fuzzy numbers. Using this method, the decision maker's fuzzy assignments with different rating viewpoints and the trade-offs among different criteria are considered in the aggregation procedure to ensure more accurate decision making (Chu, 2002). Fuzzy TOPSIS is the most frequently used method in fuzzy MCDM environment.

Analytic network process (ANP), as a multiple criteria decision making (MCDM) method, can be used to evaluate the most suitable locations for the undesirable facilities systematically. The ANP is relatively simple and systematic approach that can be used by decision makers. Essentially, it is a more general form of the analytical hierarchy process (AHP) which was first introduced by Thomas L. Saaty. The ANP is different from the AHP in that decision models can be built as complex networks of decision objectives, alternatives, scenarios, and criteria that all influence on another's priorities. It also tolerates complex interrelationships between the criteria and decision levels, but the AHP models decision making structure using uni-directional hierarchical relationships among decision levels. Furthermore, the ANP does not require strictly hierarchical structure and uses a ratio scale by human judgments instead of arbitrary scales. It also allows measuring all tangible and intangible criteria in the model (Saaty, 1996, 1999). The most important disadvantage of the ANP method is that it does not consider the uncertain human judgments. To cope with this problem, the fuzzy ANP (FANP) method can be used (Yu & Tzeng, 2006). In FANP, weights are simpler to calculate than for conventional ANP. To avoid the large number of pairwise comparisons, these fuzzy weights can be combined to determine the best alternative by using fuzzy TOPSIS. In fuzzy TOPSIS, criteria values are represented by fuzzy numbers. Using this method, the decision maker's fuzzy assignments with different rating viewpoints and the trade-offs among different criteria are considered in the aggregation procedure to ensure more accurate decision making. There are very limited studies concerned with the combination of the ANP and TOPSIS methods. Shyur and Shih (2006) and Shyur (2006) recently developed two combined ANP and TOPSIS models for strategic vendor selection and COTS evaluation and selection, respectively.

In this chapter, an undesirable location selection procedure is presented to construct an undesirable facility by using the FANP and fuzzy TOPSIS methodology. A case study was prepared for the region of Istanbul. The rest of the chapter is organized as follows. The next section describes the main emphasize of the chapter. After reviewing the fuzzy theory briefly, the basics of the FANP and fuzzy TOPSIS is described. Then, the study area and problem domain is introduced and solid waste transfer station selection as a real-world empirical example is explained. Finally, the results are provided and the chapter is concluded.

THE PURPOSE OF THE CHAPTER

The chapter proposes a combined FANP and fuzzy TOPSIS methodology for evaluating and selecting the most suitable undesirable location. Fuzzy TOPSIS is used to rank locations in terms of their overall performance with multiple criteria and the FANP is applied to calculate relative weights of criteria. The overall procedure of the study is shown in Figure 1.

In the evaluation and selection of an appropriate undesirable facility location which is

Figure 1. The overall procedure

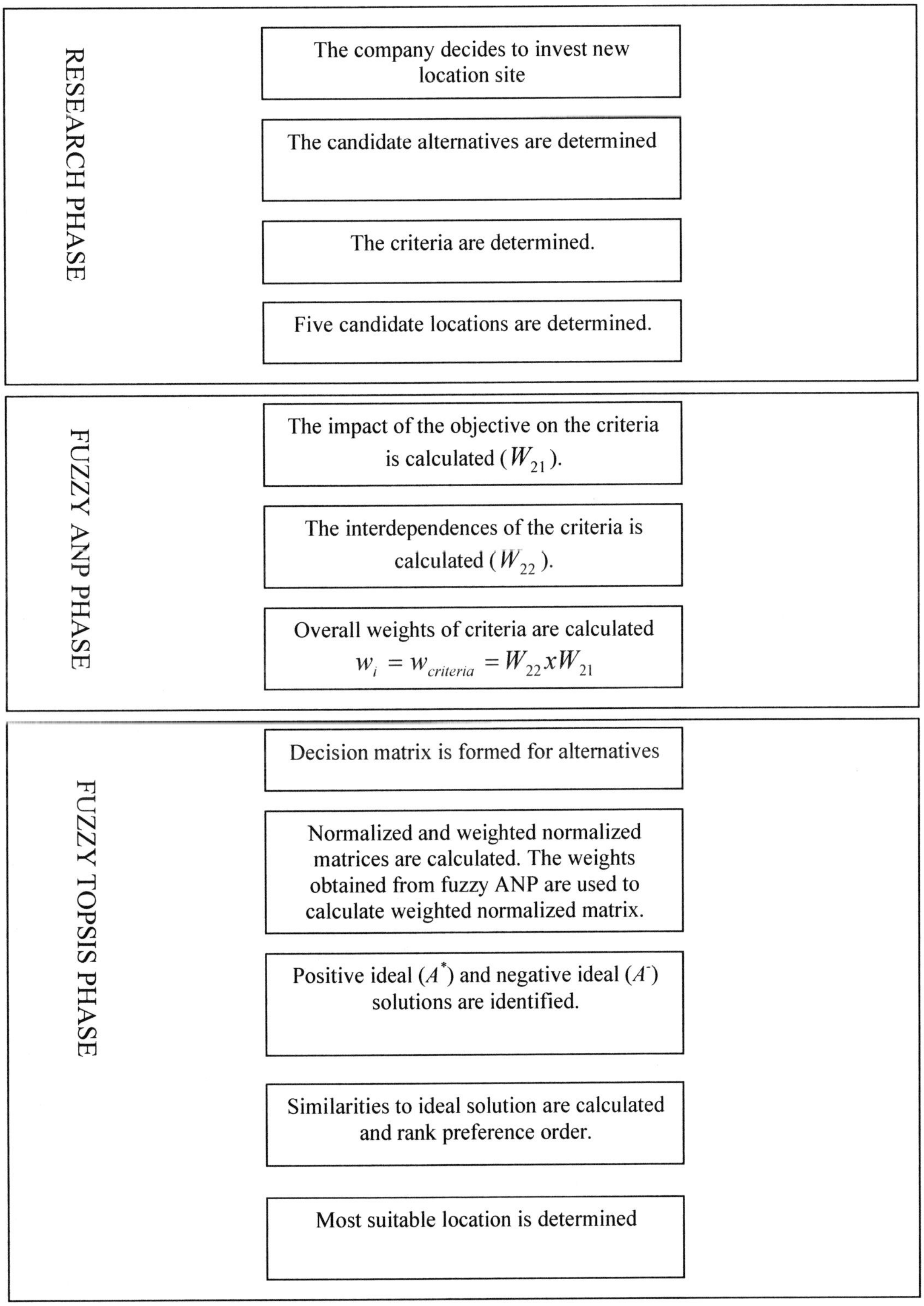

supposed to hold a huge amount of garbage, different issues of multiple hierarchy or networks may conflict with each other. These networks, which are particularly important for the decision making area, need to be assigned proper weights and the necessary trade-offs should be taken into account. The networks are required for ranking them with respect to their appropriateness. The major factors contributing to the complexity of the undesirable location selection process are constraints imposed by the municipal, governmental, environmental regulations, and so forth; multiple conflicting location selection criteria; uncertainty in the selection environment; and the wide variety of location types and models available. For these reasons the decision maker has to consider various tangible (i.e., cost-related criteria like the construction cost of a facility) and intangible (i.e., social and political criteria as image related effects) criteria. Therefore, undesirable location selection can be viewed as a MCDM problem in the presence of many quantitative and qualitative criteria. Furthermore, due to the uncertainty in the operational environment making the location choice is highly dependent on the preferences of the decision maker. Besides, it is very difficult to develop a selection criterion that can precisely describe the preference of one alternative over another. The evaluation data of location alternatives suitability for various subjective criteria, and the weights of the criteria are usually expressed in linguistic terms. This makes fuzzy logic a more natural approach to this kind of problems. For these reasons it was decided to use a fuzzy MCDM methodology to select the most appropriate undesirable facility location.

In the literature, there are many weight calculation procedures. As an efficient weight calculation method, the AHP, rather than the ANP, has been commonly used to evaluate suitable locations and transportation routes to facilities. However, a significant limitation of the AHP is the assumption of independency among various criteria of decision making. The AHP is a special case of the ANP and it doesn't contain feedback loops. Both the ANP and the AHP obtain ratio scale priorities for each element and cluster of elements by making paired comparisons of elements on a common criterion. The ANP, on the other hand, captures interdependences among the decision criteria and allows a more systematic analysis. In the location selection problem, the selection criteria are of both the types, quantitative and qualitative. These criteria also have some interdependence, which cannot be captured by the well known AHP method. Therefore, instead of using the commonly used AHP approach for solving such types of problems, we recommend the use of the ANP integrated methodology for the location selection problem.

However, the ANP method does not consider the uncertainty in the human's judgments and it is mainly used in nearly crisp decision applications. In many problems the human assessment is uncertain, and it is relatively difficult for the decision maker to provide exact numerical values for the criteria. Hence, most of the selection parameters cannot be given precisely and the evaluation data of the alternatives' suitability for various subjective criteria and the weights of the criteria are usually expressed in linguistic terms by the decision makers. In order to model uncertainty in human preference, fuzzy logic could be a more natural approach. The ANP method deals only with crisp comparison ratios. However, uncertain human judgments with internal inconsistency obstructing the direct application of the ANP are frequently found. To overcome such weaknesses, the FANP method is chosen for weighting the criteria in this chapter.

In conventional FANP method, decision maker's linguistic evaluations in fuzzy forms are first converted to crisp numbers by using different algorithms and then these crisp evaluations are used in the ANP to performed pairwise comparisons. Contrary to conventional FANP method in the literature, in our proposed method, the linguistic assessment is converted to triangular fuzzy numbers firstly. These triangular fuzzy numbers are then used to build all pairwise comparison matrices for the ANP. This is one of the main contributions of the chapter. We use triangular fuzzy numbers in all pairwise comparison matrices in the FANP.

Although one of the most important advantages of the FANP is based on pairwise comparisons with the linguistic terms, sometimes large number of pairwise comparisons should be performed by decision makers and this situation makes the usage of the FANP process impractical in some cases. As the number of criteria and alternatives is increased, the number of pairwise comparisons also increases and the performance of the decision makers decreases. To cope with these problems, in our chapter, the FANP is just used to calculate the weights of criteria and fuzzy TOPSIS technique can be used to reduce the number of pairwise comparisons and to rank the alternatives. The advantages of the integration of these two techniques are to overcome ranking problem when evaluating a number of criteria and to ease accommodating a lot of alternatives. Due to a large number of potential available undesirable facility locations in the real world applications, using a MCDM method, like the AHP or the ANP, as an efficient weighting algorithm becomes impractical in some cases. Hence, to avoid an enormously large number of pairwise comparisons, especially in the fuzzy environment, TOPSIS as an efficient ranking method is selected because of its ease of use in the fuzzy environment. This is another main contribution of this chapter.

To the authors' knowledge, there are a large number of facility location evaluation and selection models and reviews, some of which have concentrated on the selection of the undesirable facility locations exclusively. Moreover, there are also a large number of studies related with the facility location selection problems considered entirely in Turkey. When solving the problem of undesirable facility location selection, it becomes necessary to consider qualitative criteria, like image-related criteria, total opposition, and so forth. This necessity motivates us to use the MCDM methodology, which makes it possible to evaluate qualitative criteria. Although there were a limited number of publications evaluating the undesirable facility locations in the literature and some of them have been prepared using the multi attribute/multi criteria decision making methods considering human judgments, tangible, intangible, and multiple criteria, to the best of our knowledge, there is no evidence in the literature that any of them was applied to the Turkey or a region of her in connection with the evaluation of the undesirable facility locations using the ANP, the FANP, or integrated ANP and TOPSIS methodology under a fuzzy environment. These are the most important contributions of the chapter.

FUZZY THEORY

In the following, some basic important definitions of fuzzy sets from Zadeh (1965), Kaufmann and Gupta (1985), and Yang and Hung (2007) are reviewed and summarized.

Definition 1: A fuzzy set $\tilde{a}$ in a universe of discourse X is characterized by a membership function $\mu_{\tilde{a}}(x)$ which associates with each element x in X, a real number in the interval [0, 1]. The function value $\mu_{\tilde{a}}(x)$ is termed the grade of membership of x in $\tilde{a}$.

The present study uses triangular fuzzy numbers. A triangular fuzzy number $\tilde{a}$ can be defined by a triplet (a_1, a_2, a_3). Its conceptual schema and mathematical form are given by Eq. (4):

$$\mu_{\tilde{a}}(x) = \begin{cases} 0, & x \le a_1 \\ \dfrac{x - a_1}{a_2 - a_1}, & a_1 < x \le a_2, \\ \dfrac{a_3 - x}{a_3 - a_2}, & a_2 < x \le a_3 \\ 0, & x > a_3, \end{cases} \tag{1}$$

Definition 2: Let $\tilde{a}=(a_1,a_2,a_3)$ and $\tilde{b}=(b_1,b_2,b_3)$ be two triangular fuzzy numbers, then the vertex method is defined to calculate the distance between them, as Eq. (2):

$$d(\tilde{a},\tilde{b})=\sqrt{\frac{1}{3}\left[(a_1-b_1)^2+(a_2-b_2)^2+(a_3-b_3)^2\right]} \quad (2)$$

The basic operations on fuzzy triangular numbers are as follows:

$$\tilde{a}\times\tilde{b}=(a_1\times b_1,a_2\times b_2,a_3\times b_3) \text{ for multiplication} \quad (3)$$

$$\tilde{a}+\tilde{b}=(a_1+b_1,a_2+b_2,a_3+b_3) \text{ for addition} \quad (4)$$

FUZZY ANALYTIC NETWORK PROCESS

The ANP allows both interaction and feedback within clusters of elements (inner dependence) and between clusters (outer dependence). The elements in a cluster may influence other elements in the same cluster and those in other clusters with respect to each of several properties. The main object is to determine the overall influence of all the elements. In that case, first of all, properties or criteria must be organized and they must be prioritized in the framework of a control hierarchy. Then the comparisons must be performed and synthesized to obtain the priorities of these properties. Additionally, the influence of elements in the feedback system with respect to each of these properties must be derived. Finally, the resulting influences must be weighted by the importance of the properties and added to obtain the overall influence of each element (Saaty, 1999, 2003). The supermatrix representation of a hierarchy with three levels is given as follows:

$$W=\begin{matrix} Goal(G) \\ Criteria(C) \\ Alternatives(A) \end{matrix}\overset{\begin{matrix} G & C & A \end{matrix}}{\begin{pmatrix} 0 & 0 & 0 \\ W_{21} & 0 & 0 \\ 0 & W_{32} & I \end{pmatrix}} \quad (5)$$

Where W_{21} is a vector that represents the impact of the objective on the criteria, W_{32} is a vector that represents the impact of the criteria on each of the alternatives, and I is the identity matrix. W is referred to as a supermatrix because its entries are matrices. For example, if the criteria are dependent among themselves, then the (2,2) entry of W given by W_{22} would be nonzero. The interdependence is exhibited by the presence of the matrix element W_{22} of the supermatrix W (Saaty & Vargas, 1998).

$$W=\begin{pmatrix} 0 & 0 & 0 \\ W_{21} & W_{22} & 0 \\ 0 & W_{23} & I \end{pmatrix} \quad (6)$$

Since W is a column stochastic matrix, it is known that the synthesis of all the interactions among the elements of this system is given by the limit supermatrix. The overall priorities of the alternatives and the alternative with the largest overall priority are determined from the supermatrix finally.

In another words, after forming the supermatrix, if it is column stochastic, we can simply raise it to powers to obtain an answer. Otherwise, the weighted supermatrix is generated first and then raised it to limiting powers to get the global priority vector. Because the supermatrix is not column stochastic in general, the limiting matrix does not exist. Hence, stochasticity of the supermatrix can be saved by additional normalization of the columns of the submatrices (Ramik, 2006).

In the proposed methodology, the fuzzy ANP (FANP) has been used to solve undesirable location selection problem. It is very useful in situations where there is a high degree of interdependence between various attributes of the alternatives. In this approach, pairwise comparison matrices are formed between various criteria of each level with the help of triangular fuzzy numbers. Several researchers have attempted to use the FANP method for different problems. Although the ANP has also been applied to a large variety of decision making processes in the different application areas, the FANP has received much less attention in the literature (Mikhailov & Singh, 2003; Buyukozkan, Ertay, Kahraman, & Ruan, 2004; Kahraman, Ertay, & Buyukozkan, 2006; Ertay, Buyukozkan, Kahraman, & Ruan, 2005; Mohanty, Agarwal, Choudhury, & Tiwari, 2005). The FANP can easily accommodate the interrelationships existing among the functional activities (Mohanty et al., 2005). The concept of supermatrices is employed to obtain the composite weights that overcome the existing interrelationships. The values of parameters such as reliability, flexibility, performance, and so forth, are transformed into triangular fuzzy numbers and are used to calculate fuzzy values.

In the pairwise comparison of criteria, the decision makers can use triangular fuzzy numbers to state their preferences. Saaty's scale of 1-9 is precise and explicit. Even though the discrete scale of 1-9 has the advantages of simplicity and easiness for use, it does not consider the uncertainty associated with the mapping of one's perception or judgment to a number. On the other hand, decision maker's perception about the location attributes can be vague and ambiguous, and hence cannot be expressed in definite numbers. For these reasons, a scale of $\tilde{1}$ - $\tilde{9}$ can be defined for triangular fuzzy numbers instead of the scale of 1-9. When comparing criterion i with criterion j, $\tilde{1}$, $\tilde{3}$, $\tilde{5}$, $\tilde{7}$, and $\tilde{9}$ indicate equal importance among the compared criteria, moderate importance of i over j, strong importance of i over j, very strong importance of i over j and extreme importance of i over j, respectively, where $i = 1, 2, \ldots, n$, and $j = 1, 2, \ldots, m$. To evaluate the decision maker's preferences, pairwise comparison matrices are structured by using triangular fuzzy numbers (l, m, u). The $m \times n$ triangular fuzzy matrix can be given as follows:

$$\tilde{A} = \begin{pmatrix} (a_{11}^l, a_{11}^m, a_{11}^u) & (a_{12}^l, a_{12}^m, a_{12}^u) & \cdots & (a_{1n}^l, a_{1n}^m, a_{1n}^u) \\ (a_{21}^l, a_{21}^m, a_{21}^u) & (a_{22}^l, a_{22}^m, a_{22}^u) & \cdots & (a_{2n}^l, a_{2n}^m, a_{2n}^u) \\ \vdots & \vdots & \vdots & \vdots \\ (a_{m1}^l, a_{m1}^m, a_{m1}^u) & (a_{m2}^l, a_{m2}^m, a_{m2}^u) & \cdots & (a_{mn}^l, a_{mn}^m, a_{mn}^u) \end{pmatrix} \quad (7)$$

The element a_{mn} represents the comparison of component m (row element) with component n (column element). If $\tilde{A}$ is a pairwise comparison matrix, it is assumed that it is reciprocal, and the reciprocal value, that is, $1/\tilde{a}_{mn}$, is assigned to the element $\tilde{a}_{mn}$.

$$\tilde{A} = \begin{pmatrix} (1,1,1) & (a_{11}^l, a_{11}^m, a_{11}^u) & \cdots & (a_{1n}^l, a_{1n}^m, a_{1n}^u) \\ (\frac{1}{a_{11}^u}, \frac{1}{a_{11}^m}, \frac{1}{a_{11}^l}) & (1,1,1) & \cdots & (a_{2n}^l, a_{2n}^m, a_{2n}^u) \\ \vdots & \vdots & \vdots & \vdots \\ (\frac{1}{a_{1n}^u}, \frac{1}{a_{1n}^m}, \frac{1}{a_{1n}^l}) & (\frac{1}{a_{2n}^u}, \frac{1}{a_{2n}^m}, \frac{1}{a_{2n}^l}) & \cdots & (1,1,1) \end{pmatrix} \quad (8)$$

$\tilde{A}$ is also a triangular fuzzy pairwise comparison matrix. There are several methods for getting estimates for fuzzy priorities $\tilde{w}_i$, where $\tilde{w}_i = (w_i^l, w_i^m, w_i^u)$, $i = 1, 2, \ldots, n$, from the judgment matrix $\tilde{A}$ which approximate the fuzzy ratios $\tilde{a}_{ij}$ so that $\tilde{a}_{ij} \approx \tilde{w}_i / \tilde{w}_j$. One of these methods, logarithmic least squares method (Chen, Hwang, & Hwang, 1992; Ramik, 2006), is reasonable and effective, and it is used in this study. Hence, the triangular fuzzy weights for the relative importance of the criteria, the feedback of the criteria, and the alternatives according to the individual criteria can be calculated. In our proposed model, only the triangular fuzzy weights for the relative importance of the criteria and the interdependence priorities of the criteria will be used to support the fuzzy TOPSIS for selecting the best alternative. The matrix W to embed the simple case of these two matrices can be given as follows:

$$W = \begin{pmatrix} 0 & 0 \\ W_{21} & W_{22} \end{pmatrix} \quad (9)$$

The logarithmic least squares method for calculating triangular fuzzy weights can be given as follows:

$$\tilde{w}_k = \left(w_k^l, w_k^m, w_k^u\right) \qquad k = 1,2,3,\cdots,n. \quad (10)$$

where

$$w_k^s = \frac{\left(\prod_{j=1}^{n} a_{kj}^s\right)^{1/n}}{\sum_{i=1}^{n}\left(\prod_{j=1}^{n} a_{ij}^m\right)^{1/n}}, \quad s \in \{l,m,u\}. \quad (11)$$

FUZZY TOPSIS

In the following, some basic important definitions of fuzzy sets from Zimmermann (1991), Buckley (1985), Zadeh (1965), Kaufmann and Gupta (1985), Yang and Hung (2007), Chen, Lin, and Huang (2006), and Kahraman, Buyukozkan, and Ates (2007a) are reviewed and summarized. It is often difficult for a decision maker to assign a precise performance rating to an alternative for the criteria under consideration. The merit of using a fuzzy approach is to assign the relative importance of criteria using fuzzy numbers instead of precise numbers. This section extends TOPSIS to the fuzzy environment.

The problem can be described by following sets:

i. A set of J possible candidates called $A = \{A_1, A_2, \ldots\ldots\ldots\ldots A_j\}$;

ii. A set of n criteria, $C = \{C_1, C_2, \ldots\ldots\ldots\ldots C_i\}$;

iii. A set of performance ratings of A_j $(j = 1,2,3,\ldots\ldots,J)$ with respect to criteria C_i $(i = 1,2,3\ldots\ldots n)$ called $\tilde{X} = \{\tilde{x}_{ij}\ \ \mathrm{I} =\ ,2,3,\ldots\ldots,n,\ j = 1,2,3,\ldots\ldots\ldots,J\ \}$.

iv. A set of importance weights of each criterion w_i $(i = 1,2,3,\ldots\ldots,n)$

As stated above, problem matrix format can be expressed as follows:

$$\tilde{X} = \begin{bmatrix} \tilde{x}_{11} & \tilde{x}_{12} \ldots\ldots\ldots\ldots\ldots \tilde{x}_{1n} \\ \tilde{x}_{21} & \tilde{x}_{22} \ldots\ldots\ldots\ldots\ldots \tilde{x}_{2n} \\ . & . \quad \ldots\ldots\ldots \quad . \\ . & . \quad \ldots\ldots\ldots \quad . \\ . & . \quad \ldots\ldots\ldots \quad . \\ \tilde{x}_{J1} & \tilde{x}_{J2} \ldots\ldots\ldots\ldots\ldots \tilde{x}_{Jn} \end{bmatrix}$$

Considering the different importance values of each criterion, the weighted normalized fuzzy-decision matrix is constructed as:

$$\tilde{V} = [\tilde{v}_{ij}]_{n \times J} \qquad i = 1,2,\ldots,n, \qquad j = 1,2,\ldots\ldots\ldots,J$$

where $\tilde{v}_{ij} = \tilde{r}_{ij}(.)\ w_i$ (12)

According to the briefly summarized fuzzy theory above, fuzzy TOPSIS steps can be outlined as follows:

Step 1: Choose the linguistic ratings $\left(\tilde{x}_{ij}\ i = 1,2,3\ldots\ldots,n,\ j = 1.2.3\ldots\ldots\ldots,J\right)$ for alternatives with respect to criteria. To obtain normalized decision matrix $\tilde{r}_{ij}$, let $\tilde{x}_{ij} = (a_{ij}, b_{ij}, c_{ij})$, $\tilde{x}_j^- = (a_j^-, b_j^-, c_j^-)$ and $\tilde{x}_j^* = (a_j^*, b_j^*, c_j^*)$ we have

$$\tilde{r}_{ij} = \begin{cases} \tilde{x}_{ij}(\div)\tilde{x}_j^* = (\frac{a_{ij}}{a_j^*}, \frac{b_{ij}}{b_j^*}, \frac{c_{ij}}{c_j^*}) \\ \tilde{x}_j^-(\div)\tilde{x}_{ij} = (\frac{a_j^-}{a_{ij}}, \frac{b_j^-}{b_{ij}}, \frac{c_j^-}{c_{ij}}) \end{cases} \quad (13)$$

Step 2: Calculate the weighted normalized fuzzy decision matrix. The weighted normalized value $\tilde{v}_{ij}$ calculated by Eq. (12).

Step 3: Identify positive ideal (A^*) and negative ideal (A^-) solutions. The fuzzy positive-ideal solution (FPIS, A^*) and the fuzzy negative-ideal solution (FNIS, A^-) are shown in Eqs. (14) and (15).

$$A^* = \{\tilde{v}_1^*, \ldots, \tilde{v}_i^*\}$$

$$= \left\{ \left(\max_j v_j \mid i \in I \right) \right\}$$

$$i = 1,2,\ldots,n, \qquad j = 1,2,\ldots,J \quad (14)$$

$$A^- = \{\tilde{v}_1^-, \ldots, \tilde{v}_i^-\}$$

$$= \left\{ \left(\min_j v_j \mid i \in I \right) \right\}$$

$$i = 1,2,\ldots,n, \qquad j = 1,2,\ldots,J \quad (15)$$

where I is criteria.

Step 4: Calculate the distance of each alternative from A^* and A^- using Eqs. (16) and (17).

$$D_j^* = \sum_{j=1}^{n} d(\tilde{v}_j, \tilde{v}_i^*) \qquad j = 1,2,\ldots,J \quad (16)$$

$$D_j^- = \sum_{j=1}^{n} d(\tilde{v}_j, \tilde{v}_i^-) \qquad j = 1,2,\ldots,J \quad (17)$$

Step 5: Calculate similarities to ideal solution.

$$CC_j = \frac{D_j^-}{D_j^* + D_j^-} \qquad j = 1,2,\ldots,J \quad (18)$$

Step 6: Rank preference order. Choose an alternative with maximum CC_j^* or rank alternatives according to CC_j^* in descending order.

APPLICATION OF TRANSFER STATION SELECTION

The study is applied in Istanbul, which is the most populated and industrial region of Turkey. Istanbul has a surface area of 5,512 km^2, which corresponds to 0.7% of the total surface area of Turkey. According to the 2000 population census, the population of Istanbul is 10,041,477 with a population density of 1,822 persons/km^2. Istanbul has 32 district municipalities. Istanbul Metropolitan Municipality coordinates solid waste collection, transportation, treatment, and disposal activities. The current solid waste management chain consists of solid waste transfer station, a solid waste treatment (compost) plant, and regular storage fields. Since the city lies upon two different continents, namely Europe and

Asia and the continents are connected to each other with two bridges, the location selection of a regular storage field is an important and difficult issue, especially when taking into account the transportation of the solid waste material between the two sides of the city. District municipalities collect solid wastes and carries them to the nearest solid waste transfer station. These shipment activities cause a considerable consumption in time and increase in cost.

ISTAC Co., Istanbul Metropolitan Municipality Environmental Protection and Waste Materials Valuation Industry and Trade Co., is one of the Economic Enterprises of Istanbul Metropolitan Municipality. As the name denotes, ISTAC Co., within the scope of Solid Waste Project of Istanbul Metropolitan Municipality, provides services for transportation of solid wastes, production of compost fertilizer, recycling of wastes, and disposal of them via regulated storing, electric energy generation from landfills, transportation of medical waste, and their disposal via incineration. ISTAC, which is in charge of transporting, storing to sensatory to landfills, and disposing with various methods the solid wastes of Istanbul and producing compost fertilizer and electric energy from them, classifies and disposes the garbage of Istanbul under four groups, which are:

- Domestic solid wastes
- Medical solid wastes
- Hazardous solid wastes
- Construction debris and rubble

Istanbul's daily average garbage production is around 10.000 tons. According to ISTAC data, when such solid wastes as "old items" and "scraps" that can be used in the industry collected by the seekers from dump areas and the construction debris and rubble discarded illegally to empty areas are added to this amount, it can be seen that Istanbul's per capita garbage production is around one kilogram (www.istac.com.tr).

The increase in population and production in Istanbul requires the need to identify the principles to determine the best location for solid wastes. The objective of the research is to construct a decision analysis to find the optimal new transfer station for solid wastes. The proposed methodology uses fuzzy sets in describing uncertainties in the different criteria involved in transfer station selection. Each criterion is represented by a linguistic variable. Candidate locations were determined by the related municipal authorities in Istanbul. The related values, pairwise comparisons, and weights were also determined by them. The main problem encountered was the difficulty of getting correct and useful data. A considerable time was spent to collect reliable data and personal judgments. Hence, a lot of face to face interviews were held with various decision makers to develop suitable information. Furthermore, because of the lack of the systematic knowledge, the survey was conducted through the distribution of a comprehensive questionnaire to the large number of authorities.

Istanbul Metropolitan Municipality decides to invest new location sites. They already determined the candidate locations. We made face to face interviews and then determined criteria. Istanbul Metropolitan Municipality decided that the five criteria used in this study are adequate for evaluating the possible candidate locations.

In the current situation of the European side of the city, Yenibosna, Baruthane, and Halkalı transfer stations accept extra garbage. Especially Baruthane transfer station exceeds the maximum capacity 127.000 tons/year. ISTAC wants to solve this problem by setting up a new transfer station on the European side. For this reason, we determined five alternative zones with the guidance of the municipal authorities. These are:

- **Alternative 1:** Eyüp
- **Alternative 2:** Gaziosmanpaşa
- **Alternative 3:** Kağıthane
- **Alternative 4:** Sarıyer

- **Alternative 5:** Avcılar

With the aim of the selection of the new transfer station location, the transportation distances will be decreased for municipalities and also the use of energy, fuel, and the related overall costs will be reduced.

In this study, we defined five criteria for the new transfer station selection which is planning to be built. All the calculations were carried out by using Ms Excel. First of all, the corresponding weights of the criteria were calculated. Next, the pairwise comparison matrices were evaluated by using FANP. Then, the best alternative was selected by using Fuzzy TOPSIS method. According to the interviews with the related authorities, five selection criteria were identified as follows:

- **Criterion 1:** Proximity to the residential area
- **Criterion 2:** The suitability of the ground
- **Criterion 3:** The amount of solid waste
- **Criterion 4:** Cost
- **Criterion 5:** Easement of access

The fourth criterion which is defined as cost criterion will be utilized as a negative value and the others are benefit criteria. The pairwise comparisons are made to define weights of criteria. Linguistic scales and their corresponding fuzzy numbers defined by Saaty (1980). According to this scale, the pairwise comparisons are done by using Table 1.

The supermatrix which represents our study is defined as follows:

$$W = \begin{bmatrix} 0 & 0 \\ W_{21} & W_{22} \end{bmatrix}$$

As can be seen from the supermatrix, initially W_{21} and W_{22} submatrices should be calculated. In the first phase of the study, the relative fuzzy importance degrees of the individual criteria using triangular fuzzy numbers are determined and then triangular fuzzy importance weights are derived from the fuzzy pairwise comparison matrices (i.e., calculate W_{21}) by using the logarithmic least squares method (Eq.11). Table 2 shows the pairwise comparison matrices between the criteria.

The relative fuzzy importance of the individual criteria (W_{21}) is shown in Table 3. The fuzzy inter-

Table 1. Comparison scale

1, 1, 1	equal importance
2, 3, 4	weak importance (of one over the other)
4, 5, 6	strong importance
6, 7, 8	demonstrated importance over the other
8, 9, 10	absolute importance

Table 2. Pairwise comparison of the criteria

	C_1	C_2	C_3	C_4	C_5
C_1	1,1,1	6,7,8	0.25, 0.333, 0.5	4,5,6	2,3,4
C_2	0.125, 0.143, 0.167	1,1,1	0.1, 0.111, 0.125	0.25, 0.333, 0.5	0.167, 0.2, 0.25
C_3	2,3,4	8,9,10	1,1,1	6,7,8	4,5,6
C_4	0.167, 0.2, 0.25	2,3,4	0.125, 0.143, 0.167	1,1,1	0.25, 0.333, 0.5
C_5	0.25, 0.333, 0.5	4,5,6	0.167, 0.2, 0.25	2,3,4	1,1,1

dependences among the criteria (the feedback of the criteria) are subsequently specified based on the linguistic evaluation. By using the logarithmic least squares method (Eq. 11) again, triangular fuzzy importance weights are derived and these weights are arranged into the fuzzy interdependence matrix (i.e., calculate W_{22}). The data for the fuzzy feedbacks among the criteria is composed of the six pairwise comparison matrices for each criterion. Table 4 shows W_{22} calculations. We put zeroes into the main diagonal as we do not expect an impact of the criterion on itself.

W_{21} is multiplied by W_{22} and then supermatrix which shows the weights of the criteria is obtained. (i.e., $w_i = w_{criteria} = W_{22}xW_{21}$). Table 5 shows the overall weights (w_i). This supermatrix will be used at the second part to make the best alternative's choice by using fuzzy TOPSIS Method.

According to the results shown at the Table 5, the most important criterion is the proximity to the residential area. The other criterions are stand in line as the amount of solid waste, easement of access, cost, and the suitability of the ground.

The above mentioned calculations belong to the FANP phase essentially. The second phase of the study, which is called the fuzzy TOPSIS phase, starts establishing fuzzy evaluations of the alternative suppliers (A_1, A_2,…, A_5) with respect to the individual criteria by using triangular fuzzy numbers again. This is a decision matrix for ranking alternatives and indicates the performance ratings of the alternatives according to the criteria. We use the linguistic scales and their corresponding fuzzy numbers: *(1,1,1)-very poor, (2,3,4)-poor, (4,5,6)-fair, (6,7,8)-good, (8,9,10)-very good.* Table 6 shows comparison of alternatives according to the criteria. After constructing decision matrix, normalized decision matrix is calculated.

The normalized decision matrix is obtained by using Eq.(13). In our calculation, the fourth

Table 3. The relative fuzzy importance of the individual criteria (W_{21})

	W_{21}
C_1	0.213, 0.264, 0.323
C_2	0.029, 0.033, 0.039
C_3	0.426, 0.51, 0.588
C_4	0.052, 0.064, 0.079
C_5	0.112, 0.13, 0.161

Table 5. The overall weights (w_i)

	Overall weights
C_1	0.242,0.351,0.481
C_2	0.035,0.048,0.072
C_3	0.216,0.303,0.422
C_4	0.066,0.098,0.128
C_5	0.132,0.199,0.277

Table 4. W_{22} calculations

	C_1	C_2	C_3	C_4	C_5
C_1	0,0,0	0.21,0.26,0.33	0.46,0.56,0.66	0.22,0.27,0.33	0.25,0.29,0.35
C_2	0.04,0.05,0.05	0,0,0	0.05,0.06,0.07	0.04,0.05,0.06	0.04,0.04,0.06
C_3	0.58,0.65,0.73	0.46,0.56,0.66	0,0,0	0.47,0.57,0.66	0.49,0.58,0.66
C_4	0.08,0.1,0.12	0.05,0.06,0.07	0.09,0.12,0.15	0,0,0	0.07,0.09,0.1
C_5	0.17,0.2,0.24	0.09,0.12,0.15	0.21,0.26,0.33	0.09,0.11,0.14	0,0,0

Table 6. Comparison of alternatives according to the criteria

	A_1	A_2	A_3	A_4	A_5
C_1	4,5,6	8,9,10	6,7,8	2,3,4	6,7,8
C_2	4,5,6	6,7,8	4,5,6	8,9,10	2,3,4
C_3	6,7,8	8,9,10	6,7,8	4,5,6	6,7,8
C_4	6,7,8	4,5,6	4,5,6	8,9,10	2,3,4
C_5	4,5,6	6,7,8	6,7,8	2,3,4	8,9,10

Table 7. The weighted normalized decision matrix

	A_1	A_2	A_3	A_4	A_5
C_1	0.12,0.2,0.29	0.24,0.35,0.48	0.18,0.27,0.38	0.06,0.12,0.19	0.18,0.27,0.38
C_2	0.02,0.03,0.04	0.03,0.04,0.06	0.02,0.03,0.04	0.03,0.05,0.07	0.01,0.02,0.03
C_3	0.16,0.24,0.34	0.22,0.3,0.42	0.16,0.24,0.34	0.11,0.17,0.25	0.16,0.24,0.34
C_4	0.02,0.04,0.06	0.03,0.06,0.09	0.03,0.06,0.09	0.02,0.03,0.05	0.07,0.1,0.13
C_5	0.07,0.11,0.17	0.1,0.15,0.22	0.1,0.15,0.22	0.03,0.07,0.11	0.13,0.2,0.28

criterion "C_4" is defined as a cost criterion, and the others are defined as benefit criteria. An example is given as follows. The maximum value of the criterion "C_1" is fuzzy number (8.00, 9.00, 10.00) on A_2 alternative. The calculation is

$\tilde{r}_{11} = \tilde{x}_{11}(\div)\tilde{x}_1^*$=(4.00, 5.00, 6.00) / (8.00, 9.00, 10.00)=(4.00/8.00, 5.00/9.00, 6.00/10.00)= (0.5, 0.56, 0.60).

As an example, we find the cost criterion's first column value as follows. Minimum value of the cost criterion is fuzzy number (2.00, 3.00, 4.00) on A_5 alternative. The calculation for the normalization is

$\tilde{r}_{13} = \tilde{x}_3^-(\div)\tilde{x}_{13}$ =(2.00, 3.00, 4.00)/ (6.00, 7.00, 8.00) = (0.33, 0.43, 0.50).

The weighted normalized fuzzy decision matrix can be obtained multiplying the normalized decision matrix by the weights of the criteria matrix (Table 5) which is found by using fuzzy analytic network process. Table 7 shows the weighted normalized decision matrix.

The positive ideal solution (A^*) and negative ideal solution (A^-) are determined by using the weighted normalized values. Eqs. (14-15) are used to determine the positive ideal solution and negative ideal solution. The positive triangular fuzzy numbers are in the range [0,1], hence the fuzzy positive ideal reference point (FPIS, A^+) is *(1,1,1)* and fuzzy negative ideal reference point (FNIS, A^-) is *(0,0,0)*. In the last step, the relative closeness to the ideal solution is calculated. The relative closeness to the ideal solution is defined on Eqs.(16-17). Eq.(18) is used to calculate distances to ideal solutions. Table 8 summarizes the results. The higher the closeness means the better the rank, and hence the relative closeness to the ideal solution of the alternatives can be substituted as following, **$CC_2 > CC_5 > CC_3 > CC_1 > CC_4$.** Gaziosmanpaşa is defined as the best alternative

Table 8. The results

	D+	D-	CC*
A_1	4.3748	0.6666	0.13
A_2	4.0846	0.9673	0.19
A_3	4.2383	0.8073	0.16
A_4	4.5496	0.4880	0.10
A_5	4.1678	0.8788	0.17

for the transfer station in this study, planning to be built on the European side in Istanbul.

CONCLUSION

We present a useful model using both fuzzy ANP and fuzzy TOPSIS techniques for transfer station selection process. Transfer station selection process is a technique for evaluating the basic suitable centers and selecting a limited number of locations by using a detailed evaluation. The objective of this study is to analyze the potential of solid waste transfer stations and to choose the best candidate by using a multicriteria approach. If the measures are ambiguous and vague, the decision process begins to get difficult. For this reason, the usage of the fuzzy sets in describing uncertainties in different factors simplifies the complex structure of the decision phase. In other words, using linguistic preferences can be very useful for uncertain situations. Criteria weights are derived by using fuzzy ANP-based on pairwise comparison. Then, fuzzy TOPSIS approach is used for transfer station selection. The results guide municipality authorization to choose the best solid waste location among the candidate centers. For further research developing, a group decision making system can be very useful. In this way different authorities' opinions can be compromised. Also, different hierarchical and detailed objectives can be incorporated into the study. Lastly, mathematical models or metaheuristics can be combined with the existing methodology.

FUTURE RESEARCH DIRECTIONS

Using TOPSIS approach provides an efficient way to obtain satisfactory solution of such problems. Generally, TOPSIS presents a compromise solution in multiple criteria decision making problems. But further applications can be performed in this study. For further research developing a group decision making system can be very useful. In this way, different authorities' opinions can be compromised. Many decision makers believe that they are achieved in such group decision making processes as action planning and problem-solving. But, their ability to perform such techniques efficiently is often hindered by their lack of understanding of the dimensions of these group decision making processes. As a result, if group decision techniques can be applied efficiently, realistic results will be obtained. And these analyses can realize effective group decision making faster without requiring long meetings. Also other multi criteria techniques like, ELECTRE, PROMETHEE, SAW, VIKOR and so forth, can be integrated or compared to get more accurate consequences. Besides, this comparison can highlight key success factors of different methods. As another further issue, different hierarchical and detailed objectives and criteria can be incorporated into the study. It is important to focus attention on what the decision makers' requirements are. Criteria are based on these requirements. Also criterion forms are the basis for the comparison of alternatives, consequently make it easy the selection process, and obtain satisfactory results. So, different and detailed opinions can be included in evaluation process. Lastly, mathematical models or metaheuristics can be combined with the existing method. At a practical level, mathematical programming under multiple objectives is a powerful tool to assist in the process of evaluating decisions which best satisfy conflicting objectives, and there are limited number of applications for multicriteria decision making problems integrated with mathematical programming. This gap can be filled in further researches.

REFERENCES

Al-Jarrah, O., & Abu-Qdais, H. (2006). Municipal solid waste landfill siting using intelligent system. *Waste Management, 26*, 299-306.

Avella, P., Benati, S., Martinez, L.C., Dalby, K., Di Girolamo, D., Dimitrijevic, B., et al. (1998). Some personal views on the current state and the future of locational analyses. *European Journal of Operational Research, 104*, 269-287.

Bautista, J., & Pereira, J. (2006). Modeling the problem of locating collection areas for urban waste management. An application to the metropolitan area of Barcelona. *Omega, 34*, 617-629.

Buckley, J.J. (1985). Fuzzy hierarchical analysis. *Fuzzy Sets and Systems, 17*, 233-247.

Buyukozkan, G., Ertay, T., Kahraman, C., & Ruan, D. (2004). Determining the importance weights for the design requirements in the house of quality using the fuzzy analytic network approach. *International Journal of Intelligent Systems, 19*, 443-461.

Chang, N.B., & Wei, Y.L. (2000). Siting recycling drop-off stations in urban area by genetic algorithm-based fuzzy multiobjective nonlinear integer programming modeling. *Fuzzy Sets and Systems, 114*, 133-149.

Charnpratheep, K., Zhou, Q., & Garner, B. (1997). Preliminary landfill site screening using fuzzy geographical information systems. *Waste Management and Research, 15*, 197-215.

Chen, S.J., Hwang, C.L., & Hwang, F.P. (1992). Fuzzy multiple attribute decision making. *Lecture Notes in Economics and Mathematical Systems, 375*. Berlin: Springer-Verlag.

Chen, C.T., Lin, C.T., & Huang, S.F. (2006). A fuzzy approach for supplier evaluation and selection in supply chain management. *International Journal of Production Economics, 102*(2), 289-301.

Cheng, S., Chan, C.W., & Huang, G.H. (2002). Using multiple criteria decision analysis for supporting decisions of solid waste management. *Journal of Environmental Science and Health A, 37*(6), 975-990.

Cheng, S., Chan, C.W., & Huang, G.H. (2003). An integrated multi-criteria decision analysis and inexact mixed integer linear programming approach for solid waste management. *Engineering Applications of Artificial Intelligence, 16*, 543-554.

Chu, T.-C. (2002). Selecting plant location via a fuzzy TOPSIS approach. *International Journal of Advanced Manufacturing Technology, 20*, 859-864.

Chu, T.-C., & Lin, Y.-C. (2003). A fuzzy TOPSIS method for robot selection. *International Journal of Advanced Manufacturing Technology, 21*, 284-290.

Colebrook, M., & Sicilia, J. (2007). Undesirable facility location problems on multicriteria networks. *Computers and Operations Research, 34*, 1491-1514.

Erkut, E., & Neuman, S. (1989). A survey of analytical models for locating undesirable facilities. *European Journal of Operational Research, 40*, 275-29.

Erkut, E., & Neuman, S. (1992). A multiobjective model for locating undesirable facilities. *Annals of Operations Research, 40*, 209-227.

Ertay, T., Buyukozkan, G., Kahraman, C., & Ruan, D. (2005). Quality function deployment implementation based on analytic network process with linguistic data: An application in automotive industry. *Journal of Intelligent & Fuzzy Systems, 16*(3), 221-232.

Giannikos, I. (1998). A multiobjective programming model for locating treatment sites and routing hazardous wastes. *European Journal of Operational Research, 104*, 333-342.

Hwang, C.L., & Yoon, K. (1981). *Multiple attribute decision making-methods and applications: A state of the art survey.* Springer-Verlag.

Kahraman, C., Büyüközkan G., & Ateş N.Y. (2007a). A two phase multi-attribute decision-making approach for new product introduction. *Information Sciences, 177*, 1567-1582.

Kahraman, C., Cevik, S., Ateş, N.Y., & Gülbay, M. (2007b). Fuzzy multi-criteria evaluation of industrial robotic systems. *Computers & Industrial Engineering, 52*, 414-433.

Kahraman, C., Ertay T., & Buyukozkan, G. (2006). A fuzzy optimization model for QFD planning process using analytic network approach. *European Journal of Operational Research, 171*(2), 390-411.

Kao, J.J., & Lin, H.U. (1996). Multifactorial spatial analysis of landfill siting. *Journal of Environmental Engineering, 122*, 902-908.

Karsak, E.E. (2002). Distance-based fuzzy MCDM approach for evaluating flexible manufacturing system alternatives. *International Journal of Production Research, 40*(13), 3167-3181.

Kaufmann, A., & Gupta, M.M. (1985). *Introduction to fuzzy arithmetic: Theory and applications.* New York: Von Nostrand Reinhold.

Mahler, C.F., & Lima, G.S. (2003). Applying value analysis and fuzzy logic to select areas for installing waste fills. *Environmental Monitoring and Assessment, 84*, 129-140.

Mikhailov, L., & Singh, M.G. (2003). Fuzzy analytic network process and its application to the development of decision support systems. *IEEE Transactions on Systems, Man and Cybernetics, 33*(1), 33-41.

Mohanty, R.P., Agarwal, R., Choudhury, A.K., & Tiwari, M.K. (2005). A fuzzy ANP-based approach to R&D project selection: A case study. *International Journal of Production Research, 43*(24), 5199-5216.

Neaupane, K.M., & Piantanakulchai, M. (2006). Analytic network process model for landslide hazard zonation. *Engineering Geology, 85*, 281-294.

Nema, K.M, & Gupta, S.K. (1999). Optimization of regional hazardous waste management systems: An improved formulation. *Waste Management, 19*, 441-451.

Önüt, S., & Soner, S. (2008). Transshipment site selection using the AHP and TOPSIS under fuzzy environment. *Waste Management, 28*(9), 1552-1559.

Pohekar, S.D., & Ramachandran, M. (2004). Application of multi-criteria decision making to sustainable energy planning: A review. *Renewable and Sustainable Energy Reviews, 8*, 365-381.

Rakas, J., Teodorovic, D., & Kim, T. (2004). Multi-objective modeling for determining location of undesirable facilities. *Transportation Research Part D, 9*, 125-138.

Ramik, J. (2006). A decision system using ANP and fuzzy inputs. In *Proceedings of the 12th International Conference on the Foundations and Applications of Utility, Risk and Decision Theory*. Roma.

Ramuu, N., & Kennedy, W. (1994). Heuristic algorithm to locate solid waste disposal site. *Journal of Urban Planning and Development, 120*, 14-21.

Saaty, T.L. (1999, August 12-14). Fundamentals of the analytic network process. In *Proceedings of ISAHP 1999*, Kobe, Japan.

Saaty, T.L. 1996. *Decision making with dependence and feedback: The analytic network process*. Pittsburgh: RWS Publications.

Saaty, R.W. (2003). *Decision making in complex environment: The analytic hierarchy process (AHP) for decision making and the analytic network process (ANP) for decision making with dependence and feedback*. Retrieved July 8, 2008, from http://www.Superdecisions.com

Saaty, T.L., & Vargas, L.G. (1998). Diagnosis with dependent symptoms: Bayes theorem and the analytic network process. *Operations Research, 46*(4), 491-502.

Salminen, P., Hokkanen, J., & Lahdelma, R. (1998). Comparing multicriteria methods in the context of environmental problems. *European Journal of Operational Research, 104*, 485-496.

Shyur H.J. (2006). COTS evaluation using modified TOPSIS and ANP. *Applied Mathematics and Computation, 177*(1), 251-259.

Shyur, H.-J., & Shih, H.-S. (2006). A hybrid MCDM model for strategic vendor selection. *Mathematical and Computer Modeling, 44*, 749-761.

Siddiqui, M.Z., Everett, J.W., & Vieux, B.E. (1996). Landfill siting using geographic information systems: A demonstration. *Journal of Environmental Engineering, 122*, 515-523.

Stowers, C.L., & Palekar, V.S. (1993). Location models with routing considerations for a single obnoxious facility. *Transportation Science, 27*(4), 350-362.

Tuzkaya, G., Önüt, S., Tuzkaya, U.R., & Gülsün, B. (2008). The analytic network process approach for locating undesirable facilities: An example from Istanbul, Turkey. *Journal of Environmental Management, 88*(4), 970-983.

Wadhwa, V., & Ravindran, A.R. (2007). Vendor selection in outsourcing. *Computers & Operations Research, 34*, 3725-3737.

Wey, W.-M. (2005). An integrated expert system/operations research approach for the optimization of waste incinerator siting problems. *Knowledge-Based Systems, 18*, 267-278.

Yang, T., & Hung, C.-C. (2007). Multiple-attribute decision making methods for plant layout design problem. *Robotics and Computer-Integrated Manufacturing, 23*(1), 126-137.

Yeşilnacar, M.I., & Cetin, H. (2005). Site selection for hazardous wastes: A case study from the GAP area, Turkey. *Engineering Geology, 81*, 371-388.

Yu, R., & Tzeng, G.H. (2006). A soft computing method for multi-criteria decision making with dependence and feedback. *Applied Mathematics and Computation, 180*, 63-75.

Zadeh, L.A. (1965). Fuzzy sets. *Information and Control, 8*, 338-353.

Zimmermann, H.J. (1991). *Fuzzy set theory and its applications* (2nd ed.). London: Kluwer Academic.

ADDITIONAL READING

Alumur, S., & Kara, B.Y. (2007). A new model for the hazardous waste location-routing problem. *Computers & Operations Research, 34*(5), 1406-1423.

Boffey, T.B., & Karkazis, J. (1993). Models and methods for location and routing decisions relating to hazardous materials. *Studies in Locational Analysis, 5*, 149-166.

Chen, C.T. (2000). A fuzzy approach to select location of the distribution center. *Fuzzy Sets Systems, 118*, 65-73.

Chen, C.T. (2000). Extensions of the TOPSIS for group decision-making under fuzzy environment. *Fuzzy Sets and Systems, 114*, 1-9.

Chen, S.J., & Hwang, C.L. (1992). *Fuzzy multiple attribute decision-making: Methods and applications*. New York: Springer-Verlag.

Cram, S., Sommer, I., Morales, L., Oropeza, O., Carmona, E., & Gonzales-Medrano, F. (2006). Suitability of the vegetation types in Mexico's Tamaulipas state for the siting of hazardous waste treatment plants. *Journal of Environmental Management, 80*, 13-24.

Current, J., & Ratick, S. (1995). A model to assess risk, equity and efficiency in facility location and transportation of hazardous materials. *Location Science, 3*(3), 187-202.

Erkut, E., & Verter, V. (1995). *Hazardous materials logistics in facility location: A survey of applications and methods*. New York: Springer-Verlag.

Flahaut, B., Laurent, M., & Thomas, I. (2002). Locating a community recycling center within a residential area: A Belgian case study. *The Professional Geographer, 54*(1), 67-82.

Hale, T.S., & Moderg, C.R. (2003). Location science research: A review. *Annals of Operations Research, 123*, 21-35.

Hung, M., Yang, W., Ma, H., & Yang, Y. (2006). A novel multiobjective programming approach dealing with qualitative and quantitative objectives for environmental management. *Ecological Economics, 56*, 584-593.

Karagiannidis, A., & Moussiopoulos, N. (1998). A model generating framework for regional waste management taking local peculiarities explicitly into account. *Location Science, 6*, 281-305.

Liang, G.S., & Wang, M.J.J. (1991). A fuzzy multicriteria decision-making method for facility site selection. *International Journal of Production Research, 29*, 2313-2330.

List, G., & Mirchandani, P. (1991). An integrated network/planar multiobjective model for routing and siting for hazardous material and wastes. *Transportation Science, 25*, 100-114.

Meade, L. (1998). Strategic analysis of logistics and supply chain management systems using the analytical network process. *Transportation Research Part E-Logistics and Transportation Review, 34*(3), 201-215.

Meade, L.M., & Presley A. (2002). R and D project selection using the analytic network process. *IEEE Transaction on Engineering Management, 49*(1), 59-66.

Meade, L.M., & Sarkis, J. (1999). Analyzing organizational project alternatives for agile manufacturing processes an analytical network approach. *International Journal of Production Research, 37*(2), 241-246.

Meyer, C.D. (2000). *Matrix analysis and applied linear algebra*. PA, USA: Society for Industrial and Applied Mathematics SIAM.

Ölçer, A.I., & Odabaşı, A.Y. (2005). A new fuzzy multiple attributive group decision making methodology and its application to propulsion/manoeuvring system selection problem. *European Journal of Operational Research, 166*, 93-114.

Opricovic, S., & Tzeng, G. (2004). Compromise solution by MCDM methods: A comparative analysis of VIKOR and TOPSIS. *European Journal of Operational Research, 156*, 445-455.

Partovi, F.Y. (2006). An analytic model for locating facilities strategically. *Omega, 34*, 41-55.

Perez, J.A.M., Vega, J.M.M., & Verdegay, J.L. (2004). Fuzzy location problems on Networks. *Fuzzy sets and Systems, 142*, 393-405.

Ramik, J. (2007). A decision system using ANP and fuzzy inputs. *International Journal of Innovative Computing, Information and Control, 3*(4), 825-837.

Ravi, V., Shankar, R., & Tiwari, M.K. (2005). Analyzing alternatives in reverse logistics for end-of-life computers: ANP and balanced scorecard approach. *Computers & Industrial Engineering, 48*(2), 327-356.

Revelle, C., Cohon, J., & Shorbrys, D. (1991). Simultaneous siting and routing in the disposal of hazardous wastes. *Transportation Science, 25*, 138-145.

Rodriguez, J.J.S., Garcia, C.G., Perez, J.M., & Casermeiro, E.M. (2006). A general model for the undesirable single facility location problem. *Operations Research Letters, 34*, 427-436.

Ross, T.J. (2004). *Fuzzy logic with engineering applications*. John Wiley & Sons.

Saaty, T.L. (2001). *Decision making with dependence and feedback: The analytic network process*. USA: RWS Publications.

Sarkis, J. (1998). Evaluating environmentally conscious business practices. *European Journal of Operational Research, 107*, 159-174.

Sarkis, J. (1999). Methodological framework for evaluating environmentally conscious manufacturing programs. *Computers & Industrial Engineering, 36*, 793-810.

Sarkis, J. (2003). A strategic decision framework for green supply chain management. *Journal of Cleaner Production, 11*(4), 397-408.

Sener, B., Süzen, M.L., & Doyuran, V. (2006). Landfill site selection by using geographic information systems. *Environmental Geology, 49*, 376-388.

Vasiloglou, V.C. (2004). New tool for landfill location. *Waste Management Researches, 22*, 427-439.

Yurdakul, M. (2003). Measuring long-term performance of a manufacturing firm using the analytic network process (ANP) approach. *International Journal of Production Research, 41*(11), 2501-2529.

Chapter X
Sustainable Product Service Systems:
Potential to Deliver Business and Social Benefits with Less Resource Use

David Ness
University of South Australia, Australia

ABSTRACT

This chapter introduces sustainable product service systems (S-PSS) as a means of achieving both forward and reverse supply chain utilization, leading to much improved resource productivity coupled with business and social benefits. It outlines the challenge to enable economic growth, especially in developing countries, with corresponding reduction in consumption of resources, greenhouse emissions, and waste. It is argued that S-PSS can make a significant contribution, not only in greening products, but also in poverty alleviation, employment generation, and social development. An Australian, industry-based product stewardship scheme for used computers is first outlined. The potential for S-PSS to take product stewardship to a new level is then explained, with reference to several Hewlett-Packard case studies and research involving Interface modular carpets. The author hopes that the potential for S-PSS to deliver business and social benefits with less resource use may be recognized, leading to necessary further investigation and research.

INTRODUCTION

The notion of *product service systems* (PSS), whereby products are not sold to customers but are provided as part of a service or rental contract, originated in the business world due to perceived business benefits. More recently, it has been recognized that such systems may also have environmental advantages because they facilitate take-back, reuse, and recycling, thus reducing material consumption, energy, emissions, and waste. Hence, the concept of *sustainable product service*

Copyright © 2009, IGI Global, distributing in print or electronic forms without written permission of IGI Global is prohibited.

systems (S-PSS) has gained in usage, especially in Europe, and exemplifies the "service economy." However, its application to the Asia Pacific region, and especially developing countries, is a relatively unexplored area. S-PSS has the potential not just for greening of business but also for achieving economic development, improving the lives of the poor and contributing towards achievement of the UN Millennium Development Goals (see http://www.un.org/millenniumgoals/goals.html). It may become an important mechanism for advancing "Green Growth," environmentally sustainable economic growth for the benefit of all, a concept promoted by the UN (ESCAP, 2006).

This chapter examines the basic principles of S-PSS, and the potential environmental and business benefits, outlining some preliminary research at the University of South Australia. Drawing upon several case studies, it shows how PSS may be exemplified by the Hewlett-Packard (HP) approach to selling services and how this may lead to S-PSS. The chapter then highlights the exciting potential for applications in developing countries.

THE CHALLENGE: ECONOMIC GROWTH WITH LESS RESOURCE USE

As Manzini and Vezzoli (2002) have acknowledged, developing countries need to go through a process of economic growth to reach a similar standard of living of developed countries, with some increase in consumption of natural resources to be expected. The challenge is to achieve necessary growth but with less resource use and "ecological footprint," a measure of the impact of resource consumption and waste on the planet (see http://www.footprintnetwork.org/). If developing countries follow the extravagant consumption pattern of the west (footprint exceeding 5 global hectares per person) then the planet will be unable to cope with the pressure on resources.

In this regard, the western or Fordist "production-consumption model," based on growth and throughput, is not the way forward. This model exhibits a linear material flow: resource extraction-production-consumption-waste; increase of productivity only becomes possible by using more fixed capital and consuming growing quantities of matter and energy (Altvater, 1993). The business application of PSS may act as an opportunity to facilitate the process of industrialization in developing countries, by "leap-frogging" the stage characterized by individual consumption/ownership of mass produced goods towards the more advanced service economy, thus avoiding some of the mistakes made by developed countries (Manzini & Vezzoli, 2002). PSS is increasingly seen as a possible and promising solution for the sustainable development dilemma, although a major cultural shift is required (Leong, 2006). This is especially so with some consumer products, where ownership is a symbol of status and style. Perhaps the biggest potential for PSS is in business transactions, where ownership may assume less importance.

Associated with the global 3R Initiative (Japan Ministry of the Environment, 2005), involving reduce, reuse, and recycle, various countries have embraced a new economic growth mode that operates in the way of resource extraction - production - consumption - regenerated resources. This is reflected by Korea's "resource circulating society," Japan's "sound material-cycle society," Thailand's "sufficiency economy," and the "circular economy policy" of the People's Republic of China. By organizing economic activities in a closed-loop of materials, these approaches promote harmony between the economic system and the ecosystem, consistent with the notion of a "cyclical restorative economy" introduced by Hawken (1993). New types of industrialization are being pursued, with the eco-efficiency of take-back and recycling being well understood (Huisman & Stevels, 2006). Among these, product and service design to promote reduce, reuse, and recycling of materials and "sustainable product and service design" are at the leading edge of innovation. They offer the potential to achieve substantial improvements in resource productivity, such as Factor 4, where productivity grows fourfold. On the one hand, this involves doubling wealth and, on the other, halving resource use (WBCSD, 2000; von Weizsacker, Lovins, & Lovins, 1997). The Wuppertal Institute communicates Factor 4 best practices and has developed a useful indicator system enabling appraisal of "ecologic, economic and social effects" (see http://www.wupperinst.org/FactorFour/). Some have argued that even greater resource productivity is required to accompany ambitious growth targets, even Factor 10 (see Factor 10 Institute http://www.factor10-institute.org/seitenges/Factor10.htm).

Greening of business through resource or eco-efficiency is an important element of the UN "Green Growth" programme. Thus, ESCAP organized the 3rd Green Growth Policy Dialogue on "the Greening of Business and the Environment as a Business Opportunity" in June 2007 (ESCAP, 2007). It was recommended that ESCAP should promote green business growth opportunities to aid the poor in escaping the poverty trap, with governments supporting local enterprises in achieving Millennium Development Goal 1 (poverty reduction) in synergy with MDG 7 (environmental sustainability). Among other conclusions, it was recommended that the private sector should improve the eco-efficiency of resource use in processes and operations, so that services provided by products were achieved with the least materials flow throughout the product's life.

PRODUCT STEWARDSHIP AND TAKE-BACK SCHEMES

Industry is already responding to the above challenges through corporate social responsibility (CSR), environmental charters and, of special interest to this chapter, product stewardship approaches. These involve reverse supply chain management, whereby products are taken back and the parts recovered and recycled, usually on an industry sector basis (see Huisman & Stevels, 2006).

Within the information technology (IT) industry, this is exemplified by the "Byteback" programme that has operated in Victoria, Australia, since 2005 (Sustainability Victoria, 2006). Byteback is a free service, available to residents and small business owners who want to dispose of unwanted, old, and unused computers in a safe and environmentally responsible manner. Initially piloted by Sustainability Victoria in partnership with HP in June 2005, the scheme now involves the Australian Information Industry Association (AIIA) in association with HP and other partners, including Apple, Canon, Dell, Epson, Fujitsu, Fuji-Xerox, IBM, Lenovo, and Lexmark. Personal computer systems including desktops, laptops, computer mice, monitors, printers, scanners, keyboards, computer power supplies, printed circuit boards, motherboards, network and memory cards, disk and CD drives are all deposited at collection points. After collection, equipment is transported to a specialized electronic recycling and recovery centre, where it is disassembled into its parts (e.g., plastic, metals, chemicals, and glass) and sent off to various parts of Australia and the world for recovery and recycling. Since its launch, the Byteback scheme has collected close to 500 tons of "e-waste," with an overall diversion from landfill of 97%. Materials reuse vs. virgin material manufacture has resulted in a carbon offset of 2700 tons (1 ton of computer waste equates to 5.45 tons of carbon). Initially supported by the Victorian Government, it is expected to be self-supporting by late 2008. In addition to expansion of the scheme within Victoria (Hewlett-Packard, 2007), the AIIA is designing a framework for a national industry-wide IT return and recycling scheme, under a national product stewardship initiative (see EPHC, 2004), an example of extended producer responsibility at an industry level.

In terms of the 3Rs and the waste hierarchy, recycling is far preferable to disposal, but can be energy intensive. Further reductions in waste and energy may be achieved through reuse, and avoidance of waste in the first place. As Stahel (1994) pointed out, the reuse of goods slows down the flow of materials from production to recycling (or disposal), whereas recycling does not influence the speed of the flow of materials or goods through the economy. This is where reverse supply chain management may meet forward supply chain management, which emphasizes the use of fewer resources in the process and increased resource utilization. In this regard, the concept of individual producers retaining ownership of products over their life, and supplying these as part of a service, offers much promise. Product service systems (PSS) may not only incorporate design for disassembly, but also facilitate take-back and reuse, with the entire process, from cradle to grave or, preferably, cradle to cradle, having the potential to reduce consumption of materials, energy, and other resources, with less pollution and waste. The added attraction of business and social benefits mean that such schemes warrant special attention.

SUSTAINABLE PRODUCT SERVICE SYSTEMS

Product service systems (PSS) involve a shift from product ownership to use; shifting the business focus from designing and selling physical products to selling a system of products and services that are jointly capable of fulfilling specific client demands (see Manzini & Vezzoli, 2002). The basic idea is that products are seen as "service carriers" (Ayres, 1999).

The potential for PSS has been recognized for over a decade. Arguably, the "father" of PSS is Walter Stahel who recognized, in the early 1980s, that extending the "use-life" of goods was an essential part of a transition to a more sustainable society (Stahel, 1982). Later, Stahel linked product life extension to the "utilization-focused service economy," differentiating between sale, rental, and "selling system utilization" (Stahel, 1994). Around that time, Hawken highlighted the potential of the leasing concept to extend product life and conserve resources (Hawken, 1993). More recently, a significant PSS-related research effort has been underway under the 5th European Commission research framework. This is well documented under the Sustainable Consumption Research Exchange or SCORE (http://www.score-network.org), SusProNet (www.suspronet.org/) and in the methodology for product service innovation (MEPSS) developed by van Halen, Vezzoli, and Wimmer (2005). As Stoughton, Horic, and Nakao (in press) have noted, PSS research in Japan has also increased significantly, including investigations through the Business for Sustainability project through the Institute for Global Environmental Strategies (IGES), Kansai Research Centre. The U.S. Environmental Protection Agency has promoted "servicizing" (see White, Stoughton, & Feng, 1999), while the UNEP Production and Consumption Branch has also strongly advocated PSS (see http://www.uneptie.org/PC/sustain/design/pss.htm) and issued publications and a brochure (UNEP, 2002). However, J.C. Diehl and colleagues at the Technical University of Delft are among the few to have instigated research and applications involving developing countries (Diehl, 2006).

PSS approaches, whereby ownership remains with the producer, can be categorized as:

a. **Use-oriented services:** These provide consumers with access to the product and the function it provides without the need to own the product, for example, renting or leasing. Business applications to date include services such as lighting, chemicals, air comfort, paint, mobility (e.g., car sharing), floor coverings, and business equipment;

b. **Result-oriented services:** These provide a function to the customer who in turn pays for this function rather than use of, or access to, a particular product. Applications include waste and energy management, water treatment, and communications.

(See Stoughton et al., in press; van Halen et al., 2005).

PSS is not automatically sustainable. As van Halen et al. (2005, p. 2) have noted,

Although PSS strategies and sustainable development paths often coincide, there is no universal rule. PSSs need to be well-planned and developed to fully realize their sustainable development potential and to avoid negative side effects. For example, they can create extra transportation or packaging for the individualized delivery of goods/services.

To realize their full potential (S-PSS), product service systems may require reconfiguring with products being designed—in standardized, modular form—for ease of reuse, disassembly, and recycling via remanufacturing. Energy will be saved where products or their components can be reused in as close as possible to the original form. This reflects the aforementioned 3R approach (reduce, reuse, and recycle), with reduce and reuse using less energy than recycling) and, as Stahel (1982, 1994) has emphasized, leading to

Table 1. Comparison of S-PSS with product stewardship

S-PSS	Product Stewardship/recycling/take-back
Ownership of product retained by service provider	Ownership transferred to customer
Holistic management of suite of services by "solution provider" for customer leading to improved service for customer	Not normally as responsibility passes to customer with sale/ purchase
Ease of technological updating by provider for customer	Updating requires purchase of new equipment and disposal
Provider manages fleet of products for customer, leading to increased utilization, reduction in fleet, and efficiencies	Not normally
Reporting by provider on performance of fleet in meeting service outcomes	Not normally. Performance is related to levels of collection, recycling and resource recovery, at industry level
Payment can be related to performance	Not normally
Partnership between provider and customer opens up opportunities for other profit centres/increased business	Not normally
Almost certain that product will be taken back and greater chance of reuse/recycling	Depends on consumers depositing used equipment at collection points (even if free)
Provider has incentive to design product and components in robust, modular, standardized form for ease of disassembly and enabling longevity	Some incentive due to take-back and recycling
Customer pays stream of payments, not large capital cost up front	No
Employment generation including remanufacturing, services	Some employment generation in collection, sorting, disassembly, recycling, etc.
Less resource use (materials, energy, water) and emissions, waste due to products being kept in closed loop - reduced/reused resources	Recycling uses more energy than reuse

greater profitability. As will be shown later, better management of a fleet or stock of assets/products may lead to reduction in the number required to perform a service, through their more efficient utilization.

Computing and other business equipment is especially suitable for PSS due to rapid technological change in IT, with equipment quickly becoming out of date and having a relatively short life. HP, which has had recycling programmes in place for 20 years, is seeking to exemplify S-PSS, with components—as far as practicable—being kept in a closed loop, reducing consumption of new resources and waste to landfill, coupled with an emphasis on energy reduction and efficiency.

PSS solutions, and the shift from procuring products to services, require new sets of skills that are not generally present, and a culture change in procurement, "a fundamental change in the relationship between producer and consumer" (ESCAP, 2006, p. 19). They can also lead to increased management costs, reflecting the complexity of the concept. Notwithstanding these and other barriers, PSS may offer a triple win (people, planet, profit) scenario that combines sustainable concepts with powerful presence in the marketplace. The basic idea is that a company's commercial value goes beyond the spreading of material goods (Van Halen et al., 2005).

Table 1 seeks to highlight the key operational aspects of S-PSS, with comparison to reverse supply chain utilization as represented by product stewardship, recycling, and take-back.

As Hawken, Lovins, and Lovins (1999) pointed out, service leasing fits perfectly with the manufacturer's life cycle responsibility for ultimate remanufacturing. A focus on selling services or functions instead of physical products can, through remanufacturing, be a way of closing material flows (Sundin, Bjorkman, & Jacobsson, 2000). When a company decides to sell services, a closer connection with the customer can be established and better control over the products can be achieved. When this is accompanied by reuse and remanufacturing, then economic and environmental—and perhaps social—benefits can be achieved.

THE HP "SERVICE SOLUTION"

As one of a menu of procurement options available to customers, HP offers an "End User Workplace Solution" (EUWS). An example of PSS, this involves provision of business equipment to customers as part of a "service solution."

In addition to the benefits of higher service levels at a reduced cost, significant energy savings can also be generated over the lifetime usage of the IT equipment, coupled with savings in greenhouse emissions and reduced waste. To this can be added savings in embodied energy associated with the production of computing equipment, and reduced consumption of resources (materials, water, and energy).

These energy savings and other environmental benefits can be included in the Total Cost of Ownership (TCO) model which is used to quantify and calculate the benefits of moving to a S-PSS solution. Research based on a series of pilot studies is planned with the University of South Australia and the South Australian Government to fully quantify and verify these benefits.

Figure 1 introduces a roadmap approach for implementation of S-PSS solutions. Each of these individual steps can generate benefits in improved service or reduced support cost. The approach is consistent with ISO 9004: 2000, the international standard for quality management systems. Clients do not necessarily need to make a big jump to a complete service solution, but can take steps progressively and incrementally towards this. While each of these steps should lead to service benefits, the total benefits of a combined S-PSS solution are greater once all the component areas are aligned into a single solution.

Figure 1. HP roadmap to Sustainable Product Service Solution (S-PSS)

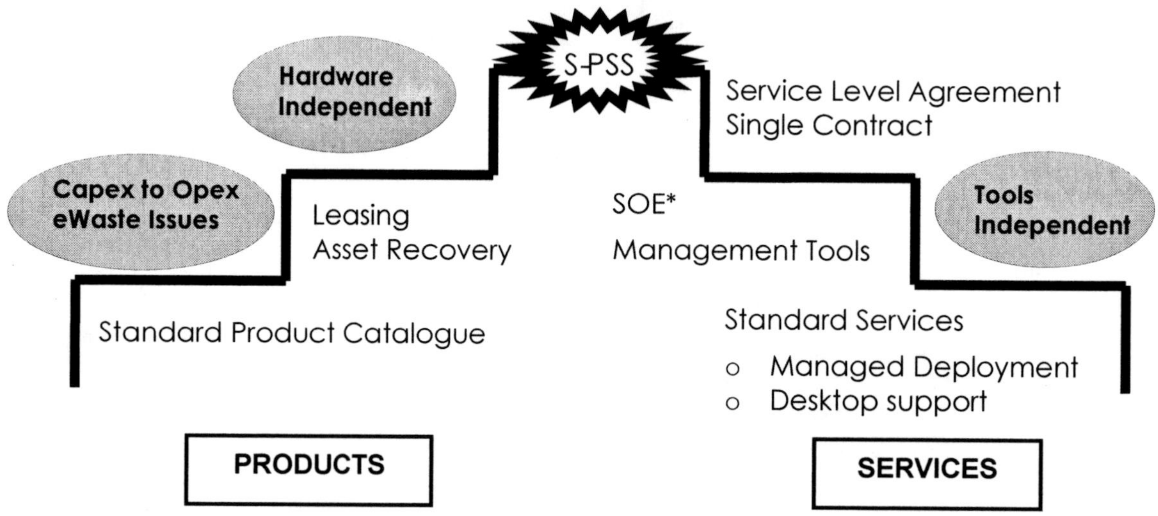

**SOE – Standard Operating Environment.*
Contains the operating system and all desktop software applications, for example, MS Office

Some Examples of HP Service Solution

Examples of HP service solutions involving several different client organisations are now presented to demonstrate how PSS has successfully delivered commercial benefits, with an indication of how it may also deliver environmental benefits (S-PSS).

Krung Thai Bank, Thailand, uses a "Desktop Lifecycle Solution," part of HP's suite of End User Workplace Solutions, to manage its 12 000 PCs. The solution provides desktop PCs and laptops, bundled with software and services as a utility, priced on a per-seat (user) per month basis for ease of procurement, ease of financing, and a single source of vendor accountability. It aims to reduce desktop Total Cost of Ownership and increase quality of service to end-users. These services span the entire life cycle of the desktops from acquisition, deployment, management, operation, maintenance right through to disposal, and "technology refresh." The service also includes a central helpdesk and a service level agreement. This enables the bank to focus more on its strategic core competencies, to be free of the burdens and risks of IT desktop management, to have flexible and cost-effective access to expertise, and to have increased agility to respond to new business opportunities.

The Universal College of Learning (UCOL), New Zealand, also chose to work with HP in an outsourced environment, procuring three HP services: Desktop Solutions, Service Desk Solutions, and Server Management. UCOL's heterogeneous desktop environment made hardware "refreshes" very labour intensive. The HP Desktop Solutions now provide full support for the assortment of end-user devices used by students and staff. Greater efficiency and utilization of the computing "fleet" has been achieved, allowing UCOL to eliminate more than 200 desktops from the network. Periodic hardware "refresh" ensures desktops stay compatible with the IT industry. Another feature is a Standard Operating Environment (SOE), with UCOL being able to upgrade and expand regularly, quickly, and uniformly across its computer fleet. Software for specific courses can be introduced readily to a group of computers. UCOL now has achieved higher levels of productivity for end users and IT staff through industry-standard technology, defined service level agreements, rapid problem resolution, and a well-documented process for change management. The results show a 133% return on investment (ROI) in 5 years.

The International Rice Research Institute (IRRI) is another organization that implemented an End-User Workplace Solution (EUWS). Cost savings resulted from the increased efficiency and productivity of users and IT management staff, and transferring PC hardware and software costs from an ownership to a service model. With a total investment in EUWS of US$2.25M over 3 years, it is estimated that IRRI will experience an ROI of 193%.

Fleet Management

An important element of the HP approach is to offer clients a "fleet management" service. HP can manage the stock of business equipment so that it is used more efficiently, reducing the number of products. For example, in the UCOL example described above, more than 200 computers could be, or were, eliminated from the network. Similarly, in the IRRI example, the number of printers was reduced, with a goal of reducing the total printers from 400 to 200. Such more efficient use not only reduces resource consumption and operating energy, but also leads to savings in IT support employee hours. Moreover, HP can report on the performance and utilization of the individual products and fleet. When combined with "remote client solutions," involving centralization of computer hardware and data, "fleet management" has the potential to achieve dramatic savings in energy and other resources, in addition to cost savings.

From PSS to S-PSS

The above examples are certainly product service systems, and provide a sound basis for sustainable product service systems (i.e., S-PSS), building upon HP's achievements in the environmental field. The HP approach relies heavily on product end-of-life management, which includes product collection, remanufacturing, recycling, and disposal. HP's global *Planet Partners* programme operates in more than 40 countries. The recycled materials are used in new HP products, as well as a range of products in other industries. In Australia, as indicated earlier, HP was the initial industry partner in the "Byteback" computer take-back and recycling scheme.

Energy Saving Settings

By 2010, HP is committed to reducing the energy consumption of its desktop and notebook product lines by 25%, relative to 2005.

All current model HP PCs and monitors are provided with energy saving settings. Compared to older models of PCs, a single PC with such power settings saves enough energy to power a 75W light bulb continuously for over a year. For every 12 consumers who keep these power settings enabled on their PCs and monitors, CO_2 emissions equivalent to removing one average automobile off the road may be avoided. In addition, power management can save up to $75 per desktop computer and monitor each year. Thus, by using less power, HP's new energy-efficient business desktop PCs are better for the environment and help consumers reduce energy costs. HP is also the first major PC manufacturer to offer 80% efficient power supplies, enabling total system power consumption to be reduced by up to 52%.

The total energy consumption of the overall computer service is also an important consideration. For example, HP established an on-campus Help Desk at UCOL. Not only did this provide an additional training opportunity for students, but it also provided a quicker response to user problems. What may be overlooked is that such an on-site facility also reduces the travel cost and associated emissions associated with a response.

There are tools available which can report on energy use/emissions for clients, to show the improvements and efficiencies gained. The "Surveyor" product from Verdiem can be used to set PC power management settings and to track the energy savings achieved (see http://www.verdiem.com).

FUTURE DIRECTIONS

Future innovations include equipment with a much lower footprint, even without the need for a monitor: The screen image can be projected with infra-red technology on to a nearby surface. Furthermore, networking of computers enables a reduction in the number of data centres, with equipment being able to be "leveraged" from others in the network. This may have particular applications in developing countries, where the smaller footprint, robust, and lower energy equipment is likely to be more affordable and reliable. The data centre can be remote, with remote villages being able to have computer access provided they are connected to the network. This has considerable potential for enabling IT access to the rural poor, aiding achievement of the MDGs.

As van Halen et al. (2005) have commented, radical new business models are required for doing business with the world's 4 billion poorest people, or 2/3 of the global population. New ICT can play an important enabling role for this "low transaction size/high volume" market by creating connectivity. This is exemplified by Microsoft's "Unlimited Potential" programme aimed at the 5 billion people for whom the opportunity to learn, connect, create, and succeed remains elusive (see http://www.microsoft.com/emerging/default.mspx). The programme may enable sustained social and economic opportunity for the poor in both developed and especially developing countries. PSS may lead to more appropriate means for poor people to access services, for example, by creating local service centres or product rental propositions.

OTHER APPLICATIONS AND WIDER POTENTIAL

The service approach has much wider applications than computer services. As indicated earlier, there are already examples of "lighting management services" (Matsushita Electric Works Ltd), "energy services companies" or ESCOs, "chemical management services," "call-a-bike," "car sharing," "subscription services for organic food products," and many more. However, while an increasing number of businesses and clients are realizing the benefits of S-PSS, the approach is still in its infancy. It is important to be able to develop and test "pilot" applications, measuring the costs and benefits, and especially comparing the costs and benefits of service solutions with sale and purchase. Further testing and research is undoubtedly required.

The service approach, moreover, has the potential to lead to economic, environmental, and social benefits when applied at a community level in poorer developing countries. Products forming part of the service system may be manufactured, maintained, and repaired within the community, generating employment for poor women. For example, solar lanterns are being assembled within communities in India, involving the Energy and Resources Institute (see Chowdhury, 2006), while conversion of petrol powered 3-wheeled vehicles to electric created an electric vehicle industry in Nepal (Dhakal, 2002). Grameen Shakti (GS), Bangladesh, has introduced soft financing options for rural people who wish to buy a solar photovoltaic (PV) system, as part of its renewable energy technologies programme and whole system approach (see http://www.gshakti.net). Of particular interest is that GS has also introduced another financial model, known as Micro-utility, in order to reach the poor. It allows those who cannot afford a solar home system by themselves to *share* the benefit and cost of one, such as one shopkeeper sharing his/her system with other shopkeepers for a fee. Diehl (2006) has pioneered PSS applications in developing countries, for example, PV lighting in Cambodia and there may be useful synergies with the Grameen approach. Thus, a service solution, where the products/equipment are shared and rented within the community, may add another important and exciting dimension towards sustainability. This is akin to taking a further step not only with the HP "roadmap," but also towards the MDGs.

RESEARCH AT THE UNIVERSITY OF SOUTH AUSTRALIA

The Interface Approach

Ray Anderson, former Chairman and Chief Executive Officer of Interface Inc., championed a "mid-course correction" in the global carpet company (see Anderson, 1998). In 1994, Interface declared its vision to embark on a sustainability journey with the goal to ultimately leave no environmental footprint (see http://www.interfacesustainability.com).

A key part of this strategy was to create products for cradle to cradle cycles, within which materials are perpetually circulated in closed loops. For example, Interface designs and manufactures its carpet tiles so that, when they are "reclaimed," the backing (bitumen or vinyl) can be detached from the face fibre (nylon). In the U.S., nylon is commercially recycled to auto components through a relationship with a car manufacturer. Vinyl backing can theoretically be recycled 100%, with other vinyl products being recycled into carpet tiles.

Interface has conducted life cycle assessment (LCA) of their products and processes, consistent with the international standard (see Standards Australia, 1998). The carbon equivalent emissions (CO_{2e}) through the life cycle of Interface carpet are summarized in Table 2. It is noteworthy that most of the emissions are associated with the raw material inputs. Interface has worked for over 10 years to minimize the impact of its own in-house processes, which is now reduced to less than 20% of the total environmental footprint of modular carpet. While it will continue to work to minimize impacts from its own mill activities, Interface is also turning its attention to influencing raw material suppliers to reduce impact, providing end of life options that ensure raw materials stay within "the loop," and reducing the need for new raw material inputs.

Anderson reasoned that if companies leased products (such as carpet) or provided them as

Table 2. Carbon equivalent (CO_{2e}) emissions through life cycle of Interface carpet

Material	*% CO_{2e} emissions*
Raw material inputs	*59*
Interface conversion	*19*
Carpet installation and use (including cleaning) for life of product	*8*
End of life (including removal, disposal and decomposition)	*14*
Total	*100*

part of a service, manufacturers would have an incentive to maximize and, ultimately, recapture the end-of-life value of their products, thereby reducing the need for virgin materials. Interface pioneered the concept of using leasing as a strategy to close material loops and, in 1995, launched a unique leasing programme for modular carpet tiles, known as the "Evergreen Lease" (Anderson, 1998; Ness, & Field, 2003). However, practical application of this leasing approach has so far proved difficult, as explained by White et al. (1999) and Fishbein, McGarry, and Dillon (2000), and it is understood that the concept of a carpet service through lease/rental has not been widely adopted by building owners and occupiers.

This motivated a group of researchers at the University of South Australia to compare rental and leasing procurement methods with the more common sale/purchase approach, from environmental and revenue perspectives, with the longer term ambition of applying the service approach to an entire office fitout, as had been envisaged by Hawken (1993), and to other sectors.

Methodology

A basic model was developed to enable exploration of the environmental ramifications of using alternative financial arrangements for procuring carpet. The model uses the criteria of revenue to the manufacturer, waste to landfill, and greenhouse gas equivalent emissions as the indicators of performance, and investigates purchase, rental, and lease-to-buy as the alternative financial arrangements. Interface Inc. kindly assisted with the provision of environmental and revenue data.

In the model, the relationship of a carpet manufacturer with the client is represented in time or "service" periods of around 7 years, corresponding to normal refurbishment intervals. At the end of each period, revenue is calculated, based on the probability that the manufacturer obtains a repeat order. The three possible methods of procurement, namely purchase, rental, and lease-to-buy each have different probabilities, with the chance of the manufacturer missing out on a repeat rental contract being very low, lease-to-buy reasonably high and re-purchase quite high, based on a hypothetical market place where all methods are available. The amount of waste to landfill and greenhouse gas emissions are also calculated accordingly for the three methods over sequential time periods. The specific components of the carpet that were considered with respect to waste and emissions were nylon, vinyl, and fibreglass.

Findings

Notwithstanding the preliminary nature of the research, the findings were promising. The model indicated not only a significant reduction in waste going to landfill when the carpet is supplied on a rental basis rather than with a lease or purchase arrangement (see Figure 2), but also similar advantages with emissions and even revenue to the manufacturer.

The model predicts this outcome due to a greater probability that the carpet supplier will remain in touch with the customer over the rental period and will be more likely to re-supply at the end of each service period. Hence, carpet can be returned to the factory for product recycling rather than being disposed of in landfill. The research has predicted similar reductions in greenhouse gas equivalent emissions. A major advantage to the carpet manufacturer is that the rental model predicts greater cumulative revenue over several carpet service periods compared with lease or purchase arrangements, resulting in a positive outcome for both the supplier and the environment (see Figure 3).

The research findings, reported to the World Sustainable Building Conference SB05 (Ness, Clement, Field, Filar, & Pullen, 2005), may be extrapolated very broadly to a wider context. If products can be taken back and fully recycled, a Factor 10 improvement in resource productivity is theoretically attainable. The research showed

Figure 2. Expected cumulative vinyl to be redirected (landfill saving) for 1,000 square metres of carpet

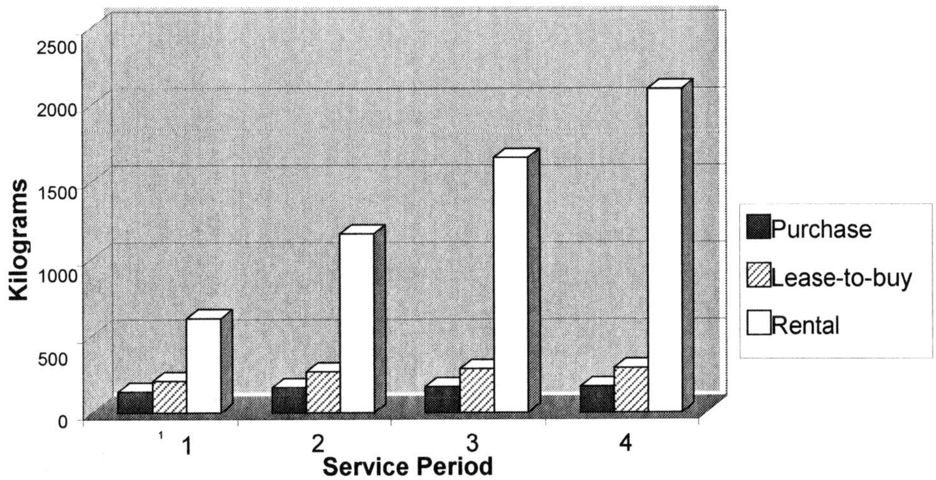

Figure 3. Expected cumulative revenue over 4 service periods for the three business models

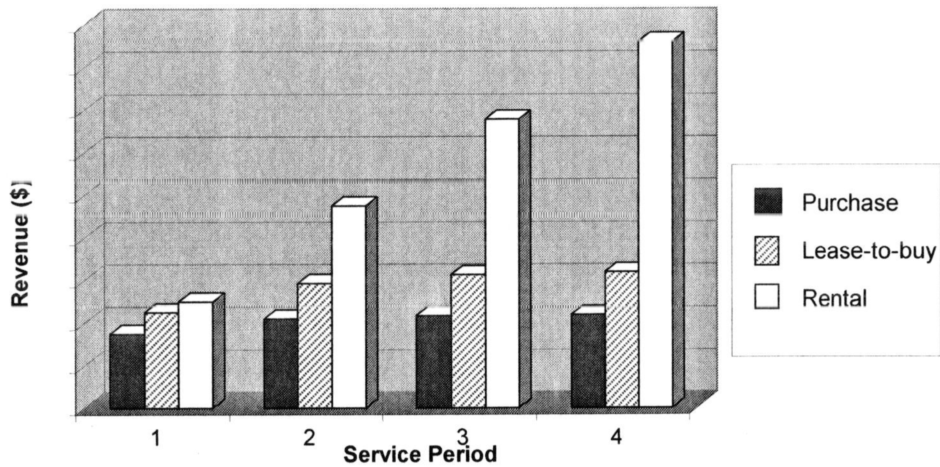

that, after four service periods (around 28 years), a seven-fold reduction in vinyl waste to landfill could be achieved, accompanied by over a doubling of revenue.

Research with HP

In association with HP and the South Australian Government, further research is planned to validate the above preliminary findings and develop an S-PSS business model and applications for public service organizations. It is hoped that this will demonstrate improved service for the government agencies as customers, profitable growth for service providers (e.g., HP), and reduced carbon footprints for both customers and service providers. The new model may then be extended to other industries and sectors.

CLOSING COMMENTS

HP is championing the S-PSS approach and is in discussion with the University of South Australia and others on how the HP End User Workplace Solution may be enhanced and its application extended. It is important that the costs and benefits of such new and innovative business models can be demonstrated, from both a financial and environmental perspective. S-PSS offers potential, beyond just the computer sector, to improve customer service with much reduced resource consumption, and with added social benefits, especially in poorer developing countries. Exemplifying "Green Growth" and eco-efficiency, it may be an important contributor to the achievement of the MDGs, a reduced ecological footprint and a Factor 4 or even Factor 10 improvement in resource productivity (ESCAP, 2006; WBCSD, 2000; von Weizsacker et al., 1997).

But there are many more steps required on the roadmap to sustainability and the implementation of a service economy. As the Asia Pacific Forum on Environment and Development (APFED, 2005) has commented: "There is a long journey ahead before the region will enjoy a resource efficient society, devoted to reuse, recycling and a service economy." Arguably, "a less materials-intensive society should be the ultimate aim, coupled with a more knowledge-based and service oriented economy" (p. 18).

FUTURE RESEARCH DIRECTIONS

Notwithstanding the progress made in Europe, Japan, and the U.S., and some preliminary research in Australia including that described above, the knowledge and application of PSS (let alone S-PSS) is in its infancy. A considerably strengthened applied research effort is required, based on universities and other research organizations, and especially those in rapidly developing countries such as PR China and India. In conjunction with governments and private companies such as HP, such a research network could act as a platform for introducing S-PSS, in a planned and staged manner. The research concentration in Europe, through the previously mentioned SCORE, could form the core of this network, in association with organizations such as the Asia Pacific Roundtable for Sustainable Consumption and Production (see http://www.aprscp.org/) and the international 3R initiative.

Research needs to demonstrate that selling services is able to deliver business and social benefits with less resource use, when compared with selling physical products, and over the life cycle of products using LCA techniques (see Standards Australia, 1998). To engage the attention of businesses and consumers and demonstrate benefits, successful pilot programmes and case studies are required, accompanied by research on behavioural change that involves the fields of humanities and management.

It is important that research and applications are related to government plans and policies, such as the 11th Five-Year Plan of the PR China, and its "Circular (or Recycling) Economy" policy. Governments can actively facilitate the introduction of S-PSS through their procurement policies, practices and "green purchasing" initiatives. For example, the research in South Australia, with the support of the government, is aimed at developing an S-PSS business model and applications for public service organizations.

A potentially exciting area of research is that related to community service systems, where S-PSS may be introduced through community organizations and cooperatives in developing countries, perhaps with support of the UN in relation to its "Green Growth" agenda.

ACKNOWLEDGMENT

I gratefully acknowledge the assistance of Mr. Michael H. Wagner, Business Development

Manager, South Pacific, End User Workplace Solutions, Hewlett-Packard Australia *michael.h.wagner@hp.com.*

REFERENCES

Altvater, E. (1993). *The future of the market.* London: Verso.

Anderson, R.C. (1998). *Mid-course correction: Towards a sustainable enterprise—the Interface model.* Atlanta, GA: The Peregrinzilla Press.

Asia Pacific Forum for Environment & Development (APFED). (2005). *Paradigm shift towards sustainability for Asia and the Pacific.* Retrieved July 8, 2008, from http://www.apfed.net/index.html

Ayres, R. (1999). *Products as service carriers: Should we kill the messenger, or send it back?* Centre for the Management of Environmental Resources. Fontainebleau, France: Zero Emissions Forum. Retrieved July 8, 2008, from http://www.unu.edu/zef/publications_e/ZEF_EN_1999_01_D.pdf

Chowdhury, F. (2006). Sun power, woman power. *Boloji.* Retrieved July 8, 2008, from http://www.boloji.com/wfs5/wfs625.htm

Dhakal, S. (2002). *Introduction of electric three-wheelers in Kathmandu, Nepal.* IGES. Retrieved July 8, 2008, from http://www.iges.or.jp/APEIS/RISPO/inventory/db/pdf/0018.pdf

Diehl, J.C. (2006). *Renewable energy in emerging countries from an end-user and business perspective.* Presentation to the Management of Technology Programme, University of California, Berkeley, in association with UN Industrial Development Organization (UNIDO). Retrieved July 8, 2008, from http://bridge.berkeley.edu/2006_Pages/PresentationArchives/2006/Panel%206/Diehl.pdf

EPHC. (2004, December). *Industry discussion paper on co-regulatory frameworks for product stewardship.* Environment Protection and Heritage Council, Australia. Retrieved July 8, 2008, from http://www.ephc.gov.au/pdf/product_stewardship/ProductStewardship_IndustryDP.pdf

ESCAP. (2006, March). *Green growth at a glance: The way forward for Asia and the Pacific.* UN Economic and Social Commission for Asia and the Pacific. Bangkok. Retrieved July 8, 2008, from http://www.unescap.org/esd/water/publications/sd/GGBrochure.pdf See also http://www.greengrowth.org

ESCAP. (2007, June 5-7). *3rd green growth policy dialogue on 'the greening of business and the environment as a business opportunity.* Bangkok. Retrieved July 8, 2008, from http://www.greengrowth.org/3ggpd_pres_media/pres-media.asp

Fishbein, B., McGarry, L., & Dillon, P. (2000). *Leasing: A step toward producer responsibility.* INFORM Inc, New York. Retrieved July 8, 2008, from http://www.informinc.org/reportpdfs/wp/Leasing.pdf

Frazao, R., & Rocha, C. (2004, October 30). *Product services in the need area "base materials.* Suspronet report. Retrieved July 8, 2008, from http://www.suspronet.org/fs_reports.htm

Hawken, P. (1993). *The ecology of commerce.* London: Weidenfield and Nicholson.

Hawken, P., Lovins, A., & Lovins, L.H. (1999). *Natural capitalism: The next industrial revolution.* London: Earthscan Publications.

Hewlett-Packard. (2007, September 6). *HP and sustainability Victoria expand their highly successful recycling programme.* Retrieved July 8, 2008, from http://h50025.www5.hp.com/ENP5/Public/Content.aspx?contentID=22821&portalID=367&pageID=1

Huisman, J., & Stevels, A.L.N. (2006, April). Eco-efficiency of take-back and recycling, a comprehensive approach. *IEEE Transactions of Electronics Packaging Manufacturing, 29*(2). Retrieved July 8, 2008, from http://www.io.tudelft.nl/live/binaries/683f3ab7-08ce-4c03-84a6-45c49d8b5127/doc/HuismanEcoefficiency.pdf

Japan Ministry of the Environment. (2005). *The 3R Initiative*. Japan. Retrieved July 8, 2008, from http://www.env.go.jp/recycle/3r/en

Leong, B.C.H. (2006, April 20-21). Is a radical systemic shift toward sustainability possible in China? In *Proceedings: Changes to Sustainable Consumption*, Copenhagen, Denmark (pp. 279-294).

Manzini, E., & Vezzoli, C. (2002, July). *Product service systems and sustainability: Opportunities for sustainable solutions*. Paris: UN Environment Program. Retrieved July 8, 2008, from http://www.uneptie.org/pc/sustain/reports/pss/pss-imp-7.pdf

Ness, D., Clement, S., Field, M., Filar, J., & Pullen, S. (2005, September 27-29). *(Approaches towards) sustainability in the built environment through dematerialization*. Paper presented at the World Sustainable Building Conference (SBO5), Tokyo, Japan.

Ness, D., & Field, M. (2003). *Cradle to cradle carpets and cities*. Paper presented at International Conference on Smart and Sustainable Built Environments, SASBE 03, Brisbane, Australia. See also http://www.bml.csiro.au/susnetnl/netwl36E.pdf

Stahel, W. (1982). *The product-life factor*. Geneva: Product-Life Institute. Retrieved July 8, 2008, from http://www.product-life.org/milestone2.htm

Stahel, W. (1994). The utilization-focused service economy: Resource efficiency and product life extension. In B.R. Allenby & D.J. Richards (Eds.), *The greening of industrial ecosystems* (pp. 178-190). Washington, DC: National Academy Press. Retrieved July 8, 2008, from http://books.nap.edu/openbook.php?record_id=2129&page=178

Standards Australia. (1998). *Environmental management life cycle assessment: Principles and framework*. AS/NZS ISO 14040.

Stoughton, M., Horie, Y., & Nakao, Y. (in press). *Service-led businesses for sustainability? Evaluating the potential of and policy for innovative product service systems in Japan*. Institute for Global Environmental Strategies (IGES), Kansai Research Centre.

Sundin, E., Bjorkman, M., & Jacobsson, N. (2000). Analysis of service selling and design for remanufacturing. In *Proceedings of the 2000 IEEE International Symposium on Electronics and the Environment,* San Francisco, CA, USA (pp. 272-277). See also http://ieeexplore.ieee.org/xpl/freeabs_all.jsp?arnumber=857661

Sustainability Victoria. (2006). *Byteback*. Retrieved July 8, 2008, from http://www.sustainability.vic.gov.au/www/html/2045-byteback.asp

UNEP. (2002). *The role of product service systems in a sustainable society.* United Nations Environment Programme, Production and Consumption Branch brochure. Retrieved July 8, 2008, from http://www.uneptie.org/pc/sustain/reports/pss/pss-brochure-final.pdf

Van Halen, C., Vezzoli, C., & Wimmer, R. (2005). *Methodology for product service innovation: How to develop clean, clever and competitive strategies for companies*. The Netherlands: Koninklijke Van Gorcum.

Von Weizsacker, E., Lovins, A.B., & Lovins, L.H. (1997). *Factor four: Doubling wealth, halving resource use*. Australia: Allen and Unwin.

WBCSD. (2000). *Eco-efficiency: Creating more value with less impact.* World Business Council for Sustainable Development. Retrieved July 8,

2008, from http://www.wbcsd.org/web/publications/eco_efficiency_creating_more_value.pdf

White, A., Stoughton, M., & Feng, L. (1999). *Servicizing: The quiet transition to extended producer responsibility*. U.S.: The Tellus Institute. Retrieved July 8, 2008, from http://www.tellus.org/b&s/publications/servicizing.pdf

ADDITIONAL READING

Bleischwitz, R. (2005). 3R business in Germany and Europe: Trends and emerging policies. In-*Proceedings of the Businesses for a Reduce-Reuse-Recycle Economy: Current Status and Future Prospects/A Japanese and German Dialogue, "Business and the Environment" International Workshop 2005* (pp. 15-23). Institute for Global Environmental Strategies (IGES), Kansai Research Centre.

Brezet, J.A., Bijma, S.A., & Silvester, S. (2001). *The design of eco-efficient services: Method, tools and review.* Dutch Ministry of Housing, Spatial Planning and the Environment (VROM) and Delft University of Technology. Retrieved July 8, 2008, from http://www.score-network.org/files//806_1.pdf

Cooper, T., & Evans, E. (2000). *Products to services*. Report for Friends of the Earth, The-Centre for Sustainable Consumption, Sheffield Hallam University, UK. Retrieved July 8, 2008, from http://www.foe.co.uk/resource/reports/products_services.pdf

Ehrenfeld, J. (2005). Designing "sustainable" product/service systems. In *EcoDesign '01: Proceedings of the 2nd International Symposium on Environmentally Conscious Design and Inverse Manufacturing*. Retrieved July 8, 2008, from http://csdl2.computer.org/persagen/DLAbsToc.jsp?resourcePath=/dl/proceedings/&toc=comp/proceedings/ecodesign/2001/1266/00/1266toc.xml&DOI=10.1109/.2001.992308

GTZ/CSCP/Wuppertal Institute. (2006, August). *Policy instruments for resource efficiency: Towards sustainable production and consumption*. Retrieved July 8, 2008, from http://www.scp-centre.org/uploads/media/GTZ-CSCP-PolicyInstrumentsResourceEfficiency_01.pdf

Heiskanen, E., & Jalas, M. (2000, August). *Dematerialization through services: A review and evaluation of the debate*. The Finnish Environment 436, Ministry of the Environment, Environmental Department. Helsinki: Edita Ltd. Retrieved July 8, 2008, from http://hkkk.fi/organisaatiot/research/programs/dema/sy436.pdf

Hertwich, E., Briceno, T., Hofstetter, P., & Inaba, A. (2005, February 10-12). Sustainable consumption: The contribution of research. In *Proceedings of Workshop*, Oslo, NTNU. Retrieved July 8, 2008, from http://www.indecol.ntnu.no/indecolwebnew/publications/reports/rapport05/rapport1_05web.pdf

IGES. (2006, August 30-September 1). *Promoting reduce, reuse and recycle in South Asia*. Synthesis Report on 3R South Asia Expert Workshop in Kathmandu, Nepal. Retrieved July 8, 2008, from http://enviroscope.iges.or.jp/modules/envirolib/view.php?docid=750

Kanda, Y., & Nakagami, Y. (2006). What is product-service systems (PSS)? A review on PSS approaches and relevant policies. *IGES Kansai Research Centre discussion paper*, Japan. Retrieved July 8, 2008, from http://enviroscope.iges.or.jp/modules/envirolib/view.php?docid=469

McDonough, W., & Braungart, M. (2002). *Cradle to cradle: Remaking the way we make things*. New York: North Point Press.

Mont, O. (2001). *Introducing and developing a product-service system (PSS) concept in Sweden*. The International Institute for Industrial

Environmental Economics, IIIE Reports 2001:6. Retrieved July 8, 2008, from http://ask.lub.lb.se/archive/00009121/01/NUTEK_rev.PDF

Mont, O. (Ed). (2003). Product service systems and sustainable consumption. Special Issue, *Journal of Cleaner Production, 11*(8). Retrieved July 8, 2008, from http://www.sciencedirect.com/science?_ob=PublicationURL&_tockey=%23TOC%236022%232003%23999889991%23434487%23FLA%23&_cdi=6022&_pubType=J&_auth=y&_acct=C000052143&_version=1&_urlVersion=0&_userid=1252936&md5=b979601230ef929a8bf104678f9f4fed

Mont, O. (2004). Trends in PSS field in European Union. In *Proceedings of the International Symposium 2004 on "Business and the Environment."* Kobe, Japan: IGES.

Ness, D., & Field, M. (2004, January 29). Cradle to cradle carpets and cities. In *CSIRO Sustainability Network,* Sustainability Network Update - 36E Glen Osmond, South Australia: CSIRO. Retrieved July 8, 2008, from http://www.bml.csiro.au/susnetnl/netwl36E.pdf

Product-Life Institute. (2004). *From manufacturing industry to a service economy, from selling products to selling the performance of products.* Retrieved July 8, 2008, from http:///www.product-life.org/executive_summary.htm

Professional Engineering Publishing. (2007). State-of-the-art in product-service systems. In *Proceedings of the Institution of Mechanical Engineers, 221*(10). Retrieved July 8, 2008, from http://journals.pepublishing.com/content/q37436107010216h/

Rifkin, J. (2000). *The age of access: How the shift from ownership to access is transforming capitalism.* London: Penguin Books.

Ritthoff, M., Rohn, H., & Liedtke, C. (2002). *Calculating MIPS: Resource productivity of products and services.* Wuppertal Special Issue 27e, Wuppertal Institute for Climate, Environment and Energy, at the Science Centre North Rhine-Westphalia. Retrieved July 8, 2008, from http://www.wupperinst.org/uploads/tx_wibeitrag/ws27e.pdf

Ryan, C. (2002, September). *Sustainable consumption: A global status report.* United Nations Environment Programme (UNEP), Paris, Division of Technology, Industry and Economics, Production and Consumption Branch. Retrieved July 8, 2008, from http://www.uneptie.org/pc/pc/pdfs/Sus_Cons.pdf

Stahel, W. (2007). Resource-miser business models. *International Journal of Environmental Technology and Management (IJETM),* 7(5/6).

Stoughton, M., Yuhta, H., & Yuriko, N. (in press). *Service-led businesses for sustainability? Evaluating the potential of and policy for innovative product service systems in Japan* (an Institute for Global Environmental Strategies Report). Kobe, Japan: IGES Kansai Research Centre.

Suspronet Coordination Team. (2004a). *Sustainable product-service systems 2004* (newsletter No. 7). Retrieved July 8, 2008, from http://www.suspronet.org/download.asp?File=documents3\susprospaspoort.pdf&Name=susprospaspoort.pdf

Suspronet Coordination Team. (2004b, June 3-4). *Sustainable product-service systems: Lessons learned* (newsletter No. 7). Report on the 2nd International Workshop, Practical Value, Brussels. Retrieved July 8, 2008, from http://www.suspronet.org/download.asp?File=documents3\nieuwsbrief6.pdf&Name=nieuwsbrief6.pdf

Tukker, A., Charter, M., Vezzoli, C., Sto, E., & Anderson, M.M. (in press). *System innovation for sustainability 1: Perspectives on radical changes to sustainable consumption and production.* Greenleaf Publishing.

Tukker, A., & van Halen, C. (2003, July 29). *Innovation scan for product service systems: A manual for the development of new product service systems for companies and intermediaries for the SME sector.* TNO, Delft/Utrecht, PriceWaterhouseCoopers. Retrieved July 8, 2008, from http://www.score-network.org/score/score_module/index.php?doc_id=827

Tukker, A., & Tischner, U. (2004, September). *New business for Old Europe: Product-service development: Competitiveness and sustainability.* Greenleaf Publishing.

Chapter XI
Strategic Decisions for Green Electricity Marketing:
Learning from Past Experiences

Marta Pérez-Plaza
Universidad Pontificia Comillas, Spain

Pedro Linares
Universidad Pontificia Comillas, Spain

ABSTRACT

Green electricity (GE) has emerged as one of the most interesting instruments for promoting renewable electricity in liberalized markets, at least in theory. Indeed, some experiences have already been carried out, mostly in the U.S. and Europe. However, most of them have been largely unsuccessful. In this chapter, we look at previous surveys and studies carried out on customer response, and provide a review of the most relevant results achieved by GE experiences, in order to learn from them. As a result, we provide what we believe are the key strategic recommendations for green electricity retailers to launch a successful GE program. Although the green electricity market remains a difficult one, several improvements can be achieved by learning from past mistakes and carefully analysing the alternatives and the boundary conditions.

INTRODUCTION

Now that the risks of the current energy mix are being recognized and awareness of the benefits of electricity production from renewable energy sources has become widely extended, there is a general consensus on the need to stimulate technical progress and development of renewable electricity sources. However, there is still controversy about which should be the instrument chosen to achieve these objectives. Indeed, a wide array of support schemes and policies

Copyright © 2009, IGI Global, distributing in print or electronic forms without written permission of IGI Global is prohibited.

have been introduced with the aim of stimulating competition with conventional technologies, the most used of which are feed-in tariffs, subsidies, or renewable energy quotas (see e.g., Del Río & Gual, 2004).

One of these instruments, which in principle is well suited to liberalized markets, is green electricity. This consists basically of the possibility for electricity retailers to offer a differentiated product, electricity produced from "green" sources, charge a premium for it in order to account for the extra cost of these green sources, and let the customer decide whether to accept the offer and pay this extra amount or to not accept it. It is a voluntary mechanism based on product differentiation and relying exclusively on market forces.

Green electricity may take the form of "green pricing" (Moskovitz, 1993) in regulated markets, whereby consumers may pay a premium to their electric utility in order to be supplied with electricity from renewable energy sources or increase the contribution of renewable energy into the system. In competitive markets, this is also known as "green power marketing," the difference being that customers may have a choice of different suppliers and products, and therefore switch between them. However, the concept is essentially the same, and hence we will consider both under the same "green electricity" name.

On first inspection, it seems that green electricity programs are then a quite straightforward and market-based approach to promoting renewables. The problem is, this is not as easy as it may seem.

A first problem is how to define "green." Usually, green means renewable electricity: hydro (large and small), wind, biomass, solar, and other minor ones such as geothermal, wave, or tidal energy. Of course, it would be arguable that some renewables are "green" in the sense that they do have large impacts on the environment. In fact, some programs exclude large hydro due to this reason. In addition, sometimes other non-renewable electricity is also included in "green" programs: co-generation is sometimes included because of the environmental benefits it provides to the system (due to its higher efficiency in energy conversion). The fact is that there may be differences in customer response depending on the type of energy included in the program, but in the end, most of the analysis applies to all types described. So, for practical purposes, we will consider "green" equivalent to "renewable."

But the major problem is that, although many experiences have been carried out with green electricity retailing in different countries, none of these experiences has been truly successful, due to the complex issues lied to this option: green energy definition and certification, customer response, specificities of the electricity markets, and compatibility with other renewable electricity support policies.

Let us put as an example the green electricity programs launched in Spain during 2004. The major Spanish utilities offered their customers the possibility of consuming electricity only from renewable sources, mostly hydro and wind, at a quite small premium (around 15%). Each of them devised large publicity campaigns and built customer service centers specially devoted to this issue. Given that Spain is one of the European countries with the largest contribution of renewable electricity, and that the electricity retail market was just being liberalized, it seemed a good business opportunity. However, after some months, the real participation in the program was less than 1%, and in fact all programs were discontinued after less than 1 year. It seems that many elements in this strategy were mistaken, as has happened with many other programs around the world.

In this chapter, we aim to learn from these experiences in order to provide recommendations on how to successfully market green electricity. We first look at the most salient of the considerable number of surveys and studies carried out regarding green electricity and consumer willingness to pay for it. Second, we provide a review of the results achieved in the most relevant real green electricity programs. By looking at these programs in the U.S. and the European Union, concrete examples of how these instruments were designed, how successful green electricity as a product was, and how much new renewable capacity was installed as a result of these markets are analyzed. The final part of the chapter provides some strategic recommendations for green electricity retailers in liberalized markets. Although the green electricity market remains a difficult one, several improvements can be achieved by learning from past mistakes and carefully analyzing the alternatives and the boundary conditions.

BACKGROUND

In principle, there are many reasons for the attractiveness of green electricity programs: they may provide benefits for utilities, for companies, and, possibly, for individual customers.

Utilities find green electricity programs interesting in that they help them improve their environmental performance and corporate image (especially interesting for those with environmental management systems or under regulatory constraints); differentiate from the competition and provide niche markets; retain or gain environmentally-minded customers; and also may be thought as a defensive strategy against critical stakeholders (usually from the environmental community) (Kotchen, Moore, & Clark, 2001; Wüstenhagen, Markard, & Truffer, 2003). They also have the potential to encourage learning processes, which are certainly welcome given the recent liberalization context.

For companies, buying green electricity is a way of signaling their concern for the environment, of reinforcing their corporate image (Fouquet, 1998). They can also help meet corporate and institutional goals related to corporate social responsibility.

Incentives for individual customers to participate, however, are less understood. Green electricity is an impure public good, in that it provides both private (electricity consumption) and public benefits (the improvement of the environment compared to the use of conventional energy). But because the latter is the essential characteristic of green electricity, it should be expected that individuals will have little incentive to provide such a public good and instead free-ride (Clark, Kotchen, & Moore, 2003). In fact, RE advocates have opposed the concept (Swezey & Bird, 2001): since this is a public good, all consumers should share the cost of RE development. A survey by Wiser (2007) reinforces this idea by showing that collective payment methods are generally preferred by consumers, that is, that consumers prefer all to pay for this good.

But then, environmental concerns, altruistic attitudes, or even egoistic reasons may exist that explain why, as will be shown in the following section, individual customers are willing to engage in these programs. Some authors (e.g., Ek, 2005) have pointed out that when people deal with public issues, they may adopt public rather than private preferences. In addition, these programs provide an opportunity for individuals to express personal preferences and thus are beneficial to them. Indeed, they may also help them form preferences, attitudes, and consumer behavior (Markard & Truffer, 2006). Green electricity programs also integrate consumers into the RE support process.

Several studies have analyzed both the willingness to pay (WTP) of individual consumers for increased renewable energy contribution in the system, and also the success of the different green electricity programs implemented. A good review of WTP estimates may be found in Menger (2003), whereas Swezey and Bird (2001), Bird, Swezey, and Aabakken (2004), Bird, Wustenhagen, and Aabakken (2004), Bird and Kaiser (2007) and Wiser, Olson, Bird, and Swezey (2004) provide good overviews of green electricity programs. In this section, we bring these two issues together, and we update them with the most recent results and findings, in order to draw meaningful recommendations for the green electricity marketer.

The Willingness to Pay for Green Electricity

As mentioned before, green electricity, although having public good characteristics, shows a certain attractiveness to consumers, which are hypothetically willing to pay a premium over normal electricity prices. In fact, empirically observed levels of provision of public goods such as green electricity usually exceed levels predicted by rational-choice theories. This is usually explained by some kind of pro-environmental behavior, derived from a combination of egoistic, social altruistic, and biocentric value orientations (Kotchen et al., 2001).

Therefore, most studies show positive WTP values. Fouquet (1998) cites a survey indicating that 5% of residential customers in the UK would pay a 20% premium for environmentally friendly electricity. In Switzerland, Truffer, Markard, and Wustenhagen (2001) state that 20% of the households are willing to pay a 10-20% premium. Farhar (1999), in a market survey, found that there is a consistent pattern for the U.S. in that 70% of residential customers would pay $5/month, 40% would pay $10/month, and 20% would pay $15/month. Wüstenhagen et al. (2003), based on results from Germany, Sweden, the UK, and Switzerland, estimates that 20% of consumers would pay a 20% premium, whereas almost none would pay a 40% premium.

These WTP estimates are averages. However, they will depend on many parameters (including those related to pro-environmental behavior mentioned above). Roe, Teisl, Levy, and Russell (2001) identified several differences in WTP across regions in the U.S. They also found that a higher income, a higher education level, and affiliation with an environmental organization would increase the hypothetical premium. These results are consistent with those obtained by Rowlands, Scott, and Parker (2003), which identified as the major drivers for WTP the following: ecological concerns, altruism, education, perceived effectiveness, age (younger people have higher WTP), income, and involvement in community services or environmental organizations.

WTP estimates may also be conditioned by the type of renewable energy offered. Borchers, Duke, and Parsons (2007) found a positive WTP for green electricity in the U.S., but also found that the energy source affects this WTP. Thus, they found that solar is better, wind is similar to a generic offer, and that biomass and biogas achieve lower WTP estimates.

Finally, most of the estimates correspond to residential customers, because no studies have been found on the WTP of firms or institutions to buy green electricity. This is unfortunate, because these clients may be powerful drivers for the green electricity market.

So, to summarize: there is a positive willingness to pay for green electricity, and this WTP will depend on some issues which should be contemplated carefully by green electricity retailers, such as the client profile, the type of renewable offered, and the premium at which the green electricity is sold.

Green Electricity Programs Across the World

As has been shown, there are a large number of households and firms willing to pay a premium for green electricity. However, when it comes to actually signing in for green electricity programs, participation rates plummet: Market penetration rates for green electricity programs around the world are generally 1% (Bird et al., 2004). Although some programs have been more successful (up to 15% in some cases), this is much lower than the rates expected from the WTP studies. Some factors which may explain this are:

- Failure in marketing research
- Overestimation of WTP due to its hypothetical nature
- Free-riding
- Education or communication failure

It should also be kept in mind that the personal attitude toward environmental or energy policy is not necessarily the same as the perception about the personal responsibility to fulfill environmental goals. This should not be considered free-riding, but rather a view on how public goods should be provided. This may also explain the different consumer response across countries with different public-private cultures. For example, in Europe, consumers usually consider the environmental impact of electricity generation as the responsibility of the regulator and utilities (Fuchs & Arentsen, 2002).

We will now review the major green electricity experiences across the world, briefly reflecting on their major characteristics. The basic data for these are summarized in Table 1.

As may be observed, most of the programs have achieved very small penetration rates. However, it may also be noticed that some of them have achieved significant rates, such as the Netherlands, Sweden, or Switzerland. We will briefly review these cases below.

The Dutch case is the most noticeable: Here market penetration rates were very large. This can be explained by a number of reasons: first, green electricity was offered at or below conventional electricity rates, due to an exemption from the common energy tax (in fact, this exemption was the major RE support mechanism); second, green electricity was liberalized well before the rest of electricity sources, that is, the Dutch government decided that, during the first stage of the liberalization process, green electricity was the only option for those customers who wanted to switch suppliers; finally, large-hydro power imported from France was in a first stage considered as green electricity by the Dutch government, and that allowed for a large supply of RE. However, the Dutch example is not usually considered a success story: most of the green electricity was imported and already existing, and therefore the growth in RE production was almost insignificant (Reijnders, 2002). In fact, partly as a result of this lack of delivery and the realization by the Dutch government that the real bottleneck was in domestic supply, not in demand, the tax exemption and the possibility to use imported hydro power were terminated in 2005, and replaced by a feed-in tariff only for domestic sources (Van Damme & Zwart, 2003; Van Rooijen & Van Wees, 2006). This also ended with the growth in green electricity share.

Sweden also features a large penetration of green electricity (9%). In this case, the major reason is the use of existing cheap hydro power, and also the large involvement of government and public companies, which signed up to a large extent for these programs (Ek, 2005). But again, in spite of the large market share, there was not a significant growth of renewable energy, because most of it was already existing power.

Finally, we should also look at the Swiss case. Here, penetration rates have not been very large (between 0 and 4.4% depending on the program), but the interesting point is that most of it is due to photovoltaic electricity, with its associated large premiums (prices 4 to 7 times higher than ordinary electricity). This case shows the possibility of using green electricity for small niches of price-insensitive, environmentally-concerned, customers (Wüstenhagen et al., 2003).

So we see that there are large differences between the different green electricity programs. Even in countries with low market shares, there are very successful programs (in the U.S., for example, there are programs which have achieved almost 5% penetration rates). It seems then that it is not only the market environment, but also how the program is designed, that really drives its success. In the next section, we review the major aspects to be considered in order to design a successful green electricity program.

Table 1. Green electricity programs in the world

	Electricity Market					Green Electricity Market							
	Total customers (mill)	**Residential customers (mill)**	**Total consumption (Bill.kWh)**	**Residential consumption (Bill kWh)**	**Cost (c€/kWh)**	**Generation Capacity (GW)**	**Number of green suppliers**	**Green customers**	**Green retail customers (%)**	**Price premium (%)**	**Market share (%)**	**New capacity installed (aprox.)**	
AUSTRALIA	8.7	7.5	205.25	46.5	12.8	37.9	20	68000	0.9	31.25	0.3	200 MW	Due to certification systems, a great amount of new capacity installed
CANADA	14.9	11.9	572.99	129.5	6	109.8	<10	6500	1	40 to 100	0.03	80 MW	Only some states offer green products
GERMANY	43.5	38.4	566.89	130.5	15.9	107.8	140	325000	0.8	4 to 50	0.2	54 MW	Lack of regulation (free access to grid). Many regional small players.
FINLAND	2.9	2.3	81.6	31	9.1	16.1	>30	8000	0.4	0 to 10	0.2	n/a	
HOLLAND	7.2	5.8	92.7	20.8	13.2	14.2	15	775000	10.8	-3 to 10	3	50 MW	Favorable fiscal system
JAPAN	71	56.8	974.4	251.8	21.2	226.4	>10	38000	0.3	30 to 40	0.003	12 MW	Limited eligibility
SWEDEN	5.2	n/a	157.6	n/a	11.2	n/a	75	n/a	n/a	0-5	10.3	n/a	Existing hydro
SWITZERLAND	3.8	3	61.97	15.1	13.1	14.6	135	48000	1.3	10(hydro) to 500 (new solar)	0.3	10 MW	Environmentally conscious retail clients
U.K.	27.3	21.8	363.17	109.6	11.7	69.9	10	45000	0.21	10 to 60	0.04	30 MW	Limited success
USA	126	101.4	3979.04	1193.4	6.64	785.9	>100	375000	1	8 to 200	0.1	650 MW	

Sources: www.greenprices.org; Markard & Truffer (2006); www.iea.org; www.eia.doe.gov/fuelelectric.html

STRATEGIC DECISIONS

As mentioned before, a careful program design and marketing can increase largely its success in customer response (Swezey & Bird, 2001): Market penetration rates beyond 10% (Bird et al., 2002) or even up to 20% (Ethier, Poe, Schulze, & Clark, 2000) are achievable under favorable conditions.

In this section, we detail a number of issues which should be carefully considered by green electricity retailers when designing their products. Basically, these issues should help counteract the little knowledge existing among consumers about green electricity, and also its additional costs due to generation, administration, and certification.

Basic Design of the Program

There are basically two types of basic green-electricity program designs, contribution-based programs (also known as voluntary contribution mechanisms or VCM), and green tariff programs (GTM).

Contribution-based programs are those whereby households donate money to finance new renewable electricity capacity. Payments are independent of electricity consumption. In contrast, GTM programs link payments for green electricity with household consumption, by setting up a specific tariff per kWh. In some cases, this tariff may apply only to a fraction of the total household consumption.

Generally, it has been shown (Kotchen & Moore, 2007) that GTMs will generate lower demand levels than VCMs. But this is only if consumers are allowed to choose the fraction of demand to be supplied by green electricity. All-or-nothing GTMs (when demand is covered 100% by green electricity) can generate either lower or higher demand levels, depending on other issues. The comparison between them will depend on the green tariff: sufficiently low or high tariffs continue to favor the VCM, whereas for mid-range tariffs the all-or-nothing GTM may be preferred (Kotchen & Moore, 2007). Some surveys (Swezey & Bird, 2001) argue that contribution programs have resulted in only small amounts of new RE capacity, except for photovoltaics.

The type of program will also have an influence on the target client: VCM contribution is affected by environmental concerns, altruistic attitudes, household income, gender, and household size. However, GTM participation is not affected by household income, but essentially by the effective price of participation (Kotchen & Moore, 2007)

In addition to these basic program features, there may also be some elements which may contribute to a greater participation rate. For example, provision point mechanisms have been shown to improve participation rates. These mechanisms consist of providing a minimum threshold of participants in the program, so that the program will only be effectively started if this threshold is attained. The major effect of this mechanism is the reduction of free-riding, and so it has been shown to better reflect actual preferences, and to increase participation rates in real programs (Ethier et al., 2000; Rose, Clark, Poe, Rondeau, & Schulze, 2002). This mechanism also increases the perceived program effectiveness, which has also been shown as a driving factor for increased participation (Rowlands et al., 2003).

Other programs have also proposed money-back guarantees: if the project is not undertaken, then money will be returned to customers. This mechanism has been strongly favored in surveys, but seems not to be significant for joining into the program (Rose et al., 2002).

Finally, a last issue is the continuity of the program: Older programs tend to achieve higher levels of success, because they are able to increase their market share with time (Wiser et al., 2004). This may have to do with different issues, such as credibility, program effectiveness, or consumer awareness.

Renewable Electricity Types

Much of the green power sold has been supplied from existing sources, both in the U.S. (Bird et al., 2002) and Europe (Chappaz, 2003), in some cases even from either amortized or supported by long-term purchase contracts. This certainly allows for lower premiums, which are in principle desirable. However, it seems that consumers are eager to pay more for newly created generation, even if its total amount is not significant (Roe et al., 2001).

In addition, if we consider the amount of new RE capacity as a measure of the success of green electricity programs, then newly created generation should be a must. In some cases, this may be mandatory, as in Australia (ICON, 2004), whereas in other countries it relies entirely on the firm's decisions.

As for the type of RE source, a study by Borchers et al. (2007) found that solar energy was able to generate larger premiums from consumers than wind energy, and that biomass and biogas were the less valued energy sources for green electricity. No data have been found for large hydro or cogeneration.

The use of biomass, cogeneration, or large hydro is worth citing: Although some clients may have problems with them, because of their "impure" renewable characteristic (which can be avoided by using eco-labeling, as mentioned below), they are required if the retailer wants to provide real-time renewable energy to the customer (i.e., to follow his or her demand curve), because they are the only technologies able to regulate their production.

The case of large hydro is also relevant because of its large volume, and because it does not usually require a premium. Therefore, many utilities are considering it for their green electricity programs. However, in most countries this is a depleted technology (i.e., with no further expansion capacity), and introducing it into green electricity programs would merely displace it from some customers to others without creating additional environmental benefits (see the section on additionality). And then there is the question of the price at which this electricity should be offered: Because most of the large hydro plants are competitive, and in addition have been almost paid off, in principle the price should be low; on the other hand, hydro should be priced at the opportunity cost of the alternative electricity, which is the marginal electricity price, but that may be difficult to explain to customers.

It is obvious that the percentage of renewable included, the type of technologies used, and whether there are new plants or not will determine the final price of the product, as well as the possibility to balance generation and demand in real time. In most cases, retailers may offer different possibilities, adapting mixes to the price sensitivity and needs of the customer.

Customer Demand Coverage

At least in principle, the type of contract that leaves more purchase flexibility to the retailer, and minimizes the need of demand forecasting, is covering with renewables the aggregate of total annual consumption (or a percentage of it), because this method removes the need for real time generation-consumption balance. Therefore, the retailer can purchase cheaper electricity by avoiding buying electricity in peak hours. The only commitment would be to acquire a quantity of renewable energy equal to that consumed by the client at the end of the year, without taking into account when it was generated or acquired.

Nonetheless, there is a fundamental drawback: A well informed client could argue that there is an excessive dependency on nonrenewable generation to follow her demand in real time. The retailers that choose this option focus on the fact that the renewable generation is intrinsically very unpredictable, and that nowadays the installed capacity is insufficient to cover demand fluctuations in real time.

Coverage in real time with renewables is a more complicated option. Previous experiences in some countries confirm that this coverage would need a suitable method of forecasting demand as well as major flexibility in the mix of technologies (e.g., the use of cogeneration or biomass, which allows dispatch). The relative weight of each technology in the mix should fluctuate according to the needs, although it is possible to establish required margins of values.

The option not to cover the total consumption with a green tariff, but, for example, to cover only 20% and the 80% remaining with a normal tariff, might be translated in a significant final price reduction. This would have economic sense in case the client was more interested in enhancing its brand image than in the environmental benefit. This might be the case of the small industry and commercial sector.

Energy Purchases

Depending on the country, the green electricity retailer may choose among different alternatives when buying renewable electricity from producers. In most cases, the most interesting option will be a combination of them.

Wholesale Market

This is the more flexible but riskier alternative. It will be advantageous if the contract specifies that total green energy generated will equal total retail supply of green electricity on an annual basis. The retailer may then obtain better prices, provided it has the flexibility to choose when to buy the green electricity (avoiding peak hours).

However, not many green electricity producers sell their output on the wholesale market. The vast majority of them prefer bilateral contract agreements or alternatively, they are owned directly by the utility or retailer.

Consumers must have confidence that those products offer genuine environmental benefits. Wholesale market electricity has no way of identification, so green labels and certificates are crucial to guarantee the greenness of the electricity purchased (see below).

The main drawback of this option is the consumer perception of this scheme as excessively dependent on nonrenewable generation, and also the need to guarantee in a credible way the origin of the electricity.

Bilateral Contracts

These contracts make it easier to guarantee the green origin of the energy supplied. Nevertheless, it would be desirable for an independent third party to certify that the generation facilities comply with the necessary requirements to be considered "green."

It is a less risky option, given that price is fixed in advance, but potential savings from buying during off-peak hours are not available. On the other hand, the reduced risk due to the long-term contract may help lower the price of this electricity.

However, given the lack of flexibility and predictability associated with renewable generation, it might be difficult to use this option to follow hourly demand if cogeneration, large hydro, or biomass is not included. Therefore, a certain trade in the wholesale market may be required.

Vertical Integration

In case the retailer does not only devote itself to green marketing, but also to generation (with any type of facilities, renewable or not) and distribution, this option would have a certain advantage when considering to acquire or to build green generation facilities, as opposed to a nonvertically integrated retailer. This initial advantage would come from the experience and the know-how in the generating business, as well as from the previous availability of the necessary means to operate the facilities. If this option is chosen, the retailer would have green energy at generating price, and it would know exactly the cost of generation. There would be no need for intermediate steps and negotiations, although risks of own capital investment must be taken into account.

Investing the profits obtained in new renewable generation to integrate vertically looks like a particularly attractive option for a green retailer, because this strategy allows putting this money at work and at the same time makes it easier to justify that clients' contribution is being used to improve the environment.

Tradable Green Certificate (TGC) Systems

There is another possibility, although only feasible in some countries: the establishment of a TGC system would allow the retailer to acquire the physical energy separately from the green certificate. The retailer should possess at the end of the year a number of TGCs equivalent to the quantity of energy consumed by clients (and to have acquired, though separately, the corresponding energy). This concept could be applied to any of the purchase options cited previously: to wholesale markets purchases (where it seems to be especially necessary), and to bilateral contracts (theoretically, it would be possible to have a bilateral contract with a nonrenewable facility, and purchase the number of equivalent certificates from another facility).

The major advantage of this system is the flexibility it provides for the retailer.

Target Clients

Different target clients may be identified, depending on the type of product to be supplied. A good analysis of the general client segments to be targeted may be found in Fuchs and Arentsen (2002).

The first customer segment to be targeted seems to be those clients more prone to pay high premiums. These are households with pro-environmental and altruistic attitudes, high income, few members, and high education levels. It has been shown that these aspects reliably predict participation in a green electricity program, according to several studies (Clark et al., 2003, Kotchen & Moore, 2007; Wiser, 2007).

Household income is important, but this depends on the type of program: For example, income does not affect participation in GTM programs, whereas for VCM programs it is the only factor influencing the amount contributed (Kotchen & Moore, 2007). Therefore, these authors propose to target households with higher income when using a VCM program, and to target households with lower electricity consumption (to lower effective prices) when using a GTM program.

Although some authors (Rowlands et al., 2003) argue that gender is not important, others (Kotchen & Moore, 2007; Wiser, 2007) have found that females tend to make larger contributions than males.

In addition to this major target group, it might also be interesting to direct efforts at the large group of "conventional" customers, because a small premium in this large group will be very significant overall. This group is usually very responsive to information, but also very sensitive to prices, although this can be modified when they are made to reflect on the low share of electricity consumption in their budget (see section on premiums).

Social and economic elites may also be interesting target groups, because of their high consumption level and their capacity to influence other groups. In addition, they are easy to target because of their small size.

Finally, private firms, governments, and institutions should also be target clients for green electricity programs. As already mentioned, they are increasingly recognizing the interest of this type of electricity for meeting their institutional goals, and can help much in the success of the program, by providing an example to residential customers, and also free advertising. In fact, non-residential customers already represent about 25% of the total green power sold in the U.S. (Swezey & Bird, 2001).

Another important issue regarding the target client is its origin: Those more prone to enter into these programs are those already buying electricity from the same utility. In fact, most green electricity clients have purchased it without switching suppliers. This is easy to explain, because, given the very low switching rates experienced in most liberalized markets, requiring the customer to switch supplier will certainly decrease her participation rate in a green electricity program.

It has to be reminded that consumers are used to receiving their electricity from monopolies, with no room or need for making choices. Many find supplier choice, and the related information analysis demand, too encumbering, and prefer to stay with the original supplier (Salmela & Varho, 2006).

Premiums

In this point, evidence looks contradictory: Whereas some studies point to the significant influence of price in customer response (Bird et al., 2002), others (Swezey & Bird, 2001; Wiser et al., 2004) argue that there is no definitive relationship between the amount of the premium and participation rates. This may also be observed by looking at the Swiss case described in the section analyzing green electricity programs across the world, where a market share similar to other countries was achieved in spite of much higher premiums. Indeed, electricity purchases represent a very small percentage of household budgets, so one should not expect a large elasticity of demand here.

However, the success of green products when offered at prices below or similar to conventional electricity cannot be denied. All in all, it seems that premiums should range from 0 to 30%. A premium of more than 30% has been considered as too high in some surveys (Truffer et al., 2001; Salmela & Varho, 2006), although again the Swiss case shows that some customers are ready to pay much more.

Here the intelligent approach seems to rely on market segmentation: If a firm only offers a single program, it could be neglecting segments of customers willing to pay more. To this extent, posted prices seem not to be desirable, because they do not allow households to select the amount which better represents their preferences. A range of products with different prices helps meet the varying WTP.

An additional, but important concern expressed by consumers regarding premiums is that they should not be dominated by administrative and marketing costs (Swezey & Bird, 2001).

Finally, it should also be considered the possibility of offering green electricity at no premium, with the utility bearing the additional costs. This might be considered as a tool for retaining customers or as a way to improve its environmental profile.

Value Creation

Green electricity is not only about pricing, it is also about providing customers with values or private benefits which will drive them to pay more for it. These values may be monetary or not. Monetary ones may be tax deductibility or protection from fuel price increases. Nonmonetary ones include personal recognition, civic pride, promoting sustainability, or educational benefits. The important thing is to make these values visible to customers.

A critical issue then is to know which are the values more prized by green electricity program participants. The major reasons cited by Kotchen et al. (2001) in their study of a program in Michigan were: health of natural ecosystems, local pollution benefits, then personal health, global warming, and finally, warm glow. Altruism toward the environment is more important than toward regional residents or health-based egoism. Local environment is also more important to them than global environment.

Therefore, marketing campaigns should highlight the positive environmental impact of buying green electricity. And these benefits should be made as personal as possible, appealing to personal health rather than to a general improvement in the environment (Rowlands et al., 2003).

The most common methods of providing non-monetary values are program updates in periodic newsletters and window decals. In addition, programs may recognize businesses through program advertisements in media, or provide customers with plaques or other recognitions (Bird et al., 2004). A large visibility of the RE projects promoted by green electricity programs is also useful for creating value (Swezey & Bird, 2001).

Being precise about objectives may also increase the value creation of the program, by providing enhanced visibility of its benefits. According to Rowlands et al. (2003), several utilities have found that programs focusing on a well-defined RE project tend to be more successful in attracting customers than those promoting RE in general.

Information to Customers

Lack of knowledge of green electricity is widespread, and this may explain to a large extent the low participation rates. In fact, consumers are frequently uninformed even of their own electricity consumption and of the related costs and environmental impacts (Fuchs & Arentsen, 2002). This is not surprising in liberalized markets, given the multiplicity of products and technologies. Therefore, any effort to increase consumer awareness will certainly improve these rates.

For example, participation rates in a New York state program were 20%, when sufficient information was provided (Ethier et al., 2000). As another example, 15% of the Australian customers provided with the right information did sign up (ICON, 2004).

An important issue is that the information provided has to be credible, and true. The information provided might be misleading when, even being true, it is not complete or sufficient, so that the advertising might be deceitful not only for what it says, but also for what it does not. Misinforming the customer may backlash against the program, as shown in some experiences (CNE, 2004).

A very interesting way of raising awareness while enhancing credibility is by teaming with environmental or community organizations in order to reinforce messages.

As for the vehicle to provide this information, most utilities perceive telemarketing as the most useful way (Bird et al., 2004). However, most of them use cheaper, but less efficient ones, such as bill inserts and media advertisements. An important point is to keep it as simple as possible, not to overburden customers with excessive information which may deter them from analyzing it.

Credibility

In order to buy green electricity, consumers must have confidence in that the product offered features genuine environmental benefits, and value for money. This requires usually a certification or legitimating process.

Sometimes utilities may not be viewed as legitimate providers of environmental benefits, and therefore the credibility of the program may be greatly enhanced by engaging in partnerships with environmental organizations. Also, green electricity purchases by government or public firms may contribute to improve credibility, as well as to the overall success of the program. These same partnerships may also provide an additional benefit, free advertising.

In the U.S., Wiser (2007) found that private providers were able to elicit higher WTP than public ones because of their higher credibility.

However, this may probably vary depending on the country, and in Europe the contrary might be expected.

Legitimacy may also be provided by eco-labeling, which can reduce the transaction costs associated to credibility issues (Truffer et al., 2001). The recognition of the eco-label will be enhanced if it is accepted as a standard not only by consumers but also by competitors, so a broadly accepted label should be sought after by green electricity programs. There are several labels applicable to renewable electricity, such as the Eugene label developed by the European Commission, which not only certify the renewable origin of electricity but also ask for additional environmental benefits, which is certainly relevant for RE sources such as hydro.

Relationship with Other RE Support Schemes

The existence of other support mechanisms for renewable electricity may have either positive or negative impacts on green electricity. For example, some authors (e.g., Markard & Truffer, 2006) argue that the existence of feed-in tariffs in Germany or Spain may be an explanation for the almost negligible role of green electricity in these markets. On the other hand, Menger (2003) argues that the amount that customers are willing to pay to prevent environmental damage is independent of the amount of damage prevented, and therefore, that there is a potential for voluntary demand in addition to mandatory support schemes.

What everybody agrees on (e.g., Menger, 2003) is that all green electricity programs should be additional: The funds collected from these programs should be clearly earmarked for new RE investments, additional to those which would have taken place anyway under the other RE support mechanisms.

This does not necessarily mean that green electricity and other RE support schemes should be incompatible. In fact, some argue (e.g., Swezey & Bird, 2001) that other support schemes should be sought by retailers in order to lower the premiums. The key point here is that this is done only to effectively lower the premium and not to increase artificially the profits of the retailer (e.g., by charging a premium for electricity which is already competitive and therefore does not need the premium to operate).

Although those plants which are economical under other support schemes might be sold without a premium, they would not comply with the requirement of being additional, because they would have been installed anyway. One possibility might be for these plants to decline to participate in the mandatory support scheme, and try to get the premium instead. That would certainly comply then with the additionality criterion. However, this should be handled with care, because such a combination of support mechanisms creates confusion among consumers, and burdens the administration of the system (Dinica & Arentsen, 2002).

Therefore, only those RE plants uneconomical under other RE support schemes, or those which decline to enter into them, should be allowed to be included in green electricity programs (e.g., by only certifying as renewable energy this type of plants). The premium in both cases should be carefully monitored so that it reflects the additional cost of the technology (plus the administrative and certification expenses required) and not undue profits for the retailer. Some countries (e.g., Spain) have already regulated these aspects for green electricity retailers, by requiring separate accounts and a specific use of premiums.

Another way of thinking of additionality is to use the premium to reduce the environmental impact of existing RE plants beyond the current regulations (e.g., helping windmills integrate in the landscape, providing additional fish stairs for small hydro). However, it is arguable whether consumers will respond equally favorably to this additionality concept, because they might argue that these measures should have been taken anyway.

SUMMARY AND CONCLUSION

Based on our review, we can conclude that there seems to be a considerable gap between being environmentally conscious and acting upon these convictions, which has hindered the success of past green electricity schemes, together with some strategic errors on the part of retailers.

Therefore, major improvements on retailing strategies are still required in order to achieve a larger penetration of green electricity, both by maximizing customer participation and also new RE development. As mentioned before, rates up to 20% may be achieved for selected market segments, when all recommendations are met. Below we summarize our major recommendations:

- Green tariff programs (GCM) are more effective, at the usual tariff levels, in providing new RE development, so they should be generally chosen to contribution-based ones (VCM).
- A provision point mechanism reduces free-riding, and can therefore increase participation rates.
- Persistence pays: Long-term programs see steady increases in customers.
- Whereas solar and wind seem to attract higher participation and premiums, they are not able to provide real-time coverage of demand. If this is the goal, biomass and cogeneration should be included. Hydro presents several problems which should be addressed carefully.
- Premiums should range between 0% and 30%. Variable premiums (based on different products) help account for the differences in WTP among clients.
- Bilateral contracts help lower costs, by reducing risks, and increase the credibility of the green origin of the electricity.
- It appears that the greater success will be obtained by targeting young-age, highly-educated households with greater concerns for the environment or stronger altruistic values.
- Teaming up with environmental and charitable NGOs may prove really useful, because that will also provide greater credibility for the program, help provide information and raise awareness, and may even provide free advertising.
- Relying on the existing utility client base enhances participation, by eliminating the switching barrier problem.
- The retailer must be able to define clearly, simply, and visibly the environmental advantages of the product, to offer something tangible that has added value and to provide arguments supporting the legitimacy of its right to receive a premium. Focusing on specific RE projects increase visibility and credibility. A local focus seems also to be more effective than broadly-based programs.
- Complete information on the characteristics and advantages of the program must be provided in a simple and effective way (e.g., via telemarketing) to consumers.

Of course, most of our conclusions are general, and therefore specific analysis should be carried out for different market conditions, because, as mentioned along this chapter, both cultural differences, energy policy, and electricity market design may influence to a large extent the issues to be considered (e.g., an analysis for the Spanish electricity market may be found in Pérez-Plaza, 2004). However, we consider them to be a necessary first step if successful green electricity programs are to be devised, and an analysis which had not been undertaken before.

FUTURE RESEARCH DIRECTIONS

There are several areas in which future research may improve significantly our knowledge of this issue, and therefore the effectiveness of green electricity programs.

First of all, an extension of the market surveys and WTP studies to other countries where green electricity programs might be implemented would be a very welcome future line of research. Most WTP studies have been carried out in the U.S., UK and northern Europe. However, many other countries show good potential for these programs, and estimations of WTP values would be the first input for the definition of marketing strategies in these countries.

Second, there is no data on the willingness to pay of firms and institutions for green electricity, in spite of the seemingly larger interest that this type of consumers may have on these programs. An extension of WTP studies to firms or institutions would therefore be very interesting.

Finally, it should be pointed out that most of the work done on the analysis of green electricity programs has been carried out from the energy policy or environmental economics fields, whereas it is clearly an issue to be studied within the marketing community, which have specific tools and methods to address this issue. Again, this research might prove critical for the success of green electricity programs.

ACKNOWLEDGMENT

This work was funded in part by Gamesa Energia. Pedro Linares also acknowledges the hospitality of Harvard Electricity Policy Group, support from Fundacion Repsol YPF and Unión Fenosa, and comments by G. Saenz de Miera. As usual, opinions and errors remain the sole responsibility of the authors.

REFERENCES

Bird, L., & Kaiser, M. (2007). *Trends in utility green pricing programs (2006)* (NREL/TP-670-42287). Golden, CO: National Renewable Energy Laboratory.

Bird, L., Swezey, B., & Aabakken, J. (2004). *Utility green pricing programs: Design, implementation and consumer response* (NREL/TP-620-35618). Golden, CO: National Renewable Energy Laboratory.

Bird, L., Wüstenhagen, R., & Aabakken, J. (2002). *Green power marketing abroad: Recent experience and trends* (NREL/TP-620-32155). Golden, CO: National Renewable Energy Laboratory.

Borchers, A.M., Duke, J.M., & Parsons, G.R. (2007). Does willingness to pay for green energy differ by source? *Energy Policy, 35*, 3327-3334.

Chappaz, C. (2003). *Green is only skin-deep* (decision brief). Cambridge, MA: Cambridge Energy Research Associates.

Clark, C.F., Kotchen, M.J., & Moore, M.R. (2003). Internal and external influences on pro-environmental behavior: Participation in a green electricity program. *Journal of Experimental Psychology, 23*, 237-246.

CNE. (2004). *Informe sobre las campañas publicitarias de energía verde*. Madrid: Comisión Nacional de la Energía.

Del Río, P., & Gual, M. (2004). The promotion of green electricity in Europe: Present and future. *European Environment, 14*, 219-234.

Dinica, V., & Arentsen, M.J. (2003). Green certificate trading in The Netherlands in the prospect of the European electricity market. *Energy Policy, 31*, 609-620.

Ek, C. (2005). Public and private attitudes towards "green" electricity: The case of Swedish wind power. *Energy Policy, 33*, 1677-1689.

Ethier, R.G., Poe, G. L., Schulze, W.D., & Clark, J. (2000). A comparison of hypothetical phone and mail contingent valuation responses for green-pricing electricity programs. *Land Economics, 76*, 54-67.

Farhar, B.C. (1999). *Willingness to pay for electricity from renewable resources: A review of utility market research* (NREL/TP.550.26148). Golden, CO: National Renewable Energy Laboratory.

Fouquet, R. (1998). The United Kingdom demand for renewable electricity in a liberalized market. *Energy Policy, 26*, 281-293.

Fuchs, D.A., & Arentsen, M.J. (2002). Green electricity in the market place: The policy challenge. *Energy Policy, 30*, 525-538.

ICON. (2004). *Electricity market in Australia: A strategic reference*. San Diego, CA: ICON Group International.

Kotchen, M.J., & Moore, M.R. (2007). Private provision of environmental public goods: Household participation in green-electricity programs. *Journal of Environmental Economics and Management, 53*, 1-16.

Kotchen, M.J., Moore, M.R., & Clark, C.F. (2001). Environmental voluntary contracts between individuals and industry: An analysis of consumer preferences for green electricity. In E. Orts & K. Deketelaere (Eds.), *Environmental voluntary contracts: Comparative approaches to regulation innovation in the United States and Europe*. London: Kluwer Law International.

Markard, J., & Truffer, B. (2006). The promotional impacts of green power products on renewable energy sources: Direct and indirect eco-effects. *Energy Policy, 34*, 306-321.

Menger, R. (2003). Supporting renewable energy on liberalised markets: Green electricity between additionality and consumer sovereignty. *Energy Policy, 31*, 583-596.

Moskovitz, D. (1993, October). Green pricing: Customer choice moves beyond IRP. *The Electricity Journal*.

Pérez Plaza, M. (2004). *Análisis de viabilidad de una comercializadora verde en el mercado eléctrico español*. Senior thesis, Universidad Pontificia Comillas, Madrid, Spain.

Reijnders, L. (2002). Imports as a major complication: Liberalisation of the green electricity market in The Netherlands. *Energy Policy, 30*, 723-726.

Roe, B., Teisl, M.F., Levy, A., & Russell, M. (2001). U.S. consumers' willingness to pay for green electricity. *Energy Policy, 29*, 917-925.

Rose, S.K., Clark, J., Poe, G.L., Rondeau, D., & Schulze, W.D. (2002). The private provision of public goods: Test of a provision point mechanism for funding green power programs. *Resource and Energy Economics, 24*, 131-155.

Rowlands, I.H., Scott, D., & Parker, P. (2003). Consumers and green electricity: Profiling potential purchasers. *Business Strategy and the Environment, 12*, 36-48.

Salmela, S., & Varho, V. (2006). Consumers in the green electricity market in Finland. *Energy Policy, 34*, 3669-3683.

Swezey, B., & Bird, L. (2001). *Utility green-pricing programs. What defines success?* (NREL/TP.620.29831). Golden, CO: NREL National Renewable Energy Laboratory.

Truffer, B., Markard, J., & Wüstenhagen, R. (2001). Eco-labeling of electricity: Strategies and tradeoffs in the definition of environmental standards. *Energy Policy, 29*, 885-897.

Van Damme, E., & Zwart, G. (2003). The liberalized Dutch green electricity market: Lessons from a policy experiment. *De Economist, 151*, 389-413.

Van Rooijen, S.N.M., & Van Wees, M.T. (2006). Green electricity policies in the Netherlands: An analysis of policy decisions. *Energy Policy, 34*, 60-71.

Wiser, R.H. (2007). Using contingent valuation to explore willingness to pay for renewable energy: A comparison of collective and voluntary payment vehicles. *Ecological Economics, 62*, 419-432.

Wiser, R., Olson, S., Bird, L., & Swezey, B. (2004). *Utility green pricing programs: A statistical analysis of program effectiveness* (NREL/TP-620-35609). Golden, CO: National Renewable Energy Laboratory.

Wüstenhagen, R., Markard, J., & Truffer, B. (2003). Diffusion of green power products in Switzerland. *Energy Policy, 31*, 621-632.

ADDITIONAL READING

Bird, L., Dagher, L., & Swezey, B. (2007). Green power marketing in the United States: A status report (10th ed., NREL/ TP-670-42502). Golden, CO: National Renewable Energy Laboratory.

Bird, L., & Kaiser, M. (2007). *Trends in utility green pricing programs (2006)* (NREL/TP-670-42287). Golden, CO: National Renewable Energy Laboratory.

Bird, L., Swezey, B., & Aabakken, J. (2004). *Utility green pricing programs: Design, implementation and consumer response* (NREL/TP-620-35618). Golden, CO: National Renewable Energy Laboratory.

Bird, L., Wüstenhagen, R., & Aabakken, J. (2002). *Green power marketing abroad: Recent experience and trends* (NREL/TP-620-32155). Golden, CO: National Renewable Energy Laboratory.

Greenprices. (2007). Retrieved July 8, 2008, from *www.greenprices.com*

Kotchen, M.J., & Moore, M.R. (2007). Private provision of environmental public goods: Household participation in green-electricity programs. *Journal of Environmental Economics and Management, 53*, 1-16.

Pérez Plaza, M. (2004). *Análisis de viabilidad de una comercializadora verde en el mercado eléctrico español.* Senior Thesis, Universidad Pontificia Comillas, Madrid, Spain.

Wiser, R.H. (2007). Using contingent valuation to explore willingness to pay for renewable energy: A comparison of collective and voluntary payment vehicles. *Ecological Economics, 62*, 419-432.

Wiser, R., Olson, S., Bird, L., & Swezey, B. (2004). *Utility green pricing programs: A statistical analysis of program effectiveness* (NREL/TP-620-35609). Golden, CO: National Renewable Energy Laboratory.

Section III
Supply Chain and Logistics Management

Chapter XII
Modeling of Green Supply Chain Logistics

Hsin-Wei Hsu
National Tsing Hua University, Taiwan, ROC

Hsiao-Fan Wang
National Tsing Hua University, Taiwan, ROC

ABSTRACT

The green supply chain management has drawn researchers' attention in recent years, but most of the proposed models for green topics on the subject are case based, and for this reason, they lack generality. In this work, the design of a supply chain network is studied. In this chapter, we try to overcome this limitation and a generalized model is proposed, in which a logistics chain network problem is formulated into a 0-1 mixed integer linear programming model and the decisions for the function of manufactures, distribution centers, and dismantlers will be suggested with minimum cost. A numerical example is provided for illustration.

INTRODUCTION

While the competition among companies has been globally and rapidly intensified, the worldwide consensus on environmental protection is increasing. In the European Union (EU), the regulations have clearly demanded the companies to meet the green criteria of their products (e.g., Schultmann, Moritz, & Otto, 2006). Among these regulations, the so called "green supply chain" (GSC) conditions are particularly emphasized because the configuration of conventional supply chain has been the one affected the most in this changes during a product's life cycle. Since it's necessary to satisfy GSC for companies under society pressure and decrees, how we can reduce the system cost from the logistics viewpoint in order to improve the company's competence has become an important issue.

Copyright © 2009, IGI Global, distributing in print or electronic forms without written permission of IGI Global is prohibited.

The GSC comprises two parts, forward supply chain and reverse supply chain. Apart from the conventional supply chain, GSC has an additional role called dismantlers which makes the functions of a green logistics possesses different behaviors, like recover and recycling. Schultmann et al. (2006), Baumgarten, Christian, Annerous, and Thomas (2003) and Lu, Vivi, Julie, and Taylor (2000) have provided excellent reviews of the related literature.

Before we proceed to our discussion, let us define the reverse logistics as below.

Definition 1 (REVLOG, 1999): Reverse logistics is the process of planning, implementing, and controlling flows of raw materials, in process inventory and finished goods, from the point of use back to a point of recovery or point of proper disposal.

Based on this concept, many researches are devoted to this issue, but they assumed the dismantlers or recover facilities' capacity to be infinite (e.g., Pochampally, Surendra, & Sagar, 2004). Because of this unrealistic assumption, we shall consider limitation of the recovery or recycling capacity in this study. In addition, it is the basic difference between conventional supply chain and green supply chain that conventional supply chain considers only forward logistics; whereas green supply chain take both forward and reverse routings into consideration. Therefore, to minimize the total operation cost, considering both routings simultaneously in one model is necessary (Fleischmann et al., 1997). To achieve these goals, a close-loop green supply chain logistics model is proposed in this study to minimize the total system's cost when the capacity and routing in the system are considered.

Due to the uncertainty of recovery and landfilling rates, sensitivity analysis will be conducted to facilitate the effective management.

BACKGROUND

Green supply chain refers to all those activities associated with the transformation and flows of goods and services, including their information flows from the sources of materials to end users. According to De Groene and Hermans (1998), integrated supply chain management aims to close material cycles and prevent leakage of the materials in the chain. Similar to integrating supply chains, green supply chain management (GSCM) refers to the integration of all these activities, both internal and external to the firm (Bowersox & Closs, 1996).

Fleischmann et al. (1997) mentioned that GSC includes the members of the forward channel (e.g., traditional manufacturers, retailers, and logistics service providers) or specialized parties (e.g., secondary material dealers and material recovery facilities). One of the key aspects to green supply chain is to improve both economic and environmental performance simultaneously throughout the chains by establishing long-term relationships between buyers and suppliers (Zhu & Raymond, 2004). Therefore, building a stable close-loop logistics in a chain to include the activities of all of involved roles is necessary when the object of minimizing the total cost is desired from both the companies and environment aspects.

A supply chain can be described by a network of suppliers, manufacturing sites, distribution centers (DCs), and customer locations through logistics. The logistics are focused on the routing of the shipping units throughout the networks. In a GSC logistics problem, there is an important module, dismantlers or recyclers, to be incorporated into a supply chain network. These dismantlers handle the recover resources into many different types for further uses or dispose (Baumgarten et al., 2003). That is, if at dismantler sites, the recycled resources can be used again, the resource should be shipped to a manufacture for reproduction; otherwise, the un-useful resources must be landfilled (e.g., Schultmann et al., 2006).

Figure 1. The framework of green supply chain logistics

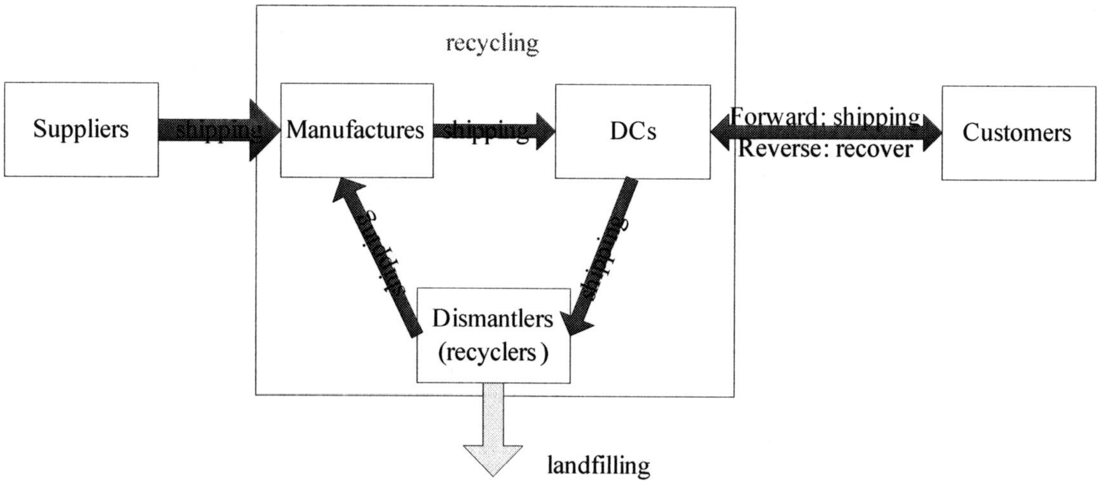

The logistics system in GSC collects the used resources for further treatment, and this behavior in the system is called *reverse logistics*. The routing in reverse logistics implies a recovery action including collecting, shipping, and allocating activities. The concepts of logistics in GSC can be shown in Figure 1.

In order to integrate the conventional supply chain and reverse supply chain, a model is developed to minimize the total operation cost of the involved roles of manufactures, DCs, and dismantlers.

MAIN THRUST OF THE CHAPTER

From the concepts we described above, we know that GSC is much different from a conventional supply chain, and the problems are more complex and the effort needed to analyze both forward and reverse logistics in GSC problem is more than double.

To measure the efficiency of the logistics in a GSC network, the cost is normally considered by a company of which a general close-loop model for GSC is lacking in the literature of study. Yeh (2005) has suggested that in multistage the supply chain network problem, the following conditions should be satisfied in modeling. Since they are also the basic conditions for GSC logistics, we shall base on them to develop our model:

1. The demand of each customer must be satisfied.
2. The flow is only allowed to be transferred between two consecutive stages.
3. The number of facilities that can be open is limited.

Furthermore, it has been noted that a close-loop mathematical model for GSC logistics problem can be viewed as the combination of multiple-choice Knapsack problem and the capacitated location-allocation problem. So this is known to be NP-hard (Gen & Cheng, 1997). The special issues in GSC are the recovery and landfilling rates, which are uncertain but can be estimated from historical data. In our model, the fourth assumption is

4. The recovery and landfilling rates are constant.

Before modeling, we define the related parameters and notations:

Indices:

I: The number of suppliers (i=1, 2,..., I)
J: The number of manufactories (j=1, 2,..., J)
K: The number of DCs (k=1, 2, ..., K)
L: The number of customers (l=1, 2, ..., L)
M: The number of dismantlers (m=1, 2, ..., M)

Parameters:

a_i: Capacity of supplier i
b_j: Capacity of manufactory j
Sc_k: Capacity of the DC k
p_d: Capacity percentage of quantity recovered in DC
p_c: Percentage for customer recovery rate
p_l: The land-filling rate
d_l: Demand of the customer l
e_m: Capacity of dismantler m
s_{ij}: Unit cost of production in manufactory j using materials from supplier i
t_{jk}: Unit cost of transportations from each manufactory j to each DC k
u_{kl}: Unit cost of transportations from DC k to customer l
v_{km}: Unit cost of transportations from DC k to dismantler m
w_{mj}: Unit cost of transportations from dismantler m to manufactory j
Ru_{lk}: Unit cost of recover in DC k from customer l
f_j: Fixed cost for operating Manufactory j
g_k: Fixed cost for operating DC k
h_m: Fixed cost for operating dismantler m
φ: Fixed cost for land-filling per unit

Variables:

x_{ij}: Quantity produced at manufactory j using raw materials from supply i
y_{jk}: Amount shipped from manufactory j to DC k
z_{kl}: Amount shipped from DC k to customer l
o_{km}: Amount shipped from DC k to dismantler m
Rd_{mj}: Amount shipped from dismantler m to manufactory j
Rz_{lk}: Quantity recovered at DC k from customer l

$$\alpha_j = \begin{cases} 1, & \text{if production takes place at manufactory } j \\ 0, & \text{otherwise} \end{cases}$$

$$\beta_k = \begin{cases} 1, & \text{if DC } k \text{ is opened} \\ 0, & \text{otherwise} \end{cases}$$

$$\delta_m = \begin{cases} 1, & \text{if dismantler } m \text{ is opened} \\ 0, & \text{otherwise} \end{cases}$$

Because the recovery and landfilling rates are the estimated proportional value of demand and recovery amount, it will cause nonintegral values in solution. In order to present this scenario, we use Gauss symbol in our mathematical model as follows:

TC means the total cost here, and the model is logic integer program (IP).

Object function is shown in Box 1.

Box 1. Equation 1 (Minimize the transportation cost and operational cost)

$$\min \ TC = \sum_i \sum_j s_{ij} x_{ij} + \sum_j \sum_k t_{jk} y_{jk} + \sum_k \sum_l u_{kl} z_{kl} + \sum_k \sum_m v_{km} o_{km} + \sum_m \sum_j w_{mj} Rd_{mj}$$
$$+ \sum_l \sum_k Ru_{lk} Rz_{lk} + \sum_j f_i \alpha_j + \sum_k g_k \beta_k + \sum_m h_m \delta_m + \phi \sum_m \left\lfloor p_l \sum_k o_{km} \right\rfloor$$

Subject to:

$$\sum_j x_{ij} \le a_i, \quad \text{for all } i \tag{2}$$

(The capacity constraint about supplier)

$$\sum_k y_{jk} \le b_j \alpha_j, \quad \text{for all } j \tag{3}$$

(The capacity constraint about manufactory)

$$\sum_i x_{ij} + \sum_m Rd_{mj} = \sum_k y_{jk}, \quad \text{for all } j \tag{4}$$

(Amount-in = Amount-out in manufactory)

$$\sum_l z_{kl} + \sum_m o_{km} \le Sc_k \beta_k, \quad \text{for all } k \tag{5}$$

(The capacity constraint about DC)

$$\sum_j y_{jk} = \sum_l z_{kl}, \quad \text{for all } k \tag{6}$$

(Amount-in = Amount-out in DC for forward logistics)

$$\sum_m o_{km} \le \lfloor p_d Sc_k \beta_k \rfloor, \quad \text{for all } k \ \lfloor\ \rfloor \text{ floor forGauss' symbol} \tag{7}$$

(The reverse capacity limit of DC)

$$\sum_l Rz_{lk} = \sum_m o_{km}, \quad \text{for all } k \tag{8}$$

(Amount-in = Amount-out in DC for reverse logistics)

$$\sum_k Rz_{lk} \ge \left\lceil p_c \sum_k z_{kl} \right\rceil, \text{ for all } l \ \lceil\ \rceil \text{ Ceiling for Gauss' symbol} \tag{9}$$

(The recovered capacity constraint about customer)

$$\sum_k z_{kl} \ge d_l, \quad \text{for all } l \tag{10}$$

(The capacity constraint about in-flow of customer or demand constraint between DC and customer)

$$\sum_j Rd_{mj} + \left\lfloor p_l \sum_k o_{km} \right\rfloor \le e_m \delta_m, \quad \text{for all } m$$

$\lfloor\ \rfloor$:floor forGauss' symbol

(11)

(The capacity constraint about dismantler)

$$\sum_k o_{km} = \sum_m Rd_{mj} + \left\lfloor p_l \sum_k o_{km} \right\rfloor, \quad \text{for all } m$$

$\lfloor\ \rfloor$:floor forGauss' symbol

(12)

(Amount-in = Amount-out in dismantler)

$$\alpha_j, \beta_k, \delta_m = \{0, 1\}, \text{ for all } j, k, m \tag{13}$$

$x_{ij}, y_{jk}, z_{kl}, o_{km}, Rd_{mj}, Rz_{lk} \ge 0$ and are integer for all i, j, k, l, m (14)

The objective is to minimize total cost of the transportation and the operations. The constraints mainly contain two types: one is for limited capacities and the other is for the law of flow conservation. Because the variables denote the basic units of logistics, therefore apart from 0-1 decision variables, all other variables must also be integer and thus for solution purposes, Gauss' symbols are introduced in the model. The floor and ceiling of Gaussian are defined below:

Definition 2: The Floor or the Ceiling of a Real number x is an integer denoted by $\lfloor x \rfloor$ and $\lceil x \rceil$, respectively, and defined as below:

$$\lfloor x \rfloor = \{\underline{x} \mid \underline{x} \ge x, \underline{x} \le y, \forall y, \underline{x} \in I\}$$
$$\lceil x \rceil = \{\overline{x} \mid \underline{x} \le x, \overline{x} \ge y, \forall y, \underline{x} \in I\}$$

Because of Gaussian, the model is a logic linear program and needed to further transform into a linear, computable model.

Integer Linear Programming

In constraint (7), the Gauss' symbol is used to present the upper limit of reverse capacity limit in DC, and we can observe that because all parameters P_d, Sc_k and β_k are known, $\lfloor p_d Sc_k \beta_k \rfloor$ is a known constant. Let $SP_k = \lfloor p_d Sc_k \rfloor$, then constraint (7) is rewritten into (7)' below :

$$\sum_m o_{km} \leq SP_k \beta_k, \quad \text{for all } k \qquad (7)'$$

Similarly, in constraint (9), the Gauss' symbol is used to present the recovery amount. Because the customer demand must be satisfied in each customer group, $\sum_k z_{kl}$ is given. In other words, $\left\lceil p_c \sum_k z_{kl} \right\rceil$ is a constant too. Let $ZP_l = \left\lceil p_c \sum_k z_{kl} \right\rceil$ and transfer constraint (9) into (9)' as below:

$$\sum_m o_{km} \leq SP_k \beta_k, \quad \text{for all } k \qquad (9)'$$

Constraints (11) and (12) are different from the situation above. Because $\sum_k o_{km}$ is a decision value that we do not know in advance. To transfer these two constraints with Gauss's symbol, three additional inequalities are needed as defined below.

$$OP_m \leq p_l \sum_k o_{km}, \quad \text{for all } m \qquad (15)$$

$$OP_m > p_l \sum_k o_{km} - 1, \quad \text{for all } m \qquad (16)$$

$OP_m \geq 0$ and are integer for all m (17)

$$\sum_j Rd_{mj} + OP_m \leq e_m \delta_m, \quad \text{for all } m \qquad (11)'$$

$$\sum_k o_{km} = \sum_m Rd_{mj} + OP_m, \quad \text{for all } m \qquad (12)'$$

Through the above processes, we can transfer a logic model with Gauss's symbol into an integer linear program (ILP) without Gauss's symbol. The final model is summarized as shown in Box 2 (Equation 1).

Subject to:

$$\sum_j x_{ij} \leq a_i, \quad \text{for all } i \qquad (2)$$

$$\sum_k y_{jk} \leq b_j \alpha_j, \quad \text{for all } j \qquad (3)$$

$$\sum_i x_{ij} + \sum_m Rd_{mj} = \sum_k y_{jk}, \quad \text{for all } j \qquad (4)$$

$$\sum_l z_{kl} + \sum_m o_{km} \leq Sc_k \beta_k, \quad \text{for all } k \qquad (5)$$

$$\sum_j y_{jk} = \sum_l z_{kl}, \quad \text{for all } k \qquad (6)$$

$$\sum_m o_{km} \leq SP_k \beta_k, \quad \text{for all } k \qquad (7)'$$

$$\sum_l Rz_{lk} = \sum_m o_{km}, \quad \text{for all } k \qquad (8)$$

$$\sum_k Rz_{lk} \geq ZP_l, \quad \text{for all } l \qquad (9)'$$

Box 2. Equation 1

$$\min \ TC = \sum_i \sum_j s_{ij} x_{ij} + \sum_j \sum_k t_{jk} y_{jk} + \sum_k \sum_l u_{kl} z_{kl} + \sum_k \sum_m v_{km} o_{km} + \sum_m \sum_j w_{mj} Rd_{mj} + \sum_l \sum_k Ru_{lk} Rz_{lk} + \sum_j f_j \alpha_j + \sum_k g_k \beta_k + \sum_m h_m \delta_m + \phi \sum_m OP_m$$

$$\sum_k z_{kl} \geq d_l, \quad \text{for all } l \qquad (10)$$

$$OP_m \leq p_l \sum_k o_{km}, \quad \text{for all } m \qquad (15)$$

$$OP_m > p_l \sum_k o_{km} - 1, \quad \text{for all } m \qquad (16)$$

$$\sum_j Rd_{mj} + OP_m \leq e_m \delta_m, \quad \text{for all } m \qquad (11)'$$

$$\sum_k o_{km} = \sum_m Rd_{mj} + OP_m, \quad \text{for all } m \qquad (12)'$$

$$\alpha_j,\ \beta_k,\ \delta_m = \{0, 1\}, \text{ for all } j, k, m \qquad (13)$$

$$x_{ij},\ y_{jk},\ z_{kl},\ o_{km},\ Rd_{mj},\ Rz_{lk} \geq 0, \text{ for all } i, j, k, l, m \qquad (14)$$

$$OP_m \geq 0, OP_m \in N, \forall m \qquad (17)$$

This kind of model can be treated as a multiple-choice Knapsack problem. However, the model cannot be divided into submodels, because the decision of which site should be opened must be considered throughout the network. If individual stages are treated by submodels, the location will not be optimal. Hence, the model's variables have 0-1 integer variables for this decision, and that's one of the points why the model is hard to solve (Gen & Cheng, 1997; Yeh, 2005). In this reverse logistics model, there are $(I+2J+4K+2L+4M)$ constraints, and $(I\times J+J\times K+K\times L+L\times K+K\times M+M\times J+J+K+2M)$ variables with additional $2M$ variables and M constraints for transformation.

Numerical Example

To illustrate the properties of the problem with the proposed model, a numerical example is provided in this section.

Tables 1 to 3 are the given data of the example of which 3 suppliers, 5 manufactories, 3 distribution centers, 4 customers and 2 dismantlers. Five types of roles are involved with the respective recovery rates, as shown in Table 1. Tables 2 and 3 list all the unit costs of transportation and operations, respectively.

In this example, with I=3, J=5, K=3, L=4 and M=2, there are (3+10+12+8+8)=41 constraints, and (15+15+12+12+6+10+5+3+4)=82 variables.

Table 1. The size and estimated constants of the example

suppliers	manufactories	DCs	customers	dismantlers	p_d	p_c	p_l	φ
3	5	3	4	2	10%	10%	10%	5

Table 2. Capacity, demand (in unit) and fixed cost (NT$)

supplier	Manufactory		DC		customer	dismantler	
capacity	capacity	fixed cost	capacity	fixed cost	demand	capacity	fixed cost
500	400	1800	870	1000	500	540	900
650	550	900	890	900	300	380	800
390	490	2100	600	1600	400		
	300	1100			300		
	500	900					

Table 3. Shipping cost of unit value for each stage (NT$1000)

supplier	manufactory				
	1	2	3	4	5
1	5	6	4	7	5
2	6	5	6	6	8
3	7	6	3	9	6
manufactory	DC				
	1	2	3		
1	5	8	5		
2	8	7	8		
3	4	7	4		
4	3	5	3		
5	5	6	6		
DC	customer				
	1	2	3	4	
1	7	4	5	6	
2	5	4	6	7	
3	7	5	3	6	
customer	DC				
	1	2	3		
1	3	7	4		
2	8	5	5		
3	4	3	4		
4	3	2	5		
DC	dismantler				
	1	2			
1	3	2			
2	2	5			
3	3	3			
dismantler	manufactory				
	1	2	3	4	5
1	2	3	4	2	5
2	3	4	6	3	4

Using software LINGO 7.0 with 1(s) elapsed time, we obtained the optimal solution as follows with logistics shown in Figure 2:

Global optimal solution found at iteration: 3135

Objective value: $29848.00

$x_{13} = 40$, $x_{15} = 460$, $x_{22} = 415$, $x_{23} = 60$, $x_{33} = 390$
$y_{22} = 550$, $y_{31} = 490$, $y_{51} = 319$, $y_{52} = 141$
$z_{12} = 109$, $z_{13} = 400$, $z_{14} = 300$, $z_{21} = 500$, $z_{22} = 191$
$o_{11} = 61$, $o_{21} = 89$
$Rd_{12} = 135$,
$Rz_{11} = 50$, $Rz_{22} = 30$, $Rz_{32} = 40$, $Rz_{41} = 11$, $Rz_{42} = 19$
$\alpha_2 = 1$, $\alpha_3 = 1$, $\alpha_5 = 1$
$\beta_1 = 1$, $\beta_2 = 1$
$\delta_1 = 1$

Therefore, from the display of the optimal logistics in Figure 2, we can realize that only 3 manufactory sites, 2 distribution centers, and one dismantler are required to open for overall demands from customer and recovery. The forward and reverse flows ensure the close system for environmental protest and economic consumption.

From this numerical example, we can clearly understand the characteristic of the network flows, and what the problem was the programming solved.

Figure 2. The pattern of optimal logistics of the example

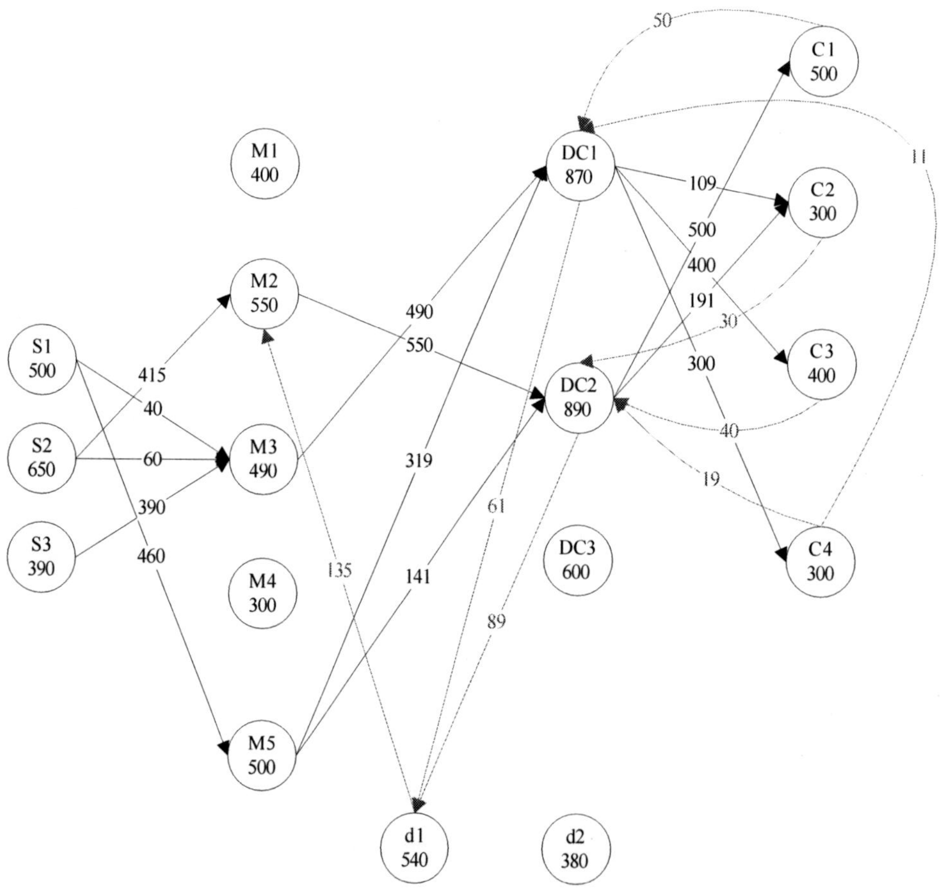

Sensitivity Analysis for Recovery and Land-Filling Rates

Recovery and land-filling rate in previous numerical example is assumed 10% of the shipping units from the distribution center, and they are the green factors we care about in our scenario. In GSC problem, the recovery and land-filling rate are the most important and uncertain factors. Therefore, sensitivity analysis is necessary to ensure the optimality.

There are two preliminary issues to cope with before sensitivity analysis. First, the close-loop model is an integer linear model, and conventional parameter analysis for real numbers fails to apply. Second, the transformed model does not have recovery rate anymore. For the later issue, we revise the model as follows.

Note that the original program with Gauss's symbol in constraint (9) can also be transferred into:

$$ZP_l^{'} \geq p_c \sum_k z_{kl}, \quad \text{for all } l \qquad (18)$$

$$ZP_l^{'} < p_c \sum_k z_{kl} + 1, \quad \text{for all } l \qquad (19)$$

$ZP_l^{'} \geq 0$ and must be integer (20)

$$\sum_k Rz_{lk} \geq ZP_l^{'}, \text{ for all } l \qquad (21)$$

Therefore :

$$\frac{ZP_l^{'}}{\sum_k z_{kl}} \geq p_c, \quad \text{for all } l \qquad (18)'$$

$$\frac{ZP_l^{'} - 1}{\sum_k z_{kl}} < p_c, \quad \text{for all } l \qquad (19)'$$

$$\frac{OP_m}{\sum_k o_{km}} \leq p_l \quad \text{for all } m \qquad (15)'$$

$$\frac{OP_m + 1}{\sum_k o_{km}} > p_l, \quad \text{for all } m \qquad (16)'$$

$$\sum_k Rz_{lk} \geq ZP_l^{'}, \quad \text{for all } l \qquad (21)$$

$$\sum_j Rd_{mj} + OP_m \leq e_m \delta_m, \quad \text{for all } m \qquad (11)'$$

$$\sum_k o_{km} = \sum_m Rd_{mj} + OP_m, \quad \text{for all } m \qquad (12)'$$

$ZP_l^{'} \geq 0$, $OP_m \geq 0$ and must be integer

In order to do the sensitivity analysis, two parameter θ_1 and θ_2 with range [-1,1] are introduced :

$$\frac{ZP_l^{'}}{\sum_k z_{kl}} \geq p_c + \theta_1 p_c^{'}, \quad \text{for all } l$$

$$\frac{ZP_l^{'} - 1}{\sum_k z_{kl}} < p_c + \theta_1 p_c^{'}, \quad \text{for all } l$$

$$\frac{OP_m}{\sum_k o_{km}} \leq p_l + \theta_2 p_l^{'} \quad \text{for all } m$$

$$\frac{OP_m + 1}{\sum_k o_{km}} > p_l + \theta_2 p_l^{'}, \quad \text{for all } m$$

$$\sum_k Rz_{lk} \geq ZP_l^{'}, \quad \text{for all } l$$

$$\sum_j Rd_{mj} + OP_m \leq e_m \delta_m, \quad \text{for all } m$$

$$\sum_k o_{km} = \sum_m Rd_{mj} + OP_m, \quad \text{for all } m$$

$ZP_l^{'} \geq 0$, $OP_m \geq 0$ and must be integer

$p_c^{'}$ and $p_l^{'}$ are the given parameters which denote the differences between max possible percentage and current recovery rate and land-filling rate, respectively.

Applying a binary search, the upper and lower bounds of these two parameters such that the optimal bases remains can be defined. The process is summarized below:

Step 1: Let θ_2=0 and θ_1=1. Use binary search in θ_1 between 0 and 1 to obtain the optimal solution. If the solution bases are not changed in θ_2=0 and

θ_1 =1, then stop, else continue the binary search until θ_1 have a value θ_1^+ that the solution bases are not changed relatively to θ_2=0 and θ_1=0 and the solution will change by increasing a small value. This step can find marginal upper bound of recovery rate.

Step 2: Let θ_2=0 and θ_1=-1. Use binary search in θ_1 between 0 and -1 to obtain the optimal solution. If the solution bases are not changed in θ_2=0 and θ_1=-1, then stop, else continue the binary search until θ_1 have a value θ_1^- that the solution bases are not changed relatively to θ_2=0 and θ_1=0 and the solution will change by decreasing a small value. This step can find marginal lower bound of recovery rate.

Step 3: Let θ_1=0 and θ_2=1. Use binary search in θ_2 between 0 and 1 to obtain the optimal solution. If the solution bases are not changed in θ_1=0 and θ_2 =1, then stop, else continue the binary search until θ_2 have a value θ_2^+ that the solution bases are not changed relatively to θ_2=0 and θ_1=0 and the solution will change by increasing a small value. This step can find marginal upper bound of land-filling rate.

Step 4: Let θ_1=0 and θ_2=-1. Use binary search in θ_2 between 0 and -1 to obtain the optimal solution. If the solution bases are not changed in θ_1=0 and θ_2=-1, then stop, else continue the binary search until θ_2 have a value θ_2^- that the solution bases are not changed relatively to θ_2=0 and θ_1=0 and the solution will change by decreasing a small value. This step can find marginal lower bound of land-filling rate.

Step 5: Let $\theta_2=\theta_2^-$ and $\theta_1=\theta_1^-$. If the solution bases are not changed relatively to θ_2=0 and θ_1=0, then go to step 6, else continue the binary search in θ_1 between 0 and θ_1^- until θ_1 have a new value θ_1^{-*} that the solution bases are not changed relatively to θ_2=0 and θ_1=0 and the solution will change by decreasing a small value. Let $\theta_1^-=\theta_1^{-*}$.

Step 6: Let $\theta_2=\theta_2^-$ and $\theta_1=\theta_1^+$. If the solution bases are not changed relatively to θ_2=0 and θ_1=0, then go to step 7, else continue the binary search in θ_1 between 0 and θ_1^+ until θ_1 have a new value θ_1^{+*} that the solution bases are not changed relatively to θ_2=0 and θ_1=0 and the solution will change by increasing a small value. Let $\theta_1^+=\theta_1^{+*}$.

Step 7: Let $\theta_2=\theta_2^+$ and $\theta_1=\theta_1^-$. If the solution bases are not changed relatively to θ_2=0 and θ_1=0, then go to step 8, else continue the binary search in θ_1 between 0 and θ_1^- until θ_1 have a new value θ_1^{-*} that the solution bases are not changed relatively to θ_2=0 and θ_1=0 and the solution will change by decreasing a small value. Let $\theta_1^-=\theta_1^{-*}$.

Step 8: Let $\theta_2=\theta_2^+$ and $\theta_1=\theta_1^+$. If the solution bases are not changed relatively to θ_2=0 and θ_1=0, then go to step 9, else continue the binary search in θ_1 between 0 and θ_1^+ until θ_1 have a new value θ_1^{+*} that the solution bases are not changed relatively to θ_2=0 and θ_1=0 and the solution will change by increasing a small value. Let $\theta_1^+=\theta_1^{+*}$.

Step 9: Let $\theta_1=\theta_1^-$ and $\theta_2=\theta_2^-$. If the solution bases are not changed relatively to θ_2=0 and θ_1=0, then go to step 10, else continue the binary search in θ_2 between 0 and θ_2^- until θ_2^- have a new value θ_2^{-*} that the solution bases are not changed relatively to θ_2=0 and θ_1=0 and the solution will change by decreasing a small value. Let $\theta_2^+=\theta_2^{-*}$.

Step 10: Let $\theta_1=\theta_1^-$ and $\theta_2=\theta_2^+$. If the solution bases are not changed relatively to θ_2=0 and θ_1=0, then go to step 11, else continue the binary search in θ_2 between 0 and θ_2^+until θ_2 have a new value θ_2^{+*} that the solution bases are not changed relatively to θ_2=0 and θ_1=0 and the solution will change by increasing a small value. Let $\theta_2^+=\theta_2^{+*}$.

Step 11: Let $\theta_1=\theta_1^+$ and $\theta_2=\theta_2^-$. If the solution bases are not changed relatively to θ_2=0 and θ_1=0, then go to step 12, else continue the binary search in θ_2 between 0 and θ_2^- until θ_2^- have a new value θ_2^{-*}

Table 4. Numerical illustration of parameter analysis

Step	θ_1	θ_2	Recovery rate	Land-filling rate	Optimal solution
1	1	0	10%	10%	29848
2	-1	0	9.4%	10%	29801
3	0	1	10%	10.9%	29855
4	0	-1	10%	8.7%	29834
5	-0.3	-0.65	9.7%	8.7%	29816
6	0	-0.65	10%	8.7%	29848
7	-0.15	0.45	9.9%	10.9%	29834
8	0	0.45	10%	10.9%	29855
9	-0.5	-0.65	9.9%	8.7%	29848
10	-0.5	0.45	9.9%	10.9%	29855
11	0	-0.65	10%	8.7%	29848
12	0	0.45	10%	10.9%	29855
13	[-0.5,0]	[-0.65,0.45]	[9.9%,10%]	[8.7%,10.9%]	[29848,29855]

that the solution bases are not changed relatively to θ_2=0 and θ_1=0 and the solution will change by decreasing a small value. Let $\theta_2^- = \theta_2^{-*}$.

Step 12: Let θ_1=θ_1^+ and θ_2=θ_2^+. If the solution bases are not changed relatively to θ_2=0 and θ_1=0, then go to step 13, else continue the binary search in θ_2 between 0 and θ_2^+ until θ_2 have a new value θ_2^{+*} that the solution bases are not changed relatively to θ_2=0 and θ_1=0 and the solution will change by increasing a small value. Let θ_2^+= θ_2^{+*}.

Step 13: Repeat step 5 to 12 until previous step θ_1^{+*}, θ_1^{-*} , θ_2^{+*} and θ_2^{-*} are equal to current step θ_1^{+*}, θ_1^{-*} , θ_2^{+*} and θ_2^{-*}, then stop and print the answer.

We can ensure that land-filling rate between $p_l + \theta_2^+ p_l^{'}$ and $p_l + \theta_2^- p_l^{'}$ and recovery rate between $p_c + \theta_1^+ p_c^{'}$ and $p_c + \theta_1^- p_c^{'}$ will have the same optimal policy. We operated the numerical example used before to test and verify that the process can obtain the optimal range. Recovery and land-filling rate in previous numerical example are assumed 10% ($p_c = p_l$ =0.1), and we assumed the max possible percentage for each rate is 12% ($p_c^{'} = p_l^{'}$ =0.02).

Apply the above process, sensitivity analysis of the example is shown in all steps in Table 4.

Therefore, by the proposed procedure we can find the exact tolerance levels of these two parameters in which we may notice that, in fact, at step 6, the correct range has been found.

Besides, from this example, we can observe two of the following features in this process.

First, these two factors are the most important parameters in the GSC. Although they are not easy to estimate correctly, the proposed process can ensure that land-filling rate between 8.7%~10.9% and recovery rate between 9.9%~10% will retain the same optimal logistic pattern in this example. However, based on the revealed information from sensitivity analysis, we also can consider two or more policies with different ranges close to the current range. In particular, when the rates out of the current ranges, we may change or know what pattern should be adopted.

Second, by comparing these two influential factors of recovery and land-filling rate, it can be noted that the recovery rate is more sensitivity than land-filling rate. Therefore, with smaller tolerance range, possible variation of the recovery rate should be paid more attention in control and management.

FURTURE TRENDS

The green issues are more and more important in recent years, and its applications to the products are around companies. Reduction of the primary resource use, pollution prevention, waste management, and sustainable products policy became the focuses of modern industrial societies and environmental policies. The green logistics is one of the most essential keys in related to the cost of the companies. In the future, conventional supply chain will be replaced by the green logistics and the main issues will be the uncertainty regarding the amount of customer demand and the recovery rate and therefore further analytical tools need to be developed for the purposes of analysis and management.

CONCLUSION

The green logistics has been an urgent issue, but the solution and the consistent principles are still lacking in both theory and practice. Most of the proposed models are cases based, and therefore their application and generalization are limited.

Based on the properties of green logistics which includes both forward and reverse logistics, in this study, we have proposed a mathematical programming model for general applications. To retain the integral properties, the model contends Gussian symbols which are not algebraically computable. Therefore, a transformation procedure was proposed to convert the model into an integer linear programming model with additional $2M$ decision variables and M constraints.

In addition, in order to cope with the uncertainty embedded in the recovery and landfill rates, an approach to perform sensitivity analysis was proposed, from which the tolerance ranges with respect to these two factors can be precisely defined to retain the optimal bases. A simple example was used to illustrate the properties of the model and the analysis and the results can be shown that the proposed model with its parametric analysis can fulfill the environment and economic requirements of a green logistics in an optimal manner.

FUTURE RESEARCH DIRECTIONS

It is noted that the model is NP hard, for real case applications, an efficient algorithm is required and this is our undergoing research. In addition, the uncertainty embedded in the demand and recovery rates should be treated in a more analytical way. Fuzzy logic can be the tool for resolving this problem. Furthermore, future research should consider the trade-offs among cost, response time, market potential, and returns in more systematic manner so that green supply chain management as a whole can be conducted more efficiently and effectively. These would be the future trends of research.

ACKNOWLEDGEMENT

The authors acknowledge the financial support from the National Science Council, Taiwan, ROC with the project number NSC95-2221-E-007-213.

REFERENCES

Baumgarten, H., Christian, B., Annerous, F., & Thomas, S.-D. (2003). Supply chain management and reverse logistics-integration of reverse logistics processes into supply chain management approaches. In *Proceedings of the International Symposium on Electronics and the Environment* (pp. 79-84).

Booker, L. (1987). Improving search in genetic algorithm. In L. Davis (Ed.), *Genetic algorithms and simulated annealing* (pp. 61-73). San Mateo, CA: Morgan Kaufmann.

Bowersox, D.J., & Closs, D.J. (1996). *Logistical management: The integrated supply chain process.* New York: McGraw-Hill.

De Groene, A., & Hermans, M. (1998). Economic and other implications of integrated chain management: A case study. *Journal of Cleaner Production, 6,* 199-221.

Fleischmann, M., Jacqueline, M. B.-R., Rommert, D., van der Laan, E., van Nunen, J.A.E.E., & van Wassenhove, L.N. (1997). Quantitative models for reverse logistics: A review. *European Journal of Operational Research, 103*(16), 1-17.

Gen, M., & Cheng, R. (1997). *Genetic algorithms and engineering design.* New York: John Wiley.

Lu, Q., Vivi, C., Julie, A.S., & Taylor, R. (2000). A practical framework for the reverse supply chain. In *Proceedings of the International Symposium on Electronics and the Environment* (pp. 266-271).

Pochampally, K.K., Surendra, M.G., & Sagar, V.K. (2004). Identification of potential recovery facilities for designing a reverse supply chain network using physical programming. *The International Society for Optical Engineering: Environmentally Conscious Manufacturing III, 5262,* 139-146.

Schultmann, F., Moritz, Z., & Otto, R. (2006). Modeling reverse logistic tasks within closed-loop supply chains: An example from the automotive industry. *European Journal of Operational Research, 171,* 1033-1050.

The European Working Group on Reverse Logistics (REVLOG). (1999). Retrieved July 9, 2008, from http://www.fbk.eur.nl/OZ/REVLOG/PROJECTS/TERMINOLOGY/def_reverselogistics.html

Tilanus, B. (1997). Introduction to information system in logistics and transportation. *Information system in logistics and transportation.* Elsevier Science.

Wang, H.F., & Jyh-Shing, H. (1996). Structural approach to parametric analysis of an IP. *European Journal of Operation Research, 92,* 148-156.

Wang, H.F., & Jyh-Shing, H. (1996). Directed purturbation analysis of an IP. *Journal of Mathematics Analysis and Applications, 201,* 447-460.

Wei-Chang, Y. (2005). A hybrid heuristic algorithm for the multistage supply chain network problem. *Internal Journal of Advanced Manufacturing Technology, 26,* 675-685.

Zhu, Q., & Raymond, P.C. (2004). Integrating green supply chain management into an embryonic eco-industrial development: A case study of the Guitang Group. *Journal of Cleaner Production, 12,* 1025-1035.

ADDITIONAL READING

Balou, R.H. (1992). *Business logistics management.* NJ: Prentice Hall.

Beomon, B.M. (1999). Design a green supply chain. *Logistics Information Management, 12*(4), 332-342.

Fleischmann, M., Bloemhof-Ruwaard, J., Beullens, P., & Dekker, R. (2003). Reverse logistics network design. In Dekker, et al. (Eds.), *Reverse logistics: Quantitative models for closed-loop supply chains* (pp. 65-94). Berlin: Springer-Verlag.

Jayaraman, V., Guide, J., & Srivastava, R. (1999). A closed-loop logistics model for re-manufacturing. *Journal of the Operational Research Society, 50*, 497-508.

Minner, S. (2001). Strategic safety stocks in reverse logistics supply chains. *International Journal of Production Economics, 71*, 417-428.

Chapter XIII
Reverse Supply Chain Design: A Neural Network Approach

Kishore K. Pochampally
Southern New Hampshire University, Manchester, USA

Surendra M. Gupta
Northeastern University, Boston, USA

ABSTRACT

The success of a reverse supply chain heavily relies on the efficiency of the collection facilities and recovery facilities chosen while designing that reverse supply chain. In this chapter, we propose a neural network approach to evaluate the efficiency of a facility (collection or recovery) of interest, which is being considered for inclusion in a reverse supply chain, using the available linguistic data of facilities that already exist in the reverse supply chain. The approach is carried out in four phases, as follows: In phase I, we identify criteria for evaluation of the facility of interest, for each group participating in the reverse supply chain. Then, in phase II, we use fuzzy ratings of already existing facilities to construct a neural network that gives impacts (importance values) of criteria identified for each group in phase I. Then, in phase III, using the impacts obtained in phase II, we employ a fuzzy TOPSIS (Technique for Order Preference by Similarity to Ideal Solution) approach to obtain the overall rating of the facility of interest, as calculated by each group. Finally, in phase IV, we employ Borda's choice rule to calculate the maximized consensus (among the groups considered) rating of the facility of interest.

MOTIVATION

Although companies tend to spend more time and money in fine-tuning their forward supply chains, in today's competitive business environment, they can no longer ignore reverse supply chains due to the two most important factors, viz., environmental regulations and profitability (Fleischmann, 2001; Gungor & Gupta, 1999). A reverse supply chain, which is the series of activities required to retrieve used products from consumers and either recover their left-over market values or

Copyright © 2009, IGI Global, distributing in print or electronic forms without written permission of IGI Global is prohibited.

dispose of them, utilizes at least the following (see Figure 1): *collection facilities* where used products are collected, *recovery facilities* where reprocessing, viz., disassembly, remanufacturing, or recycling, are performed, and *demand centers* where re-processed goods are sold. Evidently, the success of a reverse supply chain heavily relies on the efficiency of the collection facilities and the recovery facilities chosen while designing (also called strategic planning) of that reverse supply chain.

The efficiency of a collection or recovery facility depends on the participation (in the reverse supply chain) of three different groups who have multiple, conflicting, and incommensurate goals, as follows:

i. **Consumers** whose primary concern is *convenience*
ii. **Local government officials** whose primary concern is *environmental consciousness*
iii. **Supply chain company executives** whose primary concern is *profit*

Therefore, the evaluation of a facility must be based upon the maximized consensus among the three groups.

In this chapter, we propose a neural network approach to evaluate the efficiency of a facility (collection or recovery) of interest, which is being considered for inclusion in a reverse supply chain, using the available *linguistic* data of facilities that already exist in the reverse supply chain. The approach is carried out in four phases, as follows: In phase I, we identify criteria for evaluating the efficiency of the facility of interest, for each group participating in the reverse supply chain. Then, in phase II, we use fuzzy ratings (Zadeh, 1965) of existing facilities to construct a neural network that gives impacts (importance values) of criteria identified for each group in phase I. Then, in phase III, using the impacts obtained in phase II, we employ a fuzzy TOPSIS approach (Chu, 2002), that is, a combination of the fuzzy set theory (Zadeh, 1965) and the TOPSIS (Technique for Order Preference by Similarity to Ideal Solution; Triantaphyllou & Lin, 1996), to obtain the overall rating of the facility of interest, as calculated for each group. Finally, in phase IV, we employ Borda's choice rule (Hwang, 1987) to calculate the maximized consensus (among the groups considered) rating of the facility of interest.

In the next section, we review a few important papers in the literature, which propose models to design a reverse supply chain. Then, we briefly introduce the techniques, viz., the fuzzy set theory, the TOPSIS, and the Borda's choice rule used in our approach, and present the approach to evaluate the efficiency of a collection facil-

Figure 1. A generic reverse supply chain network

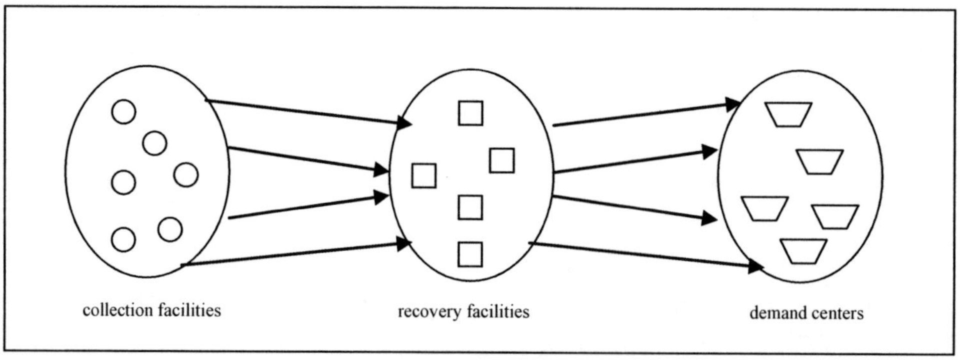

ity of interest. Next, we present the approach to evaluate the efficiency of a recovery facility of interest, give some conclusions, and present the future research directions. Finally, we give additional reading material in the field of reverse supply chain design.

LITERATURE REVIEW

Many papers in the literature propose how to design a reverse supply chain (for a good review, see Fleischmann, 2001). However, every paper assumes that all of the recovery facilities that are engaged in the supply chain are profited by reprocessing economical used products, and also that these facilities have sufficient potential to efficiently reprocess the incoming used products. Motivated by the risk of reprocessing uneconomical used products in inefficient recovery facilities, Pochampally and Gupta (2003) proposed an approach that employs linear programming to select economical used products for reprocessing in a reverse supply chain and analytic hierarchy process (AHP) (Saaty, 1980) to identify efficient recovery facilities operating in a region where that supply chain is to be designed. Furthermore, realizing the increasing enforcement of environmental consciousness by governmental regulations (Gungor & Gupta, 1999), and the developing practice of collection and reprocessing of used products being carried out by the same parties that are involved in a forward supply chain (the series of activities required to produce new products from raw material), they developed an integrated approach to design a closed-loop supply chain. To that end, they formulated a fuzzy (Zadeh, 1965) cost-benefit function that can be used to perform a multicriteria economic analysis to select economical products to process in the closed-loop supply chain (Pochampally, Gupta, & Cullinane, 2003), and proposed a fuzzy TOPSIS (Technique for Order Preference by Similarity to Ideal Solution) approach (Chu, 2002) to evaluate production facilities in a region where that closed-loop supply chain is to be designed, in terms of both environmental consciousness (mainly associated with the forward supply chain) and efficiency (mainly associated with the reverse supply chain) (Pochampally, Gupta, & Kamarthi, 2003).

Despite all of the papers cited above, there is no paper in the literature which proposes how to identify efficient collection facilities. Moreover, no one has looked at the problem of evaluating recovery facilities based upon the consensus among all of the important groups participating in the reverse supply chain, viz., the consumers, local government officials, and the supply chain company executives. This chapter attempts to fill both the voids.

The traditional/forward supply chain design models in the literature cannot be applied to designing a reverse supply chain due to the following challenges in the reverse supply chain: uncertainty in supply rate of used products, unknown condition of used products, and imperfect correlation between supply of used products and demand for reprocessed goods. For example, Talluri, Baker, and Sarkis's model (1999) that uses data envelopment analysis and integer goal programming and Talluri and Baker's (2002) model that uses multiphase mathematical programming to select partners in a traditional supply chain, do not consider the reverse flow of products after their end of use.

TECHNIQUES USED IN THIS CHAPTER

This section introduces the fuzzy set theory, the TOPSIS, and the Borda's choice rule.

Fuzzy Set Theory

Expressions such as "not very clear," "probably so," and "very likely" are often heard in daily life. The commonality in such expressions is that they are tainted with imprecision. This imprecision or vagueness of human decision-making is called "fuzziness" in the scientific literature. With different decision-making problems of varied intensity, the results can be misleading if fuzziness is not taken into account. However, since Zadeh (1965) first proposed fuzzy set theory, an increasing number of studies have dealt with imprecision (fuzziness) in problems by applying the fuzzy set theory. The concepts of the fuzzy set theory, which we utilize in this chapter, are as follows.

Linguistic Values and Fuzzy Sets

When dealing with imprecision, decision-makers may be provided with information characterized by vague language such as: high risk, low profit, and good customer service. By using *linguistic* values like "high," "low," "good," "medium," "cheap," and so forth, people are usually attempting to describe factors with uncertain or imprecise values. For example, "weight" of an object may be a factor with an uncertain or imprecise value and so, its linguistic value can be "very low," "low," "medium," "high," "very high," and so forth. The fuzzy set theory is primarily concerned with quantifying the vagueness in human thoughts and perceptions. The transition from vagueness to quantification is performed by applying the fuzzy set theory as depicted in Figure 2.

To deal with quantifying vagueness, Zadeh proposed a membership function which associates with each quantified linguistic value a grade of membership belonging to the interval [0, 1]. Thus, a fuzzy set is defined as:

$$\forall x \in X, \mu_A(x) \in [0,1]$$

where $\mu_A(x)$ is the degree of membership, ranging from 0 to 1, of a quantity x of the linguistic value, A, over the universe of quantified linguistic values, X. X is essentially a set of real numbers. The more x fits A, the larger the degree of membership of x. If a quantity has a degree of membership equal to 1, this reflects a complete fitness between the quantity and the vague description (linguistic value). On the other hand, if the degree of membership of a quantity is 0, then that quantity does not belong to the vague description.

The membership function can be viewed as an expert's opinion. We use the term "expert" because an expert usually holds some required knowledge about relative problems while a layperson may not. For example, when a financial manager is asked what a "high annual interest rate" is, the possibility of 20% being "high annual interest rate" would be higher than that of 3%, 5%, or 9%. Thus, the membership function, here, can be explained as the possibility of an interest rate being *considered* as "high." A reasonable mapping from interest rate to its degree of membership about the fuzzy set "high annual interest rate" is depicted in Figure 3. This membership function looks like a typical cumulative probability function; however, here, the value of the membership function represents

Figure 2. Application of fuzzy set theory

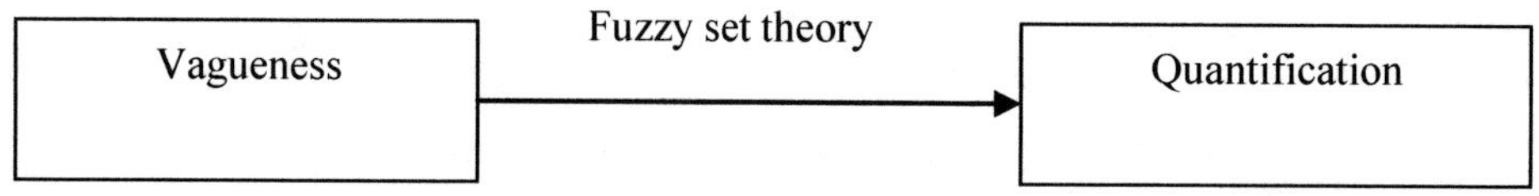

Figure 3. Mapping of quantified "high" interest values to their degrees of membership

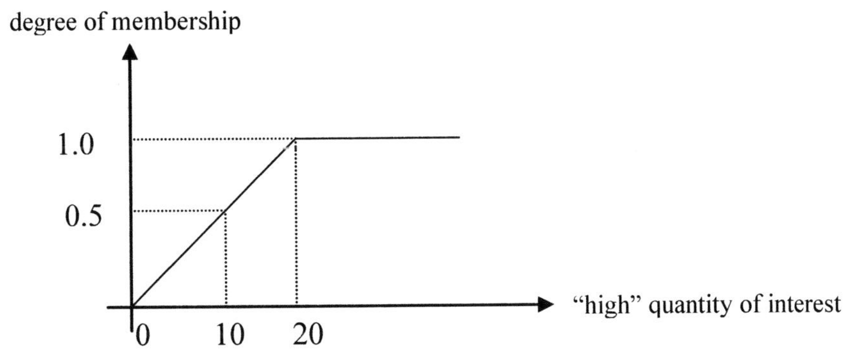

Figure 4. Triangular fuzzy number

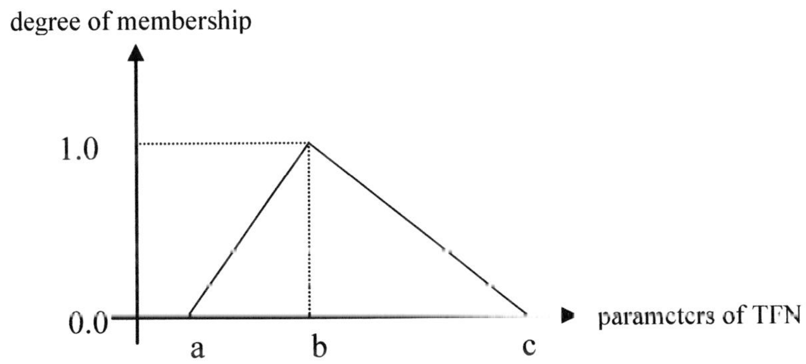

the possibility of a fuzzy event, while the value of a cumulative probability function represents the cumulative probability of a statistical event.

Triangular Fuzzy Numbers

A triangular fuzzy number (TFN) (Tsaur, Chang, & Yen, 2002) is a fuzzy set with three parameters, each representing a quantity of a linguistic value associated with a degree of membership of either 0 or 1. It is graphically depicted in Figure 4. The parameters *a, b,* and *c* respectively denote the smallest possible quantity, the most promising quantity and the largest possible quantity that describe the linguistic value.

Each TFN, *P*, has linear representations on its left and right side such that its membership function can be defined as:

$$\mu_P = 0, \qquad x < a \qquad (1)$$

$$= (x-a) / (b-a) \qquad a \leq x \leq b \qquad (2)$$

$$= (c-x) / (c-b) \qquad b \leq x \leq c \qquad (3)$$

$$= 0, \qquad x \geq c. \qquad (4)$$

For each quantity x increasing from a to b, its corresponding degree of membership linearly increases from 0 to 1. While x increases from b to c, its corresponding degree of membership linearly decreases from 1 to 0. The membership function is a mapping from any given x to its corresponding degree of membership.

The TFN is mathematically easy to implement, and more importantly, it represents the rational basis for quantifying the vague knowledge in most decision-making problems.

The basic operations on triangular fuzzy numbers are as follows (Tsaur et al., 2002):

For example, $P_1 = (a, b, c)$ and $P_2 = (d, e, f)$.

$P_1 + P_2 = (a+d, b+e, c+f)$ addition; (5)

$P_1 - P_2 = (a-f, b-e, c-d)$ subtraction; (6)

$P_1 * P_2 = (a*d, b*e, c*f)$ where $a \geq 0$ and $d \geq 0$ multiplication; (7)

$P_1 / P_2 = (a/f, b/e, c/d)$ where $a \geq 0$ and $d > 0$ division. (8)

Defuzzification

Defuzzification is a technique to convert a fuzzy number into a crisp real number. There are several methods to serve this purpose. For example, the Centre-of-Area method (Tsaur et al., 2002) converts a fuzzy number $P = (a, b, c)$ into a crisp real number Q where

$$Q = \frac{(c-a)+(b-a)}{3} + a \quad (9)$$

Defuzzification might become necessary in two situations: (i) When comparison between two or more fuzzy numbers is difficult to perform, and (ii) When a fuzzy number to be operated on has negative parameters (in other words, we make sure that upon performing an arithmetic operation on one or more TFNs, we get a TFN only; for example, squaring TFN (-1, 0, 1) using Equation 7 will lead to (1, 0, 1) that is not a TFN and so, we defuzzify (-1, 0, 1) before squaring it).

TOPSIS Method

The basic concept of the TOPSIS (technique for order preference by similarity to ideal solution) method (Triantaphyllou & Lin, 1996) is that the rating of the alternative selected as the best from a set of different alternatives, should have the shortest distance from the ideal solution and the farthest distance from the negative-ideal solution in a geometrical (i.e., Euclidean) sense.

Exhibit 1.

	Criteria				
	C1	C2	C3	....	Cn
Alternatives	w1	w2	w3	....	wn
A1	z11	z12	z13	....	z1n
A2	z21	z22	z23	....	z2n
A3	z31	z32	z33	....	z3n
.	.	.	.		.
.	.	.	.		.
.	.	.	.		.
.	.	.	.		.
Am	zm1	zm2	zm3	....	zmn

The TOPSIS method evaluates the following decision matrix, which refers to m alternatives that are evaluated in terms of n criteria as shown in Exhibit 1.

Where A_i is the ith alternative, C_j is the jth criterion, w_j is the weight (importance value) assigned to the jth criterion, and z_{ij} is the rating (e.g., on a scale of 1-10, the higher the rating, the better it is) of the ith alternative in terms of the jth criterion.

The following steps are performed:

Step 1: *Construct the normalized decision matrix.* This step converts the various dimensional measures of performance into nondimensional attributes. An element r_{ij} of the normalized decision matrix R is calculated as follows:

$$r_{ij} = \frac{z_{ij}}{\sqrt{\sum_{i=1}^{m} z_{ij}^2}} \qquad (10)$$

Step 2: *Construct the weighted normalized decision matrix.* A set of weights $W = (w_1, w_2, \ldots w_n)$ (such that $\sum w_j = 1$), specified by the decision-maker, is used in conjunction with the normalized decision matrix R to determine the weighted normalized matrix V defined by $V = (v_{ij}) = (r_{ij}w_j)$.

Step 3: *Determine the ideal and the negative-ideal solutions.* The ideal (A*) and the negative-ideal (A-) solutions are defined as follows:

$$A^* = \left\{\max_i v_{ij} \quad \text{for } i = 1, 2, 3, \ldots\ldots, m\right\} \qquad (11)$$

$$= \{p_1, p_2, p_3, \ldots\ldots, p_n\}$$

$$A- = \left\{\min_i v_{ij} \quad \text{for } i = 1, 2, 3, \ldots\ldots, m\right\} \qquad (12)$$

$$= \{q_1, q_2, q_3, \ldots\ldots, q_n\}$$

With respect to each criterion, the decision-maker desires to choose the alternative with the maximum rating (it is important to note that this choice varies with the way he or she awards ratings to the alternatives). Obviously, A* indicates the most preferable (ideal) solution. Similarly, A- indicates the least preferable (negative-ideal) solution.

Step 4: *Calculate the separation distances.* In this step, the concept of the n-dimensional Euclidean distance is used to measure the separation distances of the rating of each alternative from the ideal solution and the negative-ideal solution. The corresponding formulae are

$$S_{i*} = \sqrt{\sum (v_{ij} - p_j)^2} \quad \text{for } i = 1, 2, 3, \ldots, m \qquad (13)$$

where S_{i*} is the separation (in the Euclidean sense) of the rating of alternative i from the ideal solution, and

$$S_{i-} = \sqrt{\sum (v_{ij} - q_j)^2} \quad \text{for } i = 1, 2, 3, \ldots, m \qquad (14)$$

where S_{i-} is the separation (in the Euclidean sense) of the rating of alternative i from the negative-ideal solution.

Step 5: *Calculate the relative coefficient.* The relative closeness coefficient for alternative A_i with respect to the ideal solution A* is defined as follows:

$$C_{i*} = \frac{S_{i-}}{S_{i*} + S_{i-}} \qquad (15)$$

Step 6: *Rank the preference order.* The best alternative can now be decided according to preference order of C_{i*}. It is the one with the rating that has the shortest distance to the ideal solution. The way the alternatives are processed in the previous steps reveals that if an alternative has the rating with the shortest distance to the ideal solution, then that rating is guaranteed to have the longest distance to the negative-ideal solution. That means, the higher the C_{i*}, the better the alternative.

Borda's Choice Rule

Borda (Hwang, 1987) proposed a rank-order method for group decision-making in which marks of m-1, m-2, ……., 1, 0 are assigned to the first ranked, second ranked, ……, last ranked alternative, for each decision maker (group, in our case). That means that a larger mark corresponds to more importance. Borda score (maximized consensus rating) for each alternative is then determined as the sum of the individual marks for that alternative. Then, the alternative with the highest Borda score is declared the winner. That means that the different decision makers unanimously choose the alternative that obtains the largest Borda score as the most preferred one.

Besides the above techniques, some concepts of constructing and training a neural network are implemented in phase II of our approach. Introduction to those concepts is beyond the scope of this chapter. The reader is referred to any of the hundreds of introductory neural network books available in the literature.

EVALUATION OF EFFICIENCIES OF COLLECTION FACILITIES

In this section, we present our four-phase approach to evaluate the efficiency of a collection facility of interest, through a numerical example. Phases I, II, III, and IV are presented.

Phase-I of the Approach

We consider the following sets of criteria for the three groups, for evaluating the efficiency of a collection facility of interest:

Consumers

- Incentives from collection facility (IC) (higher incentives imply higher motivation to participate)
- Proximity to the residential area (PH) (higher proximity implies more motivation to participate)
- Proximity to roads (PR) (higher proximity implies more motivation to participate)
- Simplicity of the collection process (SP) (simpler process implies more motivation to participate)
- Employment opportunity (EO) (the more the better)
- Salary (SA) (the higher the better)

Local government officials

- Proximity to residential area (PH) (higher proximity implies greater collection and hence lower disposal)
- Proximity to roads (PR) (higher proximity implies greater collection and hence lower disposal)

Supply Chain Company Executives

- Per capital income of the people in the residential area (PI) (the higher it is, the more the number of "resourceful" used products, and the less the people will care about the incentives from the collection facility)
- Space cost (SC) (the lower the better)
- Labor cost (LC) (the lower the better)
- Utilization of incentives from local government (UI) (the higher the better)
- Proximity to residential area (PH) (higher proximity implies greater collection and hence greater profit)
- Proximity to roads (PR) (higher proximity implies greater collection and hence greater profit)
- Incentives from local government (IG) (higher incentives from local government imply higher incentives to consumers)

Phase-II of the Approach

Suppose that we have the linguistic ratings of 10 existing collection facilities, as given by an

Table 1. Conversion table for ratings

Linguistic rating	TFN	Defuzzified rating
Very Good (VG)	(7, 10, 10)	9
Good (G)	(5, 7, 10)	7.3
Fair (F)	(2, 5, 8)	5
Poor (P)	(1, 3, 5)	3
Very Poor (VP)	(0, 0, 3)	1

Table 2. Consumer ratings of existing collection facilities

Collection Facility	IC	PH	PR	SP	EO	SA	Overall
C1	1	3	5	3	5	9	5
C2	9	1	3	5	7.3	9	7.3
C3	3	1	3	1	9	1	3
C4	3	9	1	7.3	1	7.3	5
C5	5	1	3	5	1	3	7.3
C6	9	3	7.3	3	5	7.3	3
C7	5	7.3	9	1	7.3	9	1
C8	1	5	1	5	3	1	9
C9	1	5	5	9	9	5	5
C10	5	9	5	3	9	3	1

Table 3. Local government officials ratings of existing collection facilities

Collection Facility	PH	PR	Overall
C1	1	3	5
C2	9	1	7.3
C3	3	1	3
C4	3	9	5
C5	5	1	7.3
C6	9	3	3
C7	5	7.3	1
C8	1	5	9
C9	1	5	5
C10	5	9	1

Table 4. Supply chain company executives' ratings of existing collection facilities

Collection Facility	PI	SC	LC	UI	PH	PR	IG	Overall
C1	1	3	1	3	5	1	3	5
C2	9	1	3	7.3	3	5	7.3	7.3
C3	3	1	7.3	9	1	7.3	9	3
C4	3	9	5	1	5	3	1	5
C5	5	1	5	5	9	9	5	7.3
C6	9	3	9	5	3	9	3	3
C7	5	7.3	3	1	7.3	9	1	1
C8	1	5	1	3	1	3	5	9
C9	1	5	3	5	9	9	1	5
C10	5	9	1	3	5	7.3	7.3	1

expert in *each* group described in phase I. Using the fuzzy set theory, these linguistic ratings are converted into TFNs (fuzzy ratings). Table 1 shows not only one of the many ways for conversion of linguistic ratings into TFNs but also the defuzzified ratings of the corresponding TFNs. Tables 2, 3, and 4 show the defuzzified overall rating of each existing collection facility, as well as its (collection facility's) defuzzified rating with respect to each criterion, as evaluated by the consumers, the local government officials, and the supply chain company executives, respectively.

A neural network is constructed and trained *for each group,* using the defuzzified ratings of the existing collection facilities with respect to criteria as input sets, and their (collection facilities) defuzzified overall ratings as corresponding outputs. In our example, there are 10 input-output pairs for each neural network because there are 10 existing collection facilities. Also, we consider three layers in each network, with 5 nodes in the hidden layer. The number of nodes in the output layer is one (for overall rating), and that in the input layer is the number of criteria considered by the corresponding group. For example, Figure 5 shows the neural network constructed and trained for the group of consumers.

After each neural network is trained, Equation 16 (Cha & Jung, 2003) is used to calculate the impacts of criteria considered by the corresponding group. Here, absolute value of W_{vk} is the impact of the vth input node upon kth output node, n_V is the number of input nodes, n_O is the number of output nodes (one, in our case), n_H is the number of hidden nodes, I_{ij} is the connection weight from the ith input node to the jth hidden node, and O_{jk} is the connection weight from the jth hidden node to the kth output node.

$$|W_{vk}| = \frac{\sum_{j}^{nH}\left(\frac{I_{vj}}{\sum_{i}^{nV}|I_{ij}|}O_{jk}\right)}{\sum_{v}^{nV}\left(\sum_{j}^{nH}\left(\frac{I_{vj}}{\sum_{i}^{nV}|I_{ij}|}O_{jk}\right)\right)} \quad (16)$$

Tables 5, 6, and 7 show the impacts of the criteria considered by the consumers, the local government officials, and the supply chain company executives, respectively.

Figure 5. Neural network for consumers (Phase II)

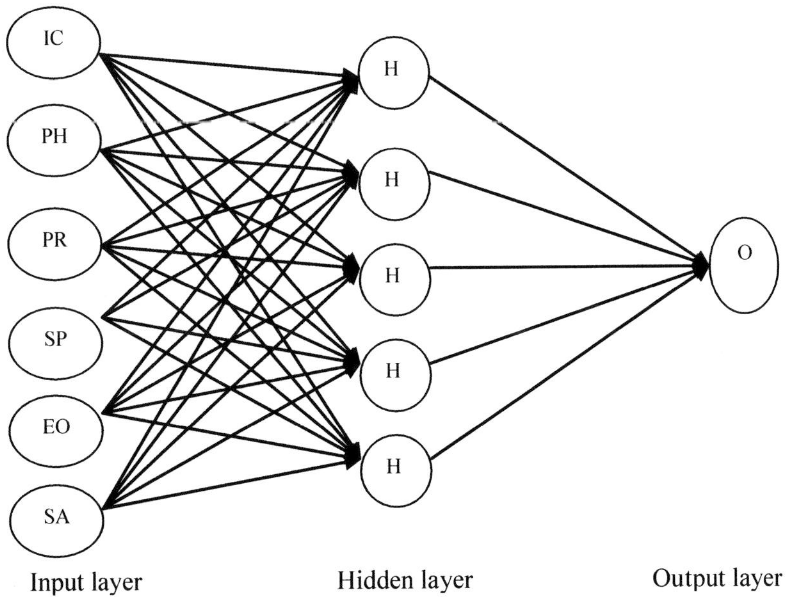

Table 5. Impacts of criteria of consumers

Criterion	IC	PH	PR	SP	EO	SA
Impact	0.01	0.13	0.06	0.18	0.19	0.43

Table 6. Impacts of criteria of local government officials

Criterion	PH	PR
Impact	0.33	0.67

Table 7. Impacts of criteria of supply chain company executives

Criterion	PI	SC	LC	UI	PH	PR	IG
Impact	0.24	0.09	0	0.18	0.25	0.1	0.13

Phase-III of the Approach

Suppose that there are three collection facilities, C11, C12, and C13, of interest. We employ a fuzzy TOPSIS (Chu, 2002) approach that uses the weights obtained in phase-II, to calculate the overall ratings of the three collection facilities.

The decision matrices formed by the consumers, the local government officials, and the supply chain company executives (with defuzzified ratings for C11, C12, and C13) in this example are shown in Tables 8, 9, and 10, respectively (we use Table 1 here too, to convert linguistic ratings given by each group into TFNs).

Now, we are ready to perform the six steps in the TOPSIS for each group. The following steps show the implementation of the TOPSIS *for the consumers*, to evaluate C11, C12, and C13.

Step 1: *Construct the normalized decision matrix.* Table 11 shows the normalized decision matrix formed by applying Equation 10 on each element of Table 8 (decision matrix formed by the consumers). For example, the normalized rating of collection facility, C12, with respect to criterion, PH (see Tables 8 and 10), is calculated using Equation 10 as follows:

$$r_{22} = \frac{1}{\sqrt{9^2 + 1^2 + 3^2}} = 0.105.$$

Step 2: *Construct the weighted normalized decision matrix.* Table 12 shows the weighted normalized decision matrix for the consumers. This is constructed using the impacts of the criteria listed in Table 5 and the normalized decision matrix in Table 11. For example, the weighted normalized rank of collection facility, C12, with

Table 8. Decision matrix formed by consumers

Collection Facility	IC	PH	PR	SP	EO	SA
C11	3	9	1	7.33	1	7.33
C12	5	1	3	5	1	3
C13	9	3	7.33	3	5	7.33

Table 9. Decision matrix formed for local government officials

Collection Facility	PH	PR
C11	3	9
C12	5	1
C13	9	3

Table 10. Decision matrix formed by supply chain company executives

Collection Facility	PI	SC	LC	UI	PH	PR	IG
C11	5	1	5	5	9	9	5
C12	9	3	9	5	3	9	3
C13	5	7.33	3	1	7.33	9	1

Table 11. Normalized decision matrix formed by consumers for collection facilities

Collection Facility	IC	PH	PR	SP	EO	SA
C11	0.278	0.943	0.125	0.783	0.192	0.679
C12	0.466	0.105	0.376	0.534	0.192	0.278
C13	0.839	0.314	0.918	0.320	0.962	0.679

Table 12. Weighted normalized decision matrix formed by consumers for collection facilities

Collection Facility	IC	PH	PR	SP	EO	SA
C11	0.004	0.122	0.007	0.140	0.036	0.294
C12	0.006	0.014	0.022	0.095	0.036	0.120
C13	0.011	0.041	0.053	0.057	0.181	0.294

Table 13. Separation distances calculated by consumers for collection facilities

Collection Facility	S*	S-
C11	0.152	0.221
C12	0.257	0.041
C13	0.116	0.233

respect to criterion, PH, that is, 0.014 (see Table 12), is calculated by multiplying the impact of PH, that is, 0.129 (see Table 5) with the normalized rating of C12 with respect to PH, that is, 0.105 (see Table 11).

Step 3: *Determine the ideal and the negative-deal solution.* Each column in the weighted normalized decision matrix shown in Table 12 has a maximum rating (found using Equation 11) and a minimum rating (found using Equation 12). They are the ideal and the negative-ideal solutions, respectively, for the corresponding criterion. For example (see Table 12), with respect to criterion, PH, the ideal solution (maximum rating) is 0.122, and the negative-ideal solution (minimum rating) is 0.014.

Step 4: *Calculate the separation distances.* The separation distances (see Table 13) for each collection facility, are calculated using Equations 13 and 14. For example, the positive separation distance for collection facility, C12 (see Table 13), is calculated using Equation 13 that contains the weighted normalized ratings of C12 (see Table 12) and the ideal solutions (obtained in step 3) for the criteria.

Step 5: *Calculate the relative closeness coefficient.* Using Equation 15, we calculate the relative closeness coefficient for each collection facility (see Table 14). For example, relative closeness coefficient (i.e., 0.137) for collection facility C12 (see Table 14) is the ratio of C12's negative separation distance (i.e., 0.041) to the sum (i.e., $0.041 + 0.257 = 0.298$) of its negative and positive separation distances (see Table 13).

Step 6: *Rank the preference order.* Since the best alternative is the one with the highest relative closeness coefficient, the preference order for the collection facilities is C13, C11, and C12 (that means, C13 is the best collection facility, *as evaluated by the consumers*).

Table 14. Relative closeness coefficients calculated byconsumers for collection facilities

Collection Facility	C*
C11	0.592
C12	0.137
C13	0.668

Table 15. Relative closeness coefficients calculated by local government and supply chain company for collection facilities

Collection Facility	Local govt.	Supply chain company
C11	0.754	0.619
C12	0.096	0.502
C13	0.354	0.415

Table 16. Marks and Borda scores of collection facilities

Collection Facility	Consumers	Local government	Supply chain company	Borda score
C11	1	2	2	5
C12	0	0	1	1
C13	2	1	0	3

The TOPSIS is implemented for the local government officials and the supply chain company executives as well. The relative closeness coefficients of the collection facilities, as calculated by those two groups, are shown in Table 15.

Phase-IV of the Approach

Table 16 shows the marks of the collection facilities as given using Borda's choice rule (Hwang, 1987) for the consumers, the local government officials, and the supply chain company executives. Borda scores (maximized consensus rating) calculated for C11, C12, and C13 (viz., 5, 1, and 3, respectively) are also shown. For example, Borda score for C12 (i.e., 1) is calculated by summing the marks of C12 for the consumers, the local government officials, and the supply chain company executives (i.e., 0 + 0 + 1). Since C11 has the highest Borda score, it is the best of the lot.

EVALUATION OF EFFICIENCIES OF RECOVERY FACILITIES

In this section, we present only the first phase of our approach to evaluate the efficiency of a recovery facility of interest because the remaining three phases are similar to the ones for a collection facility.

We consider the following sets of criteria for the three groups, for evaluating the efficiency of a recovery facility of interest:

Consumers

- Proximity to surface water (PS) (lower proximity implies more suitability, that is, less hazardous)
- Proximity to residential area (PH) (lower proximity implies more suitability, that is, less hazardous)

- Employment opportunity (EO) (the more the better)
- Salary (the higher the better)

Local government officials

- Proximity to surface water (PS) (lower proximity implies more suitability, that is, less hazardous)
- Proximity to residential area (PH) (lower proximity implies more suitability, that is, less hazardous)

Supply Chain Company Executives

- Space cost (SC) (the lower the better)
- Labor cost (LC) (the lower the better)
- Proximity to roads (PR) (higher proximity implies easier transportation)
- Quality of reprocessed products (QO) – Quality of used-products (QI) (the higher the better)
- Throughput (TP) /Supply (SU) (the higher the better)
- Throughput (TP) * Disassembly time (DT) (the higher the better)
- Utilization of incentives from local government (UI) (the higher the better)
- Pollution control (PC) (the higher the better)

Unlike in a forward supply chain, components of incoming goods (used-products) of even the same type in a recovery facility are likely to be of varied quality (worn-out, low-performing, etc.). Though the average quality of reprocessed goods (QO) is a criterion that can evaluate a recovery facility, it is not justified to use QO as an independent criterion for evaluation because QO depends on average quality of incoming products (QI). However, QI must not be taken as an independent criterion too because it cannot evaluate the recovery facility. So, the idea is to take the difference between QO and QI as a criterion for evaluation.

The only driver to design a forward supply chain is the demand for new products and so if there is low demand for new products, there is practically no forward supply chain. However, this is not the case in some reverse supply chains where even if there is a low supply of used-products (SU), reverse supply chain must be administered due to the possible drivers like environmental regulations and asset recovery. In supply-driven cases like these, it is unfair to judge a recovery facility without considering SU for evaluation. Although throughput (TP) is a criterion that can evaluate a recovery facility, it is not justified to use TP as an independent criterion because TP depends on SU. However, SU must not be taken as an independent criterion too because it cannot evaluate the recovery facility. Furthermore, a low SU might lead to a low TP and a high SU might lead to a high TP. So, the idea is to take (TP)/(SU) as a criterion for evaluation. Thus, we compensate for the effect of a low TP by dividing TP with a possibly low SU, in order not to underestimate the facility under consideration. Similarly, we dampen the effect of a high TP by dividing TP with a possibly high SU, in order not to overestimate the facility under consideration.

Average disassembly time (DT) is not exactly the inverse of TP because TP takes into account the whole reprocessing (disassembly plus recovery) time. Unlike in a forward supply chain, components of incoming goods (used-products) in a recovery facility are likely to be deformed or broken or different in number even for the same type of products. Hence, incoming products of the same type might have different reprocessing times, unlike in a forward supply chain where manufacturing time and assembly time are predetermined and equal for products of the same type. Since TP of a recovery facility depends upon the DT, it is unfair to not consider DT for evaluation. However, DT must not be taken as an independent criterion because it cannot evaluate the recovery facility. Furthermore, a high DT might lead to a low TP and a low DT might lead to a high TP.

So, the idea is to take (TP)*(DT) as a criterion for evaluation. Thus, we compensate for the effect of a low TP by multiplying TP with a possibly high DT, in order not to underestimate the facility under consideration. Similarly, we dampen the effect of a high TP by multiplying TP with a possibly low DT, in order not to overestimate the facility under consideration.

CONCLUSION

In this chapter, a neural network approach to evaluate the efficiency of a facility (collection or recovery) of interest, which is being considered for inclusion in a reverse supply chain, using the available linguistic data of facilities (collection or recovery) that already exist in the supply chain, was proposed. The approach was carried out in four phases as follows: In phase I, criteria for evaluation of the facility of interest, by each group participating in the reverse supply chain, were identified. Then, in phase II, fuzzy ratings of existing facilities were used to construct a neural network that gives impacts of criteria identified for each group in phase I. Then, in phase III, using the impacts obtained in phase II, a fuzzy TOPSIS (Technique for Order Preference by Similarity to Ideal Solution) approach was employed to obtain the overall rating of the facility of interest, as calculated by each group. Finally, in phase IV, Borda's choice rule was employed to calculate the maximized consensus (among the groups considered) rating of the facility of interest.

FUTURE RESEARCH

For their future research, the authors plan to propose quantitative models for the following additional issues faced by decision-makers in the area of reverse supply chain design:

- Selection of economical used products to reprocess in a reverse supply chain
- Optimization of transportation of goods (used and reprocessed) across a reverse supply chain
- Evaluation of marketing strategies for success of a reverse supply chain
- Selection of potential second-hand markets to sell reprocessed goods

ACKNOWLEDGMENT

The authors are indebted to Dr. Sagar V. Kamarthi for letting them use his neural network software.

REFERENCES

Cha, Y., & Jung, M. (2003). Satisfaction assessment of multi-objective schedules using neural fuzzy methodology. *International Journal of Production Research, 41*(8), 1831-1849.

Chu, T. C. (2002). Selecting plant location via a fuzzy TOPSIS approach. *The International Journal of Advanced Manufacturing Technology, 20,* 859-864.

Fleischmann, M. (2001). *Quantititative models for reverse logistics: Lecture notes in economics and mathematical systems.* Germany: Springer-Verlag.

Gungor, A., & Gupta, S. M. (1999). Issues in environmentally conscious manufacturing and product recovery: A survey. *Computers and Industrial Engineering, 36*(4), 811-853.

Hwang, C. L. (1987). *Group decision making under multi-criteria: Methods and applications.* New York: Springer-Verlag.

Pochampally, K. K., & Gupta, S. M. (2003). A multi-phase mathematical programming approach to strategic planning of an efficient reverse supply chain network. In *Proceedings of the IEEE International Symposium on the Electronics and the Environment* (pp. 72-78).

Pochampally, K. K., Gupta, S. M., & Cullinane, T. P. (2003). A fuzzy cost-benefit function to select economical used products for re-processing. In *Proceedings of the SPIE International Conference on Environmentally Conscious Manufacturing* (CD-ROM).

Pochampally, K. K., Gupta, S. M., & Kamarthi, S. V. (2003). Evaluation of production facilities in a closed-loop supply chain: A fuzzy TOPSIS approach. In *Proceedings of the SPIE International Conference on Environmentally Conscious Manufacturing* (CD-ROM).

Saaty, T. L. (1980). *The analytic hierarchy process.* New York: McGraw-Hill.

Talluri, S., & Baker, R. C. (2002). A multi-phase mathematical programming approach for effective supply chain design. *European Journal of Operations Research, 141,* 544-558.

Talluri, S., Baker, R. C., & Sarkis, J. (1999). A framework for designing efficient value chain networks. *International Journal of Production Economics, 62,* 133-144.

Triantaphyllou, E., & Lin, C. (1996). Development and evaluation of five fuzzy multi-attribute decision-making methods. *International Journal of Approximate Reasoning, 14,* 281-310.

Tsaur, S., Chang, T., & Yen, C. (2002). The evaluation of airline service quality by fuzzy MCDM. *Tourism Management, 23,* 107-115.

Zadeh, L. A. (1965). Fuzzy sets. *Information and Control, 8,* 338-353.

ADDITIONAL READING

Readers interested in the area of reverse supply chain design are referred to the following additional articles.

Alshamrani, A., Mathur, K., & Ballou, R. H. (2007). Reverse logistics: Simultaneous design of delivery routes and return strategies. *Computers and Operations research, 34,* 595-619.

Amini, M. M., Retzlaff-Roberts, D., & Bienstock, C. C. (2005). Designing a reverse logistics operation for short cycle time repair services. *International Journal of Production Economics, 96*(3), 367-380.

Ammons, J. C., Realff, M. J., & Newton, D. J. (1999). Carpet recycling: Determining the reverse production system design. *Polymer-Plastics Technology and Engineering, 38*(3), 547-567.

Barros, A. I., Dekker, R., & Scholten, V. (1998). A two-level network for recycling sand: A case study. *European Journal of Operational Research, 110,* 199-214.

Bautista, J., & Pereira, J. (2006). Modeling the problem of locating collection areas for urban waste management. An application to the metropolitan area of Barcelona. *Omega, 34*(6), 617-629.

Beamon, M. B., & Fernandes, C. (2004). Supply-chain network configuration for product recovery. *Production Planning and Control, 15*(3), 270-281.

Biehl, M., Prater, E., & Realff, M. J. (2007). Assessing performance and uncertainty in developing carpet reverse logistics systems. *Computers and Industrial Engineering, 34,* 443-463.

Dowlatshahi, S. (2005). A strategic framework for the design and implementation of remanufacturing operations in reverse logistics. *International Journal of Production Research, 43*(16), 3455-3480.

Gautam, A. K., & Kumar, S. (2005). Strategic planning of recycling options by multi-objective programming in a GIS environment. *Clean Technologies and Environmental Policy, 7*(4), 306-316.

Hu, T., Sheu, J., & Huan, K. (2002). A reverse logistics cost minimization model for the treatment of hazardous wastes. *Transportation research Part E, 38*, 457-473.

Krikke, H., Bloemhof-Ruwaard, J., & Van Wassenhove, L.N. (2003). Concurrent product and closed-loop supply chain design with an application to refrigerators. *International Journal of Production Research, 41*(16), 3689-3719.

Krikke, H., Leblanc, I., & van de Velde, S. (2004). Product modularity and the design of closed-loop supply chains. *California Management Review, 46*(2), 23-39.

Krikke, H. R., Van harten, A., & Schuur, P. C. (1999). Business case: Reverse logistic network re-design for copiers. *OR Spectrum, 21*(3), 381-409.

Kroon, L., & Vrijens, G. (1995). Returnable containers: An example of reverse logistics. *International Journal of Physical Distribution and Logistics Management, 25*(2), 56-68.

Lieckens, K., & Vandaele, N. (2007). Reverse logistics network design with stochastic lead times. *Computers and Operations Research, 34*, 395-416.

Lim, G. H., Kasumastuti, R. D., & Piplani, R. (2005). Designing a reverse supply chain network for product refurbishment. In *Proceedings of the International Conference of Simulation and Modeling.*

Listes, O. (2007). A generic stochastic model for supply-and-return network design. *Computers and Operations Research, 34*(2), 417-442.

Listes, O., & Dekker, R. (2005). A stochastic approach to a case study for a product recovery network design. *European Journal of Operational Research, 160*, 268-287.

Louwers, D., Kip, B. J., Peters, E., Souren, F., & Flapper, S. D. P. (1999). A facility location allocation model for reusing carpet materials. *Computers and Industrial Engineering, 36*(4), 855-869.

Lu, Z., & Bostel, N. (2007). A facility location model for logistics system including reverse flows: The case of remanufacturing activities. *Computers and Operations Research, 34*, 299-323.

Ravi, V., Ravi, S., & Tiwari, M. K. (2005). Analyzing alternatives in reverse logistics for end-of-life computers: ANP and balanced scorecard approach. *Computers and Industrial Engineering, 48*(2), 327-356.

Salema, M. I. G., Barbosa-Povoa, A. P., & Novais, A. Q. (2007). An optimization model for the design of a capacitated multi-product reverse logistics network with uncertainty. *European Journal of Operational Research, 179*, 1063-1077.

Savaskan, R. C., Bhattacharya, S., & Van Wassenhove, L. N. (2004). Closed-loop supply chain models with product remanufacturing. *Management Science, 50*(2), 239-252.

Savaskan, R., & Van Wassenhove, L. N. (2006). Reverse channel design: The case of competing retailers. *Management Science, 52*(1), 1-14.

Veerakamolmal, P., & Gupta, S. M. (1999). Analysis of design efficiency for the disassembly of modular electronic products. *Journal of Electronics Manufacturing, 9*(1), 79-95.

Wojanowski, R., Verter, V., & Boyaci, T. (2007). Retail-collection network design under deposit-refund. *Computers and Operations Research, 34*(2), 324-345.

Chapter XIV
System Dynamics Modeling for Strategic Management of Green Supply Chain

Ying Su
Institute of Scientific and Technical Information of China, Beijing, P.R. China

Zhanming Jin
Tsinghua University, Beijing, P.R. China

Lei Yang
South China University of Technology, Panyu, Guangzhou, P.R. China

ABSTRACT

Environmental issues are rapidly emerging as one of the most important topics in strategic manufacturing decisions. Perusal of the literature has shown many models to support executives in the assessment of a company's environmental performance. Unfortunately, none of these identifies operating guidelines on how the systems should be adapted to support the deployment of different types of green supply-chain strategies. This chapter seeks to investigate how system dynamics modeling can be supportive for management of feasible green supply-chain strategies. Besides conceptual considerations, we base our arguments on the development of efficient performance measurement systems for remanufacturing facilities in reverse supply chains, taking into account not only economic but also environmental issues. The behavior of the green supply-chain management under study is analyzed through a simulation model based on the principles of the system dynamics methodology. The simulation model can be helpful for green strategic management as an experimental tool, which can be used to evaluate alternative long-term strategies ("what-if" analysis) using total supply chain profit as measure of strategy effectiveness. Validation and numerical experimentation further illustrate the applicability of the developed methodology, while providing additional intuitively sound insights.

Copyright © 2009, IGI Global, distributing in print or electronic forms without written permission of IGI Global is prohibited.

INTRODUCTION

Environmental issues are rapidly emerging as one of the most important topics for strategic manufacturing decisions. The scarcity of natural resources and the growing concern in the market for "green" issues have forced executives to manage operations within an environmental perspective (Dimitrios Vlachos, Georgiadis, & Iakovou, 2007). Growing public awareness and increasing government interest in the environment have induced many Chinese manufacturing enterprises to adopt programs aimed at improving the environmental performance of their operations (Vincent, 2006; Zhu & Sarkis, 2004).

In the light of the strategic importance of environmental issues and of their effects on the corporate management system, a growing body of literature is focused on how companies should manage environmental issues. Two major lines of research are evident:

- Studies which analyze feasible green supply-chain strategies available to operations managers and describe how growing environmental concern impacts on the process of strategy formation; and
- General approaches aimed at supporting managers in the assessment of a company's environmental performance, such as life-cycle assessment methods, or models reporting physical indicators, environmental costs, contingent liabilities, and so forth.

Despite the availability of the various approaches to develop performance measurement systems (PMSs) in respect of distinct green supply-chain strategies, none of them attempted to quantify the effects of various environmentally friendly activities pursued by the manufacturing function. Such a shortcoming is, in our opinion, critical, since environmental behavior results from specific environment-related objectives and has its own managerial and financial implications on the corporate system.

In response to the issues identified in the above paragraphs this chapter presents a quantitative framework to:

- Define the basic green supply-chain strategies a company can implement and identify factors affecting environmental performance and their relationships for operations management
- Structure environmental performance measures hierarchically
  Quantify the effectiveness of a planned environmental strategy on environmental performance
- "What if" analysis on environmental performance and green supply-chain strategy selection

By bringing together existing contributions on strategic environmental management and performance measurement systems, the chapter aims to develop quantitative models for environmental performance measurement systems (QMEPMS) using supermatrix, cause and effect diagrams, tree diagrams, and the analytical network process. It describes how different green supply-chain strategies can be deployed and presents the technique that can be used to identify factors affecting environmental performance and their relationships, structure them hierarchically, quantify the effect of the factors on environmental performance, and express them quantitatively.

The chapter is divided into six major sections. First, we give a taxonomy of green supply-chain management (GSCM) and highlight the problem existing in a company's strategic management, describe research objectives and methodology to quantify the effect of the factors on an EPMS, and specify a quantitative model on how to structure critical factors hierarchically to support managers in the implementation for an EPMS. Then, we analyse how the suggested QMEPMS can be implemented in practice. Finally, we draw some conclusions from the suggested approach and indicate future directions for further environment-related research.

LITERATURE REVIEW

Sufficient literature exists about various aspects and facets of GSCM. Comprehensive reviews on green design (Zhang, Kuo, Lu, & Huang, 1997), repairable inventory (Guide, Jayaraman, & Srivastava, 1997, 1999), production planning and control for remanufacturing (Bras & McIntosh, 1999; Guide, 1997; Guide, Jr., 2000; Guide, Spencer, & Srivastava, 1997), issues in green manufacturing and product recovery (Guide, Spencer, & Srivastava, 1996; Gungor & Gupta, 1999), reverse logistics (RL) (Carter & Ellram, 1998; Fleischmann et al., 1997), logistics network design (Fleischmann, Beullens, Bloemhof-Ruwaard, & van Wassenhove, 2001; Fleischmann, Krikke, Dekker, & Flapper, 2000; Jayaraman, Patterson, & Rolland, 2003), and green product databases (Nimse, Vijayan, Kumar, & Varadarajan, 2007)have been published.

Earlier works and reviews have a limited focus and narrow perspective. They do not cover adequately all the aspects and facets of GSCM. Much of the work is empirical and does not focus adequately on strategic management, mathematical modeling, and network design-related issues and practices. The objective of this section is to present a comprehensive integrated view of the published literature on all the aspects and facets of GSCM, taking a "reverse logistics angle" so as to facilitate further study, practice, and research. To meet this objective, we define GSCM as "integrating environmental thinking into supply-chain management, including product design, material sourcing and selection, manufacturing processes, delivery of the final product to the consumers as well as end-of-life management of the product after its useful life." We specifically focus on strategic management, reverse logistics (RL) and mathematical modeling aspects in order to facilitate further study and research. Qualitative analysis was applied to classify the existing literature on the basis of problem context and the methodology/approach adopted. We also map the tools/techniques vis-à-vis the problem context classification.

Classification Based on Problem Context

We classify the existing GSCM literature into three broad categories based on the problem context in supply chain design: literature highlighting the strategic management; literature on green design; and literature on green operations, as shown in Figure 1, which was adapted from Srivastava (2007). Green design may be looked into from the viewpoint of environment conscious design taking lifecycle assessment of the product/process into account. Similarly, green operations involve all operational aspects related to RL and network design (collection; inspection/sorting; preprocessing; network design), green manufacturing and remanufacturing (reduce; recycle; production planning and scheduling; inventory management; remanufacturing: re-use, product and material recovery), and waste management(source reduction; pollution prevention; disposal).We purposely do not consider literature and practices related to green logistics, as we feel that the issues are more operational than strategic in nature and may not be significant in the supply chain design per se. We also do not focus in detail on empirical studies on GSCM and literature on green purchasing, industrial ecology and industrial ecosystems, as it is delimited by our research design. We focus more on RL as the establishment of efficient and effective RL networks as a prerequisite for efficient and profitable recycling and remanufacturing.

We also focus more on mathematical modeling aspects. Both of these have received less attention in the GSCM literature so far.

The classification is for the purpose of easier understanding of different problem contexts of GSCM—their interactions and relationships—in order to present a well defined and clear picture for further study and research. It is not rigid, and there may be many overlaps (e.g., reduce gets attention not only in green manufacturing and remanufacturing, but also elsewhere as in reverse logistics and waste management; green design, too, emphasizes reduced use of virgin material and other resources). Similarly, green design should take into account the whole product life-cycle cost, including those during manufacturing and remanufacturing, reverse logistics, and disposal. Figure 1 does not take account of all these complex relationships and interactions but presents a simplistic view. Further, we do not show some other relevant aspects and areas such as green purchasing, industrial ecology, and industrial ecosystems, as they are delimited by our research design.

Strategic Management

As in any emerging research area, the early literature focuses on the necessity and strategic management, defines the meaning and scope of various terms and suggests approaches to explore the area further. Fundamentals of greening as a competitive initiative are explained by Porter and van der Linde. Their basic reasoning is that investments in greening can be resource saving, waste eliminating, and productivity improving (Porter & van der Linde, 1995a, 1995b). Three approaches in GSCM, namely reactive, proactive, and value-seeking, are suggested (Hoek, 1999). In the reactive approach, companies commit minimal resources to environmental management, start labeling products that are recyclable and use "end of pipeline" initiatives to lower the environmental impact of production. In the proactive approach,

Figure 1. Classification based on problem context in supply chain design

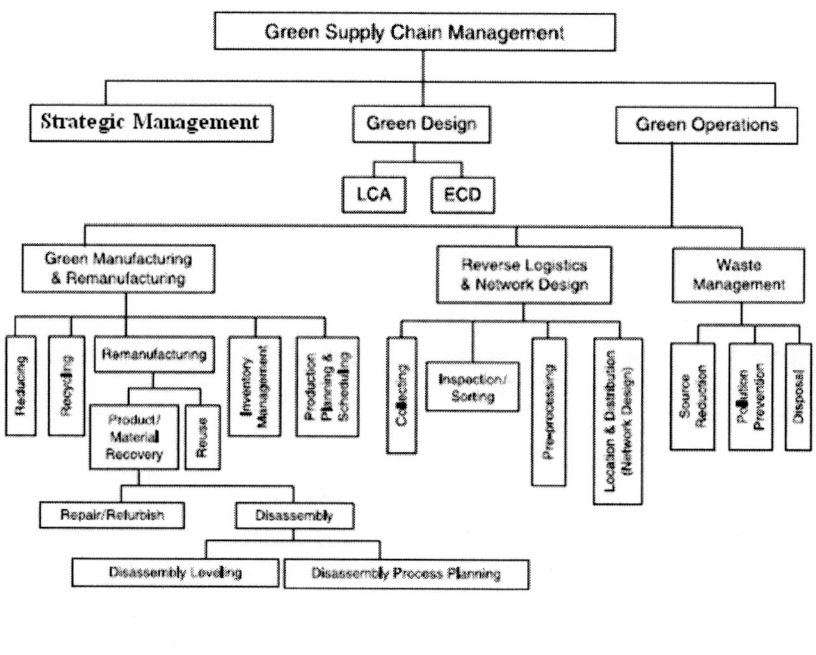

they start to preempt new environmental laws by realizing a modest resource commitment to initiate the recycling of products and designing green products. In the value-seeking approach, companies integrate environmental activities such as green purchasing and ISO implementation as strategic initiatives into their business strategy.

The perspective then changes from greening as a burden to greening as a potential source of competitive advantage (Hoek, 1999). Owen (1993) discusses environmentally conscious manufacturing. Friedman (1992), Guide, Jr., and Van Wassenhove (2002), and Gupta and Sharma (1996) discuss the changing role of the environmental manager. Interactions among various stakeholders on integrated GSCM and advantages that may accrue to them have been described by Gungor and Gupta (1999). At the end of the 1990s, integrating these issues into the mainstream was identified as the future research agenda (Angell & Klassen, 1999). In a study linking GSCM elements and performance measurement, Beamon (1999) advocates for the establishment and implementation of new performance measurement systems. He suggests that the traditional performance measurement structure of the supply chain must be extended to include mechanisms for product recovery (RL) (Beamon, 1999).

During the present decade, related and emergent issues such as consideration of stages of the product life cycle during material selection (Kaiser, Eagan, & Shaner, 2001), impact of green purchasing on a firm's supplier selection (Zhu, Geng, & Spring, 2002), waste management (Theyel, 2001), packaging and regulatory compliance (Min & Galle, 2001), greener manufacturing and operations (Sarkis, 2001), study of the environmental management system (EMS) implementation practices (Hui, Chan, & Pun, 2001), selection of environmental performance indicators (Scherpereel, van Koppen, & Heering, 2001), relationship between environmental and economic performance of firms (Wagner, Schaltegger, & Wehrmeyer, 2001), focus on third-party logistics providers (Krumwiede & Sheu, 2002; Meade & Sarkis, 2002), overview of management challenges and environmental consequences in reverse manufacturing (White, Masanet, Rosen, & Beckman, 2003) and extended producer responsibility (Spicer & Johnson, 2004), including OEM, pooled and third-party take-back, have been taken up by researchers.

Zhu and Sarkis (2004) describe empirical findings on relationships between operational practices and performance among early adopters of green supply-chain management(Zhu & Sarkis, 2004), while Bowen, Cousins, Lamming, and Faruk (2001) seek to resolve the apparent paradox between the desirability and the actual slow implementation of GSCM in practice (Bowen, Cousins, Lamming, & Faruk, 2001). Chouinard et al. (2005) deal with problems related to the integration of RL activities within a supply chain information system (Chouinard, D'Amours, & Aït-Kadi, 2005). Nagurney and Toyasaki (2005) develop a multi-tiered network equilibrium framework for e-cycling (Nagurney & Toyasaki, 2005), while Sheu et al. (2005) present an optimization based integrated logistics operational model for GSCM (Sheu, Chou, & Hu, 2005). Ravi et al. (2005) analyze alternatives in RL (Ravi, Shankar, & Tiwari, 2005), Mukhopadhyay and Setoputro (2005) derive a number of managerial guidelines for return policies of build-to-order products, while Srivastava and Srivastava (2006) suggest ways to manage end-of-life product returns. Kainuma and Tawara (2006) extend the range of supply chain to include re-use and recycling throughout the life cycle of product and services and propose a "lean and green" multiple utility theory approach to evaluate green supply chain performance from an environmental performance point of view (Kainuma & Tawara, 2006).

Green Design

The literature emphasizes both environmentally conscious design (ECD) and life-cycle assessment/analysis (LCA) of the product. The aim is to develop an understanding of how design decisions affect a product's environmental compatibility (Glantschnig, 1994; Navinchandra, 1991). Madu et al. (2002) present a very useful hierarchic framework for environmentally conscious design (Madu, Kuei, & Madu, 2002).

Sufficient literature exists on design for material and product recovery (Barros, Dekker, & Scholten, 1998; Ferrer, 1997a, 1997b; Ferrer & Whybark, 2001; Gatenby & Foo, 1990; Guide, Jr., & Van Wassenhove, 2001; Krikke, van Harten, & Schuur, 1999a, 1999b; Louwers, Kip, Peters, Souren, & Flapper, 1999; Melissen & de Ron, 1999; Seliger, Zussman, & Kriwet, 1994). Boothroyd and Alting (1992), Krikke, Bloemhof-Ruwaard, and Van Wassenhove (2003), Kroll, Beardsley, and Parulian (1996), Laperiere and ElMaraghy (1992), Lee, O'Callaghan, and Allen (1995), Moore, Gungor, and Gupta (2001), Scheuring, Bras, and Lee (1994), Seliger et al. (1994), and Taleb and Gupta (1997) discuss design for disassembly, whereas Gupta and Sharma (1996), He, Gao, Yang, and Edwards (2004), Jahre (1995), Jayaraman, Guide, and Srivastava (1999), Johnson (1998), and Sarkis and Cordeiro (2001) deal with design for waste minimization.

A common approach is to replace a potentially hazardous material or process by one that appears less problematic. This seemingly reasonable action can sometimes be undesirable if it results in the rapid depletion of a potentially scarce resource or increased extraction of other environmentally problematic materials. Several examples of such equivocal proposals are presented by Graedel (2002).

Green Operations

Some of the key challenges of GSCM such as integrating remanufacturing with internal operations (Ferrer & Whybark, 2001), understanding the effects of competition among remanufacturers (Majumder, Groenevelt, & Summer, 2001), integrating product design, product take-back, and supply chain incentives (Guide, Jr., & Van Wassenhove, 2001; Guide & van Wassenhove, 2002), and integrating remanufacturing and RL with supply chain design (Chouinard et al., 2005; Fleischmann et al., 2001; Goggin & Browne, 2000; Savaskan, Bhattacharya, & Van Wassenhove, 2004) are posed in this area.

In recent years, a lot of work related to quantitative approaches in RL has been published. Shih (2001) discusses in detail the RL system planning for recycling electrical appliances and computers in Taiwan. Hu, Sheu, and Huang (2002) present a cost-minimization model for a multi-time-step, multi-type hazardous-waste RL system. They present application cases to demonstrate the feasibility of their proposed approach. Nagurney and Toyasaki (2005) develop an integrated framework for modeling the electronic waste RL network which includes recycling, while the framework of Srivastava and Srivastava (2005) incorporates three types of rework facilities. Ravi et al. (2005) use analytical network process (ANP) and balanced score card for analysing RL alternatives for end-of-life computers. Listes and Dekker (2005) present a stochastic programming-based approach by which a deterministic location model for product recovery network design may be extended to account explicitly for uncertainties. They apply it to a representative real case study on recycling sand from demolition waste in The Netherlands. Their interpretation of the results gives useful insights into decision-making under uncertainty in a RL context. Pochampally and Gupta (2005) propose a three-phase mathematical programming approach, taking the above uncertainties into account, for strategic planning of a reverse supply chain network. Mostard and Teunter (2006) carry out a case study to derive a simple closed-form equation. They determine the optimal order quantity given the demand distribution, the probability that a sold product is returned, and all relevant revenues and costs for a single period model. Min, Ko, and Ko (2006) determine the number and location of centralized return centres using a nonlinear mixed-integer programming model and a genetic algorithm that solves the RL problem involving product returns.

Classification Based on Approach

The literature on GSCM may also be classified on the basis of methodology and approach used into: thought papers and perspectives; frameworks and approaches; empirical studies; mathematical modeling approaches; and reviews. This helps us to understand GSCM from a different perspective from the problem context described earlier. Thought papers and perspectives as well as frameworks- and approaches-related articles have been sufficiently covered in "Strategic management." Similarly, review papers have been covered in the introduction, and are not covered further. Therefore, empirical studies and mathematical modeling approaches are covered here.

Empirical Studies

Empirical research studies include case research, field surveys and interviews, field experiments, mail surveys, laboratory experiments, and game simulations. Several empirical studies in the area of GSCM have been published. They consist mainly of case studies and surveys. Most case studies deal with green design (product and logistics) and green operations (remanufacturing, recycling, RL, etc.). Goldsby and Closs (2000) describe the case study of a Michigan beverage distributor and retailer who collects empty beverage containers for recycling purposes. They discuss the reengineering of supply chain-wide processes using activity-based costing (ABC). Duhaime, Riopel, and Langevin (2000) describe value analysis and optimization of reusable containers at Canada Post. Ritchie, Burnes, Whittle, and Hey (2000) discuss the RL supply chain of a UK pharmacy. Warren, Rhodes, and Carter (2001) describe a total product system concept for a highly customized build-to-order product system. Scherpereel et al. (2001) use a case study to establish the relevance of selecting environmental performance indicators, while Khoo, Spedding, Bainbridge, and Taplin (2001) present a case study of a supply chain concerned with the distribution of aluminum. They use simulation to create a green supply chain. Tan, Yu, and Kumar (2002) take on a computer company in the Asia-Pacific region. De Koster, de Brito, and van de Vendel (2002) carry out an exploratory study with nine retailer warehouses regarding returns handling. Review of a number of case studies in RL is provided by de Brito, Flapper, and Dekker (2003). Flapper, van Nunen, and van Wassenhove (2005) address a number of case studies on closed-loop supply chains covering pharmaceuticals, electronics, breweries, containers, mail orders, tyres, photocopiers, cars, computers, cosmetics, and consumer durables.

Mathematical Modeling

A variety of tools and techniques have been used for problem formulation. A variety of the above tools and techniques have been used for problem formulation, solution, and analysis in papers published in edited books such as Dekker, Fleischmann, Inderfurth, and Van Wassenhove (2004), Dyckhoff, Lackes, and Reese (2003), and Fleishmann and Klose (2005). We map various mathematical tools/techniques vis-à-vis the contexts of GSCM. This depends much on the methodology used and also helps us to gauge their applicability/suitability. This is shown in Table 1.

Very few models have been used for strategic management of GSCM. AHP/ANP, Regression, DEA, and descriptive statistics (based on surveys/interviews) have been tried. Linear programming, nonlinear programming (NLP), and MILP have also been suggested in books but have not been used to a great extent. Green design has seen very little application in terms of mathematical

Table 1. Mapping of mathematical tools/techniques used vis-à-vis the contexts of GSCM

Mathematical tools/techniques	Strategic Management	Green Design	Green Operations
Algebraic		(Richter, 1996)	(Ashayeri, Heuts, & Jansen, 1996; Mukhopadhyay & Setoputro, 2005; Richter & Dobos, 1999)
AHP/ANP	(Sarkis, 1999)		(Madu et al., 2002; Ravi et al., 2005; Sarkis, 1998, 1999)
Computer programs			(Barros et al., 1998; Johnson & Wang, 1995; Louwers et al., 1999)
Descriptive statistics/ANOVA	(Chinander, 2001; Sarkis, 1999)		(Chinander, 2001; Haas & Murphy, 2002; Sarkis & Cordeiro, 2001; Swenseth & Godfrey, 2002)
DEA	(Sarkis, 1999, 2001)		(Haas & Murphy, 2002; Sarkis, 1999; Sarkis & Cordeiro, 2001)
Dynamic programming		(Inderfurth & van der Laan, 2001; Richter & Weber, 2001)	(Inderfurth, de Kok, & Flapper, 2001; Kiesmuller & Scherer, 2003; Klausner & Hendrickson, 2000; Richter & Sombrutzki, 2000)
Fuzzy/neuro-fuzzy			(Marx-Gomez, Rantenstrauch, Nurnberger, & Kruse, 2002)
Game theory		(Majumder et al., 2001)	(Mostard & Teunter, 2006; Nagurney & Toyasaki, 2005)
Heuristics		(Richter & Sombrutzki, 2000; Richter & Weber, 2001)	(Barros et al., 1998; Bloemhof-Ruwaard, Solomon, & Van Wassenhove, 1996; Jayaraman et al., 2003; Mourao & Amado, 2005)
I/O Model	(Ferrer & Ayres, 2000)		(Ferrer & Ayres, 2000)
LP and MILP	(Sarkis, 2001)	(Barros et al., 1998; Bloemhof-Ruwaard, Solomon et al., 1996; Bloemhof-Ruwaard, van Wassenhove, Gabel, & Weaver, 1996)	(Fleischmann et al., 2001; Haas & Murphy, 2002; Hu et al., 2002; Kroon & Vrijens, 1995) (Jayaraman & Srivastava, 1995; Louwers et al., 1999; Marin & Pelegrin, 1998) (Jayaraman et al., 1999; Jayaraman, Srivastava, & Benton, 1998; Ritchie et al., 2000; Srivastava & Srivastava, 2005)
Markov chain/queuing		(Van der Laan, Dekker, & Salomon, 1996; Van der Laan, Dekker, Salomon, & Ridder, 1996)	(Fleischmann, Kuik, & Dekker, 2002; Gupta, 1993; Kiesmuller & van der Laan, 2001; van der Laan & Salomon, 1997)
Metaheuristics			(Min et al., 2006; Minner, 2001)
Nonlinear programming	(Sarkis, 2001)		(Jayaraman et al., 1998; Richter & Dobos, 1999; Sarkis, 2001)
Petri net			(Moore, Gungor, & Gupta, 1998; Moore et al., 2001)
Regression	(Klassen, 2001; Sarkis, 2001; Zhu & Sarkis, 2004)	(Minner, 2001)	(Ferrer, 1997a; Haas & Murphy, 2002; Sarkis & Cordeiro, 2001; Zhu & Sarkis, 2004)
Scenario/sensitivity analysis			(Klausner & Hendrickson, 2000; Linton & Johnston, 2000; van der Laan, Salomon, & Dekker, 1999; van der Laan, Salomon, Dekker, & van Wassenhove, 1999)
Simulation			(Ashayeri et al., 1996; Khoo et al., 2001; Marx-Gomez et al., 2002; Vlachos & Tagaras, 2001)
Software and spreadsheets	(Nagel & Meyer, 1999)		(Krikke, Harten, & Schuur, 1998; Louwers et al., 1999)

tools, techniques, and methodologies. Lately, LP, MILP formulations, and software packages and spreadsheets for solution have been used. Green operations have used mathematical models, tools, and techniques to a much larger extent. MILP, simulation, computer programming, software packages, spreadsheets, and dynamic programming have been used extensively. Other traditional tools and techniques such as simulation, Markov chains, algebraic equations, ANOVA, heuristics, metaheuristics, and regression have also been used. Fuzzy reasoning, neuro-fuzzy, and game theory too have been tried.

One of the biggest challenges facing the field of GSCM is the developing of strategic and tactical tools. The inherent complexity of environmental issues—their multiple stakeholders, uncertain implications for competitiveness, and international importance—present significant challenges to researchers. Much research is needed to support the evolution in business strategy towards greening along the entire supply chain. Effective approaches for data sharing across the supply chain need to be developed. Researchers might take advantage of the emergent ICT for more effective collaboration and cooperation.

Although the current development in GSCM research is encouraging, a few studies link GSC strategy and performance measurement. Beamon (1999) suggests the traditional performance measurement structure of the supply chain must be extended and include mechanisms for product recovery (reverse logistics) and the establishment and implementation of new performance measurement systems. Yet, overall environmental performance measurement and supporting systems, across supply chains has not been as extensively studied (Hervani, Helms, & Sarkis, 2005).

RESEARCH OBJECTIVES AND METHODOLOGY

The objective of the research adopted under the heading of quantitative models for environmental performance measurement systems (QMEPMS) was to identify tools and techniques that would facilitate:

- Identification of factors affecting environmental performance
- Identification of the relationship between factors affecting environmental performance
- Quantification of these relationships on one another, and on the overall performance of the production processes
- Establishment of "What if" analysis on process performance and strategy selection

The introduction of a green supply-chain strategy is a very complex issue, since it presents a multidimensional impact on performance and often induces a significant modification in management procedures. In the light of these issues, it is important to analyze feasible patterns of strategic environmental behavior, under which conditions these are a sustainable option and the implications on operations management.

The introduction of factors describing a company's strategic attitude towards the environment, that is, how executives consider "green" issues, and of external variables describing the stakeholders' environment-related pressures, allows us:

- To highlight in which context(s) a specific green supply-chain strategy may be considered a sustainable option; and
- To identify the key elements of an efficient EPMS.

A company's strategic attitude heavily depends on managers' environmental awareness. For example, managers:

- Could have an ethical objective: in this case, the reduction of the company's impact on the natural environment is a more important task than the improvement of economic performance;
- May consider the environment as a means of achieving a competitive advantage: the introduction of new "green" product development procedures or the definition of a unique blend of "green" competencies identifying would be appropriate managerial solutions;
- Might concentrate on ensuring compliance with current environmental regulations or leading "green" movements/customers by developing products which are consistent with their requirements;
- May take no initiative to improve environmental performance; this behavior essentially reflects short-term vision and a resistant management.

Many authors (DePass, 2006; Rentmeester, 2005; Srivastava, 2007) have tried to identify the drivers of environmental pressures. It has been claimed that cost control, total quality management, communities, investors, and environmental regulations are the main pressures faced by companies.

Such environmental drivers do not affect a company's pattern of environmental behavior in equal measure. Their influence depends on industry- and country-specific factors. In our opinion, the major external influences concern:

- "Green" movements or regulators: specifically, the binding pressure of regulations and the importance of "green" movements are significant variables that could explain the adoption of a green supply-chain strategy; and
- The company's relationships with the other supply value chain partners (Dickinson, Draper, Saminathan, Sohn, & Williams, 1995; Hervani et al., 2005).

In the light of the above issues, we distinguish between (see Table 2).

This framework reflects the extensive literature on environmental strategies. Nevertheless, it differs from other state of the art approaches, as it introduces a more detailed taxonomy of strategic patterns of environmental behavior. The reasons for this choice are to identify precisely the operat-

Table 2. Main characteristics of the green supply-chain strategies

Strategy	Context	Characteristic
"evangelist" strategy	ethical objective and radical approach to environmental issues	Futurity
Pro-active green strategy	"systemic" initiatives affecting the whole value chain and relationships with suppliers	High bargaining power of the company Strategic perspective
Responsive strategy	bargaining power vs. suppliers/shredders is low the regulators' pressures are low	High/low bargaining power of the company Technical perspective
Reactive strategy	comply with environmental regulations or customers' environmental requirements	External oriented: High pressures from regulators and Technical perspective Market driven: High pressures of "green" customers and Technical perspective
Unresponsive strategy	limited financial resources, passive pattern of environmental behaviour and delay "green" programmes	High importance of cost based strategy

ing objectives associated with the implemented environment-related initiatives and to define the key requirements that an effective EPMS might respect in order to assess these.

Effective operating EPMSs to support the implementation of the above green supply-chain strategies and assess the resulting environmental performance might respect two general requirements:

- Measurability of the output, in order to have measures that can be used in identifying both to assess the company's "green" efficiency and to reward effective EPMSs employees;
- Long-term orientation, such a requirement is particularly important if the EPMS is adopted to support the implementation of "evangelist," pro-active, and responsive strategies.

Completeness, timeliness, and cost of the analysis are significant elements of an effective operating EPMS, but their importance varies with the different green supply-chain strategies. Completeness means the extent to which the model can take account of all the relevant performance factors in the environmental field; timeliness aims to describe how long the EPMS takes to analyze the collected data; while cost refers to the amount of time and human resources needed to implement the EPMS.

In the light of these issues, it is clear that the development of a complete and timely model represents the best solution, but this implies great computational costs. Hence, on the basis of the main characteristics of the identified green supply-chain strategies, we attempt to define EPMSs that, within each context, ensure the best trade-off between completeness, timeliness, and cost.

The six steps of the approach were developed as a result of the QMEPMS methodology implementation as depicted in Figure 2. The details of this approach have been explained through a case study.

The QMEPMS methodology, which is adopted in this research, is a modeling and simulation technique specifically designed for long-term, chronic, dynamic management problems. It focuses on understanding how the physical processes, information flows, and managerial policies interact so as to create the dynamics of the variables of

Figure 2. QMEPMS methodology implementation

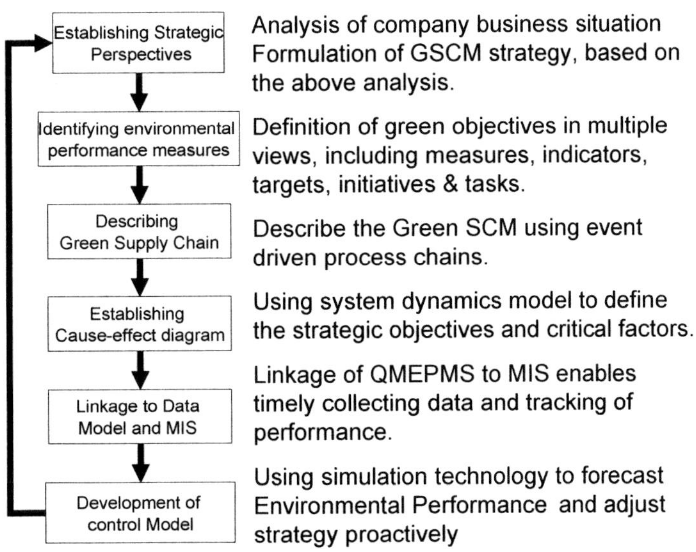

interest. The totality of the relationships between these components defines the "structure" of the system. Hence, it is said that the "structure" of the system, operating over time, generates its "dynamic behavior patterns." It is most crucial in QMEPMS that the model structure provides a valid description of the real processes. The typical purpose of a QMEPMS study is to understand how and why the dynamics of concern are generated and then search for policies to further improve the system performance. Policies refer to the long-term, macrolevel decision rules used by upper management.

In order to achieve the green supply chain, manufacturing organizations must follow the basic principles established by ISO 14000. In particular, organizations must develop procedures that focus on operations analysis, continuous improvement, measurement, and objectives. An implementation procedure for implementing the green supply chain strategy includes the following tasks:

- **Establishing strategic perspectives:** For each product within the supply chain, identify all inputs, outputs, by-products, and resources.
- **Identifying environmental performance measures:** Defining green objectives in multiple views, including measures, indicators, targets, initiatives, and tasks. Environmental performance indicators are core requirements of a GSCM/PMS when evaluating the environmental performance of activities, processes, hardware, and services. Environmental performance indicators are described in ISO 14031 (environmental management-environmental performance evaluation of the ISO 14001 accreditation guidelines). Environmental performance indicators are needed when evaluating the environmental performance of activities, processes, hardware, and services. Given the complexity of most supply chains, a single performance measure will likely be inadequate in assessing the true performance of the supply chain. Thus, a system of performance measures will be necessary. Such a performance measurement system must include measures for the three environmental categories given above, as well as existing operational measures.
- **Describing green supply chain:** Describe the Green SCM using event driven process chains (EPCs). EPCs are directed graphs, which visualize the control flow and consist of events, functions and connectors. Each EPC starts with at least one event and ends with at least one event. An event triggers a function, which leads to a new event. Three types of connectors (AND, Exclusive OR, OR) can be used to model splits and joins.
- **Establishing cause-effect diagram:** Using system dynamics model to define the strategic objectives and critical factors (Figure 4). Calculate the actual composite performance at each step in the supply chain process for each product. The composite performance, as calculated at each supply chain process step, will be a function of the performance measures developed above. The composite performance, therefore, may be a single numerical value, or (more likely) a vector of numerical values.
- **Linkage to data model and MIS:** Linkage of QMEPMS to MIS enables timely collecting, measuring of data, and tracking of performance. After all processes for all products have been measured, prioritize the process steps in order of increasing composite performance, as calculated above.
- **Development of control model:** Develop alternative simulation models for performance improvement (targeting first those process steps exhibiting the worst composite performance, based on prioritization above), and select a preferred approach. Establish

schedules and procedures for auditing and continuous improvement, including emergency and noncompliance procedures.

QUANTITATIVE MODEL FOR ENVIRONMENTAL PMS

Performance measurement systems usually involve a number of multidimensional performance measures. Neely pointed out that a problem, which arises from that situation is the integration of those several measures expressed in heterogeneous units into a single unit (Neely et al., 2000).

The key techniques of the QMEPMSs are a set of models of business object, coupling operation and system dynamics. These models are proposed based on the object-oriented approach, and are shown in Figure 3.

Business Object Models (BOMs)

Our BOMs are divided from three views and their relationships are also shown in Figure 3.

Organization View

The organizational model is a typical form of representing organizational structures. Person Type (PT) objects can be defined as a 3-tuple:

$$PT = \{(personID, roleName, prsType)\} \quad (1)$$

Where *personID* is the identifier of a human resource; *roleName* is defined as the role of a person in the business process; *prsType* is the type of a person when he processes information resources, such as listener, processor, and dispatcher.

Function View

An enterprise activity (EA) is defined as a 9-tuple:

$$EA = \{(activityID, actFunction, ,orgBelongTo) actType\} \quad (2)$$

Where activityID is the identifier of an EA; actFunction is defined as the function of EA; orgBelongTo defines the organization to which activity belongs; actType refers to the type of

Figure 3. Relationship views of the QMEPMS model

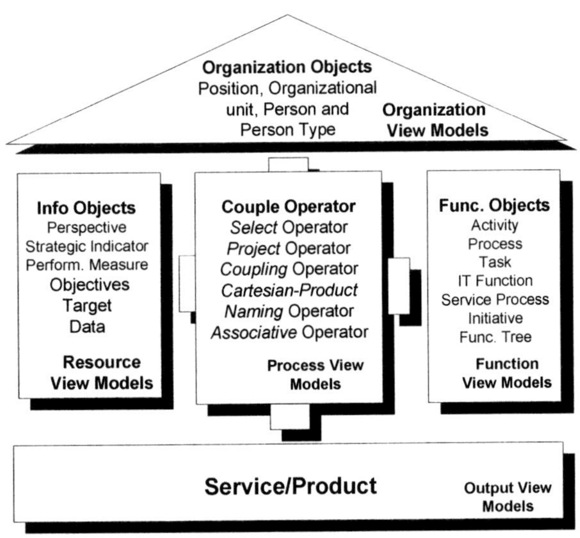

activity which can be cataloged as a structured activity and a nonstructured activity.

Info View

An info view model includes a description of the semantic data model of the field which is to be examined. An information resource (IR) can be defined as a 5-tuple:

$$IR = \{(inforResID, content, generationTime, periodOfValidity\ \ inforType)\} \quad (3)$$

Where inforResID is the identifier of IR; content includes three components: clear definition or meaning of data, correct value(s), and understandable presentation (the format represented to PTs); generationTime refers to the time when the IR comes into being; periodOfValidity refers to the age of the IR remaining valid; inforType is the type of the IR which can be classified as environmental, inner, and efferent.

Output View

An output view model includes a description of the products or services performed in a company. A product service (PS) can be defined as a 6-tuple:

$$PS = \{(ProdServID, Name, Frequency, Costs, Significance, Price)\} \quad (4)$$

Coupling Operation Models (COMs)

The coupling operation consists of a set of operations that take one or two sets as the input and produce a new set as their result. The fundamental operations in the coupling operation are select, project, Cartesian product, and associative.

The Select Operator

The select operation selects tuples that satisfy a given predicate. We use the lowercase Greek letter sigma (σ) to denote selection. The predicate appears as a subscript to σ. The argument relation is in parentheses after the σ. Thus, to select those tuples of the IR in Equation (2) object where the inforResID is "1," we write: σ inforResID = "1" (IR).

In general, we allow comparisons using =, ≠, <, ⩽, >, ⩾, ≮, ≯ in the selection predicate. Furthermore, we can combine several predicates into a larger predicate by using the connectives and (∧), or (∨), and not (¬).

The Project Operator

Suppose we want to list all names and values of IR, but do not care about the identifier of IR. The project operation allows us to produce this relation. The project operation is a unary operation that returns its argument relation, with certain attributes left out. Since a relation is a set, any duplicate rows are eliminated. Projection is denoted by the uppercase Greek letter pi (Π). We list those attributes that we wish to appear in the result as a subscript to Π. The argument relation follows in parentheses. Thus, we write the query to list all periodOfValidity of IR as: ΠperiodOfValidity (IR)

Composition of Coupling Operator

The fact that the result of a coupling operation is itself a set is important. Consider the more complicated query "Find periodOfValidity of the IR which inforResID is 1." We write:

$$\Pi_{periodOfVality}(\sigma_{\inf or \operatorname{Re} sID=1}(IR)) \quad (5)$$

The Cartesian-Product Operator

The Cartesian-product operation, denoted by a cross (×), allows us to combine information from any two objects. We write the Cartesian product of object o1 and o2 as o1×o2.

The Naming Operator

However, since the same attribute name may appear in both o1 and o2, we devise a naming operation to distinguish the object from which the attribute originally came. For example, the relation schema for R = IR × RI is shown in Box 1.

With this operation, we can distinguish IR.inforResID from RI.inforResID. For those attributes that appear in only one of the two objects, we shall usually drop the relation-name prefix. This simplification does not lead to any ambiguity. We can then write the relation schema for R as shown in Box 2.

The Associative Operator

It is often desirable to simplify certain operations that require a Cartesian product. Usually, an operation that involves a Cartesian product includes a selection operation on the result of the Cartesian product. Consider the operation "Find the contents of all IRs which come into the object of RI, along with the peridodOfValidity and generationTime." Then, we select those tuples that pertain to only the same inforResID, followed by the projection of the resulting content, generationTime, and peridodOfValidity:

$$\Pi_{\text{content, generationTime, periodOfValidity}} (\sigma_{\text{IR.inforResID=RI.inforResID}} (\text{IR} \times \text{RI})) \quad (6)$$

The associative operation is a binary operation that allows us to combine certain selections and a Cartesian product into one operation. It is denoted by the "join" symbol "⊠." The associative operation forms a Cartesian product of its two arguments, performs a selection forcing equality on those attributes that appear in both relation objects, and finally removes the duplicate attributes.

Although the definition of an associative operation is complicated, the operation is easy to apply. As an illustration, consider again the example "Find the contents of all IRs which come into the object of RI, along with the peridodOfValidity and generationTime." We express this operation by using the associative operation as following:

$$\Pi_{\text{content, generationTime, periodOfValidity}} (\sigma (\text{IR} \boxtimes \text{RI}))$$

System Dynamics Models (SDMs)

This section is a detailed discussion of the system dynamics modeling, which allows for simple representation of complex cause-and-effect re-

Box 1.

IR × RI = {(IR.inforResID, IR.content, IR.generationTime, IR.periodOfValidity, IR.inforType, RI.resInputID,RI.receiveTime, RI.activityID, RI.inforResID, RI.personID, RI.IQMeasure)}

Box 2.

IR × RI = {(IR.inforResID, content, generationTime, periodOfValidity, inforType resInputID, receiveTime, activityID, RI.inforResID, personID, IQMeasure)}

lationships. For the discussion that follows, it is important to understand that it is the levels (or state variables) that define the dynamics of a system. For the mathematically inclined, we can introduce this in a more formal way. The following equations show the basic mathematical form of the QMEPMS.

$$measures[i]_t = \int_0^T levels[j]_t dt; \quad \frac{d}{dt} measures[i]_t = levels[j]_t \qquad (7)$$

$$rates_t = g(levels_t, aux_t, data_t, const) \qquad (8)$$

$$aux_t = f(levels_t, aux_t, data_t, const) \qquad (9)$$

$$levels_0 = h(levels_0, aux_0, data_0, const) \qquad (10)$$

In these equations g, h, and f are arbitrary, nonlinear, potentially time varying, vector-valued functions. Equation represents the evolution of the system over time, equation the computation of the rates determining that evolution, equation the intermediate results necessary to compute the rates, and equation the initialization of the system.

QMEPMS differs significantly from a traditional simulation method, such as discrete-event simulation where the most important modeling issue is a point-by-point match between the model behavior and the real behavior, that is, an accurate forecast. Rather, for an EPMS model it is important to produce the major "dynamic patterns" of concern (such as exponential growth, collapse, asymptotic growth, S-shaped growth, damping or expanding oscillations, etc). Therefore, the purpose of our model would not be to predict what the total green supply chain profit level would be each week for the years to come, but to reveal under what conditions and capacity planning policies the total profit would be higher, if and when it would be negative, and if and how it can be controlled.

Model Variables

The flow variables represent the flows in the system (i.e., remanufacturing rate), which result from the decision-making process. Below, we define the model variables (stock, smoothed stock, and flow) converters and constants and cost parameters, their explanation, where necessary, and their units. We chose to keep a nomenclature consistent with the commercial software package that we employed; thus, for the variable names we use terms with underscore since this is the requirement of the software package (it does not accept spaces). The stock variables in order that they appear in the green supply chain processes are the following:

- **Raw_Materials:** Inventory of raw materials [items].
- **Serviceable_Inventory:** On-hand inventory of new and remanufactured products [items].
- **Distributors_Inventory:** On-hand inventory of the distributor [items].
- **Collected_Products:** The inventory of collected reused products [items].
- **Collection_Capacity:** The maximum volume of products handled by the collection and inspection facilities per day [items/day].

The smoothed stock variables are:

- **Expected_Distributors_Orders:** Forecast of distributor's orders using exponential smoothing with smoothing factor a_DI [items/day].
- **Expected_Demand:** Demand forecast using exponential smoothing with smoothing factor a_D [items/day].
- **Expected_Remanufacturing_Rate:** Forecast of remanufacturer rate using exponential smoothing with smoothing factor a_RR [items/day].

- **Expected_Used_Products:** Forecast of used products obtained using exponential smoothing with smoothing factor a_UP [items/day].
- **Desired_CC:** Estimation of collection capacity obtained by exponential smoothing of Used_Products with smoothing factor a_CC [items/day].
- **Production_Rate:** [items/day].
- **Products_Rejected_for_Reuse:** The flow of used products that have not passed inspection and should be disposed [items/day].
- **Controllable_Disposal:** The flow of surplus stock of reusable products to prevent the costly accumulation if there is not enough remanufacturing capacity to handle them [items/day].
- **RC_Adding_Rate:** Remanufacturing capacity adding rate [items/day/day].

Constants, converters are:

- **CC_Discrepancy:** Discrepancy between desired and actual collection capacity [items/day].
- **CC_Expansion_Rate:** Collection capacity expansion rate [items/day/day].
- **DI_Adj_Time:** Distributor's inventory adjustment time [days].
- **DI_Cover_Time:** Distributor's inventory cover time [days].
- **Pr:** Remanufacturing capacity review period [days].
- **Reuse_Ratio:** The ratio of Expected_Remanufacturing_Capacity to Expected_Used_Products [dimensionless].
- **SI_Adj_Time:** Serviceable inventory adjustment time [days].
- **SI_Cover_Time:** Serviceable inventory cover time [days].

Cause-Effect Diagram

The structure of a system in QMEPMS methodology is captured by cause-effect diagrams. A cause-effect diagram represents the major feedback mechanisms. These mechanisms are either negative feedback (balancing) or positive feedback (reinforcing) loops. A negative feedback loop exhibits goal-seeking behavior: after a disturbance, the system seeks to return to an equilibrium situation. In a positive feedback loop an initial disturbance leads to further change, suggesting the presence of an unstable equilibrium. Cause-effect diagrams play two important roles in QMEPMS methodologies. First, during model development, they serve as preliminary sketches of causal hypotheses and secondly, they can simplify the representation of a model.

The first step of our analysis is to capture the relationships among the system operations in a QMEPMS manner and to construct the appropri-

Figure 4. Cause-effect diagram of the green supply chain

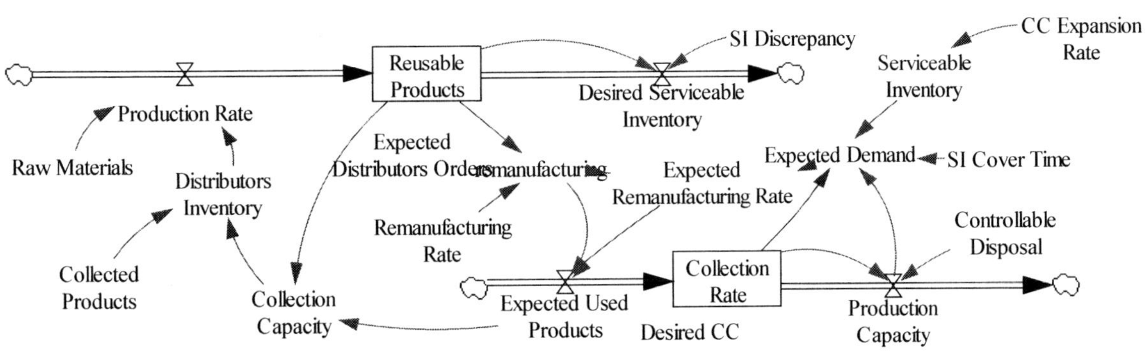

ate cause-effect diagram. Figure 3 depicts the cause-effect diagram of the system under study which includes both the forward and the reverse manufacturing process. To improve appearance and distinction among the variables, we removed underscores from the variable names and changed the letter style according to the variable type. Specifically, stock variables are written in capital letters, the smoothed stock variables are written in small italics and the flow variables are written in small plain letters. These variables may be quantitative, such as levels of inventories and capacities, or qualitative, such as failure mechanisms.

Mathematical Formulation

The next step of QMEPMS methodology includes the development of the mathematical model, also presented as a cause-effect diagram that captures the model structure and the interrelationships among the variables. The cause-effect diagram is easily translated to a system of differential equations, which is then solved via simulation.

The cause-effect diagram is a graphical representation of the mathematical model. The embedded mathematical equations are divided into two main categories: the stock equations, defining the accumulations within the system through the time integrals of the net flow rates, and the rate equations, defining the flows among the stocks as functions of time. In the remaining of this section, we present selected formulations related to important model assumptions.

The equations related to collection green supply chain policy are the following:

$$Desired\_CC(t) = \text{DELAYINF}(Used\_Products, a\_CC, 1, Used\_Products) \quad (11)$$

$$Collection\_Capacity(0) = 0 \quad (12)$$

$$Collection\_Capacity(\text{t} + \text{dt}) = Collection\_Capacity(\text{t}) + \text{dt} * CC\_Adding\_Rate \quad (13)$$

$$CC\_Adding\_Rate = \text{DELAYMTR}(CC\_Expansion\_Rate, 24, 3, 0), \quad (14)$$

$$CC\_Discrepancy = \text{PULSE}(Desired\_CC * Collection\_Capacity, 50, P_c), \quad (15)$$

$$CC\_Expansion\_Rate = \max(K_c * CC\_Discrepancy, 0), \quad (16)$$

Desired_CC is a first order exponential smoothing of Used_Products with smoothing coefficient a_CC. Its initial value is the initial value of Used_Products. Collection_Capacity begins at zero and changes following CC_Adding_Rate, which is a delayed capacity expansion decision (CC_Expansion_Rate) with an average delay time of 24 time units, an order of delay equal to 3 and initial value equal to zero at t = 0. CC_Expansion_Rate is proportional to the CC_Discrepancy between the desired and actual collection capacity, multiplied by Kc. The pulse function determines when the first decision is made (50 time units) and the review period Pc. Similar equations dictate the green supply chain policy.

The total profit per period is given from:

$$Total\_Profit\_per\_Period = Total\_Revenue\_per\_Period - Total\_Cost\_per\_Period \quad (17)$$

Where

$$Total\_Cost\_per\_Period = Investment\_Cost + Operational\_Cost + Penalty\_Cost, \quad (18)$$

$$Total\_Revenue\_per\_Period = Sales * Price, \quad (19)$$

$$Investment\_Cost = (CC\_Expansion\_rate)^{0.6} * Col\_Cap\_Construction\_Cost + (RC\_Expansion\_rate)^{0.6} * Rem\_Cap\_Construction\_Cost, \quad (20)$$

$$Operational\_Cost = Collection\_Rate * Collection\_Cost$$

$$Remanufacturing\_Rate * Remanufacturing\_Cost + Production\_Rate * Production\_Cost + Reusable\_Products * Holding\_Cost + Sales * DI\_Transportation\_Cost + Distributors\_Inventory * DI\_Holding\_Cost + Shipments\_to\_Distributor * SI\_Transportation\_Cost + Serviceable\_Inventory * SI\_Holding\_Cost, \quad (21)$$

ILLUSTRATIVE CASE

Owing to the wide set of measures and processes that must often be considered in an EPMS, the implementation of the suggested quantitative models may be complex. To understand the major models of the identified EPMSs, An example that highlights how measures must be structured at the operational level is given. In the following section, the case of FAW Toyota Changchun Engine Co. Ltd. (FTCE) in the automotive industry is analyzed.

First Auto Works (FAW) is the largest Chinese corporation in the automotive industry. It has industrial sites both in Changchun and Tianjin, and over the last few years has adopted a green manufacturing strategy aimed at reducing product costs (through innovative technology) and improving product quality. As a pioneering automobile company, FTCE has initiated multiple dimensions of GSCM practices, including internal environmental management, green purchasing, green marketing, and eco-design.

Since 2000, senior management has been committed to a reduction in the environmental impact resulting from industrial activities, and product usage. In terms of operational policy, such an interest in "green" issues has given rise to two major programmes:

- The F1 program, specifically aimed at improving the environmental performance of the production processes.
- The F2 program, which focuses on the introduction of new environmentally friendly cars. Indeed, in 1999, the group developed a new generation of recyclable cars.

In the light of these issues, it is clear that First Auto has adopted a pro-active pattern of environmental behavior, whereby it has tried to improve its ("green") image.

In the sample application, an EPMS was designed to support operations managers in assessing the results of the Crown model. The car is designed to respect recycling and dismantling techniques, and allows the company to recover all end-of-life components. Materials for engines are recycled into plastics for air ducts in the dashboard, glass is recovered to produce colored bottles; reclining seats are recycled into carpets for furnishing, and so forth. Here, the effectiveness of engine recycling is assessed, since it is the only activity that is implemented internally.

Producing environmentally sound engines is one key dimension FTCE uses to establish their environmental image, and thus gain and keep competitiveness. Within this competitive market, senior managers in the FTCE put forward a call of "Green plant, environmental engines." They have worked on furthering their environmental image by producing petrol engines with low emissions, low petrol consumption, low noise, as well as high dynamic functions and reliability. To at least maintain and potentially improve its environmental performance, FTCE has invested over 14 million RMB since 2004. The plant purchased equipment for emission purification, noise elimination and wastewater treatment, which greatly improved its internal environmental conditions. In 2006, FTCE initiated a waste water reuse project, and became the first company realizing "zero emissions" for both industrial and municipal waste water in Changchun, which is very important in a municipality that is consistently threatened with water shortages. To complete this program the plant invested 3.26 million RMB for a wastewater treatment project by using flocculation, bio-chemical, ultra-filtration, and reverse osmosis technologies.

Environmental issues are main concerns for FTCE during its product design and development. The Product Development Director in FTCE stated that environmental requirements are quickly becoming primary priorities, even over economic benefits. To help them address this management priority, the plant closely cooperates with our research methodology and models on eco-design projects. As an example of this success, since April 2007, all products produced by the FTCE meet the Europe II emission standards.

The plant has also implemented cleaner production activities in its production stages focusing on source reduction and waste prevention. The plant implements collaborative development efforts with its suppliers, which include environmental considerations, and these efforts and programs are driven by the organization's internal environmental strategy and policy. Customer collaboration is also evident here. For different types of vehicles, road conditions, and consumer characteristics, the plant and its main customer, FAW, jointly develop improved engines that consume less fuel, while maintaining suitable performance standards (including acceleration and cooling systems capabilities).

The significance of outsourcing practiced by FTCE requires them to more closely monitor supplier environmental practices to guarantee both quality and environmental performance requirements. The plant not only collects environmental information related to suppliers, but also establishes a database on environmental situations for main component suppliers. The plant jointly implements research on substitute materials and technologies to improve environmental practices with those partners and even joins in some of these innovation programs with competitors. At the same time, the plant also outsources other nonmanufacturing functions, such as logistics functions to help achieve their goals of just-in-time (JIT) production. This outsourcing requires monitoring of its distribution and transportation environmental and economic performance. JIT provides a managerial challenge since JIT's minimization of waste philosophy is environmentally sound, yet, more frequent delivery requirements weaken transportation energy efficiency, causing environmentally detrimental consequences.

Table 3. Measures expressing a company's impact on the state of natural resources

		Planned value	***Reported measure***
	Time for production	4 hours	3.5 hours
	Time for disassembling	5.8 hours	4.6 hours
	No. of different materials in the product	4	9
Volume index	Quantity of recovered plastics	6.376 tons	8.670 tons
	SOx	523 tons	532 tons
	NOx	412 tons	395 tons
Process efficiency	Electrical energy	445,000 Mwh	430,000 Mwh
	Oil	2,250 tons	2,383 tons
	COD	35,500 tons	33,000 tons
	Sulphates	368,000 tons	369,500 tons

FTCE has improved both environmental and economic performance through GSCM-related practices. It is complying with regulatory and market pressures by offering innovative and environmentally sound products. However, the plant has also faced numerous challenges. Prices for energy and raw materials have continuously increased. Emission standards have become increasingly strict. For example, the federal government recently announced plans to implement Euro III standards on emissions by the end of 2007. These continued pressures and forces will cause not only FTCE to adopt and advance GSCM innovation, but other manufacturers will need to react as well.

In line with the above discussion, the change in the main (physical) environmental performance resulting from the implementation of this program and the main drivers of shareholders' value were calculated.

The implementation of the above initiative results in the modification of design, process efficiency, and volume indices (see Table 3). Specifically, the take-back of engines leads to a reduction in the purchase of plastic raw materials and energy consumption (30% with respect to traditional plants), since the fluff resulting from the grinding of car bodies is cleaner.

From a financial perspective (see Table 4), the program affects expenditure related to the internal efficiency of operations, for example, the reduction of energy, raw materials, and environmental regulations related costs (regarding both waste water and solid wastes), as well as other operating costs associated to the take back and recycling of engines, higher labor costs to implement the recycling process internally, and increased expense for the recycling process itself. In addition, the introduction of new cars produced an increase in volume (50,000 units).

In the light of the above analysis, it can be concluded that the company respected its own targets: indeed, the increase in actual labor costs over standard costs is only marginal and, above all, the result of the growth in production volumes.

The above discussion highlights that there are significant differences in the deployment and assessment of a pro-active or a reactive green supply-chain strategy. In particular, both the design of the EPMS and the gathering of data present different operating problems which depend on the adopted pattern of environmental behavior.

In general terms, the design of an effective EPMS is more complex within pro-active companies than within reactive organizations. It must be noted that the assessment of a pro-active green

Table 4. The economic items affected by the initiative

	Forecast Value (RMB)	*Reported measure (RMB)*
Revenue		
Total Revenue per Period	2,150,000,000	2,345,000,000
Total Cost per Period		
Total Profit per Period	56,500,000,000	58,450,000,000
Operational Cost	18,250,000,000	17,750,000,000
Energy costs	5,650,000,000	5,537,000,000
Other environmental costs		
Recycling costs	435,720,000	428,780,000
Costs related to environmental regulations	593,500,000	693,000,000

supply-chain strategy requires identification of physical and economic indicators which well describe a company's potential environment-related sources of competitive advantage. This implies significant changes in the traditional systems adopted to monitor the evolution of environmental performance. Indeed, the latter were usually designed to verify compliance with existing regulations. A reactive green supply-chain strategy simply demands verification of whether environmental performance of the company's products or processes are consistent with the stakeholders', that is, regulators' or customers', requirements. The implementation of the suggested approach in FA (the reactive firm) did not in fact require the definition of new measures, as the company's EPMS already considered compliance indicators.

It is evident that, apart from managers' skills and the effectiveness of the information system, the deployment of innovation-based green supply-chain strategies (evangelist, pro-active and responsive) is more complex than passive patterns of environmental behavior. A key point in the effective assessment of innovative environmental policies is the identification of measures clarifying how the company positions itself with respect to competitors, and how the adopted programmes affect the company's profitability. In this respect, a growing body of literature highlights that the failure of some ambitious environmental strategies is a direct consequence of an incorrect selection of the indicators to be used in the EPMS.

CONCLUDING REMARKS

The suggested framework is, in our opinion, an effective tool for operations managers wishing to design EPMSs. The operational guidelines on PMS architecture and the appropriate measurement techniques provide support in devising performance indicators that best suit the intended green supply-chain strategy.

The model can be used to analyze various scenarios (i.e., to conduct various "what-if" analyses), thus identifying efficient policies and further to answer questions about the long-term operation of green supply chain using total process profit as the measure of performance. The model could further be adopted and used not only for product recovery, but also for material recycling systems. Thus, it may prove useful to policy-makers/regulators and decision-makers dealing with long-term strategic management issues along with researchers in environmental management. The benefits of the QMEPMS approach may be summarized as follows:

- Factors affecting performance can be identified and then their effects can be quantified
- Effects of multidimensional factors on performance can be aggregated into a single dimensionless unit (priority)
- Help managers to quantify the level of impact of each factor on overall performance and therefore assists in focusing improvement activities
- The relationships between factors can be clearly identified and expressed in quantitative terms
- Models can be easily altered to assists understanding the dynamic behavior of factors affecting performance
- Facilitates the reduction of the number of performance measurement reports

An important benefit gained from the QMEPMS approach is that the interaction of the factors can be clearly identified and expressed in quantitative terms. This identification will bring us one step forward in understanding the dynamic behavior of factors affecting environmental performance.

Moreover, the approach can be used in a "dynamic perspective," that is, to analyze whether to change the adopted pattern of environmental behavior from a passive/re-active to a pro-active strategic attitude. In operational terms, this implies, for example, that a reactive firm has to design an EPMS which includes indicators highlighting how the company's economic value may change with the introduction of innovation-based environmental programmes (i.e., the EPMS suggested for a pro-active manufacturing strategy).

However, the suggested framework does not solve all the problems associated to environmental performance measurement. In this respect, two directions for further research can be identified:

The integration of environmental aspects into the corporate management control system, since, in the above discussion, we considered the control of the implemented environmental programmes as an isolated problem. The design of a comprehensive PMS which includes the environmental dimension as well as the other competitive priorities (i.e., cost, quality, time, flexibility, innovation) may be difficult. A key point for future research is to avoid excessive proliferation of data, since this may hinder the use of PMS to identify how a company performs with respect to the planned objectives.

Decision-making techniques must be developed which allow physical and economical measures to be integrated into a synthetic judgment. The assessment of different "green" options requires the decision maker to identify how each alternative contributes to the reduction of environmental impact and shareholders' value creation. The definition of a synthetic indicator is of fundamental importance if the comparison of the available "green" options shows contrasting results with regards environmental performance and the financial implications of its implementation.

FUTURE DIRECTION

Research in GSCM to date may be considered compartmentalized into content areas drawn from operations strategy. The primary areas of emphasis have been quality, operations strategy, supply-chain management, and product and process technologies, which are collectively beginning to contribute to a more systematic knowledge base. It is reasonable to expect that these research areas will continue to hold the greatest promise for advance in the short term. However, more integrative contributions are needed in the longer term, including green supply chain strategy, intra- and inter-firm diffusion of best practices, green technology transfer, and environmental performance measurement.

One of the biggest challenges facing the field of GSCM is the inherent complexity of environmental issues, such as natural environment limits, multiple stakeholders, uncertain implications for competitiveness, international importance, and so forth. These present significant challenges to researchers, management academicians, and application practitioners. Much research is needed to support the evolution in business practice towards green supply chain strategy. Effective quantitative models for green supply chain need to be developed. Researchers might take advantage of the emergent mathematical modeling technologies for more effective collaboration and cooperation. Although research on intelligent GSCM is still in its infancy, there is no doubt that this will be the hottest topic in the near future. Artificial intelligence techniques, including knowledge-based systems, fuzzy systems, and neural networks, are expected to play a significant role in research and development.

Although many case studies, survey-based empirical methods, and so forth, have been carried out, they have not dealt with strategic management aspect of GSCM. Detailed empirical case studies need to be carried out in such areas as organizational function to GSCM at the firm level, selection of returns and rework facilities in alignment with competitive priorities, the influence of remanufacturing on the supply chain of a particular firm, and how service quality and recovery strategies influence consumer behavior and vice versa. The chance also exists to carry out empirical studies to find how the regulatory environment, economic considerations, and level of function influence the volume of returns. Similarly, studies to find how various uncertainties influence channel relationships within GSCM are also desired.

The product life cycle has been studied in great depth. However, more research is needed in understanding strategic management and its connection to the product life cycle. An important area for investigation would be to see how, in practice, strategic management activities do change over the life of a particular product. More information is needed about returns levels. At a strategic level, there is little published information on product return levels by product type. More study of the impact of marketing on strategies is needed. In general, theory and models need to be developed and consolidated to establish the relationship between new product sales and returns rates. Research is needed into how companies should process, store, and dispose of returned goods. Much more research is needed in understanding secondary markets, and how companies should best sell unwanted products. In addition to traditional brokers, many firms are now selling this material through online and traditional auctions.

Although the current development in GSCM research is encouraging, literature on integrated business strategy (comprising product and process design, manufacturing, marketing, RL and regulatory compliance) in the context of GSCM is at the level of thought papers and frameworks only. More research is needed in determining how companies should best select green strategies for each outlet to maximize returns, while still protecting brand integrity. Further, GSCM deserves special attention in terms of resource function within a firm/ supply chain.

GSCM seems a promising area for trying out new research techniques and for using traditional techniques for overall GSCM Strategy. The problem is complex and challenging, as a very large number of parameters, decision variables, and constraints are involved along with a large number of estimation requirements such as those of expected demands and returns and cost criteria associated with each decision. Perhaps a combination of various tools and techniques may be combined for the purpose of formulation, approximation, analysis, and solution of such complex problems.

Developing and further improving greening strategy concepts means that it will be more beneficial for manufacturing companies to implement recycling, refurbishing, and remanufacturing operations for economic reasons alone besides meeting the consumer pressures and regulatory norms. By determining the factors that most influence a firm's greening strategy undertakings, it can concentrate its limited resources in those areas. Areas and topics such as integrated logistics for network design, under which circumstances should returns be handled, stored, transported, processed jointly with forward flows and when should they be treated separately, comparing cost of remanufacturing with cost of production from virgin materials, potential attractiveness of postponement operations in greening strategy, change in a firm's green strategy for a particular product over the course of the product's life, and modeling for situation when customer returns cannot be cost minimization model may be explored for further research.

ADDITIONAL READING

Flapper, S., Wassenhove, L. V., & Nunen, J. v. (2005). *Managing closed-loop supply chains.* Berlin/Heidelberg: Springer-Verlag. This book provides a framework for analysis and design of closed-loop supply chains including technical, organizational, planning and control, information, environmental and business economic issues, as well as the interactions between them.

Sarkis, J. (2006). *Greening the supply chain*. London: Springer-Verlag. This book is a good introduction for investigating green supply chain management. The chapters of this book include work from a number of international authors from theoretical and practical backgrounds, sharing their research and experiences in the field to promote a better understanding of the environmental influence of supply chain management.

System dynamics modeling allows researchers to specify stocks and flows of resources, and the relatedness of decisions about those resources (Forrester, 1999). Relatedness may be in the font of direct or indirect feedback loops (with or without time lags) that reinforce or dampen effects from other decisions. The process of modeling strategic decision environments compels researchers to specify assumptions and variables explicitly (Crossland & Smith, 2002).

Dynamic models can be classified as white box and black box (Forrester, 2007b). Black-box models are data driven, and comparing the forecast outcome with actual outcomes can test their validity (Forrester, 2007a). White-box models are descriptive and theory-like in that they try to explain the behavior of a system. System dynamics models, which are of the white-box type, exhibit validity if their internal structure adequately represents the issues relevant to the behavior being described. Further, the internal structure cannot be validated from an entirely objective, formal, and quantitative perspective (Burgelman & McKinney, 2006). Software designed for building system dynamic models assists in clarifying the internal logic of relationships. The responsibility for the accuracy of the description of the system that is being modeled, however, remains with the researcher (Hilmola, Helo, & Ojala, 2003). The availability of system dynamics software facilitates applying concepts, such as the supply chain, to case studies. We chose Vensim® Version 5 software for our study.

Fundamentals of greening as a competitive initiative are explained by Porter and van der Linde (1995). Three strategies in GSCM, namely reactive, proactive, and value-seeking, are suggested by van Hoek (1999) and Johnson (1998). Nasr (1997) and Gungor and Gupta (1999) discuss environmentally conscious manufacturing. Friedman (1992), Guide and Van Wassenhove (2002) and Gupta and Sharma (1996) discuss the changing role of the environmental manager. Interactions among various stakeholders on integrated GSCM and advantages that may accrue to them have been described by Gungor and Gupta (1999).

ACKNOWLEDGMENT

We would like to thank NNSFC (National Natural Science Foundation of China) for supporting Ying Su with a project (70772021), Zhanming Jin with a project (70372004), and China Postdoctoral Science Foundation for supporting Ying Su with a project (20060400077) for providing additional funding.

REFERENCES

Angell, L. C., & Klassen, R. D. (1999). Integrating environmental issues into the mainstream: An agenda for research in operations management. *Journal of Operations Management, 17*(5), 575-598.

Ashayeri, J., Heuts, R., & Jansen, A. (1996). Inventory management of repairable service parts for personal computers. *International Journal of Operational and Production Management, 16*, 74-97.

Barros, A. I., Dekker, R., & Scholten, V. (1998). A two-level network for recycling sand: A case study. *European Journal of Operational Research, 110*, 199-214.

Beamon, B. M. (1999). Designing the green supply chain. *Logistics Information Management, 12*(4), 332-342.

Bloemhof-Ruwaard, J. M., Solomon, M., & Van Wassenhove, L. N. (1996). The capacitated distribution and waste disposal problem. *European Journal of Operational Research, 88*, 490-503.

Bloemhof-Ruwaard, J. M., van Wassenhove, L. N., Gabel, H. L., & Weaver, P. M. (1996). An environmental life cycle optimization model for the European pulp and paper industry. *Omega, 20*, 615-629.

Boothroyd, G., & Alting, L. (1992). Design for assembly and disassembly. *Ann. CIRP, 41*, 625-636.

Bowen, F. E., Cousins, P. D., Lamming, R. C., & Faruk, A. C. (2001). Horses for courses. *Greener Management International, 35*, 41-60.

Bras, B., & McIntosh, M. W. (1999). Product, process, and organizational design for remanufacture: An overview of research. *Robot. Comput.-Integr. Mfg, 15*, 167-178.

Burgelman, R. A., & McKinney, W. (2006). Managing the strategic dynamics of acquisition integration: Lessons from HP and COMPAQ. *California Management Review, 48*(3), 6-27.

Carter, C. R., & Ellram, L. M. (1998). Reverse logistics: A review of the literature and framework for future investigation. *Journal of Business Logistics, 19*, 85-102.

Chinander, K. R. (2001). Aligning accountability and awareness for environmental performance in operations. *Production and Operations Management, 10*, 276-291.

Chouinard, M., D'Amours, S., & Aït-Kadi, D. (2005). Integration of reverse logistics activities within a supply chain information system. *Comput. Ind., 56*, 105-124.

Crossland, P., & Smith, F. L. (2002). Value creation in fine arts: A system dynamics model of inverse demand and information cascades. *Strategic Management Journal, 23*(5), 417-434.

De Brito, M. P., Flapper, S. D. P., & Dekker, R. (2003). *Reverse logistics: A review of case studies B2--reverse logistics: A review of case studies*. The Netherlands: Erasmus University Rotterdam.

De Koster, M. B. M., de Brito, M. P., & van de Vendel, M. (2002). How to organise return handling: An exploratory study with nine retailer warehouses. *International Journal of Retail & Distribution Management,* 30, 407-421.

Dekker, R., Fleischmann, M., Inderfurth, K., & Van Wassenhove, L. N. (2004). *Reverse logistics: Quantitative models for closed-loop supply chains B2--reverse logistics: Quantitative models for closed-loop supply chains*. Berlin: Springer-Verlag.

DePass, D. (2006). Green manufacturing gets a push. *Knight Ridder Tribune Business News*, 1.

Dickinson, D. A., Draper, C. W., Saminathan, M., Sohn, J. E., & Williams, G. (1995). Green product manufacturing. *At&T Technical Journal, 74*(6), 26-35.

Duhaime, R., Riopel, D., & Langevin, A. (2000). Value analysis and optimization of reusable containers at Canada Post. *Interfaces, 30*, 3-15.

Dyckhoff, H., Lackes, R., & Reese, J. (2003). *Supply chain management and reverse logistics B2: Supply chain management and reverse logistics*. Berlin: Springer-Verlag.

Ferrer, G. (1997a). The economics of personal computer remanufacturing. *Resources, Conservation and Recycling, 21*, 79-108.

Ferrer, G. (1997b). The economics of tire remanufacturing. *Resources, Conservation and Recycling, 19*, 221-255.

Ferrer, G., & Ayres, R. U. (2000). The impact of remanufacturing in the economy. *Ecological Economics, 32*, 413-429.

Ferrer, G., & Whybark, D. C. (2001). Material planning for a remanufacturing facility. *Production and Operations Management, 10*, 112-124.

Flapper, S. D. P., van Nunen, J. E. E., & van Wassenhove, L. N. (2005). *Managing closed-loop supply chains B2: Managing closed-loop supply chains*. Berlin: Springer-Verlag.

Fleischmann, M., Beullens, P., Bloemhof-Ruwaard, J. M., & van Wassenhove, L. N. (2001). The impact of product recovery on logistics network design. *Production & Operations Management, 10*, 156-173.

Fleischmann, M., Krikke, H. R., Dekker, R., & Flapper, S. D. P. (2000). A characterization of logistics networks for product recovery. *Omega, 28*, 653-666.

Fleischmann, M., Kuik, R., & Dekker, R. (2002). Controlling inventories with stochastic item returns: A basic model. *European Journal of Operational Research, 138*, 63-75.

Fleischmann, M., van Wassenhove, L. N., van Nunen, J. A. E. E., van der Laan, E., Dekker, R., & Bloemhof-Ruwaard, J. M. (1997). Quantitative models for reverse logistics: A review. *European Journal of Operational Research, 103*, 1-17.

Fleishmann, B., & Klose, A. (2005). *Distribution logistics B2: Distribution logistics.* Berlin: Springer-Verlag.

Forrester, J. W. (1999). *Industrial dynamics.* Waltham, MA: Pegasus Communications.

Forrester, J. W. (2007a). System dynamics: A personal view of the first fifty years [dagger]. *System Dynamics Review, 23*(2/3), 345.

Forrester, J. W. (2007b). System dynamics: The next fifty years [dagger]. *System Dynamics Review, 23*(2/3), 359.

Friedman, F. B. (1992). The changing role of the environmental manager. *Business Horizons, 35*(2), 25.

Gatenby, D. A., & Foo, G. (1990). Design for X (DFX): Key to competitive, profitable products. *AT&T Technical Journal, 69*, 2-15.

Glantschnig, W. J. (1994). Green design: An introduction to issues and challenges. *IEEE Transactions on Components, Packaging and Manufacturing Technology-Part A, 17*, 508-513.

Goggin, K., & Browne, J. (2000). Towards a taxonomy of resource recovery from end-of-life products. *Computers in Industry, 42*, 177-191.

Goldsby, T. J., & Closs, D. J. (2000). Using activity-based costing to reengineer the reverse logistics channel. *International Journal of Physical Distribution & Logistics Management, 30*, 500-514.

Graedel, T. E. (2002). Material substitution: A resource supply perspective. *Resources, Conservation and Recycling, 34*, 107-115.

Guide, V. D. R. (1997). Scheduling with priority dispatching rules and drum-buffer-rope in a recoverable manufacturing system. *International Journal Production Economics, 53*, 101-116.

Guide, V. D. R., Jr. (2000). Production planning and control for remanufacturing: Industry practice and research needs. *Journal of Operations Management, 18*, 467-483.

Guide, V. D. R., Jayaraman, V., & Srivastava, R. (1997). Repairable inventory theory: Models and applications. *European Journal of Operational Research, 102*, 1-20.

Guide, V. D. R., Jayaraman, V., & Srivastava, R. (1999). Production planning and control for remanufacturing: A state-of-the-art survey. *Robot. Comput.-Integr. Mfg, 15*, 221-230.

Guide, V. D. R., Spencer, M. S., & Srivastava, R. (1996). Are production systems ready for the green revolution? *Production and Inventory Management Journal, Fourth Quarter,* 70-78).

Guide, V. D. R., Spencer, M. S., & Srivastava, R. (1997). An evaluation of capacity planning techniques in a remanufacturing environment. *International Journal of Production Research, 35*, 67-82.

Guide, V. D. R., Jr., & Van Wassenhove, L. N. (2001). Managing product returns for remanufacturing. *Production and Operations Management, 10*, 142-155.

Guide Jr, V. D. R., & Van Wassenhove, L. N. (2002). The reverse supply chain. *Harvard Business Review, 80*(2), 25-26.

Gungor, A., & Gupta, S. M. (1999). Issues in environmentally conscious manufacturing and product recovery: A survey. *Computers & Industrial Engineering, 36*(4), 811-853.

Gupta, A. (1993). Approximate solution of a single-base multi-indentured repairable-item inventory system. *Journal of the Operational Research Society, 44*, 701-710.

Gupta, M., & Sharma, K. (1996). Environmental operations management: An opportunity for improvement. *Production and Inventory Management Journal, 37*(3), 40-46.

Haas, D. A., & Murphy, F. H. (2002). Compensating for non-homogeneity in decision-making units in data envelopment analysis. *European Journal of Operational Research, 144*, 530-554.

He, C. H., Gao, Y. H., Yang, S. H., & Edwards, D. W. (2004). Optimization of the process for recovering caprolactam from wastewater in a pulsed-sieve-plate column using green design methodologies. *Journal of Loss Prevention in the Process Industries, 17*, 195-204.

Hervani, A. A., Helms, M. M., & Sarkis, J. (2005). Performance measurement for green supply chain management. *Benchmarking, 12*(4), 330-353.

Hilmola, O.-P., Helo, P., & Ojala, L. (2003). The value of product development lead time in software startup. *System Dynamics Review, 19*(1), 75-82.

Hoek, R. I. v. (1999). From reversed logistics to green supply chains. *Supply Chain Management, 4*(3), 129.

Hu, T. L., Sheu, J. B., & Huang, K. H. (2002). Reverse logistics cost minimization model for the treatment of hazardous wastes. *Transportation Research, Part E: Logistics and Transportation Review, 38*, 457-473.

Hui, I. K., Chan, A. H. S., & Pun, K. F. (2001). A study of the environmental management system implementation practices. *Journal of Cleaner Production, 9*, 269-276.

Inderfurth, K., de Kok, A. G., & Flapper, S. D. P. (2001). Product recovery in stochastic remanufacturing system with multiple reuse options. *European Journal of Operational Research, 133*, 130-152.

Inderfurth, K., & van der Laan, E. (2001). Leadtime effects and policy improvement for stochastic inventory control with remanufacturing. *International Journal of Production Economics, 71*, 381-390.

Jahre, M. (1995). Household waste collection as a reverse channel: A theoretical perspective. *International Journal Physical Distribution and Logistics Management, 25*, 39-46.

Jayaraman, V., Guide, V. D. R., & Srivastava, R. (1999). A closed-loop logistics model for remanufacturing. *Journal of the Operational Research Society, 50*, 497-508.

Jayaraman, V., Patterson, R. A., & Rolland, E. (2003). The design of reverse distribution networks: Models and solution procedures. *European Journal of Operational Research, 150*, 128-149.

Jayaraman, V., & Srivastava, R. (1995). A service logistics model for simultaneous siting of facilities and multiple levels of equipment. *Computers and Operations Research, 22*, 191-204.

Jayaraman, V., Srivastava, R., & Benton, W. C. (1998). A joint optimization of product variety and ordering approach. *Computers & Operations Research, 25*, 557-566.

Johnson, P. F. (1998). Managing value in reverse logistics systems. *Logistics and Transportation Review, 34*, 217-227.

Johnson, M. R., & Wang, M. H. (1995). Planning product disassembly of material recovery opportunities. *International Journal of Production Research, 33*, 3119-3142.

Kainuma, Y., & Tawara, N. (2006). A multiple attribute utility theory approach to lean and green supply chain management. *International Journal of Production Economics, 101*, 99-108.

Kaiser, B., Eagan, P., & Shaner, H. (2001). Solutions to health care waste: Lifecycle thinking and "green" purchasing. *Environmental Health Perspectives, 109*, 205-208.

Khoo, H., Spedding, T. A., Bainbridge, I. e. D. M. R., & Taplin. (2001). Creating a green supply chain. *Greener Management International, 35*, 71-88.

Kiesmuller, G. P., & Scherer, C. W. (2003). Computational issues in a stochastic finite horizon one product recovery inventory model. *European Journal of Operational Research, 146*, 553-579.

Kiesmuller, G. P., & van der Laan, E. A. (2001). An inventory model with dependent product demands and returns. *International Journal of Production Economics, 72*, 73-87.

Klassen, R. D. (2001). Plant level environmental management orientation: The influence of management views and plant characteristics. *Production and Operations Management, 10*, 257-275.

Klausner, M., & Hendrickson, C. T. (2000). Reverse logistics strategy for product take-back. *Interfaces, 30*, 156-165.

Krikke, H., Bloemhof-Ruwaard, J., & Van Wassenhove, L. N. (2003). Concurrent product and closed-loop supply chain design with an application to refrigerators. *International Journal Prod. Res., 41*, 3689-3719.

Krikke, H. R., Harten, A. V., & Schuur, P. C. (1998). On a medium term product recovery and disposal strategy for durable assembly products. *International Journal Prod. Res., 36*, 111-139.

Krikke, H. R., van Harten, A., & Schuur, P. C. (1999a). Business case Oce: Reverse logistic network re-design for copiers. *OR Spectrum, 21*, 381-409.

Krikke, H. R., van Harten, A., & Schuur, P. C. (1999b). Business case Roteb: Recovery strategies for monitors. *Computers & Industrial Engineering, 36*, 739-757.

Kroll, E., Beardsley, B., & Parulian, A. (1996). A methodology to evaluate ease of disassembly for product recycling. *IIE Transactions, 28*, 837-845.

Kroon, L., & Vrijens, G. (1995). Returnable containers: An example of reverse logistics. *International Journal of Physical Distribution & Logistics Management, 25*, 56-68.

Krumwiede, D. W., & Sheu, C. (2002). A model for reverse logistics entry by third-party providers. *Omega, 30*, 322-333.

Laperiere, L., & El Maraghy, H. A. (1992). Planning of products assembly and disassembly. *Annals of the CIRP, 41*, 5-9.

Lee, J. J., O'Callaghan, P., & Allen, D. (1995). Critical review of life cycle analysis and assessment techniques and their application to commercial activities. *Conservation and Recycling, 13*, 37-56.

Linton, J. D., & Johnston, D. A. (2000). A decision support system for the planning of remanufacturing at Nortel. *Interfaces, 30*, 17-31.

Listes, O., & Dekker, R. (2005). A stochastic approach to a case study for product recovery network design. *European Journal of Operational Research, 160*, 268-287.

Louwers, D., Kip, B. J., Peters, E., Souren, F., & Flapper, S. W. P. (1999). A facility location allocation model for reusing carpet materials. *Computers & Industrial Engineering, 36*, 855-869.

Madu, C. N., Kuei, C., & Madu, I. E. (2002). A hierarchic metric approach for integration of green issues in manufacturing: A paper recycling application. *Journal of Environmental Management, 64*, 261-272.

Majumder, P., Groenevelt, H., & Summer. (2001). Competition in remanufacturing. *Production and Operations Management, 10*, 125-141.

Marin, A., & Pelegrin, B. (1998). The return plant location problem: Modeling and resolution. *European Journal of Operational Research, 104*, 375-392.

Marx-Gomez, J., Rantenstrauch, C., Nurnberger, A., & Kruse, R. (2002). Neuro-fuzzy approach to forecast returns of scrapped product to recycling and remanufacturing. *Knowledge-Based Systems, 15*, 119-128.

Meade, L., & Sarkis, J. (2002). A conceptual model for selecting and evaluating third-party reverse logistics providers. *Supp. Chain Manag. Int. J., 7*, 283-295.

Melissen, F. W., & de Ron, A. J. (1999). Defining recovery practices: Definitions and terminology. *International Journal on Environmentally Conscious Manufacturing and Design, 8*, 1-18.

Min, H., & Galle, W. P. (2001). Green purchasing practices of U.S. firms. *International Journal of Operations and Production Management, 21*, 1222-1238.

Min, H., Ko, J. H., & Ko, S. C. (2006). A genetic algorithm approach to developing the multi-echelon reverse logistics network for product returns. *Omega, 34*, 56-69.

Minner, S. (2001). Strategic safety stocks in reverse logistics supply chains. *International Journal of Production Economics, 71*, 417-428.

Moore, K. E., Gungor, A., & Gupta, S. M. (1998). A petri net approach to disassembly process planning. *Comp. Indus. Engin., 35*, 165-168.

Moore, K. E., Gungor, A. K., & Gupta, S. M. (2001). Petri net approach to disassembly process planning for products with complex AND/OR precedence relationships. *European Journal of Operational Research, 135*, 428-449.

Mostard, J., & Teunter, R. (2006). The newsboy problem with resalable returns: A single period model and case study. *European Journal of Operational Research, 169*, 81-96.

Mourao, M. C., & Amado, L. (2005). Heuristics method for a mixed capacitated arc routing problem: A refuse collection application. *European Journal of Operational Research, 160*, 139-153.

Mukhopadhyay, S. K., & Setoputro, R. (2005). Optimal return policy and modular design for build-to-order products. *Journal of Operations Management, 23*, 496-506.

Nagel, C., & Meyer, P. (1999). Caught between ecology and economy: End-of-life aspects of environmentally conscious manufacturing. *Comput. Ind. Eng., 36*, 781-792.

Nagurney, A., & Toyasaki, F. (2005). Reverse supply chain management and electronic waste recycling: A multitiered network equilibrium framework for e-cycling. *Transportation Re-*

search Part E: Logistics and Transportation Review, 41, 1-28.

Nasr, N. (1997). Environmentally conscious manufacturing. *Careers and the Engineer*, 26-27.

Navinchandra, D. (1991). Design for environmentally. *Desig Theor. Methodol, 31*, 99-125.

Neely, A., Mills, J., Platts, K., Richards, H., Gregory, M., Bourne, M., et al. (2000). Performance measurement system design: Developing and testing a process-based approach. *International Journal of Operations & Production Management, 20*(10), 1119-1145.

Nimse, P., Vijayan, A., Kumar, A., & Varadarajan, C. (2007). A review of green product databases. *Environmental Progress, 26*(2), 131-137.

Owen, J. V. (1993). Environmentally conscious manufacturing. *Manufacturing Engineering, 111*(4), 44.

Pochampally, K. K., & Gupta, S. M. (2005). Strategic planning of a reverse supply chain network. *International Journal of Integrated Supply Management (IJISM), 1*(4), 421-441.

Porter, M. E., & van der Linde, C. (1995a). Green and competitive: Ending the stalemate. *Harvard Business Review, 73*(5), 120-134.

Porter, M. E., & van der Linde, C. (1995b). Toward a new conception of the environment: Competitiveness relationship. *Journal of Economic Perspectives, 9*(4), 97-118.

Ravi, V., Shankar, R., & Tiwari, M. K. (2005). Analyzing alternatives in reverse logistics for end-of-life computers: ANP and balanced scorecard approach. *Computers and Industrial Engineering, 48*, 327-356.

Rentmeester, K. (2005). Green manufacturing. *Marketplace, 17*(4), 26.

Richter, K. (1996). The EOQ repair and waste disposal model with variable setup numbers. *European Journal of Operational Research, 95*, 313-324.

Richter, K., & Dobos, I. (1999). Analysis of the EOQ repair and waste disposal problem with integer setup. *International Journal of Production Economics, 59*, 463-467.

Richter, K., & Sombrutzki, M. (2000). Remanufacturing planning for the reverse Wagner/Whitin models. *European Journal of Operational Research, 121*, 304-315.

Richter, K., & Weber, J. (2001). The reverse Wagner/Whitin model with variable manufacturing and remanufacturing cost. *International Journal of Production Economics, 71*, 447-456.

Ritchie, L., Burnes, B., Whittle, P., & Hey, R. (2000). The benefits of reverse logistics: The case of the Manchester Royal Infirmary Pharmacy. *Supply Chain Management, 5*, 226 233.

Sarkis, J. (1998). Evaluating environmentally conscious business practices. *European Journal of Operational Research, 107*, 159-174.

Sarkis, J. (1999). A methodological framework for evaluating environmentally conscious manufacturing programs. *Comput. Ind. Eng., 36*, 793-810.

Sarkis, J. (2001). *Greener manufacturing and operations: From design to delivery and back B2: Greener manufacturing and operations: From design to delivery and back*. Sheffield: Greenleaf.

Sarkis, J., & Cordeiro, J. J. (2001). An empirical evaluation of environmental efficiencies and firm performance: Pollution prevention versus end-of-pipe practice. *European Journal of Operational Research, 135*, 102-113.

Savaskan, R. C., Bhattacharya, S., & Van Wassenhove, L. N. (2004). Closed loop supply chain models with product remanufacturing. *Management Science, 50*, 239-252.

Scherpereel, C., van Koppen, C. S. A., & Heering, G. B. F. (2001). Selecting environmental performance indicators. *Greener Management International, 33*, 97-114.

Scheuring, J., Bras, B. A., & Lee, K. M. (1994). Significance of design for disassembly on integrated disassembly and assembly processes. *International Journal of Environmentally Conscious Design and Manufacturing, 3*, 21-23.

Seliger, G., Zussman, E., & Kriwet, A. (1994). Integration of recycling considerations into product design: A system approach. In S. Y. Nof (Ed.), *Information and collaboration models of integration-based on the NATO research workshop on integration, Il Crocco, Italy. Dordrecht, The Netherlands: Kluwer Academic.*

Sheu, J. B., Chou, Y. H., & Hu, C. C. (2005). An integrated logistics operational model for green supply chain management. *Transportation Research Part E, 41*, 287-313.

Shih, L. H. (2001). Reverse logistics system planning for recycling electrical appliances and computers in Taiwan. *Resour. Conserv. Recycl., 32*, 55-72.

Spicer, A. J., & Johnson, M. R. (2004). Third-party demanufacturing as a solution for extended producer responsibility. *Journal of Cleaner Production, 12*, 37-45.

Srivastava, S. K. (2007). Green supply-chain management: A state-of-the-art literature review. *International Journal of Management Reviews, 9*(1), 53-80.

Srivastava, S. K., & Srivastava, R. K. (2005). Profit driven reverse logistics. *International Journal of Business Research, 4*, 53-61.

Srivastava, S. K., & Srivastava, R. K. (2006). Managing product returns for reverse logistics. *International Journal of Physical Distribution and Logistics Management (Special Issue on 3PL, 4PL and Reverse Logistics), 36*, 524-546.

Swenseth, S., & Godfrey, M. (2002). Incorporating transportation costs into inventory replenishment decisions. *International Journal of Production Economics, 77*, 113-130.

Taleb, K. N., & Gupta, S. M. (1997). Disassembly of multiple product structures. *Comput. Ind. Engng, 32*, 949-961.

Tan, A. W. K., Yu, W. S., & Kumar, A. (2002). Improving the performance of a computer company in supporting its reverse logistics operations in the Asia-Pacific region. *International Journal of Physical Distribution & Logistics Management, 33*, 59-74.

Theyel, G. (2001). Customer and supplier relations for environmental performance. *Greener Management International, 35*, 61-69.

Van der Laan, E., Dekker, R., & Salomon, M. (1996). Product remanufacturing and disposal: A numerical comparison of alternative control strategies. *International Journal of Production Economics, 45*, 489-498.

Van der Laan, E., Dekker, R., Salomon, M., & Ridder, A. (1996). An (s, Q) inventory model with remanufacturing and disposal. *International Journal of Production Economics, 46*, 339-350.

van der Laan, E., & Salomon, M. (1997). Production planning and inventory control with remanufacturing and disposal. *European Journal of Operational Research, 102*, 264-278.

van der Laan, E., Salomon, M., & Dekker, R. (1999). An investigation of lead-time effects in manufacturing/remanufacturing systems under simple PUSH and PULL control strategies. *European Journal of Operational Research, 115*, 195-214.

van der Laan, E., Salomon, M., Dekker, R., & van Wassenhove, L. (1999). Inventory control in hybrid systems with remanufacturing. *Management Science, 45*, 733-747.

Van Hoek, R. I. (1999). From reversed logistics to green supply chains. *Supply Chain Management, 4*, 129-135.

Vincent, M. (2006). China's manufacturing capability steadily ramping, going 'green'. *Connector Specifier, 22*(5), 1-2.

Vlachos, D., Georgiadis, P., & Iakovou, E. (2007). A system dynamics model for dynamic capacity planning of remanufacturing in closed-loop supply chains. *Computers & Operations Research, 34*(2), 367.

Vlachos, D., & Tagaras, G. (2001). An inventory system with two supply modes and capacity constraints. *International Journal of Production Economics, 72*, 41-58.

Wagner, M., Schaltegger, S., & Wehrmeyer, W. (2001). The relationship between the environmental and economic performance of firms: What does theory propose and what does empirical evidence tell us? *Greener Management International, 34*, 95-108.

Warren, J. P., Rhodes, E., & Carter, R. (2001). A total product system concept. *Greener Management International, 35*, 89-104.

White, C. D., Masanet, E., Rosen, C. M., & Beckman, S. L. (2003). Product recovery with some byte: An overview of management challenges and environmental consequences in reverse manufacturing for the computer industry. *Journal of Cleaner Production, 11*, 445-458.

Zhang, H. C., Kuo, T. C., Lu, H., & Huang, S. H. (1997). Environmentally conscious design and manufacturing: A state-of-the-art survey. *Journal Mfg Systems, 16*, 352-371.

Zhu, Q. H., Geng, Y., & Spring. (2002). Integrating environmental issues into supplier selection and manage management: A study of large and medium-sized stateowned enterprises in China. *Greener Management International, 35*, 27-40.

Zhu, Q. H., & Sarkis, J. (2004). Relationships between operational practices and performance among early adopters of green supply chain management practices in Chinese manufacturing enterprises. *Journal of Operations Management, 22*(3), 265-289.

Chapter XV
A Vehicle Routing and Scheduling Model for a Distribution Center

Hsiao-Fan Wang
National Tsing Hua University, ROC

Yu-Chun Chiu
National Tsing Hua University, ROC

ABSTRACT

One key role along green supply chain is the distribution center which has the responsibility to deliver the commodities to the customers and collect the end-used products back to the center for further process. This activity requires a distributor to determine how many vehicles with what sizes along which routes to deliver commodities so that the demands from all customers will be satisfied within customers' available time with minimum operation cost. This problem can be classified into a vehicle routing and scheduling problem with multiple vehicle types and service time windows. In practice, the complexity of the problem requires a structural model to facilitate general analysis and applications. However, also because of its complexity, an efficient solution procedure is equivalently important. Therefore, in this study, we have first developed a model for a distribution center to support the decisions on vehicle types and numbers; as well as the routing route and schedule so that the overall operation cost will be minimized. Since this model of vehicle routing and scheduling problem with multiple vehicle types and multiple time windows (VRSP-MVMT) is a nondeterministic polynomial time (NP)-hard problem, we have developed a genetic algorithm (GA) for efficient solution. The efficiency and accuracy of the algorithm will be evaluated and illustrated with numerical examples.

Copyright © 2009, IGI Global, distributing in print or electronic forms without written permission of IGI Global is prohibited.

INTRODUCTION

In 1959, Dantzig and Ramser investigated the truck dispatching problem (TDP) and were considered the pioneers of the vehicle routing problem (VRP). VRP considers a given vehicle with limited or unlimited capacity which deliveries (homogenous) products from a distribution center to a set of customers with known demands. For a green supply chain, this activity is in particular emphasized by its function of recycling. The delivering planning process must take into consideration the best possible route to satisfy these customers and the environmental impact.

The VRP has many characteristics, including the information of the demand, vehicle fleet, crew requirement, and data requirement. All of these further complicate an already complicated problem, with a multitude of solutions being put forward. VRP is like the intermediate state between sophisticated theory and the real world. On one hand, we have many mathematical models proposed by many scholars to deal with different requirements. On the other hand, they have been applied to many different practical situations such as postal delivery, transportation of the handicapped, product distribution, and others. Vehicle routing problem plays an important role in green logistic management, because money distribution and green legislation go hand in hand with physical distribution. Purchasing vehicles and planning the routes of those vehicles are the most important factors affecting the cost of a physical distribution. Therefore, the number of vehicles a company needs and how to arrange the vehicle routing remain the main issues for a distribution company. In this study, we will concentrate on these two problems.

The 3R (Recycling, Reuse, and Reduction) activities in the green market keep increasing, and as a result not only the original delivery and dispatching of forward distribution need to be considered, but also the collection and recycling of reverse routing have to be planned. The prime consideration for finding an answer to the VRP is to minimize the total traveling cost and at the same time satisfy the demands of the customers. Over the years, many methods have been developed.

In this study, we investigate the combined vehicle routing and scheduling problem (VRSP). VRSP can be thought of as routing problems with the additional constraints of various activities having to be carried out within a certain time limit. However, from our observations of the operations of distribution companies, the existing model with a single time window allowance is insufficient for dealing with a competitive market. Therefore, a more flexible and more realistic model is needed for a wider range of applications.

Based on the above motivation, this study considers a vehicle routing and scheduling model with multiple vehicle types and multiple time windows (VRSP-MVMT). We will determine how to dispatch a limited number of multiple vehicle types from a distributional center to a set of customers and return to the center. Each of these customers will be offered two time intervals for receiving the services. Because each customer can set two time intervals for receiving the services, there are four possible time pairs that occur, and time windows combination cost is incurred accordingly. The first time pair (1,1) means time window 1 of former customer combines time window 1 of next customer. The second time pair (1,2) means time window 1 of former customer combines time window 2 of next customer. The third time pair (2,1) means time window 2 of former customer combines time window 1 of next customer. The final time pair (2,2) means time window 2 of former customer combines the time windows 2 of next customer. The vehicles will have to return to the center after delivery. This study will investigate the minimum operation cost including vehicles dispatched cost, traveling cost, and time window combination cost.

Although VRSP-MVMT is a relaxed variation of VRSP, the problem is not easy to formulate and remains difficult to solve. When the size of the problem increases, the solution time increases exponentially. Therefore, apart from developing a mathematical model, we shall propose an efficient solution procedure in this study.

In summary, the main purposes of our study can be outlined as follows:

1. To develop a model of VRSP-MVMT, and investigate its properties.
2. To transform the model into a simple and computational form.
3. To develop an algorithm for the proposed model and obtain a near-optimal solution at a reasonable computation time.
4. To evaluate the proposed model and algorithm on both accuracy and efficiency with existing benchmark problems.

LITERATURE REVIEW

In this session, existing research regarding vehicle routing and scheduling problems with their solutions will be reviewed.

Vehicle Routing and Scheduling Problems (VRSP)

VRSP has been studied for almost 50 years. It is an issue central to the successful management of an efficient and effective physical distribution industry.

Many models have been developed based on the factors concerned and their combinations, such as the number of depots, the number of vehicles with limited or unlimited capacities, deterministic (known) demands, directed or undirected networks, and with or without a routing time constraint. In addition, the vehicle routing problem with time window (VRP-TW) (Bodin, Golden, Assad, & Ball, 1983), and the multiple-depot vehicle routing problem (MD-VRP) (Bodin et al., 1983) all are commonly applied. Table 1 lists the related issues with references.

SOLUTION APPROACH

Due to the complexity of VRP and its variation, different solution approaches have been developed in the literature. Among them, most heuristic algorithms have shown their potential in solving a high degree of complicated problems. A meta-heuristic refers to a master strategy that guides and modifies other heuristic to produce solutions beyond those that are normally generated in a quest for local optimality (Russell & Igo, 1997).

Genetic Algorithm

Genetic algorithm (GA), an evolutionary-based mechanism for solving an optimization problem, was developed by John Holland, his colleagues, and his students at the University of Michigan in the U.S. GA are based on the mechanics of natural selection and natural genetics, derived from Darwinian evolution to create populations from generation to generation. Each generation consists of several chromosomes and each chromosome represents solution to the problem. Using three main operators of reproduction, crossover, and mutation, GA differs from conventional optimization and search produces in several fundamental ways and has four advantages to solve problem with more robustness than other mechanisms.

1. GA works with a coding of solution set, not the solutions themselves.
2. GA search from a population of solutions, not a single solution.
3. GA use payoff information (fitness, function), not derivatives or other auxiliary knowledge.
4. GA use probabilistic transition rules, not deterministic rules.

Table 1. Characteristics of routing and scheduling problems

Subject	Characteristics	Possible Options
SUPPLY	1. Size of Available Fleet	□One vehicle (Bodin, 19A83, Russell , 1979) □Multiple vehicles (Bertsimas & Ryzin, 1993, Gillett & Miller, 1974)
	2.Type of Available Fleet	□Homogeneous (only one vehicle type) (Dantzig & Ramser, 1959, Russell , 1979) □Heterogeneous (multiple vehicle types) (Bertsimas & Ryzin, 1993, Gillett & Miller, 1974) □Special vehicle types (compartmentalized, etc.) (Bodin & Berman, 1979)
	3.Housing of Vehicle	□Single depot (domicile)(Dror & Trudeau,1989) □Multiple depots(Chao, et al.,1993)
	4.Vehicle Capacity Restrictions	□Imposed(all the same) (Dantzig & Ramser, 1959, Russell , 1979) □Imposed (different vehicle capacities) (Bertsimas & Ryzin, 1993, Gillett & Miller, 1974) □Not imposed (unlimited capacity) (Bodin, 1983)
	5.Maximum Route Times	□Imposed (same for all routes)(Ho & Haugland, 2004) □Imposed (different for different routes)(Dror, et al, 1989)
	6.Operations	□Pickups only (Fabri & Recht, 2006) □Drop-offs (deliveries) only(Bodin, 1983) □Mixed (pick ups and deliveries) (Bodin, 1983) □Split deliveries (allowed or disallowed) (Dror & Trudeau, 1989; Dror & Trudeau, 1990)
DEMAND	7.Nature of Demands	□Deterministic (known) demands(Ho & Haugland, 2004, Russell , 1979) □Stochastic demand requirements(Berger & Barkaoui, 2004; Bertsimas & Ryzin, 1993] □Partial satisfaction of demand allowed(Dror & Trudeau, 1989; Dror & Trudeau, 1990)
	8.Location of Demands 9.Service Time	□At nodes (not necessarily all)(Chao, et al.,1993) □ On arcs (not necessarily all) (Golden &Wong, 1981) □mixed(Bertsimas & Ryzin, 1993) □ One time window(Solomon, 1987)
NETWORKS	10.Underlying Network	□Undirected(Lin & Kerninghan, (1973), □Directed(Ho & Haugland, 2004) □Grid(Frizzell & Giffin, 1995) □Euclidean(Bertsimas & Ryzin, 1993)
	11. Reverse	□Design(Jayaraman & Rolland., 2003;Tang & Xie, 2007) □Management(Blackburn, et al, 2004; Krikke, et al, 2004)
COST	12.Costs	□Variable or routing costs(Dror, et al, 1989) □Fixed operating or vehicle acquisition costs (Russell , 1979) □Common carrier costs (for unserviced demands) (Bertsimas & Ryzin, 1993)
	13.Objectives	□Minimize total routing costs(Ho & Haugland, 2004) □Minimize sum of fixed and variable costs (Christofides et al.,1981) □Minimize number of vehicles required (Gillett & Johnson, 1976) □Maximize utility function based on service or convenience (Dror & Trudeau, 1989) □Maximize utility function based on customer priorities(Frizzell & Giffin, 1995)

Owing to these four advantages, GA can find solutions efficiently and effectively. Although many random schemes are used, GA cannot guarantee an optimal solution, yet it has shown its ability in finding near-optimal solutions.

Tabu Search

The basic concept of Tabu Search (TS) as described by Glover (1977) is

a meta-heuristic superimposed on another heuristic. The overall approach is to avoid entrainment in cycles by forbidding or penalizing moves which take the solution, in the next iteration, to points in the solution space previously visited (hence tabu).

TS is still actively researched, and is continuing to evolve and improve (Barbarosoglu & Ozgur, 1999).

TS begins by marching to a local minimum. To avoid retracing the steps used, the method records recent moves in one or more Tabu lists. The original intent of the list was not to prevent a previous move from being repeated, but rather to ensure that it was not reversed. The Tabu lists are historical in nature and form TS memory. The role of the memory can change as the algorithm proceeds. By this, the algorithm forces other solutions to be explored.

Comparison of These Two Meta-Heuristics

Now, most of references use either TS or GA to solve VRP and its extensions. At this subsection, we summarize their features in comparison manner in Table 2.

DISCUSSION AND SUMMARY

Starting with the first vehicle routing problem, many scholars carried out research and reported their related algorithm. Because the solutions to vehicle routing and scheduling problems are always an adjusted or a relaxed version in order to respond to the rapidly changing socio-economic environment, the related VRSP study remains open to continual research. In our study, we introduce a limited number of multiple vehicle types, multiple time windows, and a single depot, so as to represent a green logistic and distribution application.

Table 2. Comparison of TS, GA, and exact procedure

	Reference	Characteristics	
Tabu Search	(Eric & Philippe, 1997; Hillier & Lieberman, 2001; Ho & Haugland, 2004)	Features	1. Tabu list, Memory; 2. neighborhood exchange slowly;
		Disadvantages	3. cannot set the proper size of tabu list; 4. cannot guarantee to get the optimal solution;
		Advantages	5. It is possible to break out of local minima; 6.elapsed time is fast for solving large-scale problem.
Genetic Algorithm	Berger & Barkaoui, 2004; Lacomme , et al., 2006; Mitsuo & Runwei, 1997)	Features	1. Reproduction, Crossover, Mutation;
		Disadvantages	2. cannot guarantee to get the optimal solution;
		Advantages	3. It is possible to break out of local minima; 4. elapsed time is fast for solving large-scale problem.
Exact Procedures	(Bodin, 1982; Christofides, et al., 1981)	Features	1. liner programming problem;
		Disadvantages	2.elapsed time is longer for solving large-scale problem;
		Advantages	3. guarantee to get the optimal solution.

Since considering these factors may reduce dispatching cost and traveling costs, and provide increased appropriate time window combinations for more customer satisfaction, we researched the related literatures. In the next section, we develop a model to cope with these factors simultaneously in order to facilitate flexible and effective routing and collecting scheduling.

Distribution Model

Time windows are a natural occurrence in problems faced by business organizations that must work on a fixed time schedule. This problem must be taken into consideration when scheduling vehicles, becomes the distribution center schedules vehicles to serve customers at specific time intervals. In other words, each location may require delivery at its own specified time. Thus, from a temporal aspect, vehicle movements must be planned precisely. The feasibility to do so is influenced by both space and time characteristics. For example, a vehicle just serves one location with an identical delivery time. This is why that particular time window does not exist in the VRP field.

In 1985, Solomon (1985) developed an algorithm to be considered in the design and analysis for VRP-TW. At the same time, he designed a problem set that included vehicle limited capacity, one distributional center, 100 customers as a set, given demand for each customer, known locations of customers, and the time interval for each customer. This model is comparatively more realistic and is used as a benchmark for VRP-SD.

Based on the literature review above, in this study, we consider a VRSP-MVMT problem for more realistic and wider applications. The problem specifically states that a fleet of multicapacitated vehicle types from a depot delivery, a given amount of homogenous products to a set of customers at one of the required two time intervals, and return to the depot with minimum operation cost which includes dispatching cost, traveling distance cost, and time windows combination cost.

In this section we shall formulate this problem into a VRSP-MVMT model, after defining the notation that is used throughout the chapter. Then, we shall use two examples modified from Solomon's data (Solomon, 1985) to illustrate our model.

For our study, all instances we modified are from Solomon of R109 (Solomon, 1985), which are widely used both for exact and heuristic methods applied to the VRP-TW. However, the benchmark data didn't include the second time window, and therefore we randomly generate it for VRSP- MVMT. Besides, the objective function for VRP-TW is to minimize the distance only; which is not sufficient to reflect the real situation. Therefore, the proposed model is aimed to minimize total operational costs, including vehicles' dispatched costs, traveling distance cost, and time windows cost.

First, we define the problem under study, and the notation used throughout the chapter.

Customer: A set, C, is given by n locations each with demand w_i, another set, N, is given by $n+1$ locations including depot. In the following model, we use number 0 to represent depot. $(coordx_i, coordy_i)$ denotes the geographical coordinates of customer i. Every pair of locations (i, j) where $i, j = 1...n$ and $i \neq j$, is associated with a traveling cost measured by distance d_{ij} and traveling time t_{ij}. Every customer i has a demand $w_i > 0$.

Vehicles: A set, V, vehicles with various capacities, is given. In this study, three types of the vehicles are considered. There are *large* vehicle $V_l, l = 1...L$ with capacity P_l and dispatching cost g_l; *medium* vehicle $V_m, m = L+1..., M$, with capacity P_m and dispatching cost g_m; and *small* vehicle $V_S, s = M+1...V$, with capacity P_s and dispatching cost g_s. Therefore, total fleet is $V = \{V_l\} \cup \{V_m\} \cup \{V_s\}$ and total capacity is $P = \{P_l\} \cup \{P_m\} \cup \{P_s\}$.

Time windows: Each customer i has two available time windows, as T_{1i}=[a_{1i}, b_{1i}], and T_{2i}=[a_{2i}, b_{2i}]. A vehicle can serve customer i at each of the two time windows. The depot also has a time window [a_0, b_0] which shows that vehicles can leave the depot no earlier than a_0, and return no later than b_0.

Without loss of generality, in this study, T_{1i} is preferred to T_{2i}. In other words, if we deliver goods for customer j after customer i, the order of consideration of the available time pairs is: (T_{1i}, T_{1j}) $\succ$ (T_{1i}, T_{2j}) $\succ$ (T_{2i}, T_{1j}) $\succ$ (T_{2i}, T_{2j}). This can be fulfilled by assigning a respective weight e_u, $u = 1,2,3,4$ such that $e_1 > e_2 > e_3 > e_4$ for cost minimization objective. One of these four time pairs will be decided to serve customer j after customer i. The decision variables $y_{1j}, y_{2j}, y_{3j}, y_{4j}$ are defined respectively such that for each u, if

$$y_{uj} = \begin{cases} 1, \text{ the } u^{th} \text{time pair of customer } j \text{ will not be chosen.} \\ 0, \text{ otherwise} \end{cases}$$

For each arc (i, j), where $i, j \in$ C, $i \neq j$, and for each vehicle k, we define x_{ijk} as

$$x_{ijk} = \begin{cases} 1, \text{ if vehicle } k \text{ traverses directly from customer } i \text{ to customer } j \\ 0, \text{otherwise} \end{cases}$$

Let the decision variable s_{1ik}, s_{2ik} denotes the first and the second time window, a vehicle k starts to serve customer i respectively. And we assume $s_{0k} = a_0$ for all k.

Model for VRSP-MVMT

Our model—VRSP-MVMT explores the relaxation version of VRSP. The additional features constructed in our model include: limited number of vehicles, different vehicle types with limited capacity and multiple time windows. The objective of VRSP-MCMT is to minimize the total traveling cost when we assign a fleet of vehicles and plan the vehicle scheduling to serve the set of customers at one of two specific time windows. Then, the VRSP-MVMT can be stated mathematically as shown in Exhibit 1.

The first term of objective function presents dispatching cost when vehicle leaves the depot, the second term presents the traveling cost when vehicle service customer j directly after customer i, and the third term presents time windows combination cost. Formula (2) states that the prerequisite for vehicle k to service customer j directly after customer i is that it must leave the depot. Formula (3) states no vehicle can stagnate some customer. Formula (4) says that a customer can only be serviced by one single vehicle. Formula (5) says that not all vehicles are forced to leave the depot, because it depends on total demand and (6) states that no vehicle delivers more goods than its capacity. Formulae (7.1)~(7.4) are time window constraints that a vehicle k cannot arrive at customer j before $s_{1k} + t_j$ or $s_{2k} + t_j$ if it is traveling directly from customer i to customer j. The constants K and M are sufficiently large numbers and the decision variables $y_{1j} \sim y_{4j}$ present all time-window combinations of which only one works as shown in Formula (8). Formulae (9.1) and (9.3) say that customer j only can choose the time-window combination 1 or 2 if customer i already selected time- window combination 1 or 3. Similarly, Formulae (9.2) and (9.4) restrict customer j to choose only the time-window combination 3 or 4 if customer i already selected time windows combination situation 2 or 4. Formulae (10.1.1) ~(10.2.3) make sure that the service time of customer j falls in s_{1jk}, s_{2jk} in a continuous manner. Formulae (11.1) and (11.2) force every vehicle to arrive at the depot before the depot's time window is closed. Formulae (13) and (14) state that whenever vehicle k starts to serve customer i it has to be a time window specified by customer i.

The number of decision variables included into this model is $4C + 2CV + NCV$ and that of constraints is $2C + 3V + 8CV + 4NCV + 9C(C-1)V + N(N-1)V$.

Exhibit 1. Model of VRSP-MVMT

$$\textbf{Min } z(x) = \sum_{j\in C}\sum_{k\in V}(g_k x_{0jk}) + \sum_{k\in V}\sum_{i\in N}\sum_{j\in N}(d_{ij}x_{ijk}) + \sum_{u=1}^{4}\sum_{j\in C}(e_u y_{uj}) \quad (1)$$

$$\textbf{Subject to } \sum_{i\in C}\sum_{j\in C} x_{ijk} \le \sum_{h\in C} M(x_{0hk}) \qquad \forall k\in V \quad (2)$$

$$\sum_{i\in N} x_{ihk} - \sum_{j\in N} x_{hjk} = 0 \qquad \forall h\in C, \forall k\in V \quad (3)$$

$$\sum_{k\in V}\sum_{i\in N} x_{ijk} = 1 \qquad \forall j\in C \quad (4)$$

$$\sum_{j\in C} x_{0jk} \le 1 \qquad \forall k\in V \quad (5)$$

$$\sum_{i\in C}\sum_{j\in C} w_i x_{ijk} \le p_k \qquad \forall k\in V \quad (6)$$

$$s_{1ik} + t_{ij} - K\,(1-x_{ijk}) \le s_{1jk} + My_{1j} \qquad \forall j\in C, \forall i\in N, \forall k\in V \quad (7.1)$$

$$s_{1ik} + t_{ij} - K\,(1-x_{ijk}) \le s_{2jk} + My_{2j} \qquad \forall j\in C, \forall i\in N, \forall k\in V \quad (7.2)$$

$$s_{2ik} + t_{ij} - K\,(1-x_{ijk}) \le s_{1jk} + My_{3j} \qquad \forall j\in C, \forall i\in N, \forall k\in V \quad (7.3)$$

$$s_{2ik} + t_{ij} - K\,(1-x_{ijk}) \le s_{2jk} + My_{4j} \qquad \forall j\in C, \forall i\in N, \forall k\in V \quad (7.4)$$

$$y_{1j}, y_{2j}, y_{3j}, y_{4j} = 0 \text{ or } 1$$

$$\sum_{j\in C}(y_{1j} + y_{2j} + y_{3j} + y_{4j}) = 3 \qquad \forall j\in C \quad (8)$$

$$1 - M(x_{ijk} - y_{1i} - 1) \ge y_{1j} + y_{2j} \ge 1 + M(x_{ijk} - y_{1i} - 1) \qquad \forall i\in C, \forall j\in C, \forall k\in V \quad (9.1)$$

$$1 - M(x_{ijk} - y_{2i} - 1) \ge y_{3j} + y_{4j} \ge 1 + M(x_{ijk} - y_{2i} - 1) \qquad \forall i\in C, \forall j\in C, \forall k\in V \quad (9.2)$$

$$1 - M(x_{ijk} - y_{3i} - 1) \ge y_{1j} + y_{2j} \ge 1 + M(x_{ijk} - y_{3i} - 1) \qquad \forall i\in C, \forall j\in C, \forall k\in V \quad (9.3)$$

continued on following page

Exhibit 1. continued

$1-M(x_{ijk}-y_{4i}-1)\geq y_{3j}+y_{4j}$ $\geq 1+M(x_{ijk}-y_{4i}-1)$	$\forall i\in C,\forall j\in C,\forall k\in V$	**(9.4)**
$s_{1jk}\geq s_{1ik}+t_{ij}+M(x_{ijk}-y_{1j}-1)$	$\forall i\in C,\forall j\in C,\forall k\in V$	**(10.1.1)**
$s_{1jk}\geq s_{2ik}+t_{ij}+M(x_{ijk}-y_{3j}-1)$	$\forall i\in C,\forall j\in C,\forall k\in V$	**(10.1.2)**
$s_{1jk}\geq a_{1j}$	$\forall j\in C,k\in V$	**(10.1.3)**
$s_{2jk}\geq s_{1ik}+t_{ij}+M(x_{ijk}-y_{2j}-1)$	$\forall i\in C,\forall j\in C,\forall k\in V$	**(10.2.1)**
$s_{2jk}\geq s_{2ik}+t_{ij}+M(x_{ijk}-y_{4j}-1)$	$\forall i\in C,\forall j\in C,\forall k\in V$	**(10.2.2)**
$s_{2jk}\geq a_{2j}$	$\forall j\in C,k\in V$	**(10.2.3)**
$s_{1ik}+t_{i0}-K\ (1-x_{i0k})\leq b_0+M((1-(y_{1i}-y_{3i})^2)$	$\forall i\in C,\forall k\in V$	**(11.1)**
$s_{2ik}+t_{io}-K\ (1-x_{i0k})\leq b_0+M(1-(y_{2i}-y_{4i})^2)$	$\forall i\in C,\forall k\in V$	**(11.2)**
$s_{10k}=a_0$	$\forall k\in V$	**(12)**
$a_{1i}\leq s_{1ik}\leq b_{1i}$	$\forall i\in C,\forall k\in V$	**(13)**
$a_{2i}\leq s_{2ik}\leq b_{2i}$	$\forall i\in C,\forall k\in V$	**(14)**
$x_{iik}=0$	$\forall i\in C,\forall k\in V$	**(15)**
$x_{ijk}\in\{0,1\}$	$\forall i,j\in N,\forall k\in V$	**(16)**

Linearization of VRSP-MVMT

Although we have proposed the mathematical model in the former section, the constraint (11.1) and (11.2) are nonlinear. To facilitate computation, in this section we transform these two nonlinear constraints in linear forms. Then, VRSP-MVMT is an integer linear programming problem (ILP) which can be solved by LINGO 9.0, if the scale of the problem is small.

First, in constraint (11.1) of

$$s_{1ik}+t_{i0}-K(1-x_{i0k})\leq b_0+M((1-(y_{1i}^2-2y_{1i}y_{3i}+y_{3i}^2)),$$

the $y_{1i}^2, y_{1i}y_{3i}$ and y_{3i}^2 are in quadratic terms. By replacing y_{1i}^2, $y_{1i}y_{3i}$ and y_{3i}^2 with $q_{1\ i}$, q_{13i} and q_{33i} respectively, Formula (11.1) is transformed into to Formula (11.1.1) are

$$s_{1ik}+t_{i0}-K(1-x_{i0k})\leq b_0+M((1-(q_{11i}-2q_{1i}q_{3i}+q_{33i}))\cdot$$

Since one decision variable of decision variables $y_{1i}\sim y_{4i}$ is allowed to be 0, if $y_{1i}=0$, that means $y_{2i}=1$, $y_{3i}=1$ and $y_{4i}=1$. Then, using Formula (11.1.2), if $y_{1i}=0$ and $y_{3i}=1$, these two inequalities will force $q_{B\ i}=0$. Similarly, Formula (11.1.3) states that $y_{1_i} = 0$, these two inequalities force $q_{11_i} = 0$; and using Formula (11.1.4), if $y_{3_i} = 1$, these two inequalities lead to $q_{33i} = 1$. With the same token, Formula (11.2) applies the same procedure to transform quadratic terms to linear forms.

After linearization, the numbers of decision variables becomes $10C + 2CV + NCV$ and that of constraints is

$10C + 3V + 8CV + 4NCV + 9C(C-1)V + N(N-1)V$.

Two properties can be revealed from this linear model, which are useful for developing solution procedures:

◆*Lemma 1. Feasibility Condition*

The model is infeasible solution if

1. Total vehicle capacity < total demand, or;
2. Each customer i cannot be reached at T_{1_i} or T_{2_i}, or;

$$s_{1ik} + t_{i0} - K(1 - x_{i0k}) \le b_0 + M((1 - (y_{1_i} - y_{3_i})^2) \quad \forall i \in C, \ \forall k \in V \quad (11.1)$$

➔ $$s_{1ik} + t_{i0} - M(1 - x_{i0k}) \le b_0 + M(1 - (q_{11_i} - 2q_{13_i} + q_{33_i})) \quad \forall i \in C \ \forall k \in V \quad (11.1.1)$$

$$y_{1_i} - M(1 - y_{3_i}) \le q_{13_i} \le y_{1_i} + M(1 - y_{3_i}) \quad \forall i \in C \quad (11.1.2)$$

$$-M \times y_{3_i} \le q_{13_i} \le M \times y_{3_i} \quad \forall i \in C \quad (11.1.3)$$

$$y_{1_i} \le q_{11_i} \le y_{1_i} \quad \forall i \in C \quad (11.1.4)$$

$$y_{3_i} \le q_{33_i} \le y_{3_i} \quad \forall i \in C \quad (11.1.5)$$

$$s_{2ik} + t_{i0} - K(1 - x_{i0k}) \le b_0 + M((1 - (y_{2_i} - y_{4_i})^2) \quad \forall i \in C, \ \forall k \in V \quad (11.2)$$

➔ $$s_{2ik} + t_{i0} - M(1 - x_{i0k}) \le b_0 + M(1 - (q_{22_i} - 2 \times q_{24_i} + q_{44_i})) \quad \forall i \in C, \ \forall k \in V \quad (11.2.1)$$

$$y_{2_i} - M(1 - y_{4_i}) \le q_{24_i} \le y_{2_i} + M(1 - y_{4_i}) \quad \forall i \in C \quad (11.2.2)$$

$$-M \times y_{4_i} \le q_{24_i} \le M \times y_{4_i} \quad \forall i \in C \quad (11.2.3)$$

$$y_{2_i} \le q_{22_i} \le y_{2_i} \quad \forall i \in C \quad (11.2.4)$$

$$y_{4_i} \le q_{44_i} \le y_{4_i} \quad \forall i \in C \quad (11.2.5)$$

3. Any customer is not served by any vehicle.

◆*Lemma 2. Optimality Condition*
The model is optimal if

1. The solution is feasible and
2. **The total operational cost is minimal.**

At the next two sections, we use two illustrative examples to explain VRSP-MVMT. The first example illustrates how the proposed model is able to dispatch vehicles to satisfy all demand of these customers; and able to effectively select time pair to save additional cost of dispatching another vehicle. The second illustrative example shows that when one vehicle cannot satisfy all demand of customers, how the proposed model will dispatch another vehicle to satisfy all demand of customers.

Illustrative Example I

In order to illustrate the proposed model, we adopted two examples which are modified from Marius M. Solomon's data R109 (Solomon, 1985) by giving an additional time window for each customer. For the proposed model, we extracted five customers from R109, including the given data geographical coordinates, demand, and one time interval and given another time interval.

There is one large vehicle available with capacity 100 units and dispatching cost \$1000, and one small vehicle available with 50 units and dispatching cost \$500. Besides, the time window combination costs are $e_1 = \$50, e_2 = \$40, e_3 = \$20, e_4 = \$10$. The given data are listed in Table 3. including locations, demand, and two time windows of each customer. Table 4 presents the distance from customer i to customer j, d_{ij}, which is calculated by Euclidean distance of

$$\sqrt{(x_1 - y_1)^2 + (x_2 - y_2)^2}$$

and the traveling distance costs. Table 5 contains traveling time from customer i to customer j, t_{ij}, which is calculated by (d_{ij} / average speed per hour:80 km/hr) ×60(minutes). In the modeling, the number of the decision variables in this example is 178, and the number of constraints is 955.

In this example, by using the software of LINGO 9.0 ILP model class, the optimal value is \$1509.48 with solution of $x_{051} = 1, x_{521} = 1, x_{241} = 1, x_{431} = 1, x_{311} = 1, x_{101} = 1$.

Table 3. Locations of all nodes

	Demand w_i	$T_{1i} = [a_{1i}, b_{1i}]$	$T_{2i} = [a_{2i}, b_{2i}]$
Customer 1 (41,49)	**10**	$T_{11} = [161,171]$	$T_{21} = [99,109]$
Customer 2 (35,17)	**7**	$T_{12} = [50,60]$	$T_{22} = [81,91]$
Customer 3 (55,45)	**13**	$T_{13} = [116,126]$	$T_{23} = [95,105]$
Customer 4 (55,20)	**19**	$T_{14} = [149,159]$	$T_{24} = [97,107]$
Customer 5 (15,30)	**26**	$T_{15} = [34,44]$	$T_{25} = [124,134]$
Depot(35,35)	**0**	$T_{01} = [0,230]$	

Table 4. Traveling cost, d_{ij} (unit: dollars)

	Customer 1	Customer 2	Customer 3	Customer 4	Customer 5
Customer 1	0	32.55764	14.56022	32.20248	32.20248
Customer 2	32.55764	0	34.40930	20.22375	23.85372
Customer 3	14.56022	34.40930	0	25	42.72002
Customer 4	32.20248	20.22375	25	0	41.23106
Customer 5	32.20248	23.85372	42.72002	41.23106	0
Depot	15.23155	18	22.36068	25	20.61553

Table 5. Traveling time, t_{ij} (unit: minutes)

	Customer 1	Customer 2	Customer 3	Customer 4	Customer 5
Customer 1	0	39.06917	17.47226	38.64298	38.64298
Customer 2	39.06917	0	41.29116	24.26850	28.62447
Customer 3	17.47226	41.29116	0	30	51.26402
Customer 4	38.64298	24.26850	30	0	49.47727
Customer 5	38.64298	28.62447	51.26402	49.47727	0
Depot	18.27786	21.6	26.83282	30	24.73863

The dispatching consequence was that vehicle departed from depot to serve customer 5 first, then followed in sequence by customer 2, customer 4, customer 3, customer 1, and finally returned to depot. The decision variables of $y_{15}=0, y_{12}=0,$ $y_{24}=0, y_{33}=0, y_{11}=0$ means the time windows combination at the former two customers is the first option, the vehicle leaves customer 2 to customer 4 is the second option for cost effectiveness. The vehicle leaves customer 4 to customer 3 is the third option for abiding by the rule of continuity. Finally, the vehicle leaves customer 3 to customer 1 is the first option for the smallest penalty cost. Our computer hardware, CPU is Pentium Inter (R) Xeon ™ CPU 3.20 GHz, 1.00GB RAM and Microsoft Windows Server 2003 to solve the problem. The elapsed runtime is 6 seconds and the solution is shown in Figure 1 and Table 6.

Illustrative Example II

There are two small vehicles available with 50 units and dispatching cost $500. Besides, the time window combination costs are $e_1=\$50$, $e_2=\$40$, $e_3=\$20$, $e_4=\$10$. The given data are the same listed in Table 2 including locations, demand, and two time windows of each customer. Table 3 are the same as example I, presents the distance from customer i to customer j, d_{ij}, which is calculated by Euclidean distance of

$$\sqrt{(x_1-y_1)^2+(x_2-y_2)^2}$$

and the traveling distance costs. Table 4 are the same as example I, contains traveling time from customer i to customer j, t_{ij}, which is calculated by (d_{ij} / average speed per hour:80 km/hr)×60(minutes).

In this example, the number of the decision variables is 173, and the number of constraints

Figure 1. Time axis of Example I

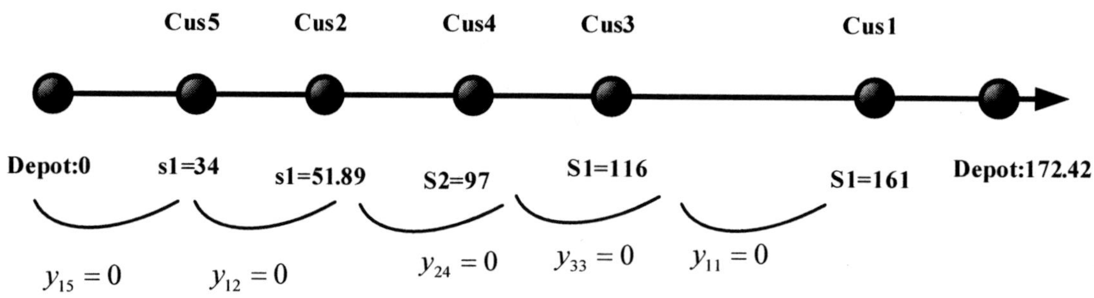

Figure 2. Time axis of Example II

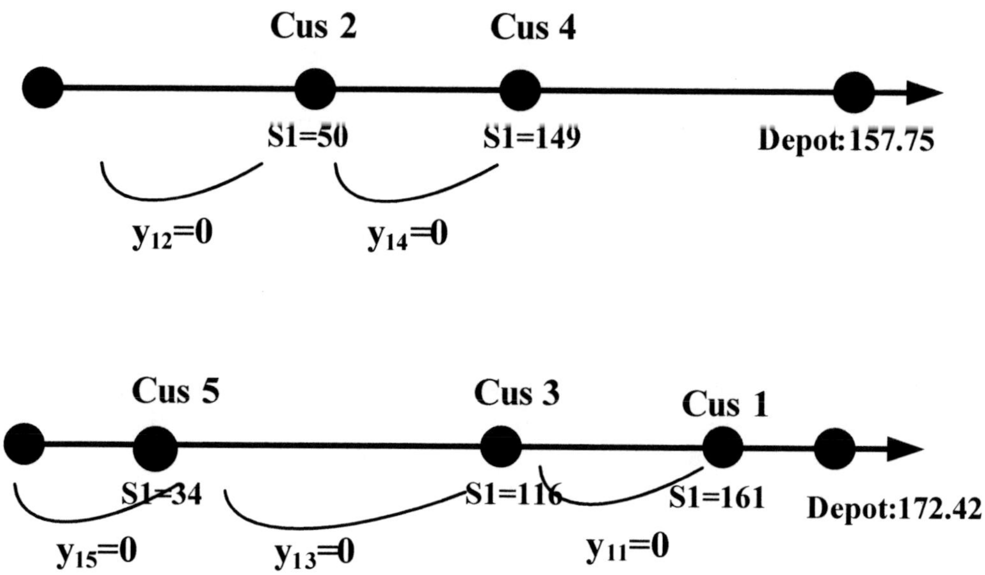

is 955. By using the software of LINGO 9.0 ILP model class, the optimal value is \$1506.35 with solution of the first vehicle $x_{021}=1$, $x_{241}=1$, $x_{401}=1$ and the second vehicle $x_{052}=1$, $x_{532}=1$, $x_{312}=1$.

The dispatching consequence was that first vehicle departed from depot to serve customer 2 first, then followed in sequence by customer 4 and finally returned to depot. The second vehicle departed from depot to serve customer 5 first, then followed in sequence by customer 3, customer 1 and finally returned to depot. The time windows combination at these five customers is the first option for the smallest penalty cost. And the decision variables of are $y_{12}=0, y_{14}=0, y_{15}=0, y_{13}=0, y_{11}=0$.

Our computer hardware, CPU is Pentium Inter (R) Xeon ™ CPU 3.20 GHz, 1.00GB RAM and Microsoft Windows Server 2003 to solve the problem. The elapsed runtime is 6 seconds and the solution is shown in Figure 2 and Table 7.

Comparison and Discussion

To show the effectiveness in considering multiple time windows, models of VRSP and VRSP-

Table 7(a). Solution of Example II

Vehicle 1.	$x_{021} = 1$	$x_{241} = 1$	$x_{401} = 1$
$y_{1j} \sim y_{4j}$	$y_{12} = 0$ $y_{22} = 1$ $y_{32} = 1$ $y_{42} = 1$	$y_{14} = 0$ $y_{24} = 1$ $y_{34} = 1$ $y_{44} = 1$	none
Time windows cost	\$70	\$70	none

Table 7(b). Solution of Example II

Vehicle 2	$x_{052} = 1$	$x_{532} = 1$	$x_{312} = 1$	$x_{102} = 1$
$y_{1j} \sim y_{4j}$	$y_{15} = 0$ $y_{25} = 1$ $y_{35} = 1$ $y_{45} = 1$	$y_{13} = 0$ $y_{23} = 1$ $y_{33} = 1$ $y_{43} = 1$	$y_{11} = 0$ $y_{21} = 1$ $y_{31} = 1$ $y_{41} = 1$	none
Time windows cost	\$70	\$70	\$70	none

TWSD were compared and the results are shown in Table 8.

From Table 8 it can be shown that our model obtained the smallest operation cost, while providing the largest flexibility in operation.

Summary

After stating the significance and necessity of the concerned problem, a model was formulated and calibrated to ensure its accuracy, and the complexity of the model was analyzed.

Due to the NP time complexity of the model, we develop a more efficient algorithm and the capabilities of the computer to bear on the routing problem at hand, while preserving a high degree of model realism. We embark on designing a genetic algorithm (GA). Although the best known results for benchmark VRPS have been obtained using Tabu search or simulated annealing, GA have seen widespread application to various combinatorial optimization problems, including certain types of vehicle routing problem, especially where time windows are included. In the next section, we shall explain how to design a GA to solve large-scaled VRSP-MVMT problems.

A GENETIC ALGORITHM FOR VRSP-MVMT

Classical optimization methods often encounter great difficulty in solving hard problems that abound in the real world. Vitally important applications in business, engineering, economics,

Table 8. Comparison of three models

	VRP (Fisher & Jaikumer, 1981)	VRP-SDTW(Ho & Haugland,2004)	VRP-MVMT
Properties:			
(1) splitting method	**(1) ☒**	**(1) ☑**	**(1) ☒**
(2) time window	**(2) ☒**	**(2) ☑**	**(2) ☑**
(3) multiple time windows	**(3) ☒**	**(3) ☒**	**(3) ☑**
(4) different types of vehicles	**(4) ☒**	**(4) ☒**	**(4) ☑**
(5) limited capacity	**(5) ☑**	**(5) ☒**	**(5) ☑**
Dispatching Route—illustrative example I	**DC→1→DC; DC→2→DC; DC→3→DC; DC→4→DC; DC→5→DC.**	**DC→5→2→3→4→DC; DC→1→DC.**	**DC→5→2→4→3→1→DC**
Number o f Required Vehicles	**5**	**2**	**1**
Cost	**$5202.41552**	**$2159.34165**	**$1509.48**
Dispatching Route—illustrative example II	**DC→1→DC; DC→2→DC; DC→3→DC; DC→4→DC; DC→5→DC.**	**DC→3→4→1→DC; DC→5→2→DC.**	**DC→2→4→DC; DC→5→3→1→DC.**
Number o f Required Vehicles	**5**	**2**	**2**
Cost	**$5202.41552**	**$1507.25**	**$1506.48**

and science cannot be tackled with any reasonable hope of success, within practical time horizons. Since VRSP-MVMT is a NP-hard problem, we cannot solve a large-scale problem by the software of LINGO 9.0 or CPLEX 9.0. Therefore, we developed a GA to cope with these large-scale problems in order to achieve both accuracy and efficiency requirements.

In this chapter, we shall first illustrate the design concept of the proposed GA procedure. In the next subsection, the proposed GA procedure is shown stage by stage in detail. Then, both the accuracy and the efficiency of the proposed GA are shown in 3 instances, respectively. These six instances demonstrate that not only for accuracy, but also for efficiency, the designed GA has convincing results.

The Proposed GA

This subsection first introduces the flowchart of proposed GA procedure and then the detailed operations will be followed.

The Structure of the Algorithm

In the beginning, the Figure 3 shows our basic concept of GA. This figure includes: STAGE 0 (Encoding), STAGE 1 (Initial solution), STAGE 2 (Crossover), STAGE 3 (Mutation), STAGE 4 (Fix), STAGE 5 (Evaluation), STAGE 6 (Selection), and STAGE 7 (Termination). The details are explained below:

STAGE 0:
Encode a solution including dispatched service sequence and selected time windows.

STAGE 1:
Generate the initial solution randomly, which is the parent for the next STAGES at generation 1.

STAGE 2:
Apply crossover method to obtain the additional offspring.

STAGE 3:
Use mutation method to obtain the additional offspring.

STAGE 4:
Based on Lemma 1 to adjust the infeasible solution to be a feasible solution.

STAGE 5:
Based on Lemma 2 to evaluate each chromosome with objective function, respectively.

STAGE 6:
Apply Roulette wheel to select 40 chromosomes to be the next parent.

STAGE 7:
Stop criterion set to be 10000 generations.

Illustration of the Procedure

STAGE 0. REPRESENTATION

At this stage we should set needed population size (pop_size), chromosome ($v_k, k = 1...pop\_size$), crossover rate (P_c), probability of selecting mutation method (p_f),mutation rate (P_m), and $\max\_gen$. For our study, the $pop\_size = 40$, the length of each chromosome=(number of customers+ number of vehicles-1), $P_c = 0.7$, $p_f = 0.5$, $P_m = 0.3$ and $\max\_gen$=10000.

Our model, VRSP-MVMT, has solution to represent dispatched sequence for a set of customers with a selected time window. For convenience, we encode the information for each chromosome. For example, we have three vehicles, the serial number is 1 to 3, the vehicle numbered 1 has large capacity with 100 units, the vehicles 2 and 3 have less capacities with 50 units, and we have five customers numbered in serial from 1 to 5 and D represents the depot, each customer can set two time intervals, with numbers 1 and 2.

Now, we have a feasible solution to a problem. Vehicle 1 serves the five customers, the dispatched sequence is 2→1→4→5→3, with requirements time windows of 1, 2, 1, 2, 2. In other words, vehicle 1 serves the first customer (customer number 2) at the first time window, serves the second customer (customer number 1) at the second time window, serves the third customer (customer number 4) at the first time window, serves the fourth customer (customer number 5) at the second time window, and serves the final customer (customer number 3) at the second time window. The encode string is 4 3 8 11 7 0 0, and 0 represents a separate point for different vehicles. The encoding string says that the serial number 2 and 3 of vehicles should not serve any customer. Figure 4 interprets our thinking of encoding a chromosome string which combines dispatched sequence and the selected time window.

Figure 3. The structure of the proposed GA

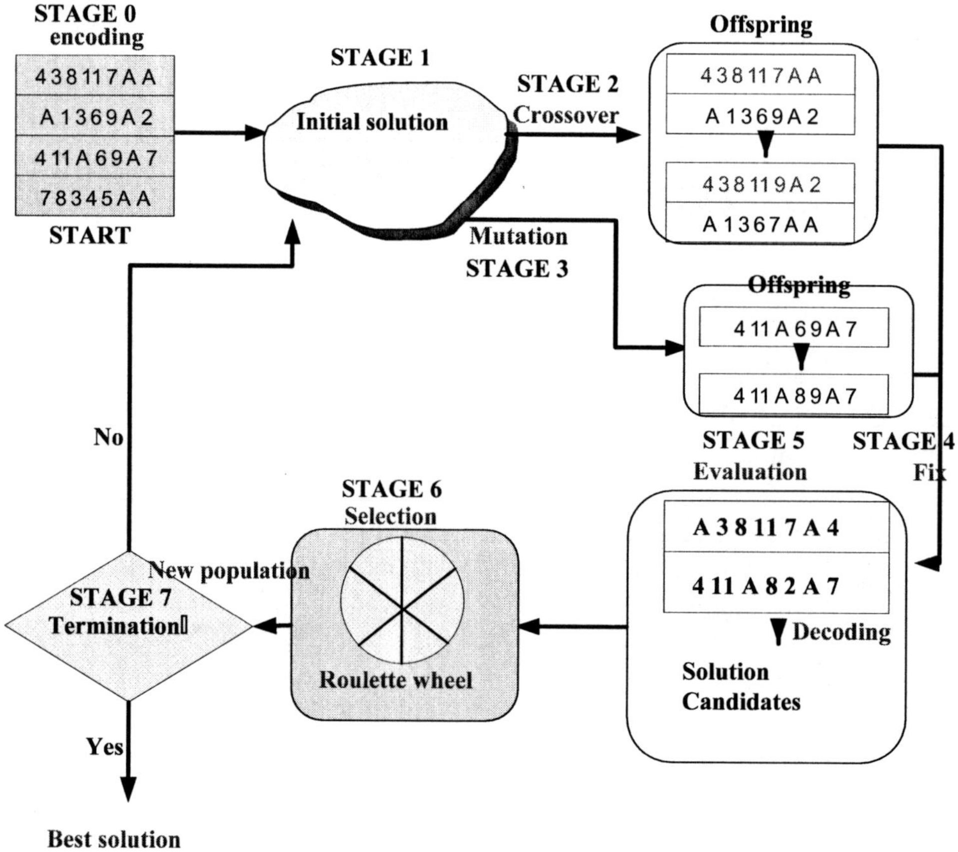

Moreover, we randomly select the gene for composing each chromosome. For said example, the gene is number 2 to number 11 and two 0 to be randomly selected for each chromosome, and each chromosome consists of seven genes.

STAGE 1. INITIALIZATION

At this stage, we should randomly generate initial population $x_k, k = 1...pop\_size$ to be the parent.

STAGE 2. CROSSOVER

At this stage, we adopt a one cut-point method (Mitsuo & Runwei, 1997) to do crossover. It operates on two chromosomes at a time and generates offspring by combining both chromosomes' features. Furthermore, crossover is used as the principle genetic operator to perform a local search in the purpose of finding an improved solution. Table 9 interprets the crossover method. When the crossover point randomly selected is 4, which means we select the left 4 genes from chromosome 1 and combine the right 3 genes from chromosome 2 to be a new chromosome 1. Similarly, we select the left 4 genes from chromosome 2 and combine the right 3 genes from chromosome 1 to be a new chromosome 2.

Figure 4. The encoding method

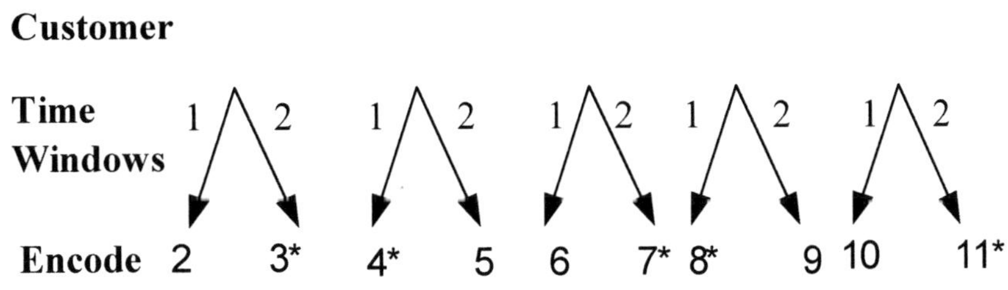

Table 9. One cut-point method

Parent Chromosome 1	Parent Chromosome 2	Crossover Point	New Chromosome 1	New Chromosome 2
4 3 8 11 7 0 0	0 1 3 6 9 0 2	4	4 3 8 11 9 0 2	0 1 3 6 7 0 0
4 11 0 6 9 0 7	7 8 3 4 5 0 0	6	4 11 0 6 9 0 0	7 8 3 4 5 0 7

STAGE 3. MUTATION

Mutation is a background operator that produces spontaneous random change to perform a random search in order to explore the area beyond local optimum.

About mutation method, we design two methods to mutate. Figure 5 shows these two mutation methods. The first mutation method is to mutate one gene randomly (Mitsuo & Runwei, 1997). That is, by referring to Table 10, if we randomly select the mutation bit as 2, we mutate the second gene for randomly selecting number 3 to number 11 and two 0 to be a new chromosome 1. The second mutation method is to swap two time windows, and is shown in Table 11. In other words, if we randomly select a gene, and the encoding number is 2, we replace 2 with 3. If the encoding number is 3, we replace 3 with 2. The method says, we interchange time window 1 and time window 2 or time window 2 to time window 1 for selected chromosomes.

STAGE 4. FIX

At this stage, we should decode each chromosome string to obtain each chromosome's related solution, $x_k, k = 1 ... pop\_size$.

For example, a chromosome string is 4,3,8,11,7,0,0, divide 2 obtain quotient as the service sequence for a set of customer, divide 2 to obtain remainder and plus 1 as the selected time window for a set of the served customer.

From the said example, we know the service sequence is D→2→1→4→5→3→D, with the related time window is 1, 2, 1, 2, 2.

However, not all of the chromosomes produce feasible solutions. As stated in Lemma 1, there are three situations that cause chromosomes to be infeasible. One is that a related solution does not cover all customers from a set of original customer based on Lemma 1 (3). The second is that the demand exceeds the capacity of any vehicle based on Lemma 1 (1). The third is that the service time is not continuous based on Lemma

Figure 5. Two mutation methods

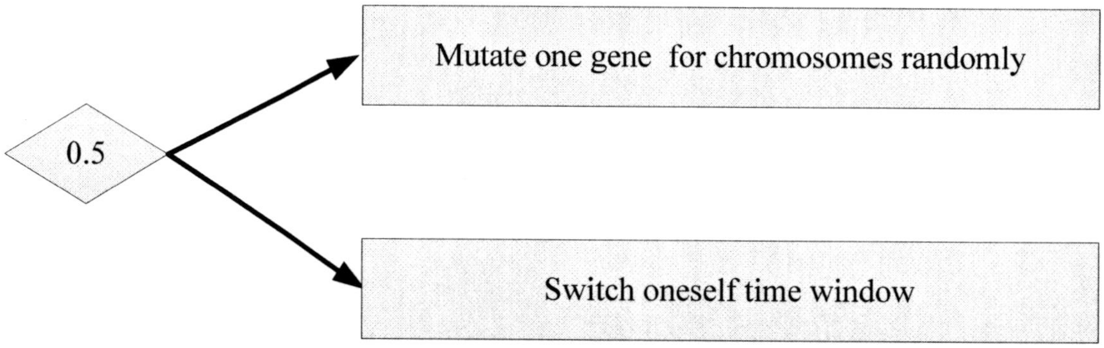

Table 10. Randomly mutate one gene for chromosomes

Parent Chromosomes 1	Mutation Bit	New Chromosomes 1
4 11 A 6 9 0 7	1	8 2 0 6 9 A 7
7 8 3 4 5 0 0	2	7 11 3 4 5 0 0

Table 11. Swap time windows

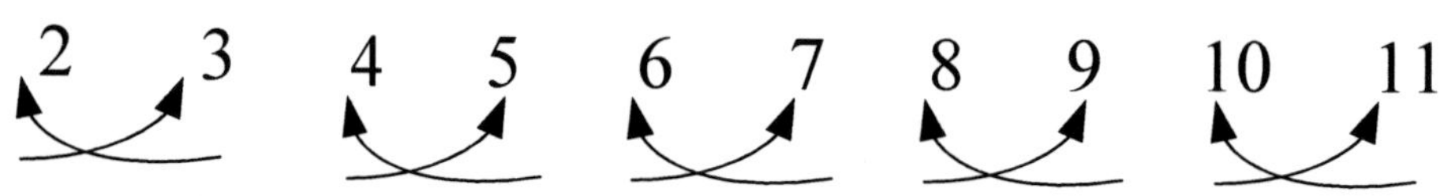

Parent Chromosomes 1	Mutation Bit	New Chromosomes 1
4 11 A 6 9 0 7	1	5 11 0 6 9 0 7
7 8 3 4 5 0 0	2	7 9 3 4 5 0 11

Table 12. The decoding method

	Chromosome string 4 3 8 11 7 0 0	
divide 2 (quotient)	2 1 4 5 3	=2 1 4 5 3
divide (remainder)	0 1 0 1 1 plus1	=1 2 1 2 2

1 (2). Therefore, we set three respective rules to fix infeasibility to feasibility are follows:

Rule 1. *Exact Services*
Rule 1: Replace the repeated customer by unserved one, and vice versa. Therefore, each customer will consist of every customer, no less no more so that each customer should appear exactly once in a solution. For example, if customer 5 is served at time window 1 and time window 2, we have to replace from time window 2 by an unserved customer, as shown in Table 13.

Rule 2. *Demand cannot Exceed Capacity*
Rule 2: If total demand of this set of customer exceeds the dispatched vehicle, the largest demand of this set of customer should be removed to another dispatched vehicle. Therefore, when a vehicle serves a set of customers, total demand of this set of customers cannot exceed the capacity of the vehicle. For example, in Table 14, vehicle 1 can serve all customers.

Rule 3. *Linearly Continuous Service Time*
Rule 3: When finish time of the former customer plus traveling time of the former customer to the next customer exceed b_1 at time window 1 $[a_1,b_1]$ or b_2 at time window 2 $[a_2,b_2]$, we should remove the next customer to another vehicle. Similarly, when finish time of the last customer of a set of customer plus traveling time to depot exceed the close time of depot, we should remove this last customer to another vehicle or change another time window. This is done after adjusting the chromosome to consist of all customers. Thus, we sort the time interval a at $[a,b]$ to obtain service sequence.

Figure 6 shows an example, because the arrival time of travel time is out of the first time interval [40,50] of customer 1, customer 1 only can be served at the second time window.

Based on these rules, we can modify the infeasible solution to feasible solution. In other words, we can pass feasible chromosomes to next STAGE.

Table 13. Rule 1: Exact services

	Chromosome string 4 3 8 11 10 0 0	
divide 2 (quotient)	2 1 4 5 5	=2 1 4 5 5
Divide (remainder)	0 1 0 1 1plus 1	=1 2 1 2 1
	Modify→ Chromosome string 4 3 8 6 10 0 0	
divide 2 (quotient)	2 1 4 3 5	=2 1 4 3 5
Divide (remainder)	0 1 0 0 0 plus 1	=1 2 1 1 1

Table 14. Rule 2: Demand cannot exceed capacity

Customer	Demand	Capacity
1	40 (Vehicle 1)	Vehicle 1=100 units
2	23 (Vehicle 1)	Vehicle 2=50 units
3	5 (Vehicle 1)	Vehicle 3=50 units
4	17 (Vehicle 1)	
5	8 (Vehicle 1)	

Figure 6. Time windows selection

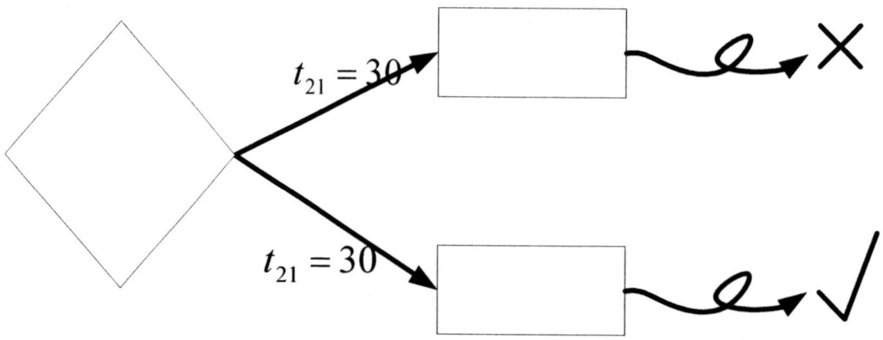

STAGE 5. EVALUATION

At this stage, we evaluate the fitness by the objective function. We take a decode string to obtain a series of the corresponding objective values. Note that in our study, we will obtain 40 solutions at each generation, and thus 40 objective values will be evaluated.

STAGE 6. SELECTION

After evaluation, we will select a better solution to be the next parent by four steps. First, we rank the 40 objective values at each generation, after the method, and the top five will be selected. Second, we calculate the total fitness for a population, and include the top five best chromosomes. Third, we calculate selection probability for each chromosome, and then we calculate cumulative probability for each chromosome. Fourth, a random number is generated from the range [0,1]. When the cumulative probability of the chromosome is larger than the random number, we select this chromosome to be the next parent.

After going through the selection procedure, we select 40 chromosomes for the next generation and keep the population so that it contains 40 chromosomes.

STAGE 7. TERMINATION

The stopping rule is set after 10000 generation. The pseudo-code of GA procedure is listed in Appendix I.

Evaluation

The heuristics described in the previous section were coded in C++ and, using a Pentium Inter (R) Xeon ™ CPU 3.20 GHz, 1.00GB RAM, and Microsoft Windows Server 2003. We test GA accuracy with three instances and GA efficiency with another three instances. These six vehicle routing problems can be downloaded from the Web site of Marius M. Solomon (Solomon, 1985) as benchmarks.

The first 3 instances are in small scales so that the accuracy of the problem can be evaluated with respect to the optimal solution produced by LINGO 9.0. Before testing 2 customers, 5 customers and 10 customers, we modify benchmark data R109 for VRSP-MVMT. For these three instances, there are three vehicles at the depot: one is a large vehicle available with capacity 100 units and dispatching cost $1000; the other is a medium vehicle available with capacity 80 units and dispatching cost $800; another is a small vehicle available with capacity 50 units and dispatching cost \$500. Besides, the time window combination costs are $e_1 = \$50, e_2 = \$40, e_3 = \$20, e_4 = \$10$.

To evaluate its efficiency of the developed GA, three instances of large scaled problems with 25 customers, 50 customers, and 100 customers from RC 205 are used. There are eight vehicles at the depot. The first two vehicles are large vehicles available with capacity 1,000 units with dispatching cost \$10,000; the third and fourth vehicles are medium vehicles available with 800 units with dispatching cost \$8,000; the final four vehicles are small vehicles available with 500 units with dispatching cost \$5,000. Besides, the time window combination costs are $e_1 = \$50, e_2 = \$40, e_3 = \$20, e_4 = \$10$. Moreover, the customers of benchmark data R205 are listed in Web site [47]. However, because the software of CPLEX 9.0 cannot solve large-scale problems as 25 nodes, 50 nodes, and 100 nodes, we set the runtime limit as 86,400 seconds for CPLEX 9.0. On the other hand, we set the 10000 generations to stop GA procedure, at the same time; we get the best value from GA procedure at an efficient time, such as 1,095.03 seconds for 25 nodes.

Evaluation of Accuracy

In this subsection, we compare the best value from GA with the optimal value from LINGO 9.0 ILP model class. The initial data are the same are used in chapter 3. Moreover, the additional problem, 10 customers with an additional 5 customers from 6th customer to 10th customer is listed in Table 14. Table 15 lists the comparison of the accuracy of designed GA and LINGO 9.0. Designed GA has a convincing result. For problems of 2 customers and 5 customers, the developed GA obtained the same values as optimal values of LINGO 9.0. For 10 customers, the error is less than 2% estimated by

$$\text{Error}=\frac{(\text{best value-optimal value})}{\text{optimal value}}\times 100\%.$$

In addition, for problems of 2 customers for LINGO 9.0 needs 3 seconds for solving the problem; the elapsed time is 0.04 seconds for GA to solve the problem. The 5 customers problem for LINGO 9.0 needs 6 seconds for solving the problem; the elapsed time is 0.19 seconds for GA to solve the problem. 10 customers problem for LINGO 9.0 needs 21720 seconds for solving the problem; the elapsed time is 240.172 seconds for GA to solve the problem.

Evaluation of Efficiency

In this subsection, we compare the feasible value from CPLEX 9.0 and best value from GA. The benchmark data RC205 are listed in Appendix II. For 25 customers, after 86,400 seconds, CPLEX 9.0 obtains a feasible solution; the designed GA obtained the best value 12398.9 with 2 small vehicles at 1,095.03 seconds. At the same time, the error is smaller than 2%. For 50 customers, CPLEX 9.0 cannot solve the large-scale problem within 86,400 seconds; yet, GA obtained the best value 19,763 with 2 small vehicles at 2,333.56 seconds. For 100 customers, GA obtained the best value 34,080.9 with 2 medium vehicles and 4 small vehicles at 6,789.53 seconds. Therefore, the developed GA has shown its capability of solving large-scale problems at efficiently.

SUMMARY

In this chapter, we have developed a GA procedure to solve VRSP-MVMT problems. Not only is the designed concept illustrated in detail; but also the performance is evaluated on both its accuracy and efficiency with those of LINGO 9.0 and CPLEX 9.0.

About accuracy of GA procedure, we properly test it with three small-scaled examples with 2 customers, 5 customers, and 10 customers. In comparison to the optimal solution of LINGO 9.0 the errors of best value of GA are smaller than

Table 15. The remaining 5 customers for 10 customers

Customer (location)	**Demand** w_i	$T_{1i} = [a_{1i}, b_{1i}]$	$T_{2i} = [a_{2i}, b_{2i}]$
Customer 6 (25, 30)	3	$T_{16} = [76,131]$	$T_{26} = [111,170]$
Customer 7 (20, 50)	5	$T_{17} = [61,110]$	$T_{27} = [106,163]$
Customer 8 (10,43)	9	$T_{18} = [75,124]$	$T_{28} = [77,134]$
Customer 9 (55,60)	16	$T_{19} = [74,129]$	$T_{29} = [147,210]$
Customer 10 (30,60)	16	$T_{110} = [107,150]$	$T_{210} = [17,100]$

Table 16. Comparison of optimal values and best values

	Scales of the problems		LINGO 9.0		GA		Error (%)
Customers	Number of decision variables	Number of constraints	Optimal value	Elapsed time(sec)	Best value	Elapsed time(sec)	
2	38	205	705.789 3		705.789	0.04	0%
5	186	985	1509.48 6		1509.48	0.19	0%
10	591	5152	2434.872	21720	2471.36	240.172	1.49%

Table 17. Comparison of feasible solutions and best values

	Scales of the problems		CPLEX 9.0		GA		Error (%)
Benchmark data	Number of decision variables	Number of constraints	Feasible value	Elapsed Time(sec)	Best value	Elapsed Time(sec)	
RC205.25	4884	61341	12198	86400	12398.9	1095.03	1.65%
RC205.50	17184	24591	----------	86400	19763	2333.56	---------
RC205.100	107177 9	61136	-----------	86400	34080.9	6789.53	---------

2%. About the efficiency of GA procedure, we also test it with three large-scaled problems with 25 customers, 50 customers, and 100 customers. For 25 customers, the difference of the feasible solution of CPLEX 9.0 and the best value of GA is still smaller than 2%. However, for 50 customers and 100 customers within 24 hours, CPLEX 9.0 cannot get any solution. GA obtained a best value of 19,763 for 50 customers at 2,333.56 seconds and obtained a best value of 34,080.9 for 100 customers at 6,789.53 seconds. Therefore, the developed GA is not only able to obtain a near-optimal but also capable for solving large-scaled problems in efficient and effective manners.

CONCLUSION

For rapidly changing socio-economic environment, distribution occurs frequently among countries, companies, and individuals. We embark on proposing a model with solution procedure to deal with the requests of the real world.

In this study, we have proposed a model, vehicle routing and scheduling problem with multiple vehicle types and multiple time windows (VRSP-MVMT) to incorporate additional yet realistic features for wider application. These features include multiple types with limited capacity, and multiple time windows. We aim at seeking the smallest operation cost that includes vehicle dispatching cost, total traveling cost, and time window combination costs. The model has been illustrated by examples and signified by comparing the operation costs with VRP and vehicle routing problem with time windows and split deliveries (VRP-SPTW).

Due to the NP time complexity of the model, we develop a more efficient algorithm by GA. We have evaluated the performance of genetic algorithm (GA) by three instances. The three small scaled instances of 2 customers, 5 customers and 10 customers are used to test accuracy. The other three large-scaled instances, including 25 customers, 50 customers, and 100 customers, are used for evaluating its efficiency. These six instances demonstrated that not only the accuracy, but also the efficiency, of GA has convincing results.

Future Trends

Future trends of studies should be placed on the heterogeneous goods, in particular, when the collection of the end-use goods is considered. In addition, for scheduling, the waiting time of each customer should be taken into account for a more realistic model.

REFERENCES

Assad, A.A., & Golden, B.L. (1998). *Vehicle routing: Methods and studies*. New York: Elsevier.

Barbarosoglu, G., & Ozgur, D. (1999). A tabu search algorithm for the vehicle routing problem. *Computers & Operations Research, 26*, 255-270.

Blackburn, J.D., Guide, V.D.R., Jr., Souza, G.C., & Van Wassenhove, L.N. (2004). Reverse supply chains for commercial returns. *California Management Review, 46*(2), 6-22.

Berger, J., & Barkaoui, M. (2004). A parallel hybrid genetic algorithm for the vehicle routing problem with time windows. *Computers & Operational Research, 31*, 2037-2053.

Bertsimas, D., & Ryzin, G.V. (1993). Stocastic and dynamic vehicle routing in the Euclidean plane with multiple capacitated vehicle. *Operations Research, 41*, 60-76.

Bodin, L.D., Golden, B.L., Assad, A.A., & Ball, M.O. (1983). Routing and scheduling of vehicles and crews. *Computers & Operations Research, 10*, 63-211.

Chao, I.M., Golden, B.L., & Wasil, E. (1993). A new heuristic algorithm for the multi-depot vehicle routing problem that improves upon best-known solutions. *American Journal of Mathematical Management Science, 13*, 371-406.

Christofides N., Mingozzi, A., & Toth, P. (1981). Exact algorithms for the vehicle routing problem, based on spanning tree and shortest path relaxations. *Mathematical Programming, 20*, 255-282.

Dantzig, G.B., & Ramser, J.H. (1959). The truck dispatching problem. *Management Science, 6*, 80-91.

Dror, M., & Trudeau, P. (1989). Savings by split delivery routing. *Transportation Science, 23*, 141-149.

Dror, M., Laporte, G., & Trudeau, P. (1989). Vehicle routing with stochastic demands: Properties and solution framework. *Transportation Science, 23*, 166-176.

Dror, M., & Trudeau, P. (1990). Split delivery routing. *Naval Research Logistics, 37*, 383-402.

Eric T., & Philippe, B. (1997). A tabu search heuristic for the vehicle routing problem with soft time windows. *Transportation Science, 31*, 170-186.

Fabri, A., & Recht, P. (2006). On dynamic pickup and delivery vehicle routing with several time windows and waiting times. *Transportation Research, Part B, 40*, 335-350.

Fisher, M.L., & Jaikumer, R. (1981). A generalize assignment heuristic for vehicle routing. *Networks, 11*, 109-124.

Frizzell, P.W., & Giffin, J.W. (1995). The split delivery vehicle scheduling problem with time windows and grid network distances. *Computers & Operations Research, 22*, 655-667.

Gillett, B., & Johnson, J. (1976). Multi-terminal vehicle-dispatch algorithm. *Omega, 4*, 711-718.

Glover, F. (1977). Heuristic for integer programming using surrogate constraints. *Decision Science, 8*, 156-166.

Golden, B., & Wong, R. (1981). Capacitated arc routing problems. *Networks, 11*, 305-315.

Hillier, F.S., & Lieberman, G.J. (2001). *Introduction to operation research* (7th ed.). Dubuque, IA: McGraw-Hill.

Ho, S.C., & Haugland, D. (2004). A tabu search heuristic for the vehicle routing problem with time windows and split deliveries. *Computers & Operations Research, 31*, 1947-1964.

Jayaraman, V., Patterson, R.A., & Rolland, E. (2003). The design of reverse distribution networks: Models and solution procedures. *European Journal of Operational Research, 150*, 128-149.

Krikke, H., Blanc, I.I., & Velde, S. (2004). Product modularity and design of closed-loop supply chains. *California Management Review, 46*(2), 23-39.

Lacomme, P., Prins, C., & Sevaux, M. (2006). A genetic algorithm for a bi-objective capacitated arc routing problem. *Computers & Operations Research, 33*, 3473-3485.

Lin, S., & Kerninghan, B. (1973). An effective heuristic algorithm for the traveling salesman problem. *Operations Research, 21*, 498-516.

Mitsuo, G., & Runwei, C. (1997). *Genetic algorithms and engineering design*. New York: John Wiley & Sons.

Russell, R., & Igo, W. (1979). An assignment routing problem. *Networks, 9*, 1-17.

Solomon, M.M. (1985). *Benchmark data*. Retrieved July 9, 2008, from http://web.cba.neu.edu/%7Emsolomon/problems.htm

Solomon, M.M. (1987). Algorithms for the vehicle routing and scheduling problems with time window constraints. *Operations Research, 35*, 254-265.

Tang, Q., & Xie, F. (2007, August 24-27). A genetic algorithm for reverse logistics network design. In *Proceedings of the Third International Conference on Natural Computation*, Haikou, China.

ADDITIONAL READING

Ali, A., & Kennington, J. (1986). The asymmetric M-traveling salesman problem: A duality based branch and bound. *Discrete Applied Mathematics, 13*, 259-276.

Baker, B.M., & Ayechew, M.A. (2003). A genetic algorithm for the vehicle routing problem. *Computers & Operations Research, 30*, 787-800.

Bertsimas D. (1992). A vehicle routing problem with stochastic demand. *Operations Research, 40*, 574-586.

Bodin, L.D., & Kursh, S. (1978). A computer-assisted system for the routing and scheduling of street sweepers. *Operations Research, 26*, 525-537.

Bodin, L.D., & Kursh, S. (1979). A detailed description of a street sweeper routing and scheduling system. *Computers & Operations Research, 6*, 181-198.

Golden, B., Magnanti, T., & Nguyen, H. (1977). Implementing vehicle routing algorithm. *Networks, 7*, 113-148.

Lu, Q., Vivi, C., Julie, A.S., & Taylor, R. (2000). A practical framework for the reverse supply chain. In *Proceedings of the International Symposium on Electronics and the Environment* (pp. 266-271).

Mokhtar, S.B., Jarvis, J.J., & Sherali, H.D. (2005). *Linear programming and network flows* (3rd ed.). John Wiley.

Pochampally, K.K., Surendra, M.G., & Sagar, V.K. (2004). Identification of potential recovery facilities for designing a reverse supply chain network using physical programming. *The International Society for Optical Engineering, 5262.*

Savaskan, R.C., Bhattacharya, S., & Van Wassenhove, L.N. (2004). Closed-loop supply chain models with product remanufacturing. *Management Science, 50*(2), 239-252.

Schultmann, F., Moritz, Z., & Otto, R. (2006). Modeling reverse logistic tasks within closed-loop supply chains: An example from the automotive industry. *European Journal of Operational Research, 171*, 1033-1050.

Wang, H.F., & Horng, J.-S. (1996). Directed perturbation analysis of an IP. *Journal of Mathematics Analysis and Applications, 201*, 447-460.

APPENDIX I GA PROCEDURE

STAGE 0. REPRESENTATION

STEP 1.Set population size pop_size, chromosome $V_k ,k = 1,2,..., pop\_size$, crossover rate P_c, mutation rate P_m, and the maximum number of generations $\max\_gen$;

STEP 2.Encode a salutation as a chromosome;

STEP 3.Set $chromosome\_size$, $chromosome\_size$ =(number of customers + number of vehicles -1);

STEP 4.Randomly select the chromosome.

STAGE 1. INITIALIZATION

STEP 1.Randomly generate initial population $x^k ,k = 1,2,..., pop\_size$.

STAGE 2. CROSSOVER

STEP 1.Set $P_C = 0.7$;

STEP 2.Use 2-point crossover to produce an offspring, in which two points in the chromosome are chosen randomly;

STEP 3.Perform uniform crossover.

STAGE 3. MUTATION

STEP 1.Set $P_f = 0.5$ to decide which method to mutate;

STEP 2. Set $P_m = 0.3$;

STEP 3.Perform random perturbation mutation.

STAGE 4. FIX

STEP 1.Decode a chromosome string;

STEP 2.Convert the chromosome's genotype to its phenotype, that is, convert chromosome string into relative solution $x^k ,k = 1,2,...pop\_size$;

STEP 3.Modify infeasible solution to feasible solution;

3.1 Test the rule 1 (serve all customer)
if (a solution consists of the same customer)
then remove the duplicate customer and correct to unserved customer
else go to the next test;

3.2 Test the rule 2
(capacity of a vehicle can serve the customers of a solution)
if (total demand of the customers is exceed capacity of the dispatched vehicle)
then remove the largest demand of the customer to another dispatched vehicle
else go to the next test

3.3 Test rule 3 (Time axis have to continuous)

3.3.1Sort the StartTime_i of the customer_i;

3.3.2// Start from the depot to the first customer
Depot + $\boldsymbol{r}_{0i}$ = CloseTime_i
if (CloseTime_i > StartTime_i)

continued on following page

APPENDIX I CONTINUED

then RealCloseTime$_i$ = CloseTime$_i$
else RealCloseTime$_i$ = StartTime$_i$
if (RealCloseTime$_i$ > EndTime$_i$ of the time interval)
then remove the customer *i* to another dispatched vehicle
else go to the next step

3.3.4// Start from the first customer *i* to the second customer *j*
RealCloseTime$_i$ + tr_{ij} = CloseTime$_j$
if (CloseTime$_j$ > StartTime$_j$)
then RealCloseTime$_j$ = CloseTime$_j$
else RealCloseTime$_j$ = StartTime$_j$
if (RealCloseTime$_j$ > EndTime$_j$)
then remove the customer *j* to another dispatched vehicle
else serve the next customer *j* + 1

3.3.5// Start from the final customer *i* to the depot
RealCloseTime$_i$ + tr_{i0} =TerminateTime$_0$
if (TerminateTime$_0$ < EndTime$_0$)
then RealTerminateTime$_0$ =TerminateTime$_0$
else dispatch one un-dispatched vehicle

3.4if (a solution after the 3 rules is still a infeasible solution)
then remove the solution from the solution candidates
else go to the next step

STAGE 5. EVALUATION

STEP 1.Evaluate the fitness by the objective function, $f(x_k)$, $k = 1,2,...,pop\_size$
eval (V_k)= $f(x_k)$,$k = 1,2,...,pop\_size$

STAGE 6. SELECTION$k = 1,2,...,pop\_size$

STEP 1. Reserve the top 5 best solution to be the next parent
STEP 2. Calculate the total fitness for the population

$$F = \sum_{k=1}^{popsize} eval(V_k)$$

STEP 3. Calculate selection probability p_k for each chromosome V_k

$$p_k = \frac{eval(V_k)}{F},\ k = 1,2,...popsize$$

STEP 4. Calculate cumulative probability q_k for each chromosome V_k

$$q_k = \sum_{j=1}^{k} p_j,\ k = 1,2,...popsize$$

STEP 5. Generate a random number r from the range [0,1]
STEP 6. if ($r < q_1$)
then select the first chromosome V_1
else select the *k*th chromosome V_2 $(2 \le k \le pop\_size)$
such that $q_{k-1} < r \le q_k$

continued on following page

APPENDIX I CONTINUED

STAGE 7. TERMINATION

STEP 1. if $(|optimalvalue - eval(V_k)| < 10^{-4})$
then stop the procedure
else go to the next iteration

APPENDIX II BENCHMARK DATA R205

Customer (location)	**Demand** w_i	$T_{1i}=[a_{1i},b_{1i}]$	$T_{2i}=[a_{2i},b_{2i}]$
Customer 1 (25,85)	20	$T_{11}=[431,911]$	$T_{21}=[613,853]$
Customer 2 (22,75)	30	$T_{12}=[30,510]$	$T_{22}=[92,332]$
Customer 3 (22,85)	10	$T_{13}=[291,771]$	$T_{23}=[411,651]$
Customer 4 (20,80)	40	$T_{14}=[674,734]$	$T_{24}=[584,824]$
Customer 5 (20,85)	20	$T_{15}=[40,520]$	$T_{25}=[40,280]$
Customer 6 (18,75)	20	$T_{16}=[393,502]$	$T_{26}=[328,528]$
Customer 7 (15,75)	20	$T_{17}=[120,600]$	$T_{27}=[240,480]$
Customer 8 (15,80)	10	$T_{18}=[397,457]$	$T_{28}=[307,547]$
Customer 9 (10,35)	20	$T_{19}=[401,461]$	$T_{29}=[311,551]$
Customer 10 (10,40)	30	$T_{110}=[535,622]$	$T_{210}=[459,699]$
Customer 11 (8,40)	40	$T_{111}=[225,285]$	$T_{211}=[135,375]$
Customer 12 (8,45)	20	$T_{112}=[43,523]$	$T_{212}-[163,403]$
Customer 13 (5,35)	10	$T_{113}=[683,743]$	$T_{213}=[593,833]$
Customer 14 (5,45)	10	$T_{114}=[35,366]$	$T_{214}=[35,275]$
Customer 15 (2,40)	20	$T_{115}=[204,264]$	$T_{215}-[114,354]$
Customer 16 (0,40)	20	$T_{116}=[204,425]$	$T_{216}=[195,435]$
Customer 17 (0,45)	20	$T_{117}=[698,827]$	$T_{217}=[643,883]$
Customer 18 (44,5)	20	$T_{118}=[306,483]$	$T_{218}=[275,515]$
Customer 19 (42,10	40	$T_{119}=[199,428]$	$T_{219}=[194,434]$
Customer 20 (42,15)	10	$T_{120}=[494,699]$	$T_{220}=[477,717]$
Customer 21 (40,5)	10	$T_{121}=[45,525]$	$T_{221}=[155,395]$
Customer 22 (40,150	40	$T_{122}=[383,486]$	$T_{222}=[315,555]$
Customer 23 (38,5)	30	$T_{123}=[231,291]$	$T_{223}=[141,381]$
Customer 24 (38,15)	10	$T_{124}=[609,872]$	$T_{224}=[621,861]$
Customer 25 (35,5)	20	$T_{125}=[821,881]$	$T_{225}=[664,904]$
Customer 26 (95,30)	30	$T_{126}=[349,829]$	$T_{226}=[469,709]$

continued on following page

APPENDIX II CONTINUED

Customer 27 (95,35)	20	$T_{127} = [138,273]$	$T_{227} = [86,326]$
Customer 28 (92,30)	10	$T_{128} = [78,339]$	$T_{228} = [89,329]$
Customer 29 (90,35)	10	$T_{129} = [132,375]$	$T_{229} = [134,174]$
Customer 30 (88,30)	10	$T_{130} = [252,359]$	$T_{230} = [186,426]$
Customer 31 (88,35)	20	$T_{131} = [50,530]$	$T_{231} = [105,345]$
Customer 32 (87,30)	10	$T_{132} = [562,799]$	$T_{232} = [561,801]$
Customer 33 (85,25)	10	$T_{133} = [71,208]$	$T_{233} = [51,291]$
Customer 34 (85,35)	30	$T_{134} = [307,787]$	$T_{234} = [427,667]$
Customer 35 (67,85)	20	$T_{135} = [655,778]$	$T_{235} = [597,837]$
Customer 36 (65,85)	40	$T_{136} = [43,186]$	$T_{236} = [43,283]$
Customer 37 (65,82)	10	$T_{137} = [377,857]$	$T_{237} = [497,737]$
Customer 38 (62, 80)	30	$T_{138} = [308,368]$	$T_{238} = [218,458]$
Customer 39 (60,80)	10	$T_{139} = [46,201]$	$T_{239} = [36,276]$
Customer 40 (60,85)	30	$T_{140} = [339,438]$	$T_{241} = [269,509]$
Customer 41 (58,75)	20	$T_{141} = [377,494]$	$T_{241} = [316,556]$
Customer 42 (55,80)	10	$T_{142} = [33,166]$	$T_{242} = [33,273]$
Customer 43 (55,85)	20	$T_{143} = [531,736]$	$T_{243} = [514,754]$
Customer 44 (55,82)	10	$T_{144} = [247,307]$	$T_{244} = [157,397]$
Customer 45 (20,82)	10	$T_{145} = [37,177]$	$T_{245} = [37,277]$
Customer 46 (18,80)	10	$T_{146} = [432,665]$	$T_{246} = [429,699]$
Customer 47 (2,45)	10	$T_{147} = [38,332]$	$T_{247} = [45,285]$
Customer 48 (42,5)	10	$T_{148} = [424,904]$	$T_{248} = [664,904]$
Customer 49 (42,12)	10	$T_{149} = [460,539]$	$T_{249} = [380,620]$
Customer 50 (72,35)	30	$T_{150} = [327,807]$	$T_{250} = [447,687]$

continued on following page

APPENDIX II CONTINUED

Customer 51 (55,20)	19	$T_{151} = [273, 498]$	$T_{251} = [266, 506]$
Customer 52 (25,30)	3	$T_{152} = [25, 505]$	$T_{252} = [115, 355]$
Customer 53 (20,50)	5	$T_{153} = [405, 465]$	$T_{253} = [315, 555]$
Customer 54 (55,60)	16	$T_{154} = [554, 767]$	$T_{254} = [541, 781]$
Customer 55 (30,60)	16	$T_{155} = [629, 698]$	$T_{255} = [539, 779]$
Customer 56 (50,35)	19	$T_{156} = [560, 673]$	$T_{256} = [497, 737]$
Customer 57 (30,25)	23	$T_{157} = [342, 571]$	$T_{257} = [337, 577]$
Customer 58 (15,10)	20	$T_{158} = [842, 902]$	$T_{258} = [662, 902]$
Customer 59 (10,20)	19	$T_{159} = [42, 522]$	$T_{259} = [42, 282]$
Customer 60 (15,60)	17	$T_{160} = [623, 884]$	$T_{260} = [634, 874]$
Customer 61 (45,65)	9	$T_{161} = [214, 421]$	$T_{261} = [198, 438]$
Customer 62 (65,35)	3	$T_{162} = [197, 257]$	$T_{262} = [107, 347]$
Customer 63 (65,20)	6	$T_{163} = [39, 316]$	$T_{263} = [39, 297]$
Customer 64 (45,30)	17	$T_{164} = [191, 310]$	$T_{264} = [131, 371]$
Customer 65 (35,40)	16	$T_{165} = [11, 140]$	$T_{265} = [11, 251]$
Customer 66 (41,37)	16	$T_{166} = [570, 681]$	$T_{266} = [506, 746]$
Customer 67 (64,42)	9	$T_{167} = [298, 358]$	$T_{267} = [208, 448]$
Customer 68 (40,60)	21	$T_{168} = [613, 730]$	$T_{268} = [552, 792]$
Customer 69 (31,52)	27	$T_{169} = [187, 247]$	$T_{269} = [97, 337]$
Customer 70 (35,69)	23	$T_{170} = [780, 930]$	$T_{270} = [690, 930]$
Customer 71 (65,55)	14	$T_{171} = [191, 410]$	$T_{271} = [181, 421]$
Customer 72 (63,65)	8	$T_{172} = [27, 507]$	$T_{272} = [87, 267]$
Customer 73 (2,60)	5	$T_{173} = [240, 451]$	$T_{273} = [226, 466]$
Customer 74 (20,20)	8	$T_{174} = [675, 735]$	$T_{274} = [585, 825]$

continued on following page

APPENDIX II CONTINUED

Customer 75 (5,5)	16	$T_{175} = [57,537]$	$T_{275} = [172,412]$
Customer 76 (60,12)	31	$T_{176} = [298,358]$	$T_{276} = [208,448]$
Customer 77 (23,3)	7	$T_{177} = [794,854]$	$T_{277} = [660,900]$
Customer 78 (8,56)	27	$T_{178} = [366,483]$	$T_{278} = [305,545]$
Customer 79 (6,68)	30	$T_{179} = [382,442]$	$T_{279} = [292,532]$
Customer 80 (47,47)	13	$T_{180} = [817,942]$	$T_{280} = [702,942]$
Customer 81 (49,58)	10	$T_{181} = [332,497]$	$T_{281} = [295,535]$
Customer 82 (27,43)	9	$T_{182} = [14,494]$	$T_{282} = [92,332]$
Customer 83 (37,31)	14	$T_{183} = [19,499]$	$T_{283} = [45,285]$
Customer 84 (57,29)	18	$T_{184} = [425,485]$	$T_{284} = [335,575]$
Customer 85 (63,23)	2	$T_{185} = [164,644]$	$T_{285} = [284,524]$
Customer 86 (21,24)	28	$T_{186} = [310,507]$	$T_{286} = [289,529]$
Customer 87 (12,24)	13	$T_{187} = [389,449]$	$T_{287} = [299,539]$
Customer 88 (24,58)	19	$T_{188} = [262,377]$	$T_{288} = [200,440]$
Customer 89 (67,5)	25	$T_{189} = [611,897]$	$T_{289} = [653,893]$
Customer 90 (37,47)	6	$T_{190} = [311,526]$	$T_{290} = [299,539]$
Customer 91 (49,42)	13	$T_{191} = [457,937]$	$T_{291} = [659,899]$
Customer 92 (53,43)	14	$T_{192} = [14,74]$	$T_{292} = [14,254]$
Customer 93 (61,52)	3	$T_{193} = [789,928]$	$T_{293} = [688,698]$
Customer 94 (57,48)	23	$T_{194} = [212,692]$	$T_{294} = [332,572]$
Customer 95 (56,37)	6	$T_{195} = [20,500]$	$T_{295} = [40,280]$
Customer 96 (55,54)	26	$T_{196} = [382,862]$	$T_{296} = [502,742]$
Customer 97 (4,18)	35	$T_{197} = [516,697]$	$T_{297} = [487,727]$
Customer 98 (26,52)	9	$T_{198} = [14,494]$	$T_{298} = [112,352]$
Customer 99 (26,35)	15	$T_{199} = [338,398]$	$T_{299} = [248,488]$
Customer 100 (31,67)	3	$T_{1100} = [870,930]$	$T_{2100} = [690,930]$
Depot (40,50)	0	$T_{1D} = [0,960]$	

Chapter XVI
A Data Envelopment Analysis Approach for Household Appliances and Automobile Recycling

Elif Kongar
University of Bridgeport, Bridgeport, CT, USA

Surendra M. Gupta
Northeastern University, Boston, USA

ABSTRACT

Rapid technological developments are leading to a significant decrease in the demand for old technology products. As a result, old technology products are rushed to their end-of-lives (EOLs) even though they still function properly and have the ability to satisfy stated needs. It is therefore important to find environmentally and economically benign ways to handle this accumulating waste to regain the value added to such products and to reduce the environmental damage. However, EOL recovery options are not always economically justifiable due to the complexity and uncertainty involved in the process. To reduce these setbacks, it is crucial to perform an analysis prior to taking any action and rank the products according to the importance of their EOL processing outcomes. To this end, this chapter proposes a data envelopment analysis (DEA) algorithm to determine the technical efficiency of end-of-life processing of household appliances and automobiles depending on various tangible and intangible performance criteria.

Copyright © 2009, IGI Global, distributing in print or electronic forms without written permission of IGI Global is prohibited.

INTRODUCTION

Advanced manufacturing technologies coupled with increased desire of customers to acquire the newest products have transformed highly technical products into time-sensitive items. With each technological enhancement, demand and need for old technology products diminish. As a result, such products are rushed to their end-of-lives (EOLs) even though they often function properly and are able to satisfy stated needs.

The severity of the problem increases as the advancement of countries increase, since the market for technological products tends to be larger in advanced nations. The population of a country is an additional factor that contributes to the size of the market, and hence the severity of the problems caused by EOL products. Thus, the United States, being one of the wealthiest nations in the world with its over 300 million residents, provides an appropriate environment for EOL product management case studies.

Automobiles are one of the most common products that are recycled in industry. The economics of their EOL processing operations has been well studied in the literature. Furthermore, in the United States, as reported by ARC, an average American family owns half a dozen major appliances (AHAM, 2007). For instance, 88.81 million households in the U.S. own at least one refrigerator and 18.19 million households own more than one refrigerator, corresponding to approximately 100% of the overall households in the United States with refrigerators (Table 1).

This fact, coupled with environmental regulations and increasing public awareness, has started to motivate many organizations and researchers to seek environmentally benign ways to manage highly technical EOL products.

As is well known, every EOL product is potentially hazardous to the environment if not handled properly. On the other hand, if proper actions are taken, there is a significant potential for savings in energy usage, virgin material usage, and reduction in air pollution, water pollution, and consumption. Among the proper actions, recycling, remanufacturing, reuse, and proper disposal are accepted as the most common and efficient ways for EOL processing.

However, economically benign ways of these actions remain a challenge for governmental and industrial organizations. Thus, it is crucial to perform some sort of decision analysis prior to taking any action and rank the products based on the importance of their EOL processing outcomes. To achieve this, various criteria can be employed, such as: scarcity and resale price of the materials content of the EOL product, difficulty level and cost of EOL processing activities, frequency of disposal, potential environmental damage of the EOL product, and so forth.

To this end, in this chapter, we propose a data envelopment analysis (DEA) algorithm to determine the technical efficiency of EOL processing of household appliances based on the above mentioned tangible and intangible performance criteria.

BACKGROUND

Data envelopment analysis is a widely applied methodology for evaluating relative efficiencies of a set of decision making units (DMUs). DEA can embody multiple outputs and inputs without a priori weights and allows introduction of both quantitative and qualitative data in different units.

Due to the above mentioned advantages, DEA has become a very popular tool among both academicians and institutions that are seeking ways to compare similar entities depending on quantitative results.

Sarkis (1999) proposed a two-stage methodology to integrate managerial preferences and environmentally conscious manufacturing (ECM) programs. In a subsequent paper, Sarkis and Cordeiro (2001) investigated the relationships

*Table 1. Appliances in U.S. households, selected years, 1980-2001**

	Survey Year								
Survey Category	**1980**	**1981**	**1982**	**1984**	**1987**	**1990**	**1993**	**1997**	**2001**
Number of Households (millions)	82	83	84	86	91	94	97	101	107
Air-Conditioners	(percent of households)								
Central	27	27	28	30	34	39	44	47	55
Individual Room Units	30	31	30	30	30	29	25	25	23
None	43	42	42	40	36	32	32	28	23
Electric Appliances									
Clothes Dryer	47	45	45	46	51	53	57	55	57
Clothes Washer	74	73	71	73	75	76	77	77	79
Computer, Personal	NA	NA	NA	NA	NA	16	23	35	56
Dehumidifier	9	9	9	9	10	12	9	NA	11
Dishwasher	37	37	36	38	43	45	45	50	53
Evaporative Cooler	4	4	4	4	3	4	3	NA	3
Fan, Ceiling	NA	NA	NA	NA	NA	NA	54	61	65
Fan, Whole House	NA	NA	8	8	9	10	4	NA	NA
Fan, Window or Ceiling	NA	NA	28	35	46	51	60	NA	NA
Freezer, Separate	38	38	37	37	34	34	35	33	32
Oven, Microwave	14	17	21	34	61	79	84	83	86
Pump for Swimming Pool	3	4	3	NA	NA	5	5	5	6
Pump for Well Water	NA	NA	NA	NA	NA	15	13	14	13
Range (stove-top burner)	54	54	53	54	57	58	61	60	60
Refrigerator (one)	86	87	86	88	86	84	85	85	83
Refrigerator (two or more)	14	13	13	12	14	15	15	15	17
Television Set (any type)	98	98	98	98	98	99	99	NA	NA
Television Set (b/w)	51	48	46	43	36	31	20	NA	NA
Television Set (color)	82	83	85	88	93	96	98	99	99
Waterbed Heaters	NA	NA	NA	10	14	15	12	8	5
Gas Appliances									
Clothes Dryer	14	16	15	16	15	16	15	16	17
Heater for Swimming Pool	(s)	(s)	(s)	1	1	1	1	1	1
Outdoor Gas Grill	9	9	11	13	20	26	29	NA	NA
Outdoor Gas Light	2	2	2	1	1	1	1	1	(s)
Range (stove-top burner)	46	46	47	45	43	42	38	39	39
Kerosene Appliance									
Portable Heater	(s)	1	3	6	6	5	3	2	2

**Energy Information Administration, Form EIA-457, Residential Consumption Survey, for each year shown*

between environmental and financial performance at the firm level. Talluri, Baker, and Sarkis (1999) applied DEA and goal programming methods to a value chain network (VCN) considering the cross efficiency evaluations of decision making units (DMUs). Sarkis (2000) compared DEA and conventional multiple criteria decision making (MCDM) tools in terms of efficiency and concluded that DEA seemed to perform well as a discrete alternative MCDM tool. Sarkis (2000) and Sarkis and Weinrach (2001) used DEA to evaluate environmentally conscious waste treatment technologies. Sarkis (2000) explained how DEA can be used to improve eco-efficiency. Kusomanen and Kortelainen (2005) employed DEA to measure the eco-efficiency scores for three towns of eastern Finland. Munksgaard, Wier, Lenzen, and Dey (2006) used DEA as a complement of input-output analysis using the example of CO_2.

Methods other than DEA have also been utilized to study materials life cycles and eco-efficiency issues. Ecological impact of the life cycle scrap has been the focus of Moyer and Gupta's (1997) study on minimization of life-cycle scrap via a comprehensive survey of previous work on environmentally conscious manufacturing practices. Further, Gupta and Isaacs (1997) investigated the alternative disposal strategies for vehicle design with varying relative proportions of materials using goal programming to analyze the tradeoffs between technological, economic, and environment factors. Isaacs and Gupta (1997) also analyzed the effects of substitution of high-grade plastics for steel where discarded products are no longer considered as scrap metal using goal programming (GP) techniques. This study is followed by Boon, Isaacs, and Gupta (2000), where the authors applied GP to examine the economic impact of aluminum intensive vehicles on the U.S. automotive recycling infrastructure. Creating a model of the automobile-recycling infrastructure, Boon et al. (2003) used the GP technique to assess the materials streams and process profitability for several different clean vehicles.

INTRODUCTION TO DATA ENVELOPMENT ANALYSIS APPROACH

DEA is a linear programming-based technique to measure the relative efficiency of organizational units. Since its development by Charnes, Cooper, and Rhodes (1978), DEA has been widely used to benchmark and evaluate performance in various industries such as healthcare, education, banking, and manufacturing due to its advantages. The most appealing advantage of DEA is that the method can accommodate multiple inputs and multiple outputs allowing these inputs and outputs to be expressed in different units of measurement. DEA also provides ease in comparing multiple decision making units (DMUs) by providing a single score for each DMU by optimizing the performance measure of each individual unit. Here, efficient units form the "efficient frontier" and inefficient units are enveloped by this frontier providing information on their improvement potential.

This single score provides the user with a more informative solution environment compared to benchmarking and ranking techniques that are available in the literature. As it will be explained in detail in the following section, any score less than 1 implies that there is a chance of improvement for the DMU compared to other units in the problem space.

Furthermore, unlike parametric approaches such as regression analysis (RA), DEA optimizes on each individual observation and does not require a single function that suits best to all observations (Charnes, Cooper, Lewin, & Seiford, 1994). Comparison of DEA and RA has been well studied in the literature. Even though there exist some studies emphasizing the advantages of both (e.g., see Thanassoulis, 1993), it is more commonly accepted in the literature that DEA is more advantageous in comparing decision making units.

Banker, Conrad, and Strauss (1986) compared estimates of technical efficiencies of individual hospitals and reported that DEA estimates were highly related to the capacity utilization, whereas translog estimates did not provide such relationship.

Bowlin, Charnes, Cooper, and Sherman (1884) compared DEA and RA using 15 hypothetical hospitals and stated that DEA also performed better in estimating and returning scale characterizations. The authors concluded that DEA outperformed RA by being able to identify the sources of inefficiencies by underlining the resources that are used in excess in inefficient hospitals.

DEA algorithms can be categorized using two criteria, namely, the "orientation" and the "optimality scale." The "orientation" criterion categorizes DEA algorithms into two depending on whether the definition of efficiency used in the algorithm is input- or output-oriented. Simply put, *input-oriented* DEA models define efficiency as "the least input for the same amount of output," whereas *output-oriented* DEA models define it as "the most output for the same amount of input." The second criterion, namely, the "optimality scale" criterion categorizes DEA models into four based on the returns to scale. If production increases, efficiency may increase, remain constant, or decrease, thus demonstrating "Increasing Returns to Scale (IRS)," "Constant Returns to Scale (CRS)," or "Decreasing Returns to Scale (DRS)," respectively. "Variable Returns to Scale (VRS)" refers to a case where both an increase and a decrease in returns to scale are observed at alternative levels of output. First introduced by Banker et al. (1984) as an extension of the CRS DEA model, the VRS model assumes that not all DMUs operate on an optimal scale. In this chapter, an output-oriented CRS DEA model is utilized. A more detailed discussion of the CRS model is presented in the following sections.

A basic DEA model allows the introduction of multiple inputs and multiple outputs and obtains an "efficiency score" of each DMU with the conventional output/input ratio analysis. Defining basic efficiency as the ratio of weighted sum of outputs to the weighted sum of inputs, the relative efficiency score of a test DMU p can be obtained by solving the following DEA ratio model (CCR) proposed by Charnes et al. (1978):

$$\begin{aligned} \max \quad & \frac{\sum_{k=1}^{s} v_k y_{kp}}{\sum_{j=1}^{m} u_j x_{jp}} & & \\ s.\ t. \quad & \frac{\sum_{k=1}^{s} v_k y_{ki}}{\sum_{j=1}^{m} u_j x_{ji}} \le 1 & \forall \text{DMUs } i & \qquad (1) \\ & v_k, u_j \ge 0 & \forall k, j. & \end{aligned}$$

where,

y_{ki} = amount of output k produced by DMU i,
x_{ji} = amount of input j produced by DMU i,
v_k = weight given to output k,
u_j = weight given to input j.
$k = 1$ to s,
$j = 1$ to m,
$i = 1$ to n,

The nonlinear problem given in Equation (1) can be converted into a linear program as follows (for further explanation on the model, please see Charnes et al., 1994):

$$\begin{aligned} \max \quad & \sum_{k=1}^{s} v_k y_{kp} & & \\ s.\ t. \quad & \sum_{j=1}^{m} u_j x_{jp} = 1 & & \qquad (2) \\ & \sum_{k=1}^{s} v_k y_{ki} - \sum_{j=1}^{m} u_j x_{ji} \le 0 & \forall \text{DMUs } i & \\ & v_k, u_j \ge 0 & \forall k, j. & \end{aligned}$$

where the $\sum_{j=1}^{m} u_j x_{jp} = 1$ constraint sets an upper bound of 1 for the relative efficiency score.

The CCR model provided in Equation (2) is run for each DMU to obtain the corresponding technical efficiencies. Using duality, the dual of the model can be represented as follows:

$$\min$$

$$s.t.$$

$$\begin{aligned} &\sum_{i=1}^{n}\lambda_i x_{ji} - \theta x_{jp} \leq 0 && \forall \text{Inputs } j \\ &\sum_{i=1}^{n}\lambda_i y_{ki} - y_{kp} \geq 0 && \forall \text{Outputs } k \\ &\lambda_i \geq 0 && \forall \text{DMUs } i. \end{aligned} \quad (3)$$

Equation (3) is the dual of the basic input-oriented CCR model assuming constant returns to scale for all the inputs and outputs. Using Talluri's (2000) notation, the dual of a basic output-oriented CRS model can be written as follows:

$$\max \quad \Phi$$

$$s.t.$$

$$\begin{aligned} &x_{jp} - \sum_i \lambda_i x_{ji} \geq 0 && \forall \text{Inputs } j \\ &-\varphi y_{kp} + \sum_i \lambda_i y_{ki} \geq 0 && \forall \text{Outputs } k \\ &\lambda_i \geq 0 && \forall \text{DMUs } i. \end{aligned} \quad (4)$$

Equation (4) could be converted into a VRS model by adding the constraint $\sum_i \lambda_i \geq 0$ to the set of constraints. According to this formulation, variable Φ is the relative efficiency score of each DMU, and $1/\Phi$ is the technical efficiency value (E) for each DMU. If the technical efficiency value (E) is 1, then DMU p is the most efficient DMU for its selected weights. In other words, DMU p is on the optimal frontier and is not dominated by any other DMU. Alternatively, if the technical efficiency value (E) is less than one, then DMU p does not lie on the optimal frontier and there exists at least one more efficient DMU.

DEA APPLICATION TO END-OF-LIFE DECISION MAKING PROCESS

This chapter considers a simplified life cycle assessment method with the help of a DEA model that would compare household appliances and automobiles in the U.S. for their technical efficiencies in end-of-life processing activities.

LCA is a technique to assess the environmental aspects and potential impacts associated with a product, process, or service, by:

- Compiling an inventory of relevant energy and material inputs and environmental releases;
- Evaluating the potential environmental impacts associated with identified inputs and releases; and
- Interpreting the results to help you make a more informed decision (EPA, 2007).

The proposed algorithm ranks considered appliances depending on their environmental and economical outcomes after these activities. Here, TVs, computer monitors, personal computers (CPUs), consumer electronics, household electronics, and automobiles are investigated. The indicators include hazardous material content removed from the EOL product, amount of recycled steel per EOL product, and quantity of EOL products (unit).

In the proposed model, each household appliance and automobile corresponds to decision making units, whereas each indicator corresponds to either an input or an output variable in DEA. There are six decision making units (five household appliances and automobiles) and three criteria are introduced. The proposed three criteria include two inputs and one output.

Here, input criteria consists of h and r, and output criterion consists of q, where,
h = hazardous material content removed per EOL product (lb/unit),

r = amount of recycled steel per EOL product (lb/unit),
q = quantity of each EOL product type (unit).

Hence, following the notation of the first DEA model, the only output formulation for each DMU i (y_{1i}) can be written as follows:

$$y_{1i} = q_i \qquad \forall \text{DMUs } i. \qquad (5)$$

The inputs are *hazardous material content removed from the EOL product* (h) and *amount of recycled steel per EOL product* (r). Therefore, with similar reasoning, equations (6) and (7) can be expressed mathematically as follows:

$$x_{1i} = h_i \qquad \forall \text{DMUs } i. \qquad (6)$$

$$x_{2i} = r_i \qquad \forall \text{DMUs } i. \qquad (7)$$

Table 2 represents the criteria for the five EOL products.

Here, hazardous material content (h_i, i = 1, 2, 3, 4, 5) indicates the lead in a CRT's funnel glass and the frit, whereas, for automobiles, this value (h_i, i = 6) includes all the hazardous material such as zinc, lead, and copper.

Using these data, the output-oriented DEA model is run and technical efficiency *(TE)* values for each EOL product in the sample is calculated.

The results of the model are presented in Table 3 in descending order of *TE* values.

As can be observed from Table 3, the most efficient EOL product is automobile, since it dominates the appliances by providing the highest benefit for both the environment and the recycler. With similar reasoning, TVs follow automobiles, whereas personal computers (CPUs) provide the least efficient recycling results. This is initiated

Table 2. Initial data for the DEA model

EOL Product	Quantity*	Hazardous material content (lb/unit)	Steel content (lb/unit)
TVs	11	23.049	22.928
Computer Monitors	5	7.089	4.254
Personal Computers	10	0	1.010
Consumer Electronics	10	0	11.525
Household Electronics	7	0	5.027
Automobiles$	30	167.002	156.308

*Adjusted from (MOOEA, 2001)
$ Estimated from (Gupta & Isaacs, 1997)

Table 3. Results of the DEA model

Rank	DMU	Score
1	Automobiles	1.00
2	TVs	0.40
3	Computer Monitors	0.25
4	Consumer Electronics	0.22
5	Household Electronics	0.14
6	Personal Computers	0.02

Table 4. Results of the DEA model

Rank	DMU	Score
1	Automobiles	1.00
1	Personal Computers	1.00
3	Computer Monitors	0.96
4	Household Electronics	0.95
5	Consumer Electronics	0.67
6	TVs	0.23

by the insignificant amount of hazardous material and steel.

The results would have naturally varied if there were additional input and output variables included in the model. For example, if the scarcity or amount of precious material content of CPUs were embedded as one of the output variables, CPUs might have climbed up in the ranking. Similarly, if monetary values were fed into the model one would easily expect a change in the results. This situation can easily be observed from Table 4.

According to the second output-oriented DEA model (Table 4), when monetary values are embedded in the model replacing the quantity indicators, technical efficiency of personal computer significantly increases and joins the automobile as one of the most efficient DMUs.

This is a good example on the importance of input and output variable selection for the EOL decision making process. However, it also proves that DEA algorithm provides meaningful results and can easily be adapted to the current environmental and economic changes. That is, if the significance of the material content of the EOL products change, the model then can easily be altered to fit the new settings.

CONCLUSION

In this chapter, an application of output-oriented DEA model is considered and applied to a sample of six EOL products to determine the relative efficiency score of each product for their end-of-life management processes. The model provides a basis to perform further investigation on the end-of-life management processes.

DEA models do not require any a priori weights for either the input or the output variables of interest. However, the results are sensitive to the choice of the data set and their reliability increases with sample size and accuracy of the data.

FUTURE RESEARCH

Model results would also vary if additional EOL products were fed into the model, providing different technical efficiencies for each EOL product. However, proposed methodology provides meaningful and reliable results providing a basis for establishing take-back policies for household appliances and automobiles. The model can easily be enriched by adding a variety of EOL products and input and output variables in the future.

However, products are different by their nature and require different handling methodologies when they reach their end-of-lives. For instance, hazardous material content might not exist for some product categories, necessitating an alteration in the proposed DEA models.

Furthermore, introducing the supply chain operations reference model (SCOR) to future study can broaden the analysis of end-of-life products.

REFERENCES

AHAM. (2007). *Recycling major home appliances*. ARIC, Appliance Recycling Information Center.

Banker, R. D., Charnes, A., & Cooper, W. W. (1984). Some models for estimating technical and scale inefficiencies in data envelopment analysis. *Management Science, 30*(9), 1078-1092.

Banker, R. D., Conrad, R. F., & Strauss, R. P. (1986). A comparative application of data envelopment analysis and translog methods: An illustrative study of hospital production. *Management Science, 32*(1), 30-44.

Boon, J., Isaacs, J. A., & Gupta, S. M. (2000). Economic impact of aluminum intensive vehicles on the U.S. automotive recycling infrastructure. *Journal of Industrial Ecology, 4*(2), 117-134.

Boon, J. E., Isaacs, J. A., & Gupta, S. M. (2003). End-of-life infrastructure economics for "clean vehicles" in the United States. *Journal of Industrial Ecology, 7*(1), 25-45.

Bowlin, W. F., Charnes, A., Cooper, W. W., & Sherman, H. D. (1984). Data envelopment analysis and regression approaches to efficiency estimation and evaluation. *Annals of Operations Research, V2*(1), 113-138.

Charnes, A., Cooper, W. W., Lewin, A. Y., & Seiford, L. M. (1994). *Data envelopment analysis: Theory, methodology, and applications*. Boston: Kluwer.

Charnes, A., Cooper, W., & Rhodes, E. (1978). Measuring the efficiency of decision-making units. *European Journal of Operational Research, 2*(6), 429-444.

EPA. (2007). Life cycle assessment: Principles and practice. *Life-cycle assessment research*. Retrieved July 9, 2008, from http://www.epa.gov/nrmrl/lcaccess/lca101.html

Gupta, S. M., & Isaacs, J. A. (1997). Value analysis of disposal strategies for automobiles. *Computers & Industrial Engineering, 33*(1-2), 325-328.

Isaacs, J. A., & Gupta, S. M. (1997). Economic consequences of increasing polymer content on U.S. automobile recycling infrastructure. *Journal of Industrial Ecology, 1*(4), 19-33.

Kuosmanen, T., & Kortelainen, M. (2005). Measuring eco-efficiency of production with data envelopment analysis. *Journal of Industrial Ecology, 9*(4), 59-72.

MOOEA. (2001). *Minnesota's demonstration project for recycling used electronics*. Minnesota Office of Environmental Assistance.

Moyer, L., & Gupta, S. M. (1997). Environmental concerns and recycling: Disassembly efforts in the electronics industry. *Journal of Electronics Manufacturing, 7*(1), 1-22.

Munksgaard, J., Wier, M., Lenzen, M., & Dey, C. (2006). Using input-output analysis to measure the environmental pressure of consumption at different spatial levels. *Journal of Industrial Ecology, 9*(1-2), 169-185.

Sarkis, J. (1999). A methodological framework for evaluating environmentally conscious manufacturing programs. *Computers & Industrial Engineering, 36*(4), 793-810.

Sarkis, J. (2000). Comparative analysis of DEA as a discrete alternative multiple criteria decision tool. *European Journal of Operational Research, 123*(3), 543-557.

Sarkis, J. (2000, November 5-8). Ecoefficiency: How data envelopment analysis can be used by managers and researchers. In *Proceedings of the SPIE International Conference on Environmentally Conscious Manufacturing*, Boston, MA (pp. 194-203).

Sarkis, J., & Cordeiro, J. J. (2001). An empirical evaluation of environmental efficiencies and firm performance: Pollution prevention versus end-of-pipe practice. *European Journal of Operational Research, 135*(1), 102-113.

Sarkis, J., & Weinrach, J. (2001). Using data envelopment analysis to evaluate environmentally conscious waste treatment technology. *Journal of Cleaner Production, 9*(5), 417-427.

Talluri, S. (2000). Data envelopment analysis: Models and extensions. *Decision Line, 31*(3), 8-11.

Talluri, S., Baker, R. C., & Sarkis, J. (1999). Framework for designing efficient value chain networks. *International Journal of Production Economics, 62*(1-2), 133-144.

Thanassoulis, E. (1993). A comparison of regression analysis and data envelopment analysis as alternative methods for performance assessments. *Journal of the Operational Research Society, 44*(11), 1129-1144.

ADDITIONAL READING

Readers interested in more information on data envelopment analysis, end-of-life processing, and environmentally conscious manufacturing are referred to the following publications.

APME. (2001). A material of innovation for the electrical and electronic industry: Insight into consumption and recovery in Western Europe 2000. Brussels, Belgium: Association of Plastic Manufacturers in Europe.

Boon, J. E., Isaacs, J. A., & Gupta, S. M. (2002). Economic sensitivity for end of life planning and processing of personal computers. Journal of Electronics Manufacturing, 11(1), 81-93.

Cooper, W. W., Seiford, L. M., & Tone, K. (2006). *Data envelopment analysis: A comprehensive text with models, applications, references and DEA-solver software*. Springer-Verlag.

Fisher, M., Kingsbury, T., & Headley, L. (2004). *Sustainable electrical and electronic plastics recycling*. Paper presented at the International Symposium on Electronics and the Environment (ISEE 04), Phoenix, AZ.

Fisher, M., & Peuch, P. (1998). *Plastics in electronic equipment: Quantifying the U.S. and European marketplace*. Paper presented at the Annual Recycling Conference (ARC 98), Chicago.

Graedel, T. E., & Allenby, B. R. (1996). *Design for environment*. Prentice Hall.

Gupta, S. M., & Lambert, A. J. D. (Eds.). (2008). *Environment conscious manufacturing*. Boca Raton, FL: CRC Press.

Kongar, E., & Gupta, S. M. (2002). A multi-criteria decision making approach for disassembly-to-order systems. *Journal of Electronics Manufacturing, 11*(2), 171-183.

Kongar, E., & Gupta, S. M. (2006a). Disassembly sequencing using genetic algorithm. *International Journal of Advanced Manufacturing Technology, 30*(5-6), 497-506.

Kongar, E., & Gupta, S. M. (2006b). Disassembly to order system under uncertainty. *OMEGA, 34*(6), 550-561.

Lambert, A. J. D., & Gupta, S. M. (2005). *Disassembly modeling for assembly, maintenance, reuse, and recycling*. Boca Raton, FL: CRC Press.

Lifset, R. (1993). Take it back: Extended producer responsibility as a form of incentive-based policy. *Journal of Resource Management and Technology, 21*(4), 163-175.

Rios, P., Stuart, J. A., & Grant, E. (2003). Plastics disassembly versus bulk recycling: Engineering design for EOL electronics resource recovery. *Environmental Science Technology, 37*, 5463-5470.

Sarkis, J. (Ed.). (2002). *Greener manufacturing and operations: From design to delivery and back*. Sheffield: Greenleaf Publications.

Tyteca, D. (1998). Sustainability indicators at the firm level: Pollution and resource efficiency as a necessary condition toward sustainability. *Journal of Industrial Ecology, 2*(4), 61-78.

Wang, T., Müller, D. B., & Graedel, T. E. (2007). Forging the anthropogenic iron cycle. *Environmental Science and Technology, 41*, 5120-5129.

Section IV
Web-Based Management Technology

Chapter XVII
Green Product Retrieval and Recommendations System

Yi-Chun Liao
Hsuan Chuang University, Taiwan, R.O.C.

ABSTRACT

This chapter introduces a preference-based recommendation procedure in a green product information retrieval system. It constructs a green information management system based on data mining technology. Green products and relevant green regulations were collected and then integrated in a content-based and collaborative filtering method to provide a preference-based query interface for green products. It is hoped that the proposed system offers consumers a green information platform when they are considering buying green products. Our proposed system recommends the best possible choices for consumers that indicate a green preference. Besides serving as a green information retrieval for the consumers, the system also assists the product designers with understanding the preference some consumers have for green products and the satisfaction they get from buying these products.

With the steadily worsening pollution and the continuous degradation of the environment, consumers are becoming more and more concerned about what they eat, the goods they purchase, and the impact it has on the environment. Jones (1994) pointed out that 94% of Italians will consider the green index when selecting a product; 77% of Americans regard the green index as an important reference for purchase and more than 40% of consumers in Europe love to purchase products with a green seal. However, in Asia green consumerism is still a very limited phenomenon, as far as the share of green consumers in the overall population is concerned, as well as the willingness to pay for green products. At the same time however, there is little useful information available on the Internet that helps consumers to make a green purchase decision.

To respond to the global environment trend, an increasing number of environmental labeling programs have been developed that identify producers and the level of environmental friendliness of their

Copyright © 2009, IGI Global, distributing in print or electronic forms without written permission of IGI Global is prohibited.

company or their product. Meanwhile, more and more companies are emphasizing green in their product as a matter of business policy. However, most of the green products that are being produced are designed to follow the international green regulations and policies, for example, WEEE, RoHS, and so forth, and few producers consider the consumers' needs and perception of green. As a result, the market share of green products remains restricted. How to increase consumer satisfaction, while being restricted by a limited budget and guided by only a set of basic green rules, is an important task for a green producer. In other words, the criteria that need to be considered for producing a green product should be identified beforehand.

Consumers often find it difficult to understand let alone make a judgment regarding the criteria of the green products in the market. Faced with the huge amount of general information available on the Internet, consumers have to spend much time and effort sorting through the results provided by all kinds of search engines, forums, advertisements, and so forth. Therefore, we will design a green product information retrieval system which provides consumers with green information, green products recommendation, and allows for feedback regarding the level of satisfaction with the recommender system.

In other words, the system will provide a green platform for the green product designers so that the producers can create green models by which to understand the expectation of consumers regarding green products.

MANAGEMENT INFORMATION SYSTEM

The Trend of E-Business

First, business and technology trends are changing rapidly. More and more enterprises increase their portion of the e-market and develop their information systems (Post & Anderson, 2003). Utilization of the Internet has changed how people network and communicate, and the worldwide Web has changed how we obtain information.

Consequently, customer-oriented interactive systems are becoming a major trend in the development of the current e-business system (Blecker et al., 2005). Information systems should support the requirements of the customers while automating the operating process, allowing customers to configure their products by specifying the attributes of the products they are looking for (Bramham & MacCarthy, 2003). In order to configure a system for a user, the system requires an accurate understanding of the customer's needs so as to create a complete description of a product that suits the consumer's individual requirements. Given a set of customer requirements and a product family description, the task of configuration is to find a valid and completely specified product among all of the alternatives (Sabin & Weigel, 1998). Up to now, the product configuration process has been a very technical-oriented process, necessitating product expertise of the customer while seldom taking into account the requirements of the customer.

When it comes to configuration knowledge, there are three important design approaches based on: (a) rule-based, (b) model-based, or (c) case-based, respectively (Sabin & Weigel, 1998). The rule-based knowledge representation method relies on rules which have the following form: "if condition then consequence," which is the most common one implemented in practice. The main assumption behind model-based reasoning is that the system's model consists of decomposable entities and interactions between their elements. For configuration problems with high product complexity, model-based approaches are more convenient than rule-based approaches. The case-based approach relies on the assumption that similar problems have similar solutions. The knowledge necessary for this type of reasoning consists of cases that record a set of configurations sold earlier to customers. The implementation of a case-based reasoning system is appropriate when the solution space consists of only a few products.

Furthermore, suppliers never stop improving the advisory quality in mass customization. Muther (2000) provided a supplier-customer model that structures the relationship between customers and suppliers in four phases: stimulation, evaluation, purchasing, and after-sales. A customer advisory is especially important during the evaluation phase in which the customer evaluates different product offers in order to decide which product to buy. In this phase, the customer must process the information about the different products that are available. To ensure a high level of customer satisfaction as well as an optimal personalized advisory, valuable data about the customers must be obtained for all of the four phases, which has to be automated and offered as an e-service today.

In the existing customer advisory systems, recommender systems have been successfully implemented in online shops. Generally, they support people who have little or no product knowledge in making a suitable choice (Resnick & Varian, 1997).

Introduction to Green Information Systems

Although everyone agrees that green information is needed and that regulations and policies need to be drawn up, few green management information systems have been proposed and even fewer have been implemented. Even if we give the query "green product" to today's most powerful search engine, Google, the result are not systematic. Google is a general search engine which has the ability to find any information you are interested in; however, Google does not emphasize a specified object or area.

In order to develop a specific green information system, Anderl, Daum, John, and Putter (1997) developed a cooperative Web-based information system for green products. Different departments within a company cooperate on the proposed platform during the early design phases to minimize any harmful effect on the environment. Middendorf, Hoppner, and Teller (1997) implemented a closed loop economic network connecting various companies and created the IDEE (Information Network for Recycling of Electronic Equipment) for exchanging information on products, processes, and economic factors, from the recycler to the producer. Kurakawa et al. (1996) developed a green browser, an Internet-based information sharing tool for the design of a product life cycle, to support designers and specialists collaborating when considering the trade-off relationships among the requirements for a product over its life cycle. These above systems only provide the required information for the producers, but they are not necessarily useful to the needs of the customers.

Therefore, the Green Electronics Council (2006) built up an assessment system (Electronic Product Environmental Assessment Tool, EPEAT) to help purchasers compare and select desktop computers, notebooks, and monitors based on their environmental attributes. This system also provides a clear and consistent set of performance criteria for the design of products. Based on this formation, the manufacturers are able to secure market recognition of their computer products and reduce their environmental impact. Although the products database collected by EPEAT grows constantly, it can only offer the users a list of green products for browsing, but it cannot provide any suggestions to the consumer regarding the use of the product based on the user's preference.

Compared to a general search engine, our proposed system focuses on specific green products. We collect the green information and any relevant green regulations, on the product, and then we analyze their characteristics. This allows us to provide a preference-based interface for green products queries based on the data mining technology and the collected green database. In addition, the system recommends other or better choices to the consumers for their green product purchase.

DESIGN OF THE CUSTOMER-ORIENTED RETRIEVAL SYSTEM

Basic Concept of Information Retrieval

Information retrieval (IR) is developed for finding documents with a high degree of relevance, not simply finding a match to a pattern. The effective retrieval of relevant information is directly affected by both the user and the logical view of the documents (information) adopted by the retrieval system (Baeza-Yates & Riberio-Neto, 1999).

The user of a retrieval system has to translate his or her need into a query in the language provided by the system. With an information retrieval system, this implies the need of specifying a set of words which convey the semantics of the information. With a data retrieval system, a query is used to convey the conditions that must be satisfied by objects in the answer. In both cases, the user searches for useful information by executing a retrieval task.

On the other hand, documents in a collection are frequently represented through a set of index terms or keywords. Such keywords might be extracted directly from the text of the documents or specified subjectively. No matter whether these keywords are derived automatically or generated by a specialist, they provide a logical reference to the document.

Retrieval system design depends on the retrieval model. Three classic models in information retrieval are: Boolean, Vector, and probabilistic (Baeza-Yates & Riberio-Neto, 1999). In the Boolean model, documents and queries are represented as sets of index terms. In the vector space model, documents and queries are represented as vectors in an n-dimensional space. In the probabilistic model, the framework for modeling documents and query representations is based on the probability theory. In the applications of information retrieval, the library was the first case to adopt IR systems. In the beginning, library systems consisted basically of an automation of previous technologies (such as card catalogs) and only allowed searchers based on author names and titles. Currently, the focus is on improved graphical interfaces, electronic forms, hypertext features, open system architectures, and so forth.

Due to the rapid development of Internet technology, several advanced applications have been developed, including product search, entertainment search, academic search, healthcare search, travel search, job search, and others. The search mechanism is changing from keywords to objects and the search content is changing from documents to images and multimedia.

Weight-Based Information Retrieval System Design

In the development process of a retrieval system, the search engine attracts most of the attention. However, there are four issues that concern the user the most.

a. **Global search**. To make the query process efficient, many researches focused on developing a personalized search engine or agent for reducing the size of the information space used in data mining approaches (Aggarwal, Gates, & Yu, 1998; Cutting, Karger, Pedersen, & Tukey, 1992; Jonesa, Walkerb, & Robertson, 2000; Leuski, 2001; Willet, 1988; Zamir, Etzioni, Madani, & Karp, 1997). However, the global search mechanism was not satisfactory. As a result, the common drawback of this system is that it provides incomplete information.

b. **Excessive-amount of query results**. Although complete information with a ranked listing is desirable, too much information is still hard for users to go through within a limited period of time. These issues have been discussed in the literature with the consideration of using data mining and optimization techniques (Glover, Lawrence, Gordon, Birmingham, & Giles, 1999, 2001). However, the required amount of information varies from user to user. Therefore, how to provide the appropriate amount of relevant information according to each user's need remains a concern.

c. **Automatic adjustment of the search structure.** Some studies on query expansion provided users the refined results from online feedback (Billerbeck, Scholer, Williams, & Zobel, 2003; Kim, Kim, & Kim, 2001; Lin, Wang, & Chen, 2006). The common draw backs for these methods are summarized as follows:
   - First, the re-query process requires addtional query terms from the user or is preference based on the previous retrieved results.
   - Second, this system cannot make use of the query experience of previous users to help new users.
   - Third, the existing search system cannot change its search structure based on the actions of the user, such as downloading a related document or accessing a Web site. Therefore, designing a self-learning search engine that can automatically adjust its search structure to a user's query behavior is both important and valuable.

d. **Ranking improvement.** Users usually realize their desired information after reviewing many of the displayed search results. Although it is a learning process, spending too much time often discourages a user. Because "time is money," how to improve the ranking mechanics of the search results is important. Based on the preference of the users, genetic algorithms have been applied to try and improve the search queries (Gordon, 1988; Yang & Korfhage, 1993). However, they didn't consistently provide a satisfactory evaluation of scoring and ranking the retrieved information.

A weight-based approach to information retrieval and relevance feedback is proposed (Liao, 2006). This approach is built according to the vector space model (Grossman & Frieder, 1998) of which the weight matrix based on keywords is constructed for all documents, as per Table 1.

Table 1. Weight matrix of documents

		Keywords				
		k_1	k_2 ...	k_j	...	k_M
Documents	d_1	w_{11}	w_{12}			w_{1M}
	d_2	w_{21}	w_{22}			
	⋮					
	d_i			w_{ij}		
	⋮					
	d_N	w_{N1}				w_{NM}

Deciding the weight is the next importance issue in this model. Salton (1970) first studied weight collection by considering term frequency (*tf*) and inverse document frequency (*idf*). tf_{ij} is defined as the number of occurrences of keyword k_j in document d_i, and idf_j is defined as $\log(N/df_j)$ in which N is the total number of documents and df_j the number of documents containing keyword k_j. Based on Salton's concept, several researchers further modified the formulas into various forms (Buckley, Singhal, & Mitra, 1995; Horng & Yeh, 2000; Lochbaum & Streeter, 1989; Salton & Buckley, 1988). Due to the consideration of trade-off between precision and time, Salton and Buckly's (1988) method described below has been adopted in the present study.

$$w_{ij} = \frac{(\log tf_{ij} + 1.0) \times idf_j}{\sum_{j=1}^{m} [(\log tf_{ij} + 1.0) \times idf_j]^2}, \quad j = 1,\ldots,M \text{ and } i = 1,\ldots,N \qquad (2.1)$$

Based on Formula (2.1), a weight matrix of all the documents with respect to the keywords can be set up. Then, a query vector $Q \equiv [q_j, j = 1, \ldots, M]$ corresponding to these keywords is defined by binary numbers of which the element $q_j = 1$, if any of the query terms given by a user matches the *j*th keyword in the keywords set; otherwise $q_j = 0$.

After the preliminary preparation of the weight matrix, we shall propose the method for our retrieval system by looking at the issues mentioned above.

For issue (a), to avoid providing incomplete search information, a global search approach is adopted by using a technique of cylindrical extension (Klir & Folger, 1988; Zimmermann, 1991) on the weight matrix, as defined below:

Definition 2.1: Let Q be a vector of size M and $Q_{CE} = [\overline{q}_{ij}]$ be an N×M matrix. Then, Q_{CE} is a *cylindrical extension* of Q defined by $\overline{q}_{ij} = q_j, \forall i = 1,\ldots,N$ as below and Q is the *base* of Q_{CE}.

$$Q = [q_1, q_2, \ldots, q_M]_{1\times M} \xrightarrow{\text{Cylindrical Extension}} Q_{CE}$$

$$= \begin{bmatrix} q_1 & q_2 & \cdots & q_M \\ \vdots & \vdots & \cdots & \vdots \\ q_1 & q_2 & \cdots & q_M \end{bmatrix}_{N\times M}$$

The cylindrical extension guarantees that all information that is included in the base will be employed in the determination of the extended relation. Then, the weight of the importance of a document will be measured according to the degree of fitness (DF) of the document with respect to the query vector with a min-operator defined as matrix F below:

$$F = [f_{ij}]_{N\times M}, \text{ where } f_{ij} = \min(w_{ij}, \overline{q}_{ij}), \quad 1 \le i \le N, 1 \le j \le M \qquad (2.2)$$

Then, we retrieve the documents by a specific weight threshold ($\overline{w}$) given by the system calculated from (2.3). The average weight value defined as formula (2.3) will be taken as a default weight threshold.

$$\overline{w} = \frac{\sum_{i=1}^{M}\sum_{j=1}^{N} w_{ij}}{M \times N}, \text{ where } w_{ij} > 0 \qquad (2.3)$$

Any weight component of matrix F greater than the threshold will be retained, which contributes to matrix C, as shown in (2.4). Based on this matrix, the system will calculate the scores, sco_i, of all documents, which are defined as the largest weighting value of each corresponding vector in formula (2.5).

$$C = [c_{ij}]_{N\times M}, \text{ where}$$

$$\begin{cases} c_{ij} = f_{ij}, & \text{if } f_{ij} \ge \overline{w} \\ c_{ij} = 0, & \text{if } f_{ij} < \overline{w} \end{cases}, 1 \le i \le N, 1 \le j \le M \qquad (2.4)$$

$$sco_i = \max_{1 \le j \le m}\{c_{ij}\}, \quad 1 \le i \le N \tag{2.5}$$

Document d_i is retrieved if sco_i is greater than zero and is added into the retrieved documents set, D, as shown in (2.6). After a query is made by a user, the system ranks the retrieved documents in order of sco_i and recommends in such order.

$$D = \{d_i \mid \text{if } sco_i > 0, 1 \le i \le N\} \tag{2.6}$$

Furthermore, to resolve issue (b), parameter α is introduced which allows users to retrieve the desired amount of documents by the following operations. If more information is desired, the users can click the "more" button. Then, in order to enlarge the number of the nonzero value in matrix C, the system will decrease the weight threshold by setting a value α >1 to adjust $\overline{w}$ by

$$\overline{w} = (\overline{w})^{\alpha}. \tag{2.7}$$

The larger α is, the larger the reduced range of the threshold is and the larger the amounts of retrieved documents are. The default value set in the system is α=1.5. On the other hand, if a lesser amount of documents is expected, especially when users don't have much time to filter a large amount of documents, the users can click the "Less" button and the system will increase the weight threshold for this setting 0<α <1 in (2.7). The smaller α is, the larger the incremental range of the threshold will be, and the smaller the amount of retrieved documents. For this case, α=0.9 is the default value.

The search engine provides an automatic adjustment mechanism for the users based on their preferences, and thus issue (b) in the introduction is resolved.

Finally, for issue (c) of self-learning, the keywords set K provided by the documents and the weight values will be updated by the feedback of the users. First, any new query term not belonging to K will be added and a new column of weight values will be computed and expanded automatically. Next, if any retrieved document d_i is downloaded by the users, the corresponding weight values with respect to the query keywords will be increased by formula (2.8) below. The default value of β=0.8 is set to increase the corresponding weight values.

$$w_{ij} = (w_{ij})^{\beta}, \quad \text{where } 0 < \beta < 1, i \in \{i \mid d_i \in D\} \text{ and } j \in \{j \mid q_j = 1\} \tag{2.8}$$

Therefore, the search structure is modified if more users make queries and download documents. Consequently, issue (c) is resolved. If a user gives the same query terms, the rank of the previous downloaded documents will be raised to achieve the goal of ranking improvement and solve the issue (d) in the introduction.

Based on these resolution concepts, we summarize the procedure as per the following flowchart and the detailed algorithm shown in the appendix.

An Example for Green Products Retrieval

In this section, a simple example of green products retrieval will illustrate the proposed weight-based retrieval system model.

Step 1. Twenty desktop products (documents) are picked for illustrating our proposed procedure from the Green Electronics Council Web site (2006). Eight green indices (keywords) are used to evaluate the greenness of the products, as per Table 2.2.

Step 2. We obtain the weight matrix of the products by computing their greenness, as per Table 2.3.

Step 3. Suppose a user makes a query that includes two indices, g1 (Reduction/ elimination of environmentally sensitive materials) and g5 (Energy conversation). The query vector will be

Figure 2.1. Flow chart of the proposed procedure

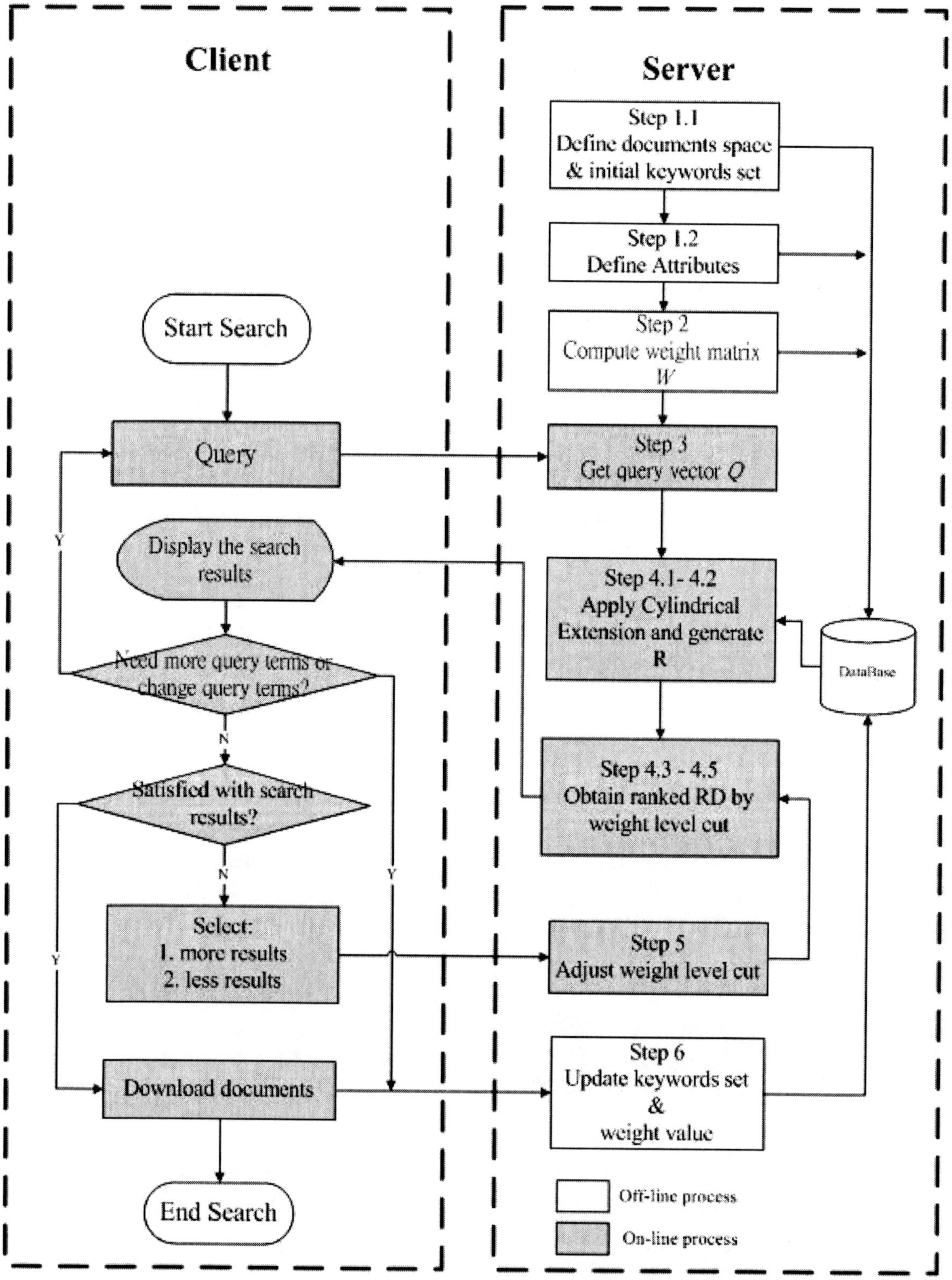

Table 2.2 Green index

Green index	Description
g_1	Reduction/elimination of environmentally sensitive materials
g_2	Materials selection
g_3	Design for end of life
g_4	Product longevity/life cycle extension
g_5	Energy conversation
g_6	End of life management
g_7	Corporate performance

Table 2.3. Weight (Greenness) matrix

Product	Product Name	g_1	g_2	g_3	g_4	g_5	g_6	g_7	g_8
P1	Apple Mac Pro	1	0.5	1	1	1	1	0.8	0.86
P2	ThinkCentre A51	0.71	0.5	1	1	0.25	1	0.71	0.86
P3	ThinkCentre A52(small)	1	0.5	1	1	0.25	1	0.71	0.71
P4	HP Compaq dc7700	0.86	0.5	1	1	0.8	0.67	1	0.57
P5	HP Compaq dc5750	0.86	0.5	1	1	0.8	0.67	1	0.57
P6	ThinkCentre M55 (Small Desktop)	0.71	0.5	1	1	0.25	1	0.71	0.71
P7	ThinkCentre M55p (Desktop)	0.71	0.5	1	1	0.25	1	0.71	0.71
P8	ThinkCentre A55 (Tower)	0.71	0.5	1	1	0.25	1	0.8	1
P9	OptiPlex GX620 USFF	0.71	0.5	1	1	0.25	1	1	0.57
P10	OptiPlex 745 USFF	0.71	0.5	1	1	0.25	1	1	0.57
P11	OptiPlex GX520 SFF	0.71	0.5	1	1	0.9	1	0.86	0.57
P12	OptiPlex 210L DT	0.71	0.5	1	1	0.8	1	0.86	0.57
P13	OptiPlex 210L MT	0.71	0.5	1	1	0.8	1	0.71	0.57
P14	Precision 490	0.71	0.5	1	1	0.7	1	0.71	0.57
P15	Precision 690	0.71	0.5	1	1	0.25	1	0.71	0.57
P16	OptiPlex GX620 DT	0.71	0.5	1	1	0.25	1	1	0.57
P17	Lenovo 3000 J100 (Tower)	0.86	0.5	1	1	0.25	1	0.8	0.71
P18	Lenovo 3000 J105 (Tower)	0.71	0.5	1	1	0.25	1	0.71	0.71
P19	Precision 390	0.71	0.5	1	1	0.25	1	0.71	0.71
P20	Meridian SL700	0.71	0.5	1	1	0.25	1	0.71	0.71

Table 2.4. Cylindrical extension matrix Q_{CE}

1	0	0	0	1	0	0	0
1	0	0	0	1	0	0	0
1	0	0	0	1	0	0	0
1	0	0	0	1	0	0	0
1	0	0	0	1	0	0	0
1	0	0	0	1	0	0	0
1	0	0	0	1	0	0	0
1	0	0	0	1	0	0	0
1	0	0	0	1	0	0	0
1	0	0	0	1	0	0	0

Q=[1, 0, 0, 0, 1, 0, 0, 0] and the extended matrix Q_{CE} is obtained, as shown in Table 2.4.

Step 4. From Formula (2.2), matrix F is generated. From formula (2.3), the weight threshold of $\overline{w}$ =0.755 is obtained, and then matrix C is obtained from Formula (2.4). Therefore, the retrieved set is D={pl, p3, p4, p5, p11, p12, p13, p17}.

Step 5. If the user wants more green products, s/he can select the "more" button. Then, after reducing the weight threshold based on the given α=1.5, the updated weight threshold is computed as 0.656 by Formula (2.7), and the retrieved set is D={pl, p2, 3, p4, p5, p6, p7, p8, p11, p12, p13, p14, p16, p17, p20}, where p2, p6, p7, p8, p14, p16 and p20 are added. On the other hand, if the user selects the "less" button, then, after increasing the weight threshold based on the given α=0.7, the updated weight threshold is computed as 0.821 by Formula (2.7) and the retrieved set is D={ pl, p3, p4, p5, p11, p17}, where p12 and p13 are eliminated.

RECOMMENDING SYSTEM DESIGN FOR BOTH CUSTOMER AND PRODUCER

Concepts of Recommenders

Many recommender systems for advising customers have been implemented in online marketing. In general, they help customers in making an appropriate choice in products buying or information acquisition. The main goal is to provide users with a product proposal that will meet their needs. Recommender systems can be regarded as information agents who serve their users, trying to provide them with the information that best serves their needs (Paulson & Tzanavari, 2002).

Schafer, Konstan, and Riedl (1999) provided a classification of recommender systems. They mainly distinguish between two techniques, namely personalized and nonpersonalized systems. Nonpersonalized recommender systems do not offer individual recommendations that meet the customer's individual interests. Recommendations are generated on the basis of an average rating of a wide range of customers who have previously expressed their preferences with respect to the products. For instance, the products that have the highest ratings attributed by other users are suggested to the customers. Nonpersonalized recommender systems cannot adequately support customers during the product configuration process in mass customization. However, personalized recommender systems make product suggestions according to the customers' individual preferences and are good candidates to provide the required customer assistance in mass customization. In this category of recommender systems, a distinction can be made between content-based filtering and collaborative filtering systems.

Content-based filtering is a technique that evaluates the attributes of the offered products with respect to the user model that holds the preferences of the individual customer. The objects with attributes that are not relevant for the individual customer are excluded from the recommendation. This method is especially appropriate if customers have a clear idea as to their interest and needs. However, it can be disadvantageous if the user does not reach many other products in the product assortment. A pure content-based system has several shortcomings (Balabanovic & Shoham, 1997). First, in some domains, the items are not amenable to any useful feature extraction methods with the current technology (such as movies, music, restaurants). A second problem, which has been studied extensively both in this domain and in others, is that of overspecialization. When the system can only recommend items scoring highly against a user's profile, the user is restricted to seeing only items similar to those already rated.

Collaborative filtering generates recommendations on the basis of similarities between customers. If there are similarities, for example, in their buying behavior, it is likely that there are also similarities between their preferences and interests. Therefore, products bought by other customers may be relevant for a particular user with similar preferences. Contrary to content-based filtering, collaborative filtering can also recommend products that are not directly related to the customer's profile or product's attributes. Therefore, it is popular to apply the recommender system of an enterprise, for example, Amazon, eBay, CDNOW, and so forth. There are some limitations when applying collaborative filtering techniques (Hung, 2005). The first limitation is the *sparsity* problem. Conventional collaborative filtering recommendation systems require users to explicitly input preference ratings about many products. The number of ratings received is relatively small compared to the number of ratings required for prediction. Consequently, the predicted ratings accuracy degrades significantly when the received ratings are sparse. The second limitation is the *scalability* problem. As the number of customers and products increase, the computation time of the algorithms, which perform product comparisons, grows accordingly. Another problem occurs on "cold start." A new user who did not provide ratings for all products cannot obtain any recommendation because the recommender system cannot find any neighbor with him.

There are other advanced techniques or hybrid approaches for personalized product recommendation that have been already implemented:

- **Demographic systems:** In addition to the user ratings, these systems collect demographical and social information about the users to determine their preferences (Pazzani, 1999).
- **Utility-based systems:** They use information about features and utility functions of the items that describe user preferences (Burke, 2002).
- **Knowledge-based systems:** They use knowledge about how a particular item meets a particular user's need. On this basis, the system can reason about the relationship between a need and a possible recommendation (Burke, 2002).

Green Products Recommender Design for Both Customers and Producers

Even though there are many firms who have claimed that their products possess green characteristics, their products may only meet part of the environmental protection regulations. For different catalogs of products, the green indices may have slight differences. For example, 3C (Computers, Consumers electronics, and Communications) products will emphasize the qualification in WEEE (Waste Electrical and Electronic Equipment), RoHS (the Restriction of the use of certain Hazardous Substances in electrical and electronic equipment), and so forth. Farm products focus on the satisfaction of Certified Agricultural Standards (CAS), including high quality agriculture and safe agriculture.

In this section, we propose a green retrieval system both for the customers and for the producers, based on Liao's study (2007). The proposed system mainly provides two functions in green product information sharing. One of them is to support designers and specialists to understand the green preferences of consumers and how satisfied they are with a green produced product. The other role of this system is to serve as a green information retrieval for the customers. It collects and displays the green levels of the products on the Internet and provides consumers the appropriate green products by product ingredient and the degree of user satisfaction in using these products. Meanwhile, customers may give their opinions according to their experience with using these green products, which will be used to update the degree of user satisfaction. Through the self-learning mechanism, the proposed green information retrieval system can provide proper information of the green products for both the companies and the customers. Through the green information retrieval system, the product designers can also collect the feedback from the customers and so understand what the customer tends to focus on. Furthermore, they can design the products based on the customers' feedback in order to reduce the gap between designer and the customer.

We propose to integrate two methods to recommend green products. For the content-based filtering, we mainly consider the greenness of the product. Therefore, the products with the higher level of greenness will have a higher probability of being recommended to the consumers. We shall collect the green indices and the corresponding green score for each product. Regarding collaborative filtering, we shall collect the user's rating for each product after s/he has used the system so that a high-rating product has a higher possibility of being recommended.

Before establishing our green recommendation system, we first collect and define the information of each product's greenness. For a specific category of products, we define N green indices with a set of $\{g_1, \ldots, g_j, \ldots, g_N\}$, where each is specified by a number of criteria, R_j. That is to say, there are R_j criteria in index g_j. For each product, p_i, $i=1,\ldots, M$, all R_j criteria will be assessed to be satisfactory or not for green index, g_j, $j=1,\ldots,N$. Thus, we have the *qualified vector* $C_{ij} = [c_{ij}^1, c_{ij}^2, \cdots, c_{ij}^r, \cdots, c_{ij}^{R_j}]$, where $c_{ij}^r = 1$ if the green criterion r is satisfied with product p_i and $c_{ij}^r = 0$, otherwise the level of greenness for each product corresponding to each green index is computed as per formula (3.1).

$$w_{ij} = \frac{\sum_{r=1}^{R_j} c_{ij}^r}{R_j} \qquad (3.1)$$

The recommendation mechanism for green information is built according to the vector space model (Grossman & Frieder, 1998) of which the weight matrix based on the green indices are constructed for all green products, as per Table 3.1. Each row vector denotes the degree of greenness for each individual product with respect to a different index. Therefore, the weight value, w_{ij}, in the weight matrix will be assigned as the greenness formula (3.1).

Table 3.1. The (weight) greenness matrix of the green product-attribute

	g_1	...	g_j	...	g_N
p_1	w_{11}				w_{1N}
⋮					
p_i	w_{i1}		w_{ij}		w_{iN}
⋮					
p_M	w_{M1}		w_{Mj}		w_{MN}

A user can choose multiple indices when searching for the green products s/he is interested in. The system will recommend the products by his/her preference for the chosen green indices. First, the user can choose the preferred indices, then s/he can select the emphasized degree for each chosen index. The emphasized degree generally denotes the user's preference in green consuming. The system will retrieve the green products based on the user's preference. For the green indices, the *preference vector* $V=[v_1,\ldots, v_j,\ldots,v_N]$ is defined and collected, $v_j = 0,1,3,5,7,9$, where if g_j is chosen, then v_j is given by the user and denotes the corresponding preference degree, otherwise v_j=0, which means the user is not interested in index g_j. Following the proposed *Cylindrical Extension* technique, we can obtain V_{CE}, a cylindrical extension of the preference vector V (Definition 2.1).

To prevent the fact that no products are retrieved for each selected index, in addition to the user's preference degree, we consider the maximum weight among all products in computing the weight threshold. Therefore, the system sets a weight threshold, $\overline{w}_j$ as per formula (2).

$$\overline{w}_j = \frac{v_j}{10} \times w_j^{\max}, \text{for } j=1,\ldots,N. \quad (3.2)$$

where $w_j^{\max}$ is the maximum weight among all products for index *j*.

The recommender will retrieve the green products with higher greenness according to the chosen indices and the corresponding preference degree. The higher the preference degree is, the larger the weight threshold is. The products with higher greenness in the chosen indices will be retrieved and defined as set $\overline{p}$.

On the other hand, to offer consumers a green preference and satisfaction of using the green products that have already been used by consumers, the system will ask the users to offer the rating and satisfaction of the recommended result, that is, to assess whether it is helpful when consumers want to buy this green product. To reach this goal, the recommender considers the existing users' ratings, r_i, i=1,...,M, for the recommended products, where $-10 \le r_i \le 10$. The users' rating is defined as the degree a recommended product satisfies them. The system provides 5 rating levels as: very poor(-10), poor(-5), no opinion(0), good(5) and very good(10) for the user's choice. After a user uses the system, s/he can provide a subjective rating, r'_i for product p_i. The existing rating will then be updated by three rules:

- **Rule 1:** The new rating is better than the existing rating. Therefore, the existing rating will be increased. If both the existing rating and the new rating are positive or both the two ratings are negative, we update r_i as $r_i = r_i + \delta\,|\,r'_i\,|$. δ is the increasing rate and set as 1/10 by experience. If the existing rating is negative and the new rating is positive, we shall double the increasing rate.

- **Rule 2:** The new rating is worse than the existing rating. Therefore, the existing rating will be reduced. If both the existing rating and the new rating are positive or both the two ratings are negative, we update r_i as $r_i = r_i - \delta\,|\,r'_i\,|$. δ is the increasing rate and set as 1/10 by experience. If the existing rating is negative and the new rating is positive, we shall double the increasing rate.
- **Rule 3:** The new rating is equal to the existing rating. The existing rating remains unchanged.

Finally, to consider the advantage of collaborative filtering, the recommend model will integrate both characters of the content-based and the collaborative filtering concepts. The recommended list will be ranked by the weighted score (*ws*), which is computed with the preference degree provided by the user and the existing rating as formula (3.3).

$$ws_i = \alpha \sum_{j=1}^{N} v_j w_{ij} + \beta r_i, \text{ for } p_i \in \overline{p} \qquad (3.3)$$

where α is the weight of the content-base method and β(=1-α) is the weight of collaborative filtering, respectively.

The proposed algorithm is described as follows:

1. Initialization
   a Set the initial product set, $P=\{p_1, p_2, \ldots, p_i, \ldots, p_M\}$.
   b Define the green index set, $G=\{g_1, g_2, \ldots, g_j, \ldots, g_N\}$ as the base for the weight values of the attributes of the products with respect to each product class. Initialize the evaluated criteria set for each green index g_j.
2. Compute the weight value
   a For each p_i, $i=1,2,\ldots,M$, evaluate if the criteria is satisfied and obtain the satisfaction vector $C_{ij} = [c_{ij}^1, c_{ij}^2, \cdots, c_{ij}^r, \cdots, c_{ij}^{R_j}]$ with respect to index g_j, $j=1,2,\ldots,N$.
   b Compute the greenness for each product p_i with respect to index g_j as formula (3.1)
   c Define a ratng r_i for each product p_i, where r_i -10□ r_i □10
3. Record the preference vector $V=[v_1, \ldots, v_j, \ldots, v_N]$ from the input of user with the preferred indices.
4. Compute the weight threshold, $\overline{w}$, and obtain the retrieved set, $\overline{p}$.
5. Compute the weighted scores for the retrieved green products as per formula (3.3), respectively.
6. Recommend the top-N products according to the weighted scores.
7. Collect the rating, r'_i for recommended products after the user uses the system and update the existing rating.

An Example of Green Recommendation

In this section, the example of 20 desktops is picked for illustration of our proposed procedure from the EPEAT Web site. Eight green indices used to evaluate the greenness of the products and the corresponding numbers of criteria are displayed in Table 3.2.

For each product, the weight (greenness) can be obtained by the number of satisfied criteria for each index. For example, a product, Apple Mac Pro (Desktop, produced by Apple Inc.), is assessed and the numbers of satisfied criteria are 7, 3, 11, 4, 1, 3, 4, and 6, respectively. Therefore, the weight (greenness) values are 1, 0.5, 1, 1, 0.25, 1, 0.8, and 0.86 corresponding to 8 green indices. Following the rule, the weight of other products can be obtained, as per Table 2.3.

If a user emphasizes the importance of indices, g_1, g_6, and g_8, and the corresponding preference ratings are 7, 9, 7, respectively, then the preference rating vector is [7, 0, 0, 0, 0, 9, 0, 7]. The threshold

Table 3.2. Green index

Green index	Regulations From	No. of Criteria
g_1	Reduction/elimination of environmentally sensitive materials	11
g_2	Materials selection	6
g_3	Design for end of life	11
g_4	Product longevity/life cycle extension	4
g_5	Energy conversation	4
g_6	End of life management	3
g_7	Corporate performance	5
g_8	Packaging	7

Table 3.3. Top 5 recommended green products

Rank	Product No.	g1	g2	g3	g4	g5	g6	g7	g8
1	P1	1	0.5	1	1	0.25	1	0.8	0.86
2	P8	0.71	0.5	1	1	0.25	1	0.8	1
3	P3	1	0.5	1	1	0.25	1	0.8	0.71
4	P2	0.71	0.5	1	1	0.25	1	0.8	0.86
5	P17	0.86	0.5	1	1	0.25	1	0.8	0.71

will be computed from formula (3.2) as [0.602, 0, 0, 0, 0, 0.9, 0, 0.602].The retrieved result is obtained based on the weight threshold. Any product will be retrieved with the weight value of index 1 greater than 0.602, the weight value of index 6 greater than 0.9 and the weight value of index 8 greater than 0.602 and the retrieved set, $\bar{p} = \{p1, p2, p3, p6, p7, p8, p17, p18, p19, p20\}$. Finally, the recommended list will be provided by the rank of the weighted score (formula 3.3) with initial zero rating, r_i and 0.8 for α. Table 3.3 shows the recommended top five green products.

From the recommended list, the greenness of the products with respect to index g1, g6, or g8 are indeed higher than those of other products.

The users can offer their assessment rating and their level of satisfaction after reviewing the recommended products online to the producers. After the system collects more ratings from the users, the recommending models will be adjusted as formula (3.3) and the recommended results will be changed.

CONCLUDING REMARKS

The green information retrieval system mainly intends to help customers with making a decision while purchasing green products, and to help the producers design the green products by incorporating the user's preferences. In this chapter, we introduced the latest in information technologies and the popular methods of information retrieval. Then, we proposed a search mechanism with an illustrated example to construct the green information retrieval system. The proposed system allows users to set different levels of importance for each selected indices of their green preference. In addition, the rating of others is also integrated into the recommendation mechanism. The users, apart from gaining more green information, can obtain a list of recommendations based on their green preferences. For the manufacturer, by collecting the preference rating on each index, they can further understand the users' green preferences for the different products. The product designers can collect the users' preferences and become aware of what the users focus on. Furthermore, they can then not only consider the international green regulations, but they can design their products based on the users' preferences so as to reduce the gap between the designer and the user.

Future Research Directions

Al Gore, the former vice present of the United States, drew the world's attention to the dangers of global warming and won the 2007 Nobel Peace Prize. More and more green regulations are released and more and more people emphasize the green consumption today. The green industry is both a trend and an opportunity. Future research may be focused on the following topics: 1) the determination of the green indices. The green indices are collected from the related green regulations. However, different products may have different green properties or the related rules. How to determine the green indices and the corresponding criteria is another important and complicate work ; 2) collection of more categories of products. In our research, we first focus on 3C products. Expanding our study to other categories of products is our next topic; 3) integration of the customers' feedback. The customers' feedback reflects the recommender's performances; therefore, how to integrate the customers' feedbacks to our recommendation model is our next point. We believe it will have better recommendation to the consumers; and 4) connection to the green enterprise. Besides providing the customers' feedback to the enterprises, we shall try to build a Web platform connecting the main companies such that their green products can be updated and make sure the green information is the newest.

ACKNOWLEDGMENT

The author acknowledges the financial support from National Science Council, ROC with project number NSC 95-2221-E-364-004.

REFERENCES

Aggarwal, C.C., Gates, S.C. & Yu, P.S. (1998, November). On the merits of building categorization system by supervised clustering. In *Proceedings of the Fifth ACM SIGKDD International Conference on Information and Knowledge Management*, Bethesda, MD (pp. 3-7).

Anderl, R., Daum, B., John, H., & Putter, C. (1997). Cooperative product data modeling in life cycle networks. In F.L. Krause & G. Seliger (Eds.), *Life cycle networks* (pp. 435-446). London: Chapman & Hall.

Baeza-Yates, R., & Ribeiro-Neto, B. (1999). *Modern information retrieval.* MA: Addison-Wesley Longman.

Balabanovic, M., & Shoham, Y. (1997). Fab: Content-based, collaborative recommendation. *Communications of the ACM, 40*(3), 66-72.

Billerbeck, B., Scholer, F., Williams, H. E., & Zobel, J. (2003). Query expansion using associated queries. In *Proceedings of the 12th International*

Conference on Information and Knowledge Management, New Orleans, LA (pp. 2-9).

Blecker, T., Friedrich, G., Kaluza, B., Abdelkafi, N., & Kreutler G. (2005). *Information and management systems for product customization.* Boston: Springer-Verlag.

Bramham, J., & MacCarthy, B.L. (2003, October). Matching configurator attributes to business strategy. In *Proceedings of the MCPC 2003, 2nd Interdisciplinary World Congress on Mass Customization and Personalization.* Munich: Technische Universitaet Muenchen.

Buckley, C., Singhal, A., & Mitra, M. (1995). New retrieval approaches using SMART: TREC 4. In *Proceedings of the Fourth Text Retrieval Conference* (pp. 25-48). Gaithersburg, MD: National Institute of Standards and Technology.

Burke, R.D. (2002). Hybrid recommender systems: Survey and experiments. *User Modeling and User-Adapted Interaction, 12*(4), 331-370.

Cutting, D.R., Karger, D.R., Pedersen, J.O., & Tukey, J.W. (1992). Scatter/Gather: A cluster-based approach to browsing large document collection. In *Proceedings of the 15th Annual International ACM/SIGIR Conference*, Copenhagen, Denmark.

Glover, E.J., Lawrence, S., Gordon, M.D., Birmingham, W.P., & Giles, C.L. (1999). Recommending Web documents based on user preferences. In Proceedings of the *SIGIR 99 Workshop on Recommender Systems*, Berkeley, CA.

Glover, E.J., Lawrence, S., Gordon, M.D., Birmingham, W.P., & Giles, C.L. (2001). Web search—your way. *Communications of the ACM, 44*(12), 97-102.

Gordon, M. (1988). Probabilistic and genetic algorithms for document retrieval. *Communications of the ACM, 31*(10), 1208-1218.

Grossman, D.A., & Frieder, O. (1998). *Information retrieval: Algorithms and heuristics.* Boston: Kluwer.

Green Electronics Council. (2006). *Electronic product environmental assessment tool (EPEAT).* Retrieved July 9, 2008, from URL:http://www.epeat.net/

Horng, J.T., & Yeh, C.C. (2000). Applying genetic algorithms to query optimization in document retrieval. *Information Processing and Management, 36*(5), 737-759.

Hung, L.P. (2005). A personalized recommendation system based on product taxonomy for one-to-one marketing online. *Expert Systems with Applications, 29*, 383-392.

Jones, L.P. (1994). Taste and the greening of design: The role of design imagery in a post-acquisitive society. *Leonardo, 27*(4), 317-325.

Jonesa K.S., Walkerb, S., & Robertson, S.E. (2000). A probabilistic model of information retrieval: Development and comparative experiments: Part 2. *Information Processing and Management, 36*(6), 809-840.

Kim, B.M., Kim, J.Y., & Kim, J. (2001). Query term expansion and reweighting using term co-occurrence similarity and fuzzy inference. In *Proceedings of the Joint Ninth IFSA World Congress and 20th NAFIPS International Conference*, Vancouver, Canada.

Klir, G.J., & Folger, T.A. (1988). *Fuzzy sets: Uncertainty, and information.* Englewood Cliffs, NJ: Prentice Hall.

Kurakawa, K., Kiriyama, T., Baba, Y., Umeda, Y., Tomiyama, T., & Kobayashi, H. (1997). The green browser: An information sharing tool for product life cycle design. In F.L. Krause & G. Seliger (Eds.), *Life cycle networks* (pp. 454-466). London: Chapman & Hall.

Leuski, A. (2001, November). Evaluating document clustering for interactive information retrieval. In *Proceedings of the 2001 ACM CIKM International Conference on Information and Knowledge Management*, Atlanta, GA, USA.

Liao, Y.C. (2006). A weight-based approach to information retrieval and relevance feedback. *Expert Systems with Applications* (accepted).

Liao, Y.C. (2007). A weight-based approach to green products recommendation. In *Proceedings of the Sixth International Conference on Information and Management Sciences*, Lhasa, Tibet, China.

Lin H.C., Wang, L.H., & Chen, S.M. (2006). Query expansion for documents retrieval based on fuzzy rules and user relevance feedback techniques. *Expert Systems with Applications, 31*, 397-405.

Lochbaum, K.E., & Streeter, L.A. (1989). Comparing and combining the effectiveness of latent semantic indexing and the ordinary vector space model for information retrieval. *Journal of Information Science, 6*, 25-33.

Middendorf, A., Hoppner, W., & Teller, M. (1997). IDEE-Information network for closed loop economy: Life cycle networks. In F.L. Krause & G. Seliger (Eds.), *Life cycle networks* (pp. 447-453). London: Chapman & Hall.

Muther, A. (2000). *Electronic customer care: die Anbieter-Kunden-Beziehung im informationszeitalter* (2nd ed.). Berlin: Springer-Verlag.

Paulson, P., & Tzanavari, A. (2002). *Combining collaborative and content-based filtering using conceptual graphs* (Tech. Rep. No. 5). Lefkosia: University of Cyprus, Department of Computer Science.

Pazzani, M.J. (1999). A framework for collaborative, content-based and demographic filtering. *Artificial Intelligence Review, 13*, 393-408.

Post, G.V., & Anderson, D.L. (2003). *Management information systems: Solving business problems with information technology.* Boston: McGraw-Hill.

Resnick, P., & Varian, H.R. (1997). Recommender systems. *Communications of the ACM, 40*(3), 56-58.

Sabin, D., & Weigel, D. (1998). *Managing the hidden costs of complexity* (whitepaper). Boston Consulting Group.

Salton, G. (1970). Automatic text analysis. *Science, 168*(3929), 335-342.

Salton, G., & Buckley, C. (1988). Term-weighting approaches in automatic text retrieval. *Information Proceeding and Management, 24*(5), 513-523.

Schaefer, J.B., Konstan, J.A., & Riedl, J. (1999), Recommender systems in E-commerce. In *Proceedings of the ACM Conference on Electronic Commerce*, Denver, CO.

Willet, P. (1988). Recent trends in hierarchical document clustering: A critical review. *Information Processing and Management, 24*(5), 577-597.

Yang, J.J., & Korfhage, R.R. (1993). Query optimization in information retrieval using genetic algorithms. In *Proceedings of the Fifth ICGA*, Urbana, Champaign, IL, USA.

Zamir, O., Etzioni, O., Madani, O., & Karp, R.M. (1997). Fast and intuitive clustering of Web documents. In *Proceedings of the KDD '97,* Newport Beach, CA.

Zimmermann, H.J. (1991). *Fuzzy set theory—and its applications.* Boston: Kluwer Academic Publishers.

ADDITIONAL READING

Anderl, R., Daum, B., John, H., & Putter, C. (1997). Cooperative product data modeling in life cycle networks. In F.L. Krause & G. Seliger (Eds.), *Life cycle networks* (pp. 435-446). London: Chapman & Hall.

Baeza-Yates, R., & Ribeiro-Neto, B. (1999). *Modern information retrieval*. MA: Addison-Wesley Longman.

Balabanovic, M., & Shoham, Y. (1997). Fab: **Content-based, collaborative recommendation.** *Communications of the ACM, 40*(**3), 66-72.**

Blecker, T., Friedrich, G., Kaluza, B., Abdelkafi, N., & Kreutler G. (2005). *Information and management systems for product customization*. Boston: Springer-Verlag.

Cutting, D.R., Karger, D.R., Pedersen, J.O., & Tukey, J.W. (1992). Scatter/Gather: A cluster-based approach to browsing large document collection. In *Proceedings of the 15th annual International ACM/SIGIR Conference*, Copenhagen, Denmark.

Eagan, P., & Weinberg, L. (1999) Application of analytic hierarchy process techniques to streamlined life-cycle analysis of two anodizing processes. *Environ Sci Technol, 33*(9), 1495-1500.

Glover, E.J., Lawrence, S., Gordon, M.D., Birmingham, W.P., & Giles, C.L. (1999). Recommending Web documents based on user preferences. In *Proceedings of the SIGIR 99 Workshop on Recommender Systems*, Berkeley, CA.

Grossman, D.A., & Frieder, O. (1998). *Information retrieval: Algorithms and heuristics*. Boston: Kluwer.

Hung, L.P. (2005). A personalized recommendation system based on product taxonomy for one-to-one marketing online. *Expert Systems with Applications, 29*, 383-392.

Hur, T., Kim, I., & Yamamoto, R. (2004) Measurement of green productivity and its improvement. *Journal of Cleaner Production, 12*, 673-683.

Kennedy, M.L. (1997). *Total cost assessment for environmental engineering and managers*. New York: John Wiley & Sons.

Kobayashi, H. (2003, December 8-11). Idea generation and risk evaluation methods for life cycle planning. In *Proceedings of the Third International Symposium on Environmentally Conscious Design and Inverse Manufacturing, Ecodesign03*, Tokyo, Japan.

Kurakawa, K., Kiriyama, T., Baba, Y., Umeda, Y., Tomiyama, T., & Kobayashi, H. (1997). The green browser: An information sharing tool for product life cycle design. In F.L. Krause & G. Seliger (Eds.), *Life cycle networks* (pp. 454-466). London: Chapman & Hall.

Liu, C.C., & Chen, J.L. (2001). Development of product green innovation design method. In Proceedings of Eco-Design, *Second International Symposium on Environmentally Conscious Design and Inverse Manufacturing*, Tokyo, Japan (pp.168-173).

Middendorf, A., Hoppner, W., & Teller, M. (1997). IDEE-Information network for closed loop economy: Life cycle networks. In F.L. Krause & G. Seliger (Eds.), *Life cycle networks* (pp. 447-453). London: Chapman & Hall.

Min, H., & Galle, W.P. (1997). Green purchasing strategies: Trends and implications. *International Journal of Purchasing Material Management, 33*(3), 10-17.

Nagel, M.H. (2000). Environmental supply chain management versus life cycle analysis (LCA) method eco-indicator '95: A relative business perspective versus an absolute environmental perspective. In *Proceedings of the 2000 IEEE International Symposium on Electronics and the Environment* (pp. 118-123).

Ottman, J.A. (1998). *Green marketing: Opportunity for innovation* (2nd ed.). McGraw-Hill.

Pazzani, M.J. (1999). A framework for collaborative, content-based and demographic filtering. *Artificial Intelligence Review, 13*, 393-408.

Pineda-Hensen, R., Culabe, A., & Mendoza, G.A. (2002). Evaluating environmental performance of pulp and paper manufacturing using the analytic hierarchy process and life cycle assessment. *Journal Ind Ecol, 6*(2), 15-28.

Post, G.V., & Anderson, D.L. (2003). *Management information systems: Solving business problems with information technology.* Boston: McGraw-Hill.

Russel, T. (1998). *Greener purchasing: Opportunities and innovations.* Sheffield: Greenleaf Publishing, Interleaf Productions Limited.

Salton, G., & Buckley, C. (1988). Term-weighting approaches in automatic text retrieval. *Information Proceeding and Management, 24*(5), 513-523.

Schott, H., & Birkhofer, H. (1995). Global engineering network-applications for green design. In F. Krause & H. Jansen (Eds.), *Life cycle modelling for innovative products and processes: Proceedings of PROLAMAT '95* (pp. 93-105). IFIP.

Willet, P. (1988). Recent trends in hierarchical document clustering: A critical review. *Information Processing and Management, 24*(5), 577-597.

APPENDIX: THE DETAILED ALGORITHM OF SECTION 2.2

Step 1. Initialization

Step 1.1 Set the initial document set, $D_0=\{d_1, d_2,\ldots,d_N\}$ and collect the initial keywords set, $K=\{k_1, k_2, \ldots,k_M\}$.

Step 1.2 Define a set A, with the attributes of the documents as, $A=\{A_1, A_2\}$, where A_1 is the publishing year and A_2 is the properties of documents, including journal, conference, patent, thesis.

Step 1.3 Set β=0.8.

Step 2. Compute weight matrix

Step 2.1 Compute the term frequency (tf)

For each k_j in K

For each d_i in D_0

Find the number tf_{ij}

Step 2.2 Compute the inverse document frequency (idf)

For j=1 to M

Set n_j =0

For i=1 to N

If tf_{ij} >0 then $n_j = n_j +1$

$idf_j = \log(N/n_j)$

Step 2.3 Compute the weight matrix

For j=1 to M

For i=1 to N

Compute w_{ij} as formula (2.1)

Step 2.4 Compute the threshold $\overline{w}$ as formula (2.3)

Step 3. Make a query through online interface.

Step 3.1 If a user selects the attributes of A, filter N documents by A_1 and A_2, and obtain N' documents.

Step 3.2 Define query vector Q

For each k_j in K

If (k_j matches the query terms) then q_j =1

Else q_j = 0

Step 4. Retrieve documents

Step 4.1 Extend Q to Q_{CE}, an N' by M matrix by the cylindrical extension

Step 4.2 Generate matrix F

For i=1 to N'

For j=1 to M

$f_{ij} = \min(w_{ij}, \overline{q}_{ij})$

Step 4.3 Generate matrix C by the weight threshold $\overline{w}$ in Step 1.4

For i=1 to N'

For j=1 to M

If $f_{ij} >= \overline{w}$, then $c_{ij} = f_{ij}$

Else $c_{ij} = 0$

continued on following page

APPENDIX: CONTINUED

Step 4.4 Compute the scores and generate D, the set of retrieved documents

For i=1 to N'

$sco_i = \max(c_{ij})$ for j=1 to M

IF $sco_i > 0$ then

Add d_i into D

Step 4.5 Display the retrieved documents according to the rank of the related scores.

For d_i in D

Sort sco_i and display

Step 5. Adjust the amount of results

If a user is looking for a greater amount of documents, then after he or she clicks the "more" button, the system will decrease $\overline{w}$.

Set α=1.5 and Compute $\overline{w}$ as formula (2.7)

Go to Step 4.3

Else, if a user is looking for a less amount of documents, then "less" button is clicked for increasing $\overline{w}$ in the system.

Set α=0.9 and Compute $\overline{w}$ as formula (2.7)

Go to Step 4.3

Else, if a user re-query or stop querying, then

Go to step 6.

Step 6. Update weight values and keywords set

Step 6.1 Update weight values

For i=1 to N' and $d_i \in D$

If d_i is downloaded

For j=1 to M and q_j=1

Update w_{ij} as formula (2.8)

Step 6.2 Update K

For any query term q_k not in K, then

Add q_k into K

For i=1 to N, j=M+1

Compute w_{ij} as formula (2.1)

Step 6.3 if the user re-query, then

Go to Step 3.

Else, Stop.

Chapter XVIII
Applying Web-Based Collaborative Decision-Making in Reverse Logistics: The Case of Mobile Phones

Giannis T. Tsoulfas
University of Piraeus, Greece

Costas P. Pappis
University of Piraeus, Greece

Nikos I. Karacapilidis
University of Patras, Greece

ABSTRACT

The increasing environmental concerns and the technological advances have boosted the post-use treatment of nearly all kinds of products and a new area for research and application has emerged described by the term "reverse logistics." In this chapter, parameters that may affect reverse logistics operation are discussed from a decision-making perspective, so that alternative design options may be proposed and evaluated. In particular, these parameters are used for the qualitative evaluation of the reverse supply chain of mobile phones in Greece. For this purpose, we present an illustrative application of a Web-based decision support tool that may assist collaborative decision-making in conflicting environments, where diverse views, perspectives, and priorities shared among stakeholders have to be considered.

Copyright © 2009, IGI Global, distributing in print or electronic forms without written permission of IGI Global is prohibited.

INTRODUCTION

The increasing environmental concerns and the technological advances have boosted the post-use treatment of nearly all kinds of products, regardless of their size, composition, and initial value. Relevant legislative frameworks have been enforced in developed countries aiming at apportioning the responsibilities related to the recovery of end-of-life products. In addition, specific targets regarding product design and recovery rates are set, networks' requirements are suggested and, last but not least, voluntary schemes are applauded. As a result, further extensions in research and applications of supply chain management have emerged described by the term "reverse logistics." De Brito and Dekker (2004) defined reverse logistics as "the process of planning, implementing and controlling backward flows of raw materials, in process inventory packaging and finished goods, from a manufacturing, distribution or use point, to a point of recovery or point of proper disposal." In this definition both economic and environmental dimensions of reverse logistics are implied, indicating the potential benefits that companies would have by adopting such practices.

Reverse logistics is a multidisciplinary area of research. For example, operations research, environmental analysis, marketing, and informatics have all a significant role to play in order to assist decision-making regarding the design and operation of reverse supply chains. Moreover, reverse logistics is often regarded in conjunction with forward logistics, since they are interrelated. However, the distinguishing characteristics of reverse supply chains introduce new dimensions in decision-making aspects. In particular, the main differences between forward and reverse supply chains, as stated by Fleischmann, Krikke, Dekker, and Flapper (1999) and Krikke, Pappis, Tsoulfas, and Bloemhof-Ruwaard (2002), are the following:

- In contrast to forward supply chains, in reverse supply chains there are a lot of sources of "raw materials" (used products), which may enter the reverse flow at low or no cost at all, and significantly fewer "customers" (recyclers, remanufacturers, etc.).
- The economic value of inputs in reverse supply chains is lower than the one in the case of forward supply chains.
- In the case of reverse supply chains, offer does not follow demand.
- The economic efficiency of reverse supply chains is precarious, since it is not sure that there will be markets to exploit their outputs.
- Reverse supply chains are characterized by higher uncertainty regarding issues like quality, volumes, and composition of reverse flows.

From this perspective, it is important to identify the parameters that may affect reverse logistics operation so that alternative design options are proposed and evaluated. In Tsoulfas, Dasaklis, and Pappis (2007), a first attempt to define and categorize them is presented. Given these parameters, in this chapter we discuss a qualitative evaluation of the reverse supply chain of mobile phones in Greece, as presented by Pappis, Tsoulfas, and Dasaklis (2006). For this purpose, we make use of a Web-based decision support tool that may assist collaborative decision-making (CDM) in conflicting environments, where diverse views, perspectives, and priorities shared among stakeholders have to be considered.

The remainder of the chapter is structured as follows: First, the parameters affecting reverse logistics operation are discussed. Then, the reverse supply chain of mobile phones in Greece is briefly presented. Next, the CDM tool is presented, followed by its illustrative application regarding the reverse supply chain of mobile phones in Greece. Finally, some concluding remarks are outlined.

PARAMETERS AFFECTING REVERSE LOGISTICS OPERATION

Three major categories of parameters that may affect reverse logistics operation are identified: product-dependant, organizational, and social. These parameters, which cannot be addressed independently since they may interact with each other, may form a nonexhaustive basis for analysis in the following decision-making situations:

a. When assessing the current situation regarding the operation of reverse supply chains;
b. When exploring alternative options for the reverse supply chain activities, as well as their interaction with the external environment.

Generally speaking, reverse supply chains may be considered as the conjunction of two major sessions of activities: acquisition and exploitation. The first one refers to the activities that aim at the physical transportation of used products and the second one includes the activities targeting final value extraction or environmentally sound management. Although exploitation follows acquisition when the materials' flows are regarded, it may be considered as a necessary condition for the acquisition in the causal chain. To be more specific, the ability to exploit used products may trigger their acquisition. Otherwise, it would be purposeless to acquire used products without having in mind how to treat them. In addition, information exchange between these sessions is bidirectional and repeated. The relationships between the two major sessions of reverse supply activities are illustrated in Figure 1, where the parameters affecting these operations are regarded as influential factors.

Product-Dependent Parameters

Product-dependant parameters refer to the particular characteristics of products that determine their post-use treatment from a technical and an economic point of view. In particular:

- *The weight or the volume of used products and the infrastructure needed* is a decisive criterion for the development of reverse logistics activities, since several operations, such as collection, storage, and transportation, may be affected. Generally speaking, large products may require special machinery and equipment for handling, transportation, and so forth, whereas small products may call for big quantities to be collected before being transported.

Figure 1. The various flows between the two major sessions of reverse supply activities

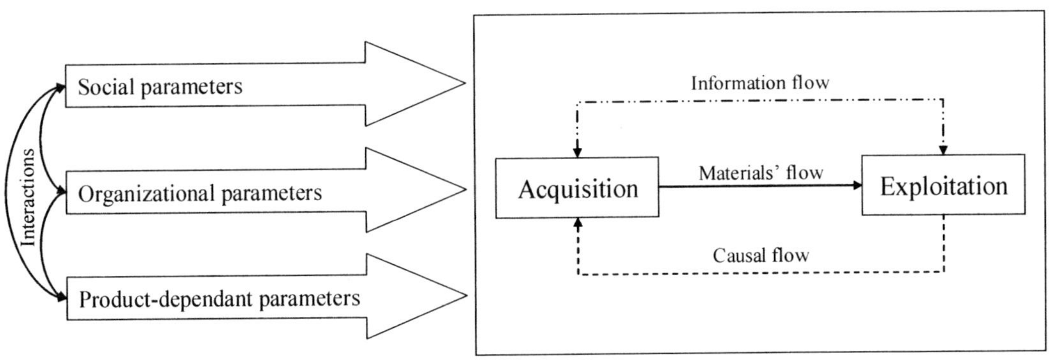

- *The composition and the technical characteristics of used products* may be another decisive issue, since they determine the ways used products should be treated in order to preserve their value and to prevent them from harming the environment.
- *The way used products are replaced by new ones* is another important parameter for the implementation of reverse logistics. It is obvious that replacements, which occur in the same place or using the same distribution means for the return of used products, have positive effects on the reverse supply chain operation, both from an economic and an environmental perspective.
- *The remaining value of used products* is considered to be a very significant issue for consumers and manufacturers, since they can both benefit from the post-use treatment of used products. Consumers may achieve reduced prices for new products replacing used ones, while manufacturers can extract value from used products by refurbishing, reusing, or recycling them.
- *Direct reuse or reuse after minor treatment* is a situation commonly perceived in the case of packaging materials and may offer significant benefits to companies and the environment, as the useful life cycle of used products is extended and the production of new ones is avoided.
- *The capability to change the usage of used products or to provide them to different markets (e.g., second hand)* may be another important criterion. Generally, in such situations no special treatments are necessary and the life cycle of products is extended.

Organizational Parameters

Organizational parameters refer to issues regarding the stakeholders involved in the recovery of used products. In particular:

- *The recovery networks structure* is a decisive element for reverse logistics activities. Generally speaking, companies have two options: either they will handle the recovery processes themselves (even by using outsourcing practices), or they will participate in wider networks, usually by financially supporting them. The first option is commonly adopted when companies can achieve significant return rates, whereas the second scheme is preferred, especially when used products are widely dispersed.
- *Asset control policies* that are adopted by some companies can contribute to the effective operation of reverse logistics. Such cases are often met, for example, in the automotive sector and in the electronics industry. By using such practices, companies actually sell services rather than the product itself. As a result, they can have improved control of their products and, at the same time, fulfill their customers' needs, with whom they can easier communicate.
- *Marketing* is a very important criterion for the implementation of reverse logistics. Companies may participate in campaigns for promoting collection of used products and they can indicate recovery options in the products themselves or in their packages.
- *Economic motivation* is a means used in many industrial sectors in order to involve consumers in the recovery activities. Usually, consumers prepay a certain amount of money as a deposit and they get it back when they return the product or the package to collection facilities.

Social Parameters

Social parameters involve attitudes and values prevailing in societies that may determine practices regarding recovery of used products. In particular:

- *Social habits* may significantly affect the results of reverse logistics activities, since individual attitudes are often affected by mainstreams. Recovery of used products seems to find a more fertile ground in big cities rather than in small communities.
- *Legislation* is a decisive parameter affecting the recovery of used products. In particular, the principle of shared responsibility and the "cradle to grave" perspective have been elevated in legislative frameworks around the world. Furthermore, explicit targets are posed and certain benefits are offered in some cases (e.g., tax relieves, improved financial eligibility, etc.).
- *Social awareness* is a critical issue regarding reverse logistics practices, especially with respect to consumers' attitudes. In developed countries, the environmental standards stemming from social demand are higher. Education is of particular importance regarding this parameter, not solely in schools, but also in corporate environments.

THE REVERSE SUPPLY CHAIN OF MOBILE PHONES IN GREECE

Facts

In 2002, the total number of mobile phones in use worldwide exceeded the number of land-lines (Donner, 2005). According to the International Telecommunication Union the mobile subscribers in 2006 were more than 2.5 billions (International Telecommunication Union, 2007). According to the same source, the subscribers in Greece were around 11 million.

Typically, mobile phones are used for only 1½ years before being replaced (Fishbein, 2002). These obsolete mobile phones are mainly replaced due to fashion trends and the rapid technological improvements, as new features are added in mobile phones. Other reasons for replacement are the incompatibility with a new provider, or the fact that they no longer function. Less than 1% of mobile phones retired and discarded annually are recycled and the majority is accumulated in consumers' desk drawers, store rooms, or other storage, awaiting disposal (Most, 2003). Of this small percentage recovered, some are refurbished and put into use or used for replacement parts. If these options are not possible, some metals are recycled. The refurbishment process can significantly aid to the prolongation of a mobile phone's life cycle and therefore prevent it from early entry into the waste stream. The recycling process keeps discarded phones out of disposal facilities and reduces the need for raw materials used to make new products.

In the case of Greece, Appliances Recycling S.A. is the authorized collective take-back and recycling organisation for all electrical and electronic waste in Greece (Pappis et al., 2006). Actually, all service providers and importers are obliged by law to cooperate with Appliances Recycling S.A., since they are the only authorized take-back organisation in Greece right now. The program relies on in-store collection and special bins have been installed in retail stores. In addition, several bins have been put on central city spots, as the result of cooperation with local municipalities. Recycling Appliances S.A. aimed at covering 67% of Greek mobile phones population by the end of 2006, while their corresponding target for 2008 is 90% (http://www.electrocycle.gr). The used mobile phones collected have been destined only abroad for further treatment, since no appropriate facilities exist in Greece. In the recycling process, the plastic parts of mobile phones are incinerated and utilised as a fuel to melt the metal mixture. Then metals are separated using electrolytic refining and mechanical (e.g., magnetic segregation) procedures.

The possible routes of used mobile phones and the affected activities in the forward supply chain (grey color) are illustrated in Figure 2.

Major Concerns

Mobile phones contain a great number of metals such as copper, aluminium, iron, nickel, silicon, lead, antimony, beryllium, arsenic, silver, tantalum, and zinc. Some of these metals are toxic and hazardous for mankind and the environment. This variety of valuable metals raises very significant issues regarding the gradual exhaustion of natural resources. In addition, the side effects of this exhaustion are also important. For example, the mining of tantalum has been identified as a serious threat to gorillas clinging to survival in the Democratic Republic of Congo (Macey, 2005). Apart from metals, mobile phones contain also brominated flame retardants, which are used in the plastic parts and cables in order to reduce the risk of fire. When burned in incinerators, these substances have the potential to pollute the air and to pose threats for the workers in recycling facilities, since dioxins and furans can be formed. When buried in landfills, they may leach into soil and drinking water.

The environmental impact of the substances mentioned above is of great concern because some of them, like flame retardants and lead, are considered to be persistent, bioaccumulative, and suspected carcinogens. Relative legislation enforcement in the European Union aims at the restriction of the use of certain hazardous substances in electrical and electronic equipment, such as mobile phones (RoHS Directive) (European Union, 2003a). In addition, the WEEE Directive draws the frame regarding the post-use treatment of electrical and electronic equipment (European Union, 2003b).

Apart from the environmental concerns related to the treatment of used mobile phones, there are some important economic issues as well. Indeed, many substances contained in mobile phones are valuable as it is relatively more expensive to acquire them as primary raw materials (e.g., lead, zinc).

Figure 2. The possible routes of used mobile phones and the affected activities in the forward supply chain (grey color)

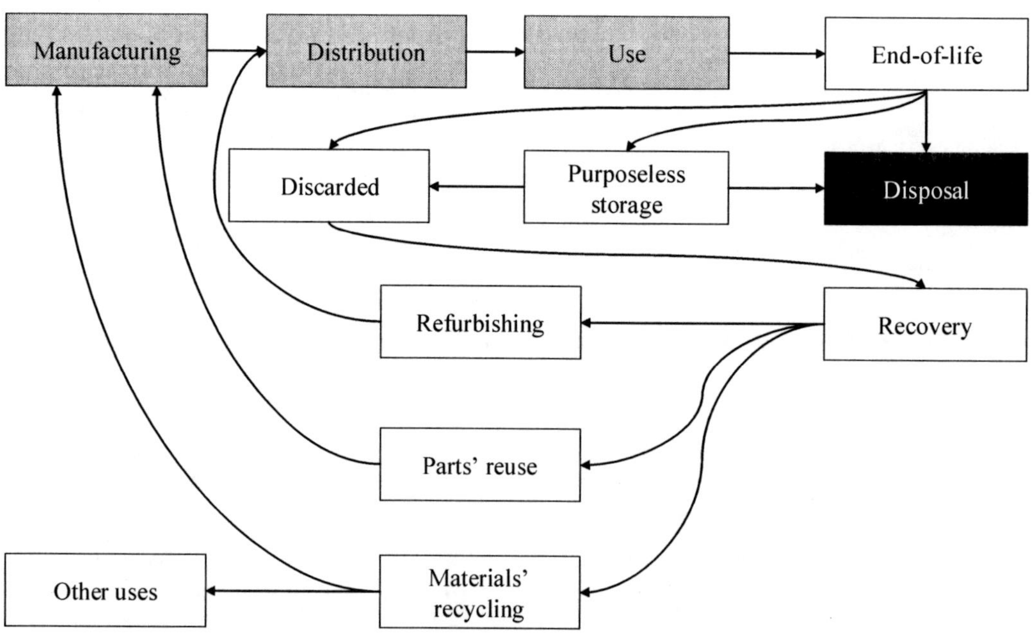

It is obvious that decision-making procedures regarding the operation of reverse supply chains get more complicated, due to the involvement of diverse parties. For example, in the case of mobile phones, manufacturers, distributors, service providers, recovery operators, and recyclers would be the participants of such a decision-making situation. Moreover, even different departments of these stakeholders might have diverse views of the situation.

The Decision-Making Situation

From an OEMs' perspective, reverse logistics implementation in the case of mobile phones is determined by their interaction with several stakeholders, as shown in Figure 3.

Thus, reverse logistics managers are responsible for taking into account and coordinating all stakeholders' requirements. Correspondingly, similar actions are necessary among the different departments within a company. Consequently, a conflicting decision-making environment is formed, where the factors "place" and "time" may pose restrictions. Such decision-making situations may be dealt with Web-based CDM tools and a corresponding approach is presented in the sequel.

A WEB-BASED TOOL FOR COLLABORATIVE DECISION-MAKING

Approaching Conflicting Decision-Making Situations

Choices in decision-making cannot generally be addressed by individuals working alone or even by several people working separately and then merging their pieces of work. Instead, they have to be addressed through collaborative work among stakeholders with diverse views, perspectives, and priorities.

Information and Communication Technology (ICT) infrastructure to support people working in teams has been the subject of interest for quite a long time (Fjermestad & Hiltz, 2000). Such systems aim at facilitating group decision-making processes by providing forums for expression of opinions, as well as qualitative and quantitative tools for aggregating proposals and evaluating their impact on the issue in hand. They may exploit intranet or Internet technologies to connect decision-makers in a way that encourages dialogue and, at the same time, stimulates the exchange of knowledge. Accordingly, recent computer-based knowledge management systems (KMS) focus on providing a corporate memory, that is, an explicit, disembodied, and persistent representation of the knowledge and information in an organization,

Figure 3. OEMs and their interactions with stakeholders in reverse logistics activities

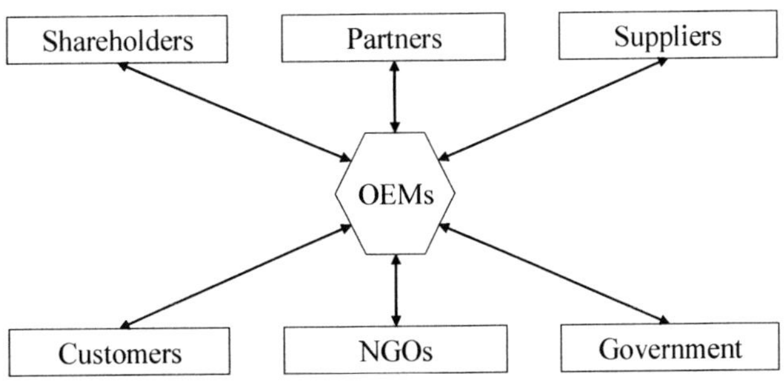

as well as mechanisms that improve the sharing and dissemination of knowledge by facilitating interaction and collaboration among the parties involved (Bolloju, Khalifa, & Turban, 2002).

CDM may provide a means for a well-structured decision-making process. Usually, CDM is performed through debates and negotiations among the parties involved. Conflicts of interest are inevitable and support for achieving consensus and compromise is required. Decision-makers may adopt and suggest their own strategy that fulfils some goals at a specific level and may have arguments supporting or against alternative solutions. In addition, they have to confront the existence of insufficient information. Generally speaking, efficient and effective use of information technology in the collection and dissemination of information and knowledge produced by diverse sources, the evaluation of alternative schemes, the construction of shared meanings, and the associated feedback learning process are critical factors for the decision-making process (Clases & Wehner, 2002).

The Web-Based Tool

Given the above issues, a Web-based tool has been implemented that supports the collaboration conducted in decision-making situations, by facilitating the creation, leveraging, and utilization of the relevant knowledge. This tool is based on an argumentative reasoning approach, where discourses about complex problems are considered as social processes and they may result in the formation of groups whose knowledge is clustered around specific views of the problem (Karacapilidis, Adamides, & Pappis, 2004). In addition to providing a platform for group reflection and capturing of organizational memory, this approach augments teamwork in terms of knowledge elicitation, sharing, and construction, thus enhancing the quality of the overall process. This is due to its structured language for conversation and its mechanism for evaluation of alternatives. Taking into account the input provided by the individual experts, the proposed tool constructs an illustrative discourse-based knowledge graph that is composed of the ideas expressed so far, as well as their supporting documents. Moreover, through the integrated decision support mechanisms, experts are continuously informed about the status of each discourse item asserted so far and reflect further on them according to their beliefs and interests on the outcome of the discussion. In addition, the overall approach aids group sense-making and mutual understanding through the collaborative identification and evaluation of diverse opinions.

The proposed tool builds on a server-client network architecture. It is composed of two basic components, namely the *collaboration visualization module* and the *collaborative decision making module*. The former provides a shared Web-based workspace for storing and retrieving the messages and documents deployed by the discussion participants, using the widely accepted XML document format (http://www.w3.org/XML). This module actually provides the interfaces through which participants get connected with the system via Internet (by using a standard Web browser; there is no need of installation of any specific software in order to use the tool). Exploitation of the Web platform renders, among others, low operational cost and easy access to the system. The knowledge base of the system maintains all the above items (messages and documents), which may be considered, appropriately processed and transformed, or even re-used in future discussions. Storage of documents and messages being asserted in an ongoing discussion takes place in an automatic way, upon their insertion in the discussion. On the other hand, retrieval of knowledge is performed through appropriate interfaces, which aid participants in exploring the contents of the knowledge base and exploit previously stored or generated knowledge for their current needs. In such a way, our approach builds a "collective memory" of a particular community. On the other hand, the collaborative decision-making module is responsible for the reasoning and evaluation purposes of the system. Alternative mechanisms for these purposes can be invoked each time, upon the participants' wish and context under consideration. These mechanisms follow well-defined and broadly accepted algorithms (based on diverse decision making approaches, such as multi-criteria decision-making, argumentation-based reasoning, utility theory, risk assessment, etc.), which are stored in the tool's model base.

The basic discourse elements in the proposed tool are *issues, alternatives, positions,* and *preferences*. In particular, issues correspond to problems to be solved, decisions to be made, or goals to be achieved. They are brought up by users and are open to dispute (the root entity of a discourse-based knowledge graph has to be an issue). For each issue, the users may propose alternatives (i.e., solutions to the problem under consideration) that correspond to potential choices. Nested issues, in cases where some alternatives need to be grouped together, are also allowed. Positions are asserted in order to support the selection of a specific course of action (alternative), or avert the users' interest from it by expressing some objection. A position may also refer to another (previously asserted) position, thus arguing in favor or against it. Finally, preferences provide individuals with a qualitative way to weigh reasons for and against the selection of a certain course of action. A preference is a tuple of the form (position, relation, position), where the relation can be "more important than" or "of equal importance to" or "less important than." The use of preferences results in the assignment of various levels of importance to the alternatives in hand. Like the other discourse elements, they are subject to further argumentative discussion.

These four types of elements enable users to contribute their knowledge on the particular problem (by entering issues, alternatives, and positions) and also to express their relevant values, interests and expectations (by entering positions and preferences). In such a way, the tool supports both the rationality-related dimension and the social dimension of the underlying collaborative decision-making process. Moreover, the tool continuously processes the elements entered by the users (by triggering its reasoning mechanisms each time a new element is entered in the graph), thus enabling users to become aware of the elements for which there is (or there is not) sufficient (positive or negative) evidence, and accordingly conduct the discussion in order to reach consensus.

ASSESSING THE OPERATION OF THE REVERSE SUPPLY CHAIN OF MOBILE PHONES IN THE CASE OF GREECE

An illustrative application of the Web-based tool presented earlier is conducted regarding the qualitative assessment of the operation of the reverse supply chain of mobile phones in the case of Greece. In this application, decision-makers A, B, and C explore interventions in the operation of the chain as well as their possible interaction with the external environment. The parameters that affect reverse logistics operations are used as a basis for the discourse. The decision-making process may reveal flaws of current practices as well as improvement potentials and areas to focus on.

Figures 4 and 5 correspond to instances of collaboration concerning the *"Recovery network structure,"* and *"Marketing,"* respectively. In these instances, the stakeholders participate in an argumentation-based decision-making process. More specifically, in the instance shown in Figure 4, the issue under consideration is *"Priorities in improving the recovery network's structure,"* while three alternatives, namely *"Extended cooperation with local municipalities," "Collection bins in super markets,"* and *"Collection programs in schools,"* have been proposed so far (by C,

Figure 4. Instances of collaboration concerning "Priorities in improving the recovery network's structure"

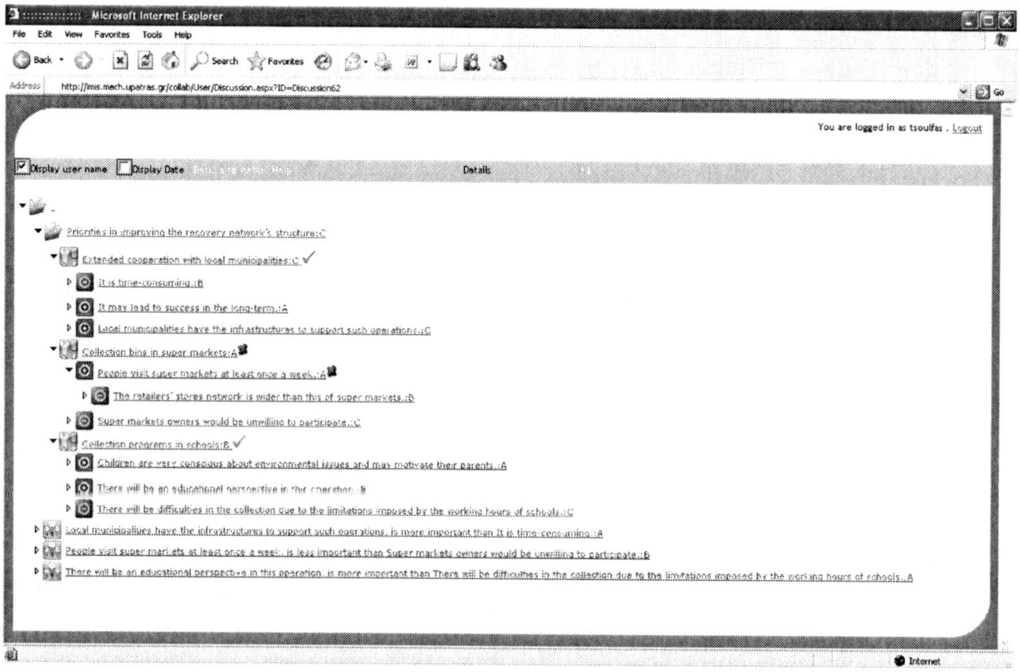

Figure 5. Instances of collaboration concerning "Marketing interventions"

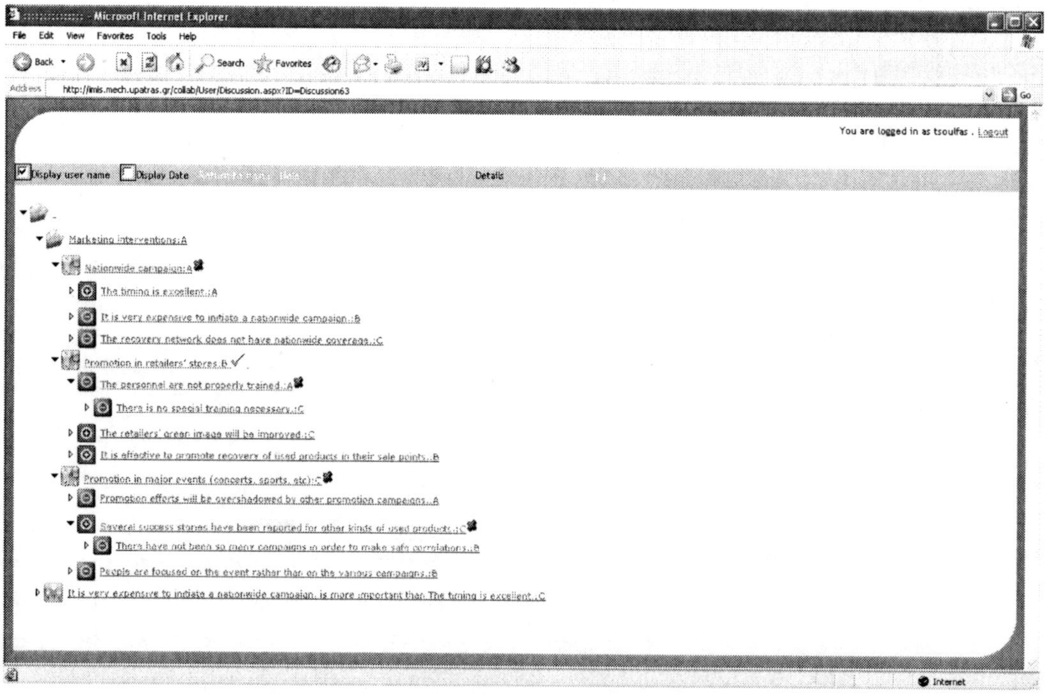

A, and B, respectively). The three stakeholders have argued about them by expressing positions speaking in favor or against them.

For instance, *"People visit super markets at least once a week"* is a position (asserted by A) that argues in favor of the second alternative, while *"It is time-consuming"* is a position (asserted by B) that argues against the first alternative. As also shown in Figures 4 and 5, argumentation can be conducted in multiple levels. Furthermore, users may also assert preferences about positions already expressed. As shown in Figure 5, user C has expressed a preference concerning the relative importance between the positions *"It is very expensive to initiate a nationwide campaign"* and *"The timing is excellent,"* arguing that the first position is of bigger importance for him. Users may also express their arguments in favor or against a preference.

When clicking on a discourse item, detailed information about it is provided in a dedicated window of the basic interface of the tool. More specifically, this part contains information about the user who submitted the selected discussion element, its submission date, any comments that the user may have inserted, as well as links to related Web pages and multimedia documents that the user may have uploaded to the tool in order to justify this element and aid his/her peers in their contemplation.

Further to the argumentation-based structuring of a discourse, the tool integrates a reasoning mechanism that determines the status of each discourse item in order to keep users aware of the discourse outcome. More specifically, alternatives, positions, and preferences of a graph have an *activation label* (it can be *"active"* or *"inactive"*) indicating their current status (inactive entries are indicated with a red "x"). This label is calculated according to the argumentation underneath and the type of evidence specified for them. In the instance of Figure 4, the position "*People visit super markets at least once a week*" is inactive because, according to the argumentation rule holding for this specific discussion, it has been defeated by the position "*The retailers' stores network is wider than this of super markets.*" Activation in the tool is a recursive procedure; a change of the activation label of an element is propagated upwards in the discourse graph. Depending on the status of positions and preferences, the mechanism goes through a scoring procedure for the alternatives of the issue. A detailed presentation of more technical details concerning the argumentation-based reasoning and scoring mechanisms of the tool can be found in Karacapilidis and Papadias (2001).

At each discourse instance, the tool informs users about what is the most prominent (according to the underlying argumentation) alternative solution (this is shown by a green "tick" sign). In the instance shown in Figure 4, *"Extended cooperation with local municipalities"* and *"Collection programs in schools"* are equally justified as best solutions, while in the instance shown in Figure 5 *"Promotion in retailers' stores"* is the better justified solution so far. However, this may change upon the type of the future argumentation; each time an alternative is affected during the discussion, the issue it belongs to is updated, since another alternative solution may be indicated by the tool.

CONCLUSION

The introduction of reverse logistics in supply chain management has created new decision-making dimensions. Consequently, parameters that may affect the operation of reverse supply chains should be evaluated. In this chapter, a qualitative approach has been discussed with respect to such parameters, aiming at facilitating and augmenting decision-making in reverse supply chains. In such cases, several stakeholders get involved, including governments, producers, distributors, and customers. As a result, decision-making procedures get more complicated due to increased levels of conflicts of interests but also due to practical reasons. For example, it is not always easy to get all stakeholders together in a round table. As it has been illustrated in this chapter, ICT may support decision-making procedures in conflicting environments by providing the means to structure dialogue, disseminate information, and last but not least, facilitate the associated reasoning process.

FUTURE RESEARCH DIRECTIONS

The parameters affecting reverse logistics operation may guide decision-makers towards identifying possible modifications in supply chain activities as well as in other corporate issues, such as marketing and supplier selection. Further research should be devoted to explore the interactions among these parameters and the ways they affect the reverse supply chains' operation and success. In addition, research efforts should also focus on how reverse supply chains may interact with forward supply chains and on relevant expedient strategies that aim at making the extended supply chains more efficient. Moreover, the qualitative evaluation of the reverse supply chains of different products may reveal the determinant parameters for each case, helping to create a body of knowledge based on thorough observations. In particular, it is important to identify the circumstances under which reverse supply chains are impeded and the options to improve their operation. Such knowledge may be exploited in developing organizational memory, a process which, beyond storing individual and collective knowledge, is related to organizational learning, decision-making, and competitive capability issues.

Apart from economic criteria, additional criteria (environmental, social, etc.) get increasingly involved in decision-making problems, leading to more complex decision-making situations. Moreover, such problems may not be usually addressed by formal models or methodologies. Instead, an argumentative practical reasoning approach seems to offer a more convenient solution. Thus, decision-making tools should focus on facilitating the cooperation of the different parties involved towards well-structured decision-making processes. The corresponding technologies should further exploit the advances in ICT in order to deliver applications of enhanced performance to decision-makers, while efficiently and effectively addressing communication and collaboration requirements. In particular, it is important to develop a more human-centric view of the problem, which appropriately structures and manages the underlying human interaction. The CDM tool discussed previously in this chapter may be exploited in order to retrieve useful information and knowledge, as well as to reason according to previous cases or predefined rules. The proposed tool may be enhanced with intelligent agent technologies, which are able to facilitate a variety of decision-makers' tasks and actions by acting on their behalf, as well as to automate system's processes.

ACKNOWLEDGMENT

The project is co-funded by the European Social Fund and national resources - EPEAEK II.

REFERENCES

Bolloju, N., Khalifa, M., & Turban, E. (2002). Integrating knowledge management into enterprise environments for the next generation decision support. *Decision Support Systems, 33*(2), 163-176.

de Brito, M. P., & Dekker, R. (2004). A framework for reverse logistics. In R. Dekker, K. Inderfurth, L. N. van Wassenhove, & M. Fleischmann (Eds.), *Quantitative approaches to reverse logistics* (pp. 3-27). Berlin, Germany: Springer-Verlag.

Clases, C., & Wehner, T. (2002). Steps across the border: Cooperation, knowledge production and systems design. *Computer Supported Cooperative Work, 11*(1-2), 39-54.

Donner, J. (2005, June 7-8). *Research approaches to mobile use in the developing world: A review of the literature.* Paper presented at the International Conference on Mobile Communication and Asian Modernities, Hong Kong. Retrieved July 9, 2008, from http://www.jonathandonner.com/donner-mobrev.pdf

European Union. (2003a). Directive 2002/95/EC of the European Parliament and of the Council of 27 January 2003 on the restriction of the use of certain hazardous substances in electrical and electronic equipment. *Official Journal of the European Union.*

European Union. (2003b). Directive 2002/96/EC of the European Parliament and of the Council of 27 January 2003 on waste electrical and electronic equipment (WEEE). *Official Journal of the European Union.*

Fishbein, B. K. (2002). *Waste in the wireless world: The challenge of cell phones.* INFORM Inc., New York, USA. Retrieved July 9, 2008, from http://www.informinc.org/reportpdfs/wp/WasteintheWirelessWorld.pdf

Fjermestad, J., & Hiltz, S. R. (2000). Group support systems: A descriptive evaluation of case and field studies. *Journal of Management Information Systems, 17*(3), 115-159.

Fleischmann, M., Krikke, H. R., Dekker, R., & Flapper, S. D. P. (1999). *Logistics network (re)-design for product recovery and reuse* (Management Report 17). Rotterdam, The Netherlands: Erasmus University of Rotterdam.

International Telecommunication Union. (2007). *Basic indicators: Population, GDP, total telephone subscribers and total telephone subscribers per 100 people.* Retrieved July 9, 2008, from http://www.itu.int/ITU-D/icteye/Indicators/Indicators.aspx

Karacapilidis, N., Adamides, E., & Pappis, C. P. (2004, September 20-25). An IS framework to support the collaborative design of supply chains. In M. Negoita, R. J. Howlett, & L. C. Jain (Eds.), *Knowledge-based intelligent information and engineering systems: Proceedings of the 8th International Conference, KES 2004,* Wellington, New Zealand, Part II (pp. 62-70). Berlin/Heidelberg, Germany: Springer-Verlag.

Karacapilidis, N., & Papadias, D. (2001). Computer supported argumentation and collaborative decision making: The HERMES system. *Information Systems, 26*(4), 259-277.

Krikke, H. R., Pappis, C. P., Tsoulfas, G. T., & Bloemhof-Ruwaard, J. (2002). Extended design principles for closed loop supply chains: Optimising economic, logistic and environmental performance. In A. Klose, M. G. Speranza, & L. N. Van Wassenhove (Eds.), *Quantitative approaches to distribution logistics and supply chain management* (pp. 61-74). Berlin/Heidelberg, Germany: Springer-Verlag.

Macey, R. (2005, March 10). Mobile phones kill great apes. *Sydney Morning Herald.*

Most, E. (2003). *Calling all cell phones: Collection, reuse, and recycling programs in the U.S.* INFORM Inc., New York, USA. Retrieved July 9, 2008, from http://www.informinc.org/reportpdfs/wp/Calling%20All%20Cell%20Phones.pdf

Pappis, C. P., Tsoulfas, G. T., & Dasaklis, T. (2006, July 2-5). *Assessing alternative reverse logistics policies for the recovery of used mobile phones.* Paper presented at the EURO XXI Conference, Reykjavik, Iceland.

Tsoulfas, G. T., Dasaklis, T., & Pappis, C. P. (2007, May 9-11). Identifying success factors for reverse logistics activities. In *Proceedings of the 2nd International Conference ECO-X 2007,* Vienna, Austria (pp. 39-46).

http://www.electrocycle.gr

http://www.w3.org/XML

ADDITIONAL READING

Adamides, E., & Karacapilidis, N. (2006). A knowledge centred framework for collaborative business process modelling. *Business Process Management Journal, 12*(5), 557-575.

Ahn, H. J., Lee, H. J., Chob, K., & Park, S. J. (2005). Utilizing knowledge context in virtual collaborative work. *Decision Support Systems, 39*(4), 563-582.

Álvarez-Gil, M. J., Berrone, P., Husillos, F. J., & Lado, N. (2007). Reverse logistics, stakeholders' influence, organizational slack, and managers' posture. *Journal of Business Research, 60*(5), 463-473.

Angell, L. C., & Klassen, R. D. (1999). Integrating environmental issues into the mainstream: An agenda for research in operations management. *Journal of Operations Management, 17*(5), 575-598.

Boons, F. (2002). Greening products: A framework for product chain management. *Journal of Cleaner Production, 10*(5), 495-505.

Bowen, F. E., Cousins, P. D., Lamming, R. C., & Faruk, A. C. (2001). The role of supply management capabilities in green supply. *Production and Operations Management, 10*(2), 174-189.

Chouinard, M., D'Amours, S., & Aït-Kadi, D. (2005). Integration of reverse logistics activities within a supply chain information system. *Computers in Industry, 56*(1), 105-124.

Courtney, J. (2001). Decision making and knowledge management in inquiring organizations: Toward a new decision-making paradigm for DSS. *Decision Support Systems, 31*(1), 17-38.

Dowlatshahi, S. (2000). Developing a theory of reverse logistics. *Interfaces, 30*(3), 143-155.

Eichner, T., & Pethig, R. (2001). Product design and efficient management of recycling and waste treatment. *Journal of Environmental Economics and Management, 41*(1), 109-134.

Evangelou, C., Karacapilidis, N., & Tzagarakis, M. (2006). On the development of knowledge management services for collaborative decision making. *Journal of Computers, 1*(6), 19-28.

Fleischmann, M., Krikke, H. R., Dekker, R., & Flapper, S. D. P. (2000). A characterization of logistics networks for product recovery. *Omega, 28*(6), 653-666.

Forgionne, G., Gupta, J., & Mora, M. (2002). Decision making support systems: Achievements, challenges and opportunities. In M. Mora, G. Forgionne, & J. Gupta (Eds.), *Decision making support systems: Achievements and challenges for the new decade* (pp. 392-403). Hershey, PA: Idea Group.

Georgiadis, P., & Vlachos, D. (2004). The effect of environmental parameters on product recovery. *European Journal of Operational Research, 157*(2), 449-464.

Gungor, A., & Gupta, S. M. (1999). Issues in environmentally conscious manufacturing and product recovery: A survey. *Computers & Industrial Engineering, 36*(4), 811-853.

Handfield, R., Sroufe, R., & Walton, S. (2005). Integrating environmental management and supply chain strategies. *Business Strategy and the Environment, 14*(1), 1-19.

Karacapilidis, N. (2006). An overview of future challenges of decision support technologies. In J. Gupta, G. Forgionne, & M. Mora (Eds.), *Intelligent decision-making support systems: Foundations, applications and challenges* (pp. 385-399). London: Springer-Verlag.

Khanna, M., & Anton, W. Q. (2002). Corporate environmental management: Regulatory and market-based pressures. *Land Economics, 78*(4), 539-558.

Liebowitz, J., & Megbolugbe, I. (2003). A set of frameworks to aid the project manager in conceptualizing and implementing knowledge management initiatives. *International Journal of Project Management, 21*(3), 189-198.

Malhotra, Y. (2005). Integrating knowledge management technologies in organizational business processes: Getting real time enterprises to deliver real business performance. *Journal of Knowledge Management, 9*(1), 7-28.

Mora, M., Forgionne, G., Gupta, J., Cervantes, F., & Gelman, O. (2003, September 3-5). A framework to assess intelligent decision-making support systems. In V. Palade, R. J. Howlett, & L. C. Jain (Eds.), *Knowledge-based intelligent information and engineering systems: Proceedings of the 7th International Conference, KES 2003, Oxford, UK, Part II* (pp. 59-65). Berlin/Heidelberg: Springer Verlag.

Muckstadt, J., Murray, D., Rappold, J., & Collins, D. (2001). Guidelines for collaborative supply chain system design and operation. *Information Systems Frontiers, 3*(4), 427-453.

Nonaka, I. (1994). A dynamic theory of organizational knowledge creation. *Organization Science, 5*(1), 14-37.

Provis, C. (2004). Negotiation, persuasion and argument. *Argumentation 18*(1), 95-112.

Ravi, V., & Shankar, R. (2005). Analysis of interactions among the barriers of reverse logistics. *Technological Forecasting and Social Change, 72*(8), 1011-1029.

Richey, R. G., Chen, H., Genchev, S. E., & Daugherty, P. J. (2005). Developing effective reverse logistics programs. *Industrial Marketing Management, 34*(8), 830-840.

Rogers, D. S., & Tibben-Lembke, R. S. (1999). *Going backwards: Reverse logistics trends and practices.* Pittsburgh: Reverse Logistics Executive Council.

Shapiro, J. (2001). Modeling and IT perspectives on supply chain integration. *Information Systems Frontiers, 3*(4), 455-464.

Shim, J. P., Warkentin, M., Courtney, J. F., Power, D. J., Sharda, R., & Carlsson, C. (2002). Past, present and future of decision support technology. *Decision Support Systems, 33*(2), 111-126.

Tibben-Lembke, R. S., & Rogers, D.S. (2002). Differences between forward and reverse logistics in a retail environment. *Supply Chain Management, 7*(5), 271-282.

Tsoulfas, G. T., & Pappis, C. P. (2006). Environmental principles applicable to supply chains design and operation. *Journal of Cleaner Production, 14*(18), 1593-1602.

Compilation of References

Abramson, H., et al. (1997). *Technology transfer systems in the United States and Germany* (pp. 241-348). Washington, DC, USA: National Academy Press.

Adda, S., Dahl, T., Gjerstad, T. B., Lamvik, T., Miljeteig, G., Molden, T. H., et al. (2002, November 1). *Environmental/social cost/value assessment methodology* (AEOLOS D4.1). WP4 D4.1, Version 2.

Aggarwal, C.C., Gates, S.C. & Yu, P.S. (1998, November). On the merits of building categorization system by supervised clustering. In *Proceedings of the Fifth ACM SIGKDD International Conference on Information and Knowledge Management*, Bethesda, MD (pp. 3-7).

AHAM. (2007). *Recycling major home appliances*. ARIC, Appliance Recycling Information Center.

Akkermans, H., Bogerd, P., & van Dorenmalen, J. (2004). Travail, transparency and trust: A case study of computer-supported collaborative supply chain planning in high tech electronics. *European Journal of Operational Research, 153*(2), 445-456.

Alaja, S. (1998). *Structuring effects in environmental decision models*. Unpublished master's thesis, Helsinki University of Technology, Helsinki.

Alesina, A., & La Ferrara, E. (2000). *The determinants of trust* (working paper 7621). Cambridge: National Bureau of Economic Research.

Al-Jarrah, O., & Abu-Qdais, H. (2006). Municipal solid waste landfill siting using intelligent system. *Waste Management, 26*, 299-306.

Allan, J. A. (1997). *Virtual water: A long-term solution for water-short Middle Eastern economies*. Retrieved July 6, 2008, from www.soas.ac.uk/waterissues/occasionalpapers/OCC03.PDF

Aloisi de Larderel, J. (1998, October 14). *What is a sustainable enterprise?* Paper presented at the UNEP Workshop, Paris, France.

Altvater, E. (1993). *The future of the market*. London: Verso.

Amanor-Boadu, V., & Starbird, A. (2004). Minimizing the value of anonymity in supply chains. In Hofstede et al. (Ed.), *Hide or confide, the dilemma of transparency* (pp. 35-40). The Hague: Reed Business Information.

American Electronic Association (AeA). (2004). *Update: International environmental regulations affecting high-tech companies*. Retrieved July 8, 2008, from http://www.aeanet.org/GovernmentAffairs/gaet_EnvUpdate042704.asp?bhcp=1

Anderl, R., Daum, B., John, H., & Putter, C. (1997). Co-operative product data modeling in life cycle networks. In F.L. Krause & G. Seliger (Eds.), *Life cycle networks* (pp. 435-446). London: Chapman & Hall.

Anderson, R. C. (1998). *Mid course correction: Toward a sustainable enterprise: The Interface model*. Atlanta, USA: The Peregrinzilla Press.

Andersson, K., Eide, M. H., Lundqvist, U., & Mattsson, B. (1998). The feasibility of including sustainability in LCA for product development. *Journal of Cleaner Production, 6*(3-4), 289-298.

Andersson, R., Aronsson, M., Bucht, E., Le Clerq, L., Ebbersten, S., Edling, P., et al. (1993). *Agriculture from*

Copyright © 2009, IGI Global, distributing in print or electronic forms without written permission of IGI Global is prohibited.

a scientific perspective. Stockholm: The Federation of Swedish Farmers, Det Naturliga Steget.

Andrae, A. S. G. (2005). *Environmental life-cycle assessment in microelectronic packaging*. ISBN 91-7291-607-9, doctoral dissertation, Chalmers University of Technology, Gothenburg, Sweden.

Angell, L. C., & Klassen, R. D. (1999). Integrating environmental issues into the mainstream: An agenda for research in operations management. *Journal of Operations Management, 17*(5), 575-598.

Ashayeri, J., Heuts, R., & Jansen, A. (1996). Inventory management of repairable service parts for personal computers. *International Journal of Operational and Production Management, 16*, 74-97.

Ashford, N. (2005). Pathways to sustainability: Evolution or revolution? In M. Geenhuizen, D. Gibson, & M. Heitor (Ed.), *Regional development and creation for innovation in the network society* (pp. 35-59). West Lafayette, IN, USA: Purdue University Press.

Asia Pacific Forum for Environment & Development (APFED). (2005). *Paradigm shift towards sustainability for Asia and the Pacific*. Retrieved July 8, 2008, from http://www.apfed.net/index.html

Assad, A.A., & Golden, B.L. (1998). *Vehicle routing: Methods and studies*. New York: Elsevier.

Avella, P., Benati, S., Martinez, L.C., Dalby, K., Di Girolamo, D., Dimitrijevic, B., et al. (1998). Some personal views on the current state and the future of locational analyses. *European Journal of Operational Research, 104*, 269-287.

Ayres, R. (1999). *Products as service carriers: Should we kill the messenger, or send it back?* Centre for the Management of Environmental Resources. Fontainebleau, France: Zero Emissions Forum. Retrieved July 8, 2008, from http://www.unu.edu/zef/publications_e/ZEF_EN_1999_01_D.pdf

Ayres, R.U., & Simonis, U.E. (Eds.). (1994). *Industrial metabolism*. Tokyo, Japan: United Nations University Press.

Azapagic, A., & Clift, R. (1995). Life cycle assessment and linear programming environmental optimization of product systems. *Computers and Chemical Engineering, 19*, 229-234.

Azapagic, A., & Clift, R. (1999). Life cycle assessment and multiobjective optimization. *Journal of Cleaner Production, 7*, 135-143.

Baeza-Yates, R., & Ribeiro-Neto, B. (1999). *Modern information retrieval*. MA: Addison-Wesley Longman.

Balabanovic, M., & Shoham, Y. (1997). Fab: Content-based, collaborative recommendation. *Communications of the ACM, 40*(3), 66-72.

Bana e Costa, C. A., Stewart, T. J., & Vansnick, J.-C. (1997). Multicriteria decision analysis: Some thoughts based on the tutorial and discussion sessions of the ESIGMA meetings. *European Journal of Operational Research, 99*(1), 28-37.

Banker, R. D., Charnes, A., & Cooper, W. W. (1984). Some models for estimating technical and scale inefficiencies in data envelopment analysis. *Management Science, 30*(9), 1078-1092.

Banker, R. D., Conrad, R. F., & Strauss, R. P. (1986). A comparative application of data envelopment analysis and translog methods: An illustrative study of hospital production. *Management Science, 32*(1), 30-44.

Barbarosoglu, G., & Ozgur, D. (1999). A tabu search algorithm for the vehicle routing problem. *Computers & Operations Research, 26*, 255-270.

Barros, A. I., Dekker, R., & Scholten, V. (1998). A two-level network for recycling sand: A case study. *European Journal of Operational Research, 110*, 199-214.

Barry, M.J.A., & Linoff, G.S. (1997). *Data mining technique for marketing, sale, and customer support*. Wiley Computer.

Baumann, H., & Cowell, S. (1999). An evaluative framework for conceptual and analytical approaches used in environmental management. *The Journal of Corporate Environmental Strategy and Practice, 26*, 109-122.

Baumgarten, H., Christian, B., Annerous, F., & Thomas, S.-D. (2003). Supply chain management and reverse logistics-integration of reverse logistics processes into supply chain management approaches. In *Proceedings of the International Symposium on Electronics and the Environment* (pp. 79-84).

Bautista, J., & Pereira, J. (2006). Modeling the problem of locating collection areas for urban waste management. An application to the metropolitan area of Barcelona. *Omega, 34*, 617-629.

Bazaraa, M.S., & Shetty, C.M. (1990). *Nonlinear programming, theory and algorithms.* John Wiely & Sons.

Beamon, B. M. (1999). Designing the green supply chain. *Logistics Information Management, 12*(4), 332-342.

Belton, F., Ackermann, F., & Shepherd, I. (1997). Integrated support from problem structuring through to alternative evaluation using COPE and V.I.S.A.. *Journal of Multi-Criteria Decision Analysis, 6*, 115-130.

Belton, V., & Vickers, S. (1990). Use of a simple multi-attribute value function incorporating visual interactive sensitivity analysis for multiple criteria decision making. In C.A. Bana e Costa (Ed.), *Readings in multiple criteria decision aid* (pp. 319-334). Berlin: Springer-Verlag.

Bergendahl, C. G., Lichtenvort, K., Johansson, G., Zackrisson, M., & Nyyssonen, J. (2005). Environmental and economic implications of a shift to halogen-free printed wiring boards. *Circuit World, 31*(3), 26-31.

Berger, J., & Barkaoui, M. (2004). A parallel hybrid genetic algorithm for the vehicle routing problem with time windows. *Computers & Operational Research, 31*, 2037-2053.

Bertsimas, D., & Ryzin, G.V. (1993). Stocastic and dynamic vehicle routing in the Euclidean plane with multiple capacitated vehicle. *Operations Research, 41*, 60-76.

Bezdek, J.C. (1973). *Fuzzy mathematics in pattern classification.* Unpublished doctoral dissertation, Cornell University.

Billerbeck, B., Scholer, F., Williams, H. E., & Zobel, J. (2003). Query expansion using associated queries. In *Proceedings of the 12th International Conference on Information and Knowledge Management,* New Orleans, LA (pp. 2-9).

Bird, L., & Kaiser, M. (2007). *Trends in utility green pricing programs (2006)* (NREL/TP-670-42287). Golden, CO: National Renewable Energy Laboratory.

Bird, L., Swezey, B., & Aabakken, J. (2004). *Utility green pricing programs: Design, implementation and consumer response* (NREL/TP-620-35618). Golden, CO: National Renewable Energy Laboratory.

Bird, L., Wüstenhagen, R., & Aabakken, J. (2002). *Green power marketing abroad: Recent experience and trends* (NREL/TP-620-32155). Golden, CO: National Renewable Energy Laboratory.

Blackburn, J.D., Guide, V.D.R., Jr., Souza, G.C., & Van Wassenhove, L.N. (2004). Reverse supply chains for commercial returns. *California Management Review, 46*(2), 6-22.

Blecker, T., Friedrich, G., Kaluza, B., Abdelkafi, N., & Kreutler G. (2005). *Information and management systems for product customization.* Boston: Springer-Verlag.

Bloemhof-Ruwaard, J. M., Solomon, M., & Van Wassenhove, L. N. (1996). The capacitated distribution and waste disposal problem. *European Journal of Operational Research, 88*, 490-503.

Bloemhof-Ruwaard, J. M., van Wassenhove, L. N., Gabel, H. L., & Weaver, P. M. (1996). An environmental life cycle optimization model for the European pulp and paper industry. *Omega, 20*, 615-629.

Bodin, L.D., Golden, B.L., Assad, A.A., & Ball, M.O. (1983). Routing and scheduling of vehicles and crews. *Computers & Operations Research, 10*, 63-211.

Boersma, M.F. (1999). *Developing trust in international joint ventures.* Doctoral thesis on Systems, Organization and Management, Groningen, Rijksuniversiteit.

Bohlen, G.M., Schlegelmilch, B.B., & Diamantopoulos, A. (1993a). Consumer perceptions of the environmental impact of an industrial service. *Marketing Intelligence & Planning, 11*(1), 37-48.

Bohlen, G.M., Schlegelmilch, B.B., & Diamantopoulos, A. (1993b). Measuring ecological concern: A multi-construct perspective. *Journal of Marketing Management*, 415-430.

Bolloju, N., Khalifa, M., & Turban, E. (2002). Integrating knowledge management into enterprise environments for the next generation decision support. *Decision Support Systems, 33*(2), 163-176.

Booker, L. (1987). Improving search in genetic algorithm. In L. Davis (Ed.), *Genetic algorithms and simulated annealing* (pp. 61-73). San Mateo, CA: Morgan Kaufmann.

Boon, J. E., Isaacs, J. A., & Gupta, S. M. (2003). End-of-life infrastructure economics for "clean vehicles" in the United States. *Journal of Industrial Ecology, 7*(1), 25-45.

Boon, J., Isaacs, J. A., & Gupta, S. M. (2000). Economic impact of aluminum intensive vehicles on the U.S. automotive recycling infrastructure. *Journal of Industrial Ecology, 4*(2), 117-134.

Boothroyd, G., & Alting, L. (1992). Design for assembly and disassembly. *Ann. CIRP, 41*, 625-636.

Borcherding, K., Eppel, T., & von Winterfeldt, D. (1991). Comparison on weighting judgments in multiattribute utility measurement. *Management Science, 37*(12), 1603-1619.

Borchers, A.M., Duke, J.M., & Parsons, G.R. (2007). Does willingness to pay for green energy differ by source? *Energy Policy, 35*, 3327-3334.

Bots, P.W.G., & Hofstede, G.J. (2004). The Takeover Trio. *Simulation and Gaming, an International Journal of Theory, Practice, and Research, 35*(4), 505-516.

Bottomley, P.A., & Doyle, J.D. (2001). A comparison of three weight elicitation methods: Good, better and best. *Omega, 29*, 553-560.

Boulding, K.E. (1966). The economics of the coming spaceship Earth. In H. Jarrett (Ed.), *Environmental quality in a growing economy* (pp. 3-14). Baltimore, MD: John Hopkins Press.

Bouwer, H. (2000). Integrated water management: Emerging issues and challenges. *Agricultural Water Management, 45*, 217-228.

Bouyssou, D. (1990). Building criteria: A prerequisite for MCDA. In C.A. Bana e Costa (Ed.), *Readings in multiple criteria decision aid* (pp. 58-80). Berlin: Springer-Verlag.

Bowen, F. E., Cousins, P. D., Lamming, R. C., & Faruk, A. C. (2001). Horses for courses. *Greener Management International, 35*, 41-60.

Bowersox, D.J., & Closs, D.J. (1996). *Logistical management: The integrated supply chain process*. New York: McGraw-Hill.

Bowlin, W. F., Charnes, A., Cooper, W. W., & Sherman, H. D. (1984). Data envelopment analysis and regression approaches to efficiency estimation and evaluation. *Annals of Operations Research, V2*(1), 113-138.

Bramham, J., & MacCarthy, B.L. (2003, October). Matching configurator attributes to business strategy. In *Proceedings of the MCPC 2003, 2nd Interdisciplinary World Congress on Mass Customization and Personalization*. Munich: Technische Universitaet Muenchen.

Brans, J.-P., & Vincke, P. (1985). A preference ranking organization method. *Management Science, 31*, 647-656.

Bras, B., & McIntosh, M. W. (1999). Product, process, and organizational design for remanufacture: An overview of research. *Robot. Comput.-Integr. Mfg, 15*, 167-178.

Brattebø, H. (1996). *Industrial ecology — interdisciplinary perspectives and challenges. NTVA-report 2: Industrial ecology and sustainable product design*. Trondheim, Norway: The Norwegian Academy of Technological Science.

Broman, G., Byggeth, S. H., & Robèrt, K.-H. (2002). Integrating environmental aspects in engineering education. *International Journal of Engineering Education, 18*(6), 717-724.

Broman, G., Holmberg, J., & Robèrt, K.-H. (2000). Simplicity without reduction: Thinking upstream towards the sustainable society. *Interfaces, 30*(3), 13-25.

Brown, H.L., Hamel, B.B., & Hedman, B.A. (1985). *Energy analysis of 108 industrial processes*. U.S. Department of Energy.

Brundtland, G.H. (1987). *Our common future*. Oxford, UK: Oxford University Press.

Bucciarelli, L. (1998). Project-oriented learning as part of the curriculum development. *Industrial ecology and curriculum*. Troyes, France: NTVA (Norwegian Academy of Technological Science).

Buckley, C., Singhal, A., & Mitra, M. (1995). New retrieval approaches using SMART: TREC 4. In *Proceedings of the Fourth Text Retrieval Conference* (pp. 25-48). Gaithersburg, MD: National Institute of Standards and Technology.

Buckley, J.J. (1985). Fuzzy hierarchical analysis. *Fuzzy Sets and Systems, 17*, 233-247.

Buckminster Fuller, R. (1963). *Operating manual for spaceship Earth*. New York: Dutton & Co.

Buehner, F.W., & Rossiter, A.P. (1996, April). Minimize waste by managing process design. *Chemtech, 26*, 64-72.

Bufardi, A., Gheorghe, R., Kiritsis, D., & Xirouchakis, P. (2004). A multicriteria decision-aid approach for product end-of-life alternative selection. *International Journal of Production Research, 42*(16), 3139-3157.

Bufardi, A., Sakara, D., & Kiritsis, D. (2002, March 14). *Environmental/social cost/value software methodology and tool* (AEOLOS D4.2). WP4 D4.2, Version 1.

Burgelman, R. A., & McKinney, W. (2006). Managing the strategic dynamics of acquisition integration: Lessons from HP and COMPAQ. *California Management Review, 48*(3), 6-27.

Burke, R.D. (2002). Hybrid recommender systems: Survey and experiments. *User Modeling and User-Adapted Interaction, 12*(4), 331-370.

Buyukozkan, G., Ertay, T., Kahraman, C., & Ruan, D. (2004). Determining the importance weights for the design requirements in the house of quality using the fuzzy analytic network approach. *International Journal of Intelligent Systems, 19*, 443-461.

Byggeth, S. H. (2001). *Integration of sustainability aspects in product development*. Unpublished Licentiate, Göteborg University, Göteborg, Sweden.

Byggeth, S. H., Broman, G. I., & Robert, K. H. (2007). A method for sustainable product development based on a modular system of guiding questions. *Journal of Cleaner Production*, (15), 1-11.

Camper, C. D., & Turcanu, C. (2007). On the governmental use of multi-criteria analysis. *Ecological Economics, 62*, 298-307.

Canbolat, Y.B., Chelst, K., & Garg, N. (2007). Combining decision tree and MAUT for selecting a country for a global manufacturing facility. *Omega, 35*(3), 312-325.

Carter, C. R., & Ellram, L. M. (1998). Reverse logistics: A review of the literature and framework for future investigation. *Journal of Business Logistics, 19*, 85-102.

Cha, Y., & Jung, M. (2003). Satisfaction assessment of multi-objective schedules using neural fuzzy methodology. *International Journal of Production Research, 41*(8), 1831-1849.

Chambers, R., Herendeen, R., Joyce, J., & Penner, P. (1979). Gasohol: Does it or doesn't it produce positive net energy? *Science, 206*, 790-795.

Chang, N.B., & Wei, Y.L. (2000). Siting recycling drop-off stations in urban area by genetic algorithm-based fuzzy multiobjective nonlinear integer programming modeling. *Fuzzy Sets and Systems, 114*, 133-149.

Chao, I.M., Golden, B.L., & Wasil, E. (1993). A new heuristic algorithm for the multi-depot vehicle routing problem that improves upon best-known solutions.

American Journal of Mathematical Management Science, 13, 371-406.

Chapman, P.F., & Roberts, F. (1983). *Metal resources and energy*. London: Butterworth.

Chappaz, C. (2003). *Green is only skin-deep* (decision brief). Cambridge, MA: Cambridge Energy Research Associates.

Charnes, A., Cooper, W. W., Lewin, A. Y., & Seiford, L. M. (1994). *Data envelopment analysis: Theory, methodology, and applications*. Boston: Kluwer.

Charnes, A., Cooper, W., & Rhodes, E. (1978). Measuring the efficiency of decision-making units. *European Journal of Operational Research, 2*(6), 429-444.

Charnpratheep, K., Zhou, Q., & Garner, B. (1997). Preliminary landfill site screening using fuzzy geographical information systems. *Waste Management and Research, 15*, 197-215.

Chen, C.T., Lin, C.T., & Huang, S.F. (2006). A fuzzy approach for supplier evaluation and selection in supply chain management. *International Journal of Production Economics, 102*(2), 289-301.

Chen, J. L., & Chien, H. W. (2004). Simple LCA by response surface method for multidisciplinary design of eco-product. In H. Reichl, H. Griese, & H. Potter (Eds.), *2004 Proceedings of the Electronics Goes Green: Driving Forces for Future Electronics* (pp. 515-520). Stuttgart, Germany: Fraunhofer IRB, IRB Staz-und Druckcenter.

Chen, S.J., Hwang, C.L., & Hwang, F.P. (1992). Fuzzy multiple attribute decision making. *Lecture Notes in Economics and Mathematical Systems, 375*. Berlin: Springer-Verlag.

Cheng, S., Chan, C.W., & Huang, G.H. (2002). Using multiple criteria decision analysis for supporting decisions of solid waste management. *Journal of Environmental Science and Health A, 37*(6), 975-990.

Cheng, S., Chan, C.W., & Huang, G.H. (2003). An integrated multi-criteria decision analysis and inexact mixed integer linear programming approach for solid waste management. *Engineering Applications of Artificial Intelligence, 16*, 543-554.

Chinander, K. R. (2001). Aligning accountability and awareness for environmental performance in operations. *Production and Operations Management, 10*, 276-291.

Choo, E. U., Schoner, B., & Wedley, W. C. (1999). Interpretation of criteria weights in multicriteria decision making. *Computers & Industrial Engineering, 37*(3), 527-541.

Chouinard, M., D'Amours, S., & Aït-Kadi, D. (2005). Integration of reverse logistics activities within a supply chain information system. *Comput. Ind., 56*, 105-124.

Chowdhury, F. (2006). Sun power, woman power. *Boloji*. Retrieved July 8, 2008, from http://www.boloji.com/wfs5/wfs625.htm

Christiansen, K. (1997). *Simplifying LCA: Just a cut?* Brussels, Belgium: SETAC (Society of Environmental Toxicology and Chemistry)-Europe.

Christofides N., Mingozzi, A., & Toth, P. (1981). Exact algorithms for the vehicle routing problem, based on spanning tree and shortest path relaxations. *Mathematical Programming, 20*, 255-282.

Christopher, M., Deshmukh, A., & Wang, B. (1996). Green quality function deployment. In *Proceedings of the 4th International Conference on Environmentally Conscious Design and Manufacturing* (pp. 297-304).

Chu, T. C. (2002). Selecting plant location via a fuzzy TOPSIS approach. *The International Journal of Advanced Manufacturing Technology, 20*, 859-864.

Chu, T.-C., & Lin, Y.-C. (2003). A fuzzy TOPSIS method for robot selection. *International Journal of Advanced Manufacturing Technology, 21*, 284-290.

Chung, J., Lee, H., Koh, Y., & Hur, T. (2003). Web based ecodesign supporting system for electronic product. In *Proceedings of the 2003 IEEE International Symposium on Electronics and the Environment* (pp. 246-250). The Institute of Electrical and Electronics Engineers, Inc.

Clark, C.F., Kotchen, M.J., & Moore, M.R. (2003). Internal and external influences on pro-environmental behavior: Participation in a green electricity program. *Journal of Experimental Psychology, 23*, 237-246.

Clases, C., & Wehner, T. (2002). Steps across the border: Cooperation, knowledge production and systems design. *Computer Supported Cooperative Work, 11*(1-2), 39-54.

Clemen, R.T. (1991). *Making hard decisions: An introduction to decision analysis*. Boston: PWS-Kent Publishing Company.

CNE. (2004). *Informe sobre las campañas publicitarias de energía verde*. Madrid: Comisión Nacional de la Energía.

Colebrook, M., & Sicilia, J. (2007). Undesirable facility location problems on multicriteria networks. *Computers and Operations Research, 34*, 1491-1514.

Cook, D. (2004). *The natural step towards a sustainable society*. Dartington, UK: Green Books.

Cooper, J. (2003). Life-cycle assessment and sustainable development indicators. *Journal of Industrial Ecology, 7*(1), 12-15.

Côté, R., & Hall, J. (1995). Industrial parks as ecosystems. *Journal of Cleaner Production, 3*(1-2), 41-46.

Crossland, P., & Smith, F. L. (2002). Value creation in fine arts: A system dynamics model of inverse demand and information cascades. *Strategic Management Journal, 23*(5), 417-434.

Cutting, D.R., Karger, D.R., Pedersen, J.O., & Tukey, J.W. (1992). Scatter/Gather: A cluster-based approach to browsing large document collection. In *Proceedings of the 15th Annual International ACM/SIGIR Conference*, Copenhagen, Denmark.

Dale, V. H., & English, M. R. (Eds.). (1999). *Tools to aid environmental decision making*. New York: Springer-Verlag.

Daniels, P. L., & Moore, S. (2002). Quantifying the metabolism of physical economies, Part I: Methodological overview. *Journal of Industrial Ecology, 5*(4), 69-93.

Dantzig, G.B., & Ramser, J.H. (1959). The truck dispatching problem. *Management Science, 6*, 80-91.

Das, S., & Yedlarajiah, D. (2002). An integer programming model for prescribing material recovery strategies. In *Proceedings of the 2002 IEEE International Symposium on Electronics and the Environment* (pp. 118-122). The Institute of Electrical and Electronics Engineers, Inc.

de Brito, M. P., & Dekker, R. (2004). A framework for reverse logistics. In R. Dekker, K. Inderfurth, L. N. van Wassenhove, & M. Fleischmann (Eds.), *Quantitative approaches to reverse logistics* (pp. 3-27). Berlin, Germany: Springer-Verlag.

De Brito, M. P., Flapper, S. D. P., & Dekker, R. (2003). *Reverse logistics: A review of case studies B2--reverse logistics: A review of case studies*. The Netherlands: Erasmus University Rotterdam.

De Groene, A., & Hermans, M. (1998). Economic and other implications of integrated chain management: A case study. *Journal of Cleaner Production, 6*, 199-221.

De Koster, M. B. M., de Brito, M. P., & van de Vendel, M. (2002). How to organise return handling: An exploratory study with nine retailer warehouses. *International Journal of Retail & Distribution Management*, 30, 407-421.

Dekker, R., Fleischmann, M., Inderfurth, K., & Wassenhove, L.N. (Eds.). (2004). *Reverse logistics: Quantitative models for closed-loop supply chains*. Heidelberg, Germany: Springer-Verlag.

Del Río, P., & Gual, M. (2004). The promotion of green electricity in Europe: Present and future. *European Environment, 14*, 219-234.

Delucchi, M. A., Murphy, J. J., & McCubbin, D. R. (2002). The health and visibility cost of air pollution: A comparison of estimation methods. *Journal of Environmental Management, 64*, 139-152.

DePass, D. (2006). Green manufacturing gets a push. *Knight Ridder Tribune Business News*, 1.

Dewulf, W., & Duflou, J. (2004). Estimating environmental impact scores and related uncertainties using the Eco-Pas methodology. In H. Reichl, H. Griese, & H. Potter (Eds.), *2004 Proceedings of the Electronics Goes Green: Driving Forces for Future Electronics* (pp. 447-452). Stuttgart, Germany: Fraunhofer IRB, IRB Staz-und Druckcenter.

Dhakal, S. (2002). *Introduction of electric three-wheelers in Kathmandu, Nepal*. IGES. Retrieved July 8, 2008, from http://www.iges.or.jp/APEIS/RISPO/inventory/db/pdf/0018.pdf

Diakoulaki, D., Mavrotas, G., & Papayannakis, L. (1995). Determining objective weights in multiple criteria problems: The critic method. *Computers and Operations Research, 22*(7), 763-770.

Diamantopoulos, A., Schlegelmilch, B.B., Sinkovics, R.R., & Bohlen, G.M. (2003). Can socio-demographics still play a role in profiling green consumers? A review of the evidence and an empirical investigation. *Journal of Business Research, 56*(6), 465-480.

Dickinson, D. A., Draper, C. W., Saminathan, M., Sohn, J. E., & Williams, G. (1995). Green product manufacturing. *At&T Technical Journal, 74*(6), 26-35.

Dickinson, D. A., Mosovsky, J. A., & Houthuysen, S. D. (2003). Assessing integrated circuit manufacturing for environmental performance and sustainability: A full scale IC business application. In *Proceedings of the 2003 IEEE International Symposium on Electronics and the Environment* (pp. 214-219). The Institute of Electrical and Electronics Engineers, Inc.

Diehl, J.C. (2006). *Renewable energy in emerging countries from an end-user and business perspective*. Presentation to the Management of Technology Programme, University of California, Berkeley, in association with UN Industrial Development Organization (UNIDO). Retrieved July 8, 2008, from http://bridge.berkeley.edu/2006_Pages/PresentationArchives/2006/Panel%206/Diehl.pdf

Dinica, V., & Arentsen, M.J. (2003). Green certificate trading in The Netherlands in the prospect of the European electricity market. *Energy Policy, 31*, 609-620.

Donnelly, K., & Boehm, T. (2003). Implementing DFE through a product-based environmental management system. In *Proceedings of the 2003 IEEE International Symposium on Electronics and the Environment* (pp. 111-113). The Institute of Electrical and Electronics Engineers, Inc.

Donner, J. (2005, June 7-8). *Research approaches to mobile use in the developing world: A review of the literature*. Paper presented at the International Conference on Mobile Communication and Asian Modernities, Hong Kong. Retrieved July 9, 2008, from http://www.jonathandonner.com/donner-mobrev.pdf

Doyle, J.R., Green, R.H., & Bottomley, P.A. (1997, April). Judging relative importance: Direct rating and point allocation are not equivalent. *Organizational Behavior and Human Decision Processes, 70*(1), 65-72.

Dreborg, K. H. (1996). Essence of backcasting. *Futures, 28*(9), 813-828.

Dror, M., & Trudeau, P. (1989). Savings by split delivery routing. *Transportation Science, 23*, 141-149.

Dror, M., & Trudeau, P. (1990). Split delivery routing. *Naval Research Logistics, 37*, 383-402.

Dror, M., Laporte, G., & Trudeau, P. (1989). Vehicle routing with stochastic demands: Properties and solution framework. *Transportation Science, 23*, 166-176.

Dubreuil, Gaillard, G., & Muller-Wenk, R. (2007). Key elements in a framework for land use impact assessment within LCA. *International Journal of Life Cycle Assessment, 12*, 5-15.

Duhaime, R., Riopel, D., & Langevin, A. (2000). Value analysis and optimization of reusable containers at Canada Post. *Interfaces, 30*, 3-15.

Dyckhoff, H., Lackes, R., & Reese, J. (2003). *Supply chain management and reverse logistics B2: Supply chain management and reverse logistics*. Berlin: Springer-Verlag.

Eikelenberg, N. L. W., Kok, I. C., & Tempelman, E. (2004). Implementation ecodesign for EEE-products. In H. Reichl, H. Griese, & H. Potter (Eds.), *2004 Proceedings of the Electronics Goes Green: Driving Forces for Future Electronics* (pp. 469-474). Stuttgart, Germany: Fraunhofer IRB, IRB Staz-und Druckcenter.

Ek, C. (2005). Public and private attitudes towards "green" electricity: The case of Swedish wind power. *Energy Policy, 33*, 1677-1689.

Electrolux. (1994). *Electrolux annual report 1994*. Stockholm: Electrolux.

Environmental Protection Agency (EPA), U.S. (1995). An introduction to environmental accounting as a business management tool: Key concepts and terms. Retrieved July 8, 2008, from http://www.epa.gov

Environmental Protection Agency (EPA), U.S. (2002). *The Toxics Release Inventory (TRI) and factors to consider when using TRI data*. Retrieved July 8, 2008, from http://www.epa.gov/tri

Envirowise, Electronics Sector. (2005). *Relevant legislation/regulations*. Retrieved July, 8, 2008, from http://www.envirowise.gov.uk/page.aspx?o=Ref165

EPA. (2007). Life cycle assessment: Principles and practice. *Life-cycle assessment research*. Retrieved July 9, 2008, from http://www.epa.gov/nrmrl/lcaccess/lca101.html

EPHC. (2004, December). *Industry discussion paper on co-regulatory frameworks for product stewardship*. Environment Protection and Heritage Council, Australia. Retrieved July 8, 2008, from http://www.ephc.gov.au/pdf/product_stewardship/ProductStewardship_IndustryDP.pdf

Eric T., & Philippe, B. (1997). A tabu search heuristic for the vehicle routing problem with soft time windows. *Transportation Science, 31*, 170-186.

Ericsson Corporation. (2004). *Ericsson sustainability report: Bridging the digital divide with communication for all*. Stockholm, Sweden.

Erkut, E., & Neuman, S. (1989). A survey of analytical models for locating undesirable facilities. *European Journal of Operational Research, 40*, 275-29.

Erkut, E., & Neuman, S. (1992). A multiobjective model for locating undesirable facilities. *Annals of Operations Research, 40*, 209-227.

Ertay, T., Buyukozkan, G., Kahraman, C., & Ruan, D. (2005). Quality function deployment implementation based on analytic network process with linguistic data: An application in automotive industry. *Journal of Intelligent & Fuzzy Systems, 16*(3), 221-232.

ESCAP. (2006, March). *Green growth at a glance: The way forward for Asia and the Pacific*. UN Economic and Social Commission for Asia and the Pacific. Bangkok. Retrieved July 8, 2008, from http://www.unescap.org/esd/water/publications/sd/GGBrochure.pdf See also http://www.greengrowth.org

ESCAP. (2007, June 5-7). *3rd green growth policy dialogue on 'the greening of business and the environment as a business opportunity.* Bangkok. Retrieved July 8, 2008, from http://www.greengrowth.org/3ggpd_pres_media/pres-media.asp

Ethier, R.G., Poe, G. L., Schulze, W.D., & Clark, J. (2000). A comparison of hypothetical phone and mail contingent valuation responses for green-pricing electricity programs. *Land Economics, 76*, 54-67.

European Union. (2003). Directive 2002/95/EC of the European Parliament and of the Council of 27 January 2003 on the restriction of the use of certain hazardous substances in electrical and electronic equipment. *Official Journal of the European Union.*

European Union. (2003). Directive 2002/96/EC of the European Parliament and of the Council of 27 January 2003 on waste electrical and electronic equipment (WEEE). *Official Journal of the European Union.*

Evan, H.Z. (1974). Socio-economic and labour aspects of pollution control in the chemical industries. *Journal for International Labour Review, 110*(3), 219-233.

Everard, M., Monaghan, M., & Ray, D. (2000). *2020*

vision series No2: PVC and sustainability. The Natural Step UK/UK Environment Agency.

Fabri, A., & Recht, P. (2006). On dynamic pickup and delivery vehicle routing with several time windows and waiting times. *Transportation Research, Part B, 40*, 335-350.

Farhar, B.C. (1999). *Willingness to pay for electricity from renewable resources: A review of utility market research* (NREL/TP.550.26148). Golden, CO: National Renewable Energy Laboratory.

Feldmann, K., Meedt, O., Trautner, S., Scheller, H., & Hoffman, W. (1999). The "Green Design Advisor": A tool for design for environment. *Journal of Electronics Manufacturing, 9*(1), 17-28.

Ferrer, G. (1997). The economics of personal computer remanufacturing. *Resources, Conservation and Recycling, 21*, 79-108.

Ferrer, G. (1997). The economics of tire remanufacturing. *Resources, Conservation and Recycling, 19*, 221-255.

Ferrer, G., & Ayres, R. U. (2000). The impact of remanufacturing in the economy. *Ecological Economics, 32*, 413-429.

Ferrer, G., & Whybark, D. C. (2001). Material planning for a remanufacturing facility. *Production and Operations Management, 10*, 112-124.

Field, F. R. (1985). *Application of multi-attribute utility analysis to problems in materials selection.* Doctoral dissertation, Massachusetts Institute of Technology, Cambridge, MA.

Figueira, J., & Roy, B. (2002). Determining the weights of criteria in the ELECTRE type methods with a revised Simos's procedure. *European Journal of Operational Research, 139*(2), 317-326.

Fiksel, J. (Ed.). (1996). *Design for environment: Creating eco-efficient products and processes.* McGraw-Hill.

Finnveden, G., & Moberg, A. (2005). Environmental systems analysis tools: An overview. *Journal of Cleaner Production, 13*(12), 1165-1173.

Fishbein, B. K. (2002). *Waste in the wireless world: The challenge of cell phones.* INFORM Inc., New York, USA. Retrieved July 9, 2008, from http://www.informinc.org/reportpdfs/wp/WasteintheWirelessWorld.pdf

Fishbein, B., McGarry, L. S., & Dillon, P. S. (2000). *Leasing: A step toward producer responsibility.* New York: Inform.

Fisher, M.L., & Jaikumer, R. (1981). A generalize assignment heuristic for vehicle routing. *Networks, 11*, 109-124.

Fjermestad, J., & Hiltz, S. R. (2000). Group support systems: A descriptive evaluation of case and field studies. *Journal of Management Information Systems, 17*(3), 115-159.

Flapper, S. D. P., van Nunen, J. E. E., & van Wassenhove, L. N. (2005). *Managing closed-loop supply chains B2: Managing closed-loop supply chains.* Berlin: Springer-Verlag.

Fleischmann, M. (2001). *Quantititative models for reverse logistics: Lecture notes in economics and mathematical systems.* Germany: Springer-Verlag.

Fleischmann, M., Beullens, P., Bloemhof-Ruwaard, J. M., & van Wassenhove, L. N. (2001). The impact of product recovery on logistics network design. *Production & Operations Management, 10*, 156-173.

Fleischmann, M., Jacqueline, M. B.-R., Rommert, D., van der Laan, E., van Nunen, J.A.E.E., & van Wassenhove, L.N. (1997). Quantitative models for reverse logistics: A review. *European Journal of Operational Research, 103*(16), 1-17.

Fleischmann, M., Krikke, H. R., Dekker, R., & Flapper, S. D. P. (2000). A characterization of logistics networks for product recovery. *Omega, 28*, 653-666.

Fleischmann, M., Krikke, H. R., Dekker, R., & Flapper, S. D. P. (1999). *Logistics network (re)-design for product recovery and reuse* (Management Report 17). Rotterdam, The Netherlands: Erasmus University of Rotterdam.

Fleischmann, M., Kuik, R., & Dekker, R. (2002). Controlling inventories with stochastic item returns: A basic model. *European Journal of Operational Research, 138*, 63-75.

Fleishmann, B., & Klose, A. (2005). *Distribution logistics B2: Distribution logistics.* Berlin: Springer-Verlag.

Forrester, J. W. (1999). *Industrial dynamics.* Waltham, MA: Pegasus Communications.

Forrester, J. W. (2007). System dynamics: A personal view of the first fifty years [dagger]. *System Dynamics Review, 23*(2/3), 345.

Forrester, J. W. (2007). System dynamics: The next fifty years [dagger]. *System Dynamics Review, 23*(2/3), 359.

Fouquet, R. (1998). The United Kingdom demand for renewable electricity in a liberalized market. *Energy Policy, 26*, 281-293.

Frankl, P., & Rubik, F. (2000). *Life-cycle assessment in industry and business: Adoption patterns, applications and implications.* Heidelberg, Germany: Springer-Verlag.

Frazao, R., & Rocha, C. (2004, October 30). *Product services in the need area "base materials.* Suspronet report. Retrieved July 8, 2008, from http://www.suspronet.org/fs_reports.htm

Friedman, F. B. (1992). The changing role of the environmental manager. *Business Horizons, 35*(2), 25.

Frischknecht, R. et al. (2005). The ecoinvent database: Overview and methodological framework. *International Journal of Life Cycle Assessment, 10*(1), 3-9.

Frizzell, P.W., & Giffin, J.W. (1995). The split delivery vehicle scheduling problem with time windows and grid network distances. *Computers & Operations Research, 22*, 655-667.

Frosch, R.A., & Gallopoulos, N.E. (1989, September). Strategies for manufacturing. *Scientific American, 261*, 144-152.

Fruhbrodt, E. (2001). *LCA software review: An up-to-date overview of European market.* Germany: Heidelberger Druckmaschinen AG.

Fuchs, D.A., & Arentsen, M.J. (2002). Green electricity in the market place: The policy challenge. *Energy Policy, 30*, 525-538.

Gao, T., Sirgy, M.J., & Bird, M.M. (2005). Reducing buyer decision-making uncertainty in organizational purchasing: Can supplier trust, commitment, and dependence help? *Journal of Business Research, 58*, 397-405.

Gatenby, D. A., & Foo, G. (1990). Design for X (DFX): Key to competitive, profitable products. *AT&T Technical Journal, 69*, 2-15.

Geiser, K. (2001). *Materials matter: Toward a sustainable materials policy.* Cambridge, MA, USA: MIT Press.

Gen, M., & Cheng, R. (1997). *Genetic algorithms and engineering design.* New York: John Wiley.

Gheorghe, R., Bufardi, A., & Xirouchakis, P. (2004). Construction of a two-parameters outranking relation from fuzzy evaluations. *Fuzzy Sets and Systems, 143*, 391-412.

Giannikos, I. (1998). A multiobjective programming model for locating treatment sites and routing hazardous wastes. *European Journal of Operational Research, 104*, 333-342.

Gillett, B., & Johnson, J. (1976). Multi-terminal vehicle-dispatch algorithm. *Omega, 4*, 711-718.

Glantschnig, W. J. (1994). Green design: An introduction to issues and challenges. *IEEE Transactions on Components, Packaging and Manufacturing Technology-Part A, 17*, 508-513.

Glover, E.J., Lawrence, S., Gordon, M.D., Birmingham, W.P., & Giles, C.L. (1999). Recommending Web documents based on user preferences. In Proceedings of the *SIGIR 99 Workshop on Recommender Systems*, Berkeley, CA.

Glover, E.J., Lawrence, S., Gordon, M.D., Birmingham, W.P., & Giles, C.L. (2001). Web search—your way. *Communications of the ACM, 44*(12), 97-102.

Glover, F. (1977). Heuristic for integer programming using surrogate constraints. *Decision Science, 8*, 156-166.

Goedkoop, M., & Spriensma, R. (2000): *The Eco-indicator 99: A damage oriented method for life cycle impact assessment: Methodology report* (2nd rev. ed). Amersfoort, The Netherlands: PRé Consultants.

Goedkoop, M., Oele, M., & Effting, S. (2004). Simapro *6 database manual: Methods library*. PRé.

Goggin, K., & Browne, J. (2000). Towards a taxonomy of resource recovery from end-of-life products. *Computers in Industry, 42*, 177-191.

Golden, B., & Wong, R. (1981). Capacitated arc routing problems. *Networks, 11*, 305-315.

Goldsby, T. J., & Closs, D. J. (2000). Using activity-based costing to reengineer the reverse logistics channel. *International Journal of Physical Distribution & Logistics Management, 30*, 500-514.

González-Pachón, J., & Romero, C. (1999). Distance-based consensus methods: A goal programming approach. *Omega, 27*, 341-347.

Gordon, M. (1988). Probabilistic and genetic algorithms for document retrieval. *Communications of the ACM, 31*(10), 1208-1218.

Gordon, S. (2004, March 15). *The natural step and Whistler's journey towards sustainability*. Retrieved July 6, 2008, from www.whistler.ca

Gore, A. (2006). *An inconvenient truth* (Dutch version). Amsterdam: Meulenhoff.

Graedel, T. E. (1998). *Streamlined life-cycle assessment*. Upper Saddle River, NJ: Prentice Hall.

Graedel, T. E. (2002). Material substitution: A resource supply perspective. *Resources, Conservation and Recycling, 34*, 107-115.

Graedel, T. E., & Allenby, B. (1996). *Design for environment*. NJ: Prentice Hall.

Graedel, T.E., & Allenby, B.R. (1995). *Industrial ecology*. Englewood Cliffs, NJ: Prentice Hall.

Green Electronics Council. (2006). *Electronic product environmental assessment tool (EPEAT)*. Retrieved July 9, 2008, from URL:http://www.epeat.net/

Green, P.E., Tull, D.S., & Albaum, G. (1993). *Research for marketing decisions* (5th ed.). Prentice Hall.

Grossman, D.A., & Frieder, O. (1998). *Information retrieval: Algorithms and heuristics*. Boston: Kluwer.

Grossmann, I. E. (2004). Challenges in the new millennium: Product discovery and design, enterprise and supply chain optimization, global life cycle assessment. *Computers and Chemical Engineering, 29*, 29-39.

Groth, R. (1999). *Data mining: Building competitive advantage*. Prentice Hall.

Grubstrom, R.W. (2007). *The international logistics management game*. Retrieved July 7, 2008, from http://www.ipe.liu.se/rwg/ilmg/ilmg.htm

Guide Jr, V. D. R., & Van Wassenhove, L. N. (2002). The reverse supply chain. *Harvard Business Review, 80*(2), 25-26.

Guide, V. D. R. (1997). Scheduling with priority dispatching rules and drum-buffer-rope in a recoverable manufacturing system. *International Journal Production Economics, 53*, 101-116.

Guide, V. D. R., Jayaraman, V., & Srivastava, R. (1997). Repairable inventory theory: Models and applications. *European Journal of Operational Research, 102*, 1-20.

Guide, V. D. R., Jayaraman, V., & Srivastava, R. (1999). Production planning and control for remanufacturing: A state-of-the-art survey. *Robot. Comput.-Integr. Mfg, 15*, 221-230.

Guide, V. D. R., Jr. (2000). Production planning and control for remanufacturing: Industry practice and research needs. *Journal of Operations Management, 18*, 467-483.

Guide, V. D. R., Jr., & Van Wassenhove, L. N. (2001). Managing product returns for remanufacturing. *Production and Operations Management, 10*, 142-155.

Guide, V. D. R., Spencer, M. S., & Srivastava, R. (1996). Are production systems ready for the green revolution? *Production and Inventory Management Journal, Fourth Quarter*, 70-78).

Guide, V. D. R., Spencer, M. S., & Srivastava, R. (1997). An evaluation of capacity planning techniques in a remanufacturing environment. *International Journal of Production Research, 35*, 67-82.

Guinee, J. B. (Ed.). (2002). *Handbook on life cycle assessment: Operational guide to the ISO standards.* Dordrecht, The Netherlands: Kluwer.

Guinée, J.B., Heijungs, R., Udo de Haes, H.A., & Huppes, G. (1993). Quantitative life cycle assessment of products 2: Classification, valuation and improvement analysis. *Journal of Cleaner Production, 1*(2), 81-91.

Guinée, J.B., Udo de Haes, H.A., & Huppes, G. (1993). Quantitative life cycle assessment of products 1: Goal definition and inventory. *Journal of Cleaner Production, 1*(1), 3-13.

Gungor, A., & Gupta, S. M. (1999). Issues in environmentally conscious manufacturing and product recovery: A survey. *Computers and Industrial Engineering, 36*(4), 811-853.

Gupta, A. (1993). Approximate solution of a single-base multi-indentured repairable-item inventory system. *Journal of the Operational Research Society, 44*, 701-710.

Gupta, M., & Sharma, K. (1996). Environmental operations management: An opportunity for improvement. *Production and Inventory Management Journal, 37*(3), 40-46.

Gupta, S. M., & Isaacs, J. A. (1997). Value analysis of disposal strategies for automobiles. *Computers & Industrial Engineering, 33*(1-2), 325-328.

Haas, D. A., & Murphy, F. H. (2002). Compensating for non-homogeneity in decision-making units in data envelopment analysis. *European Journal of Operational Research, 144*, 530-554.

Hageluken, M., & Schichke, K. (2004). Welcome to the jungle: Survival of the fitted environmental screening indicators. In H. Reichl, H. Griese, & H. Potter (Eds.), *2004 Proceedings of the Electronics Goes Green: Driving Forces for Future Electronics* (pp. 501-508). Stuttgart, Germany: Fraunhofer IRB, IRB Staz-und Druckcenter.

Harte, J.M., & Koele, P. (1995, October). A comparison of different methods for the elicitation of attribute weights: Structural modeling, process tracing, and self-reports. *Organizational Behavior and Human Decision Processes, 64*(1), 49-64.

Hartman, F. (2000, June 21-24). The role of trust in project management: Managing business by projects. In *Proceedings of the PMI Research Conference*, Paris.

Hawken, P. (1993). *The ecology of commerce*. London: Weidenfield and Nicholson.

Hawken, P. A., & Lovins, H. L. (1999). *Natural capitalism: Creating the next industrial revolution.* Snowmass, CO, USA: Rocky Mountain Institute.

Hawken, P., Lovins, A., & Lovins, L.H. (1999). *Natural capitalism: The next industrial revolution.* London: Earthscan Publications.

He, C. H., Gao, Y. H., Yang, S. H., & Edwards, D. W. (2004). Optimization of the process for recovering caprolactam from wastewater in a pulsed-sieve-plate column using green design methodologies. *Journal of Loss Prevention in the Process Industries, 17*, 195-204.

Heijungs, R. (1994). A generic method for the identification of options for cleaner products. *Ecological Economics, 10*, 69-81.

Heijungs, R., & Suh, S. (2002). *The computational structure of life cycle assessment.* Dordrecht, The Netherlands: Kluwer.

Heinrich, A. B., & Klopffer, W. (2002). Integrating a new section in International Journal of LCA. *International Journal of Life Cycle Assessment, 7*(6), 315-316.

Heiskanen, E. (2000). Institutionalization of life-cycle thinking in the everyday discourse of market actors. *Journal of Industrial Ecology, 4*(4), 31-45.

Hendrickson, C. T., Lave, L. B., & Matthews, H. S. (2006). *Environmental life cycle assessment of goods and services. An input-output approach.* Washington, DC: RFF Press.

Herman, R. Ardekani, S.A., & Ausubel, J.H. (1990). Dematerialization. *Technological Forecasting and Social Change, 38*, 333-347.

Herrmann, C., Eyerer, P., & Geidiga, J. (2004). Economic and ecological materials index for end-of-life and design of electronic products. *IEEE Transactions on Electronics Packaging Manufacturing, 27*(1), 2-8.

Hertwich, E. G., & Hammitt, J. K. (2001). A decision-analytic framework for impact assessment, part 2: Midpoints, endpoints and criteria for method development. *International Journal of Life Cycle Assessment, 6*(5), 265-272.

Hervani, A. A., Helms, M. M., & Sarkis, J. (2005). Performance measurement for green supply chain management. *Benchmarking, 12*(4), 330-353.

Hewlett-Packard. (2007, September 6). *HP and sustainability Victoria expand their highly successful recycling programme*. Retrieved July 8, 2008, from http://h50025.www5.hp.com/ENP5/Public/Content.aspx?contentID=22821&portalID=367&pageID=1

Hillier, F.S., & Lieberman, G.J. (2001). *Introduction to operation research* (7th ed.). Dubuque, IA: McGraw-Hill.

Hillier, F.S., & Lieberman, G.J. (2005). *Introduction to operations research* (8th ed.). McGraw-Hill.

Hilmola, O.-P., Helo, P., & Ojala, L. (2003). The value of product development lead time in software startup. *System Dynamics Review, 19*(1), 75-82.

Hischier, R., Waeger, P., & Gauglhofer, J. (2005). Does WEEE recycling make sense from an environmental perspective? The environmental impacts of Swiss take-back and recycling systems for waste electrical and electronic equipment (WEEE). Environmental Impact Assessment Review, 25, 525-529.

Ho, S.C., & Haugland, D. (2004). A tabu search heuristic for the vehicle routing problem with time windows and split deliveries. *Computers & Operations Research, 31*, 1947-1964.

Hoagland, N. T. (2001). Non-traditional tools for LCA and sustainability. *The International Journal of Life Cycle Assessment, 6*(2), 110-113.

Hoek, R. I. v. (1999). From reversed logistics to green supply chains. *Supply Chain Management, 4*(3), 129.

Hofstede, G.J., & Trienekens, J.H. (2000). Food for thought. In J.H. Trienekens & P.J.P. Zuurbier (Eds.), *Proceedings of the Fourth International Conference on Chain Management in Agribusiness and the Food Industry*, Wageningen Pers (pp. 41-45).

Hofstede, G.J., Kramer, M., Meijder, S., & Wijdemans, J. (2001). A chain game for distributed trading and negotiation. In *Proceedings of the IFIP Conference/Workshop Games in Production Management*, Madrid.

Hokkanen, J., & Salminen, P. (1994). The choice of a solid waste management system by using the ELECTRE III decision-aid method. In M. Paruccini (Ed.), *Environmental management: Applying multiple criteria aid for decision to environmental management* (Vol. 3, pp. 111-153). Dordrecht, Germany: Kluwer Academic Publishers.

Hokkanen, J., Lahdelma, R., & Salminen, P. (2000). Multicriteria decision support in a technology competition for cleaning polluted soil in Hilsinki. *Journal of Environment Management, 60*(4), 339-348.

Holmberg, J. (1998). Backcasting: A natural step in operationalising sustainable development(*). *Greener Management International*, (23), 30-52.

Holmberg, J., & Robèrt, K.-H. (2000). Backcasting: A framework for strategic planning. *International Journal of Sustainable Development and World Ecology, 7*(4), 291-308.

Holmberg, J., Lundqvist, U., Robèrt, K.-H., & Wackernagel, M. (1999). The ecological footprint from a systems perspective of sustainability. *International Journal of Sustainable Development and World Ecology, 6*(1), 17-33.

Holmberg, J., Robèrt, K.-H., & Eriksson, K.-E. (1996). Socio-ecological principles for sustainability. In R.

Costanza, O. Segura, & J. Martinez-Alier (Eds.), *Getting down to Earth: Practical applications of ecological economics, International Society of Ecological Economics* (pp. 17-48). Washington DC, USA: Island Press.

Horng, J.T., & Yeh, C.C. (2000). Applying genetic algorithms to query optimization in document retrieval. *Information Processing and Management, 36*(5), 737-759.

http://www.electrocycle.gr

http://www.w3.org/XML

Hu, T. L., Sheu, J. B., & Huang, K. H. (2002). Reverse logistics cost minimization model for the treatment of hazardous wastes. *Transportation Research, Part E: Logistics and Transportation Review, 38*, 457-473.

Hui, I. K., Chan, A. H. S., & Pun, K. F. (2001). A study of the environmental management system implementation practices. *Journal of Cleaner Production, 9*, 269-276.

Huisman, J. (2003). The QWERTY/EE concept, quantifying recyclability and eco-efficiency for end-of-life treatment of consumer electronic products. Doctoral dissertation, Delft University of Technology, The Netherlands.

Huisman, J., & Stevels, A.L.N. (2006, April). Eco-efficiency of take-back and recycling, a comprehensive approach. *IEEE Transactions of Electronics Packaging Manufacturing, 29*(2). Retrieved July 8, 2008, from http://www.io.tudelft.nl/live/binaries/683f3ab7-08ce-4c03-84a6-45c49d8b5127/doc/HuismanEcoefficiency.pdf

Hung, L.P. (2005). A personalized recommendation system based on product taxonomy for one-to-one marketing online. *Expert Systems with Applications, 29*, 383-392.

Hussey, D. M., Eagan, P. D., & Pojasek, R. B. (2002). A performance model for driving environmental improvement down the supply chain. In *Proceedings of the 2002 IEEE International Symposium on Electronics and the Environment* (pp. 107-112). The Institute of Electrical and Electronics Engineers, Inc.

Hwang, C. L. (1987). *Group decision making under multi-criteria: Methods and applications.* New York: Springer-Verlag.

Hwang, C.L., & Yoon, K. (1981). *Multiple attribute decision making-methods and applications: A state of the art survey.* Springer-Verlag.

IBM Corporation. (2002). *IBM Corporation responsibility report.* USA.

ICON. (2004). *Electricity market in Australia: A strategic reference.* San Diego, CA: ICON Group International.

IFIAS. (1973). *Report of the International Federation of Institutes for Advanced Study* (Workshop n° 6 on Energy Analysis). Guldsmedshyttan, Sweden.

Imperial-Chemical-Industries-(ICI). (2007). *ICI sustainability review 2006.* London, UK: ICI.

Inderfurth, K., & van der Laan, E. (2001). Leadtime effects and policy improvement for stochastic inventory control with remanufacturing. *International Journal of Production Economics, 71*, 381-390.

Inderfurth, K., de Kok, A. G., & Flapper, S. D. P. (2001). Product recovery in stochastic remanufacturing system with multiple reuse options. *European Journal of Operational Research, 133*, 130-152.

INFORM, Inc. (2003). *Electric appliance recycling in Japan* (pp. 1-3).

Intel Corporation. (2005). *Intel Corporate responsibility report.* USA.

International Telecommunication Union. (2007). *Basic indicators: Population, GDP, total telephone subscribers and total telephone subscribers per 100 people.* Retrieved July 9, 2008, from http://www.itu.int/ITU-D/icteye/Indicators/Indicators.aspx

International-Organization-for-Standardization-(ISO). (1997). *Environmental management-life-cycle assessment: Principles and framework. ISO 14040.* Geneva, Switzerland: ISO.

International-Organization-for-Standardization-(ISO). (2000). *Environmental management--lifecycle assessment–lifecycle interpretation. ISO 14043.* Geneva, Switzerland: ISO.

IPC (Association Connecting Electronics Industries). (2005). *Legislation and regulation.* Retrieved July 8, 2008, from http://leadfree.ipc.org

Isaacs, J. A., & Gupta, S. M. (1997). Economic consequences of increasing polymer content on U.S. automobile recycling infrastructure. *Journal of Industrial Ecology, 1*(4), 19-33.

ISO 14040. (1997). *Environmental management: Life cycle assessment—principles and framework, ISO 14040: 1997(E).* Geneva, Switzerland: International Organization for Standardization.

ISO 14040. (2006). *Environmental management—life cycle assessment—principles and framework.* Geneva, Switzerland: International Organisation for Standardisation.

ISO 14044. (2006). *Environmental management—life cycle assessment—requirements and guidelines.* Geneva, Switzerland: International Organisation for Standardisation.

ISO 14047. (2003). *Environmental management—life cycle assessment—examples of the application of ISO 14042.* Geneva, Switzerland: International Organisation for Standardisation.

ISO 14048. (2002). *Environmental management—life cycle assessment—data documentation format.* Geneva, Switzerland: International Organisation for Standardisation.

Jaccard, J., Brinberg, D., & Ackerman, L.J. (1986). Assessing attribute importance: A comparison of six methods. *Journal of Consumer Research, 12*(4), 463-468.

Jahre, M. (1995). Household waste collection as a reverse channel: A theoretical perspective. *International Journal Physical Distribution and Logistics Management, 25*, 39-46.

James, S., & Lahti, T. (2004). *The natural step for communities: How cities and towns can change to sustainable practices.* Gabriola Island, British Columbia, Canada: New Society Publishers.

Japan Ministry of the Environment. (2005). *The 3R Initiative.* Japan. Retrieved July 8, 2008, from http://www.env.go.jp/recycle/3r/en

Jasch, C. (2006). How to perform an environmental management cost assessment in one day. *Journal of Cleaner Production, 14(*14), 1194-1213.

Jayaraman, V., & Srivastava, R. (1995). A service logistics model for simultaneous siting of facilities and multiple levels of equipment. *Computers and Operations Research, 22*, 191-204.

Jayaraman, V., Guide, V. D. R., & Srivastava, R. (1999). A closed-loop logistics model for remanufacturing. *Journal of the Operational Research Society, 50*, 497-508.

Jayaraman, V., Patterson, R. A., & Rolland, E. (2003). The design of reverse distribution networks: Models and solution procedures. *European Journal of Operational Research, 150*, 128-149.

Jayaraman, V., Srivastava, R., & Benton, W. C. (1998). A joint optimization of product variety and ordering approach. *Computers & Operations Research, 25*, 557-566.

Johnson, M. R., & Wang, M. H. (1995). Planning product disassembly of material recovery opportunities. *International Journal of Production Research, 33*, 3119-3142.

Johnson, P. F. (1998). Managing value in reverse logistics systems. *Logistics and Transportation Review, 34*, 217-227.

Johnson, R. (2004). *Interview with director of Environmental Affairs at IKEA during 1989-1998.*

Johnsson, J. (1999). *A monetary valuation weighting method for life cycle assessment based on environmental taxes and fees.* Master thesis, Natural Resource Management, Stockholm University, Sweden.

Jolliet, O. et al. (2004). The LCIA midpoint-damage framework of the UNEP/SETAC life cycle initiative. *International Journal of Life Cycle Assessment, 9*(6), 394-404.

Jones, L.P. (1994). Taste and the greening of design: The role of design imagery in a post-acquisitive society. *Leonardo, 27*(4), 317-325.

Jonesa K.S., Walkerb, S., & Robertson, S.E. (2000). A probabilistic model of information retrieval: Development and comparative experiments: Part 2. *Information Processing and Management, 36*(6), 809-840.

Kahn, H., & Wiener, A.J. (1967). *The year 2000: A framework for speculation on the next thirty-three years.* New York: MacMillan.

Kahraman, C., Büyüközkan G., & Ateş N.Y. (2007). A two phase multi-attribute decision-making approach for new product introduction. *Information Sciences, 177*, 1567-1582.

Kahraman, C., Cevik, S., Ateş, N.Y., & Gülbay, M. (2007). Fuzzy multi-criteria evaluation of industrial robotic systems. *Computers & Industrial Engineering, 52*, 414-433.

Kahraman, C., Ertay T., & Buyukozkan, G. (2006). A fuzzy optimization model for QFD planning process using analytic network approach. *European Journal of Operational Research, 171*(2), 390-411.

Kainuma, Y., & Tawara, N. (2006). A multiple attribute utility theory approach to lean and green supply chain management. *International Journal of Production Economics, 101*, 99-108.

Kaiser, B., Eagan, P., & Shaner, H. (2001). Solutions to health care waste: Lifecycle thinking and "green" purchasing. *Environmental Health Perspectives, 109*, 205-208.

Kao, J.J., & Lin, H.U. (1996). Multifactorial spatial analysis of landfill siting. *Journal of Environmental Engineering, 122*, 902-908.

Karacapilidis, N., & Papadias, D. (2001). Computer supported argumentation and collaborative decision making: The HERMES system. *Information Systems, 26*(4), 259-277.

Karacapilidis, N., Adamides, E., & Pappis, C. P. (2004, September 20-25). An IS framework to support the collaborative design of supply chains. In M. Negoita, R. J. Howlett, & L. C. Jain (Eds.), *Knowledge-based intelligent information and engineering systems: Proceedings of the 8th International Conference, KES 2004,* Wellington, New Zealand, Part II (pp. 62-70). Berlin/Heidelberg, Germany: Springer-Verlag.

Karlsson, S. (1999). Closing the technospheric flows of toxic metals: Modeling lead losses from a lead-acid battery system for Sweden. *Journal of Industrial Ecology, 3*(1), 23-40.

Karsak, E.E. (2002). Distance-based fuzzy MCDM approach for evaluating flexible manufacturing system alternatives. *International Journal of Production Research, 40*(13), 3167-3181.

Katz, J., Rifer, W., & Wilson, A. R. (2005). EPEAT: Electronic product environmental tool: Development of an environmental rating system of electronic products for governmental/institutional procurement. In *Proceedings of the 2005 IEEE International Symposium on Electronics and the Environment* (pp. 1-6). The Institute of Electrical and Electronics Engineers, Inc.

Kaufmann, A., & Gupta, M.M. (1985). *Introduction to fuzzy arithmetic: Theory and applications.* New York: Von Nostrand Reinhold.

Keeney, R. L., & Raiffa, H. (1976). *Decisions with multiple objectives: Preferences and value tradeoffs.* New York: John Wiley & Sons.

Keeny & Raiffa. (1976). *Decision with multiple objectives: Preferences and value tradeoffs.* New York: John Wiley.

Khélifa, S. B., Martel, J. -M., & Kiss, L. N. (1997). Synthesizing decision-makers' preferences by taking into account their relative importance. In *Proceedings of the IEEE International Conference on Systems, Man and Cybernetics* (Vol. 2, pp. 1896-1899).

Khoo, H., Spedding, T. A., Bainbridge, I. e. D. M. R., & Taplin. (2001). Creating a green supply chain. *Greener Management International, 35*, 71-88.

Kiesmuller, G. P., & Scherer, C. W. (2003). Computational issues in a stochastic finite horizon one product recovery inventory model. *European Journal of Operational Research, 146*, 553-579.

Kiesmuller, G. P., & van der Laan, E. A. (2001). An inventory model with dependent product demands and returns. *International Journal of Production Economics, 72*, 73-87.

Kim, B.M., Kim, J.Y., & Kim, J. (2001). Query term expansion and reweighting using term co-occurrence similarity and fuzzy inference. In *Proceedings of the Joint Ninth IFSA World Congress and 20th NAFIPS International Conference*, Vancouver, Canada.

Kim, J., Hwang, Y., Matthews, H. S., & Kwangho, P. (2004). Methodology for recycling potential evaluation criterion of waste home appliances considering environmental and economic factor. In *Proceedings of the 2004 IEEE International Symposium on Electronics and the Environment* (pp. 68-73). The Institute of Electrical and Electronics Engineers, Inc.

Kiritsis, D., Bufardi, A. & Xirouchakis, P. (2003). Research issues on product lifecycle management and information tracking using smart embedded systems. *Advanced Engineering Informatics, 17*(3-4), 189-202.

Kiritsis, D., Bufardi, A., & Xirouchakis, P. (2005). Multi-criteria decision aid for product end of life options selection. In *Proceedings of the 2005 IEEE International Symposium on Electronics and the Environment* (pp. 48-53). The Institute of Electrical and Electronics Engineers, Inc.

Klassen, R. D. (2001). Plant level environmental management orientation: The influence of management views and plant characteristics. *Production and Operations Management, 10*, 257-275.

Klausner, M., & Hendrickson, C. T. (2000). Reverse logistics strategy for product take-back. *Interfaces, 30*, 156-165.

Klir, G.J., & Folger, T.A. (1988). *Fuzzy sets: Uncertainty, and information*. Englewood Cliffs, NJ: Prentice Hall.

Klopffer, W. (2003). Life-cycle-based methods for sustainable product development. *The International Journal of Life Cycle Assessment, 8*(3), 157-159.

Klöpffer, W., & Rippen, G. (1992). Life cycle analysis and ecological balance: Methodological approach to the assessment of environmental aspects of products. *Environment International, 18*(1), 55-61.

Kneese, A.V., Ayres, R.U., & D'Arge, R.C. (1974). Economics and the environment: A materials balance approach. In H. Wolozin (Ed.), *The economics of pollution*. Morristown: General Learning Press.

Kolter, P. (1997). *Marketing management: Analysis, planning and control* (9th ed.). NJ: Prentice Hall.

Korhonen, J. (2004). Industrial ecology in the strategic sustainable development model: Strategic applications of industrial ecology. *Journal of Cleaner Production, 12*(8-10), 809-823.

Kotchen, M.J., & Moore, M.R. (2007). Private provision of environmental public goods: Household participation in green-electricity programs. *Journal of Environmental Economics and Management, 53*, 1-16.

Kotchen, M.J., Moore, M.R., & Clark, C.F. (2001). Environmental voluntary contracts between individuals and industry: An analysis of consumer preferences for green electricity. In E. Orts & K. Deketelaere (Eds.), *Environmental voluntary contracts: Comparative approaches to regulation innovation in the United States and Europe*. London: Kluwer Law International.

Krikke, H. R., Harten, A. V., & Schuur, P. C. (1998). On a medium term product recovery and disposal strategy for durable assembly products. *International Journal Prod. Res., 36*, 111-139.

Krikke, H. R., Pappis, C. P., Tsoulfas, G. T., & Bloemhof-Ruwaard, J. (2002). Extended design principles for closed loop supply chains: Optimising economic, logistic and environmental performance. In A. Klose, M. G. Speranza, & L. N. Van Wassenhove (Eds.), *Quantitative approaches to distribution logistics and supply chain management* (pp. 61-74). Berlin/Heidelberg, Germany: Springer-Verlag.

Krikke, H. R., van Harten, A., & Schuur, P. C. (1999). Business case Oce: Reverse logistic network re-design for copiers. *OR Spectrum, 21*, 381-409.

Krikke, H. R., van Harten, A., & Schuur, P. C. (1999). Business case Roteb: Recovery strategies for monitors. *Computers & Industrial Engineering, 36*, 739-757.

Krikke, H., Blanc, I.I., & Velde, S. (2004). Product modularity and design of closed-loop supply chains. *California Management Review, 46*(2), 23-39.

Krikke, H., Bloemhof-Ruwaard, J., & Van Wassenhove, L. N. (2003). Concurrent product and closed-loop supply chain design with an application to refrigerators. *International Journal Prod. Res., 41*, 3689-3719.

Krikke, H.R. (1999). Ketenlogistiek. In de Boer (Ed.), *Vraagbaak Inkoop en Logistiek*. Deventer: Kluwer.

Krikke, H.R., Bloemhof-Ruwaard, J.B., & Van Wassenhove, L.N. (2003). Concurrent product and closed loop design with an application of refrigerator. *International Journal of Production Research, 41*(16), 3689-3719.

Kroll, E., Beardsley, B., & Parulian, A. (1996). A methodology to evaluate ease of disassembly for product recycling. *IIE Transactions, 28*, 837-845.

Kroon, L., & Vrijens, G. (1995). Returnable containers: An example of reverse logistics. *International Journal of Physical Distribution & Logistics Management, 25*, 56-68.

Krumwiede, D. W., & Sheu, C. (2002). A model for reverse logistics entry by third-party providers. *Omega, 30*, 322-333.

Kuosmanen, T., & Kortelainen, M. (2005). Measuring eco-efficiency of production with data envelopment analysis. *Journal of Industrial Ecology, 9*(4), 59-72.

Kuosmanen, T., & Kortelainen, M. (2005). Measuring eco-efficiency of production with data envelopment analysis. *Journal of Industrial Ecology, 9*(4), 59-72.

Kurakawa, K., Kiriyama, T., Baba, Y., Umeda, Y., Tomiyama, T., & Kobayashi, H. (1997). The green browser: An information sharing tool for product life cycle design. In F.L. Krause & G. Seliger (Eds.), *Life cycle networks* (pp. 454-466). London: Chapman & Hall.

Lacomme, P., Prins, C., & Sevaux, M. (2006). A genetic algorithm for a bi-objective capacitated arc routing problem. *Computers & Operations Research, 33*, 3473-3485.

Lambert, A. J. D. (2001). Life-cycle chain analysis, including recycling. In J. Sarkis (Ed.), *Greener manufacturing and operations: From design to delivery and back* (pp. 36-55). Sheffield, UK: Greenleaf Publishing.

Lambert, A.J.D., Boelaarts, H.M., & Splinter, M.A.M. (2004). Optimal recycling system design: With an application to sophisticated packaging tools. *Environmental and Resource Economics, 28*, 273-299.

Lambert, A.J.D., Jansen, M.H., & Splinter, M.A.M. (2000). Environmental information systems based on enterprise resource planning. *Integrated Manufacturing Systems, 11*(2), 105-111.

Lamprecht, J. L. (1997). *ISO 14000: Issues and implementation guidelines for responsible environmental management*. American Management Association.

Langabeer, J., & Rose, J. (2001). *Creating demand driven supply chains*. Oxford: Chandos Publishing.

Laperiere, L., & El Maraghy, H. A. (1992). Planning of products assembly and disassembly. *Annals of the CIRP, 41*, 5-9.

Leadbitter, J. (2002). PVC and sustainability. *Progress in Polymer Science, 27*(10), 2197-2226.

Lee J. (2006, December). *Ecodesign movement in the Korean industries*. Paper presented on EcoDesign at the 2006 Asia Pacific Symposium, Tokyo, Japan.

Lee, J. J., O'Callaghan, P., & Allen, D. (1995). Critical review of life cycle analysis and assessment techniques and their application to commercial activities. *Conservation and Recycling, 13*, 37-56.

Lee, J., & Whang, J. (2006). *Identifying complementary measures to ensure the maximum realization of benefit from the liberalization of trade in environmental goods and serves case study: Korea.* OECD Trade and Environment Working Paper No. 2004-03 (JT03212028).

Leong, B.C.H. (2006, April 20-21). Is a radical systemic shift toward sustainability possible in China? In *Proceedings: Changes to Sustainable Consumption*, Copenhagen, Denmark (pp. 279-294).

Leuski, A. (2001, November). Evaluating document clustering for interactive information retrieval. In *Proceedings of the 2001 ACM CIKM International Conference on Information and Knowledge Management*, Atlanta, GA, USA.

Lewicki, R.J., McAllister, D.J., & Bies, R.J. (1996). Trust and distrust: New relationships and realities. *The Academy of Management Review, 23*(3), 438-458.

LG Electronics Corporation. (2004). *LG 2004 environmental report.* Seoul, Korea.

Liao, Y.C. (2006). A weight-based approach to information retrieval and relevance feedback. *Expert Systems with Applications* (accepted).

Liao, Y.C. (2007). A weight-based approach to green products recommendation. In *Proceedings of the Sixth International Conference on Information and Management Sciences*, Lhasa, Tibet, China.

Lin H.C., Wang, L.H., & Chen, S.M. (2006). Query expansion for documents retrieval based on fuzzy rules and user relevance feedback techniques. *Expert Systems with Applications, 31*, 397-405.

Lin, S., & Kerninghan, B. (1973). An effective heuristic algorithm for the traveling salesman problem. *Operations Research, 21*, 498-516.

Linares, P., & Romero, C. (2002). Aggregation of preferences in an environmental economics context: A goal-programming approach. *Omega, 30*, 89-95.

Lindfors, L.-G., Christiansen, K., Hoffman, L., Virtanen, Y., Juntilla, V., Hanssen, O.-J., et al. (1995). *The Nordic guidelines for life-cycle assessment. Nord 1995:20.* Copenhagen, Denmark: Nordic Council of Ministers.

Linton, J. D., & Johnston, D. A. (2000). A decision support system for the planning of remanufacturing at Nortel. *Interfaces, 30*, 17-31.

Listes, O., & Dekker, R. (2005). A stochastic approach to a case study for product recovery network design. *European Journal of Operational Research, 160*, 268-287.

Liu, L., Liu, Z., & Fung, R. (2003). "The most of the most:" Study on a new LCA method. In *Proceedings of the 2003 IEEE International Symposium on Electronics and the Environment* (pp. 177-182). The Institute of Electrical and Electronics Engineers, Inc.

Lochbaum, K.E., & Streeter, L.A. (1989). Comparing and combining the effectiveness of latent semantic indexing and the ordinary vector space model for information retrieval. *Journal of Information Science, 6*, 25-33.

Louwers, D., Kip, B. J., Peters, E., Souren, F., & Flapper, S. W. P. (1999). A facility location allocation model for reusing carpet materials. *Computers & Industrial Engineering, 36*, 855-869.

Lowe, E.A., & Evans, L.K. (1995). Industrial ecology and industrial ecosystems. *Journal of Cleaner Production, 3*(1-2), 47-53.

Lu, Q., Vivi, C., Julie, A.S., & Taylor, R. (2000). A practical framework for the reverse supply chain. In *Proceedings of the International Symposium on Electronics and the Environment* (pp. 266-271).

Lummus, R.R., & Vokurka, R.J. (1999). Managing the demand chain through managing the information flow: Capturing "moment of information." *Production and Inventory Management Journal, 1*, 16-20.

Macey, R. (2005, March 10). Mobile phones kill great apes. *Sydney Morning Herald.*

Madu, C. N., Kuei, C., & Madu, I. E. (2002). A hierarchic metric approach for integration of green issues in manufacturing: A paper recycling application. *Journal of Environmental Management, 64*, 261-272.

Magistrat der Stadt Wien (Ed.). (2005). *Öko Business Das Buch- die Besten der Wiener Wirtschaft 2005.*

Unpublished material, Wiener Umweltschutzabteilung, Vienna, Austria.

Mahler, C.F., & Lima, G.S. (2003). Applying value analysis and fuzzy logic to select areas for installing waste fills. *Environmental Monitoring and Assessment, 84,* 129-140.

Majumder, P., Groenevelt, H., & Summer. (2001). Competition in remanufacturing. *Production and Operations Management, 10,* 125-141.

Malakooti, B., & Subramanian, S. (1999). Generalized polynomial decomposable multiple utility functions for ranking and rating multiple criteria discrete. *Applied Mathematics and Computation, 106,* 69-102.

Manzini, E., & Vezzoli, C. (2002, July). *Product service systems and sustainability: Opportunities for sustainable solutions.* Paris: UN Environment Program. Retrieved July 8, 2008, from http://www.uneptie.org/pc/sustain/reports/pss/pss-imp-7.pdf

Marin, A., & Pelegrin, B. (1998). The return plant location problem: Modeling and resolution. *European Journal of Operational Research, 104,* 375-392.

Markard, J., & Truffer, B. (2006). The promotional impacts of green power products on renewable energy sources: Direct and indirect eco-effects. *Energy Policy, 34,* 306-321.

Marx-Gomez, J., Rantenstrauch, C., Nurnberger, A., & Kruse, R. (2002). Neuro-fuzzy approach to forecast returns of scrapped product to recycling and remanufacturing. *Knowledge-Based Systems, 15,* 119-128.

Masanet, E. R, & Horvath, A. (2004). A decision-support tool for the take-back of plastics from end-of-life electronics. In *Proceedings of the 2004 IEEE International Symposium on Electronics and the Environment* (pp. 51-56). The Institute of Electrical and Electronics Engineers, Inc.

Matsushita. (2002). *Environmental sustainability report 2002.* Osaka, Japan: Matsushita Electric Industrial.

Max-Neef, M., Elizalde, A., Hopenhayn, M., Herrera, F., Zemelman, H., Jataba, J., et al. (1989). Human scale development: An option for the future. *Development Dialogue Journal, 1989*(1).

McCutcheon, D., & Stuart, F.I. (2000). Issues in the choice of supplier alliance partners. *Journal of Management, 18*(3), 279-301.

Meade, L., & Sarkis, J. (2002). A conceptual model for selecting and evaluating third-party reverse logistics providers. *Supp. Chain Manag. Int. J., 7,* 283-295.

Meadows, D.H., Meadows, D.L., & Randers, J. (1972). *The limits to growth: A report for the Club of Rome's project on the predicament of mankind.* New York: Universe books.

Melissen, F. W., & de Ron, A. J. (1999). Defining recovery practices: Definitions and terminology. *International Journal on Environmentally Conscious Manufacturing and Design, 8,* 1-18.

Meng, Z., Hu, Q., Dang, C., & Yang, X. (2004). An objective penalty function method for nonlinear programming. *Applied Mathematics Letters, 17,* 683-689.

Menger, R. (2003). Supporting renewable energy on liberalised markets: Green electricity between additionality and consumer sovereignty. *Energy Policy, 31,* 583-596.

Menke, D. M., Davis, G. A., & Vigon, B. (1996). *Evaluation of life cycle tools.* Ottawa, Ontario: Environmental Canada, Hazardous Waste Branch.

Middendorf, A., Hoppner, W., & Teller, M. (1997). IDEE-Information network for closed loop economy: Life cycle networks. In F.L. Krause & G. Seliger (Eds.), *Life cycle networks* (pp. 447-453). London: Chapman & Hall.

Mikhailov, L., & Singh, M.G. (2003). Fuzzy analytic network process and its application to the development of decision support systems. *IEEE Transactions on Systems, Man and Cybernetics, 33*(1), 33-41.

Min, H., & Galle, W. P. (2001). Green purchasing practices of U.S. firms. *International Journal of Operations and Production Management, 21,* 1222-1238.

Min, H., Ko, J. H., & Ko, S. C. (2006). A genetic algorithm approach to developing the multi-echelon reverse logistics network for product returns. *Omega, 34,* 56-69.

Ministry of Environment (MOE), Japan. (2002). *Environmental accounting guidelines*. Tokyo, Japan.

Minner, S. (2001). Strategic safety stocks in reverse logistics supply chains. *International Journal of Production Economics, 71*, 417-428.

Mintzberg, H., Lampel, J., & Ahlstrand, B. (1998). *Strategy safari: A guided tour through the wilds of strategic management*. New York: Free Press.

Mitsuo, G., & Runwei, C. (1997). *Genetic algorithms and engineering design*. New York: John Wiley & Sons.

Miyamoto, T., & Rexha, N. (2004). Determinants of three facets of customer trust: A marketing model of Japanese buyer–supplier relationship. *Journal of Business Research, 57*, 312-319.

Mohanty, R.P., Agarwal, R., Choudhury, A.K., & Tiwari, M.K. (2005). A fuzzy ANP-based approach to R&D project selection: A case study. *International Journal of Production Research, 43*(24), 5199-5216.

MOOEA. (2001). *Minnesota's demonstration project for recycling used electronics*. Minnesota Office of Environmental Assistance.

Moore, K. E., Gungor, A. K., & Gupta, S. M. (2001). Petri net approach to disassembly process planning for products with complex AND/OR precedence relationships. *European Journal of Operational Research, 135*, 428-449.

Moore, K. E., Gungor, A., & Gupta, S. M. (1998). A petri net approach to disassembly process planning. *Comp. Indus. Engin., 35*, 165-168.

Moskovitz, D. (1993, October). Green pricing: Customer choice moves beyond IRP. *The Electricity Journal*.

Most, E. (2003). *Calling all cell phones: Collection, reuse, and recycling programs in the U.S.* INFORM Inc., New York, USA. Retrieved July 9, 2008, from http://www.informinc.org/reportpdfs/wp/Calling%20All%20Cell%20Phones.pdf

Mostard, J., & Teunter, R. (2006). The newsboy problem with resalable returns: A single period model and case study. *European Journal of Operational Research, 169*, 81-96.

Motorola, Inc. (2004). *Motorola global corporate citizenship report* (RC-99-2067). Schaumburg, Illinois.

Mourao, M. C., & Amado, L. (2005). Heuristics method for a mixed capacitated arc routing problem: A refuse collection application. *European Journal of Operational Research, 160*, 139-153.

Mousseau, V. (1995). Eliciting information concerning the relative importance of criteria. In P. M. Paradalos, Y. Siskos, & C. Zpounidis (Eds.), *Advances in multicriteria analysis: Nonconvex optimization and its applications* (pp. 17-43).

Moyer, L., & Gupta, S. M. (1997). Environmental concerns and recycling: Disassembly efforts in the electronics industry. *Journal of Electronics Manufacturing, 7*(1), 1-22.

Mueller, J., Griese, H., Hageluken, M., Middendorf, A., & Reichl, H. (2003). X-free mobile electronics-strategy for sustainable development. In *Proceedings of the 2003 IEEE International Symposium on Electronics and the Environment* (pp. 13-18). The Institute of Electrical and Electronics Engineers, Inc.

Mukhopadhyay, S. K., & Setoputro, R. (2005). Optimal return policy and modular design for build-to-order products. *Journal of Operations Management, 23*, 496-506.

Munksgaard, J., Wier, M., Lenzen, M., & Dey, C. (2006). Using input-output analysis to measure the environmental pressure of consumption at different spatial levels. *Journal of Industrial Ecology, 9*(1-2), 169-185.

Muther, A. (2000). *Electronic customer care: die Anbieter-Kunden-Beziehung im informationszeitalter* (2nd ed.). Berlin: Springer-Verlag.

Nagel, C., & Meyer, P. (1999). Caught between ecology and economy: End-of-life aspects of environmentally conscious manufacturing. *Comput. Ind. Eng., 36*, 781-792.

Nagurney, A., & Toyasaki, F. (2005). Reverse supply chain management and electronic waste recycling: A multitiered network equilibrium framework for e-cycling. *Transportation Research Part E: Logistics and Transportation Review, 41*, 1-28.

Nasr, N. (1997). Environmentally conscious manufacturing. *Careers and the Engineer,* 26-27.

Nattrass, B. (1999). *The natural step: Corporate learning and innovation for sustainability.* Unpublished doctoral thesis, The California Institute of Integral Studies, San Francisco, California, USA.

Nattrass, B., & Altomare, M. (2002). *Dancing with the tiger.* Gabriola Island, British Columbia, Canada: New Society Publishers.

Navinchandra, D. (1991). Design for environmentally. *Desig Theor. Methodol, 31*, 99-125.

Neaupane, K.M., & Piantanakulchai, M. (2006). Analytic network process model for landslide hazard zonation. *Engineering Geology, 85*, 281-294.

Neely, A., Mills, J., Platts, K., Richards, H., Gregory, M., Bourne, M., et al. (2000). Performance measurement system design: Developing and testing a process-based approach. *International Journal of Operations & Production Management, 20*(10), 1119-1145.

Nema, K.M, & Gupta, S.K. (1999). Optimization of regional hazardous waste management systems: An improved formulation. *Waste Management, 19*, 441-451.

Ness, D., & Field, M. (2003). *Cradle to cradle carpets and cities.* Paper presented at International Conference on Smart and Sustainable Built Environments, SASBE 03, Brisbane, Australia. See also http://www.bml.csiro.au/susnetnl/netwl36E.pdf

Ness, D., Clement, S., Field, M., Filar, J., & Pullen, S. (2005, September 27-29). *(Approaches towards) sustainability in the built environment through dematerialization.* Paper presented at the World Sustainable Building Conference (SBO5), Tokyo, Japan.

Nesterov, Y. (1997). Interior-point methods: An old and new approach to linear programming. *Mathematical Programming, 79*, 285-297.

Nimse, P., Vijayan, A., Kumar, A., & Varadarajan, C. (2007). A review of green product databases. *Environmental Progress, 26*(2), 131-137.

Nokia Corporation. (2004). *Environmental report of Nokia Corporation.* Finland.

Nonhebel, S. (2005). Renewable energy and food supply: Will there be enough land? *Renewable and Sustainable Energy Reviews, 9*, 191-201.

Nonhebel, S. (2007). Energy from agricultural residues and consequences for land requirements for food production. *Agricultural Systems, 94*, 586-592.

Ny, H., Byggeth, S. H., MacDonald, J. P., Robèrt, K.-H., & Broman, G. (2007). *Introducing templates for sustainable product development through case study of televisions at Matsushita Electric Group.* Submitted.

Ny, H., MacDonald, J. P., Broman, G., Yamamoto, R., & Robèrt, K.-H. (2006). Sustainability constraints as system boundaries: An approach to making life-cycle management strategic. *Journal of Industrial Ecology, 10*(1).

Oberender, C., & Birkhofer, H. (2004). Designing environmentally friendly products in conformity with the market: A holistic analysis of product characteristics. In H. Reichl, H. Griese, & H. Potter (Eds.), *2004 Proceedings of the Electronics Goes Green: Driving Forces for Future Electronics* (pp. 481-486). Stuttgart, Germany: Fraunhofer IRB, IRB Staz-und Druckcenter.

Ogallachoir, B., Oleary, F., Bazilian, M., Howley, M., & Mckeogh, E. J. (2006). Comparing primary energy attributed to renewable energy with primary energy equivalent to determine carbon abatement in a national context. *Journal of Environmental Science and Health, Part A, 41*, 923-937.

Oliverio, J. L. (2006). Technological evolution of the Brazilian sugar and alcohol sector: Dedini's contribution. *International Sugar Journal, 108*, 120-126.

Önüt, S., & Soner, S. (2008). Transshipment site selection using the AHP and TOPSIS under fuzzy environment. *Waste Management, 28*(9), 1552-1559.

Ottman, J.A. (1998). *Green marketing: Opportunity for innovation* (2nd **ed.).** Lincolnwood, IL: NTC Business Books.

Owen, J. V. (1993). Environmentally conscious manufacturing. *Manufacturing Engineering, 111*(4), 44.

Padberg, M. (2000). Approximating separable functions via mixed zero-one programs. *Operations Research Letters, 27*, 1-5.

Palme, U., & Tillman, A. M. (2007). Sustainable development indicators: How they are used in Swedish water utilities? *Journal of Cleaner Production*. In press.

Pappis, C. P., Tsoulfas, G. T., & Dasaklis, T. (2006, July 2-5). *Assessing alternative reverse logistics policies for the recovery of used mobile phones.* Paper presented at the EURO XXI Conference, Reykjavik, Iceland.

Parikka, M. (2004). Global biomass fuel resources. *Biomass and Bioenergy, 27*, 613-620.

Park, P., Lee, K., & Wimmer, W (2006). Development of an environmental assessment method for consumer electronics by combining top-down and bottom-up approaches. *International Journal of Life Cycle Assessment, 11*(4), 254-264.

Pascual, O., Boks, C., & Stevels, A. (2003). Communicating eco-efficiency in industrial contexts: A framework for understanding the lack of success and applicability of eco-design. In *Proceedings of the 2003 IEEE International Symposium on Electronics and the Environment* (pp. 303-308). The Institute of Electrical and Electronics Engineers, Inc.

Pauli, G. (1998). *UpSizing: The road to zero emissions, more jobs, more income, and no pollution.* Sheffield, United Kingdom: Greenleaf Publishing.

Paulson, P., & Tzanavari, A. (2002). *Combining collaborative and content-based filtering using conceptual graphs* (Tech. Rep. No. 5). Lefkosia: University of Cyprus, Department of Computer Science.

Pazzani, M.J. (1999). A framework for collaborative, content-based and demographic filtering. *Artificial Intelligence Review, 13*, 393-408.

Pennington, D. W., Potting, J., Finnveden, G., Lindeijer, E., Jolliet, O., Rydberg, T., et al. (2004). LCA Part 2: Current impact assessment practice. *Environment International, 30*, 721-739.

Pérez Plaza, M. (2004). *Análisis de viabilidad de una comercializadora verde en el mercado eléctrico español.* Senior thesis, Universidad Pontificia Comillas, Madrid, Spain.

Pochampally, K. K., & Gupta, S. M. (2003). A multiphase mathematical programming approach to strategic planning of an efficient reverse supply chain network. In *Proceedings of the IEEE International Symposium on the Electronics and the Environment* (pp. 72-78).

Pochampally, K. K., & Gupta, S. M. (2005). Strategic planning of a reverse supply chain network. *International Journal of Integrated Supply Management (IJISM), 1*(4), 421-441.

Pochampally, K. K., Gupta, S. M., & Cullinane, T. P. (2003). A fuzzy cost-benefit function to select economical used products for re-processing. In *Proceedings of the SPIE International Conference on Environmentally Conscious Manufacturing* (CD-ROM).

Pochampally, K. K., Gupta, S. M., & Gupta, S. K. (2004). Selection of collection centers and recovery facilities for designing a reverse supply chain. In *Proceedings of SPIE: The International Society for Optical Engineering* (Vol. 5583, pp. 127-137).

Pochampally, K. K., Gupta, S. M., & Kamarthi, S. V. (2003). Evaluation of production facilities in a closed-loop supply chain: A fuzzy TOPSIS approach. In *Proceedings of the SPIE International Conference on Environmentally Conscious Manufacturing* (CD-ROM).

Pochampally, K.K., Surendra, M.G., & Sagar, V.K. (2004). Identification of potential recovery facilities for designing a reverse supply chain network using physical programming. *The International Society for Optical*

Engineering: Environmentally Conscious Manufacturing III, 5262, 139-146.

Pohekar, S.D., & Ramachandran, M. (2004). Application of multi-criteria decision making to sustainable energy planning: A review. *Renewable and Sustainable Energy Reviews, 8,* 365-381.

Porter, M. E., & Krammer, M. R. (2006, December). *Strategy and society: The link between competitive advantage and corporate social responsibility* (pp. 1-17). Harvard Business Review.

Porter, M. E., & van der Linde, C. (1995). Green and competitive: Ending the stalemate. *Harvard Business Review, 73*(5), 120-134.

Porter, M. E., & van der Linde, C. (1995). Toward a new conception of the environment: Competitiveness relationship. *Journal of Economic Perspectives, 9*(4), 97-118.

Post, G.V., & Anderson, D.L. (2003). *Management information systems: Solving business problems with information technology.* Boston: McGraw-Hill.

Potra, F.A., & Wright, S.J. (2000). Interior-point methods. *Journal of Computational and Applied Mathematics, 24,* 282-302.

Quella, F., & Schmidt, W.-P. (2003). Integrating environmental aspects into product design and development: The new ISO TR 14062, Part 2: Contents and practical solutions. In *Proceedings of the 2003 Gate to EHS: Life Cycle Management – Design for Environment* (pp. 1-7).

Rakas, J., Teodorovic, D., & Kim, T. (2004). Multi-objective modeling for determining location of undesirable facilities. *Transportation Research Part D, 9,* 125-138.

Ramik, J. (2006). A decision system using ANP and fuzzy inputs. In *Proceedings of the 12th International Conference on the Foundations and Applications of Utility, Risk and Decision Theory.* Roma.

Ramuu, N., & Kennedy, W. (1994). Heuristic algorithm to locate solid waste disposal site. *Journal of Urban Planning and Development, 120,* 14-21.

Ravi, V., Shankar, R., & Tiwari, M. K. (2005). Analyzing alternatives in reverse logistics for end-of-life computers: ANP and balanced scorecard approach. *Computers and Industrial Engineering, 48,* 327-356.

Rees, W. E., & Wackernagel, M. (1994). Ecological footprints and appropriated carrying capacity: Measuring the natural capital requirement of the human economy. In A. M. Jansson, H. M., C. Folke, & R. Costanza (Eds.), *Investing in natural capital: The ecological economics approach to sustainability.* Washington, DC, USA: Island Press.

Reijnders, L. (2002). Imports as a major complication: Liberalisation of the green electricity market in The Netherlands. *Energy Policy, 30,* 723-726.

Rentmeester, K. (2005). Green manufacturing. *Marketplace, 17*(4), 26.

Resnick, P., & Varian, H.R. (1997). Recommender systems. *Communications of the ACM, 40*(3), 56-58.

Resort-Municipality-of-Whistler-(RMOW). (2005). *Whistler 2020: Moving toward a sustainable future.* RMOW.

Richter, K. (1996). The EOQ repair and waste disposal model with variable setup numbers. *European Journal of Operational Research, 95,* 313-324.

Richter, K., & Dobos, I. (1999). Analysis of the EOQ repair and waste disposal problem with integer setup. *International Journal of Production Economics, 59,* 463-467.

Richter, K., & Sombrutzki, M. (2000). Remanufacturing planning for the reverse Wagner/Whitin models. *European Journal of Operational Research, 121,* 304-315.

Richter, K., & Weber, J. (2001). The reverse Wagner/Whitin model with variable manufacturing and remanufacturing cost. *International Journal of Production Economics, 71,* 447-456.

Ritchie, L., Burnes, B., Whittle, P., & Hey, R. (2000). The benefits of reverse logistics: The case of the Manchester Royal Infirmary Pharmacy. *Supply Chain Management, 5,* 226-233.

Robèrt, K.-H. (1994). *The natural challenge*. Stockholm: Ekerlids Publisher.

Robèrt, K.-H. (1997, June 5-7). *ICA/Electrolux: A case report from 1992*. Paper presented at the 40th CIES Annual Executive Congress, Boston, MA.

Robèrt, K.-H. (2000). Tools and concepts for sustainable development: How do they relate to a general framework for sustainable development, and to each other? *Journal of Cleaner Production, 8*(3), 243-254.

Robèrt, K.-H. (2002). *The natural step story: Seeding a quiet revolution*. Gabriola Island, British Columbia, Canada: New Society Publishers.

Robèrt, K.-H., Broman, G., Waldron, D., Ny, H., Byggeth, S. H., Cook, D., et al. (2004). *Strategic leadership towards sustainability* (3rd ed.). Karlskrona, Sweden: Psilanders grafiska.

Robèrt, K.-H., Daly, H. E., Hawken, P. A., & Holmberg, J. (1997). A compass for sustainable development. *International Journal of Sustainable Development and World Ecology, 4*, 79-92.

Robèrt, K.-H., Holmberg, J., & Weizsacker, E. U. v. (2000). Factor X for subtle policy-making. *Greener Management International*, (31), 25-38.

Robèrt, K.-H., Schmidt-Bleek, B., Aloisi de Larderel, J., Basile, G., Jansen, J. L., Kuehr, R., et al. (2002). Strategic sustainable development: Selection, design and synergies of applied tools. *Journal of Cleaner Production, 10*(3), 197-214.

Robèrt, M. (2005). Backcasting and econometrics for sustainable planning: Information technology and individual preferences of travel. *Journal of Cleaner Production, 13*(8), 841-852.

Roberts, J. A. (1996). Green consumers in 1990s: Profile and implications for advertising. *Journal of Business Research, 36*, 217-231.

Robinson, J. B. (1982). Energy backcasting: A proposed method of policy analysis. *Energy Policy, 10*(4), 337-344.

Robinson, J. B. (1990). Future under glass: A recipe for people who hate to predict. *Futures, 22*(9), 820-843.

Roe, B., Teisl, M.F., Levy, A., & Russell, M. (2001). U.S. consumers' willingness to pay for green electricity. *Energy Policy, 29*, 917-925.

Rogers, M., & Bruen, M. (1998). A new system for weighting environmental criteria for use within ELECTRE III. *European Journal of Operational Research, 107*(3), 552-563.

Romm, J. (1994). *Lean and clean management*. New York: Kodansha International.

Rose, C. M., Stevels, A., & Ishii, K. (2000). A new approach to end-of-life design advisor (ELDA). In *Proceedings of the 2000 IEEE International Symposium on Electronics and the Environment* (pp. 99-104). The Institute of Electrical and Electronics Engineers, Inc.

Rose, S.K., Clark, J., Poe, G.L., Rondeau, D., & Schulze, W.D. (2002). The private provision of public goods: Test of a provision point mechanism for funding green power programs. *Resource and Energy Economics, 24*, 131-155.

Rowlands, I.H., Scott, D., & Parker, P. (2003). Consumers and green electricity: Profiling potential purchasers. *Business Strategy and the Environment, 12*, 36-48.

Roy, B. (1978). ELECTRE III: Algorithme de classement basé sur une représentation floue des préférences en présence des critères multiples. *Cahiers du* CERO, *20*, 3-24.

Roy, B. (1996). *Multicriteria methodology for decision aiding*. London: Kluwer Academic Publishers.

Roy, B. (2000). Supplement No. 1: A French-English decision aiding glossary. *Newsletter of the European Working Group "Multicriteria Aid for Decisions," Series, 3*(1), 1-10.

Russell, R., & Igo, W. (1979). An assignment routing problem. *Networks, 9*, 1-17.

Saaty, R.W. (2003). *Decision making in complex environment: The analytic hierarchy process (AHP) for decision making and the analytic network process (ANP) for decision making with dependence and feedback*. Retrieved July 8, 2008, from http://www.Superdecisions.com

Saaty, T. L. (1980). *The analytic hierarchy process*. New York: McGraw-Hill.

Saaty, T. L. (1996). *Decision making with dependence and feedback: The analytic network process*. Pittsburgh, PA: RWS Publications.

Saaty, T.L. (1999, August 12-14). Fundamentals of the analytic network process. In *Proceedings of ISAHP 1999*, Kobe, Japan.

Saaty, T.L., & Vargas, L.G. (1998). Diagnosis with dependent symptoms: Bayes theorem and the analytic network process. *Operations Research, 46*(4), 491-502.

Sabin, D., & Weigel, D. (1998). *Managing the hidden costs of complexity* (whitepaper). Boston Consulting Group.

Sakao, T., Kaneko, K., Masui, K., & Tsubaki, H. (2004). Analysis of the characteristics of QFDE and LCA for ecodesign support. In H. Reichl, H. Griese, & H. Potter (Eds.), *2004 Proceedings of the Electronics Goes Green: Driving Forces for Future Electronics* (pp. 495-500). Stuttgart, Germany: Fraunhofer IRB, IRB Staz-und Druckcenter.

Sako, M. (1992). *Prices, quality and trust*. Cambridge, UK: Cambridge University Press.

Salmela, S., & Varho, V. (2006). Consumers in the green electricity market in Finland. *Energy Policy, 34*, 3669-3683.

Salminen, P., Hokkanen, J., & Lahdelma, R. (1998). Comparing multicriteria methods in the context of environmental problems. *European Journal of Operational Research, 104*, 485-496.

Salton, G. (1970). Automatic text analysis. *Science, 168*(3929), 335-342.

Salton, G., & Buckley, C. (1988). Term-weighting approaches in automatic text retrieval. *Information Proceeding and Management, 24*(5), 513-523.

Samsung Electronics Co. Ltd. (2004). *Samsung electronics 2004 green management report: Respecting nature serving communities*. South Korea.

Sarkis, J. (1998). Evaluating environmentally conscious business practices. *European Journal of Operational Research, 107*, 159-174.

Sarkis, J. (1999). A methodological framework for evaluating environmentally conscious manufacturing programs. *Computers & Industrial Engineering, 36*(4), 793-810.

Sarkis, J. (2000). Comparative analysis of DEA as a discrete alternative multiple criteria decision tool. *European Journal of Operational Research, 123*(3), 543-557.

Sarkis, J. (2000, November 5-8). Ecoefficiency: How data envelopment analysis can be used by managers and researchers. In *Proceedings of the SPIE International Conference on Environmentally Conscious Manufacturing*, Boston, MA (pp. 194-203).

Sarkis, J. (2001). *Greener manufacturing and operations: From design to delivery and back B2: Greener manufacturing and operations: From design to delivery and back*. Sheffield: Greenleaf.

Sarkis, J., & Cordeiro, J. J. (2001). An empirical evaluation of environmental efficiencies and firm performance: Pollution prevention versus end-of-pipe practice. *European Journal of Operational Research, 135*(1), 102-113.

Sarkis, J., & Weinrach, J. (2001). Using data envelopment analysis to evaluate environmentally conscious waste treatment technology. *Journal of Cleaner Production, 9*(5), 417-427.

Satty, T. L., & Vargas, L. G. (2001). *Models, methods, concepts & applications of the analytic hierarchy process*. Kluwer Academic Publishers.

Savaskan, R. C., Bhattacharya, S., & Van Wassenhove, L. N. (2004). Closed loop supply chain models with product remanufacturing. *Management Science, 50*, 239-252.

Schaefer, J.B., Konstan, J.A., & Riedl, J. (1999), Recommender systems in E-commerce. In *Proceedings of the*

ACM Conference on Electronic Commerce, Denver, CO.

Scherpereel, C., van Koppen, C. S. A., & Heering, G. B. F. (2001). Selecting environmental performance indicators. *Greener Management International, 33*, 97-114.

Scheuring, J., Bras, B. A., & Lee, K. M. (1994). Significance of design for disassembly on integrated disassembly and assembly processes. *International Journal of Environmentally Conscious Design and Manufacturing, 3*, 21-23.

Schlegelmilch, B.B., Bohlen, G.M., & Diamantopoulos, A. (1996). The link between green purchasing decisions and measures of environmental consciousness. *European Journal of Marketing, 30*(5), 35-55.

Schmidt, I., Meurer, M., Saling, P., Kicherer, A., Reuter, W., & Gensch C. O. (2004). SEEbalance: Managing sustainability of products and processes with the socio-eco-efficiency analysis by BASF. *Greener Management International, 45*, 79-94.

Schmidt, W.-P., & Sullivan, J. (2002). Weighting in life cycle assessment in a global context. *International Journal of Life Cycle Assessment, 7*(5), 5-10.

Schmidt-Bleek, F. (1997). *MIPS and factor 10 for a sustainable and profitable economy*. Wuppertal, Germany: Wuppertal Institute.

Schoemaker, P.J.H., Waid, C., & Carter, W.C. (1982). An experimental comparison of different approaches to determining weights in additive utility models. *Management Science, Linthicum, 28*(2), 182-196.

Schoenung, J. M., Ogunseitan, O. A., Saphores, J-D. M., & Shapiro, A. A. (2005). Adopting lead-free electronics: Policy differences and knowledge gaps. *Journal of Industrial Ecology, 8*(4), 59-85.

Schultmann, F., Moritz, Z., & Otto, R. (2006). Modeling reverse logistic tasks within closed-loop supply chains: An example from the automotive industry. *European Journal of Operational Research, 171*, 1033-1050.

Scrutz M., Graulich, K., & Ebinger, F. (2004). Mind your steps towards sustainability: Developing product sustainability indicators for cellular phones. In H. Reichl, H. Griese, & H. Potter (Eds.), *2004 Proceedings of the Electronics Goes Green: Driving Forces for Future Electronics* (pp. 453-458). Stuttgart, Germany: Fraunhofer IRB, IRB Staz-und Druckcenter.

Seliger, G., Zussman, E., & Kriwet, A. (1994). Integration of recycling considerations into product design: A system approach. In S. Y. Nof (Ed.), *Information and collaboration models of integration-based on the NATO research workshop on integration, Il Crocco, Italy. Dordrecht, The Netherlands: Kluwer Academic.*

Sen, P. (2001). Communicating preferences in multiple-criteria decision-making: The role of the designer. *Journal of Engineering Design, 12*(1), 15-24.

Seppala, J. (2003). *Life cycle impact assessment based on decision analysis*. Doctoral dissertation, Helsinki University of Technology, Finland.

Seppala, J., Basson, L., & Norris, G. A. (2002). Decision analysis frameworks for life cycle impact assessment. *Journal of Industrial Ecology, 5*, 45-68.

SETAC (Society of Environmental Toxicology and Chemistry) - Europe Working Group. (1993). *Life cycle assessment and conceptually related programs*. CRP Report.

SETAC (Society of Environmental Toxicology and Chemistry). (1998). *Evolution and development of the conceptual framework and methodology of life cycle impact assessment*. SETAC Press.

Shah, N. (2005). Process industry supply chains: Advances and challenges. *Computers and Chemical Engineering, 29*, 1225-1235.

Sheu, J. B., Chou, Y. H., & Hu, C. C. (2005). An integrated logistics operational model for green supply chain management. *Transportation Research Part E, 41*, 287-313.

Shih, L. H. (2001). Reverse logistics system planning for recycling electrical appliances and computers in Taiwan. *Resour. Conserv. Recycl., 32*, 55-72.

Shyur H.J. (2006). COTS evaluation using modified TOPSIS and ANP. *Applied Mathematics and Computation, 177*(1), 251-259.

Shyur, H.-J., & Shih, H.-S. (2006). A hybrid MCDM model for strategic vendor selection. *Mathematical and Computer Modeling, 44*, 749-761.

Siddhaye, S., & Sheng, P. (2000). Environmental impact and design parameters in electronics manufacturing: A sensitivity analysis approach. In *Proceedings of the 2000 IEEE International Symposium on Electronics and the Environment* (pp. 39-45). The Institute of Electrical and Electronics Engineers, Inc.

Siddiqui, M.Z., Everett, J.W., & Vieux, B.E. (1996). Landfill siting using geographic information systems: A demonstration. *Journal of Environmental Engineering, 122*, 515-523.

Siemens Corporation. (2003). *Siemens corporate responsibility report*. Berlin/Munich, Germany.

Simos, J. (1990). *Evaluer l'impact sur l'environement: Une approche originale par l'analyse multicritère et la négociation*. Lausanne, Presses Polytechniques et Universitaires romandes.

Singhal, P., Ahonen, S., Rice, G., Stutz, M., Terho, M., & van der Wel, H. (2004). Key environmental performance indicators (KEPIs): A new approach to environmental assessment. In H. Reichl, H. Griese, & H. Potter (Eds.), *2004 Proceedings of the Electronics Goes Green: Driving Forces for Future Electronics* (pp. 697-702). Stuttgart, Germany: Fraunhofer IRB, IRB Staz-und Druckcenter.

Society for Environmental Toxicology and Chemistry. (1991). *A technical framework for life cycle assessments*. Washington, D.C.

Solomon, M.M. (1985). *Benchmark data*. Retrieved July 9, 2008, from http://web.cba.neu.edu/%7Emsolomon/problems.htm

Solomon, M.M. (1987). Algorithms for the vehicle routing and scheduling problems with time window constraints. *Operations Research, 35*, 254-265.

Sonnemann, G., Castells, F., & Schumacher, M. (2004). *Integrated life-cycle and risk assessment for industrial processes*. Lewis Publishers.

Sony Corporation. (2006). *Corporate social responsibility report*. Japan.

Spicer, A. J., & Johnson, M. R. (2004). Third-party demanufacturing as a solution for extended producer responsibility. *Journal of Cleaner Production, 12*, 37-45.

Srivastava, J., Connolly, T., & Beach, L.R. (1995, July). Do rank suffice? A comparison of alternative weighting approaches in value elicitation. *Organizational Behavior and Human Decision Process, 63*(1), 112-116.

Srivastava, S. K. (2007). Green supply-chain management: A state-of-the-art literature review. *International Journal of Management Reviews, 9*(1), 53-80.

Srivastava, S. K., & Srivastava, R. K. (2005). Profit driven reverse logistics. *International Journal of Business Research, 4*, 53-61.

Srivastava, S. K., & Srivastava, R. K. (2006). Managing product returns for reverse logistics. *International Journal of Physical Distribution and Logistics Management (Special Issue on 3PL, 4PL and Reverse Logistics), 36*, 524-546.

Stahel, W. (1982). *The product-life factor*. Geneva: Product-Life Institute. Retrieved July 8, 2008, from http://www.product-life.org/milestone2.htm

Stahel, W. (1994). The utilization-focused service economy: Resource efficiency and product life extension. In B.R. Allenby & D.J. Richards (Eds.), *The greening of industrial ecosystems* (pp. 178-190). Washington, DC: National Academy Press. Retrieved July 8, 2008, from http://books.nap.edu/openbook.php?record_id=2129&page=178

Standards Australia. (1998). *Environmental management life cycle assessment: Principles and framework*. AS/NZS ISO 14040.

Steen, B. (1999). *A systematic approach to environmental priority strategies in product development (EPS): Ver-*

sion 2000—general system characteristics. Sweden: Chalmers University.

Sterman, J. (1992, October). Teaching takes off: Flight simulators for management education. *OR/MS Today,* 40-44.

Stewart, T.J. (1996). Robustness of additive value function methods in MCDM. *Journal of Multi-Criteria Decision Analysis, 5*(4), 301-310.

Stoughton, M., Horie, Y., & Nakao, Y. (in press). *Service-led businesses for sustainability? Evaluating the potential of and policy for innovative product service systems in Japan.* Institute for Global Environmental Strategies (IGES), Kansai Research Centre.

Stowers, C.L., & Palekar, V.S. (1993). Location models with routing considerations for a single obnoxious facility. *Transportation Science, 27*(4), 350-362.

Straughan, R.D., & Roberts, J.A. (1999). Environmental segmentation alternatives: A look at green consumer behavior in the new millennium. *The Journal of Consumer Marketing, 16*(6), 558-575.

Sundin, E., Bjorkman, M., & Jacobsson, N. (2000). Analysis of service selling and design for remanufacturing. In *Proceedings of the 2000 IEEE International Symposium on Electronics and the Environment,* San Francisco, CA, USA (pp. 272-277). See also http://ieeexplore.ieee.org/xpl/freeabs_all.jsp?arnumber=857661

Sustainability Victoria. (2006). *Byteback.* Retrieved July 8, 2008, from http://www.sustainability.vic.gov.au/www/html/2045-byteback.asp

Suzuki, M. (2000). The zero emission concept in the 21st century. In U.-E. Simonis (Ed.), *Ecology yearbook 2001* (pp. 129-135). Munich, Germany: Verlag C. H. Beck.

Swenseth, S., & Godfrey, M. (2002). Incorporating transportation costs into inventory replenishment decisions. *International Journal of Production Economics, 77,* 113-130.

Swezey, B., & Bird, L. (2001). *Utility green-pricing programs. What defines success?* (NREL/TP.620.29831). Golden, CO: NREL National Renewable Energy Laboratory.

Symposium fact sheets. (2005, October 27-28). *Symposium on public initiatives to promote environmental business performance: Greening the local economy.*

Takahashi, K. I., Tatemichi, H. T., Tanaka, N. S., & Kunioka, T. (2004). Environmental impact of information and communication technologies including rebound effects. In *Proceedings of the 2004 IEEE International Symposium on Electronics and the Environment* (pp. 13-16). The Institute of Electrical and Electronics Engineers, Inc.

Taleb, K. N., & Gupta, S. M. (1997). Disassembly of multiple product structures. *Comput. Ind. Engng, 32,* 949-961.

Talluri, S. (2000). Data envelopment analysis: Models and extensions. *Decision Line, 31*(3), 8-11.

Talluri, S., & Baker, R. C. (2002). A multi-phase mathematical programming approach for effective supply chain design. *European Journal of Operations Research, 141,* 544-558.

Talluri, S., Baker, R. C., & Sarkis, J. (1999). Framework for designing efficient value chain networks. *International Journal of Production Economics, 62*(1-2), 133-144.

Tamura, S., Higuchi, K., & Tanaka, K. (1971). Pattern classification based on fuzzy relations. *IEEE Trans. SMC, 1,* 61-66.

Tan, A. W. K., Yu, W. S., & Kumar, A. (2002). Improving the performance of a computer company in supporting its reverse logistics operations in the Asia-Pacific region. *International Journal of Physical Distribution & Logistics Management, 33,* 59-74.

Tan, R. R. (2005). Application of symmetric fuzzy linear programming in life cycle assessment. *Environmental Modelling and Software, 20,* 1343-1346.

Tan, R. R., Culaba, A. B., & Aviso, K. B. (2008). A fuzzy linear programming extension of the general matrix-based life cycle model. *Journal of Cleaner Production, 16,* 1358-1367.

Tan, R. R., Culaba, A. B., & Purvis, M. R. I. (2004). Carbon balance implications of coconut biodiesel utilization in the Philippine automotive transport sector. *Biomass and Bioenergy, 26*, 579-585.

Tang, Q., & Xie, F. (2007, August 24-27). A genetic algorithm for reverse logistics network design. In *Proceedings of the Third International Conference on Natural Computation*, Haikou, China.

Tanner, C., & Kast, S.W. (2003, October). Promoting sustainable consumption: Determinants of green purchases by Swiss consumers. *Psychology & Marketing, 20*(10), 883-902.

Thanassoulis, E. (1993). A comparison of regression analysis and data envelopment analysis as alternative methods for performance assessments. *Journal of the Operational Research Society, 44*(11), 1129-1144.

The European Working Group on Reverse Logistics (REVLOG). (1999). Retrieved July 9, 2008, from http://www.fbk.eur.nl/OZ/REVLOG/PROJECTS/TERMINOLOGY/def_reverselogistics.html

Theyel, G. (2001). Customer and supplier relations for environmental performance. *Greener Management International, 35*, 61-69.

Tilanus, B. (1997). Introduction to information system in logistics and transportation. *Information system in logistics and transportation*. Elsevier Science.

Tilikidou, I. (2007). The effect of knowledge and attitudes upon Greeks' pro-environmental purchasing behaviour. *Corporate Social Responsibility and Environmental Management, 14*(3), 121-134.

Tilikidou, I., & Delistavrou, A. (2001). Utilization of selected demographics and psychographics in recycling behavior understanding: A focus on materialism. *Greener Management International, 34*, 75-93.

Tillman, A., Ekvall, T., Baumann, H., & Rydberg, T. (1994). Choice of system boundaries in life cycle assessment. *Journal of Cleaner Production, 2*(1), 21-29.

Todd, J. A. (1996). Streamlining. In M. A. Curran (Ed.), *Environmental life cycle assessment* (pp. 4.1-4.17). New York: McGraw-Hill.

Triantaphyllou, E., & Lin, C. (1996). Development and evaluation of five fuzzy multi-attribute decision-making methods. *International Journal of Approximate Reasoning, 14*, 281-310.

Triantaphyllou, E., Shu, B., Sanchez, S. N., & Ray, T. (1998). Multi-criteria decision making: An operations research approach. In J. G. Webster (Ed.), *Encyclopedia of electrical and electronics engineering* (pp. 175-186). New York: John Wiley & Sons.

Truffer, B., Markard, J., & Wüstenhagen, R. (2001). Eco-labeling of electricity: Strategies and tradeoffs in the definition of environmental standards. *Energy Policy, 29*, 885-897.

Tsaur, S., Chang, T., & Yen, C. (2002). The evaluation of airline service quality by fuzzy MCDM. *Tourism Management, 23*, 107-115.

Tsoulfas, G. T., Dasaklis, T., & Pappis, C. P. (2007, May 9-11). Identifying success factors for reverse logistics activities. In *Proceedings of the 2nd International Conference ECO-X 2007*, Vienna, Austria (pp. 39-46).

Tuzkaya, G., Önüt, S., Tuzkaya, U.R., & Gülsün, B. (2008). The analytic network process approach for locating undesirable facilities: An example from Istanbul, Turkey. *Journal of Environmental Management, 88*(4), 970-983.

Udo de Haes, H. A., Heijungs, R., Suh, S., & Huppes, G. (2004). Three strategies to overcome the limitations of LCA. *Journal of Industrial Ecology, 2*(3), 19-32.

Udo de Haes, H. A., Jolliet, O., Finnveden, G., Hauschild, M., Krewitt, W., & Mueller-Wenk, R. (1999). Best available practice regarding impact categories and category indicators in life-cycle impact assessment, Part 1. *International Journal of Life-Cycle Assessment, 4*, 66-74.

Ueno, K., et al. (2001, December). *Efforts to improve the eco-efficiency for products of Mitsubishi electronic corporation: Factor X by using MET indicators.* Paper presented at the 2001 EcoDesign Conference, Tokyo, Japan.

UNEP. (2002). *The role of product service systems in a sustainable society.* United Nations Environment Programme, Production and Consumption Branch brochure. Retrieved July 8, 2008, from http://www.uneptie.org/pc/sustain/reports/pss/pss-brochure-final.pdf

Vaccari, G., Tamburini, E., Sgualdino, G., Urbaniec, K., & Klemeš, J. (2005). Overview of the environmental problems in beet sugar processing: Possible solutions. *Journal of Cleaner Production, 13*(5), 499-507.

van Berkel, R., Willems, E., & Lafleur, M. (1997). The relationship between cleaner production and industrial ecology. *Journal of Industrial Ecology, 1*(1), 51-66.

van Calker, K.J., Berentsen, P.B.M., Romero, C., Giesen, G.W.J., & Huirne, R.B.M. (2006). Development and application of a multi-attribute sustainability function for Dutch dairy farming systems. *Ecological Economics, 57*, 640-658.

Van Damme, E., & Zwart, G. (2003). The liberalized Dutch green electricity market: Lessons from a policy experiment. *De Economist, 151*, 389-413.

van der Laan, E., & Salomon, M. (1997). Production planning and inventory control with remanufacturing and disposal. *European Journal of Operational Research, 102*, 264-278.

Van der Laan, E., Dekker, R., & Salomon, M. (1996). Product remanufacturing and disposal: A numerical comparison of alternative control strategies. *International Journal of Production Economics, 45*, 489-498.

Van der Laan, E., Dekker, R., Salomon, M., & Ridder, A. (1996). An (s, Q) inventory model with remanufacturing and disposal. *International Journal of Production Economics, 46*, 339-350.

van der Laan, E., Salomon, M., & Dekker, R. (1999). An investigation of lead-time effects in manufacturing/remanufacturing systems under simple PUSH and PULL control strategies. *European Journal of Operational Research, 115*, 195-214.

van der Laan, E., Salomon, M., Dekker, R., & van Wassenhove, L. (1999). Inventory control in hybrid systems with remanufacturing. *Management Science, 45*, 733-747.

Van Halen, C., Vezzoli, C., & Wimmer, R. (2005). *Methodology for product service innovation: How to develop clean, clever and competitive strategies for companies.* The Netherlands: Koninklijke Van Gorcum.

Van Hoek, R. I. (1999). From reversed logistics to green supply chains. *Supply Chain Management, 4*, 129-135.

Van Leeuwen, G. (2006). *Trust inside the NetChain game: The role of trust in the simulation of supply chain collaboration.* Masters thesis, Tilburg University.

Van Rooijen, S.N.M., & Van Wees, M.T. (2006). Green electricity policies in the Netherlands: An analysis of policy decisions. *Energy Policy, 34*, 60-71.

Vincent, M. (2006). China's manufacturing capability steadily ramping, going 'green'. *Connector Specifier, 22*(5), 1-2.

Vincke, P. (1992). *Multicriteria decision-aid.* New York: John Wiley & Sons.

Vlachos, D., & Tagaras, G. (2001). An inventory system with two supply modes and capacity constraints. *International Journal of Production Economics, 72*, 41-58.

Vlachos, D., Georgiadis, P., & Iakovou, E. (2007). A system dynamics model for dynamic capacity planning of remanufacturing in closed-loop supply chains. *Computers & Operations Research, 34*(2), 367.

Von Weizsacker, E., Lovins, A.B., & Lovins, L.H. (1997). *Factor four: Doubling wealth, halving resource use.* Australia: Allen and Unwin.

Wadhwa, V., & Ravindran, A.R. (2007). Vendor selection in outsourcing. *Computers & Operations Research, 34*, 3725-3737.

Wagner, M., Schaltegger, S., & Wehrmeyer, W. (2001). The relationship between the environmental and economic performance of firms: What does theory propose and what does empirical evidence tell us? *Greener Management International, 34*, 95-108.

Waldron, D. (2005). *A new education: Strategic leadership towards sustainability*. In Paper presented at the Seminar on Education for Sustainable Development, Stockholm, Sweden.

Waldron, D., Byggeth, S. H., Ny, H., Broman, G., & Robèrt, K.-H. (2004). *Structured comprehension for systems thinking, learning and leadership towards sustainability: Environmental Management for Sustainable Universities (EMSU)*. Tecnológico de Monterrey, Mexico.

Walters, D., & Rainbird, M. (2004). The demand chain as an integral component of the value chain. *The Journal of Consumer Marketing, 21*(7), 465-475.

Wang, H.F., & Jyh-Shing, H. (1996). Directed purturbation analysis of an IP. *Journal of Mathematics Analysis and Applications, 201*, 447-460.

Wang, H.F., & Jyh-Shing, H. (1996). Structural approach to parametric analysis of an IP. *European Journal of Operation Research, 92*, 148-156.

Wang, M.L., & Wang, H.F. (2005). Web mining system for mobile-phone marketing. In K. Voges & K.L. Nige (Eds.), *Business applications and computational intelligence* (pp.113-129). Hershey, PA: Idea Group Publishing.

Wang, Y.-M., Yang, J.-B., & Xu, D.-L. (2006). Environmental impact assessment using the evidential reasoning approach. *European Journal of Operational Research, 174*(3), 1885-1913.

Warren, J. P., Rhodes, E., & Carter, R. (2001). A total product system concept. *Greener Management International, 35*, 89-104.

WBCSD. (2000). *Eco-efficiency: Creating more value with less impact*. World Business Council for Sustainable Development. Retrieved July 8, 2008, from http://www.wbcsd.org/web/publications/eco_efficiency_creating_more_value.pdf

Wei-Chang, Y. (2005). A hybrid heuristic algorithm for the multistage supply chain network problem. *Internal Journal of Advanced Manufacturing Technology, 26*, 675-685.

Weisz, P. B., & Marshall, J. F. (1979). High grade fuels from biomass farming: Potentials and constraints. *Science, 206*, 24-29.

Wenzel, H., Hauschild, M., & Alting, L. (1997). *Environmental assessment of products, volume 1: Methodology, tools and case studies in product development*. London, UK: Chapman & Hall.

Wernick, I.K., Herman, R., Govind, S., & Ausubel, J.H. (1996). Materialization and Dematerialization: Measures and Trends. *Daedalus, 125*(3), 171-198.

Wey, W.-M. (2005). An integrated expert system/operations research approach for the optimization of waste incinerator siting problems. *Knowledge-Based Systems, 18*, 267-278.

White, A., Stoughton, M., & Feng, L. (1999). *Servicizing: The quiet transition to extended producer responsibility*. U.S.: The Tellus Institute. Retrieved July 8, 2008, from http://www.tellus.org/b&s/publications/servicizing.pdf

White, C. D., Masanet, E., Rosen, C. M., & Beckman, S. L. (2003). Product recovery with some byte: An overview of management challenges and environmental consequences in reverse manufacturing for the computer industry. *Journal of Cleaner Production, 11*, 445-458.

Whitehead, J. C., Pattanayak, S. K., Van Houtven, G. L., & Gelso, B. R. (2005). *Combining revealed and stated preference data to estimate the nonmarket value of ecological services: An assessment of the state of the science*. Series Working Paper (No. 05-19). Department of Economics, Appalachian State University, USA.

Widheden, J. (2002). *Methods for environmental assessments: Useful to the DANTES project*. Retrieved July 6, 2008, from http://www.dantes.info/Publications

Willet, P. (1988). Recent trends in hierarchical document clustering: A critical review. *Information Processing and Management, 24*(5), 577-597.

Williamson, O.E. (1993). *The economic institutions of capitalism: Firms, markets, relational contracting.* New York: Free Press.

Wiser, R., Olson, S., Bird, L., & Swezey, B. (2004). *Utility green pricing programs: A statistical analysis of program effectiveness* (NREL/TP-620-35609). Golden, CO: National Renewable Energy Laboratory.

Wiser, R.H. (2007). Using contingent valuation to explore willingness to pay for renewable energy: A comparison of collective and voluntary payment vehicles. *Ecological Economics, 62*, 419-432.

Wrisberg, N., Udo de Haes, H. A., Triebswetter, U., Eder, P., & Clift, R. (Eds.). (2002). *Analytical tools for environmental design and management in a systems perspective* (Vol. 10). Dordrecht, The Netherlands: Kluwer Academic Publishers.

Wüstenhagen, R., Markard, J., & Truffer, B. (2003). Diffusion of green power products in Switzerland. *Energy Policy, 31*, 621-632.

Yang, J.J., & Korfhage, R.R. (1993). Query optimization in information retrieval using genetic algorithms. In *Proceedings of the Fifth ICGA*, Urbana, Champaign, IL, USA.

Yang, T., & Hung, C.-C. (2007). Multiple-attribute decision making methods for plant layout design problem. *Robotics and Computer-Integrated Manufacturing, 23*(1), 126-137.

Yeşilnacar, M.I., & Cetin, H. (2005). Site selection for hazardous wastes: A case study from the GAP area, Turkey. *Engineering Geology, 81*, 371-388.

Yin, R.K. (2003). *Case study research: Design and methods* (3rd ed.). Thousand Oaks, CA: Sage Publications.

Yu, R., & Tzeng, G.H. (2006). A soft computing method for multi-criteria decision making with dependence and feedback. *Applied Mathematics and Computation, 180*, 63-75.

Zackrisson, M., Enroth, M., & Wilding, A. (1999). *Environmental management systems: Paper tiger or powerful tool. IVL-Report B 1351.* Stockholm: IVL Swedish Environmental Research Institute.

Zadeh, L. A. (1965). Fuzzy sets. *Information and Control, 8*, 338-353.

Zamir, O., Etzioni, O., Madani, O., & Karp, R.M. (1997). Fast and intuitive clustering of Web documents. In *Proceedings of the KDD '97*, Newport Beach, CA.

Zeleny, M. (1982). *Multiple criteria decision making.* New York: McGraw-Hill.

Zhang, H. C., Kuo, T. C., Lu, H., & Huang, S. H. (1997). Environmentally conscious design and manufacturing: A state-of-the-art survey. *Journal Mfg Systems, 16*, 352-371.

Zhou, X., & Schoenung, J. M. (2006). Integrating eco-design into the university curriculum. In *Proceedings of the 2006 Ecodesign Asia and Pacific Symposium*, Tokyo, Japan (pp. 105-110).

Zhou, X., & Schoenung, J. M. (2007). An integrated impact assessment and weighting methodology: Evaluation of the environmental consequences of computer display technology substitution. *Journal of Environmental Management, 83*(1), 1-24.

Zhou, Z., & Shi, Y. (1997). An ODE method of solving nonlinear programming. *Computers & Mathematics with Applications, 34*(1), 97-102.

Zhu, Q. H., & Sarkis, J. (2004). Relationships between operational practices and performance among early adopters of green supply chain management practices in Chinese manufacturing enterprises. *Journal of Operations Management, 22*(3), 265-289.

Zhu, Q. H., Geng, Y., & Spring. (2002). Integrating environmental issues into supplier selection and manage management: A study of large and medium-sized stateowned enterprises in China. *Greener Management International, 35*, 27-40.

Zhu, Q., & Raymond, P.C. (2004). Integrating green supply chain management into an embryonic eco-industrial development: A case study of the Guitang Group. *Journal of Cleaner Production, 12*, 1025-1035.

Zhu, Z. (2005). A feasible interior-point algorithm for non-convex nonlinear programming. *Applied Mathematics and Computation, 163*, 745-753.

Zimmermann, H.J. (1991). *Fuzzy set theory and its applications* (2nd ed.). London: Kluwer Academic.

About the Contributors

Hsiao-Fan Wang is the Tsing Hua chair professor and the vice dean of the College of Engineering of National Tsing Hua University, Taiwan, Republic of China. She has been teaching at the Department of Industrial Engineering and Engineering Management at the same university, NTHU, after she graduated from Cambridge University, UK, in 1981. She used to be the head of the Department of IEEM, NTHU, president of the Chinese Fuzzy Systems Association, vice president of International Fuzzy Systems Association, and Erskine Fellow of Canterbury University, NZ. Also, she has been awarded the Distinguished Research Award from National Science Council of Taiwan, ROC, Distinguished Contracted Research Fellow of NSC, and Distinguished Teaching Award of Engineering College, NTHU. She used to be the editor-in-chief of the *Journal of Chinese Industrial Engineering Association*, and also of the *Journal of Chinese Fuzzy Set and Theories*, and now is the area editor of several international journals. Her research interests are in multicriteria decision making, fuzzy set theory, and operations research.

****

Ruud Brekelmans (1972) is researcher at the Department of Econometrics & Operations Research, Tilburg University. His main field of interest is in the theory and applications of stochastic models with specialization in inventory management, simulation, and optimization methods. He obtained his PhD on stochastic models at Tilburg University in 2000. From 2000 until 2006 he worked for CentER Applied Research at Tilburg University. During those years he combined working on applied projects and doing fundamental research. His main goal is to develop models and actually apply them in practice.

Göran Broman is professor and head of research in mechanical engineering at Blekinge Institute of Technology, Karlskrona, Sweden. Parallel to his engineering education, he has undertaken extensive studies in ecology, economy, physical resource theory, and other subjects relevant to his commitment in sustainability. He has been instrumental in the development of the framework for strategic sustainable development and he has integrated sustainability aspects in mechanical engineering education and research. For this pioneering work he has received, for example, The Blekinge County Council Environmental Award and The Swedish Association of Environmental Managers Award. His present research interests are efficient and sustainable product development.

Ahmed Bufardi received his PhD in science from the Free University of Brussels (ULB) in April 2000. In March 2001, he joined the Computer-Aided Design and Production Laboratory (LICP) of the Swiss Federal Institute of Technology in Lausanne (EPFL), where he had different teaching, supervision,

Copyright © 2009, IGI Global, distributing in print or electronic forms without written permission of IGI Global is prohibited.

and research activities until February 2007. In November 2007, he joined the Environmental Engineering Department of the Swiss Federal Institute of Aquatic Science and Technology (EAWAG) in Dübendorf. He has published about 30 papers, mainly in the domains of preference modeling and multiple criteria decision aid and their applications. Dr. Bufardi is also referee for several scientific journals and conferences in his domains of interest.

Yu-Chun Chiu is an MSc of the Department of Industrial Engineering and Engineering Management, National Tsing Hua University, Hsinchu, ROC. Currently, she is working as an engineering assistant of TSMC, Taiwan.

Alvin B. Culaba is a professor of the Mechanical Engineering Department and currently the director of the Center for Engineering and Sustainable Development Research at De La Salle University-Manila in the Philippines. He has an MEng degree from the Asian Institute of Technology and a PhD from the University of Portsmouth. Professor Culaba is one of the pioneers of the use of life cycle assessment and related methodologies in the Philippines.

Hein Fleuren (1960) is professor in the application of Operations Research (OR) in practice at Tilburg University and he has his own consultancy OR Coach. During his career, he has been working at the edge of science and practice. Until 2006, he was director of the CentER for Applied Research at Tilburg University. From 1995 until 1999, he was manager of the Operations Research Group at the consultancy bureau Centre for Quantitative Methods (CQM BV) in Eindhoven, The Netherlands. From 1988 until 1995, he was a senior consultant at CQM, with specialization in vehicle routing, supply chain planning, and discrete event simulation of production systems.

Satomi Furukawa is a researcher at the Fuluhashi Environmental Institute, Nagoya, Japan. She holds a MA in planning from the School of Community and Regional Planning, University of British Columbia, Vancouver, Canada, and a MA from the Graduate School of International Development, Nagoya University, Nagoya, Japan. As the primary coordinator, she has led the pilot projects of PIUS-Check implementation in the Chubu Region, Japan. She is the primary coordinator of international activities of the company. She has been engaged in research and writing reports on environmental policies and programs promoting environmental management internationally.

Surendra M. Gupta, PE, is a professor of mechanical and industrial engineering and director of the Laboratory for Responsible Manufacturing at Northeastern University in Boston, Massachusetts, USA. He received his BE in electronics engineering from Birla Institute of Technology and Science, MBA from Bryant University, and MSIE and PhD in industrial engineering from Purdue University. He has authored and co-authored over 350 technical papers published in prestigious journals, books, and conference proceedings. Dr. Gupta is a recipient of the Outstanding Research Award and the Outstanding Industrial Engineering Professor Award (in recognition of teaching excellence) from Northeastern University. His recent activities can be viewed at http://www1.coe.neu.edu/~smgupta/

Hsin-Wei Hsu is a PhD candidate of the Department of Industrial Engineering and Engineering Management, National Tsing Hua University, Hsinchu, Taiwan, ROC. His research interest is in green supply chain management, reverse logistics.

Zhanming Jin is a professor of strategic management in the Department of Business Strategy and Policy at Tsinghua University. Zhanming received his BS from Jilin University in 1980, his MS from the Chinese Institute of Agriculture and Mechanic in 1986, and a PhD from Chinese University of Mining and Technology in 1989. He worked as a postdoctoral fellow from Tsinghua University in 1991. Professor Jin's research interests include strategic management, strategic selection under green supply-chain management, military strategy, and enterprise competition.

Selin Soner Kara is a PhD candidate in industrial engineering at the Yildiz Technical University, Turkey. She has an MSc in industrial engineering. She is also a research assistant in the Industrial Engineering Department. Her main research areas are waste management, reverse logistics, and the design of logistics networks.

Nikos Karacapilidis, computer engineer, PhD, is a professor in management information systems at the Department of Mechanical Engineering and Aeronautics, University of Patras. Before joining the University of Patras, he worked as a research associate in several organizations. His published work has appeared in *Fuzzy Sets and Systems, Decision Support Systems, International Transactions in Operational Research, Journal of Operational Research, European Journal of Operational Research, Computers and Operations Research Journal, Knowledge Based Systems, Knowledge and Process Management, International Journal of Business Intelligence and Data Mining, International Journal of Knowledge and Learning, Knowledge Management Research and Practice, Business Process Management Journal,* and so forth.

Dimitris Kiritsis got his diploma (1980) and PhD (1987) in mechanical engineering from the University of Patras, Greece. Since 1989, he has been with the Computer-Aided Design and Production Laboratory (LICP) of the Swiss Federal Institute of Technology in Lausanne (EPFL). He is active in teaching and research in the domain of modeling methods and techniques for integrated product-process-resource planning, product lifecycle information modeling, and transformation to knowledge. His principal investigations include: 1) an original method for integrated and dynamic manufacture/assembly/disassembly process planning modeling and simulation using Petri nets, and 2) product life cycle information modeling and management. Dr. Kiritsis is the initiator and scientific coordinator of the FP6-IP-507100 PROMISE and he is leading other international research projects in the domain of Integrated Product Design, Computer Aided Process Planning Modeling, Closed-Loop Product Lifecycle Modeling, and so forth. Dr. Kiritsis is also an active member of ASME and IFIP WG5.7, and referee of well-known scientific journals and conferences in his domains of interest. He has more than 80 publications in book chapters, scientific journals, and scientific and business conferences.

Elif Kongar is an assistant professor at the Departments of Mechanical Engineering and Technology Management at the University of Bridgeport, Bridgeport, Connecticut. She received her BS and MS in industrial engineering from Yildiz Technical University, and PhD in industrial engineering from Northeastern University. She has co-authored several technical papers presented at various national and international conferences and published in their respective proceedings. Dr. Kongar is a member of the Scientific Research Society, Sigma Xi, the Industrial Engineering Honor Society, Alpha Pi Mu, the Phi Beta Delta Honor Society, and the Phi Kappa Phi Honor Society. Her recent activities can be viewed at http://www.bridgeport.edu/~kongar/

Harold Krikke (1967) has been a member of the Department of Organization and Strategy at Tilburg University since 2002. He first studied industrial engineering and management at Twente University of Technology in Enschede. At the same university, he completed his PhD in 1998 in the field of reverse logistics. Since then, he has worked as an assistant professor at Erasmus University Rotterdam, and he also as a business consultant at Tebodin consultants. As of 2002, he is a project manager of CentER Applied Research and later became associate professor of economics and BA of Tilburg University.

Cindy Kuijpers (1968) is lecturer at the Department of Organization and Strategy, Tilburg University. Her main field of interest is in the theory and applications of operations research in healthcare, humanitarian management, and logistics. She obtained her PhD in 2000 at the Faculty of Applied Mathematics of Twente University of Technology. After spending time in Spain, from 2001 until 2005 she worked for CentER Applied Research at Tilburg University.

Ir. A.J.D. (Fred) Lambert is an assistant professor of industrial ecology in the Department of Technology Management at the University of Technology at Eindhoven, The Netherlands. He received MSc and his PhD in technical physics from the University of Technology at Eindhoven, all in The Netherlands. He has published papers on various topics, including energy systems modeling, process integration, materials flow modeling, and disassembly sequencing. He has published more than 30 research papers in various scientific journals and has made contributions to numerous books, conference proceedings, and professional papers.

Yi-Chun Liao received the BSci in industrial engineering from the University of Tsing-Hua in 1992. He received a master's in industrial engineering from the University of Tsing-Hua in 1994 and obtained PhD at University of Tsing Hua in 2000. His research interests include data mining, mathematical programming, genetic algorithm, and information system. He is an assistant professor at the Institute of Business Administration, Hsuan Chuang University.

Pedro Linares is associate professor of industrial organization at Universidad Pontificia Comillas, Madrid, and Research Associate at the J.F. Kennedy School of Government (Harvard U.) and FEDEA. He holds a MS and PhD in agricultural economics from U. Politécnica, Madrid. His research focuses on the relationship between energy, economics, and environment, and specifically on sustainable energy, renewable energy and environmental policy, and multicriteria methods applied to resource allocation. He has published about these issues in most journals relevant in the field. He has also been a consultant for several private and public institutions in Spain, Europe, and Latin America.

Jamie P. MacDonald currently serves as senior policy advisor to the Ontario provincial Minister of the Environment in Canada. He is focused on public policy related to solid waste, recycling, green product development, and a toxics reduction strategy for Ontario. Jamie has a masters of environmental studies focused on corporate environmental management systems, and past research has focused on the greening of public sector procurement, sustainable product development, and corporate environmental management systems.

David Ness is an adjunct senior research fellow at the University of South Australia. After practising as an architect and obtaining a masters degree in urban and regional planning, he gained his PhD in 2003. David advises the SA Government on strategic asset management, focusing on buildings and infrastructure, and prepared the background paper for a UN Expert Group Meeting on sustainable urban infrastructure. He convened an SA Product Stewardship Group and was Resource Person for a UN Policy Dialogue on "*Greening of Business*," in addition to being engaged by the UN to evaluate the Kitakyushu Initiative for a Clean Environment.

Henrik Ny is a PhD researcher and sessional instructor at Blekinge Institute of Technology, Karlskrona, Sweden. He holds a masters in chemical engineering from Lund Institute of Technology, Lund, Sweden, and a masters in environmental management and policy from the International Institute for Industrial Environmental Economics at Lund University, Lund, Sweden. He has worked with environmental issues at the Swedish chemical company Perstorp AB. This work focused on the integration of lifecycle assessment into the company environmental management system and the waste treatment and recycling efforts. His research interests include tool integration for sustainable product development.

Nobutaka ODAKE, is an associate professor at the Department of Techno-business Administration, Nagoya Institute of Technology since 2003, and holds a PhD in engineering from that university. He graduated in 1974 in chemical engineering from the University of Tokyo and finished the master's course in 1976. He experienced various kinds of jobs, including plant engineer for Toray Industries, Inc, sales and management for an electric wholesaler, and senior researcher of a regional think tank. At present, he is primarily responsible for education and research in the following fields: regional economic development, especially on development of clusters, and innovation system. Recently, he focused on intermediary or agent system for knowledge creation and technology transfer.

Semih Onut received his BS in mechanical engineering from Yildiz Technical University, Turkey, MS in computer integrated manufacturing from Strathclyde University, Scotland, UK, and PhD in industrial engineering from Yildiz Technical University. He is assistant professor at Yildiz Technical University. His main research areas are supply chain management, computer-integrated manufacturing, reverse logistics, waste management, and energy management.

Costas P. Pappis, mechanical and electrical engineer, Dipl. Management Studies, PhD, is professor in operations management at the Department of Industrial Management and Technology, University of Piraeus. Prior to entering academia, he had been employed for several years as a manager/consultant/research analyst. His published work has appeared in *Fuzzy Sets and Systems, International Journal of Production Economics, Resources, Conservation and Recycling, Ecological Indicators, Journal of Cleaner Production, IEEE Systems, Man and Cybernetics, European Journal of Operational Research, Journal of the Operational Research Society, Computers in Industry, Decision Support Systems, International Transactions in Operational Research*, and so forth.

Marta Pérez Plaza is a project finance manager in the Energy Department of Banco Popular Español. She analyses business plans for energy projects, such as biodiesel plants, wind farms, biomass, and waste treatment and solar thermal plants, and provides the necessary financing for these plants. She holds an industrial engineering degree from ICAI, Madrid. She has also worked as an analyst for several energy companies in Spain.

Kishore K. Pochampally is an assistant professor of quantitative studies and operations management in the School of Business at Southern New Hampshire University in Manchester, New Hampshire, USA. His prior academic experience is as a post-doctoral fellow at the Massachusetts Institute of Technology in Cambridge, Massachusetts, USA. He received his PhD in industrial engineering from Northeastern University in Boston, Massachusetts, USA. He has authored and co-authored several technical papers published in journals, books, and conference proceedings. Dr. Pochampally is also a Six Sigma Green Belt and a certified Project Management Professional (PMP®).

Michael R. I. Purvis is professor emeritus of the Department of Mechanical Engineering at the University of Portsmouth in the United Kingdom. His extensive body of work includes biomass combustion, life cycle assessment, and the development of international academic programs on sustainable technologies.

Karl-Henrik Robèrt is an adjunct professor of mechanical engineering at Blekinge Institute of Technology, Karlskrona, Sweden. Until 1993, he was an associate professor at Karolinska Institutet, headed the Division of Clinical Hematology and Oncology at the Department of Medicine at the Huddinge Hospital, Stockholm, Sweden, and was the editor of Reviews in Oncology. He founded The Natural Step Foundation in 1989. Between 1995 and 2001, he was an adjunct professor of physical resource theory at Chalmers University of Technology, Gothenburg, Sweden. In 1999, Dr. Robèrt received the Green Cross Millennium Award for International Environmental Leadership, and in 2000, he won the Blue Planet Prize for development of The Natural Step Framework. In 2005, he was named the inaugural winner of the prestigious global award, the Social Responsibility Laureate Medal. His present research interest is sustainability assessment as support for sustainable product development.

Julie M. Schoenung is a professor in the Department of Chemical Engineering and Materials Science at the University of California, Davis. Dr. Schoenung received her graduate degrees (MS and PhD) in materials engineering from the Massachusetts Institute of Technology and her bachelor of science in ceramic engineering from the University of Illinois at Champaign-Urbana. Dr. Schoenung has many years of experience in studying the materials selection process for a variety of material classifications, including electronic, ceramic, composite, and polymeric materials, and a variety of applications, including electronic, automotive, aerospace, and consumer products. Her research focuses on the analysis of factors that lead the materials selection decision-making process, such as economics, environmental impact, cost-performance trade-offs, and market potential. Dr. Schoenung uses both computer modeling and management theory in her approach to understanding these decision factors.

Ying Su received a BS at the Department of Mechanical Engineering in 1992 from Jinling Institute of Technology, Nanjing, Jiangsu Province, China. From 1992 to 1996, he was an engineer and technologist at an iron and steel plant. In 1999, he received an MS in mechanical engineering from Southeast

University, Nanjing, Jiangsu Province, China. In 2006, he received a PhD from the Department of Precision Instruments and Mechanology at the Tsinghua University, Beijing. Since 2006, he has worked at the School of Economics and Management as a postdoctoral fellow from Tsinghua University. He is an author of many scientific and research papers. His current research interests include green supply-chain management, information quality, discrete-event simulation, business process modeling, and enterprise resource planning.

Raymond R. Tan is an associate professor of the Chemical Engineering Department at De La Salle University-Manila in the Philippines. He has a PhD in mechanical engineering from the same university, and his research interests include life cycle assessment, process integration, pinch analysis, and renewable energy systems. He is the recipient of multiple awards from the National Academy of Science and Technology of the Republic of the Philippines.

Joel Q. Tanchuco is an assistant professor of the Economics Department at De La Salle University-Manila in the Philippines. He has an MA in economics from the University of the Philippines, and he specializes in energy and natural resource economics. He is currently using input-output techniques to analyze carbon emissions in Philippine industrial sectors.

Derya Tekin received his BS in industrial engineering from Yildiz Technical University, Turkey. She is still working as a process improvement assistant in Garanti Assurance, Inc. Her main research areas are waste management and supply chain management.

Giannis T. Tsoulfas, Mechanical Engineer, PhD, is employed as a scientific consultant at the Presidency of the Hellenic Republic. Prior to this he has worked as a consultant engineer in various engineering companies. His published work has appeared in *Resources, Conservation and Recycling, Ecological Indicators, Journal of Cleaner Production*, etc.

Miao-Ling Wang received the PhD in industrial engineering from National Tsing-Hua University in 1995. Her PhD dissertation was on tolerance of multiobjective programming. She was the vice manager of Episil Technologies, Inc., from 1994 until 1996. She was a vice professor at the Department of Industrial Engineering and Management of Chin Min Institute of Technology from 1996 until 2000, and she was also a dean of academic affairs from 1998 to 2000. She is now a vice professor at the Department of Industrial Engineering and Management, Ming-Hsin University of Science & Technology. Her research interests include data mining, multiobjective linear programming, fuzzy theory, and decision analysis.

Lei Yang received a BS from Shandong Normal University in 2001, and PhD from Wuhan University in 2006. He is currently a postdoctoral fellow in School of Economics and Management at Tsinghua University of China. His primary research interest is competitive analysis, supply chain management, risk management, and disruption management. He is a member of Operations Research Society of China (ORSC).

Xiaoying Zhou, PhD, graduated from the Department of Chemical Engineering and Materials Science at the University of California, Davis. She received her MS in statistics from University of California, Davis and BS in materials processing engineering from the University of Science and Technology, Beijing, P.R. China. Her dissertation focuses on the interdisciplinary research of materials system analysis and industrial ecology, modeling for the life cycle assessment of materials selection, end-of-life strategy, and environmentally benign manufacturing issues for electronic consumer product systems. Her current research activities mainly involve the integrated application of the analytic decision-making tools for the multi-objective optimization; extended producer responsibility confronting the emerging international and regional environment policy; assessing source reduction and pollution prevention in specified industry sectors; and green chemistry for sustainability and the pertinent issues. Dr. Zhou has published 11 journal and conference papers on the topics of sustainable product performance assessment methods. She is also a member of IMAPS, TMS, POMS, and AIChE.

Index

A

activity-based costing (ABC) 307
allocation problems 34
analytical hierarchy process (AHP) 213, 214
analytical network process (ANP) 306
analytic hierarchical process (AHP) 115
analytic hierarchy process (AHP) 82, 285
analytic network process (ANP) 82, 214
an end-of-life of product systems (AEOLOS) 101
anthropogenic materials flows 21

B

benchmarking type tools 101
bi-objective model construction 189
bi-objective nonlinear problem 182
bill of materials (BOM) 118
biofuels 1
biofuels, production of from agricultural crops 6
Borda's choice rule 283, 285, 290, 296
business object models (BOMs) 313

C

Certified Agricultural Standards (CAS) 390
checklist 97
chlorofluorocarbons (CFCs) 40
cleaner production (CP) 2
clustering analysis 188
coconut oil ethyl ester (CEE) 7
collaborative decision-making (CDM) 402
compact fluorescent lamps (CFLs) 57
conceptual life-cycle 20
Constant Returns to Scale (CRS) 372
consumption processes 26
corporate social responsibility (CSR) 234
cost-benefit analysis (CBA) 102
cost benefit analysis (CBA) 75
coupling operation models (COMs) 314
criteria, definition of 79
criteria, representation of 79
criteria, selection of relevant 84
criteria, weighting of 83
customer-oriented retrieval system, design of the 382
customer demand coverage 257
customer features, and classification 184

D

data envelopment analysis (DEA) 117, 368, 369
decision maker (DM) 185
decision making units (DMUs) 369, 371
Decreasing Returns to Scale (DRS) 372
defuzzification 288
dematerialization 55
der ÖkoBusinessPlan Wien 129
design for environment (DfE) 98
design for environment (DfE), aid tools 98
die Effizienz Agentur NRW (EFA) 129, 130
Directive 2002/95/EC on the Restriction of certain Hazardous Substances Directive (RoHS) 107
Directive 2002/96/EC on Waste Electrical and Electronic Equipment (WEEE) 107
direct rating (DR) 186
disassembly processes 28
distribution centers (DCs) 269

Copyright © 2009, IGI Global, distributing in print or electronic forms without written permission of IGI Global is prohibited.

E

e-business, trend of 380
echnique for order preference by similarity to ideal solution (TOPSIS) 213
eco-efficiency (EE) 102
Eco Business Plan Vienna (EBP) 129
EcoBusinessPlan Vienna (EBP), activities of the 137
EcoBusinessPlan Vienna (EBP), concept of 137
EcoScan® 99
ecosystem, cycles in the 21
ecosystem quality (EQ) 86
ELECTRE 83, 212
ELECTRE III 212
electronic product environmental assessment tool (EPEAT 105
Electronic Product Environmental Assessment Tool (EPEAT) 381
end-of-life (EOL) 75
end-of-life (EOL), oriented tools 100
end-of-life design advisor (ELDA) method 101
end-of-lives (EOLs) 368, 369
end-of-pipe processes 27
End User Workplace Solution (EUWS) 237
energy, forms and kinds 33
energy conservation measures 39
energy flow indicators 97
energy purchases 258
energy savings settings 239
environmental accounting (EA) 102
environmental design of industrial products (EDIP) 115
environmental impact assessment (EIA) 94
environmentally conscious design (ECD) 305
environmentally conscious manufacturing (ECM) 369
environmental risk assessment (ERA) 102
EOL Treatment Cost (C) 86
European Foundation for Quality Management (EFQM) 102
European Union Directive on End-of-Life Vehicles (ELV Directive) 75
European Union Directive on Waste Electrical and Electronic Equipment (WEEE Directive) 75
evaluation criteria 78
event driven process chains (EPCs) 312
extended producer responsibility (EPR), legislation on 3

F

factory gate pricing 150
fleet management 239
Fuluhashi Environmental Institute Co., Ltd. (FEI) 133
fuzzy analytic network process 218
fuzzy analytic network process (FANP) 208
fuzzy set theory 285
fuzzy theory 217
fuzzy TOPSIS 208, 220, 283, 284

G

geographical information system (GIS) 213
German Green Party (Die Grün) 131
global energy flows 21
global physical flows 21
goal programming (GP) 186, 371
Greece, mobile phones in 401
green corporate practices 1
green electricity (GE) 250
green electricity, credibility 261
green electricity, information to customers 261
green electricity, premiums 260
green electricity, relationship with other RE support schemes 262
green electricity, value creation 260
green electricity, willingness to pay for 253
green information platform 379
green information retrieval 379
green information systems, introduction to 381
greening the local economy 141
green operations 306
green products 182, 379
green products recommender Design, for both customers and producers 390
green products retrieval, example of 385
green quality function deployment (GQFD) 99
green supply-chain management (GSCM) 302
green supply-chain strategies 301
green supply chain (GSC) 268
green supply chain management 268

green supply chain management (GSCM) 269
green tariff programs (GTM) 256
gross domestic product (GDP) 108
gross energy requirement (GER) 34

H

Hewlett-Packard (HP) 233
Hewlett-Packard case 232
HP "SERVICE SOLUTION" 237
HP Service Solution, examples of 238
human health (HH) 86
hybrid electric vehicle (HEV) 198

I

impact pathway analysis (IPA) 102
Imperial-Chemical-Industries (ICI) 64
Increasing Returns to Scale (IRS) 372
industrial ecology 17, 18
industrial ecology, origin of 17
industrial metabolism 18
industrial metabolism, main characteristics of 18
industrial symbiosis 18
Information and Communication Technology (ICT), infrastructure 407
Information Network for Recycling of Electronic Equipment (IDEE) 381
information retrieval (IR), basic concept of 382
Institute for Global Environmental Strategies (IGES) 235
integer linear programming 273
international legislative focus 106
International Organization for Standardization (ISO) 106

K

key environmental performance indicators (KEPIs) 97

L

land-filling rate 277
lead (Pb) 108
life-cycle approach 20
life-cycle approach, origin of 20
life-cycle assessment (LCA) 39, 51, 52
life-cycle assessment (LCA), and eco-indicator 39
life-cycle assessment (LCA), calculations 34
life-cycle assessment/analysis (LCA) 305
life-cycle management (LCM) 52
life-cycle management, rationale for strategic 55
life cycle assessment (LCA) 3, 75, 94, 102, 150, 152
life cycle assessment, historical development of 3
life cycle assessment, methodology 4
life cycle assessment principles 1
life cycle costing (LCC) 99
life cycle engineering (LCE) 103
linguistic values, and fuzzy sets 286

M

management information system 380
material flow analysis (MFA) 102
materials flow indicators 96
methodology for product service innovation (MEPSS) 235
mixed integer linear programming model 268
mobile phones, reverse supply chain of in Greece 405
multi-attribute decision theory (MADT) 114
multi-attribute utility theory (MAUT) 185
multiattribute utility theory (MAUT) 183
multiple attribute decision making (MADM) 210
multiple attribute utility theory (MAUT) 82
multiple criteria decision making (MCDM) 74, 185, 198, 208, 210, 214, 371
multiple objective decision making (MODM) 210

N

NetChain Game (NCG) 151, 153
neural network 292
nongovernmental organization (NGO) 54
nongovernment organizations (NGOs) 102
nonlinear problem, solution procedure of the 190
nonlinear programming 186
nonlinear programming (NLP), 307

nternational Rice Research Institute (IRRI) 239

O

OneDFE 98
optimal part disposal (OPD) model 101
orth Rhine-Westphalia (NRW) 130

P

percentage of all species present in ecosystem under toxic stress (PAF) 110
performance, and sustainability 155
performance measurement systems (PMSs) 302
personal computers (CPUs) 373
photovoltaic (PV) 240
physical flows, in industry 23
physical life-cycle 20
physical systems 19
PIUS-Check 131
pollution prevention (P2) 2
polyvinylchloride (PVC) 58
preference-based recommendation procedure 379
problem context, classification based on the 303
process disaggregation 25
product-dependant parameters 403
product embedded information devices (PEIDs) 87
production processes 25
product market combinations (PMCs) 154
product recovery (RL) 305
product service systems (PSS) 232, 235
product stewardship, and take-back schemes 234
product waste, processing of 28
Produktionsintegrieter Umweltschutz (PIUS) 130
PROMETHEE 83, 212

Q

qualify function deployment (QFD) 99
quality function deployment for environment (QFDE) 99
quantitative models for environmental performance measurement systems (QMEPMS) 302, 309
quotes for environmentally weighted recyclability (QWERTY) 100

R

recovery facilities, evaluation of efficiencies of 296
Registration, Evaluation, and Authorization of Chemicals (REACH) 107
regression analysis (RA) 371
renewable electricity 250
renewable electricity, types 257
residual products 25
resource and environmental profile analysis (REPA) 3, 39
resource productivity (RP) 102
resources (R) 86
Restriction of the use of certain Hazardous Substances in electrical and electronic equipment (RoHS) 390
return on investment (ROI) 239
reverse logistics 270, 401
reverse logistics (RL) 303
reverse logistics operation, parameters that may affect 403
reverse product-process chain 27
reverse supply chain 283

S

scenario planning 53
SEEbalance® 102
Simple weighted addition (SWA) 212
small- and medium-sized enterprises (SMEs) 129
SMART 212
Social Democratic Party of Germany (SPD) a 131
Society for Promotion of Life-cycle Assessment Development (SPOLD) 40
Society of Environmental Toxicology and Chemistry (SETAC) 3, 39
strategic life-cycle management (SLCM) 53
strategic management 304
supply-derived market 184
supply chain dynamics 153

supply chains 1
supply chains, measuring environmental impact of 152
surface mounted devices (SMDs) 44
sustainability, how trust impacts 149
sustainability principles (SPs) 54
sustainability target method (STM) 102
sustainable product assessment methods, teaching 119
sustainable product service systems 235
sustainable product service systems (S-PSS) 232
system, and universe 19
system conditions (SCs) 54
system dynamics modeling 301
systems approach 19
system structure 19

T

technical efficiency (TE) 374
technique for order preference by similarity to ideal solution (TOPSIS) 288
technosystem, and ecosystem 20
templates for sustainable product development (TSPDs) 65
The Natural Step (TNS) 54
threshold criteria 78
TOPSIS 212
TOPSIS method 289
toxicity potential indicator (TPI) 100
toxic release inventory (TRI) system 97
tradable green certificate (TGC) 259
transfer station selection, application of 221
triangular fuzzy number (TFN) 287
trust, and green supply chains 151
trust, and performance 152
trust, different kinds of 151
trust, impact of 157

U

U.S. Environmental Protection Agency (EPA) 97
United Nations Division of Sustainable Development (UN DSD) 112
University of South Australia, research project 242
utility function construction 189

V

value chain network (VCN) 371
Variable Returns to Scale (VRS) 372
Vienna Business Promotion Institute (VBPI) 138
Vienna City Government 138
voluntary contribution mechanisms (VCM) 256

W

Waste Electrical and Electronic Equipment (WEEE) 390
wastes 25
Watson Implosion Technology (WIT) 101
Web-based decision support tool 401
Web-based tool 408
Web-based tool, for collaborative decision making 407
weight-based information retrieval system design 382
weighted product (WP) 212
weight elicitation 189
willingness to pay (WTP) 252